The Great Bronze Age of China

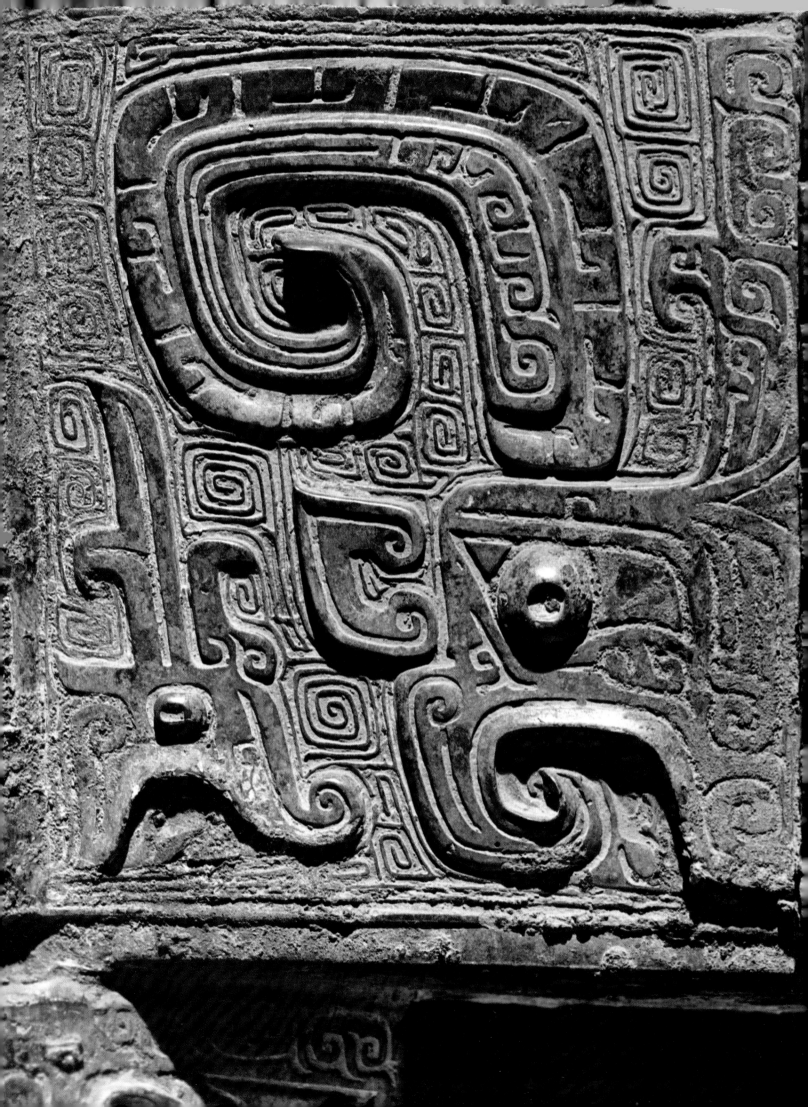

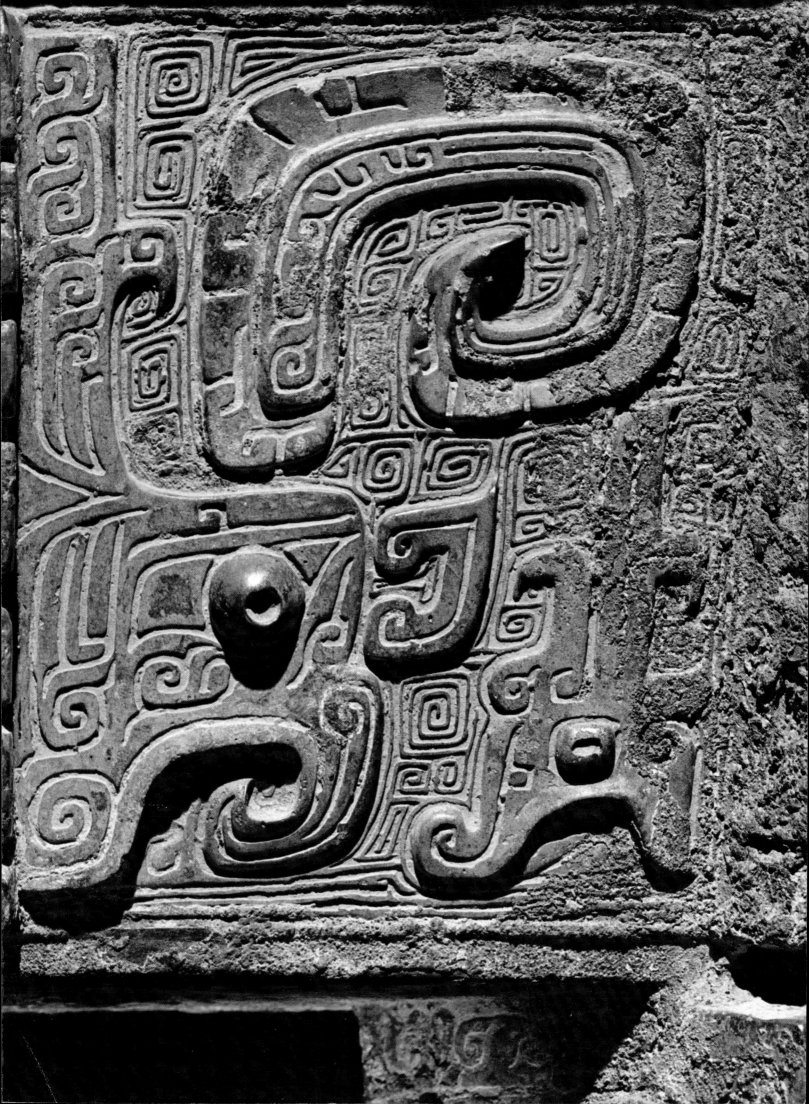

INTRODUCTORY ESSAYS BY:

Ma Chengyuan
Curator, Shanghai Museum

Wen Fong
Edwards Sanford Professor of Art and Archaeology, Princeton University,
and Special Consultant for Far Eastern Affairs, The Metropolitan Museum of Art

Kwang-chih Chang
Professor of Anthropology, Harvard University

Robert L. Thorp
Assistant Professor, Department of Art and Archaeology, Princeton University

CATALOGUE BY:

Robert W. Bagley
Research Assistant, Department of Fine Arts, Harvard University

Jenny F. So
Research Assistant, Department of Fine Arts, Harvard University

Maxwell K. Hearn
Assistant Curator, Department of Far Eastern Art, The Metropolitan Museum of Art

THE GREAT BRONZE AGE OF CHINA

An Exhibition
from the
People's Republic of China

Edited by Wen Fong

THE METROPOLITAN MUSEUM OF ART
New York
ALFRED A. KNOPF, INC.

The exhibition was made possible by grants from The Coca-Cola Company and the National Endowment for the Humanities, Washington, D.C., a federal agency.

Under the Arts and Artifacts Indemnity Act, indemnity was granted by the Federal Council on the Arts and Humanities.

The color photographs, made especially for this exhibition, were taken in China by Seth Joel. The color photographs of the gilt-bronze lamp no. 94 and the excavation of the terracotta figures (p. 335) were taken by Wang Yugui, Cultural Relics Bureau, Beijing.

Published in conjunction with the exhibition
The Great Bronze Age of China held at:

The Metropolitan Museum of Art, New York, April 12–July 9, 1980
Field Museum of Natural History, Chicago, August 20–October 29, 1980
Kimbell Art Museum, Fort Worth, December 10, 1980–February 18, 1981
Los Angeles County Museum of Art, April 1–June 10, 1981
Museum of Fine Arts, Boston, July 22–September 30, 1981

The Metropolitan Museum of Art, New York
Bradford D. Kelleher, Publisher
John P. O'Neill, Editor in Chief
Lauren Shakely and Rosanne Wasserman, Editors
Gerald Pryor and Andrius Balukas, Designers
Phyllis Ward: Maps, Charts, Drawings

Library of Congress Cataloging in Publication Data

New York (City). Metropolitan Museum of Art.
   The Great bronze age of China : an exhibition from the People's Republic of China.

   Catalogue of an exhibition to be held at the Metropolitan Museum of Art, New York, and at four other cities during the period, 1980–1981.
   Bibliography: p. 382
   1. Bronzes, Chinese—Exhibitions.   I. Bagley, Robert W.   II. So, Jenny F.   III. Hearn, Maxwell K. IV. Fong, Wen.   V. Title.
NK7983.A1N48 1980   730'.0951'074013   79-27616
ISBN 0-87099-226-0 (MMA)
ISBN 0-394-51256 (AAK)

Frontispiece: Detail, decor of Fu Hao *fang ding* no. 32

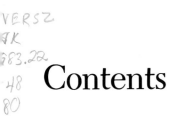

Contents

Preface

Chinese civilization is among the oldest of the world. The bronze objects of the Shang and Zhou periods represent the level of cultural development achieved during the early times of Chinese slave society. They possess a unique national style, distinctive characteristics of their time, and an outstanding degree of artistic achievement. By the Qin and Han periods, bronze vessels with inlays of gold and silver had reached a new brilliance, which today makes them artistic treasures.

Since the founding of the People's Republic of China, the many important bronze vessels discovered throughout the country have contributed invaluable scientific material for the study of political, economic, and cultural aspects of the long period of Chinese slave society. The eighty-five bronze objects displayed here are gathered from fifteen provincial and municipal museums and archaeological organizations, including those of Beijing, Shanghai, Shaanxi, Henan, and others. Through these bronze artifacts—the finest selected from the large quantity of objects archaeologically excavated in China during the last thirty years—a comprehensive picture of the bronze art of ancient China emerges.

The eight terracotta figures and terracotta horses were selected from among the thousands of burial figures recently excavated on the eastern side of the tumulus of First Emperor Qin Shihuangdi (third century B.C.). The animation of their forms, the maturity of technique, and their heroic demeanor make them unique among the painted terracotta sculpture of ancient China. They reflect the high level of sculptural art in the Qin period.

In 1974–75, cultural relics unearthed in China and, in 1976–77, copies of wall paintings of the Han and Tang were exhibited in the United States and received the warm welcome and appreciation of the American people. As a result of the establishment of Sino-American diplomatic relations, new prospects for relations between our two countries have been opened. This group of historic treasures has been gathered especially for presentation to the American people. We hope that this exhibition will make a contribution toward increased cultural exchange and friendly relations between China and the United States, and will advance the mutual friendship and understanding between the peoples of the two countries.

The Committee for the
Preparation of Exhibitions of
Archaeological Relics,
People's Republic of China

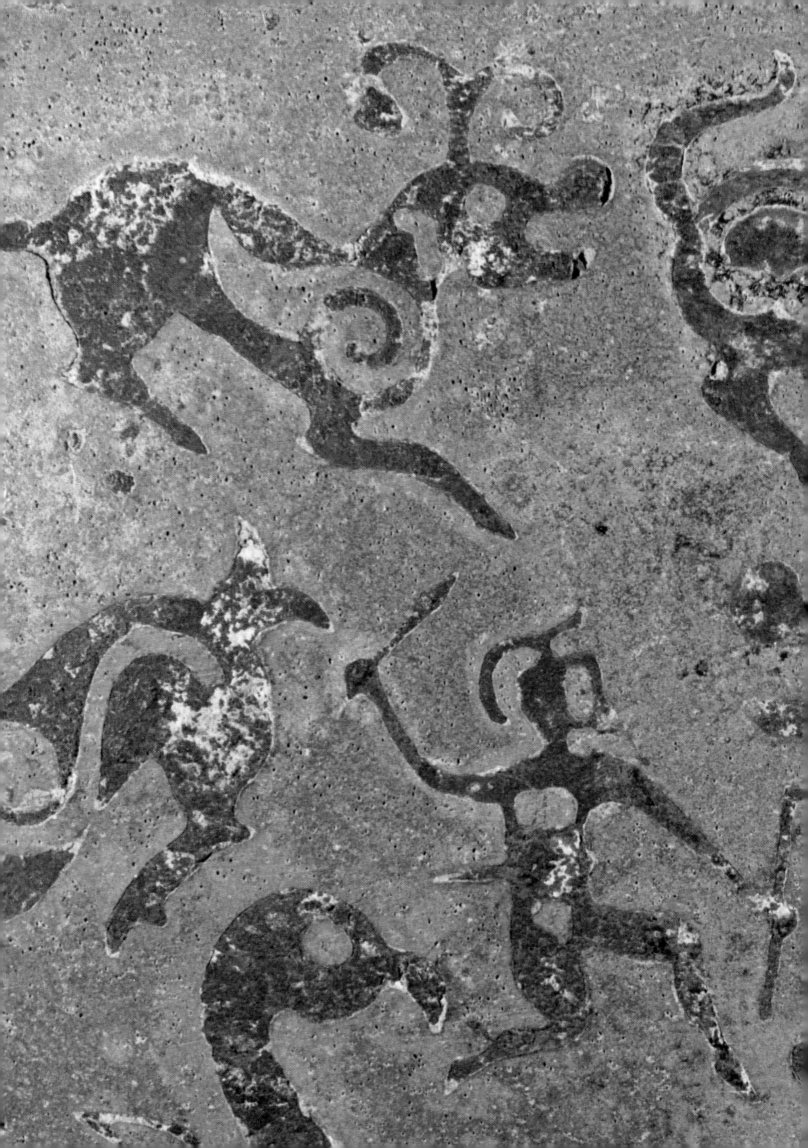

Foreword

Archaeology in China today promises to disclose the secrets of ancient China in much the same way that nineteenth-century archaeology revealed the ancient Greek world, both by refuting cherished notions of the later historians and by restoring myths and vanished kingdoms to history. The 105 exhibits in the present exhibition sent by the People's Republic of China, carefully selected for their aesthetic and historical importance, summarize the most brilliant achievements in recent Chinese Bronze Age archaeology.

The advent of bronze metallurgy in any ancient civilization assured the creation of better tools for increased productivity, and more effective weapons for making war. In ancient China, however, bronze technology was put to a third important use, the one with which this exhibition is primarily concerned, namely, the casting of imposing drinking vessels and food containers. These objects were created for rituals in ancestral temples by kings and nobles whose rank and order were measured by the size and the number of their bronzes. Such bronzes display the incredible range of inventive genius of the ancient Chinese, who successfully combined art and industry to form some of the most accomplished and enduring works of art the world knows. Splendid works in bronze and jade, these objects stand as eloquent and tangible testimony to the great early civilizations of China. The ultimate importance of such works of art lies not only in their revealing the extraordinary skill and genius of the earliest Chinese artisans, but also in their role as keystones in the reconstruction of ancient Chinese history.

Legend has it that after King Yu of the Xia dynasty controlled the flood, about 2200 B.C., he divided his land into nine provinces, and had nine *ding* (cauldrons) cast to represent them. Thus, the "nine *ding*," also called the "Heavy Vessels of the State" or the "Auspicious Bronzes of the State," became symbols of power and prestige. When the Xia dynasty fell, it is recorded, the "nine *ding*" passed to the Shang dynasty, and, in turn, to the Zhou when they conquered the Shang.

Whether weapons or ritual vessels, bronze objects meant power for those who possessed them. In times of war, the bronze from ritual vessels could be used to make weapons; in times of peace weapons might be transformed into ceremonial objects. After the First Emperor of Qin unified China in 221 B.C., he ordered that all the bronze vessels and weapons captured from his vanquished enemies be melted down and made into twelve colossal bronze statues to adorn his palaces. The real purpose of this grandiose act was to keep weapons out of the hands of his subjects, but, eventually, the giant bronze statues were melted down and recast into weapons by enemy invaders.

The Great Bronze Age of China, the exhibition that the People's Republic of China has lent to five United States museums, makes a unique contribution to Western understanding of the greatness of ancient Chinese civilizations. It opens with the earliest known Chinese bronze vessel and concludes with the extraordinary terracotta soldiers and horses that were recently excavated from the burial complex of the First Emperor of Qin. Unlike the first Chinese exhibition of archaeological finds that toured the United States in 1974–75, which consisted of a general sampling of objects dating from the Neolithic

◁ Decor of *dou* no. 70

through Yuan periods, the present show has a unified theme: it presents us with a thorough review of the most brilliant latest achievements in Chinese Bronze Age archaeology with discoveries that have fundamentally changed our knowledge of ancient Chinese history and art.

The recent reopening of diplomatic relations between the People's Republic of China and the United States insured that the planning and organization of the exhibition would become a reality. Many of the spectacular objects included are of such outstanding importance that there was some doubt at first that the Chinese government would permit them to leave the country. Equally unprecedented is the unstinting cooperation of the Chinese in the preparation of a major scholarly catalogue. With contributions by Ma Chengyuan of the Shanghai Museum, and by a team of American scholars led by Professor Wen Fong of Princeton University and The Metropolitan Museum of Art, the catalogue is a full summary by scholars both in China and in the West of current interpretations of the latest Chinese Bronze Age finds.

I had the personal pleasure of joining the exhibition's work team in China in February 1979. The sheer magnificence and beauty of these ancient art objects, especially when seen in their original setting, left me with a profound and lasting impression. Their transcendent beauty cannot fail to move and quicken the senses of the American public. Moreover, the warm reception and unfailing support that we received from His Excellency Wang Yeqiu, Director of the State Administrative Bureau of Museums and Archaeological Data, and the staff of the Committee for the Preparation of Exhibitions of Archaeological Relics will be remembered long after the exhibition closes and the artifacts return to China.

It was, we remember, the remarkable Burlington House exhibition of Chinese art in London, in 1935–36, that stimulated an entire generation of art historians and enthusiasts in Europe and the Americas. I am certain that the current exhibition of Chinese Bronze Age art will open a new era in the appreciation and understanding of ancient Chinese art and archaeology in the West.

Philippe de Montebello
Director
The Metropolitan Museum of Art

Acknowledgments

The Metropolitan Museum of Art is delighted to have the opportunity of presenting a loan exhibition of major scholarly importance from the People's Republic of China. His Excellency Chai Zhemin, Chinese Ambassador to the United States, took a personal interest in the exhibition and lent powerful support to the negotiations. The Honorable Xie Qimei, Counselor of the Chinese Embassy in Washington, D.C., not only was instrumental in getting the initial negotiations for the exhibition under way, but also guided the project through its various stages. The Chinese Embassy's First Secretary for Cultural Affairs, Zhang Wenying, always efficient and affable, made all our dealings with that embassy pleasurable and rewarding.

But it is to the active interest and support of His Excellency Wang Yeqiu, a scholar and Director of China's State Administrative Bureau of Museums and Archaeological Data, and to the unfailing cooperation of the members of the Bureau's Committee for the Preparation of Exhibitions of Archaeological Relics that we owe the successful accomplishment of this undertaking of unusual complexity and magnitude. Mr. Wang personally guided the selection of the objects. The Bureau's Foreign Affairs Section Chief, Guo Laowei, an extraordinary diplomat, solved many difficult problems with skill and graciousness. We must express our deep gratitude to the Bureau's Office for the Preparation of Exhibition Materials, especially its chief Yu Jian and its deputy chief Qiu Zhenbang, for the kind and patient assistance given to our photographer and researchers during their long stays in Beijing, as well as for supplying the large number of excellent photographic and illustrative materials used in the exhibition and catalogue. We also thank the heads and the curators of the many distinguished institutions that we visited, especially: Xia Nai, Director of the Institute of Archaeology, Beijing; Yang Zhenya, Director of the Historical Museum, Beijing; Peng Yan, Deputy Director of the Palace Museum, Beijing; Shen Zhiyu, Director of the Shanghai Museum; Liu Wenlin, Deputy Director of the Xi'an Provincial Museum; Chen Mengdong of the Shaanxi Cultural Relics Bureau; and Xiong Chuangxin of the Hunan Provincial Museum. Their warm help and advice greatly enriched our knowledge of the field.

We are profoundly grateful to the scholars of the Committee for the Preparation of Exhibitions of Archaeological Relics, who carefully read and checked the manuscript of the catalogue for accuracy and sent us thoughtful comments on our work. Arriving too late to appear in this catalogue, Ma Chengyuan's expanded essay "The Splendor of Ancient Chinese Bronzes" is published in the Chinese language catalogue of the exhibition.

We are most grateful to the Honorable Leonard Woodcock, the United States Ambassador in Beijing; the Honorable Stapleton Roy, the Deputy Chief of Mission; and John Thomson, First Secretary at the Embassy, for granting us every courtesy and help in matters relating to the project.

At the Metropolitan Museum, the entire administrative staff has for the past two years given its best effort to the planning and mounting of the exhibition. We wish to thank in particular the Director, Philippe de Montebello, who led the research and photographic expedition in China in February 1979 and successfully negotiated the inclusion of some of the most important objects in the exhibition. William Macomber, President; James Pilgrim, Deputy Director; John Buchanan, Registrar; and other members of the administration played essential roles in many matters relating to the budget, application for indemnification, and logistical planning. We also want to thank the catalogue editors, Lauren Shakely and Rosanne Wasserman, who did a remarkably skillful and sensitive job in coordinating and unifying the works of seven different authors. Within the Metropolitan Museum's Far Eastern Art Department, everyone connected with the project has worked countless hours, but special mention should be made of Maxwell K. Hearn and Alfreda Murck, who managed and supervised the physical production of the exhibition at the Museum. Alfreda Murck and Robert L. Thorp were responsible for the translation of Ma Chengyuan's essay. Julia K. Murray, now at the Freer Gallery of Art, Washington, D.C., did preliminary research and coordinated the project while she was on the staff of The Metropolitan Museum of Art. For the installation design we are grateful to Lucian Leone, Assistant Manager for Design. While at the Metropolitan Museum the exhibition is presented in The Sackler Exhibition Hall.

We are deeply indebted to those who have made this exhibition possible: the National Endowment for the Humanities and The Coca-Cola Company. In turn, we thank both the National Endowment for the Humanities and the American Council of Learned Societies for the funding of the symposium to be held in conjunction with the exhibition at the Metropolitan Museum.

Wen Fong
Edwards Sanford Professor of Art and Archaeology,
Princeton University,
and Special Consultant for Far Eastern Affairs,
The Metropolitan Museum of Art

Editor's Note

Chinese Bronze Age archaeology is a field that is constantly being enriched by dramatic new discoveries by Chinese archaeologists, by theoretical contributions and reinterpretations by scholars around the world, and by the exchange of ideas represented in part by this catalogue. In offering a wide range of informed opinions on and approaches to the subject, the catalogue includes a number of ideas in controversy. Of the several chronologies that scholars have used to date the Bronze Age of China, Kwang-chih Chang favors the traditional dates and terminology for the Xia and Shang dynasties, while the other authors follow the revised dates (see Chronology of Bronze Age China, below). Ma Chengyuan and Robert W. Bagley present different versions of the reconstruction of the bronze-casting process (cf. "The Splendor of Ancient Chinese Bronzes" and chap. 2). Further remarks on some issues raised in the catalogue by the Committee for the Preparation of Exhibitions of Archaeological Relics of the People's Republic of China have been summarized at the back of the catalogue.

We have followed the *pinyin* system of transliterating Chinese characters into the Latin alphabet. (Peking, for example, becomes Beijing in *pinyin*.) For those familiar with Chinese, a glossary gives the Chinese characters for most of the *pinyin* words used in the catalogue. For other readers we give the following short list of *pinyin* pronunciations that differ radically from the pronunciation of those letters in English:

$$c = ts$$
$$q = ch$$
$$x = sh$$
$$z = dz$$
$$zh = j.$$

W.F.

Chronology of Bronze Age China

The earliest date upon which various sources agree is 841 B.C. Dates before that year vary as much as a century depending upon which genealogical list of rulers and their reign lengths is consulted.

The cornerstone for all Shang dynasty dates is the year in which the Shang were conquered by the Zhou. One traditional chronology gives 1122 B.C. as the year for this event, a date derived from the computations of Han dynasty scholars using a calendar prepared after 105 B.C. —many centuries after the event occurred. Another set of dates is taken from the *Zhu shu ji nian* (Bamboo Annals), which was compiled for the ruler of the feudal state of Wei in the early third century B.C. and discovered in his tomb in A.D. 281. According to this work, which was lost during the Sung dynasty (960–1279) but which survives in fragmentary form as citations in extant works, the Zhou conquered the Shang in 1027 B.C. This date can be approximately confirmed by other methods of computation, including one that estimates the average generation lengths of Western Zhou rulers (giving as a date for the conquest 1030–1020 B.C.) and another that makes reference to the reigns of the dukes of the feudal state of Lu as recorded in the *Shi Ji* (Historical Records) of Sima Qian (ca. 145–86 B.C.; see Ping-ti Ho, *The Cradle of the East*, Hong Kong, 1975, pp. 1–12).

The *Shi Ji* also lists the Shang kings who ruled at Anyang (see Table 1, p. 7), a list that has received a measure of confirmation from inscribed oracle bone texts found at that site. No such contemporary records confirm the identity or date of earlier Shang kings or the locations of their capitals. Thus, while surviving fragments of the Bamboo Annals state that the Shang kings ruled at Anyang for 273 years, that the entire Shang dynasty lasted 496 years, and that the preceding Xia dynasty lasted 471 years, these time spans are so far unverifiable (David N. Keightley, "The Bamboo Annals and Shang-Chou Chronology," *Harvard Journal of Asiatic Studies* 38 [1978], pp. 423–38). Carbon-14 dating suggests that these figures may be too low, but the margin of error for such dates is so great that this method offers little more than a general confirmation of the relative age of any given site as inferred from archaeological correlation of that site's strata with those of other sites and from the stylistic analysis of each site's contents.

	Revised Chronology	*Traditional Chronology*
Xia dynasty	21st century–16th century B.C.	2205–1760 B.C.
Period of Erlitou culture	19th century–16th century B.C.	
Shang dynasty	16th century–11th century B.C.	1766–1122 B.C.
Period of Erligang culture (Zhengzhou phase)	16th century–14th century B.C.	
Period of Yinxu culture (Anyang phase)	13th century–11th century B.C.	1388–1122 B.C.
Zhou dynasty	11th century–256 B.C.	1122–256 B.C.
Western Zhou	11th century–771 B.C.	1122–771 B.C.
Eastern Zhou	770–256 B.C.	
Spring and Autumn period	770–476 B.C.	
Warring States period	475–221 B.C.	
Qin dynasty	221–206 B.C.	
Han dynasty	206 B.C.–A.D. 220	

INTRODUCTORY ESSAYS

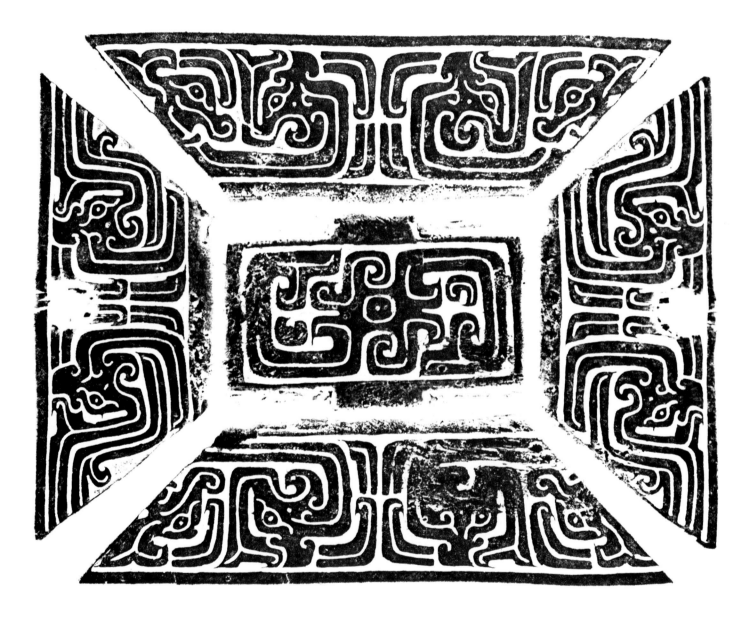

I

The Splendor of Ancient Chinese Bronzes
Ma Chengyuan

China has a long history and a vast territory. The culture established by the ancestors of the Chinese people laid a firm foundation for an enduring civilization. Like a bubbling spring the culture of the Shang and Zhou dynasties flowed over China's earth, creating a fertile environment that has brought forth much fruit. Bronzes were the preeminent artistic accomplishment of the Shang and Zhou culture and for this reason Chinese scholars have paid great attention to research on the Bronze Age objects. Because conditions for archaeological work have been excellent and archaeology has produced rich material for research, we have been able to produce steady results. Scholars in other countries have made valuable contributions in the study of the Chinese Bronze Age as well. The present exhibition of Chinese bronzes includes some of the most important archaeological finds unearthed since the establishment of the People's Republic of China and is offered to the great people of the United States of America so that they may share our appreciation of the accomplishments of ancient Chinese civilization. We also extend sincere good wishes to American scholars for new achievements in their studies of the Bronze Age culture of China.

The Use of Copper in Early Chinese Society

The material culture of the Chinese Bronze Age is well known, but for a long time the precise origins of the use of copper have been unclear. The rarity of traces of copper in early sites has added to the complexity of the problem. Recently the discovery of pieces of copper in Yangshao culture sites has been discussed, but the circumstances of this find must await a formal report before any definite conclusions can be drawn.[1] Copper artifacts have been found in sites of the Majiayao culture of Gansu Province, which is a later regional culture (ca. 3000 B.C.) that shares a common origin with the Yangshao. In October 1977 archaeologists of the Gansu Provincial Museum discovered a corroded copper blade at a depth of 1.2 meters in a stratum of a Majiayao site in Dongxiang Xian, Gansu. The knife was 12.6 centimeters long, with a straight sharp-ground blade, a convex back, and a broad handle with traces of hammering. This indubitable archaeological discovery pushes back the beginnings of the use of copper in China to 5,000 years ago. Fragmentary bronze blades—according to preliminary analysis an alloy of copper and tin[2]—have been discovered in Machang sites of Gansu Province, which date to about 2300–2000 B.C., and copper and bronze ornaments and small tools from the Qijia culture of slightly before 2000 B.C. have been discovered on several occasions.

An especially significant discovery for dating the first uses of bronze in China was made at the principal sites of the Longshan culture in Shandong Province on the lower reaches of the Yellow River. In an early Longshan culture site in Sanlihe in Jiao Xian, Shandong Province, two bronze awls were discovered,[3] which have a carbon-14 dating of 4,100 (plus or minus 90) years ago. In a late Longshan culture site at Dachengshan, Tangshan Xian, Hebei Province, two trapezoidal pieces of bronze were found as well.

Although archaeological evidence for the use of copper and bronze in early Chinese history is still fragmentary, the general trend has been for evidence of this sort to appear continually as archaeological work progresses. The efforts of archaeologists have already produced data on the origins and use of copper in early Chinese society, which is at the present concentrated primarily in the Yellow River watershed.

The Erlitou Culture Phase

For a long time, both from the perspective of historical development and from that of field archaeology, a gap in information existed for the period between the Longshan culture and the culture known from remains at Zhengzhou in the Central Plains of North China called Erligang. Before the early Shang phase at Erligang was uncovered, there were no artifactual remains that could be placed in this stage in history. In traditional Chinese history, the Xia dynasty bridged this gap. Both historical records and legend suggest that the Xia was the first slave state founded on the system of private ownership of property to be established in ancient China, but no consensus has been reached on the probability of the Xia's existence or the kinds of artifacts they might have left. Traces of a previously unknown culture were discovered at several sites in Henan Province—such as Lodamiao, Zhengzhou—as archaeological work progressed. Among the standard artifacts of this culture were: ceramic *ding* with flat legs; *ding* in the form of jars with small mouths; primitive *jue* vessels; *jiao* with spouts; *jia* with cone-shaped legs; *pan* with wide feet; and *zun* with shoulders, short necks, and everted mouths. The early artifacts of this culture were similar to those of the Longshan culture in some respects, while the later artifacts were clearly the ancestors of the types known from the Erligang culture. They were the intermediary link between the Longshan and Erligang cultures, and their discovery aroused considerable interest.

On the basis of this clue, Chinese archaeologists conducted explorations and surveys in the area of southern Shanxi Province and western and central Henan Province, which, according to historical texts, was the "Waste of the Xia." Traditionally, the fertile plain between the Yi and Luo Rivers in central Henan has been an important area of activity for the ancient people of the Xia. The *Shi Ji* (Historical Records of Sima Qian, ca. 100 B.C.) reports the words of King Wu of Zhou: "From the Luo to the Yi, dwelling sites are easy to find and secure; this was the home of the Xia." The Institute of Archaeology of the Chinese Academy of Social Sciences, Beijing, chose Erlitou in Yanshi, Henan Province, to carry out its excavations. The finds there were rich, and, after research and analysis, the stratigraphy of this site was divided into four periods. The name "Erlitou culture" was coined to apply to artifacts that conformed to those from this site.[4] Archaeologists in both Shanxi and Henan Provinces have since done considerable work in the "Waste of Xia" region. Erlitou culture sites have now been identified in over one hundred locations in western Henan Province, along the Yi and Luo Rivers in central Henan, near Zhengzhou, and in southern Shanxi.[5]

From the remains themselves, especially from the characteristics of the quantity of surviving ceramics, it appears that the periods designated as I and II had a close connection, but that, while periods III and IV were clearly related to I and II, they reveal some new elements as well. In style, some of the ceramics approach those of the early Shang found at Erligang. From estimates based on carbon-14 datings, period I at Erlitou is dated about 1900 B.C., while the latest period, period IV, is dated about 1600 B.C.[6] According to one point of view, all four periods were the Xia culture, and their dissimilarities were simply different stages of the Xia culture's development. Another position is that, while periods I and II can be considered Xia, periods III and IV were clearly Shang.[7] We know that the Xia and the Shang were successive dynasties, and that the sixteenth century B.C. was the period of transition between them, while the late eleventh century was the period of transition from Shang to Zhou. Although different historical sources give different accounts of the length of the Shang dynasty, none gives a duration of over 600 years. On the basis of the carbon-14 datings alone, all four periods of the Erlitou culture fall within the Xia period and not within the Shang; but the crucial issue of whether periods III and IV at Erlitou were Xia or predynastic Shang is complex and must await further study. Chinese archaeologists have nearly accepted the existence of the Xia, but have resisted drawing premature conclusions: much archaeological work must still be done on the character of these finds.

Bronze slag has been found in early Erlitou culture sites in Henan, and fragmentary pieces of bronze have been discovered at Xiawanggang in Xichuan, Henan, a site of the same date as the period I stratum at Erlitou. Complete bronze objects have only been discovered in the period III stratum at Erlitou, however. The cultural deposits in this stratum are fairly rich and include a formal palatial compound built on a terrace that measures 10,000 square meters in plan. From a study of the post holes and remnants of walls, the general appearance of this palace has been reconstructed. An outer wall ran around the terrace enclosing the palace. Near the terrace were found bronze tools; large bronze weapons, such as *ge* dagger-axes, *qi* axes, and arrow points; a bell with a single flange; and a round bronze object inlaid with pieces of turquoise. The most important discoveries here were bronze *jue*, three-legged cups with handles and long pouring spouts used for wine (no. 1). From the several *jue* excavated, it is apparent that some simply imitated ceramic *jue* forms and were crudely cast. Others have fairly thin walls and are true cast-bronze *jue*. The Erlitou bronzes show traces of the seams of the piece molds used in casting, and remnants of ceramic crucibles have been found with them. The use of piece-mold casting, essential for the production of such complicated forms, makes it clear that this technique had already had a long history by this time.

At this early stage the most important cast-bronze objects were tools, but a tool—an ax, for example—can also be an effective weapon. By the time of the Erlitou culture, the bronze weapons were already differentiated and mature in form, indicating that bronze weaponry was in military use by the state at this time. The Erlitou bronze weapons were quite well cast and are decorated with modified animal motifs. One large bronze *ge* imitates a jade *ge*, and, like a jade *ge*, it has a raised ridge on its haft. Naturally, bronze weapons were much sharper than their stone counterparts. According to metallurgical analysis, one bronze *jue* from Erlitou was 92 percent copper and 7 percent tin, a true bronze alloy.[8]

A bronze-casting industry as sophisticated as that of period III at Erlitou could not have appeared suddenly, and it is probably only a matter of time until bronzes are discovered in periods I and II. With Erlitou we have a confirmation of traditional historical accounts about the location and time period of the Xia dynasty. The stories of how Yu, the founder of the Xia, cast nine *ding* and of how his son Qi mined ore and cast bronze are given substance by these finds.

At the same time that bronze casting developed at Erlitou, the art of working jade reached a high level of craftsmanship (nos. 2, 3). Although the technical background for jade working had been established in the late Neolithic period, this unique art evolved only in conjunction with the development of bronze casting. Jade ritual forms at Erlitou—like the *gui*, the *zhang*, and the *zong*—were already excellently worked and their surface decoration well developed. On a jade handle from Erlitou are carved three animal heads, a forerunner of the animal-mask design of the Shang and Zhou bronzes.[9] Some *kui* dragons have been discovered on Erlitou ceramics as well, which resemble Shang and Zhou vessels in their basic forms. The bronze weapons, ritual vessels, and jades of Erlitou are the ancestors of their Shang equivalents, and the similarities between them may indicate a historical and cultural continuity between the two.

Shang

The Shang was one of the oldest tribes of ancient China, concentrated mainly along the lower reaches of the Yellow River in Hebei Province. Later they extended their influence into northern and central Henan Province to become one of the strongest states of eastern North China. In the sixteenth century B.C., Tang, the Shang leader, banded together several tribes to defeat Jie, the Xia leader, and become the first Shang king. The fortunes of the Shang dynasty met with vicissitudes over the next five hundred years, but its political power continued. Shang history can be divided into two stages: in the Early Shang, from the sixteenth to the fourteenth or thirteenth century, the political power of the dynasty was insecure and periods of stability were so short that the capital was moved five times. In the Late Shang period, the dynasty saw a great development of slave society. Pan Geng moved the capital to Yin—the name by which we know this phase of the dynasty—modern Yinxu at

Anyang, Henan Province. There it remained for 273 years until the last Shang king burned to death in his palace and the dynasty collapsed. During this fairly long period of political stability, the Shang state grew strong.

The Yinxu site is more than 24 square kilometers in area and contains large-scale palaces, temples, enormous royal tombs, tombs of the elite class, and evidence of slaves sacrificed at burials. (In one excavation at only one cemetery site, the skeletons of about two thousand slaves were discovered.) In addition, excavators have unearthed various workshops and numerous beautiful bronzes, jades, and ceramics, as well as over 10,000 divination bones and shells with inscriptions, used by the kings for every sort of divination. The material culture of Yinxu reveals the high level of civilization achieved during the period of Chinese slave society.

The area of dynastic activity and influence of the Shang was rather large, extending north of the Great Wall, south of the Wuling Mountains, east to the ocean, and west to the upper reaches of the Yellow River. Shang sites and artifacts have been discovered in all of these areas.

The study of Shang and Zhou ritual vessels by scholars has itself had a long history, but knowledge of the existence of Early Shang bronzes has come only since the founding of New China. In 1952, scientific techniques were employed to excavate pre-Yinxu Shang habitations and burials at Renmin Park and Baijiazhuang near Zhengzhou. These finds were later verified by many other discoveries. In the well laid-out ancient city of Zhengzhou, for example, remains of a still extant pre-Yinxu Shang wall were found, as well as a large palace site and workshops for ceramics, bone working, and bronze casting. With the discovery of ritual bronzes, ceramics, and oracle bones, Chinese archaeologists have begun to unravel this pre-Yinxu phase of the Shang dynasty through its material culture.

The Erligang culture of Zhengzhou was first considered, correctly, to be the culture of the Early Shang. Later, when the Erlitou culture was wrongly identified as Early Shang, the Erligang culture was reclassified as Middle Shang. Since, according to recent carbon-14 datings, the latest of the Erlitou periods, period IV, dates to the sixteenth century B.C.—the

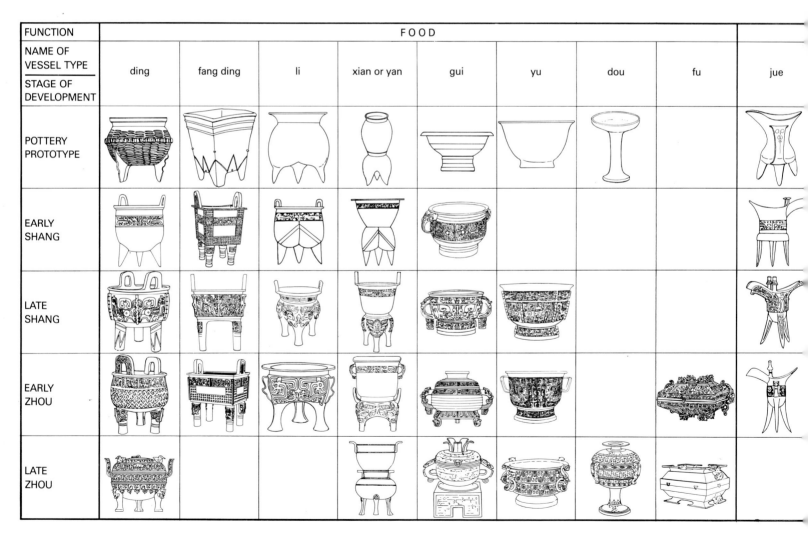

Fig. 1 Development of bronze vessel types. Drawing by Phyllis Ward

Xia-Shang transition period—the Early Shang culture must be considered the Erligang culture and not the Erlitou culture, and the period before 1600 B.C. the predynastic period before Tang established the Shang. Many early Shang culture sites have been found in other areas of Henan Province. Recently, an Early Shang site with a palace district, tombs of the elite class, and many bronzes and jades of high artistic quality was discovered at Panlongcheng, in Huangpi Xian, Hubei Province.[10] There have also been discoveries of Early Shang culture in Shandong and Anhui Provinces and in Qingjiang, Jiangxi Province.[11]

A wide range in the variety and types of cast-bronze artifacts already existed in Early Shang. Judging from the large number of ceramic molds of tools found in excavated sites, the casting of tools for labor and agriculture was an important aspect of the bronze industry. The discovery of tools has been reported only rarely, but this fact belies their real importance. Because bronze was a valuable metal, tools were no doubt melted down and reused, and because tools were not usually used as grave goods, they have not been as systematically preserved as other kinds of objects. Weapons were also cast in large quantities. At Panlongcheng, for example, many sets of bronze weapons were found. Other important objects cast in bronze were the ritual vessels, which indicated the status of their users and their exclusive right to perform sacrifices and ritual ceremonies. These vessels included cooking vessels, food vessels, wine containers, wine-drinking vessels, and washing vessels. The clan structure of the Shang-Zhou ruling class especially emphasized sacrifices to the ancestors, and those sacrifices required a large number of implements. In burial rites, many vessels had to be interred in the graves, and most of the extant bronze vessels are those originally placed in tombs. This demand for ritual vessels on the part of the elite class made bronzes an important element of the Shang-Zhou society.

Most of the bronze ritual vessels of the Shang period had either three feet or one round foot. The early Shang period *ding, li, jue, gui,* and *gu* were all tripod and round-footed vessels unique to the repertoire of Chinese bronzes. The forms of some of these vessels continued or

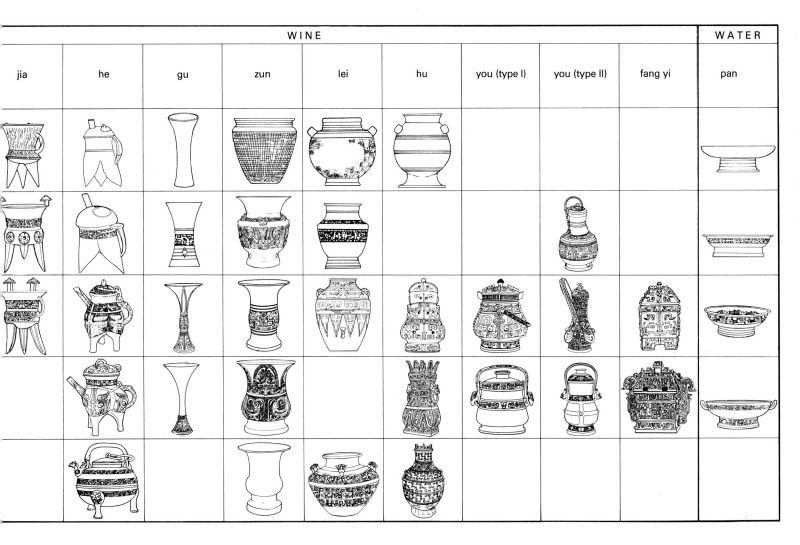

WINE										WATER
jia	he	gu	zun	lei	hu	you (type I)	you (type II)	fang yi		pan

5

further developed ceramic types of the Neolithic and pre-Shang periods that long since had achieved the exquisite simplicity of utilitarian craft objects, providing a good aesthetic basis for the process of copying, transplanting, and recreating bronzes from ceramics (see Fig. 1). The techniques for creating early Shang bronzes were simple and direct, and the relationship between the vessel body and its appendages was balanced so that each part of the vessel contributed to the whole. The result was a form charged with energy. At the same time, because the bronze casters did not follow strict rules for forms and carved decoration, the style of the early bronze vessels is relatively natural and crude. Vessels were cast with thin walls, some so thin that the vessels are extremely lightweight. The early Shang bronzes present a marked contrast to the solemn and formal shapes of the late period vessels.

In the Early Shang period, ritual bronze casting was at an early stage, and the vessel designs exhibit some primitive characteristics. For example, of the two lugs on the *ding, jia,* and other tripods, one lug is usually aligned directly over one leg, creating an imbalance in the design of the piece. In addition, the casters had not yet mastered the technique for enclosing the core of the legs, so the legs are hollow and open to the bowl of *ding* vessels.

By the Early Shang period the basic system of ritual types for bronze vessels was established, and the *ding, li, gui,* and other cooking and food storage vessels, as well as *jia, jue, gu, zun, hu, he,* and other wine storage and drinking vessels, were already in use. This system of forms dictated the later development of bronze vessel shapes.

Decorative ornament was already fairly common on early Shang vessels as well. The most important element in the decoration of that period was the animal mask. This motif represents the head of an animal or an imaginary beast with its body extending to both sides, its tail curling up, and its claws and legs parallel to the body in two registers. The motif is symmetrical and, if divided vertically at the nose, it appears to be two animals seen in profile with a common, frontally oriented face. The main feature of the motif is the eyes, and the simplest animal mask is merely a pair of eyes. Usually rendered in flat carving with bold, straight lines and feathery, hooked lines, the motif is abstract. The artisan was not trying to capture the real qualities of an animal but to portray a symbolic one; the result is a style that is expressive, reverential, and imposing.

Animal masks may also be composed of dragons, *kui* dragons, and other composite creatures of the imagination, which represent man's primeval response to the elemental forces of nature. During the Yinxu period, the art of bronze casting flourished because political control was stabilized after the transfer of the capital to Yin. King Wu Ding campaigned against the Guifang, Tufang, and other border states of the northwest and expanded the area of Shang control. He employed large-scale concentrated slave labor forces, advancing the slave society economy. Great progress was made in all kinds of crafts based on agricultural production. Palace and city building expanded, many divinations were recorded on the oracle bones, and bronze and jade craftsmanship advanced. All of these aspects of Shang society are important manifestations of the maturity of the Yin culture.

Based on years of experience excavating at Yinxu, Chinese archaeologists have divided the cultural development of the site into four periods: period I, before Wu Ding; period II, from Wu Ding to Zu Jia; period III, from Lin Xin to Wen Ding; and period IV, the reigns of Di Yi and Di Xin[12] (see Table 1). Although this periodization in some ways reflects the overall progress of the Yin material culture and the beginning and end of each period can be taken as a relative standard for dividing cultural developments, the chronology is in fact a continuum. Period I is generally called the Early Yin period; period II, the Middle Yin period; and period IV, the Late Yin period. The height of cultural development was reached in the Middle Yin period.

Ritual bronzes were fully developed by the Early Yin period, and many new types joined the standard forms, most notably new types of wine vessels. In addition to the *jue, gu, jia, zun,* and small, long-necked *hu* with a bail handle, the *lei* with shoulder, the *pou,* the tall *hu,* and other wine vessels appeared at this time. The forms most often found in large scale are the *zun* with a shoulder, the *lei,* the *pou,* and the *jia,* and most such large vessels are of the Early Yin period. Wine vessels predominate among the ritual bronze vessels. The shapes of the vessels evolved from the thin, simple, and lightweight style of the Early Shang period to a heavy, severe style that gives the vessels a ponderous, imposing feeling.

TABLE 1

THE ANYANG KINGS

Periods	Generations	
I	1	Pan Geng—Xiao Xin—Xiao Yi
II	2	Wu Ding
	3	Zu Geng—Zu Jia
III	4	Lin Xin—Kang Ding
	5	Wu Yi
	6	Wen Ding
IV	7	Di Yi
	8	Di Xin

The bronze industry of the Middle Yin period was extremely well developed, and casting techniques were fully refined. The casting of wine vessels was especially outstanding. The bird-shaped or bird-and-animal-shaped *zun* and *guang*, which cleverly combined the forms of animals with the utilitarian requirements of the vessel, appeared in the Middle Yin (see nos. 29, 30). *Fang yi* were also abundant in this period, and even the old shapes underwent revision, especially the *zun* and the *lei*. The most important cooking vessel of this period, the *ding*, grew more ample, and the three-lobed *li ding* was added to the repertoire. The *fang ding* was especially favored by the Yin royal house in the Middle Yin period, and examples range from the ox and deer *fang ding* to the monumental Si Mu Mou *fang ding*, which weighs 875 kilograms, stands 133 centimeters tall, and is the largest example of the Shang period. The Si Mu Mou *fang ding* can be dated to the end of the Middle Yin period since it bears an inscription offering sacrifice from King Wen Ding to his mother. Another *fang ding*, the Si Mu Xin from Yinxu, is, at 79.6 centimeters, the largest *fang ding* to have been excavated at Yinxu since the founding of New China (no. 28).

In the Late Yin period, wine vessels were still important, with the *jue, gu,* cylindrical *zun* with trumpet mouth, and the *you* with handle being exceptionally common. They seem to have replaced the earlier wide-mouthed, oval-bodied *hu* and the *zun* with shoulders. Most of the vessel forms of the Middle Yin period continued in use in the Late Yin period with modifications only in minor details of design. This was also true with the food vessels, of which the most common were the round-mouthed, straight-bodied *ding* with animal legs (e.g., no. 32), and the two-handled *gui*.

Because bronze ritual vessels reflected the relative status of their users, we would expect to find several different combinations of forms that would represent different ranks within the elite class. Unfortunately, the severe damage sustained by burial sites over the centuries has meant that very few complete sets of ritual vessels have remained intact. The fragmentary nature of the evidence has posed real difficulties for research in bronze studies. Tomb 5 at Yinxu, found in 1976, was the first complete tomb discovered since excavations began there (nos. 28–40). Among the sets of ritual vessels found in the tomb were *ding, fang ding, xian, gui,* double *fang yi, fang yi,* bird-shaped *zun, guang,* four-legged animal-shaped *guang, hu, fang hu,* flattened *hu, pou, fou, jia, fang jia, he, jue, gu,* and *fang gu*—a total, not counting fragments, of 217 vessels in 21 forms. Among them were 40 food vessels and three times as many—117 or more—wine vessels. The *jue* and *gu* accounted for 90 of the wine vessels. This inventory tells us something about the character of the ritual vessels, primarily, that wine vessels played the dominant role. Among the food vessels the *ding* were the most important, numbering more than thirty-seven, including three large, twelve medium-size, and seven small round *ding*. Only five *gui*, food storage vessels, were found, and each has a different shape. In fact, a general characteristic of the Yin ritual vessels is that the wine vessels are more uniform in shape than the food vessels.

The actual date of Tomb 5 is now the object of much discussion. About half of the 210 vessels found in the tomb bear the name of Fu Hao, a consort of a Shang king. In the oracle bones of the Wu Ding period, many records tell of the activities of a Fu Hao, an able woman who even led armies into battle. The Fu Hao of Tomb 5 is generally thought to have been the Fu Hao of Wu Ding's court, but certain evidence calls the attribution into question. Besides the bronzes with early characteristics are many that have later forms and kinds of decoration. Furthermore, the period IV oracle bones mention a Fu Hao, giving rise to another school of opinion that holds that the bronzes are from the Wu Yi to Wen Ding reigns of period III.[13] All theories on the date of the Fu Hao tomb agree that it falls within the Middle Yin period, but a more specific date in the early or late part of the period has yet to be determined.

With the Yinxu bronzes, the Bronze Age decor reached its peak. In addition to the animal mask, which continued as the principal motif, there were introduced many strange, beautiful decorative motifs. After the Yin kings established their capital at Anyang, bronze art developed rapidly. Not only did many new vessel forms appear, but the overall appearance of the decoration also greatly changed. A single animal mask in the Early Shang period was crude and simple, with little variety from vessel to vessel, and little impact of expression. In the Early Yinxu period, the style underwent great change to become a minutely detailed, bold decor organized in a system of strict symmetry (see colorplate, detail, no. 32). The *leiwen* or *huiwen* (dense spiral pattern) assumed a more important position. At the same time, knife-sharp lines arranged neatly together became an alternating element with the *leiwen*, thus giving the motionless decor a feeling of rhythmic movement. The two eyes on either side of the center became more prominent, disproportionately large for the size of the mask. On the three-ram *lei* in the Palace Museum, Beijing (no. 14), the eyes were enlarged so that they stare fixedly at the viewer, as if focusing the maximum amount of power in the expression of mystery (Fig. 2). The feeling is of both peace and fierceness: the peaceful quality inspiring reverence, the fierce aspect awe—the very social effects that the decoration was designed to achieve. The style can be seen not only on Shang bronzes, but also on other objects, such as white pottery and carved bones. The Shang slave-master elite worshiped the spirits with fanatic zeal, and the consciousness of the society was permeated with reverence for and delusions of the superhuman forces of nature. The oracle bone inscriptions make it clear that the Shang believed that natural forces could have either a beneficial or disastrous effect on society and that they dominated human thought and action. Essentially, any myth is a metaphor for the conquest of nature or a concrete interpretation of the imaginary forces of nature. This sensibility undoubtedly dominated Shang art. The bronze decoration characterized by the animal-mask motif is a description and a pictorialization of such imagined forces of nature. The principal motifs, such as the dragon and the phoenix, are symbolic, representing such ideas as those recorded in the *Kaogongji* of the fifth century B.C.: "Water by the dragon, mountains by the roebuck, fire by the circle." This is the earliest documentation of the pairing of natural forces with types of decoration. Although the *Kaogongji*, a record concerning building and crafts from the state of Qi, dates to the late Spring and Autumn period, this kind of thinking originated in antiquity. The dragon was the water spirit, and traditional myths report that Yu of the Xia used a dragon's tail to furrow the land and so control the waters. The roebuck was the mountain spirit, and the circle the fire spirit. Circular forms in bronze decoration were formerly called "whorls" (see Fig. 5), but they are actually a pictorialization of the graph ⊠ , meaning "brightness of fire." When spoken rapidly, this graph and the name of the fire spirit Zhurong sound the same. According to oracle bone inscriptions and ancient texts, the phoenix was the wind spirit. Toads, which also appear on bronze decor, were moon spirits in the old myths and illustrate the power of imaginary beings to take on real forms. Merely to explain the significance of this kind of decoration is extremely difficult; to understand it completely is impossible. In general, these images are primeval conceptions that suggest the barbaric. As decor they are straightforward, unconcealed, and intense.

In the Middle Yin period, the animal-mask motif developed still further, and several new types were added to the standard form. Some were based on the heads of real animals, such as tigers, bears, oxen, and rams; some are fantastic composite beasts, such as the dragon and the *kui* dragon. Although the tiger, bear, and ox were based on real animals, they were not rendered realistically. The rams on the four-ram *zun* (no. 20) certainly do not resemble tame animals, and the ox-head decoration on other vessels, moreover, is especially savage-looking. The bronze artisans have endowed this ordinary animal with an aura of mystery. Even more numerous are the many composite animals, made from special features of different animals to form a new, imaginary one. An animal mask could have several kinds of horns, some even in the form of snakes. Dragons and *kui* dragons of the Middle Yin bronzes have a snake or lizard head with ox or other kind of horns. On the dragons of the four-ram *zun* (no. 20) a pair of bottle horns is mounted on the triangular area of the head of a poisonous snake, signifying its special nature. These are but a few of the types of composite animals, which manifest the variety and richness of the mythological imagination.

Another feature of Middle Yin bronze vessels that has gained attention is the introduction into the repertoire at this time of groups of animals as decoration. An average vessel of this kind had five or six types of animals, with a maximum of ten or so animals on a single vessel. Eventually, the bronze artist cleverly filled every part of the vessel with animal groups, sometimes even covering the bottom of the vessel. Clearly, therefore, bronze decoration initially was not applied purely for its beauty. Such groups had their origin in the Early Shang period. Some of the shouldered *zun* have as many as three or four types of decoration, but this rare combination can be seen only on large vessels. The mode did not become common until the Yin culture, especially the Middle Yin period, when small as well as large vessels carried dense animal-group decoration, as on the four-ram *zun* (no. 20) and the elephant *zun* (no. 24).

For the origins of this special approach to decoration, we have no documentary sources on which to rely, though a story recorded in the *Zuo Zhuan* offers some inspiration. When King Zhuang of Chu was on campaign against the Rong barbarians in Luhun, it says, he camped near Luoyi and reviewed his troops as a show of strength. Encountering an old military commander

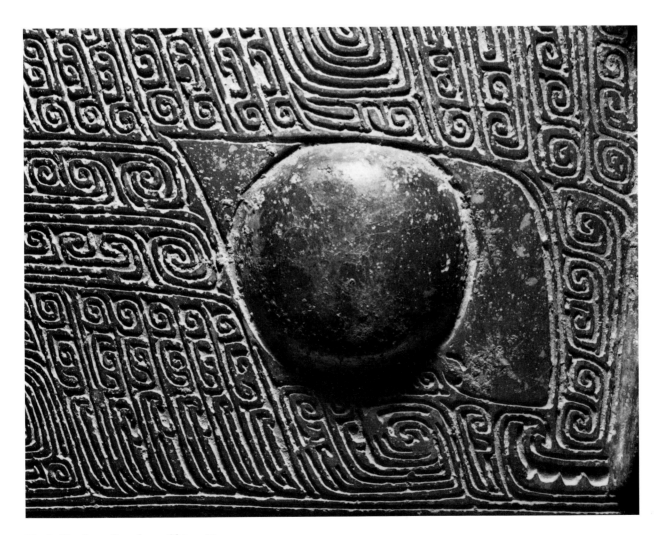

Fig. 2   Detail, eye from decor of *lei* no. 14

of the Zhou king Ding, he asked him the weight and sizes of the nine *ding* used as a symbol of royal power. An insult to the Zhou royal house, the question signified that the king of Chu coveted the royal power. The nine *ding* were said to have been cast by Yu of the Xia and were a treasure handed down from the Xia to the Shang to the Zhou. The commander replied with these words:

> Anciently, when the Xia rulers were the inheritors of virtues, creatures of distant regions were depicted. The metals of the nine provinces were used to cast tripods with representations of these creatures on them. All the myriad creatures were represented to teach the people about spirits and evil forces. Thus, the people, when they went among the rivers, marshes, hills, and forests did not meet with injurious things, and the spirits of the hills, monstrous things, and water spirits did not meet with the people [to do them injury].[14]

The creatures represented on the *ding* were thus the spirits of distant mountains, streams, and other forms of nature. Each was responsible for some aspect of the natural spirits. Like a shamanistic talisman the decoration could avert evil and attract good fortune. While the historical existence of the nine *ding* of Yu cannot of course be proven or disproven, the story of casting animals on the *ding* is known at least from the early Zhou period, when the nine *ding* were transferred to Zhou after the conquest of the Shang. To identify the creatures of the nine *ding* story with the many animals on Shang bronzes and to identify them as nature spirits brings the bronzes before us to life. Since the bronzes of the Erlitou culture bear only a few kinds of simple decoration (e.g., no. 1), it seems unlikely that the artisans of that time had reached the necessary level of accomplishment to produce designs as complicated as those related in the tale. The story does show, however, that the customs of the Shang were closely related to their bronze decor. The phrase, "All the myriad creatures were represented" is a hyperbolic description of the elaborateness of the decoration. The most complicated animal designs on Yinxu bronzes show that these words were not exaggerated.

The decoration of the Late Yin bronzes continued in the style of the Middle Yin. A few innovations in decoration appeared, such as the curling *kui* dragon and several kinds of birds. In casting, the handling of relief became generally thicker and less severe. In comparison with fully decorated vessels of this period, those with no ground patterns appear simple and clean. With the exception of a few bronzes, the carving of most vessel decoration was not as fine as it had been previously, as if the prolific spirit had achieved its peak and had lost momentum.

Cast inscriptions appeared on most Middle Yin period bronzes, but they were very simple, sometimes consisting of the clan name of the owner or of the name of the deceased used in the sacrifices with the vessel, such as Fu Yi and Mu Xin (nos. 28, 29, 46). In the late period, longer inscriptions with texts that narrate historical events appeared, but these are rare. With their terse inscriptions, the Shang vessels contrast strongly with those of the Zhou, who delighted in placing lengthy records of events on their ritual vessels. This indirectly reflects the differences between Shang and Zhou ritual vessels.

The bronze art of the Yin period is one of the most outstanding achievements of the Xia and Shang cultures. Given the particular characteristics of the period and its historical position, the quality is almost peerless.

Casting Problems of Shang Dynasty Bronze Vessels

The first step in bronze casting is to open a mine and refine the ore. The quality of copper ore in China was generally not very high, and if the copper in Shang bronzes had been refined at the foundry, a great deal of slag would remain. So far no trace of copper or smelting has yet been found among the remains of Shang dynasty casting sites, indicating that the refining was most likely carried out at the mine.

Scholars both inside and outside China have proposed theories about ancient copper mining and smelting for many years, basing their research for the most part on historical records. Until recently, no concrete evidence had been found and not one ancient mine had been discovered. However, a discovery of this kind was finally made in 1974, when an ancient mine of enormous scale was found in the mining district of Daye, Hubei Province, at Tonglüshan.[15] The mine is several dozen meters beneath the mountaintop and contains many vertical shafts and horizontal tunnels. The method of mining was to dig a vertical shaft down to the lowest part of the deposit, then to follow veins of ore, excavating tunnels and extracting the ore. After the ore was within the tunnel, it was passed up through the shaft to the ground level. Since tunnels were excavated from bottom to top, the discarded earth and rubble from the upper levels could be deposited in the tunnels on the lower level. This method not only increased the speed of mining, but also the safety of production. The varying levels of the tunnels resulted in air flowing along the passageways. Wooden supports were used throughout the tunnels; the earliest frameworks could accommodate only a single miner crawling into the mine, while during the Iron Age the shafts were enlarged so that a person of medium height could enter upright. In an excellently preserved early area of the mine, mining implements of bronze and wood including wooden gondolas and buckets used in removing the ore, were found. According to estimations, the oldest section of the mine is not later than the Spring and Autumn period. Ancient mines were often in operation for many years, during which time the skills varied and the depth of mining changed. Iron implements of the Han period excavated from the old Tonglüshan mine show that it continued in use until the Han dynasty.

The initial work of refining the ore of the old Tonglüshan mine was carried out at the site. The entire mountainside is wasted, and slag from the refining process is piled up to an estimated weight of 360,000 metric tons. Also discovered were substantial numbers of abandoned refining furnaces; research toward the reconstruction of furnaces is now in progress. The discovery of the ancient mine at Tonglüshan opens a new area for Chinese bronze-casting research.

In the early Shang dynasty fairly large-scale workshops for the bronze-casting industry were already in existence. At Nanguanwai and Zijingshan, near Zhengzhou, remains of early Shang bronze vessel casting were found along with a quantity of ceramic molds.[16] A significant aspect of this find was the large number of molds for tools in contrast to a small number of molds for ritual implements, indicating that tools for production and farming predominated. Indeed, these bronze tools and farming implements are indicators of the development of the forces of production of Bronze Age China. Traces of many cast-bronze vessels have been found within the Yinxu environs, and the largest foundry remains, excavated at Yinxu, covered 5,000 square meters and yielded numerous cast-bronze objects.[17] Many unearthed relics verify that in casting Shang dynasty bronze objects ceramic piece molds were used. Based on extensive research on ceramic molds, we can outline the piece-mold process. First, a model of the bronze vessel to be cast was sculpted from high quality clay. Then, following the necessary divisions, pieces of molds were pressed onto the surface of the model. Mortises and tenons were made on the pieces of the mold to join them. The broad design of the decor was carved on the model and transferred to the mold, on which the finer details were added. Thereafter, a surface layer was shaved from the clay model. The portion removed would exactly represent the thickness of the cast-bronze vessel, and the remaining clay model became the inner core. After the outer and inner parts of the clay model assembly were dried, they were fired to form ceramic molds. The bronze casters had only to join the pieces of the mold together according to the fit of the mortises and tenons. Then the molten bronze could be poured into a hole left for that purpose. When the bronze was cool, the mold was removed and with some filing and polishing the bronze vessel became an excellent cast-bronze object. The greatest advantage of casting bronze vessels with ceramic piece molds lies in the superb clarity that one can achieve on the cast article; ceramic molds are capable of reproducing exquisite craftsmanship and delicate precision. Because the pottery molds were porous, the air bubbles produced when the molten bronze did not flow smoothly were reduced to a minimum, and the quality of casting was kept high.

Ancient bronze objects from Europe were cast by the lost-wax method, in which wax was used to build a model, which was then surrounded with clay. When the clay was fired, the wax melted and flowed out, leaving hollow the form to be cast. Molten metal was poured into this mold to produce the object. This method emerged in China rather late: according to excavated evidence, objects cast by the lost-wax method began to appear during the transition from the Spring and Autumn to the Warring States periods. But during the Shang and Zhou dynasties the piece-mold technique was the major method, and one that became quite sophisticated. On most Shang and Zhou bronze objects, the seams where the pottery molds were joined are visible to a greater or lesser extent; if the pieces were slightly out of position, the less-than-tight fit caused irregularities at the joins which allowed seams to form during the casting process. Recently, molds for tools made of sandstone have been found among the Shang period remains unearthed at Qingjiang, Jiangxi Province. The special sandstone of Jiangxi is relatively porous and can be substituted for clay, but sandstone is not so good as clay for moldmaking. Moreover, sandstone is not available everywhere, so casting with sandstone molds did not become widespread.

Western Zhou

In the eleventh century B.C., King Wu of the Zhou took advantage of the favorable opportunity presented by the absence of the Yin king Zhou's main military force, which was in the southeast attacking the Yi people. He united the tribes who were discontented with the rule of the Yin king Zhou and invaded the Yin subsidiary capital Zhaoge. The hastily formed defensive force, primarily slaves impressed into service, quickly joined the attackers. The defeat of King Zhou's soldiers and his self-immolation brought to an end the authority of the Shang slave-owning royal house, the longest dynasty in Chinese history. King Wu of Zhou founded the Zhou dynasty.

On the substantial foundation inherited from Shang culture, the culture of the Zhou people grew in vigor, and Chinese slave society reached its height during this period. In the development of the bronze art, Western Zhou can be divided broadly into early, middle, and late periods. The early period extends from the reigns of King Wu to King Zhao; the middle period covers approximately the reigns of King Mu through King Xiao; and the late period roughly the reigns of King Yi through King You.

The early Western Zhou period began in the early eleventh century B.C. and lasted four generations, for close to one hundred years. Both in shape and in decoration, the character of bronze vessels during this period remained fundamentally the same as the later Shang. In fact, some vessels of the Shang and Zhou eras, especially the early Zhou, cannot be differentiated as to date. The reason for this is that the Zhou people were an agricultural tribe from western China who rose to power only during the last decades of the Yin period. Their cultural development was consequently not substantial, and their bronze craftsmanship had not advanced sufficiently to permit them to form their own distinct style. The breadth and depth of Shang bronze cultural influence was unprecedented. Sites at the center of Zhou territory before the conquest, such as the Qishan district on the Zhou plain and the Wei River valley, have yielded bronze vessels of the early Shang, early Yinxu, and middle Yinxu styles.[18] To the Zhou people these few bronzes were the most precious of objects. After King Wu of the Zhou conquered the Shang, he acquired bronze-casting slave artisans—craftsmen whose traditional skills had been handed down for generations.

Although bronze vessels were still cast by the same method, there were fundamental changes in the relative proportions of ritual bronze vessel types. We know that wine vessels still constituted the largest portion of the vessels at the end of the Yin period, far outnumbering food vessels. During the early Western Zhou this proportion was exactly reversed. Many more *ding* (cooking tripods) and *gui* (food storage vessels) were found than wine vessels, probably as the result of changing customs and politics. Texts by Zhou kings often mention that the Shang king Zhou "debauched and indulged in atrocities.... Everyone was drunk and the stench could be smelled above. Heaven visited misfortune upon the Yin."[19] The inscription on the Da Yu *ding*, made during the reign of King Kang, says, "I have heard that when Yin lost the Mandate [of Heaven] it was only because the Lords on the borders of Yin and those at court indulged in drunkenness and therefore lost their army." Zhou proclamations clearly stipulated that if officials of the Zhou house met in drinking bouts, they would be punished by death, and the Zhou responded to the reports of Yin drunkenness with nothing but exhortations.[20] Clearly, the politically inspired prohibitions of the Zhou against group drinking resulted in the radically decreased number of ritual wine vessels. The Zhou certainly did not oppose proper banquets and drinking per se, nor the use of wine as a sacrifice to the ancestors, but types of vessels for wine were restricted, perhaps as a demonstration of "holding the failings of the Yin as a warning."

During the Shang dynasty the *jue* and the *gu* were the most frequently encountered of the wine vessels, but in the Zhou their percentage rapidly diminished. In the early Zhou the most common wine vessels were the *zun*, *you*, *hu*, and *zhi*. Most of the *zun* popular during the early Western Zhou period were of the late Yin style, with a tall round foot, a cylindrical body, and a flaring trumpetlike mouth. But the He *zun* (no. 42), with its high projecting flanges and imposing form, can be said to represent the character of the bronze art of the Zhou. The bronze *you* is the most frequently encountered wine vessel of the early Zhou (see no. 50). The form of Yinxu *you* vessels, ordinarily a flattened oval in section, evolved by the early Zhou to an elliptical vessel. In the Yin and Zhou periods, the cylindrical-bodied *you*, such as the Luan Bo *you* (no. 43), is rare: the period of popularity of this type seems to have been brief. Bird and animal *you*, *zun*, and *guang* (no. 45) were still manufactured, all modeled on the Yin style, with some modifications.

The Western Zhou aristocracy made lavish displays of bronzes in their ancestral temples. In the last thirty years, enormous bronze *ding*—the most important of Zhou vessels—have been discovered in Shaanxi Province (no. 52), and many *fang ding* have also been uncovered.[21]

During the early Western Zhou more *gui* were made than other food vessels, and, of the early Zhou vessels, the *gui* saw the greatest changes and developed the most special characteristics. Although the basic features of the *gui* persisted, one development occurred that strengthened the form: the bottoms of the two handles were extended to become long earlobes. Besides the double-handled *gui* was a four-handled version of the type, a complete departure from the repertoire of the late Shang period, but a form that became ubiquitous in the early Zhou. Another invention was the extension of the lobes of the four handles of this type to form four supports and eliminate the round foot, leaving the bottom of the bowl suspended (no. 57). Three-handled *gui* have also been discovered. On other early Zhou *gui*, as early as the reign of King Wu, a square pedestal was added to the round foot. Cast only shortly after the conquest of the Shang by King Wu, the Li *gui* (no. 41) bears an inscription that records the event. The Li *gui* has a pedestal, as does the Tian Wang *gui* (the Da Feng *gui*), also of the reign of King Wu. The pedestaled *gui* marks an important step in the development of Zhou culture. Originally, the *gui* vessels were probably placed on a square base, not cast of bronze onto the base of the *gui* but made of wood or some other perishable material.[22] Two-handled *gui* with pedestals are the most common, but some pedestaled *gui* have four handles.

The *yu* type of vessel was not first made by the Zhou. They are occasionally discovered among Shang vessels, but they reached their height of popularity in the Western Zhou period. The *yu* is a large food container with a flared mouth, straight or slightly slanted sides that descend to a round foot, and two handles. The handles are essential, since the largest of these relatively large vessels must be lifted by two people. The Yan Hou *yu* (no. 53) is medium size. The *yu*, which held cooked millet, was probably used as a set with the *gui*, which held uncooked millet, although the large *yu* are often found alone. The capacity of one *yu* vessel is several to ten times greater than that of a *gui*.

Beginning in the middle of the Western Zhou period, the art of bronze vessels gradually changed. Vessel forms no longer strive for beauty, but are straightforward and ordinary in their features rather than unusual.

After the first one hundred years of the early Western Zhou period, the Zhou finally assimilated the bronze art of the Shang; and through transformation and development the special characteristics of the Zhou culture emerged. Among the food vessels, the *ding* showed variations in form, like the shallow-basin *ding* and the shallow *ding* with a constricted waist. The *fang ding* so prevalent in the early period declined in popularity, but the *li* food vessel continued to make new advances and its use continued to increase. While for the most part the *gui* vessels continued in the style of the early period, a new type of *gui* emerged, with no constricted rim at the lip, a lid, and a short round foot—a contrast to the high round foot type of the early period. Above the round foot there are often three short animal feet. The pair of handles are in the form of animals or rings. This type of *gui* flourished through the late Western Zhou into the Spring and Autumn era, and was the final stylistic development of the bronze *gui*. Shortly after the middle of the Western Zhou, the *xu* vessel emerged. The *xu* is a rectangular vessel with rounded corners used for holding grain. Its lid can be inverted to function as a food bowl. The early vessels of this type are called *gui* in their inscriptions; and the *xu* is probably a modification of the *gui*. In the late Western Zhou the *fu*, a rectangular vessel with slightly slanting sides and identical top and bottom, was popular (no. 63). It was usually used for food but also for grain storage.

Although the *fang yi* and *zun* persisted, the *hu* became the most important wine vessel of the middle Western Zhou period. Most bronze *guang* were used as wine-mixing vessels, and at this time inscriptions on *guang* refer to them as *he*,[23] a vessel used for diluting wine with water. After the middle Western Zhou period, the *guang* came to be used as a water vessel, and its name was changed to *yi*. It was paired with the *pan* basin, and together they served as vessels for ablutions during rituals.

The bronze ritual vessels of the middle Western Zhou period tended to be simple, and their style direct and straightforward. New creations in bronze musical instruments also appeared. All bronze musical instruments of the Shang and Zhou were percussive. In the Shang there were two kinds of percussive musical instruments: one was a set formed by three oval-shaped bells of graduated size called *nao*, which were held by a handle and have a light and clear tone when struck. In Tomb No. 5 at Yinxu near Anyang a set of five *nao* bells were found, marking an advance in musical possibilities. Most large *nao* bells have been found singly; perhaps they were used to strike a note for pitch. The second kind were the *zhong* bells which were also oval in shape (nos. 77–90). When *nao* and *zhong* bells are struck, the vibration pattern of the primary frequency is produced around the curved rim of the bell. The secondary frequency is produced along the narrow areas on the sides of the bell and is higher than the primary frequency. In every set of bells it is possible to produce two sets of musical tones. Thus, three *nao* bells would produce six tones. On the basis of the development of the *nao* bell sets, *bianzhong* (sets of graduated *zhong* bells) emerged during the middle Western Zhou period. This type of graduated bronze bell set is suspended from a frame and struck. In 1954, in a small Western Zhou tomb at Puducun, Chang'an, Shaanxi Province, a set of three *bianzhong* were discovered for the first time. This tomb dates to the middle of the Western Zhou period.[24] In 1975 at Fufeng, Shaanxi, among a cache of bronze objects of the Wei clan five remnants of five sets of Wei Xing *bianzhong* were found. Of the fourteen bells the Zha *zhong* set of eight is the most complete.[25] It too is incomplete, however, for at the very least a set should have nine bells. According to our tests of the frequencies of many Western Zhou *zhong* bells, each bell has two frequencies—one at the rim and a second at the middle of the bell. The relationship of the two frequencies is for the most part either three steps higher or lower. Therefore, if a set of Western Zhou *bianzhong* had nine or more bells, it would have eighteen musical notes, which would be a more than adequate number for performing relatively sophisticated musical compositions. Without a doubt these discoveries represent great progress in the music of antiquity.

The artistic decor of Western Zhou bronze vessels forms a striking contrast to that of the Yinxu bronzes. The bronze art of the early Western Zhou was fundamentally a continuation of the Shang period with some modifications. The use of bird designs in the decor was increased; dense patterning of the entire vessel surface was done less often; and composite masses of repeated animal designs were used less frequently. Judging from the research materials presently at hand, the great change began in the reign of the Zhou king Mu. Beginning in that reign, designs became more and more simplified until they flowed together in a continuous band of decor. There are obvious changes in the decor on several representative vessels of that period, specifically, the great simplification or transformation of the animal mask and of animal designs. The basic elements of the animal mask dissolved and became unrecognizable dismembered forms. The eye of the animal disintegrated, and its feeling of solemnity and mystery were lost. Designs like the *kui* dragon and elephant masks became paired, and the entire bodies are no longer shown. Symbolic eyes appear between the animal decor, indicating that these patterns are still zoomorphic. Traditionally, scholars of ancient bronze vessels and epigraphy called these kinds of dramatic transformations *qie qu wen* or *qiong qu wen* (curved patterns). From the point of view of design development it was a new compositional device. The band design was created from a coiled dragon with two tails: the heads of the two-tailed dragon were eliminated, the tails linked together, and the empty space in the middle of the coil enlarged (see, e.g., Fig. 86). The so-called double register pattern, which is clearly evolved from the bodies of dragons and snakes, also appeared in the middle and late Western Zhou period.

Social change caused the Zhou bronze style to evolve away from the Shang. The bronze art that the Zhou inherited from the Yin was permeated with somber religious meaning. Although the Heavenly Mandate was central to the religious thought of both the Shang and Zhou, the Shang worshiped ancestors and reverenced spirits to a fanatical degree. While the Zhou were ardent in the worship of ancestors, they were not as zealous as the Shang in the worship of ghosts and spiritual forces, in accord with the precept of Confucius: "Respect ghosts and spirits but keep them at a distance." Likewise, the Zhou could not completely accept Shang bronze tradition, because it was so strongly determined by religion. While the Zhou bronze ritual vessels upheld the status system and religious thought, they did not emphasize beautiful decoration. According to the inscriptions, most of the vessels were made to commemorate an event or to record a merit to be reported to the ancestors by sacrifice—thus boasting of the glory of their slave-owning hereditary house. All aristocrats were members of a clan, and relations within clans were controlled by clan law, which emphasized the right of inheritance by the eldest son of the principal wife. Legally, the head of the clan was the member who had the right to sacrifice to the ancestors, since the conducting of sacrifices was an expression of power and position. A noble clan with the same ancestor could divide into many branches, and these branches could again divide into individual extended families. Within the clan both the position and power of important individuals were intimately related to their hereditary house, and sacrifice to a father or ancestor was therefore extremely important to the Zhou. When the individual aristocrat reported to his ancestors in an inscription cast in a *ding*, he upheld the position and power of his hereditary house, as well as his own prestige and power. The Zhou recorded on bronze vessels many important historical events relating to the politics, military affairs, economy, and every sort of institutional system and activity of the nobility of the time. The large amount of detailed information contained in the inscriptions makes them especially valuable in the investigation of ancient history.

Even as art objects the inscriptions are important, because they show the early manifestations of what was to become the unique art of Chinese calligraphy. Beginning with the script on oracle bones of the Shang period, calligraphy grew as a special art form. From the time when relatively long inscriptions began to appear in the late Shang period, bronze inscriptions came into their own as calligraphic expressions. China's calligraphic art stresses the composition of the entire inscription, as well as the formal beauty and stylistic variety of individual characters. In the bronze inscriptions of the period between the Shang and Zhou dynasties, these elements are already present. By the middle Western Zhou period, bronze inscriptions were already fairly mature examples of calligraphic art. Bold and wavelike, round and smooth, or simple and bold, the elegant script developed in a variety of styles. As precursors of Chinese calligraphy, the Western Zhou inscriptions have been praised to the present day.

Spring and Autumn and Warring States Periods

As the slave society of China passed through the long development of the three dynasties of Xia, Shang, and Zhou, it generated unresolvable internal contradictions; the relations of production severely blocked the development of the forces of production. As a result of the long period of disruption, the populace came to distrust both the Mandate of Heaven and the authority of the king. Sharp ethnic contradictions of the late Western Zhou period resulted in the assassination of King You, who was attacked by the Quan Rong barbarians beneath Mount Li. After this, the Zhou could no longer maintain political control over their territory. In 770 B.C., when the rule of the dynasty had in fact already collapsed, King Ping moved the Zhou capital east to Luoyang. This marked the beginning of the period of struggle for hegemony between the great states and feudal lords, which is known as the Spring and Autumn period.

In the late Western Zhou bronze art reached a plateau of development and in the early Spring and Autumn period it began to decline. No new social conditions arose to stimulate a new style, and bronze vessels continued to repeat the style of the late Western Zhou, both in shapes and in decor. A detailed description of the bronzes of this period is therefore unnecessary; the only real change in Spring and Autumn period bronzes was in the identity of those who commissioned them. Since the political and cultural center of the Western Zhou was in the court of the king, most bronze vessels of the Western Zhou period were ordered by the king and his ministers. Bronze vessels reflect the collapse of the centralized royal power and the struggle for hegemony by feudal lords; most of the Spring and Autumn period vessels were manufactured for feudal lords and their high officials. In the Spring and Autumn period the feudal lords of every locality sponsored bronze workshops that manufactured vessels, including some rather large examples. Although the art of making bronzes was stagnant, the bronze-casting industry was gaining a wider distribution, preparing an essential foundation for the revival of bronze art under new social conditions.

Eventually the slave system deteriorated, and feudal relations of production were gradually brought about by the new forces of production. The state ownership of land in the slave period was eliminated. Land was bought and sold, more land came into private ownership, and the slaves who worked the land became serfs. In this new system, the level of productivity rose greatly. All feudal states had to conform to the developing system of private land ownership. In 594 B.C. the state of Lu instituted the "first tax the *mou* [1,347 m.^{2}]" system.[26] The state fixed the amount of taxes to be collected from private landowners, thus formally recognizing the private ownership of land. Feudal relations of production, that is, the system of renting land to tenant farmers, became widespread, and the advance in productive relations in agriculture rapidly advanced the agricultural economy. With this new foundation, a new handicraft industry began to flourish successively in each feudal state. We can see by examination of the great number of archaeological remains that, at least by the second half of the sixth century B.C., there was a great improvement in craftsmanship over the earlier part of the period. As the slave system gradually evolved into the feudal system in political, economic, and cultural spheres, the technique of forging iron was discovered and China entered the Iron Age.[27] The arrival of the Iron Age did not mean the immediate decline of the bronze-casting industry, however. On the contrary, the development of productive forces in the late Spring and Autumn period stimulated all aspects of craft production, bronze art among them.

Progress in bronze casting was aided by great advances in technique. The method of casting separate pieces onto an object made the work of casting complicated forms simpler, and improvements in the quality of clay molds permitted a new level of precision in the pouring of bronze vessels. It can be stated without exaggeration that it was entirely possible during this period to cast a large surface area with crisp patterns and hairline details, a level of quality that can be observed in some of the most ordinary of bronze objects.

Modern chemical analysis shows that in the late Spring and Autumn period extremely effective advances also occurred in the composition of the bronze alloy, which had previously been made up of all sorts of dissimilar proportions, each with its special features. By steadily improving the viscosity of the molten metal so that it more closely adhered to the clay mold, the bronze caster raised the quality of his product. New techniques for casting together metals of different composition also appeared. In Gou Jian's sword, for instance, the beautiful decorative pattern on the body of the sword is shown by chemical analysis to be high in tin and lead, but with a small amount of iron cast together with the bronze.[28] The precise details of this technology are currently under investigation. In a new type of inlay casting a bronze inlay relatively low in tin, and therefore relatively soft, was cast onto a bronze weapon relatively high in tin, and therefore relatively hard, to improve its flexibility, making it less breakable and consequently of higher quality.

Finally, as late as the transition between the Spring and Autumn and Warring States periods, the lost-wax technique came into regular use. In Sui Xian, Hubei Province, in 1978, a group of bronzes was discovered in the tomb of the marquis of Zeng (Fig. 89). Some were made in the lost-wax technique, others of a combination of lost-wax and piece-mold techniques. Their complicated decor is awe-inspiring and leads one to the conclusion that an art so mature must have had its origins at least slightly earlier than the fifth-century date of the tomb.

Besides the various casting techniques described above, bronze casters of the Spring and Autumn and Warring States periods had at their disposal such new finishing processes as welding and riveting. In the tomb of the marquis of Zeng and in the tombs of the Zhongshan

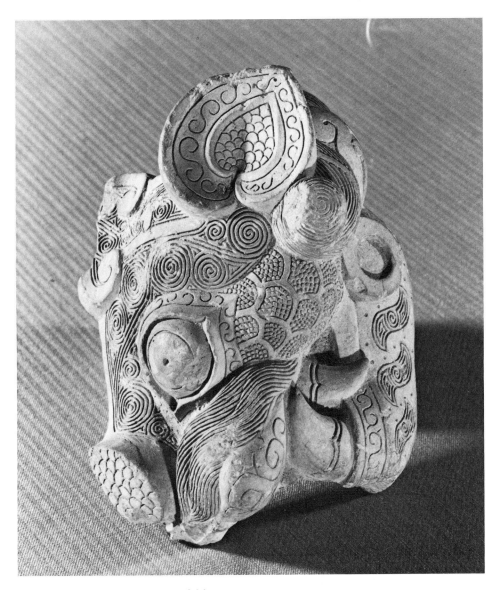

Fig. 3 Fragment of a clay casting model from
ancient bronze foundry at Houma,
Shanxi Province. Photograph courtesy
of Cultural Relics Bureau, Beijing

kings in Pingshan, Hebei,[29] some extremely fine bronze objects using high quality welding and riveting techniques have been found (no. 92).

On the whole, however, the bronze vessels of the late Spring and Autumn and Warring States periods were still cast with the piece-mold technique, by this time greatly improved. Among the remains of an enormous bronze foundry of the state of Jin, at Houma, Shanxi Province—under excavation since 1959—have been unearthed tens of thousands of clay molds, along with some master models (Figs. 3, 91–93). More than one hundred of the clay molds could be completely reassembled. These clay molds are a great discovery, unprecedented in the history of metallurgy, providing valuable material for the study of late Spring and Autumn piece-mold casting.

In the late Spring and Autumn period, bronze vessels were used less often for ritual observances and more often for practical concerns. Because ritual vessels reflected the class system of slave society and because the decaying social system was in the process of collapse, the so-called ritual vessels simply preserved their names but no longer served the same social function. Freed from the constraints of old regulations, bronze artisans attempted many new vessel forms and types of decoration, vying for novelty. Replacing the old slave-owning aristocracy as the ruling class was the newly risen landlord class, which avidly pursued the enjoyment of life and used great quantities of fine bronze vessels. While the feudal lords fought incessantly for supremacy among themselves, bronze art became increasingly more refined. Although inspired on one hand by the needs of the ruling class, the advances in bronze art also reflect the development of the forces of production. The sixty-four bells unearthed from the early Warring States tomb of the marquis of Zeng required 2,500 kilograms of bronze. The same tomb yielded large, exquisite bronze wine vessels and a number of other bronze vessels, a remarkable output for a state as small as Zeng. The magnitude of a project like the manufacture of the Zeng bells reveals the hidden strength of the development of production, which was albeit subservient to a small ruling class.

The era also produced a rich variety of complex bronze vessel forms, from types revived from earlier times to new types that appeared constantly as a result of the lifting of restrictions. So many vessel shapes were created that it is difficult to name them all. Most of them are vessels of daily life, not sacrificial vessels meant to be arrayed in ancestral halls. The number of weapons cast was extremely large, and mirrors, belt hooks, and even more mundane items were cast in bronze.

The new developments in bronze art of this period can be measured not only chronologically, but geographically, in the large range of regional variations and innovations. *Ding* vessels, for example, were generally made with short feet, round bodies, and lids in the three Jin (i.e., the Han, Wei, and Zhao territories), but with tall feet in the state of Chu. Some areas produced special shapes unknown in the other regions. In 1923 a group of late Spring and Autumn bronze vessels with rarely seen forms and decor was unearthed in Liyu, Hunyuan, Shanxi (no. 69). We now know that what European scholars call the Liyu style is in fact a bronze vessel style dating from relatively late in the Spring and Autumn period and located in the region dominated by the state of Jin, in the middle of the Yellow River valley. Similarly, the hoard of bronzes unearthed in 1923 at Xinzheng, which contained a mixture of old and new vessel types, was formerly called the Xinzheng style (no. 67). Ultimately dissatisfied with the Xinzheng style, craftsmen broke away from the customs followed since Shang and Zhou times and produced vessels with decorative themes from daily life: bronzes showed such activities as hunting, picking mulberries, feasting and dancing, and even land and water battles. This shift in style was especially marked, an illustration of the final eradication of the conservative slave-owning consciousness of the past. Art was awakened from primitive illusions and emerged from a mystical labyrinth. Escaping from a preoccupation with spiritual ideas, art became humanized and began to focus on the life of the everyday world. No longer were the spirits expressed as savage beasts, but as human beings, taking art into a completely new intellectual realm. As products of particular social conditions, with forms that manifested them, bronze artifacts underwent a series of changes during the Warring States period, adding a glorious new chapter to the history of ancient Chinese art.

Han

The early Western Han bronze art continued the high level of that of the Warring States period. The same fine workmanship is seen, for example, on the gold- and silver-inlaid Bo Shan incense burner and the bird-script *hu*—both unearthed from the tomb of the Han prince Liu Sheng at Mancheng, Hebei—from the second century B.C. (nos. 95, 96). The use of gold and silver for inlay was widespread by the Han period, and craftsmen were relatively skillful at applying it. A distinctive touch was to decorate the most beautiful objects by incising the surface with a pattern and then filling it with gold and silver. Another advance was in the casting of bronze mirrors. The precision and delicacy of decorative patterns on Han mirrors can be compared only with expert modern casting techniques. Yet such fine casting in Han mirrors is almost commonplace, an excellent testament to the quality of art of the time.

The most striking change in Han dynasty bronze vessels is the appearance of a plainly realistic representational style. The renowned Changxin palace lamp (no. 94) is a lifelike palace lady. Other bronzes are figures and animals modeled with simplicity and assurance, such as the Eastern Han galloping horses, which express a sense of freshness and vitality. This new spirit was found not only in bronzes, of course, but in all of the arts of the Han dynasty. In this era the bronze vessels culminated their long historical development, offering a final glimpse of the extraordinary magnificence of ancient Chinese society.

NOTES

1. Tang Lan, "Zhongguo qingtongqi de qiyuan yu fazhan" [The Origin and development of Chinese bronzes], *Gugong Bowuyuan Yuankan* 1979/1, pp. 4–10.

2. The materials cited here are from the author's own examination of the objects provided by the Gansu Provincial Museum; a formal report will be issued later.

3. "Shandong Jiao Xian Sanlihe yizhi fajue jianbao" [Brief report of the excavation of the Sanlihe site, Jiao Xian, Shandong], *Kaogu* 1977/4, pp. 262–67.

4. "1959 nian Henan Yanshi Erlitou shijue jianbao" [Brief report of trial excavations at Erlitou, Yanshi, Henan, in 1959], *Kaogu* 1961/2, pp. 82–93; "Henan Yanshi Erlitou zao Shang gongdian yizhi fajue jianbao" [Brief report of the excavation of the Early Shang palace site at Erlitou, Yanshi, Henan], *Kaogu* 1974/4, pp. 234–48; "Henan Yanshi Erlitou yizhi san ba qu fajue jianbao" [Excavation of Zones 3 and 8 at Erlitou, Yanshi, Henan], *Kaogu* 1975/5, pp. 302–9.

5. "1975 nian yu xi kaogu diaocha" [Archaeological explorations in western Henan in 1975], *Kaogu* 1978/1, pp. 23–34.

6. Xia Nai, "Tan-14 ceding niandai he Zhongguo shiqian kaogu xue" [Carbon-14 dating and Chinese prehistory], *Kaogu* 1977/4, pp. 217–32.

7. Zou Heng, "Guanyu tantao Xia wenhua de jige wenti" [Several problems concerning the discussion of the Xia culture], *Wenwu* 1979/3, pp. 64–69; Zheng Jieyang, "Erlitou wenhua shangque" [A Critical discussion of the Erlitou culture], *Henan Wenbo Tongxun* 1978/4; "Yanshi Erlitou yizhi xin faxian di tongqi he yuqi" [Newly discovered bronzes and jades from the Erlitou site, Yanshi], *Kaogu* 1976/4, pp. 259–63; Yin Weizhang, "Erlitou wenhua tantao" [A Discussion of Erlitou culture], *Kaogu* 1978/1, pp. 1–4.

8. See *Kaogu* 1975/5, pp. 302–9.

9. See *Kaogu* 1976/4, pp. 259–63.

10. "Panlongcheng 1974 nian du tian ye kaogu jiyao" [Summary of field work at Panlongcheng for 1974], *Wenwu* 1976/2, pp. 5–15.

11. "Jiangxi Qingjiang Wucheng Shang dai yizhi fajue jianbao" [Excavation of the Shang site at Wucheng, Qingjiang, Jiangxi], *Wenwu* 1975/7, pp. 51–71.

12. Zou Heng, "Shilun Yinxu wenhua fenqi" [A Preliminary discussion of the periodization of the Yinxu culture], *Beijing Daxue Xuebao* 1964/4–5.

13. "Anyang Yinxu wuhao mu di fajue" [Excavation of Tomb 5 at Yinxu, Anyang], *Kaogu Xuebao* 1977/2, pp. 57–98; "Anyang Yinxu wuhao mu zuotan jiyao" [Summary of the symposium on Tomb 5, Yinxu, Anyang], *Kaogu* 1977/5, pp. 341–50; "Anyang Yinxu wuhao mu di niandai wenti" [The Problem of the date of Tomb 5, Yinxu, Anyang], *Kaogu* 1979/2, pp. 165–70.

14. See *Zuo Zhuan*, *Xuan Gong*, 3rd year, King Sun Man's conversation with King Zhuang of Chu.

15. "Hubei kuangye yizhi diaocha" [An Investigation of a mining and smelting site in Hubei], *Kaogu* 1974/4, pp. 251–54; "Hubei Tonglüshan Chunqiu Zhanguo gu Kuangyejing yizhi fajue jianbao" [Brief report on an ancient mining site of the Spring and Autumn and Warring States periods at Tonglüshan in Hubei], *Wenwu* 1975/2, pp. 1–12.

16. "Zhengzhou Shang dai yizhi di fajue" [Excavation of Shang sites at Zhengzhou], *Kaogu Xuebao* 1957/1, pp. 53–74.

17. "1958–1959 nian Yinxu fajue jianbao" [Brief report of excavations at Yinxu for 1958–1959], *Kaogu* 1961/2, pp. 63–76.

18. A cache of bronzes that ought to date from the early Shang to the early Yinxu period was discovered in Qishan Xian. See Wang Guangyung, "Shaanxi sheng Qishan Xian faxian Shang dai qingtongqi" [Shang bronzes discovered at Qishan Xian, Shaanxi], *Wenwu* 1977/12, pp. 86–87. Sites along the Wei River have also yielded these kinds of bronze objects, which are on display in a local museum there.

19. *Shang Shu: Tai Shi.*

20. *Shang Shu: Jiu Gao.*

21. Waishu *ding*: height 89.5 cm., diameter at mouth 61.3 cm., "Qishan faxian Xi Zhou shidai da ding" [A Large *ding* of the Western Zhou discovered at Qishan], *Wenwu* 1959/10, pp. 84–85. Animal mask *ding*: height 85 cm., diameter at mouth 63 cm., "Shaanxi Chang'an Xinwangcun, Mawangcun chutu di Xi Zhou tongqi" [Western Zhou bronzes unearthed at Xinwangcun and Mawangcun, Chang'an, Shaanxi], *Kaogu* 1974/1, pp. 1–5. Lu *ding*: height 75.6 cm., diameter at mouth 56.1 cm.

22. A *gui* with a wooden pedestal has already been archaeologically discovered in the Zhou plain. The wooden pedestal had disintegrated, but the shell decorations from its sides remained.

23. See the Zhen He inscription, "Shaanxi sheng Qishan Xian Dongjiacun Xi Zhou tongqi yaoxue fajue jianbao" [Excavation of Western Zhou bronzes at Dongjiacun, Qishan, Shaanxi], *Wenwu* 1976/5, pp. 26–44.

24. "Chang'an Puducun Xi Zhou mu di fajue" [Excavation of a Western Zhou tomb at Puducun, Chang'an], *Kaogu Xuebao* 1957/1, pp. 75–85.

25. "Shaanxi Fufeng Zhuangbo yihao Xi Zhou qingtongqi yaocang fajue jianbao" [Excavation of Storage Pit No. 1 of Western Zhou bronzes at Zhuangbo, Fufeng, Shaanxi], *Wenwu* 1978/3, pp. 1–18.

26. *Zuo Zhuan: Xuan Gong*, 15th year.

27. Li Zhong, "Zhongguo fengjian shehui qianqi gangtie yelian zhishu fazhan di tantao" [The Development of iron and steel technology in ancient China], *Kaogu Xuebao* 1975/2, pp. 1–22.

28. "Hubei Jiangling sanzuo Chu mu chutu dapi zhongyao wenwu" [A Large number of important cultural relics unearthed from three tombs at Jiangling, Hubei], *Wenwu* 1966/5, pp. 33–55.

29. Huang Shengzhang, "Guanyu Zhanguo Zhongshan guo mu cang yiwu ruogan wenti panjeng" [Discussion of several problems on remains from the Warring States period tombs of the Zhongshan state], *Wenwu* 1979/5, pp. 43–45; Wu Hung, "Tan jijian Zhongshan guo qiwu zaoxing yu zhuangshi" [Discussion of the manufacture and decor of several implements of the Zhongshan state], *Wenwu* 1979/5, pp. 46–50; Li Xueqin and Li Ling, "Pingshan sanqi yu Zhongshan guo shi de ruogan wenti" [Three bronze vessels of Pingshan and some problems concerning the history of the Zhongshan state], *Kaogu Xuebao* 1979/2, pp. 147–70; Yu Haoliang, "Zhongshan sanqi mingwen kao" [Notes on the inscriptions of three bronze vessels of the Zhongshan state], *Kaogu Xuebao* 1979/2, pp. 171–84; "Hebei sheng Pingshan Xian Zhanguo Shiqi Zhongshan guo mu cang fajue jianbao" [Excavation of the tombs of the Zhongshan state in the Warring States period at Pingshan Xian, Hebei Province], *Wenwu* 1979/1, pp. 16–31; Liu Laicheng and Li Xiaodong, "Shi tan Zhanguo Shiqi Zhongshan guo lishi shang de jige wenti" [Discussion of several questions in the history of the Zhongshan state of the Warring States period], *Wenwu* 1979/1, pp. 32–36; Li Xueqin, "Pingshan mu cang qun yu Zhongshan guo de wenhua" [The Buried storage pit at Pingshan and the culture of the Zhongshan state], *Wenwu* 1979/1, pp. 37–41; Ju Dexi and Qiu Xigui, "Pingshan Zhongshan wang mu tongqi mingwen de chubu yanqiu" [Preliminary research on the bronze vessel inscriptions from the tombs of the Zhongshan kings at Pingshan], *Wenwu* 1979/1, pp. 42–52.

II

The Study of Chinese Bronze Age Arts: Methods and Approaches

Wen Fong

Both historiography and archaeology, our two approaches to ancient history, have had a long and distinguished tradition in China. With a zeal almost without parallel in Western cultures, Chinese scholars have amassed a vast store of knowledge about the past. In archaeology, serious research was begun nearly one thousand years ago, as artifacts were recovered and collected. "During the era of Jia You [1056–63]," writes the historian Ouyang Xiu (1007–72),

> Liu Chang was prefect of Yongxing. Since Chang'an [near modern Xi'an] was the ancient capital of the Qin and Han dynasties, many ancient objects and unusual vessels were buried in old building foundations and cemeteries. There they were frequently discovered by farmers and herdboys, and became collector's items in people's homes. Mr. Liu was fond of these ancient vessels and amassed quite a collection of them.[1]

Liu Chang owned eleven ancient bronze vessels, once used for ritual purposes. He had draftsmen copy the inscriptions and make drawings of the vessels. Then he commissioned engravings of the drawings in stone and composed an essay to accompany them entitled "A Record of Ancient Vessels from the Former Qin Dynasty." In his preface to this work, he described his method of studying ancient vessels. From experts on rituals, he said, he learned the vessels' governing principles; through etymology, he examined the inscriptions; and through the study of imperial lineages, he determined the dates of the posthumous titles mentioned in the inscriptions.[2]

Ouyang Xiu composed one of the earliest works on epigraphy, *Jigu lu* (Collection of ancient inscriptions), completed in 1061. In 1092, Lü Dalin compiled *Kaogu tu* (Illustrated record of ancient objects), which describes 211 bronzes and 13 jade objects, giving illustrations, measurements, provenance when known, and annotated transcriptions of inscriptions. And, in 1111, *Xuanhe bogu tu* (Illustrated catalogue of antique objects in the Xuanhe collection), the catalogue of the archaeological collection of the Northern Sung emperor Huizong, published 836 objects in 20 categories, with introductory essays, illustrations, transcriptions on inscriptions, and measurements and weight of the objects.

Although these works are more antiquarian than archaeological in nature, some early Chinese writers, in the tradition of Chinese skeptical rationalism, approached their subject with a method similar to that of modern science. Shen Gua (1031–95), for example, correctly criticized the imaginary reconstructions of ancient ritual vessels in the illustrated books on rituals of his day by observing and describing unearthed objects.[3]

Nevertheless, traditional Chinese studies of ancient artifacts, known as *jinshi xue*, or "studies of bronzes and stones," largely concentrated on the recording and analysis of inscriptions, both as documents supplementing recorded history and as models of ancient calligraphy. Modern scientific archaeology, based on field work, began in earnest only in the early twentieth century. Archaeological study of the early historical period of China made its significant debut between 1928 and 1937, when the "ruins of Yin" near Anyang were scientifically excavated under the auspices of the Institute of History and Philology, Academia

Sinica. The Second Sino-Japanese War brought activities to a halt, and it was only in 1949 that field work was resumed and expanded to a national scale.

In 1949, Guo Moruo (1892–1978; Fig. 4), the well-known scholar of bronzes, oracle bones, and ancient Chinese society, was appointed a vice premier of the People's Republic Central Government, simultaneously holding the titles of chairman of the National Committee on Culture and Education and director of the National Academy of Sciences (Zhongguo Kexue Yuan). At Guo's instigation, the late premier Zhou Enlai, as head of the State Council, created a Bureau of Cultural Relics (Wenwuju, also known as State Administrative Bureau of Museums and Archaeological Data), under the Ministry of Culture. At the same time, an Institute of Archaeology (Kaogu Yanjiu Suo) was established under the Academy of Sciences. Thus, for the first time, all archaeological activities in China were coordinated under a central government agency and a national research institution. The Institute of Archaeology supervised important field work, as well as publications of excavation results. The first director of the Bureau of Cultural Relics and the first director of the Institute was Zheng Zhenduo, later a vice minister of culture. A learned bibliophile, Zheng worked tirelessly to build national collections of books and cultural objects, but his career ended tragically with a fatal airplane accident in 1958.[4] He was succeeded by the present director, Wang Yeqiu, under whose leadership the Bureau's activities burgeoned, so that it now oversees what is perhaps the world's largest single complex of museums and archaeological excavations. Today the Bureau is one of China's most important agencies, reporting directly to the State Council and functioning as a ministry of its own.

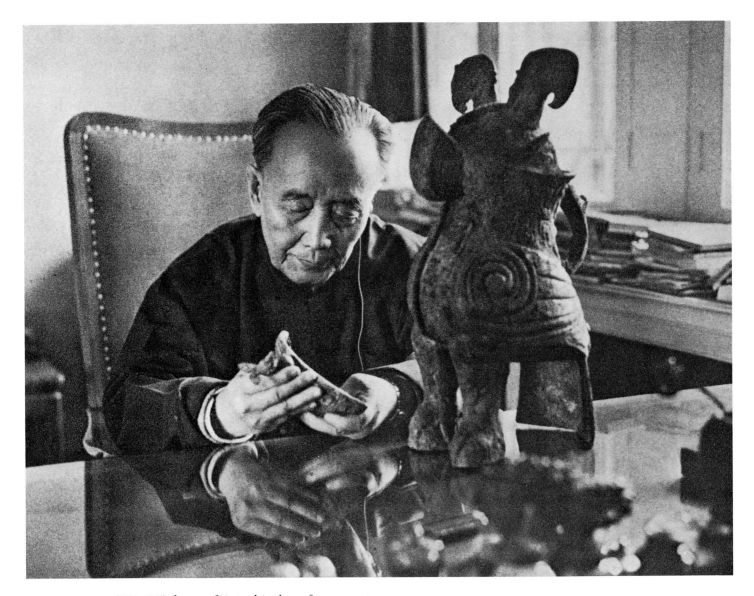

Fig. 4   Guo Moruo (1892–1978), director of National Academy of
Sciences, studying bird-shaped *zun* no. 29. Photograph after
China Pictorial 1977/6, p. 26

The career of the scholar-statesman Guo Moruo was a remarkable one.[5] As a student of Western medicine in Japan between 1913 and 1923, he studied modern scientific methodology in research and adopted the Marxist theory of dialectical materialism. During his years of exile in Japan, in 1927–37, he devoted himself to the study of archaeology and ancient history, especially the oracle bone texts and bronze inscriptions. While in Japan, in 1929, Guo Moruo translated into Chinese Adolf Michaelis's *Ein Jahrhundert kunstarchäologischer Entdeckungen* (Leipzig, 1908), which he felt had taught him the methods of archaeology.[6]

Guo published his well-known work *Zhongguo qudai shehui yanjiu* (A Study of ancient Chinese society) in 1930. In 1932 *Liang Zhou jinwenci daxi* (Collections of the bronze inscriptions from the two Zhou periods), his major work on the Zhou bronze inscriptions, classified 251 vessels (323 in the expanded edition) by determining provenance and date according to a method that employs epigraphy, history, and style: "In determining the dates of the bronzes, those vessels with dated inscriptions are used first to relate to those vessels with historical names and events, then together they are studied with reference to their calligraphic and literary styles, decorative patterns and vessel shapes."[7]

In 1956, at a conference on archaeological work held under the joint auspices of the Academy of Sciences and the Ministry of Culture, Guo Moruo and Zheng Zhenduo addressed the problems facing China's archaeological endeavors. Guo began by praising the ancient tradition of archaeological scholarship:

> Although the *Kaogu tu* and *Bogu tu* [Northern Sung archaeological texts] dealt principally with bronze vessels, these two works made a rather systematic investigation of the decorative patterns, vessel shapes, measurements, dates, and inscriptions of the bronzes; and their discussions covered history and geography, craftsmanship and techniques. It is fair to say that they presented us with a well-disciplined field of learning . . . .
>
> Since the Northern Sung period, we have not only failed to make further progress in this field, but indeed have allowed it to decline. It was only recently, chiefly with the introduction of Western archaeology, that we have gradually regained our interest in this area of research.[8]

Though he went on to list achievements, to praise Beijing University for graduating 341 field workers, and to express appreciation for his colleagues' efforts, Guo concluded with a stern exhortation: "Chinese archaeology holds a deep meaning for the entire world. Our knowledge of human history and world history still has enormous gaps. We must fill some of these gaps with the buried and hidden cultural riches beneath the earth of China."

In his speech, Zheng Zhenduo proposed a program for China's archaeological research, based on five principles:

> (1) Archaeology is the science of man's material culture. It must be founded on dialectical materialism and historical materialism.
> (2) Research must be increased. Everyone must work for the goal of catching up with the highest standards of modern archaeology within a twelve-year period.
> (3) We must coordinate archaeological work with the socialist nation's industrial and agricultural developments. Specifically, this means that archaeological work must precede, rather than follow, engineering programs.
> (4) We must coordinate archaeological work with the people, and mobilize the energies of the masses for archaeological work.
> (5) We must improve archaeology in minority regions, and cultivate minority archeological workers.[9]

Zheng's principle of involving the people established a pattern for future archaeological discovery and preservation work. As early as 1950, the State Council of the People's Central Government had established a set of laws for the "protection of revolutionary historical and artistic cultural objects" on the provincial and local levels. Gradually, in each province and major city, a Committee on Administration of Cultural Objects (Wenwu Guanli Weiyuanhui), a Bureau of Culture (Wenhuaju) or Bureau of Cultural Relics (Wenwuju), or a museum, or sometimes all three, were set up.

In the fall of 1977, when I first visited the People's Republic as a member of the United States Delegation on Chinese Painting from the Committee on Scholarly Communication with the People's Republic of China, one of our hosts told me that, besides Beijing University, which now plans a Department of Archaeology, eight other universities or colleges had special archaeology programs attached to their history departments. In addition, archaeological workers are being trained by numerous provincial and local museums. The Nanjing Museum, for instance, has a department of archaeology and a department of calligraphy, painting, and crafts, each with about thirty staff members. The museum has a docent program (*jiangjie yuan*) as well as a program for high school trainees, who are sent to the countryside to lecture, with lantern slides and other educational materials, to workers on the farms. When chance discoveries are made by farmers and workers, they are immediately reported to local cultural bureaus or museums, which in turn pass on the information to the central authorities in Beijing for evaluation. With the people's awareness of archaeological objects thus heightened, China today seems to be a nation of archaeologists dedicated to the discovery and preservation of its cultural heritage.

*   *   *

Around the turn of the century—when Michaelis wrote *Ein Jahrhundert kunst-archäologischer Entdeckungen*, which Guo Moruo so greatly admired—the study of art and archaeology was becoming established as a scientific discipline. In his concluding chapter, "Discoveries and Science," Michaelis described the advantages of the stylistic approach: "Instead of depending upon a scaffolding supposed to be firm, because [it is] derived from literary tradition, but really flimsy and scanty, we now have a structure rich in form and color.... The work of art has a language of its own, which it is our task to understand and explain."[10]

It is no accident that the development of scientific theories of stylistic analysis coincided with the expansion of the Western art historian's interest from the classical phases of Western art to the nonclassical (late Roman, Baroque) styles, industrial (rugs, basket weaving) and non-Western (Egyptian, Oriental) art forms. The methods and techniques that the stylistic historian uses to analyze a work of art are independent of country, race, or period. Through its claims to universal validity through objectivity, scientific stylistic analysis treats the formal peculiarities of a work of art as specific solutions to generic problems.

Seeking to study the genesis of art, Gottfried Semper (1803–79) attempted to derive general principles of art by studying and organizing the data represented by individual works.[11] Semper believed that primitive ornaments resulted from a plaiting or weaving technique and theorized that the origins of art lay in the interplay of material, practical purpose or function, tools, and techniques. He explained the style of a work of art largely in terms of the mechanical properties of the material and the technical problems of manufacture.

Reacting against Semper's "pernicious materialistic philosophy," Alois Riegl (1858–1905), in his *Stilfragen* (Berlin, 1893), advocated the concept of *Kunstwollen*, or "artistic volition," by which he saw the artist's mental activity as the principal source of art.[12] Riegl's *Kunstwollen* also helped to persuade his contemporaries to devote objective and impartial attention to all kinds and all phases of art. As textile curator of the Kunstgewerbemuseum (Museum for Applied Art), Vienna, Riegl wrote a textbook on ancient Oriental rugs (*Altorientalische Teppiche*, Leipzig, 1891). Riegl saw the history of art as an evolution, with each epoch culminating in a more advanced stage, from haptic (tactile, concrete) to optic (visual, fused) apprehension of reality—which corresponded, in a psychological sense, to the progression from an objective to a subjective outlook.

According to Paul Frankl (1878–1962), it was Jakob Burckhardt (1818–97) who first "sought to approach the works of art themselves, not mere ideas or mere forms ... [which are] concepts that were not aesthetic but had to do with the *scholarly* study of art [*Kunstwissenschaft*]."[13] Burckhardt was followed by Konrad Fiedler (1841–95), who argued that art is form, which he further defined as *Gestaltlung*, "artistic shaping." Then, Adolf von Hilderbrand (1847–1921), a sculptor, declaring that "art is shaping for the eye," proceeded to investigate the psychological process of seeing in sculpture and architecture. As Frankl summarized, "Fiedler merely pointed out that there was something as yet unexplored, Hilderbrand offered a few new concepts while remaining one-sided in evaluating styles, but Wölfflin produced a wealth of new insights and really gave the critics something to provoke them into action."[14]

Heinrich Wölfflin (1864–1945), Riegl's younger contemporary, became the most articulate spokesman for stylistic history. Instead of emphasizing materials and techniques, Wölfflin stressed study of the basic language of art: line, contour, plane, volume, mass, movement, modeling, light and shade, and relationship between the part and the whole. Wölfflin's *Principles of Art History,* which first appeared in 1915, remains today the most influential work on stylistic analysis.[15] Echoing Riegl's concept of *Kunstwollen,* Wölfflin points out that "men have always seen what they wished to see." He concludes that there is no such thing as objective vision: just as every person has his own individual personality, every nation and every period has a distinctive style. At the same time, the style or form of a work of art of a given country or period depends on a certain mode of representation, or visual schema, which the individual artist perfects and uses for his own ends. The history of art, for Wölfflin, is the history of seeing, or visualization—both a mental and spiritual activity. Form for him is not merely form but the form of something that has meaning: "The visible world is crystallized for the eye in certain forms. In each new crystal form, however, a new facet of the content of the world will come to light. . . . Vision itself has its history, and the revelation of these visual strata must be regarded as the primary task of art history."[16]

As universal forms of representation, which he saw in all forms of art—painting, sculpture, and architecture—Wölfflin found five sets of opposing stylistic modes. The first is "linear" versus "painterly." The movement from the linear to the painterly—or from the haptic to the optic, as Riegl had it—was to Wölfflin "psychologically intelligible, . . . the relinquishment of the physically tangible for the mere visual appearance."[17] Finding these basic forms in the arts of fifteenth-, sixteenth-, and seventeenth-century Europe, Wölfflin equates the period names Early Renaissance, High Renaissance, and Baroque, with three stages of stylistic development—archaic, classic, and baroque—but rejects the biological analogy of bud, bloom, and decay (or rise, height, and decline), because of the implied value judgment. He suggests that as basic development, the archaic-classic-baroque schema applies not only to other periods of Western art, such as the ancient and the Gothic, but also to other national arts; and that the development once completed may be renewed, "as if it had been possible to begin again at the beginning."[18]

Wölfflin has been criticized for neglecting the question of human genius (Hermann Voss summed up the issue in the title of his 1920 essay "History of Artists or History of Art Without Names"[19]), but such a quibble was irrelevant to Wölfflin's central concern. He was not interested in individual attributions or techniques—problems that he left to connoisseurs, collectors, museum curators, and dealers.

More important than his categories of style, Wölfflin bequeathed to art history a new way of looking at works of art. His history of seeing was a successful mode of thought that enabled the art historian to grapple directly with the mechanics of the artist's visualization. It is not important how complete are his theories of historical change; what matters is that many of his more profound insights are now taken for granted as common property of the modern art historical discipline.

*　　*　　*

Western scholars of Chinese art have adopted the methods of art history only by gradual absorption and after long and spirited debate. Many came to Chinese art through other disciplines, such as philology, history, or literature, and their first attempts at stylistic analysis often ignored the very art historical principles upon which their borrowed techniques had been based. Yet, in the last thirty years, Western study of Chinese art has not only made notable contributions to the field, but also gained status as a respected academic discipline in Western universities, especially in the United States.

It was less than fifty years ago that against the prevailing atmosphere of extreme scientific skepticism, the history of early Chinese art began its long process of reconstruction, literally from the ground up. Bernhard Karlgren (1889–1978), of Sweden, was an important pioneer in this effort, beginning in the 1930s to examine Chinese bronzes. A philologist and historian, Karlgren began his monumental labor by compiling inscriptions from bronze vessels of the Shang and Zhou periods. For his research he relied heavily on Guo Moruo's *Liang Zhou jinwenci daxi* of 1932. Karlgren first began to classify the inscriptions separately, establishing a literary chronology he then hoped to use to classify the vessels.[20] But, while Zhou inscriptions are valuable historical documents and useful for dating bronzes, Shang inscriptions are limited in number, usually brief, and rarely datable. In his "New Studies on Chinese Bronzes" of 1937, which concentrates on the vessels of the "archaic" (Late Shang and early Western Zhou) period, Karlgren considers "typology quite independently of the inscriptions," concentrating mainly on "the décor of the body of the vessels." "The main idea underlying my present work," he wrote, "is that we shall have to carry on our research in a *statistical* way."[21] Basing his work on 1,285 specimens, he proposed classifying bronze decor elements in three categories: two mutually exclusive styles—an A, or primary style, and a B, or secondary style—and a neutral style, C, combining with either A or B. He established his system on the assumption that the "true, realistic" *taotie* (a design recognizable as an "animal" mask) of the A style was earlier than the "dissolved" pattern of the B style. In two further articles, published in 1959 and 1960, he sought to corroborate his earlier theories by taking into account the relationship between decor arrangement and vessel shape.[22] Again examining "as many specimens as possible," he enumerated the recurrence of certain decorative motifs on vessels of certain types and profiles.

The years from 1935 to 1937 were exciting ones for students of early Chinese art. The Burlington House exhibition of Chinese art, which brought many important bronzes to the West for the first time, opened in London in November 1935, while the discoveries at Anyang were reported in articles such as H. J. Timperley's "The Awakening of China in Archaeology" in *The Illustrated London News* (4 April 1936). H. G. Creel's *Birth of China*, the first dependable and popular history of early China, was published in 1936. And numerous exciting, original, and controversial scholarly contributions, in addition to those by Karlgren, appeared in learned journals around the world.[23]

A number of scholars disagreed entirely with Karlgren's view, maintaining that abstract bronze decor designs had preceded, rather than followed, the well-developed zoomorphic motifs. To stylistic historians like Ludwig Bachhofer, Max Loehr, and J. LeRoy Davidson, Karlgren's statistical analysis of decorative motifs was meaningless, and his conclusions historically irrelevant. As Davidson pointed out in 1937, Karlgren's research had focused on the decorative motifs, which are the elements "most easily copied by later imitators."[24] Davidson reviewed Karlgren's "New Studies" in 1940 and made a more detailed critique, declaring that the "dissolved" *taotie* (B1 style) actually antedated the A style, while the "detailed" bird (B3) definitely evolved from the A style. "Karlgren's B style is actually composed of two different styles," Davidson concluded, "one of which [B1] we may call early Shang, antedating the A and C Styles, and the other [B3] a style which develops from the early Chou [Zhou] period. It is this secondary B style that formed the foundation for the abstract patterns and interlaceries of the Middle Chou period."[25]

It was Ludwig Bachhofer (1894–1976), a distinguished student of Wölfflin's, who began to develop the first coherent interpretation of Chinese bronze art development. As he suggested in his "On the Origin and Development of Chinese Art" of 1935, the evolution of style progressed from a simple, archaic type to a noble, classical style, which eventually became expansively baroque, "the ornaments losing their rigid angularity and spreading their long flowing elements over the whole surfaces of the bronzes."[26] Not only could this development be traced on bronzes, Bachhofer maintained, it could be observed as well in both shapes and ornaments of ivories, bone implements, and pottery. Over the years Bachhofer expanded and refined this theory, proposing in 1944 that the archaic, classic, and baroque phases could be equated with graphic, plastic, and ornate styles, and that a fourth "severe," or neoclassical, style appeared during the early Western Zhou period.[27] In 1946, stating that stylistic changes "revealed themselves as so many phases of a logical, orderly and organic evolution,"[28] he divided the history of Chinese bronze art into four cycles of stylistic development. In the first period, which embraced the first cycle of development from the archaic, the classic to the baroque, was Shang art. The Zhou regime marked the beginning of the next period, which opened with the creation of simple tectonic forms of the "severe" style and ended with complex atectonic forms. The third period, roughly covering the Spring and Autumn period, from about 772 to about 481 B.C., began with the Xinzheng and ended with the late Liyu style, when the animal of the decoration becomes unrecognizable. The rise of the Jincun style signaled the beginning of the fourth period, which extended from the Warring States period (ca. 481–221) to the end of the Western Han dynasty in 8 A.D.[29]

Unfortunately, in the years immediately following the Second World War, Bachhofer's bold stylistic vision aroused the old Anglo-Saxon positivistic instinct, which is perhaps basically distrustful of Germanic abstract speculations. His scheme had implied a deterministic historicism, which saw "style" moving as if it were an irresistible, autonomous force according to preordained evolutionary "laws." In a 1947 review of Bachhofer's *Short History of Chinese Art*, Benjamin Rowland, Jr., wrote that Bachhofer's "method is in the final analysis a typological one . . . a kind of genetic history of style abstracted from historical reality." "There is," Rowland pointed out, "first of all an a priori framework on which works of art in evolutionary progression are made to fit. This is no more nor less than the concept of the development of styles of art through periods of growth, maturity and decay which Geoffrey Scott once demolished as the 'biological fallacy.'"[30] Rowland concluded that Bachhofer's theories could not be applied to Chinese art, since they did not take into account its special nature and origin.

Moreover, Bachhofer's apparent low regard for inscriptional criteria brought on a renewed controversy between philologists and art historians. Otto Maenchen-Helfen, in "Some Remarks on Ancient Chinese Bronzes" of 1945, pointed out a great diversity in styles of vessels associated by their inscriptions. Objecting to Bachhofer's "purely typological approach," Maenchen observed, "A unilinear development leaves no room for bronzes with widely different dates but in the same style, or bronzes in distinctly different styles but with inscriptions that would assign them to the same date."[31] In a similar vein, John A. Pope, in "Sinology or Art History: Notes on Methods in the Study of Chinese Art" of 1947, criticized Bachhofer's system, noting that the bronzes he discusses far exceed the scope of his classification.[32]

Ironically, while Bachhofer's expressed concern was with form rather than with inscriptions, he was nevertheless the most successful at analysis when dated monuments were available to him.[33] Some of Bachhofer's concise and penetrating analyses of Chinese sculptural styles, which have more precise datings than bronzes, remain today among the best on the subject. While Bachhofer borrowed Wölfflin's stylistic categories to plot the development of Chinese art, Wölfflin himself had never intended his broad stylistic concepts to be criteria for dating works of art. Again, the accuracy or completeness of Bachhofer's knowledge of Chinese art is not important—in the 1940s everyone was more or less groping in the dark—what matters is that where he applied Wölfflin's "seeing," Bachhofer achieved unusually lucid stylistic comprehension.

Bachhofer's eminent pupil Max Loehr, recognizing that Wölfflin's general concepts alone could not describe specific stylistic developments,[34] avoided Bachhofer's literal application of Wölfflin's principles to Chinese art. In 1953, using the excavated materials made available in Li Chi's *Studies of Hsiao-t'un Bronzes* of 1948, Loehr proposed the division of the Anyang bronzes into five styles, progressing from a linear threadlike pattern to a bold plastic design (see chap. 4, p. 182, for a résumé of Loehr's "Five Styles"). He cites J. LeRoy Davidson's "perspicacious hypothesis" of identifying the thread-relief decor (Loehr's Style I) as "the first style of ornamental bronze in China"; and mentions the inclusion of his Styles III and IV in Bachhofer's "graphic style" category.[35] Loehr's sequence reverses the order proposed by Karlgren: as the tables at the end of Loehr's article demonstrate, Karlgren's "early" A-style elements appear only in Loehr's later phases (IV and V), while the "later" B-style elements are scattered throughout Loehr's five styles.

In plotting the development of the five styles of the Anyang bronzes, Loehr sees "an unbroken, steady and coherent process." Bachhofer's general idea of a graphic-to-plastic progression is transformed into a compelling step-by-step account of technical and stylistic development: the simple, abstract patterns of linear character of Style I become in Styles II and III complicated designs that cover a surface evenly and densely. In Style IV, part of the elements recede to become background patterns, bringing the principal motifs into stronger focus. By Style V the motifs become further clarified, giving the look of power and vigor that Karlgren had associated with early origins.

Predictably, Loehr's new formulation was met with strong opposition from habitual dissenters. "A confident art historian has even seen fit to establish six [sic] successive 'styles' in Anyang," noted Karlgren, who, quoting Loehr's statement "a style cannot be approached by way of statistics; large numbers cannot actually tell us more about a style than does *one* example, thoroughly analyzed and understood, . . ." declared it "foolish."[36]

But it was in the very years of the 1950s that archaeological support for Loehr's early bronze styles began to appear in the newly excavated Shang remains at Zhengzhou in Henan Province, which the historians soon came to identify as the site of one of the pre-Yinxu (pre-Anyang) Shang capital cities, Ao.[37] In 1974 a series of excavations carried out at Panlongcheng in Hubei Province brought to light bronzes that are in perfect correspondence with those found at Zhengzhou; they belong mostly to Loehr's Style II (nos. 5–7). Also in 1974, two great *fang ding* with Loehr Style I thread-relief design (no. 11) were found at Zhengzhou. Finally, one of the *jue* found at Erlitou in 1975 (no. 1), which is among the earliest known bronze vessels, shows a narrow band of simple Loehr Style I thread-relief design.

By the 1960s scholars were persuaded to applaud Loehr's analysis. Alexander C. Soper, for example, wrote in 1966:

> The vessel forms and most of the ornamental motifs that [Loehr] selected from the enormous confusion of known bronze holdings check perfectly with the new Chinese evidence. The accumulated weight of archaeological data makes it far more certain than before that the I and II phases are not merely interesting and authentic but show the closest view we have as yet of the beginnings of the bronze vessel art in China.[38]

*   *   *

If Michaelis's first "century of archaeological discoveries" had been inspired by "a desire to see and study glorious Hellas," archaeology's second century has profited equally from Guo Moruo's call to reveal "the buried and hidden cultural riches beneath the earth of China." But the task of recapturing China's cultural riches, both above and beneath the ground, is an exceedingly difficult and complex one. The philologist must have at his command more than 2,500 years of exegetical and hermeneutical literature. The art historian must understand different forms of art as languages of their own; he must learn not only to classify and compare works of art, and to theorize about their stylistic development, but also to interpret style in its broadest possible social and cultural context. The work has barely begun in this field. In spite of the immense amount of materials with which we must contend, reliable evidence on most subjects, both from ancient and more recent dynastic periods, is either far from complete, or, if available, still insufficiently understood.

In his preface to the 1954 edition of his *Jinwen congkao* (Studies on bronze inscriptions), Guo Moruo modestly referred to his epochal work on Zhou bronzes, *Liang Zhou jinwenci daxi*, as a "tool" book, lamenting the lack of a systematic corpus of early bronzes.[39] Similarly, Zheng Zhenduo, whose interests ranged from later dynastic woodcut illustrations to dramatic plays and novels, always referred to his scholarly works as *zi liao*, or "research materials." In his active years as the first director of the State Bureau of Cultural Relics (Wenwuju), Zheng had little time for scholarship, but he encouraged the editing and reprinting of old books. In a letter to a friend Zheng complained:

> [Scholarship] seems easy, as if anyone could do it; yet it is rarely done well and without too much error. . . . If we fail our ancient authors, we also fail our contemporary audience. If we are irresponsible to our ancient authors, we also become irresponsible to our own audience.[40]

In the United States, after the great methodological debate over Bachhofer's *Short History of Chinese Art* in the late 1940s, most younger scholars of Chinese art seem to have heeded Rowland's warning that "there certainly is no future in attempting to classify Chinese [art] entirely on the basis of *Stilgeschichte* on a Wölfflinian model,"[41] and turned instead to safer grounds of data gathering and research on specific topics. The turning away from theoretical speculation helped remove the impression that Chinese art history was being viewed through Western analogies, allowing Chinese art studies to become independent. But the techniques developed by stylistic historians have remained the only tool available to the modern student. When definitions of fundamental concepts are sound, the skillful use of stylistic techniques can result in penetrating criticism, but when the theoretical principles are ignored or misunderstood, the refinement of techniques alone cannot hope to lead to a profound treatment of the subject.

Yesterday's hypothesis becomes today's method. Loehr's stylistic structure for Shang bronze art, now supported by archaeology, has become an accepted method for classifying Shang art. The history of Zhou bronze styles has yet to be written, but the beginning of a coherent account is found in Bachhofer's *Short History*, where a logically comprehensible stylistic sequence is given. New insights into the problems of the provincial predynastic Zhou and other local bronze traditions have already produced a better understanding of the diversity of Western Zhou bronzes, as well as those of the lingering survivals and revivals of the Shang inheritance. To Bachhofer's Eastern Zhou stylistic sequence of Xinzheng-Liyu-Huai-Jincun have been added important materials from Shangcunling of western Henan Province, Houma of Shaanxi, Jingshan and Pingshan of Hebei, Sui Xian of Hubei, Shou Xian of Anhui, and other areas of the south.

The incredible find of the terracotta army of the First Emperor of Qin (nos. 98–105) now firmly establishes the existence of a well-developed monumental sculptural tradition by the late third century B.C. Bachhofer's description of the large stone sculpture at the tomb of the Han general He Qubing, who died in 117 B.C., then thought to be the earliest monumental sculptures in China, had not been flattering. He referred to their "rather shocking primitiveness,"[42] a feature he found to be in contrast with an earlier small bronze figure of a boy dancing on a toad (Bachhofer, *Short History*, fig. 53), datable to before the end of the third century B.C., which he praised for its expression of "swift and easy movement."[43] The perceived difference between the skillfully rendered small sculptures and the "crude" large ones proves to be illusory now that the magnificently sculpted life-size soldiers and horses of the Qin emperor have come to light.

Though the Qin figures were a startling discovery, their methods of manufacture do not require a modification of our conceptual scheme for Chinese figural representation. Bachhofer's description of archaic Chinese sculpture as adhering to rigid symmetry, or the "Law of Frontality," applies equally to the Qin figures. A psychological explanation of this so-called Law of Frontality, known in archaic figural representations of several different cultures, was given in 1900 by Emanuel Loewy. He theorized that archaic artists created according to "memory pictures," presenting the form as it could best be distinguished from other forms.[44] In all of these representations, certain common features may be observed: the figures are shown to the spectator with each of their parts in its more characteristic aspect, namely, in either the profile or the frontal view; elements break up into fractional parts, each a schematic motif, there being neither a grasp of the organic whole nor organic connectives such as neck, wrist, or ankle; foreshortening is avoided, and thus diagonal recession is distorted to keep motifs in the frontal plane; and power to move does not lie in the figure, which is two-dimensional and nonorganic, but in the rhythm of the silhouette.[45]

In Chinese figural representation, the archaic mode of linear, two-dimensional, and largely frontal forms lasted about one thousand years, from the late Eastern Zhou period (sixth century B.C.) to the late Six Dynasties period (ca. A.D. 550). At that time, a transitional style of cylindrical forms appeared, and, with it, organic relationships between parts of a figure suddenly developed. Finally, during the Tang period in the late seventh and early eighth centuries, a fully developed mode of well-articulated, three-dimensional human bodies with naturalistic drapery folds was reached. This stylistic sequence can be documented by dated Buddhist sculptures almost decade by decade and is followed by figure paintings of the period as well.

Max Loehr, as already noted, went beyond Bachhofer's literal adherence to Wölfflinian theories of cyclical structure and immanent and inexorable dynamics of style. Quoting Arnold Hauser's definition of style as "a dynamic relational concept with continually varying content," Loehr points to the continuously "changing nature of the style" in the history of Chinese art. According to Loehr, from Neolithic through Zhou periods, style was "the formal substance (as in protorepresentational images)"; and from Han through the Southern Song, style served as "a tool [used] like an instrument to record or capture reality."[46] Unlike his precise formulation of the stylistic sequence of the Shang bronzes, Loehr's broad theories about the "changing nature of the style" in Chinese art history do not help to describe stylistic changes. Although Loehr's theories are too complex to be fully discussed here, it is important to note his position in promoting the distinction between ornamental and representational art.[47] Pointing out that in Chinese antiquity "it is not representation (or the plastic facsimile) but ornamental design alone that is endowed with artistic feeling and may be called art," Loehr writes, "throughout [Chinese] antiquity, there is no trace of a pictorial art but only some representational non-art (on the level of diagrams)."[48] Loehr has made a useful contribution to Chinese art history by demonstrating that ornament ultimately succumbs to pictorial forms, but his idea of a "representational non-art" properly falls into the realm of aesthetics rather than of art history. In a stylistic history, it is not possible to separate ornament (geometric or stylized form) from representation.[49]

In Loehr's opinion, the ornaments of Shang bronzes came into being without direct allusion to reality and are therefore "sheer design ... meaningful only as pure form." Quoting Suzanne Langer's statement that "a comparative study of decorative art and primitive representational art suggests forcibly that *form is first*, and the representational function accrues to it," Loehr believes that the earliest zoomorphic images "consisting of nothing but spirals and eyes or pairs of eyes ... were by no means abstractions, but sheer design.... Quite possibly these ornaments were iconographically meaningless, or meaningful only as pure forms."[50] In the present catalogue two different views on the origin and meaning of the bronze decor are presented. Ma Chengyuan, citing late Spring and Autumn period sources in his essay "The Splendor of Ancient Chinese Bronzes" holds that zoomorphic decorations on Shang vessels with an apotropaic significance had meaning, while Robert Bagley, a student of Loehr's, agrees with Loehr that Shang decoration may be an art of pure design (chap. 2).

Since Shang bronzes are a form of industrial art, it is natural that we should consider, in Semper's words, "technique, insofar as this determines the law of artistic development."[51] Wilma Fairbank has suggested that one method of studying Chinese bronze design might be to examine the technical determinants, such as the possibilities and limitations of the mold assembly. Thus, the flanges of a vessel were developed to deal with leaks of molten bronze through the mold joins; the basic principle of apposition in bronze decor reflected the piece-mold segmentation; and, finally, the eyes in the rudimentary *taotie* might "have been [boss-heads] used to support or center the decorated mold segments on the model surface." "If so," Fairbank reasons, "their exploitation by the craftsman-designer as eyes for front-face and profile animal motifs on the bronzes may be assumed to have evolved by suggestion."[52]

But, as Riegl pointed out, the actual artistic process could well be just the opposite of what the technicalist theorist had supposed: instead of form always following technique, technique could be invented to serve the form the artist had in mind.[53] Loehr sees the fully zoomorphic form of the late Shang bronze decor as an outgrowth of the "rudimentary and vaguely suggested, semi-geometric form" of the early Shang bronzes, which, in turn, according to him, derives from the matrix of the small spirals, the lozenge, serration and zigzags, meanders, and other geometric patterns of the late Neolithic pottery.[54] In effect, Loehr would agree with Fairbank, though for different reasons, that the zoomorphic images "evolved by suggestion." The Shang artist saw a zoomorphic image in the pure design as in a Rorschach test and ultimately developed it into the full-fledged *taotie* as in Loehr Style V (nos. 27, 32).

A great fifth-century Chinese scholar gave an accepted Chinese view of this problem. According to Yan Yanzhi (A.D. 384–456) there were three kinds of *tu*, or images: "The first is the representation of principles [*tu li*]: forms of the hexagram [of the *Yi Jing*, or Book of Changes] are such. The second is the representation of concepts [*tu shi*]: the study of written characters has to do with this. The third is the representation of [natural] forms [*tu xing*]: this is painting."[55] By Yan's definition, no image or picture [*tu*] could ever be "sheer design ...

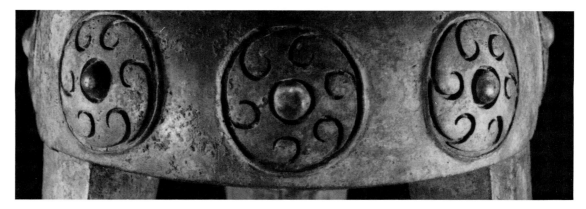

Fig. 5 Detail of whorl-circles, *jia* no. 6

meaningful only as pure form." As Ma Chengyuan points out, the familiar bronze decorative motif known as the "whorl-circle" (no. 6; Fig. 5) may be in fact a pictorialization of the graph 　　　 meaning "brightness of fire," described by the fifth-century B.C. text *Kaogongji* as "fire represented by a circle."[56] If so, the little-understood bronze decor elements, as a mixture of the "representation of principles" and the "representation of forms," may yet shed light on the origins of Chinese script, the "representation of concepts," and vice versa.[57]

We may also venture to place Loehr's five types of Shang bronze decor—as an authentic sequence of styles—into a Chinese cultural context. Shang bronze casting was a two-part process: the making of the mold, a ceramic phase; and the casting of the object, a metallurgical phase.[58] All the technical aspects of the bronze decor can be understood within the ceramic phase of working between the model and the mold. The carving of the mold (negative) and the model (positive) to achieve the desired decor (positive) on the finished bronze vessels was but the earliest of several ancient Chinese crafts that involved the transference of carved designs from one surface to another. There was, for instance, the carving of seals (negative image in relief or intaglio) to be impressed in clay (positive image with relief or intaglio pattern reversed) or on paper (positive image with relief or intaglio pattern the same as the carving). The carving of calligraphy in stone or wood (positive image mostly in intaglio but occasionally in relief) to be made into rubbings (positive image with the same pattern) was another. Finally, there was the carving of printing blocks (negative image in relief) for printing books (positive image). From Shang to Zhou bronzes; through monumental calligraphic stele of Han, Six Dynasties, and Tang; and the great collections of calligraphic anthologies of the subsequent periods; to the *Mustard Seed Garden Painter's Manual* of 1679 and its subsequent editions, the carver's art has been a vital and continuous tradition. In the more than two thousand years of the history of calligraphy, experts learned to transfer readily calligraphic images from brush to carving, and from carving to brush, thus developing an intimate relationship between brush and knife techniques. The carver must possess, above all, a highly refined sensitivity for the silhouetted form and a lively familiarity with, and love for, the interplay between the positive and negative design patterns.

In his 1953 article Loehr writes of an "atypical" example of Shang bronze art: "It may be argued that this chüeh [*jue*] shows the Styles I and II to be coeval; that they overlap; that they differ only technically."[59] If the thread lines of Style I were cut in the mold and the broad bands of Style II were cut in the model, then Styles I and II would correspond respectively to the *yin* (negative or intaglio) and *yang* (positive or relief) techniques in seal carving. If so, Styles I and II as coeval, complementary techniques suggest a dualistic way of thinking that would see not only Style III as a natural synthesis and development of Style I and II ideas, but Styles IV and V, at their time of inception, as yet another set of coeval and complementary techniques.

Bagley seems convinced, from technical observations, that Style II patterns were still carved in the mold, but all three Style II objects in the exhibition (nos. 5–7) seem, to my eye, to show designs cut into the surface of the model rather than the mold. The surface of the decor on the ax no. 7 (Fig. 24) is flush with the surface of the blade, which would make the task of carving a raised thread pattern on the mold almost unthinkable. There are other indications of an intaglio technique in the model: the way the knife stroke enters and exits; the occasional wiggle or rough edge in the incised line where the hand slips slightly or the clay crumbles at the square-headed knife's edge. To scoop out the ribbon pattern with a flat bottom from the arched surface of the mold would be exceedingly difficult, if not impossible. The smooth, rounded surfaces of the "whorl-circles" on the *jia* no. 6 (see Fig. 5), for example, would have to have been refinished after the bronze was cast.

Regardless of the technique actually used, there can be no doubt of the importance of the *yin-yang* interplays, permutations, and complementalities throughout the integral process of bronze casting and decoration—from matrix to mold, clay to bronze, image to reflection, craft to ritual, material to spirit. In this light, the principles of dualism, symmetry, reversibility, and complementality appear to be the cause, rather than the effect, of the piece-mold technology. Loehr's Style III, marked by an expanded *taotie* mask covering a large area of the body of the vessel, shows an increasingly dualistic interplay between raised and flush patterns, relief and intaglio carvings, done perhaps in both the model and the mold. In the Panlongcheng *you* no. 9, which Bagley assigns to early Style III, the main frieze of an elaborated Style II *taotie* pattern around the body is framed by two narrow Style I borders with raised small circles, and Style I bowstrings, as well as a band of Style I thread relief, decorate the neck and the shoulder of the vessel. In the main *taotie* design, the artist mixes the relief and intaglio patterns by adding some free lines on the relief surfaces, while turning the sculpted crevices between the relief patterns into narrow flowing lines with occasionally unattached flourishes; the total effect is of two fluent, energetic, almost mazelike patterns surging and swirling around the two protruding eyes. In the *pou* no. 13 from Gaocheng in Hebei Province, the main features of the *taotie* mask—nose, face, mouth, horns, and ears—stand out in relief against a background of Style III spirals and quills, and are either decorated with relief or intaglio designs, or left blank. Along the shoulder of the vessel, the band of dense and schematized Style II patterns is framed by narrow Style I borders with raised small circles. And, on the *lei* no. 14, the protruding ram faces are decorated with incised designs, while the body shows Style II raised spirals and quill decor.

Perhaps the most dramatic example of interacting *yin-yang* forces—vigorous yet harmonious, complex yet orderly interpenetration of the solid and the void, the raised and the recessed, the relief and the intaglio—is seen in the *hu* no. 21 (Fig. 6) from Shaanxi. In his 1953 article Loehr describes a similar vessel in the Avery Brundage Collection, M. H. de Young Memorial Museum, San Francisco, as an "atypical example" that displays features of Styles II through V.[60] One possible explanation for the mixture of styles in these two *hu* is that, since both are from Shaanxi, they represent an "eccentric" regional style. But, in other ways, they also offer valuable clues for the inceptions of Styles IV and V. Viewed as a development from the Hebei *pou* no. 13, they show a further clarification of the main features of the *taotie* mask against the background spirals. The ears and eyes protrude above the vessel's surface; the face, the cicada, and the background spirals are flush with the vessel; and the rows of teeth and the openings of the mouth recede into the surface. The total design is a masterly exercise in the subtle interplay of positive and negative images: the raised U-shaped ears are echoed by the similarly shaped sunken rows of teeth; the smooth solid surface of the face in the upper half of the vessel contrasts with the carved spiral-filled void spaces in the lower half; and the solid face is covered with lightly incised relief as well as intaglio patterns, while the spiral-filled void is punctuated by delicate as well as bold solid shapes of the cicada and the ears, the former lightly incised and the latter left blank. If the face and cicada, together with the spiral background, denote Style IV and the ears foreshadow Style V, both are but complementary aspects of the same development.

*   *   *

There is no doubt, as Loehr puts it, of the "compatibility, consistency, and logicality" in the stylistic properties of the materials confronting the art historian. The vast increase of knowledge of specimens, even of regional varieties, since Loehr's 1953 article, has only modified, and not changed, his conception of the beginning and growth of Shang bronze styles. The discovery of authentic stylistic sequences—when such sequences are not self-

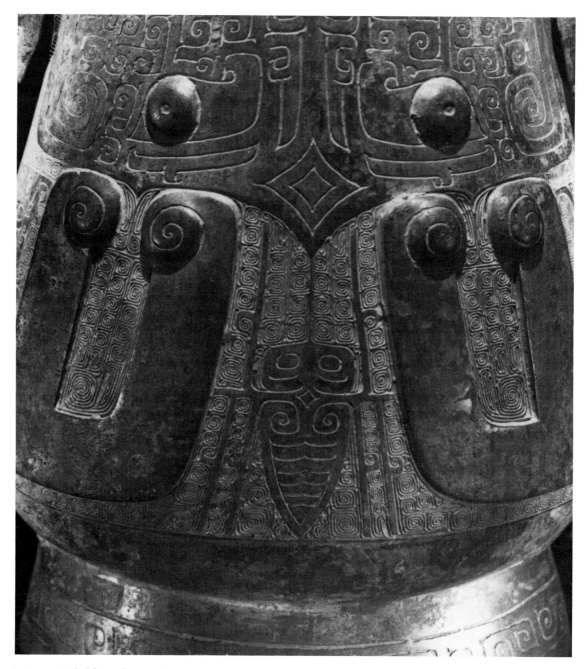

Fig. 6   Detail of decor, *hu* no. 21

evident by virtue of documented examples—appears feasible only under special circumstances: when a stylistic goal, or motivation, is clearly discernible, and when the sequence stands at the beginning of a development, and thus is little complicated by the ever-present problems of survivals and revivals. In the history of Chinese art these circumstances have converged at least three times. The stylistic sequence of Shang bronzes following the development of the *taotie* as described by Loehr is one. The development of figural representation between the fifth and the ninth centuries, as described by Bachhofer, is another. The third is the development of landscape painting from the ideographic motifs of the pre-Tang period (sixth century) to the conquest of illusionistic space in the Yuan period (fourteenth century).[61]

For describing the history of Chinese art, we need a structure that will serve for other kinds of cultural activities, such as literature and thought. A brief survey of the histories of figure painting, landscape painting, calligraphy, poetry, prose, and thought in China will show that they shared a common pattern of development: after a primary evolutionary phase, each went through successive *fugu*, or "return to the archaic," movements. In the history of

Chinese art, I see two recurrent types of *fugu*, or revival impulses: one tries to recreate greatness through a critical study of the past, and the other is a psychologically reticent and introverted retreat into a schematic, archaistic idiom.[62] As stylistic history, such a structure as I have proposed allows us to describe stylistic changes, as well as to interpret styles in changing social, political, and cultural contexts.

One of the axioms of Chinese art history is that while motifs remain or are revived, styles change constantly. In 1953 Loehr wrote, "Indeed we shall have to reckon with a continually widening repertory of motifs: perpetuated older ones existed side by side with the new ones and did not necessarily recede as these later were invented."[63] As regional developments enter the picture, the situation becomes ever more complicated. On a *hu* from Shaanxi (no. 22), for instance, the stylized Style II band could be evidence of either provincialism or conscious revival. Only the joint efforts of archaeologists and historians of style will establish firmer contexts for stylistic oddities.

NOTES

1. Quoted in Zhu Jianxin, *Jinshi xue* [Study of bronzes and stones], preface dated 1938; repr. ed. (Hong Kong, 1964), p. 21. See also Robert Poor, "Notes on the Sung Dynasty Archaeological Catalogs," *Archives of the Chinese Art Society of America* 19 (1965), pp. 33–44.

2. Zhu, *Jinshi xue*, p. 21.

3. Xia Nai, "Shen Gua he kaogu xue" [Shen Gua and archaeology], *Kaogu Xuebao* 1974/2, pp. 1–17.

4. For Zheng Zhenduo's career, see essays by Xia Nai in *Kaogu* 1959/12, pp. 682–83; Wu Yan in *Wenwu* 1961/11, pp. 1–3.

5. Xia Nai, "Guo Moruo tongzhi duiyou Zhongguo kaogu xue dizhuoyue gong xian" [Comrade Guo Moruo's distinguished contributions to Chinese archaeology], *Kaogu* 1978/4, pp. 217–22.

6. *Meishu kaogu yi shiji* [A Century of artistic archaeology], trans. Guo Moruo, rev. ed. (Shanghai, 1954).

7. See Xia, "Guo Moruo," p. 218.

8. "Jiao liu jing yan tigao kaogu gongzo di shuiping" [Exchange experiences and raise the standards of archaeological work], *Kaogu Tongxun* 1956/2, pp. 5–9.

9. "Kaogu shiye di chengjiu he jinhou nuli di fangxiang" [The Accomplishments of our archaeological enterprises and the direction of our future endeavors], *Kaogu Tongxun* 1956/2, pp. 9–16.

10. Adolf Michaelis, *A Century of Archaeological Discoveries*, trans. Bettina Kahnweiler (London, 1908), pp. 304–40.

11. Gottfried Semper, *Der Stil in den technischen Künsten* (Munich, 1878), vol. I, pp. viii ff.

12. Riegl's ideas are subtle and complex. The best presentation of them is found in Hans Sedmayr's introduction to Riegl's *Gesammelte Aufsätze* (Augsburg and Vienna, 1929).

13. Paul Frankl, *The Gothic: Literary Sources and Interpretations through Eight Centuries* (Princeton, 1960), p. 608.

14. Ibid., p. 626.

15. Heinrich Wölfflin, *Principles of Art History*, trans. M. D. Hottinger, repr. ed. (New York, 1950).

16. Ibid., p. 11.

17. Ibid., p. 229.

18. Ibid., p. 234.

19. Hermann Voss, "Kunstlergeschichte oder Kunstgeschichte ohne Namen," *Kunstchronik und Kunstmarkt*, 31/1/22 (1920), p. 435.

20 Bernhard Karlgren, "Yin and Chou in Chinese Bronzes," *Bulletin of the Museum of Far Eastern Antiquities* [Stockholm] 8 (1936).

21. Bernhard Karlgren, "New Studies on Chinese Bronzes," *Bulletin of the Museum of Far Eastern Antiquities* [Stockholm] 9 (1937), pp. 11 ff.

22. Bernhard Karlgren, "Marginalia on Some Bronze Albums, Part I," *Bulletin of the Museum of Far Eastern Antiquities* [Stockholm] 31 (1959), pp. 289 ff.; ibid., "Part II," 32 (1960), pp. 1–25.

23. Ludwig Bachhofer, "On the Origin and Development of Chinese Art," *The Burlington Magazine* 393 (December 1935), pp. 251–63; Perceval Yetts, "The Bronzes," *The Burlington Magazine* 68/384 (January 1936), pp. 15–22; Max Loehr, "Beiträge zur Chronologie der älteren chinesischen Bronzen," *Ostasiatische Zeitschrift* 22 (January-April 1936), pp. 1–41; H. G. Creel, "Notes on Professor Karlgren's System for Dating Chinese Bronzes," *Journal of the Royal Asiatic Society of G. B. & I.* (July 1936); J. Leroy Davidson, "Toward a Grouping of Early Chinese Bronzes," *Parnassus* 9/4 (April 1937), pp. 29–34, 51.

24. Davidson, "Toward a Grouping of Early Chinese Bronzes," p. 30.

25. J. Leroy Davidson, "Notes on Karlgren's 'New Studies on Chinese Bronzes,'" *The Art Bulletin* 22/3 (September 1940), pp. 165–66. See also Catherine Grassl, "New Researches on Chinese Bronzes," ibid. 25/1 (March 1943), pp. 65–78.

26. Bachhofer, "On the Origin and Development of Chinese Art," p. 257.

27. Ludwig Bachhofer, "The Evolution of Shang and Early Chou Bronzes," *The Art Bulletin* 26/2 (June 1944), pp. 107–16.

28. Ludwig Bachhofer, *A Short History of Chinese Art* (New York, 1946), preface.

29. Ibid., pp. 53–54.

30. Benjamin Rowland, Jr., review of Ludwig Bachhofer's *A Short History of Chinese Art*, *The Art Bulletin* 29/2 (June 1947), pp. 139–41.

31. Otto Maenchen-Helfen, "Some Remarks on Ancient Chinese Bronzes," *The Art Bulletin* 27/4 (December 1945), p. 239.

32. John A. Pope, "Sinology or Art History: Notes on Methods in the Study of Chinese Art," *Harvard Journal of Asiatic Studies* 10 (1947), pp. 388–417.

33. Ibid.

34. Loehr writes: "Wölfflin's 'grundbegriffe' ... if indeed they were taken to be recurrent and typical visual modes, could not be reckoned as historical categories at all" ("Some Fundamental Issues in the History of Chinese Painting," *The Journal of Asian Studies* 23/2 [February 1964], p. 186).

35. Max Loehr, "The Bronze Styles of the Anyang Period (1300–1028 B.C.)," *Archives of the Chinese Art Society of America* 7 (1953), pp. 42–53.

36. Karlgren, "Marginalia..., Part I," p. 290 n. 2.

37. *Wenwu* 1955/10, pp. 22-42; *Kaogu Xuebao* 1957/1, pp. 53–73.

38. Alexander C. Soper, "Early, Middle, and Late Shang: A Note," *Artibus Asiae* 28 (1966), p. 7.

39. Guo Moruo, *Jinwen congkao* [Studies on bronze inscriptions] (Beijing, 1954).

40. *Wenwu* 1961/11, p. 3.

41. Benjamin Rowland, Jr., "The Problem of Hui-tsung," *Archives of the Chinese Art Society of America* 5 (1951), p. 5.

42. Bachhofer, *Short History*, p. 61.

43. Ibid., p. 59.

44. Emanuel Loewy, *The Rendering of Nature in Early Greek Art*, trans. John Fothergill (London, 1907), p. 12.

45. On the basis of Loewy's "memory picture," George Rowley (1893–1962) of Princeton University characterized archaic Chinese art as "ideational" visualization. (See discussion by Alexander C. Soper, "Life-Motion and the Sense of Space in Early Chinese Representational Art," *The Art Bulletin* 30 [1948], pp. 167–86.) For Rowley's ideas about interpreting period styles in terms of the "growth of the mind," see Rowley, "Art and History," *Record of The Art Museum, Princeton University* 19 (1960), pp. 76–83.

46. Loehr, "Some Fundamental Issues," p. 186.

47. Loehr, "The Fate of the Ornament in Chinese Art," *Archives of Asian Art* 21 (1967/68), pp. 8–19.

48. Loehr, "Some Fundamental Issues," p. 192.

49. Although Riegl treated the subject of ancient Oriental rugs, which is an industrial and ornamental art, his theories of *Kunstwollen* and stylistic movement between two poles haptic and optic applied equally to the history of representational art. Likewise, Wölfflin's stylistic concepts "can be interpreted both in the decorative and in the imitative sense" *(Principles,* pp. 16, 230).

50. Max Loehr, *Ritual Vessels of Bronze Age China* (New York, 1968), pp. 12–13.

51. Semper, *Der Stil*, vol. I, p. viii.

52. Wilma Fairbank, "Piece-mold Craftsmanship and Shang Bronze Design," *Archives of the Chinese Art Society of America* 16 (1962), p. 15. Fairbank summarizes many of the ideas found in Noel Barnard, *Bronze Casting and Bronze Alloys in Ancient China*, Monumenta Serica Monograph XIV (Tokyo, 1961).

53. See Frankl, *The Gothic*, p. 628.

54. Loehr, *Ritual Vessels*, p. 12.

55. Zhang Yanyuan, *Lidai minghua ji*, trans. William R. B. Acker, *Some T'ang and Pre-T'ang Texts on Chinese Painting* (Leiden, 1954), pp. 65–66.

56. See the essay above by Ma Chengyuan, "The Splendor of Ancient Chinese Bronzes," p. 8.

57. In a recent paper, "Concepts of *Lei* and *Kan-lei* in the Early Chinese Art Theory," written for a Conference on Theories of the Arts in China sponsored by the American Council of Learned Societies and held on 6–12 June 1979, Kiyohiko Munakata discusses the importance of *kan-lei (gan lei)*, "response of the [like] kinds" or sympathetic response, in magic and art. Munakata makes a convincing attempt to interpret the meaning of the decoration on a Jincun bronze vessel in the Minneapolis Institute of Arts.

58. Fairbank, "Piece-mold Craftsmanship," p. 10.

59. Loehr, "Bronze Styles," p. 50.

60. Ibid., p. 49.

61. See Wen Fong, "Towards a Structural Analysis of Chinese Landscape Painting," *Art Journal* 28/4 (Summer 1969), pp. 388–97; idem, "How to Understand Chinese Painting," *Proceedings of the American Philosophical Society*, 115/4, August 1971, pp. 282–92; idem, *Summer Mountains: The Timeless Landscape* (New York, 1975).

62. See Wen Fong, "Archaism as a 'Primitive' Style," in *Artists and Traditions: Uses of the Past in Chinese Culture*, ed. Christian F. Murck (Princeton, 1976), pp. 89–109.

63. Loehr, "Bronze Styles," p. 50.

III

The Chinese Bronze Age:
A Modern Synthesis[1]

Kwang-chih Chang

The thirty years since the founding of New China have witnessed phenomenal progress in the country's archaeology, but one could assert that the most significant result to date in this field is the new knowledge of the formative stages of Chinese civilization, namely, the Chinese Bronze Age. Other archaeological finds may be more spectacular, such as the clay figures of warriors and horses next to the mausoleum of the First Emperor, Qin Shihuangdi, or they may be more consequential with regard to specific aspects of culture, such as the discovery of Qin legal documents at Yunmeng or that of Han books at Changsha. But these finds have merely enhanced and enriched our knowledge of Chinese history, whereas Bronze Age archaeology has fundamentally changed it. I may go so far as to say that thirty years ago we knew not how Chinese history began, and now we know or at least begin to know. This knowledge has been derived from the accumulation of a number of large and small archaeological finds made during the last thirty years from the Chinese Bronze Age.

We refer to the Chinese Bronze Age as the period in which bronzes had a significant presence in the archaeological record. We recognize a significant presence when we find artifacts of such kinds and of such numbers that there can be no question that the manufacture and use of bronzes had a central position in Chinese life. Metal objects (including bronze objects) appeared much earlier than the beginning of the Bronze Age, but by the time of the Erlitou culture the significant presence became unmistakable, and it is now believed that the Chinese Bronze Age began not later than about 2000 B.C. The ending of it was a prolonged and gradual process, beginning in the late Spring and Autumn period but not completed until the Qin dynasty of the third century B.C. According to the present archaeological record, then, the Chinese Bronze Age lasted at least 1,500 years, although toward the end it overlapped with the Iron Age for several centuries.

Whether or not one uses the term "Bronze Age" to describe the period from 2000 to 500 B.C., it was indeed an important segment in Chinese history: some refer to it as the slave society,[2] others as the formative stage of Chinese civilization.[3] If the segment of Chinese history characterized by the significant presence of bronzes coincides with the segment of history characterized by other important criteria, then bronzes could very well serve as a criterion for cultural and social definitions.

When the term "Bronze Age" was first coined in the West by Christian Jurgensen Thomsen (1788–1865), curator of the National Museum of Denmark, it was the second of the three ages representing a new classification of the collections in the museum: Stone, Bronze, and Iron Ages. "The Age of Bronze," in Thomsen's *A Guide to Northern Antiquities* (*Ledetraad til Nordisk Oldkyndighed*, Copenhagen, 1836), is the age "in which weapons and cutting implements were made of copper or bronze."[4] In his Huxley Memorial Lecture in 1944, V. Gordon Childe interpreted the three archaeological ages as "a series of consecutive stages in technological development, in the evolution of forces of production."[5] The Bronze Age, Childe further divided into three "modes." In Mode 1, weapons and ornaments were made from copper and its alloys, but no "mutant" tools and few implements were adapted exclusively for industrial use. Stone tools continued to be made with care. In Mode 2, copper and bronze were regularly used in handicraft, but neither in husbandry nor in rough work. The metal types included knives, saws, and specialized axes, adzes, and chisels. Mode 3 is characterized by the introduction of metal implements in agriculture and for heavy labor, shown in the archaeological record by metal sickles, hoe blades, and even hammerheads. Cautioning that these modes did not follow in the same order in all locations, Childe nevertheless strongly implied that the adoption of bronze implements was significant primarily in the realm of production. In "The Bronze Age," Childe again defined the concept as "a technological stage in which metal—actually copper more often than the alloy of copper and tin—first came to be used regularly for the *principal cutting tools and weapons* to replace or supplement the earlier equipment of stone, bone, and wood."[6] But he added that "Bronze Age means much more than a technological stage": he saw the manufacture and use of the metal to be connected with a series of interrelated changes that were either causes or effects of the new technological regime. These changes included: the emergence of more efficient means of production and weapons, especially metal saws suitable for the making of wheels; the practical sciences of smelting and ore prospecting; the initiation of organized international trade involving copper and other ores; and the emergence of full-time specialists. These represent fresh and more sophisticated insights, but Childe stresses bronze metallurgy as an industry geared around productive activities.

If, as we have noted, the Chinese Bronze Age essentially coincided in its commencement and its termination with a stage of Chinese social and cultural history characterized by other criteria, how can this be explained? What is in the bronzes that seems to make them the symbol of an age? Can our answers to these questions reinforce the conclusions reached by Childe on the basis of Near Eastern and European data or, perhaps, can they add to them some still newer insights? Before considering these questions we must first examine a few essential features of the Chinese Bronze Age civilization.

*   *   *

The ancient Chinese may have used metal for a long time before the Bronze Age. A small piece of metal was found at the Banpo site of the Yangshao culture, a site in Xi'an, Shaanxi Province, now firmly dated to about 5000 B.C.[7] It is a small, amorphous piece of uncertain content. Another piece, a small disc, was found lodged in the surface of a house floor at Jiangzhai, a Yangshao culture site close to Banpo and of comparable age, and it has been found to contain 65 percent copper and 25 percent zinc.[8] This is rather odd, since zinc supposedly did not find its way into ancient Chinese alloys until much later.[9] But the association is believed firm, and a copper-zinc alloy has also been reportedly identified in a metal piece at a Longshan culture (3000–2200 B.C.) site in Shandong.[10] Relatively pure copper, or copper in accidental or purposeful combination with a variety of other metals (zinc, tin, and lead), may have been used to a limited extent quite early in Chinese prehistory, at least during the periods when the kiln temperature of the Chinese potters reached a level sufficient to smelt the ores bearing these metals in some form.[11] Convincing evidence of the occurrence of metals is available for the period just before 2000 B.C., at sites in Gansu of the Qijia culture and in western Liaoning of the Lower Xiajiadian culture. Ornaments and small objects of copper have been found at several sites.[12] These cultures were roughly contemporary with many of the Longshan cultures of the Yellow River valley, which have long been thought to have used metal because of the "metallic" appearance of some pottery vessels (especially the "rivet"-like shapes at the base of handles, thought to be ceramic imitations of metallic rivets).[13] In fact, the discovery of such vessels in the Qijia culture itself, a culture with known finds of copper artifacts, has given rise to the speculation that metal vessels, perhaps at least partly smithied, were either produced by the Qijia culture or served as prototypes for Qijia vessels of pottery.[14] The existence of a "Copper Age" as a significant technological period in Chinese prehistory is a thesis long espoused by the Japanese scholar Dōno Tsurumatsu but thought to be laid on very dubious grounds.[15] There may be a subperiod of the Chinese Bronze Age that is characterized by copper vessels as well as implements, but sufficient archaeological evidence is not available for us to discuss it seriously.

The first well-established, significant presence of metal—cast-bronze ritual vessels and weapons found at archaeological centers associated with the aristocratic class—is in the Erlitou culture of western Henan Province. In the Erlitou culture (so named because it was first recognized among the archaeological finds at a village called Erlitou, in Yanshi, in 1959),[16] bronze was also employed for small tools and implements, such as knives and awls, as well as ornaments. Copper was used in the Qijia culture for axes, knives, awls, and other implements and tools, but in Qijia no trace has been found of an aristocratic locus associated with bronze ritual vessels and weapons as in the Erlitou culture. This difference in cultural and social levels associated with different classes of metal (tools, implements, and ornaments, on one hand; and weapons and ritual vessels, on the other) gives us the first clue to the real significance of bronze in the Chinese Bronze Age.

So far, four ritual vessels, all *jue* cups for wine service, have been found at the Erlitou site[17] (e.g., no. 1; Fig. 15). These vessels are small, thin (about 1 millimeter), plain, and flat-bottomed, but their seams indicate that they were cast in at least four piece molds. A distinctive ancient Chinese technique, the piece-mold casting of bronzes requires several steps. A model of the desired vessel is first built of clay and dried. Then a layer of wet clay is added onto several pieces, and the pieces are removed. A thin layer of clay is next scraped from the surface of the model, so that when the piece molds are fitted back onto it a hollow space is created between the reduced model (now a "core") and the outer molds. Decorative designs are either incised or engraved on the model so that the molds carry such designs in reverse, or are later executed on the inner surfaces of the molds. The core and the piece molds are then dried and hardened by fire. When they are reassembled and perhaps tied together, they are ready to receive the molten metal, which is poured into the hollow cavity through a pour hole. Air inside the cavity escapes through an air hole or two. After the metal hardens the molds are removed and the core is broken into fragments and taken out. The bronze vessel is then polished and retouched. Vessels of complex forms and large size required a complicated, delicate operation, with careful design and cooperative handling, but the basic principles are the same. Such principles probably held true for the making of almost all ritual metal vessels of Bronze Age China, from the smallest (such as an Erlitou *jue* only 12 centimeters high) to the largest (such as a four-legged cauldron found in Anyang, measuring 133 centimeters high and weighing 875 kilograms). Not only were all of the Erlitou *jue* vessels cast in this tradition, but they were all true bronzes: when one of the cups was analyzed with a spectrograph, it was found to have a chemical content of 92 percent copper and 7 percent tin.[18] Along with the *jue* were found bronze *ge* halberds. Thus, the Erlitou finds possess the essential distinctive features of ancient Chinese bronzes: piece-mold casting, copper-tin alloy, the use of distinctive forms such as the *jue* cups and *ge* halberds, the prominent use of bronze vessels for wine service, and the use of bronze for weapons.

The Erlitou site is the first in Chinese history, so far as has been established by archaeology, to contain a societal component characterized as aristocracy. In recent years many Chinese archaeologists have come to believe that society was significantly ranked in the Dawenkou culture in Shandong Province, as well as in the Longshan culture of both Henan and Shandong,[19] but, so far at least, the Erlitou marks the first Chinese culture to manifest archaeologically a clearly defined power center—an urban complex consisting of rammed-earth foundations that once supported houses of "palatial" proportions, smaller dwellings, workshops (including bronze foundries), as well as burials furnished with jades and cinnabar. These finds yielded bronze vessels and weapons, and inscribed pottery sherds. In contrast, houses and storage pits apparently used by members of the lower strata of society contained stone, bone, and antler implements and gray pottery typologically linked with the Neolithic pottery of the Longshan culture.

The culture represented by the Erlitou site is now known in a rather wide area, in northwestern Henan Province as far east as Zhengzhou and in southwestern Shanxi.[20] Two other sites of the culture were intensively excavated in recent years—the Wangchenggang site near Dengfeng, Henan Province, and Dongxiafeng near Xia Xian, in Shanxi Province.[21] A rammed-earth town wall was found to surround both sites, the Henan town about 100 meters square and the Shanxi town about 140 meters square. Both are located near the legendary sites of capital cities of the Xia dynasty, the first of the Three Dynasties, which, in traditional historiography, constitute the beginning phase of Chinese history. Since the distribution of the Erlitou culture remains largely coincides with the traditional sphere of activities of the Xia dynasty, and since radiocarbon dates now available for the Erlitou and Dongxiafeng sites establish their dates as the late third and early second millennia B.C., support is growing for the identification of this archaeological culture with the Xia (2205–1766 B.C.), although many archaeologists still insist that Erlitou (or at least its later phase) was in fact Shang, the second of the Three Dynasties.[22]

As far as we now know, the Erlitou culture was not literate. Many Erlitou potsherds were inscribed with characters, some of which are recognizable, but these are probably identifying marks rather than records of contemporary events. Classic texts alleged to date from the Xia dynasty are commonly regarded as later records and at best contain only fragments of Xia history. Among these are legends concerning Yu, the dynasty's founder and a hero who helped control primordial floods, and Gun, his father, first builder of walled towns. Fourteen generations of Xia kings are said to have reigned, ending with the infamous Jie, an oppressive despot who lost the kingdom to Tang, founder of the Shang dynasty.

The Shang is much better known than the Xia, through both archaeological remains and available documentary evidence.[23] Several dozen Shang sites are now known, grouped into two phases. Middle Shang sites, represented by the Shang city at Zhengzhou, northern Henan Province, have now been found in a wide area from Beijing in the north to northern Jiangxi in the south, and from central Shandong in the east to central Shaanxi in the west. This Shang phase is characterized by certain pottery forms, and especially by bronze vessels that resemble those of Erlitou but are now adorned with bands of animal profiles composed of thin lines and ribbons. Aristocratic centers associated with bronze vessels and weapons of Middle Shang are larger, more complex, again encircled by rammed-earth walls, but evidence of ritual human sacrifice is seen for the first time. Members of the lowest stratum of society not only supplied ritual victims, but their bones also provided the material for bone artifacts. Late Shang sites, represented by the famed sites in Anyang, northern Henan Province, are seen in an even larger area of China.[24] New styles of bronze vessels developed in this phase are characterized by large designs consisting of animal profiles and background spirals. Most important for historians, Late Shang archaeological finds produced inscribed oracle bones, which not only record the religious practices of the Shang kings, but also provide numerous clues to the nature of the Shang society, government, and economy.[25]

The Shang oracle bone inscriptions at Anyang leave no doubt that the kings who ruled with Anyang as their state capital in fact were kings of the last phase of the Shang dynasty, traditionally placed between 1766 and 1122 B.C.[26] Thirty kings are believed to have ruled under the Shang dynasty; the last twelve from a capital near Anyang. Zhengzhou is believed by some scholars to be a royal capital (perhaps the Ao or Xiao referred to in later histories) in the middle portion of the dynasty. Early Shang, representing the initial third of the Shang's rule, is at the moment archaeologically uncertain. Most historians, in an attempt to reconstruct the Shang's legendary route of migrations, believe that they came from the eastern parts of northern Chinese plains, and the archaeological remains of both Middle and Late Shang do show them to share important customs with the Neolithic antecedents in Shandong.[27] Predynastic and early dynastic Shang history, however, remains to be archaeologically explored. Eastern Henan, the legendary area of the Early Shang, is now covered by many meters of silt, the result of flooding during the historic period, and it is the least archaeologically known area of North China. But the Middle and Late Shang phases suffice to show that the Shang civilization was an important component of the Chinese civilization of the Bronze Age coming from the east to conquer the Xia in the eighteenth century B.C. Some six hundred years later, the Shang in their turn were conquered by the Zhou from the west.

The Zhou, the last of the Three Dynasties, is known by its own legends to have been for generations a people of the Wei River valley in central Shaanxi Province, but the archaeology of the Zhou people before their conquest of Shang—an event traditionally said to have occurred in 1122 B.C.—is now only beginning. Important excavations are now under way in Qishan and Fufeng (in an area long believed to be a predynastic capital, referred to in some texts as Zhou Yuan, the Plains of the Zhou), promising to yield new data that can be used to rewrite the early parts of the Zhou history. At Fengchu village in Jingdang People's Commune, Qishan, a cluster of more than thirty rooms built on rammed-earth foundations has already been excavated. These rooms adjoin one another to form a U-shape, with the open end facing south and a huge hall running the length of the opposite side of the courtyard. From a storage pit in a room in the western arm of the U came, in 1977, more than a thousand pieces of oracle bones, at least over two hundred of them inscribed. South of the foundations is a large burial area of many tombs, some containing bronzes.[28]

Although excavations in Zhou Yuan are continuing, enough is known to show that the Zhou had attained a level of social and cultural development comparable to the Shang well prior to the conquest of 1122. The capital of the Zhou, however, had been moved from Zhou Yuan to Feng and Hao, west of the present city of Xi'an, shortly before the conquest, and it was from Hao that the conquest was launched. Unfortunately, despite many years of archaeological reconnaissance in the area, only scattered Zhou remains have been found, and the capital sites have not yet been identified.[29]

Following the conquest, the archaeological manifestation of the Zhou civilization (traditionally, 1122–221 B.C.) is seen in two segments: Western Zhou (1122–771 B.C.), the period of Zhou history when Hao, near Xi'an, was the royal capital, and Eastern Zhou (after 771), when the royal house, under pressure from nomads to the north, had to move to Luoyang in western Henan, the ancient center of the Erlitou culture or probably the Xia civilization. Western

Fig. 7   Storage pit of Western Zhou bronzes at Beidongcun, Kezuo
Xian, Liaoning Province. The *fang ding* no. 54 and the lid of the
lei no. 55 are visible at the top right and top center.

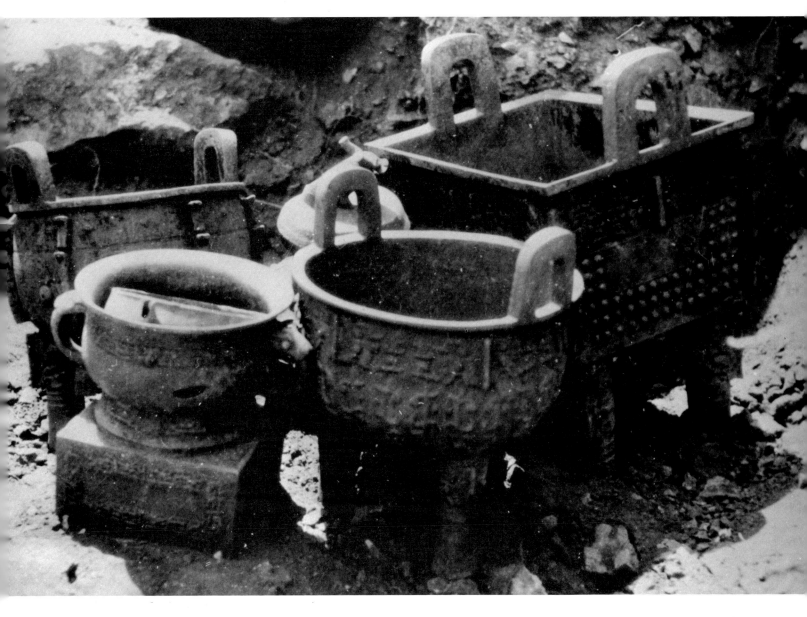

Zhou finds include large and small hoards of bronze vessels (Fig. 7), many cast with inscriptions, some quite long. For the Eastern Zhou period a number of city sites have been excavated, providing excellent information on the settlement patterns, political hierarchy, and economy of the period.[30] Bronze continued to be used for ritual vessels and weapons throughout the Zhou period, but iron tools and implements appeared shortly after the beginning of the Eastern Zhou phase, including, significantly, plowshares.[31] Throughout the Chinese Bronze Age, metal was not the principal material for the manufacture of productive implements, which continued to be made of stone, wood, antler, and bone. When iron was introduced, it was at once used on a large scale to make productive implements. Since cast iron was a relatively inexpensive metal, suitable for mass production, it exerted an immediate and profound influence upon Chinese culture and society. The beginning of the Chinese Iron Age—and therefore the end of the Chinese Bronze Age—may be said to be around 500 B.C., although significant use of bronze vessels and some weapons continued for several centuries. The unification of China under the First Emperor of the Qin dynasty in 221 B.C. probably resulted from the political and social consequences of the commencement of the Chinese Iron Age, but even then bronze remained important for weaponry. Actual bronze weapons were carried by the terracotta warriors guarding the emperor's tomb in Lintong, Shaanxi Province.[32]

Thus, the Chinese Bronze Age was the age of the Three Dynasties, extending from before 2000 B.C. to after 500 B.C. During this age, China was the stage of contending states, in parallel development, but these states formed highly stratified hierarchies, their pattern of stratification changing with the dynasties. During the Xia dynasty, the state of Xia, centered in northwestern Henan and southwestern Shanxi, was apparently of the highest rung of the ruling ladder. During the Shang dynasty, the Shang state, originating in the low plains of the Yellow River in eastern Henan and Shandong Provinces, was the supreme ruler, and in the early half of the Zhou dynasty the Zhou state from the middle and lower Wei River valley of Shaanxi became the most powerful. The Three Dynasties had shifting centers of political and ritual power, but according to the available textual and archaeological evidence all three dynastic periods are characterized by a common Chinese civilization. This is true not only for the earlier phases of the civilization—Xia and Shang—when the Chinese civilization covered a relatively small geographic area, but also for the later stages, when, as proved by the wide distribution of bronzes, the realm extended throughout China, including vast areas in South China.

*   *   *

Bronze artifacts of the Chinese Bronze Age may be approached from several different directions. They may—and should—be looked at and appreciated for their intrinsic properties as technology[33] and as art.[34] Their specific uses could be understood in the context of the activities in which they participated, such as those during meals, rituals, and battles.[35] Bronzes may also be examined for the roles they played in holding together the society in which they occurred. The key to understanding the Chinese bronzes in societal terms is the power structure of the Three Dynasties. The Chinese civilization of the Bronze Age depended on the way that the material wealth of that time was distributed, and power was used to insure that wealth be so distributed. Chinese bronzes were part of that political power.

Let us first take a look at the social units that constituted the framework for the distribution of wealth and power. At the center of the social framework was the city, the physical locus of the patrilineage. A typical city[36] during the Chinese Bronze Age consisted of an enclosure, often square or rectangular, arranged according to the cardinal directions. The enclosure was achieved through a city wall built of rammed layers of yellow earth. Inside the city was an area with large, presumably tall, houses built on rammed-earth foundations, with large columns of timber and large gates facing the south. Elsewhere in the city, inside the walls and outside, were scattered workshops, pit houses, and tombs. The loessic landscape of North China was dotted by hundreds to thousands of such cities, of varying sizes and scales of elaboration and complexity, forming hierarchical networks. Each network had one, two, three, or more levels, with the capitals of the states at the top.

The city hierarchy regulated the flow of material resources in the form of food, industrial products, and precious goods. Detailed records of economic transactions did not appear prominently in the known archives of the states. Here lies one of those East-West differences that some writers have been fond of talking about. Recent studies in both China[37] and the Near East[38] have shown that archaic forms or protoforms of writing can be traced back to the Neolithic period, when they were used for accounting in the Near East and for kinship identification in China. Much economic information occurred in ancient Chinese texts only incidentally, as it referred to religious, ritual, and political information. But enough documentation of the flow of material resources is available to indicate that the flow was heavily one-sided—mainly in the direction of the center of the state and the upper stratum of society.

For illustrating the uneven distribution of wealth—in many ways the foundation of ancient civilizations—the Shang dynasty is our best example from the Chinese Bronze Age. Information about the Xia is too scanty to be useful; *Yu Gong*, an ancient document alleged to detail the kinds of tributes that the court of the Great Yu had received from various parts of China, may contain a few facts about the Xia, but it is generally regarded as a late Zhou composition. On the other hand, the Zhou data base is vast and diverse, lacking clarity and simplicity. Data for the Shang system falls somewhere between.

At Anyang, the last Shang capital, where the divination records were kept in oracle bone inscriptions and where the best archaeological evidence avails, incoming traffic of economic resources was heavy, including mainly grains, game and domestic animals, industrial products, and services; and the outgoing flow was lighter, primarily gifts to provincial lords and the king's prayers for their well-being.

Of the incoming goods and services, grain, primarily millet, was probably the most important. The divination records show that the king took an interest in the harvest of the four quarters (East Land, West Land, North Land, and South Land) of his kingdom; he was interested in the harvests in the lands of his consorts, his princes, and his lords, but he showed no concern about the millet harvests of the alien states. Such records allow the inference that the king had a share in the grain harvests throughout his state. In addition, the king received other goods from various lords within the state, and sometimes these incomes were recorded on the bridges of turtle shells, or at the bottom of the sockets or along the flat edges of cattle shoulder blades.[39] From these we know that turtle shells, cattle shoulder blades, cowrie shells, cattle, horses, elephants, war captives, members of the Qiang people in the west, and so forth, were "entered" by or "came" from this or that lord. These recorded items probably represent a tiny proportion of the many scarce goods sent by the provinces to the capital.

The king did not just wait for gifts and tributes to roll in from his lords, however; he also went out to pick them up. The royal hunt, by all indications in the divination records an important event in which the king frequently participated, was probably one of the king's means of exploiting his provinces as well as a sport, and the gain was sometimes considerable. The king also made all sorts of journeys into the provinces, not to mention his military campaigns against his neighbors.[40] On these journeys the king and his large party undoubtedly enjoyed the "hospitality" of his subjects. Divination records tell of the *qu* ("taking") of horses, cattle, and sheep; some of these may have occurred on the king's trips.[41] At the end of successful military operations, captives in large or small numbers were taken, contributing to the wealth of the capital as both laborers and sacrificial victims.

As for outgoing wealth, the only significant items recorded are the royal gifts to the king's provincial lords. Such records occur only occasionally in the oracle bone inscriptions, but, since a royal gift of cowries or bronze often led to the commemorative casting of ritual vessels, the event was sometimes recorded in bronze inscriptions. In a catalogue of Shang and Zhou bronzes consisting of more than 4,000 inscribed bronzes, as many as 50 objects of supposedly Shang date bear inscriptions commemorating the royal gift giving.[42] Clearly, such gifts represent a "redistribution" of the state's wealth only at the top stratum of society.

In fact, the balance sheets, incomplete as they are, show that wealth in grains, meat, goods, and services consistently passed into the hands of members of the upper stratum of Shang society and of the large towns of the settlement network (especially the largest of them all, the capital). The archaeological remains of the ground houses and the royal tombs in Anyang illustrate this well. An inventory of the goods buried in one royal tomb alone, the tomb of Lady Hao (see nos. 28–40), a consort of King Wu Ding, fourth Shang king at Anyang,[43] is a staggering list:

> Wooden chamber and lacquered wooden coffin
> 16 sacrificial human victims
> 6 sacrificial dogs
> Almost 7,000 cowries
> More than 200 bronze ritual vessels
> 5 large bronze bells and 18 small bronze bells
> 44 bronze implements (27 of them knives)
> 4 bronze mirrors
> 1 bronze spatula
> More than 130 bronze weapons
> 4 bronze tigers or tiger heads
> More than 20 bronze artifacts of other descriptions
> More than 590 jade and jadelike objects
> More than 100 jade beads, discs, and pieces
> More than 20 opal beads
> 2 quartz crystal objects
> More than 70 stone sculptures and other stone objects
> 5 bone implements
> More than 20 bone arrowheads
> More than 490 bone hairpins
> 3 ivory carvings
> 4 pottery vessels and 3 clay whistles.

These offerings were gathered from beyond the Shang state territory as well as from within it, where they were manufactured by countless workers in countless workshops, probably both in Anyang and elsewhere in the state. Members of the opposite social stratum, whose pit houses and graves were numerous in the archaeological remains but whose contents warranted only brief or even statistical accounts, did not command any wealth of such proportions. The lives of the lower classes did not appear in the divination records, but some of the Zhou poems in the *Shi Jing* (Classic of Poetry) described it well:

> Kan-kan, you hew the *t'an* wood.
> You place it on the bank of the River.
> The waters of the River are clear and wavy.
> If you do not sow and do not reap
> How can you bring in three hundred yard-fulls of grain?
> If you do not chase and do not hunt
> How can we see suspended badgers in your courtyard?
> That nobleman, indeed he does not eat the food of idleness!
> ("Fa t'an")[44]

> Big rat, big rat,
> Do not gobble our millet!
> Three years we have slaved for you,
> Yet you take no notice of us.
> At last we are going to leave you
> And go to that happy land;
> Happy land, happy land,
> Where we shall have our place.
> ("Shuo shu")[45]

> In the seventh month the Fire ebbs;
> In the ninth month I had out the coats.

In the days of the First, sharp frosts;
In the days of the Second, keen winds.
Without coats, without serge,
How should they finish the year...?

In the days of the First we hunt the raccoon
And take those foxes and wild-cats
To make furs for our Lord.
In the days of the Second is the Great Meet;
Practice for deeds of war.
The one-year-old we keep;
The three-year-old we offer to our Lord....

In the seventh month, out in the wilds;
In the eighth month, in the farm;
In the ninth month, at the door.
In the tenth month the cricket goes under my bed.
I stop up every hole to smoke out the rats,
Plugging the windows, burying the doors:
Come, wife and children,
The change of the year is at hand.
Come and live in this house.
                    ("Qi yue")[46]

"Kio" sings the oriole
As it lights on the thorn-bush.
Who went with Duke Mu to the grave?
Yen-hsi of the clan Tzu-chü.
Now this Yen-hsi
Was the pick of all our men;
But as he drew near the tomb-hole
His limbs shook with dread.
That blue one, Heaven,
Takes all our good men.
Could we but ransom him
There are a hundred would give their lives.
                    ("Huang niao")[47]

The contrast between the tomb of Lady Hao and the peasants' life depicted in these poems makes clear that the gap between rich and poor was great. How this uneven sharing of wealth, a phenomenon first occurring in the Three Dynasties period, was maintained is not clear. Precise figures on population and productivity may never become available for the periods before and after the beginning of the Bronze Age, but clearly no qualitative technological transformation occurred in this time insofar as food production is concerned. Digging sticks, stone hoes, and stone sickles were the main agricultural implements both before and after. Nothing suggests that the societal change was technologically induced. With productive technology remaining essentially constant, the only potential variable is a reshuffling of resources to make them more accessible to some people than to others. This required not only a mere division of the population into economic groups, but a rigorous system of control on the part of the group on top to maintain a potentially unstable structure. The heart of the system seems to lie in *zhaomu*, *zongfa*, and *fengjian*, the three key institutions of ancient Chinese society. Wang Guowei, the great early twentieth-century historian of ancient China, believed that *zhaomu*, *zongfa*, and *fengjian* were the institutions that the Zhou invented to separate themselves from their Shang predecessors.[48] In fact, as new data and new research have made abundantly clear, these were the central institutions during much of the Chinese Bronze Age. Using more familiar anthropological terms as provisional definitions for these terms, *zhaomu* is dualistic leadership; *zongfa*, the segmentary lineage system; and *fengjian*, the incorporation in new towns of segmentary lineages.

Zhaomu

At the top of the Chinese society of the Bronze Age sat the king and his dynastic group, which consisted of all his male relatives who were either themselves eligible to be heirs or directly related to those who were eligible, and their female spouses. This unit was most likely closed and partially endogamous. According to recent studies of Xia and Shang kingship,[49] the succession to kingship during all three dynasties—except for the later Zhou period—may have rotated among a number of heir-producing units within the endogamous royal group, which was divided into two main—dualistic—divisions. In the royal ancestral temples this dualistic division was reflected in the *zhaomu* system as recorded in Zhou texts—ancestors of the *zhao* generation were placed in *zhao* temples placed to the left—east—of the founding ancestor in the middle, and those of the *mu* generation in *mu* temples to the right. It should be noted that this rotation idea is only one possible explanation of the *zhaomu* system of temple arrangement, and scholars of early China are by no means agreed as to its validity.

Zongfa

The royal dynasty was at the apex of an agnatic clan whose members claimed common descent from a single mythological ancestor. The clan consisted of a number of lineages whose members were genealogically related, and within each lineage members divided according to their genealogical distance from the main line, which was made up of the primary sons by the primary wives of each generation. A lineage member's political and ritual status was determined by his membership in primary, secondary, tertiary, and subsequent branches of lineage segments. A large lineage was thus a highly stratified society within itself.[50]

Fengjian

As lineage segments branched off from the stem of agnatic descent, the heads of the segments were dispatched to their own lands with their lineage members and wealth to establish walled cities and corporate political spheres. When these new lineages were the king's own relatives (most often brothers), they became the provincial lords of the kingdom, whose political hierarchy thus coincided with the segmentary lineage network. Agnatic lineages and their clan superstructures were usually exogamous, and the segmentary lineages had to be coupled with kinship units from other clans to form the political state.[51]

The interplay of the three institutional systems had several results. First, cities multiplied and spread out, forming among themselves stratified hierarchies parallel to the stratified hierarchies of the segmentary lineages. Their interrelationship was not always on an equal basis: within a state there was a head city—the capital—and, at the other end of the spectrum, many small cities of lowly status. Second, within each city and cluster of cities, the population was again segregated further into classes, in accordance with the degree of respective access to the main line of descent and, correspondingly, to the state's wealth and resources. Thus, within each state, dominated by a single clan but inhabited by members of many clans and their lineage subdivisions, the population formed a status continuum, with a large base and a small apex. The privileged people at the top were the rulers, controlling the resources and the armed forces. Under them were, in order of diminishing status, the small nobility, the craftsmen, and, finally, the farmers, who occupied the base of the pyramid as well as the pit houses.

When states dominated by different clans came into contact, several factors determined their respective statuses, which were constantly shifting. Marriage not only served to bond states together but also to help determine, or else reflect, the relative statuses of the intermarrying states. Relative status could also be decided by war, and captives formed the bottom stratum of society.

*   *   *

Rituals to sanction the kinship organization, both actual and fictitious, and wars were, in the words of the *Zuo Zhuan*, "the principal affairs of the state" (*guo zhi dashi zai si yu rong*). The characteristic feature of the Chinese Bronze Age is that the use of that metal was inseparable from ritual and from war. In other words, bronze *was* political power.

If in the scheme of the European Bronze Age the new metal was noted for its use for "weapons and cutting implements," it was weapons alone that seemingly dominated the minds of the ancients. Both Feng Hu Zi, the Eastern Zhou philosopher, and Lucretius, the Latin poet, described the succession of different materials used to fashion ancient weapons.[52] The ancients probably knew that the adoption of a new metal offered a more decisive advantage in weapons than anything else. In Bronze Age China, all the known major weapons had their cutting or piercing parts made of bronze: bronze-tipped arrow; spear; halberd, a bronze blade mounted perpendicularly onto a long wooden shaft; broad-blade ax and long knife, again mounted onto long wooden shafts; and sword and dagger.[53] Bows and arrows and the long arms were used primarily in conjunction with the horse-drawn chariot, and the swords and daggers were not widely in use until warriors were mounted on horseback during the latter half of the Zhou dynasty. Most of the weapons were used in war between the states, but a few, such as ax and long knife, were chiefly tools of execution. A scholarly opinion derives the ancient Chinese character for king, *wang*, from a pictograph of a bronze ax, symbol of the king who "had weapon to wage war without and had penal code to ensure order within."[54] Since bronze was not widely used for agricultural implements, the Bronze Age was not achieved primarily through a revolution in productive technology. If there was a revolution, it was in the realm of social organization. Because human labor was at the base of agricultural production, however, and because bronze weapons were instrumental in the acquisition of fresh productive labor as well as the insurance of its sustained exploitation, bronze did represent an indirect, though quite real, breakthrough in productive technology.

The other principal use of bronze—for ritual vessels—served to place bronze as a symbol of both aristocratic authority and sumptuary rules. During the Three Dynasties these vessels underwent many, sometimes conspicuous, changes of form and decorative style, but their major functions—to serve at rituals and to symbolize the legitimacy of the aristocratic rule of chosen groups of kin—were never changed. At the highest levels certain bronze vessels were made to symbolize the dynastic rule of a state, beginning (so the legend goes) with the Xia, and when dynasties changed hands so did the vessels:

> Anciently, when Xia was distinguished for its virtue, the distant regions sent pictures of the [remarkable] objects in them. The nine pastors sent in the metal of their provinces, and the tripods were cast, with representations on them of those objects.... When the virtue of Jie [the last Xia monarch] was all-obscured, the tripods were transferred to Shang, for 600 years. Zhou [last king] of Shang proved cruel and oppressive, and they were transferred to Zhou [the new dynasty]. When the virtue is commendable and brilliant, the tripods, though they were small, would be heavy; when it gives place to its reverse, to darkness and disorder, though they were large, they would be light. [*Zuo Zhuan*, bk. VII, year 3][55]

It is not known whether such symbols of dynastic legitimacy are to be found among the tens of thousands of existing bronze tripods from the Three Dynasties, but every bronze vessel—whether a tripod or other form—served as a part of the symbolic regalia and paraphernalia that accompanied aristocratic status at every level (see Figs. 8–10). Bronze vessels and weapons were among the symbolic gifts bestowed upon a royal relative sent by the king to his own land to establish his own town and political domain, and when the provincial lineages became further segmented they were again a part of the gifts handed down the aristocratic line. Bronze vessels acquired such significance because they were associated with rituals of ancestor worship, which sanctified the kinship-based aristocracy, but also because, as

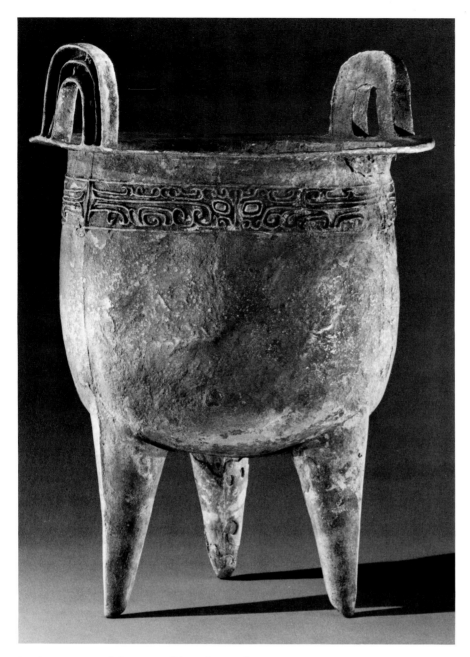

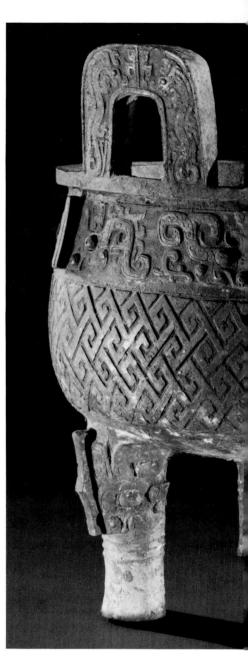

Fig. 8 Bronze tripod *ding* no. 4 of Shang dynasty, from
Lijiazui, Panlongcheng, Huangpi Xian, Hubei Province

Fig. 9 Bronze tripod *ding* no. 52 of
Western Zhou dynasty, from
Chang'an Xian, Shanxi Province

objects of precious materials that could be acquired only by those in control of vast technological and political machinery, they were suitable as symbols for sumptuary rule. Ultimately, bronze vessels were associated only with people of high status, and the number and kinds of vessels used in connection with their rituals were differentiated according to their varying statuses within the aristocracy.

There were many sources of copper and tin ores within the areas ruled by the Three Dynasties,[56] but the large-scale production of such technologically sophisticated bronzes as these must have required multistage operations by many kinds of specialists, who must have been organized and supervised by the state. Ores had to be mined and then smelted near the source. As Toguri remarked, even the richest ores contain not more than 5 percent metal.[57] Considering the number and the sizes of the bronze vessels, the demand for ores must have been enormous, and small mines must have been exhausted often and new sources constantly explored. Ingots of metals had to be transported over varying distances from the mines to the foundries and workshops, and again the transport routes had to be garrisoned. Bronzesmiths had then to initiate and complete the casting process. As Ursula Franklin has pointed out, "the beginnings of bronze production in China indicate the presence of a social order with sufficient organization and force to generate and replenish the required reservoir of forced labor."[58] At

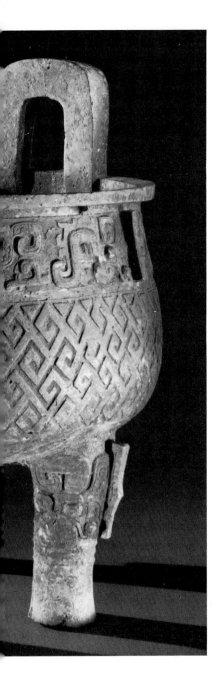
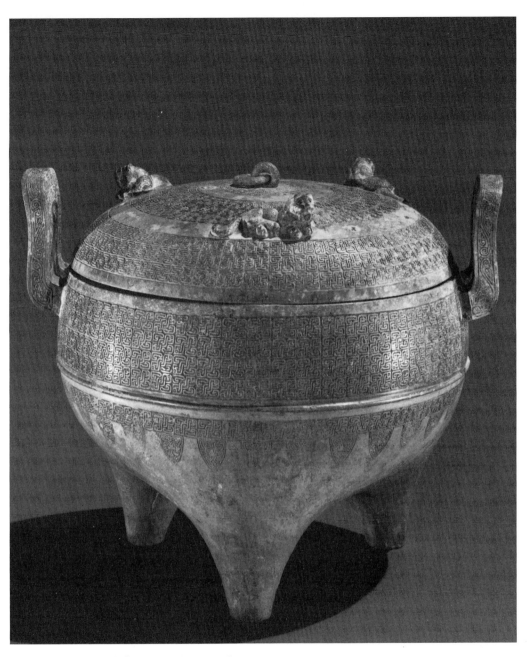

Fig. 10   Bronze tripod *li ding* no. 68 of Eastern Zhou
dynasty, from Liyu, Hunyuan, Shanxi Province

the same time, because the bronze production depended on such a social order, the bronze products assumed the role of symbols of that order and then came to reinforce it.

*   *   *

Having outlined current archaeological data of early Chinese civilization, we can return to the concept of the Bronze Age and briefly examine its usefulness—at least in the Chinese context—in relation to a few of the concepts currently or traditionally fashionable in archaeology, such as the state, urbanism, and civilization.

Unquestionably, each of these concepts has its uses. At the same time, each is limited to the area for which it was first formulated. The word "state," to begin with, is a typological category of government, and it is usually used in one of two senses. In the first sense, and at a lower level, "state" refers to a political entity with spatial borders, like a town or province. In the second sense, at a higher level, "state" is a type of society that is given certain characteristics in the political arena. In this sense, the term is a static characterizing abstraction that has no precise temporal or spatial boundary. There has been much discussion of late among archaeologists pertaining to the definition and origin of the state.[59] Such a concept is essential in archaeological studies for the understanding of the macroevolutionary process of the human society but is not suitable for a realistic grasp of the microevolutionary processes of particular histories and prehistories. Once such a characterizing abstraction has been made, however, we tend to give it a misplaced concreteness that, unfortunately, defeats our purpose. A "state" could easily be identified in an archaeological context, but that does not permit us to equate a "state society" with a realistic entity, a block of space and of time with specific dimensions and boundaries. Confusion over the two state concepts has resulted in endless debate over such false issues as the precise distinction between the chiefdom and the state in chronological sequence and the classification of one archaeological state as primary (pristine) and another as secondary. Since social evolution is continuous and cumulative, the line between chiefdom and state cannot—and need not—be precisely drawn across any actual sequence. Since developmental sequences in adjoining regions or areas are continuously interactive, the designations of one as pristine and the other as secondary are always misleading and often inaccurate. As I have had recent occasion to state, states never emerged singly; they come about in pairs or in a network of multiple components.[60] In the Chinese Bronze Age, for example, Xia, Shang, Zhou, and other political powers rose in parallel, competitive development. Archaeologists may find states in archaeological data but cannot look for the state society directly on the ground. They study their data, characterize the developments they thus come to recognize, and then may display such developments against some chosen abstract model and declare them state or not. The concept of the Bronze Age—by virtue of its reference to archaeological data close to the ground, its broadly inclusive scope, and its valid classificatory foundation (at least in the Chinese case)—is, thus, useful as a first step in any processing of archaeological data for higher generalization. It appears that, for China at least, the state form of government occurred for the first time in the Bronze Age, as the result of interrelated and interactive developments of several regional cultures.

Urbanism comes with cities, and cities can be identified on the ground, although what constitutes a city is not a question without questions. I define a city not by its size, but by its position within the political and economic system, and cities can exist only in systems that are stratified (hierarchical) and differentiated, both politically and economically. The Chinese experience shows plainly that urbanism began when the Bronze Age began and was an essential feature of the society of the Bronze Age.

Civilization—a concept that focuses on values, aesthetic quality, and ideological tradition—may be more difficult to place in contemporary American archaeology, which is preoccupied with such features as the exploitation of resources and state systems. Here, I think the Chinese archaeological experience provides some interesting food for thought. A "Chinese" civilization can be characterized on the basis of kinds and styles of artifacts for a geographical area ranging from outside the Great Wall in the north to beyond the Yangzi River in the south, an area that exhibited environmental heterogeneity and embraced within it all the political states known from archaeology or from documentary history for the Three Dynasties period. The concepts of the Chinese Bronze Age and the ancient Chinese civilization have a basic congruence that borders on interchangeability. Bronzes, of course, were themselves the outstanding features of the ancient Chinese civilization, and the reasons for their own preeminence were precisely the same factors that account for the rise of that civilization.

NOTES

1. This essay was delivered on 7 March 1979 as the annual Hume Lecture, under the auspices of the Council on East Asian Studies, Yale University, New Haven. Earlier works of synthesis include: Guo Moruo, *Qingtong shidai* [Bronze Age] (Chongqing, 1945); Guo Baojun, *Zhongguo qingtongqi shidai* [Chinese Bronze Age] (Beijing, 1963); Li Chi, "The Bronze Age of China," in *The Beginnings of Chinese Civilization* (Seattle, 1957), pp. 39–59.

2. Guo Moruo, *Nuli zhi shidai* [The Age of slavery] (Beijing, 1972).

3. Kwang-chih Chang, *Early Chinese Civilization* (Cambridge, 1976).

4. Quoted in Glyn Daniel, *The Origins and Growth of Archaeology* (Baltimore, 1967), p. 94.

5. V. Gordon Childe, "Archaeological Ages as Technological Stages," *Journal of the Royal Anthropological Institute of*

Great Britain and Ireland 74 (1944), pp. 1–19.

6. V. Gordon Childe, "The Bronze Age," *Past and Present* 12 (1957), p. 1.

7. Xia Nai, "Tan-14 ceding niandai he Zhongguo shiqian kaogu xue" [Carbon-14 dating and Chinese prehistory], *Kaogu* 1977/4, pp. 217–32.

8. Tang Lan, "Zhongguo qingtongqi di qiyuan yu fazhan" [The Origin and development of Chinese bronzes], *Gugong Bowuyuan Yuankan* 1979/1, p. 4.

9. H. T. Chang, "The Beginning of the Using of Zinc in China," *Bulletin of the Geological Society of China* 2 (1923), nos. 1/2, pp. 17–27; ibid., "New Research on the Beginning of Using Zinc in China," 4 (1925), no. 2, pp. 125–32.

10. Xia Nai and An Zhimin, verbal communication.

11. Li Jiazhi, "Wuoguo gudai taoqi he ciqi gongyi fazhan guocheng di yanjiu" [Research on the technical development of ancient ceramics and porcelain], *Kaogu* 1978/3, pp. 179–88; Zhou Ren et al., "Wuoguo Huanghe liuyu xinshiqi shidai he Yin Zhou shidai zhi tao gongyi di kexue zongjie" [Scientific summary of ceramic technology in the Yellow River valley, in the Neolithic, Yin, and Zhou periods], *Kaogu Xuebao* 1964/1, pp. 1–27. According to these works, kilns at the Neolithic sites were capable of producing a sustained temperature of 1000 degrees Centigrade, or a bit more, which is quite sufficient for smelting most pertinent ores.

As far as the unlikely combination of copper and zinc is concerned, Earle Caley's speculation about the occasional instances of early prehistoric alloys of copper and zinc in Europe and the Mediterranean is noteworthy:

> Bronze may be easily produced by an analogous process in primitive apparatus from a mixture of copper and tin ores, but brass cannot be produced by this general method for making alloys because a temperature high enough to reduce the copper and zinc ores would also be high enough to vaporize and oxidize practically all the zinc before it could alloy with any copper formed by reduction.... The formation of a copper-zinc alloy by cementation appears to be the only way by which the prehistoric alloys were produced. In this method, ... thin bars or small pieces of copper are buried in a mixture of zinc ore and charcoal contained in a crucible. On heating the crucible and its charge to a sufficiently high temperature some of the zinc formed by reduction is vaporized and lost, but most of it is trapped in the hot surface of the copper to form a copper-zinc alloy. By the subsequent fusion of the metal, and by stirring, a homogeneous alloy is produced. [*Orichalcum and Related Ancient Alloys* (New York, 1964), pp. 11–12]

I thank Linda Ellis of Harvard University for bringing this passage to my attention.

12. From the Qijia culture: "Gansu Yongjing Dahezhuang yizhi fajue baogao" [Excavation of the Qijia culture site at Dahezhuang, Yongjing, Gansu], *Kaogu Xuebao* 1974/2, pp. 53–54; "Gansu Yongjing Qinweijia Qijia wenhua yizhi" [Excavation of a Qijia culture site at Qinweijia, Yongjing, Gansu], *Kaogu Xuebao* 1975/2, pp. 74, 87; "Gansu Wuwei Huangniangniangtai yizhi fajue baogao" [Excavation at Huangniangniangtai, Wuwei, Gansu], *Kaogu Xuebao* 1960/2, pp. 59–60. From the Xiajiadian culture: "Chifeng Yaowangmiao Xiajiadian yizhi shijue baogao" [Exploratory excavations at Yaowangmiao and Xiajiadian in Chifeng], *Kaogu Xuebao* 1974/1, p. 127; Zheng, Shaozong, "Yuguan Hebei Changcheng Quyu yuanshi wenhua leixing di taolun" [A Discussion of primitive cultural types in the region of the Great Wall, Hebei], *Kaogu* 1962/12, p. 666; "Aohanqi Dadianzi yizhi 1974 nian shijue jianbao" [Exploratory excavation in 1974 at Dadianzi, Aohan Banner, Liaoning], *Kaogu* 1975/2, p. 99; "Hebei Tangshan Dachengshan yizhi fajue baogao" [Excavation at Dachengshan, Tangshan, Hebei], *Kaogu Xuebao* 1959/3, pp. 17–34.

13. Liang Ssu-yung, "The Lung-shan Culture: A Prehistoric

Phase of Chinese Civilization," *Proceedings of the Sixth Pacific Science Congress* 4 (1939), pp. 59–79.

14. Robert W. Bagley, "P'an-lung-ch'eng: A Shang City in Hupei," *Artibus Asiae* 39 (1977), nos. 3/4, pp. 197–99.

15. Noel Barnard, *Bronze Casting and Bronze Alloys in Ancient China*, Monumenta Serica Monograph XIV (Tokyo, 1961), p. 184.

16. Xu Xunsheng, "1959 nian xia Yu xi diaocha Xiaxu di chubu baogao" [In Quest of Xia remains in western Henan, summer 1959], *Kaogu* 1959/11, pp. 592–600.

17. "Henan Yanshi Erlitou yizhi san ba qu fajue jianbao" [Excavation of Zones 3 and 8 at Erlitou, Yanshi, Henan], *Kaogu* 1975/5, p. 304; "Yanshi Erlitou yizhi xin faxian di tongqi he yuqi" [Newly discovered bronzes and jades from the Erlitou site, Yanshi], *Kaogu* 1976/4, p. 260; "Erlitou yizhi chutu di tongchi he yuchi" [Bronzes and jades unearthed at Erlitou], *Kaogu* 1978/4, p. 270.

18. "Henan Yanshi Erlitou," p. 304.

19. "Tantan Dawenkou wenhua" [Notes on Dawenkou culture], *Wenwu* 1978/4, pp. 1–4.

20. Yin Weizhang, "Erlitou wenhua tantao" [A Discussion of Erlitou culture], *Kaogu* 1978/1, pp. 1–4.

21. Chou Yung-chen, "The Search for Hsia Culture," *China Reconstructs* 27 (1978), pp. 48–50.

22. Tong Zhuchen, "Cong Erlitou leixing wenhua shi lun Zhongguo di guojia qiyuan wenti" [A Preliminary discussion of the origins of the state in China in light of Erlitou culture], *Wenwu* 1975/6, pp. 29–33; Chang Kwang-chih, "Yin Shang wenming qiyuan yanjiu shang di yige guanjian wenti" [A Pivotal problem in research on the origins of Shang civilization], in *Shen Gangbo xiansheng bazhi rongching lunwen ji* [Essays congratulating Mr. Shen Gangbo on his eightieth birthday] (Taipei, 1976), pp. 151-69; Zou Heng, "Zhengzhou Shang cheng ji Tang du Bo shuo" [The Theory that the Shang city Zhengzhou was King Tang's capital Bo], *Wenwu* 1978/2, pp. 69–71; Wu Ruzuo, "Guanyu Xia wenhua ji qi laiyuan di chubu tansuo" [Notes on Xia culture and its origins], *Wenwu* 1978/9, pp. 70–73.

23. For two recent syntheses of the Shang civilization, see K. C. Chang, *Shang Civilization* (New Haven, 1980); Xia Nai, "The Slaves Were the Makers of History," *China Reconstructs* 24 (1975), no. 11, pp. 40–43.

24. See Li Chi, *Anyang* (Seattle, 1977).

25. David N. Keightley, *Sources of Shang History* (Berkeley and Los Angeles, 1978), pp. 134–56.

26. For alternate chronologies of the Shang dynasty, see K.C. Chang, *Shang Civilization*, chap. 7.

27. Chang [K. C.], "Yin Shang wenming qiyuan yanjiu shang," pp. 151–69.

28. "Shaanxi Chishan Fengchucun Xi Zhou jianzhu jizhi fajue jianbao" [Brief report of the excavations of Western Zhou building foundations at Fengchucun, Chishan, Shaanxi], *Wenwu* 1979/10, pp. 27–34.

29. Wang Bohong et al., *Feng xi fajue baogao* [Report of excavations west of the Feng River] (Beijing, 1962).

30. For Zhou archaeological finds, see Cheng Te-k'un, *Chou China* (Cambridge, 1962); Kwang-chih Chang, *The Archaeology of Ancient China*, 3rd ed. (New Haven, 1977).

31. Huang Zhanyue, "Jin nian chutu di Zhanguo liang Han tie qi" [Recently excavated iron implements from the Warring States and Han periods], *Kaogu Xuebao* 1957/3, pp. 93–108.

32. "Lintong Xian Qin yung keng shijue di yi hao jianbao" [Excavation of the Qin dynasty Pit No. 1 of pottery figures at Lintong Xian], *Wenwu* 1975/11, pp. 1-18; "Qin Shihuang ling dong ce er hao bing ma yung keng zuantan shi jue jianbao" [Exploratory excavation of Pit No. 2 of pottery warriors and horses to the east of Qin Shihuang's burial mound], *Wenwu* 1978/5, pp. 1–19.

33. Shi Zhangru, "Yin dai di zhu tong gongyi" [Bronze-casting technology of the Yin period], *Zhongyang Yanjiuyuan Lishi Yuyan Yanjiusuo Ji Kan* 26 (1955), pp. 95–129; Noel Barnard, *Bronze Casting and Bronze Alloys*; Wilma Fairbank, "Piece-mold Craftsmanship and Shang Bronze Design," *Archives of the Chinese Art Society of America* 16 (1962), pp. 8–15; R. J. Gettens, *The Freer Chinese Bronzes II. Technical Studies* (Washington, D.C., 1969); Noel Barnard and Sato Tamotsu, *Metallurgical Remains of Ancient China* (Tokyo, 1975).

34. See the essay by Wen Fong, "The Study of Chinese Bronze Age Arts: Methods and Approaches," above.

35. For use at meals, see Kwang-chih Chang, "Food and Food Vessels in Ancient China," *Transactions of the New York Academy of Sciences*, 2d ser. 35 (1973), pp. 495–520.

36. See K. C. Chang, "Towns and Cities in Ancient China" in *Early Chinese Civilization*, pp. 61–71.

37. Kwang-chih Chang, "Prehistoric and Shang Pottery Inscriptions: An Aspect of the Early History of Chinese Writing and Calligraphy" (Paper presented at Conference on Traces of the Brush: Studies in Chinese Calligraphy, Yale University, New Haven, 8–10 April 1977).

38. Denise Schmandt-Besserat, "The Earliest Precursor of Writing," *Scientific American* 238, no. 6 (1978), pp. 50–59.

39. Hu Houxuan, "Wu Ding shi wu zhong ji shi ke ci kao" [Examination of five kinds of notation inscriptions of the Wu Ding era] in *Jia gu xue Shang shi lun cong* [Collected studies of Shang history based on oracle bone studies], vol. I (Chengdu, 1944).

40. Dong Zuobin, "Wu Ding ri pu" [Date tables of the Wu Ding reign] in *Yin li pu* [Calendrical tables of the Yin dynasty], pt. II, vol. 9 (Lizhuang, 1945).

41. Chen Mengjia, *Yin xu puci zong shu* [Comprehensive study of Yin divination inscriptions] (Beijing, 1956), p. 318.

42. Chang Kwang-chih et al., *Shang Zhou gingtongqi yu mingwen di zong he yanjiu* [A General investigation of Shang and Zhou bronze vessels and their inscriptions], Zhongyang Yanjiuyuan Lishi Yuyan Yanjiusuo Zhuankan, no. 62 (Taipei, 1972).

43. "Anyang Yinxu wuhao mu di fajue" [Excavation of Tomb 5 at Yinxu, Anyang], *Kaogu Xuebao* 1977/2, pp. 57–98.

44. Bernhard Karlgren, trans., *The Book of Odes* (Stockholm, 1974), pp. 71–72.

45. Arthur Waley, trans., *The Book of Songs* (New York, 1960), p. 309.

46. Ibid., pp. 164–66.

47. Ibid., p. 311.

48. Wang Guowei, "Yin Zhou zhidu lun" [A Discussion of Yin and Zhou institutions] in *Guan Tang ji lin*, vol. 10, 1921.

49. Kwang-chih Chang, "Shang wang miao hao xin kao" [A New study of designations of the Shang kings], *Zhongyang Yanjiuyuan Minzuxue Yanjiusuo Ji Kan* 15 (1963), pp. 65–95; idem, "Tan Wanghai yu Yiyin di ji ri bing zai lun Yin Shang wang zhi" [The Days of offering to Wanghai and Yiyin with a discussion of Shang kingship], ibid. 35 (1973), pp. 111-27.

50. Ding Shan, *Jia gu wen suo jian shizu ji qi zhidu* [Clans and lineages as seen in oracle bone inscriptions and their system] (Beijing, 1956); Zhang Zhenglang, "Gudai Zhongguo di shi jin zhi shizu zuzhi" [Decimal clan organization in ancient China], *Lishi Jiaoxue* 2 (1951), pp. 85–91, 122–25, 194–97; K. C. Chang, "The Lineage System of the Shang and Chou Chinese and Its Political Implications" in *Early Chinese Civilization*, pp. 72–92.

51. Hu Houxuan, "Yin dai fengjian zhidu kao" [Study of the Yin period feudal system] in *Jia gu xue*, vol. I; Ding Shan, *Yin Shang shizu fang guo zhi* [Clan and lineage system and alien states in Yin Shang] (Beijing, 1956).

52. K. C. Chang, *The Archaeology of Ancient China*, p. 2.

53. Hayashi Minao, *Chūgoku Inshō jidai no buki* [Weapons of the Yin and Zhou periods] (Kyoto, 1972).

54. Lin Yun, "Shuo wang" [Etymology of the character *wang*], *Kaogu* 1965/6, pp. 311–12.

55. James Legge, trans., *The Ch'un Ts'ew, with the Tso Chuen*, The Chinese Classics, vol. 5 (Oxford, 1872), p. 293.

56. Shi Zhangru, "Yin dai di zhu tong gongyi"; Amano Motonosuke, "Indai sangyō ni kansuru jakkan no mondai" [Certain problems relating to Yin period industry], *Tōhōgakuhō* (Kyoto) 23 (1953), pp. 231–58.

57. Quoted in Ursula Franklin, "On Bronze and Other Metals in Early China" (Paper presented at a Conference on the Origins of Chinese Civilization, University of California at Berkeley, June 1978), p. 17. For more precise figures on percentage of metal yield for various minerals, see C. Hurlbut, *Dana's Manual of Mineralogy* (New York, 1971).

58. Franklin, "On Bronze and Other Metals," p. 17.

59. Some examples of recent discussions are: Elman R. Service, *Origins of the State and Civilization: The Process of Cultural Evolution* (New York, 1975); Henry T. Wright, "Recent Research on the Origin of the State," *Annual Review of Anthropology* 6 (1977), pp. 379–97; R. Cohen and E. Service, eds., *The Origins of the State: The Anthropology of Political Evolution* (Philadelphia, 1978).

60. Kwang-chih Chang, "Sandai Archaeology and the Formation of States in Ancient China: Processual Aspects of the Origins of Chinese Civilization" (Papers presented at a Conference on the Origins of Chinese Civilization, University of California at Berkeley, June 1978); idem, "Shang Civilization," 1980.

IV

Burial Practices of Bronze Age China

Robert L. Thorp

Most of the objects in this exhibition were uncovered during recent archaeological excavations, and those not discovered under these controlled conditions were nonetheless taken from the ground. While only the life-size human figures and horses from trenches near the tomb of the First Qin Emperor (nos. 98–105) were undeniably made for burial, most of the objects shown here ultimately became part of the furnishings of a tomb. The ritual bronze vessels and jades, though not examples of mortuary art, survived because of the burial practices of the Shang and Zhou periods, and burial customs can therefore be used to establish a context for these works of art.

A Sinitic tradition of burial can be recognized as early as the fifth millennium B.C. at sites such as Banpo and Jiangzhai near Xi'an, Shaanxi Province, where well-preserved villages and cemeteries of the early Yangshao culture have been excavated.[1] Most Neolithic sites in North China have the cemetery laid out like those in these two villages—segregated from the dwellings, with the graves arranged with care in a common and consistent orientation. Inhumation burial was favored, as were simple rectangular trenches for graves and a supine, extended-leg posture for the corpse. Single burials holding a selection of grave goods that included pottery, jewelry, and stone tools were common. The concern for the dead manifested by such habits suggests that even at this early date rites of burial and perhaps even a concern for an afterlife formed a significant aspect of the community life.

The immediate ancestors of the Shang civilization, the first period of the Chinese Bronze Age, were the late Neolithic cultures of central and eastern North China, and burial customs document the links between the two. The Neolithic Dawenkou cemetery in southern Shandong Province typifies the origins of Shang practices.[2] At this cemetery, graves were occasionally equipped with a log chamber (*guo*) to house the corpse and some of the burial goods. The large and varied assortment of pottery vessels typical of this culture was placed on a ledge or step (*ercengtai*) inside the four walls of the trench. The people of Dawenkou differentiated grave goods according to the gender of the deceased: sewing needles and spindle whorls were interred with females, and ax heads and other tools with males. Animals, usually pigs, were sacrificed at the grave, and many corpses held the teeth of the roebuck deer in their hands. The fine pottery from these graves, some of it painted and much of it elegant in shape, may have been a ceremonial ware used in burial rites. Each of these aspects of the Dawenkou graves anticipates Shang burial customs.

Erlitou

The most important early Shang (or possibly Xia) site, Erlitou in Yanshi Xian, Henan Province, provides only meager evidence for burial customs. What evidence there is shows little advance over the long-standing traditions of the Neolithic period. While archaeologists have yet to uncover any proper cemetery district, they did find small graves and other burials that may have been sacrificial scattered throughout the several tracts systematically explored. The substantial earthen terrace of the palace foundation contained burials that both predate and postdate the construction of the compound. Some of those burials may have been connected to the construction of the palace. Only a handful of the burials were more than simple trenches modestly furnished. The bronze *jue* (no. 1) and the two jade blades (nos. 2, 3) here may have been taken from a burial, but their precise context is uncertain.

The few rich graves at Erlitou clearly presage later Shang burial practices. The richest grave found so far, K3, was located about 550 meters north of the palace.[3] The grave was oriented almost precisely north-south, the direction traditionally employed by the Shang for important buildings as well. The trench was rectangular with an inner ledge on three sides. The ledge, in turn, enclosed a smaller and narrower trench for the wooden coffin. Covering the base of this area was a 5 to 6 centimeter layer of cinnabar, a typical feature of many Shang burials that accounts for the red coloration of small artifacts taken from Shang graves (cf. nos. 34–40, the small jades from the tomb of Fu Hao). The grave furnishings, while modest by later standards, included both a gray pottery *he* (similar to no. 5) and a bronze *jue* (cf. no. 1), each a wine vessel type favored by the Shang. The grave also contained a selection of weapons in bronze and jade, a stone musical chime, pieces of turquoise originally inlaid in a perishable material, and cowries. This array of grave furnishings represents the range of objects found in tombs throughout the Shang period, furnishings that were emblems of status, power, and wealth.

Zhengzhou and Panlongcheng

Middle Shang sites offer better evidence for burial practices and demonstrate a growing sophistication in tomb structures and furnishings. Paralleling the ritual bronzes from Zhengzhou and Panlongcheng, the burials at the two sites betray no significant differences in style or content. At both sites, large graves (or tombs) were placed outside the Shang walls. At Zhengzhou, large tombs from areas west and northeast of the Shang city wall are reported, and a similar distribution was found at Panlongcheng.

The Middle Shang tombs exhibit several important structural innovations. A double chamber in Tomb 2 at Lijiazui, east of Panlongcheng, provided two housings around the coffin.[4] The timbers of these chambers were carved with motifs seen on contemporary bronze vessels (cf. nos. 4–9, 11) and painted in red and black lacquer. In some areas, the incised lines of the design appeared in black and the surrounding ground in red. The available photographs suggest that this decoration was segmented into units centered on paired eyes, just as the bronze decor was executed in such units corresponding to mold sections. These paired, symmetrical motifs were not confined to bronze vessels and tomb chamber walls. A jade handle (*bing*) found at Erlitou near K3 bears three registers of animal masks with their eyes displayed on adjoining faces of the handle. Apparently, the bronze casters and other artisans shared a common artistic vocabulary even in Early and Middle Shang.

The Panlongcheng and Zhengzhou tombs are also the earliest yet found with sets of ritual vessels used in the funeral rites. Tomb 2 at Lijiazui had two dozen bronze ritual vessels, including types for wine storage, heating, and serving, as well as for the preparation and presentation of other offerings. Wine vessels in this tomb were placed around the coffin within the inner chamber, but food vessels were found between the walls of the inner and outer chambers (Fig. 11). The small pit at the base of the tomb shaft (called by convention a "waist pit," *yaokeng*, since it underlies the waist of the corpse) contained the bones of a sacrifice and a *ge* dagger-ax blade (cf. no. 10) broken into three pieces. The combination of a sacrifice, either a dog or a human victim, and a *ge* blade broken in pieces was a common feature of later Shang burials as well.

The earliest known proof that human victims were sacrificed at funerals of the Shang elite comes from these Middle Shang sites. Tomb 2 at Lijiazui had two human victims, an adult and a child, lying in the space between the inner and outer chambers on the west side, and a third victim of uncertain age, probably originally placed on the roof of the outer chamber. Tombs at Zhengzhou and Hui Xian of Middle Shang date revealed similar evidence, and at Zhengzhou the site of a workshop where human bones were carved has also been excavated.

Some excavated ritual vessels apparently did not come from proper burials. The large *fang ding* (no. 11) from Duling, Zhengzhou, was one of a pair of vessels taken from a pit on a hill

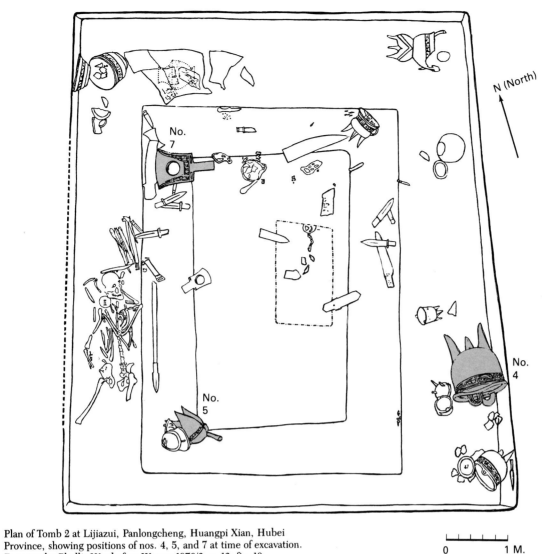

N (North)

Fig. 11   Plan of Tomb 2 at Lijiazui, Panlongcheng, Huangpi Xian, Hubei
Province, showing positions of nos. 4, 5, and 7 at time of excavation.
Drawing by Phyllis Ward after *Wenwu* 1976/2, p. 12, fig. 10

0   1 M.

about 300 meters west of the Shang wall.[5] The pair were found side by side 6 meters below
ground. Since one of the two was taller than the other, it was placed slightly deeper so that the
tops of the two *ding* were level. These are not the first paired *fang ding* excavated: both Tomb
1004 at Xibeigang and the tomb of Fu Hao at Anyang had such pairs in their shafts, and pairs are
also known from early Zhou graves such as that near Lingtai, Gansu Province, which yielded
the *he* (no. 44). It seems likely that a pair of *ding* was used for some particular rite or part of a
funeral. It is also possible that vessels were occasionally buried as part of sacrifices not tied to
burials; this may account for the *fang ding* from Duling. Such sacrifices probably also account
for random finds of Shang vessels in South China, such as the elephant *zun* (no. 24) from Liling
and the *you* (no. 25) from Ningxiang, both in Hunan Province. The Ningxiang *you* held some
300 pieces of jade when it was found.

Anyang

The Late Shang sites near Anyang in northern Henan Province have long dominated all
aspects of Shang art and archaeology. These sites may represent a cult center at the heart of an
extensive necropolis of large tombs and graves extending in virtually every direction from that
center. From the numerous oracle bone texts found at Anyang it is clear that the Shang kings
devoted an inordinate amount of time to divination, consulting the spirits of the ancestors. The
archaeological evidence also demonstrates that the Shang expended considerable wealth and
human life on their burials. The countless artifacts found at Anyang, both the humble and the
important works of art, testify to the importance of the cult that, in fact, provided the *raison
d'être* for the creation of many of them.

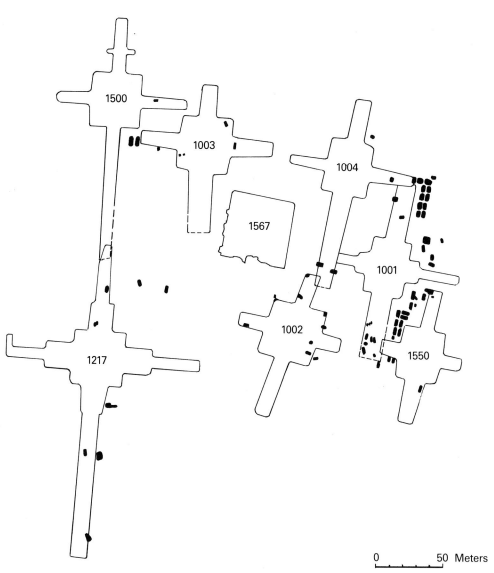

Fig. 12 Plan of large tombs and accompanying sacrificial pits at
Xibeigang, Anyang, Henan Province. After Li Chi, *Anyang*
(Seattle, 1977), fig. 9, and *Kaogu* 1977/1, p. 13, fig. 1, p. 21, fig. 2

0 _____ 50 Meters

Among the important sites near Anyang are two clusters of large tombs north of the Huan
River at Xibeigang, another cemetery tract also north of the river near the village of
Dasikongcun, a mix of large tombs and small graves south of the river at Hougang, the cult
center itself northeast of Xiaotun, and still more cemeteries to the south and west of Xiaotun.
The number of burials at these several sites certainly totals in the thousands. Tomb looting
may have taken place here as early as pre-Han times and in more recent centuries was a
consequence of the antiquarian taste for archaic vessels. In spite of such depredations, the site
is by no means exhausted.

Since the prewar Anyang excavations first gained world attention, the large tombs at
Xibeigang have been commonly considered the royal cemetery.[6] In fact, all of those tombs
were so thoroughly ransacked before Chinese archaeologists came to them that almost
anything that could be used to attribute these burials to the Shang kings had already been
removed. The large tombs excavated before the war revealed that huge looters' pits dug
directly over the shafts had destroyed almost all traces of the burial chambers and tomb
furnishings. The finds from these large tombs came either from the disturbed earth used to
refill the pits or from the periphery of the tombs, which remained untouched before the
controlled excavations. Some of the artifacts, such as the marble sculptures, were broken and
their pieces found deposited in the fill of different tombs. Thus, while it is reasonable to
suppose that such large burials were royal, any attempt to attribute specific tombs to individual kings known from the oracle bone inscriptions is highly speculative. More large tombs have
been excavated than Shang kings of the Yin period can be attested from the oracle bone

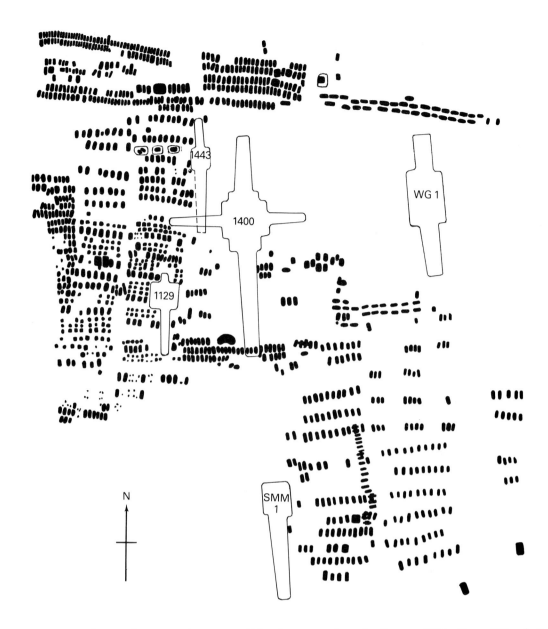

inscriptions, and more large tombs may still be discovered in the future. If Fu Hao of Tomb 5, west of Xiaotun, was a consort of the king Wu Ding, her tomb must be one of the earliest large tombs excavated to date. The oracle bone inscriptions provide no evidence that any kings before Wu Ding divined (and reigned?) at Anyang, so if the early date of this tomb is accepted it provides a benchmark for a relative chronology of the Anyang finds.

The large tombs at Xibeigang (Fig. 12) were located some distance north of the Xiaotun cult center, and other large tombs have been found both to the east and to the west of Xiaotun. None of the tombs had an earthen mound aboveground, but stone plinths above Tomb 5 suggest that sometimes small buildings, possibly mortuary temples, surmounted the tomb shafts. All of the large tombs were aligned roughly along a north-south axis, from 7 to 17 degrees east of magnetic north. The oracle bone inscriptions provide evidence that the Shang revered the four directions and had special names for them. Such careful alignment assured a harmonious relationship between burials and foundations and the spirits of the four quarters.

The large tombs at Anyang are characterized by sloping ramps (*mudao*), which descended from ground level to the base of the tomb shaft (Fig. 13). Tombs with one, two, and four ramps have been excavated; the south ramp provided access to the burial chamber and the others descended only to the rammed-earth ledges that embraced the chamber and were level with the top of it. At Tomb 1217, Xibeigang, the south ramp measured over 60 meters in length. The shafts of the large tombs were roughly square, averaging about 18 meters on a side and 12 meters in depth. The removal of so much earth must have been a major engineering feat, compounded by the Shang construction technique of rammed earth (*hangtu*). The walls of the

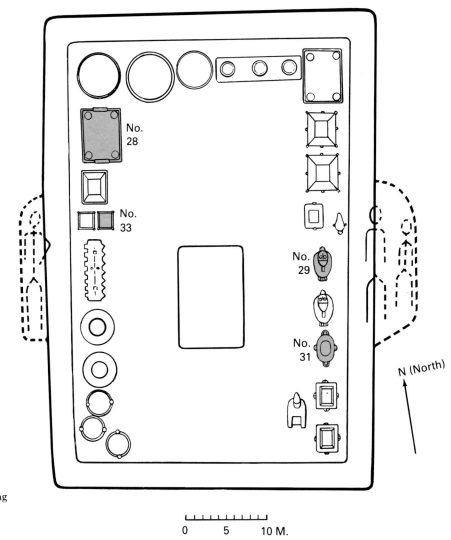

Fig. 13 Plan of Tomb 5 (tomb of Fu Hao) at Xiaotun, Anyang, Henan Province, showing a tentative reconstruction of the positions of major vessels, including nos. 28, 29, 31, and 33. Drawing by Phyllis Ward after *Kaogu Xuebao* 1977/2, p. 61, fig. 3

No. 28

No. 33

No. 29

No. 31

N (North)

0   5   10 M.

shafts were rammed hard, as was the earth used for the ledges and for the fill of the shafts and ramps replaced after the funeral. Like the city wall at Zhengzhou, the Xibeigang tombs reflect the power of the elite to muster large labor forces.

The wooden burial chambers of the large Shang tombs have not survived; in a few cases we are fortunate enough to have their imprints in the loess soil that was rammed hard around them. The chambers were large rectangular boxes with extensions from the sides that met the ramps. This cruciform shape has been dubbed "*yaxing*," because it resembles the form of the same name often found in Shang bronze inscriptions. No trace of doors or of internal partitions in the chambers has yet been found, and no coffin has been reported intact. The impressions left in the soil show that some chambers were carved with elaborate decor resembling the designs on bronzes, painted with lacquer and even inlaid with ivory and turquoise. The artisans who carved the walls of the tomb chamber as well as the bronze casters adopted a style of rendering surface decor in which major motifs were played off against a contrasting ground, another example of the unity of Shang artistic traditions.

Human sacrifice was pervasive at the late Shang sites centered on Anyang, where this custom was a part of funerals, ceremonies conducted for the ancestors, and the construction of some buildings. The late Shang oracle bones make it clear that the ancestors derived their strength in part from offerings of wine, flesh, and blood, and it was in these rites that the ritual vessels served the Shang elite. The rows of sacrificial trenches near the supposed temples at Xiaotun and the large tombs at Xibeigang demonstrate how important it was to the upper echelon of society to assuage the ancestral spirits. Such archaeological evidence is the concrete counterpart of the oracle bone texts, which document the Shang kings' relations with the ancestors.

Human victims in the large tombs around Anyang have not been found consistently, but were probably usual in a Shang funeral. Tomb 5 had sixteen victims, some in niches in the side walls of the shaft and others in the fill over the chamber. Tomb 1001, on the other hand, had human victims in several different areas of the tomb, fulfilling different functions. Nine males, possibly guardians, were buried in the base of the shaft, one in a waist pit at the center under the chamber, and two in each corner of the shaft. All were accompanied by dogs and weapons. On the ledges, in areas not disturbed by the looters' pits, were more skeletons, dignified by coffins, that may have been the remains of female attendants or concubines. In the south ramp, almost sixty decapitated skeletons were found with a larger number of skulls. In other such burials an ax has been found nearby (see no. 23). The oracle bone inscriptions note that Qiang tribesmen from the territories west of the Shang domain were sacrificed on such occasions.

While Tomb 5 was not looted, its wooden chamber had thoroughly disintegrated and was waterlogged.[7] The larger ritual vessels were lined up next to the walls of the chamber on three sides, leaving an opening on the south, which may have been a doorway, and an area in the center for the coffin (Fig. 13). Several of the vessels in this exhibition (nos. 28, 29, 31, 33) were found near the walls, but the remaining 200 bronzes found in this tomb and the hundreds of bronze weapons, and stone and jade carvings must have filled the chamber to capacity. The small jades (nos. 34–40) were concentrated in the center of the chamber among the sherds of lacquer from the coffin. A marble cormorant with a notch in its back, in the southeast corner, calls to mind the marble owl and tiger from the prewar excavations. The notch in the back of all three sculptures suggests that the marbles supported standards. Other Shang tombs have revealed imprints of canopies painted in black, white, red, and yellow. Since so many perishable items like these have been lost, we can scarcely reconstruct the appearance of the entire chamber at the time of the funeral.

While the large tombs were repositories of great wealth, during the middle and late Anyang period less costly substitute objects were buried in small graves.[8] Bronze *gu* and *jue* are normally found in pairs in Shang graves, and it appears they were the most universal ritual equipment. The substitutes were modeled in the shapes of *gu* and *jue*, but were made of a soft, low-fired pottery. Over time, their forms became increasingly crude and consequently less suited for actual use in libations or sacrifices.

Such parsimony was the opposite of the Shang trend in burial customs, which required extravagance and waste. Bronze vessels were sometimes cast especially for the funeral and then left in the tomb, as with the *fang ding* no. 28 and *guang* no. 30 from the tomb of Fu Hao. Both pieces bear the posthumous appellation of Fu Hao, the name by which she was addressed in sacrifices made on her behalf by her sons. The penchant for committing every implement used in the funeral to the tomb accounts for the preservation of most of the Shang pieces in this exhibition.

The Shang burial traditions were the foundation for burial practices in ancient China and established a standard of practice that endured long after the extinction of the Shang polity, its cult, and many of its artistic traditions. So many links between Shang burials and those of later times can be observed in the archaeological evidence that one must conclude that this culture made a lasting contribution to what we today call Chinese civilization.

Zhou Dynasty Burials

The burial customs of the Shang were largely shared by the Zhou, the subsequent dynasty, although differences of emphasis and of degree set the two apart. Archaeological exploration of the area of the Western Zhou capital, near Xi'an, Shaanxi Province, has been disappointing, and none of the tombs excavated there or at any other site is likely to be assigned to members of the royal Zhou line. The only example of an early Zhou cemetery that in its scale and the design of its tombs approaches the putative royal Shang tombs at Xibeigang is the site at Xincun in Xun Xian, Henan Province.[9] This site was a cemetery for the elite of the state of Wei and in fact has proved richer in bronze artifacts than cemetery tracts near the Zhou capital. Among eighty burials excavated at this site, eight were large-scale tombs with ramps on the north and south after the Shang fashion. Most early Zhou burials, however, are more modest in their structures and furnishings than the large Xincun examples. Moreover, as the examples here demonstrate, early Zhou ritual bronzes are as likely to be found in caches as in burials.

Like medium-size Shang graves, Zhou burials consisted of a rectangular trench with an earth ledge around the four walls, a waist pit in the base of the shaft, and one or more wooden chambers for the coffin and tomb furnishings. Ritual vessels are usually found between the coffin and the surrounding chamber walls, clustered near the head of the corpse. The *he* (no. 44) from Lingtai Xian, Gansu Province, was found in a tomb that had four layers of furnishings carefully placed around the chamber, each layer separated by woven matting.[10] The ritual vessels across the head end of the chamber were topmost, with weapons and other items at lower levels. At this and other intact early Zhou burials a large number of weapons were found around the coffin, a circumstance that has led some scholars to speculate that the weapons were intended to protect the deceased from malevolent spirits.

The most important way in which early Zhou funerals differed from their Shang antecedents was in the reduced number of human sacrifices. Whereas the large Shang tombs near Anyang consumed the lives of many victims, no early Zhou tombs have been excavated with similarly large numbers. Instead, lords and ladies of the Zhou elite were "accompanied in death" (*xunzang*) by a few concubines and other members of the household. (The small coffins from the ledges of Tomb 1001 suggest this custom may also have had Shang roots.) A pair of tombs of Western Zhou date at Rujiazhuang, near Baoji, Shaanxi Province, are examples of the Zhou custom.[11] From inscribed bronzes found in the tombs the excavators inferred that the deceased were a husband and wife, and that the man was accompanied in death by his concubine. The husband and concubine, if so she was, were buried at the same time, while the wife was buried slightly later. Nine other members of the household lost (or took) their lives during the two funerals and were buried in simple coffins on the ledges around the burial chambers.

Innovations in tomb furnishings indicate that early Zhou funeral rites differed in other ways from those of the Shang. The surrogates made for burial during the late Shang period at Anyang were not a feature of Zhou burials. Rites involving the *gu* and *jue* vessels (see nos. 46, 47), whether of pottery or bronze, must have declined in importance for the Zhou. The gradual disappearance of these two forms in bronze during the Western Zhou period strengthens this hypothesis. The grave ceramics favored by the Zhou were instead utilitarian wares indistinguishable from types found in habitation sites. Such wares were in effect pressed into service as tomb furnishings and are found in stereotyped sets that gradually evolved over time. Detailed typological studies of such assemblages have been a key tool in dating Zhou burials.[12]

Differences of kind rather than of degree characterize burials of the Warring States period, beginning approximately in the fifth century B.C. The widespread innovations of this period reflect the diversity of late Zhou China, the interchange between the various states and non-Zhou neighboring peoples, and the manifold social and economic changes then taking place. Cemetery tracts and large tombs of this period are found both outside walled cities, as traditional from Shang times, and within the walls. The additon of intramural burial grounds, known both from the Eastern Zhou capital near modern Luoyang, Henan Province, and from outlying areas, may have been motivated by a desire to protect the graves from desecration, a result of the incessant warfare that gave the period its name.

The inception of burial mounds in China can also be dated to the Warring States period. The earliest reported examples of mounds built from rammed earth over tomb shafts are from the northeast, modern Hebei Province, the territories of the states of Yan and Zhao.[13] Such mounds required foundations of rammed earth surrounding the mound itself; no traces of such foundations were found either at Xibeigang or at Xincun. Sekino Takeshi suggested long ago that the custom of raising a mound over a tomb may have come to China from the steppes, where it is known at equally early tombs, such as those at Pazyryk.[14] Like cavalry warfare, burial mounds could have been transmitted to North China from those states in contact with steppe peoples. The *Book of Rites*, a late Zhou text edited in Western Han, quotes several ancient worthies on this new feature. In the words of Confucius: "I have heard that the ancients made graves only and built no mounds over them. But I am a man who will be travelling east, west, south and north. I cannot do without something by which I can remember the place."[15] Novel customs were usually sanctioned in this text by crediting the duke of Zhou or a similar figure with the idea.

New concepts in tomb structures constitute one of the most progressive steps of the late Zhou period. The walls of the tomb shafts, in addition to being rammed hard, were sometimes baked hard, plastered, and painted to resemble curtains or parapets. Investments of sand, charcoal, and sticky clay were laid in the base of the shaft to protect the wooden chamber from moisture and decay. These techniques were especially well developed in the state of Chu, where many well-preserved tombs, rich with lacquerwares and textiles, have been discovered. Stone walls also appeared in tombs at this time, usually rising from foundations covering the base of the shaft.[16]

Two trends proceeded simultaneously in the elaboration of the wooden burial chamber. The great majority of tombs continued the Shang custom of a coffin within a simple boxlike chamber. The number of chambers and coffins were regulated in accordance with the rank of the deceased. Zhou texts tell us that, in theory, the Son of Heaven was to be buried in seven layers of chambers and coffins, while a feudal lord had five, a high minister three, and a lowly official merely one chamber and one coffin. The burial chambers also became more sophisticated, with lacquer wall painting and inlays of jade or stone plaques.

The largest late Zhou tombs, however, approached palaces in their size and appearance. The large Xibeigang tombs were already sizeable, with chambers large enough to walk in, so this trend may also have had Shang origins. The wooden chamber of Tomb 1 at Changtaiguan in Xinyang Xian, Henan Province, was almost 8 meters square and 2.5 meters tall.[17] The chamber had seven rooms, a single transverse space across the front, and two rows of three rooms each in the middle and rear. Since the furnishings included a full-size lacquered wooden bed, the rooms of the Changtaiguan tomb may have been intended to simulate those of a palace.

The two large tombs near Pingshan, Hebei Province, attributed to lords of the state of Zhongshan, offer still more evidence of the trend to model tomb structures after palaces.[18] Tomb 1 at Pingshan (Fig. 14) had a stepped mound with a tile-roofed gallery of about 50 meters on a side running around the mound on its second level. Some of the tiles for this gallery's roof had ornaments in the form of the graph *shan* used for the bronze trident no. 92. Tomb 6 at Pingshan is the most elaborate late Zhou tomb ever excavated. The ramp leading to the shaft of this tomb had two levels, the lower descending to a stone-walled burial chamber and the upper giving access to a five-bay square wooden structure built on top of the burial chamber. Post-and-beam construction supported the wooden structure, and imprints of the posts and beams were found in the surrounding earth of the mound. The wooden building was nearly 25 meters square and 4.6 meters tall. To each side of the burial chamber in each of these tombs was a treasury in one of which the trident (no. 92) was found.

The notion of graded perquisites for burials also applied to tomb furnishings. The iconoclastic thinker Mo Di (ca. 479–438 B.C.) castigated the elite of his time for their lavish burials:

If we follow the rules of those who advocate elaborate funerals and lengthy mourning and apply them to the state, then, we are told, the funeral of a king or high minister will require several inner and outer coffins, a deep grave, numerous grave clothes, a large amount of embroidery for decorating the coffins, and a large grave mound. If the family of the deceased happens to be humble commoners the wealth of the family will be exhausted, and if they are feudal lords their treasuries will be emptied.[19]

Throughout Chinese history, the debate on the merits of extravagant funerals and burials (*houzang*) continued, with neither proponents nor critics ever winning the argument.

Long-lasting modifications in tomb furnishings were initiated in the Warring States period. The great bulk of the grave ceramics found in tombs from the fifth century B.C. and later were made of soft, low-fired, fine paste pottery distinct from the ware used at the same time at habitation sites.[20] These shapes and especially the decoration of these vessels imitated ritual bronzes. A variety of techniques were employed to simulate the surface effects of bronze: cold painting, lacquer painting, tin foil, glass paste, and stamped and appliqué

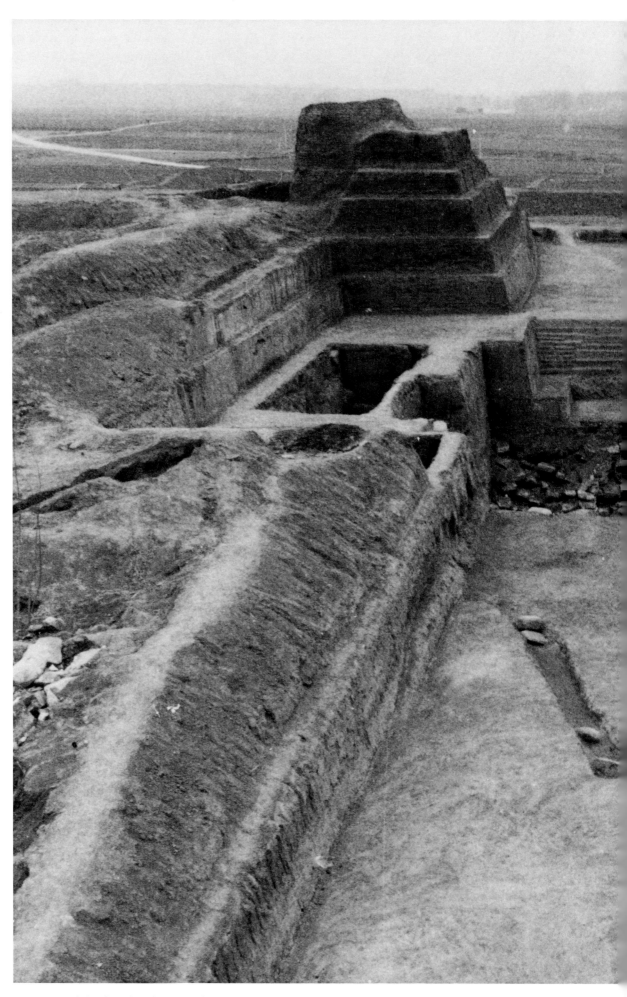

Fig. 14 Burial chamber of Tomb 1 at Pingshan Xian, Hebei Province.
Photograph courtesy of Cultural Relics Bureau

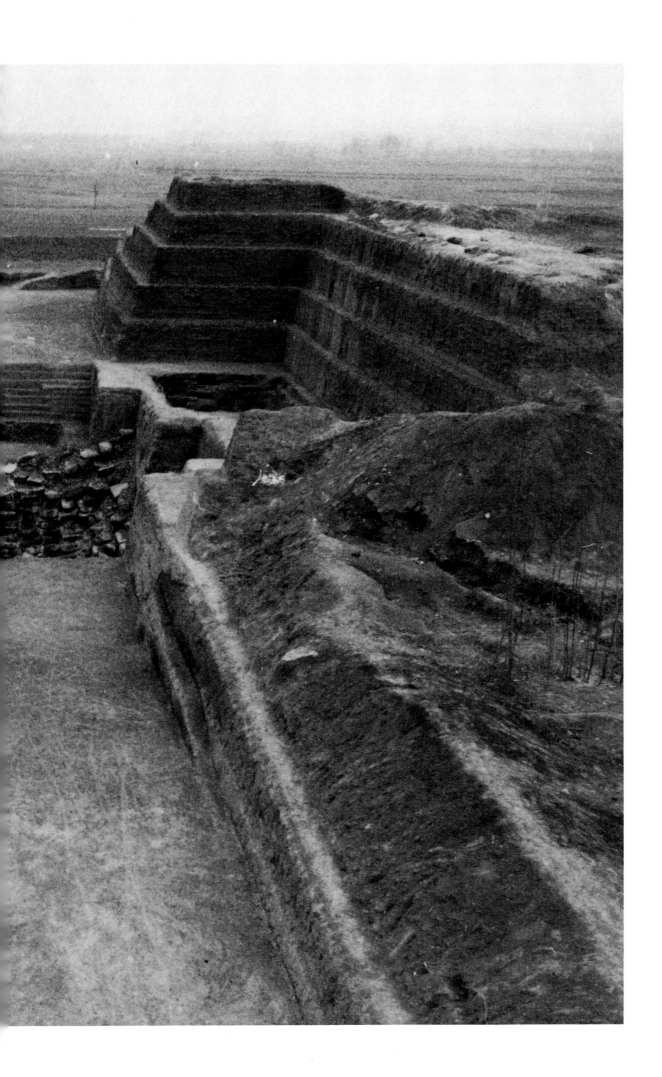

designs. Both in form and substance these vessels contrast with grave ceramics known from the early and middle Zhou periods. The development of a separate ceramic tradition for exclusive burial use parallels the rise of surrogates in the Late Shang period. Unlike the Shang surrogates, however, the late Zhou grave ceramics form the first chapter of a long-lived practice, which continued to late traditional times.

Unlike the Shang examples, surrogates were not confined to humble late Zhou graves, nor were they strictly nonutilitarian. Elaborately crafted surrogates from large, richly endowed tombs appear regularly in late Zhou, and have been found in tombs in the far north and the south.[21] The great tomb at Wangshan near Jiangling, Hubei Province, which yielded the superlative belt hook (no. 76) held a surrogate *hu* vessel that resembles the formidable *fang hu* from Xinzheng, Henan Province (no. 67). The most elaborate surrogates of the period are the vessels from Tomb 16 at Xiadu, the site of the capital of the state of Yan. Such vessels were not merely inexpensive substitutes, but rather stood side by side with bronze ritual vessels as a complement of ritual equipment made exclusively for the dead. Surrogates, moreover, now had functional roles to play in the funeral rites. Charred animal bones from offerings are sometimes found in ceramic *ding*, and alcoholic spirits were found in *hu* from the Pingshan site. The late Zhou texts refer to these objects as "inauspicious" (*xiong*) or "spirit" vessels (*mingqi*), terms that designate them as burial goods.

Ritual texts allude to the custom of placing model human figurines in tombs during the late Zhou, but the archaeological evidence for this practice is still exiguous. In the *Book of Rites* Confucius extols the virtues of the crude figurines for fear that really lifelike ones would tempt people to sacrifice human victims. Since the Anyang excavations, human sacrifice has been attested from Shang times forward, so this remark attributed to the sage has the ring of a pious rationalization that overlooks the long history of human sacrifice before late Zhou.

Figurines crude enough to satisfy Confucius are now known from a handful of sites across North China. These examples are modeled either in the expressive poses of dancers and performers or in the composed, reverential postures of servants in attendance. The bodies combine simple geometric shapes—a conelike skirt with a tubular torso and spherical head—but details were generally provided by painting. The figurines from Linzi, Shandong Province, can be dated to the fifth century, and the examples from Fenshuiling, Shanxi Province, are only slightly later.[22] While the Linzi figurines are some 10 centimeters tall, those from Fenshuiling are only half that size. Both types, however, are reminiscent of the so-called Hui Xian figurines, which have been identified as modern fakes.[23] The Hui Xian pieces thus probably followed authentic models. The best-documented of the figurines were found in the graves of women who followed their lords in death, and so may have been the perquisites of low-ranking persons. The use of clay figurines began in North China even as human victims continued to be consumed by funeral rites. The Chu tombs of South China, also of late Zhou date, are notable for their simply carved wooden figurines of considerably larger scale. But neither the clay examples from the north nor the wooden pieces from the south can compare with the life-size warriors found near the tomb of the First Qin Emperor, the next significant instance of figurines made for burial.

Qin and Han Tombs

The tomb of the First Qin Emperor was an unprecedented achievement in the mortuary traditions of ancient China, a fusion of diverse trends of the late Zhou on a scale never before attempted. The wonders of this tomb have been well known since the Western Han historian Sima Qian (ca. 145–86 B.C.) provided an account of its construction in his *Shi Ji* (Historical Records).[24] The discovery of an underground army of life-size figurines (nos. 98–105) east of the tomb mound in 1974 only confirmed the unique character of this remarkable funerary complex.

The tomb is situated east of Xi'an on the flat plain of the Wei River. Mountains face the south flank of the tomb, while the Wei River flows to the north. Nearby Mount Li (Li Shan), renowned in ancient times as a source of gold and jade, gave its name to the site. Sima Qian described the outfitting of the tomb in detail (see pp. 356–57). Other aspects of the tomb structure are suggested either by additional textual sources or by comparative archaeological evidence. Two texts state that the chamber was built of stone, possibly in the plan of a palace. A phrase in the Sima Qian account led some commentators to believe that a cast-metal sheathing or barrier was part of the tomb, and other sources indicate that the chamber was at least partly of wood. Late Zhou tombs with stone walls and wooden interiors are known from such sites as Pingshan, Hebei Province, and the three large tombs at Guweicun in Hui Xian, Henan Province.[25] The stone foundation built in the base of the shaft of Tomb 2 at Guweicun was 1.6 meters thick. North and south walls on that foundation rose 12 meters to ground level, and stone buttresses flanked the chamber area. The interior of the chamber was lined with courses of stacked timbers, referred to by texts as "yellow intestines" after the bright color of freshly planed cypress timbers. The chamber of the First Emperor's tomb was probably very similar to the Pingshan and Guweicun tombs.

In its aboveground components, the First Emperor's mortuary complex at Mount Li introduced a new plan (Fig. 117). The mound is a four-sided truncated pyramid of rammed earth with a height of 43 meters and base dimensions on each side of about 350 meters.[26] The mounds of Yan and Zhao may have inspired the First Emperor's architect. References in textual sources to temples at the site and traces of a foundation north of the mound recall the mortuary temples erected above the three Guweicun tombs, which were aligned in a row along an east-west axis. Each had stone plinths in a grid, tile roof sherds, and stone-paved paths above their shafts. The tomb precinct, a rammed-earth terrace 2 meters high, was 150 meters (east-west) by 135 meters (north-south) in plan. By contrast, the First Emperor's tomb site was surrounded by an outer wall 2,150 meters deep (north-south) and 940 meters wide (east-west). An inner wall enclosing the mound was 1,350 meters deep and 600 meters wide, with gates on several sides.

The Han emperors copied the Qin standard of burial if the textual sources are accurate, but such continuity accounts for only a small part of the history of burials in the Han.[27] While no imperial tomb of Qin or Han has yet been opened, about a dozen tombs of the Han imperial princes are known. Some of the princely tombs follow the central plan of the Guweicun examples, but others adopted an altogether new plan. The most spectacular of the new axial plan tombs are the pair on Lingshan near Mancheng, Hebei Province, renowned for their jade burial suits sewn with gold thread, which also yielded the incense burner (no. 95) and *hu* with bird script (no. 96).[28] The furnishings of these two Han tombs are perhaps the most lavish ever discovered, dramatic proof of an extreme shift toward the ostentatious in burial style.

Since the Lingshan tombs were carved out of the rocky mountainside, sturdy stone-cutting tools, probably of iron, must have been available. The passageway leading from the face of the mountain to the interior was blocked in each case by iron barriers poured on the spot. The excavated caverns included two lengthy side rooms at right angles to the passage, one a stable for horses and chariots and the other a storehouse containing food (Fig. 112). The main room of Tomb 1 was outfitted with a tile-roofed structure that transformed the rock-cut cavern into a palatial setting. Freestanding curtains further enhanced the ambience. The rear room of Tomb 1 was a stone house with a gabled roof; it held the coffin and included a mock bathing room. The Lingshan tombs apparently carried the imitation of palatial settings even further than the Pingshan tombs of the late Zhou. At the same time, by carving the tombs in a rock mountain, they achieved a secure and imposing siting without parallel in earlier times.

The Han was a great age of experimentation and innovation in tomb structures and furnishings. During the first century B.C. and the first century A.D., the burial practices of ancient times were revolutionized by brick chamber vaulted tombs, a wide selection of ceramic surrogates of new types and functions, and a significant tradition of tomb decoration. Even so, the underlying continuities between the new burial traditions of imperial times and the tested traditions of antiquity demonstrate the profound debt of early imperial China to its remote ancestors. The pattern of synthesizing diverse sources to create an original custom, prominent in the Shang and the late Zhou periods, also characterized the Han, when, after an initial burst of creativity and experimentation, the canonical traditions of imperial times emerged.

NOTES

1. For the Neolithic sites, see Kwang-chih Chang, *The Archaeology of Ancient China* (New Haven, 1977), chaps. 3,4. For Banpo and Jiangzhai, see: Shi Xingbang et al., *Xi'an Banpo* (Beijing, 1963); "1972 nian chun Lintong Jiangzhai yizhi fajue jianbao" [Brief excavation report of the site at Jiangzhai, Lintong, for spring 1972], *Kaogu* 1973/3, pp. 134–45; "Shaanxi Lintong Jiangzhai yizhi di er, san ci fajue de zhuyao shouhuo" [Important finds from the second and third seasons of excavations at the site at Jiangzhai, Lintong, Shaanxi], *Kaogu* 1975/5, pp. 280–84, 263.

2. *Dawenkou* (Beijing, 1974).

3. For K3, see "Yanshi Erlitou yizhi xin faxian de tongqi he yuqi" [Newly discovered bronzes and jades from the Erlitou site, Yanshi], *Kaogu* 1976/4, pp. 259–63. For this and other Shang sites, see K. C. Chang, *The Archaeology of Ancient China*, chap. 6.

4. For Panlongcheng, see Robert W. Bagley, "P'an-lung-ch'eng: A Shang City in Hupei," *Artibus Asiae* 39 (1977), nos. 3/4, pp. 165–219. For Tomb 2 at Lijiazui, see "Panlongcheng yijiuqisi niandu tianye kaogu jiyao" [Summary of field work at Panlongcheng for 1974], *Wenwu* 1976/2, pp. 5–15.

5. "Zhengzhou xin chutu de Shang dai qianqi da tong ding" [Large bronze *ding* of the Early Shang period newly unearthed at Zhengzhou], *Wenwu* 1975/6, pp. 64–68.

6. For the Anyang excavations and the Xibeigang tombs, see Li Chi, *Anyang* (Seattle, 1977); Liang Siyong and Gao Quxun, *Houjiazhuang* (Nangang, 1962–68), vols. 2–6.

7. "Anyang Yinxu wuhao mu de fajue" [Excavation of Tomb 5 at Yinxu, Anyang], *Kaogu Xuebao* 1977/2, pp. 57–98.

8. "1969–1977 nian Yinxu xichu muzang fajue baogao" [Brief excavation report of burials in the western districts of Yinxu for 1969–77], *Kaogu Xuebao* 1979/1, pp. 27–118, esp. pp. 108–13.

9. Guo Baojun, *Xun Xian Xincun* (Beijing, 1964), pp. 7–8.

10. "Gansu Lingtai Baicaopo Xi Zhou mu" [Western Zhou tombs at Baicaopo, Lingtai, Gansu], *Kaogu Xuebao* 1977/2, pp. 99–129.

11. "Shaanxi sheng Baoji shi Rujiazhuang Xi Zhou mu fajue jianbao" [Brief excavation report of Western Zhou tombs at Rujiazhuang, Baoji, Shaanxi], *Wenwu* 1976/4, pp. 34–56.

12. Wang Bohong et al., *Feng xi fajue baogao* [Report of excavations west of the Feng River] (Beijing, 1962), pp. 129–31; Su Bingqi et al., *Luoyang Zhongzhou lu xi gongduan* [Report of excavation at the west end of Zhongzhou Road, Luoyang] (Beijing, 1959), pp. 128–30, 140–46.

13. "Hebei Yi Xian Xiadu gu cheng kancha he shijue" [Survey and trial diggings at the ancient city of Xiadu, Yi Xian, Hebei], *Kaogu Xuebao* 1965/1, pp. 83–106; "Hebei Handan Baijiacun Zhanguo mu" [Warring States tombs at Baijiacun, Handan, Hebei], *Kaogu* 1962/12, pp. 613–34.

14. Sekino Takeshi, "Origins and Development of the Burial Mound in China," in *Chūgoku kōkogaku kenkyū* (Tokyo, 1963).

15. James Legge, trans., *Li Ki: The Book of Rites*, repr. ed. (New York, 1967), vol. I, p. 123.

16. "Linzi Langjiazhuang yihao Dong Zhou xun ren mu" [Eastern Zhou Tomb 1 with accompanying victims at Langjiazhuang, Linzi], *Kaogu Xuebao* 1977/1, pp. 73–104.

17. "Wo guo kaogu shi shang de kongqian faxian: Xinyang Changtaiguan fajue yizo Zhanguo da mu" [An Unprecedented discovery in the history of Chinese archaeology: A Large Warring States tomb excavated at Changtaiguan, Xinyang], *Wenwu* 1957/9, pp. 21–22; *Henan Xinyang Chu mu chutu wenwu tulu* [Catalogue of artifacts unearthed from the Chu tombs at Xinyang, Henan] (Henan, 1959).

18. "Hebei sheng Pingshan Xian Zhanguo shiqi Zhongshan guo muzang fajue jianbao" [Brief excavation report of Warring States burials of the state of Zhongshan at Pingshan, Hebei], *Wenwu* 1979/1, pp. 1–31.

19. Burton Watson, trans., *Mo Tzu: Basic Writings* (New York, 1963), p. 67.

20. See note 12 above.

21. "Hebei Yi Xian Yan Xiadu dishiliuhao mu fajue" [Excavation of Tomb 16 at Yan Xiadu, Yi Xian, Hebei], *Kaogu Xuebao* 1965/2, pp. 79–101; "Hubei Jiangling sanzo Chu mu chutu da pi zhongyao wenwu" [A Large group of important artifacts unearthed from three Chu tombs at Jiangling, Hubei], *Wenwu* 1966/3, pp. 33–55. For the Jiangling tombs, see also Annette Juliano, "Three Large Ch'u Graves Recently Excavated in the Chiang-ling District of Hupei Province," *Artibus Asiae* 34 (1972), pp. 5–28.

22. For the Linzi figurines, see note 16 above. For Fenshuiling, see "Shanxi Changzhi Fenshuiling gu me de qingli" [Clearing ancient tombs at Fenshuiling, Changzhi, Shanxi], *Kaogu Xuebao* 1957/1, pp. 103–18.

23. S. J. Fleming and E. H. Sampson, "The Authenticity of Figurines, Animals and Pottery Facsimiles of Bronze in the Hui-hsien Style," *Archaeometry* 14/2 (1977), pp. 237–44.

24. Sima Qian, *Shi Ji* [Historical Records] (Beijing, 1959), 6, p. 265.

25. For the Pingshan tombs, see note 18 above. For the Guweicun tombs, see Guo Baojun et al., *Hui Xian fajue baogao* [Report of excavations at Hui Xian] (Beijing, 1956), pp. 69–109.

26. "Qin shihuang ling diaocha jianbao" [Brief report of an investigation of the tomb of the First Qin Emperor], *Kaogu* 1962/8, pp. 407–11. See also chap. 10 below.

27. For a more detailed history of Qin and Han burials and their ancient roots and precedents, see Robert L. Thorp, "The Mortuary Art and Architecture of Early Imperial China," (Ph.D. diss., University of Kansas, 1979).

28. "Mancheng Han mu fajue jiyao" [Summary of the excavation of Han tombs at Mancheng], *Kaogu* 1972/1, pp. 8–18; *Mancheng Han mu* [The Han tombs at Mancheng] (Beijing, 1978).

CATALOGUE

1

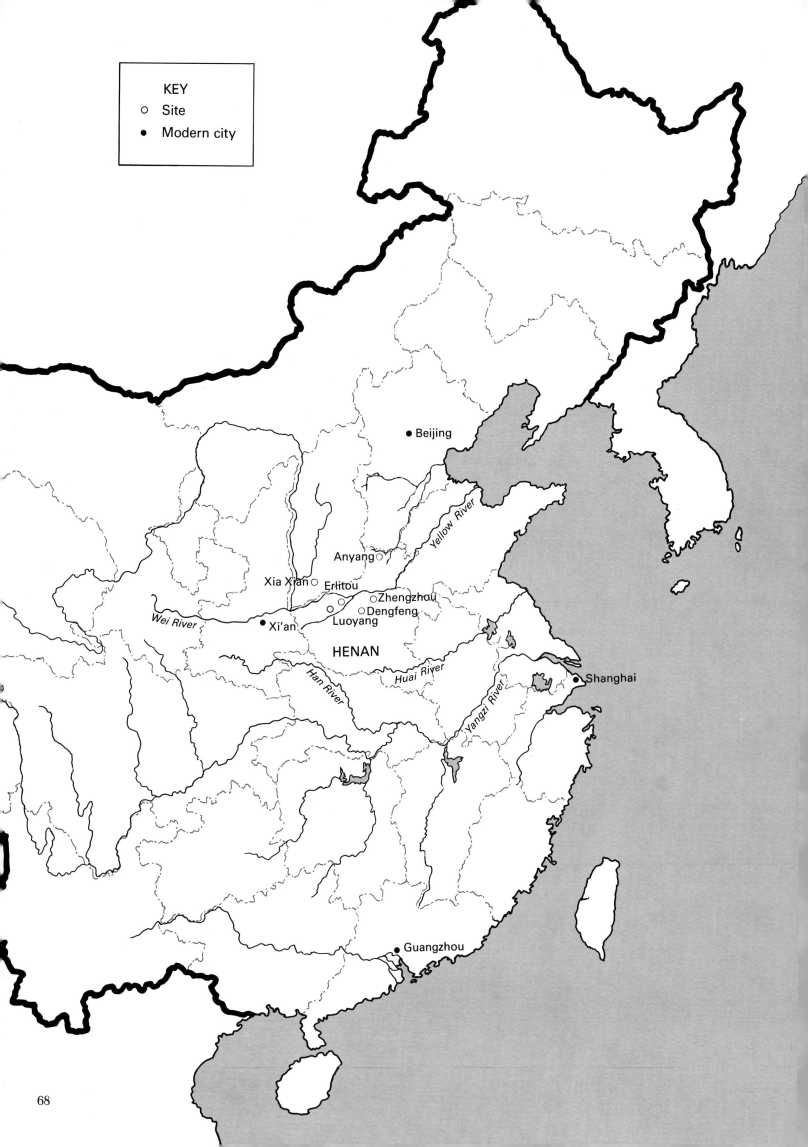

KEY
○ Site
● Modern city

● Beijing

Yellow River

Anyang ○

Xia Xian ○ Erlitou
                 ○ ○Zhengzhou
                 ○ ○Dengfeng
Wei River   ● Xi'an Luoyang

HENAN

Han River   Huai River

Yangzi River   ● Shanghai

● Guangzhou

1 The Beginnings of the Bronze Age: The Erlitou Culture Period

Robert W. Bagley

The origins of the Bronze Age in China are still obscure. There are indications, based partly on new radiocarbon dates, that metal was in use before 2000 B.C.; but the first substantial metal artifacts so far unearthed have come from the earliest sites of the Shang dynasty, several centuries later. At this time Chinese civilization emerges, and with it the full range of cultural achievements that the word "civilization" calls to mind—among them, writing, cities, the use of metals, and a highly stratified society ruled by an all-powerful king. But while these basic features are shared with Bronze Age societies elsewhere in the ancient world, Chinese civilization was distinctly individual from the first. Excavation of Shang sites has revealed a cultural tradition already recognizably Chinese and directly linked with the civilization of later historical times. The individuality of one facet of the Chinese Bronze Age—its artistic side—is to be seen everywhere in the present exhibition.

Shang was not the first ruling house to be accorded the status of a dynasty in later Chinese historical writings; that dignity belongs to the Xia. Nevertheless, although the search for Xia remains is actively under way, archaeologists have yet to find conclusive evidence for a dynasty of that name. With Shang we are on firmer ground, for the last capital of the dynasty, occupied by the Shang kings for nearly three centuries, has been found. Located at Anyang in Henan Province, it was first investigated in 1928, and, apart from wartime interruptions, the site has been more or less continuously under excavation ever since. Inscribed animal bones that record divinations made on behalf of the Shang kings were found in great numbers at Anyang. These divination inscriptions are the only written records that survive from Shang times; their discovery removed the Shang dynasty from the realm of historical legend and identified beyond doubt the site of its last capital.

Only the final and most opulent stage of Shang culture is represented at Anyang (see chap. 4). Until the 1950s, sites belonging to the earlier part of the Bronze Age remained unknown. Then, in the 1950s and 1960s, the archaeological record was enlarged by the discovery of two major pre-Anyang sites, both south of the Yellow River in Henan Province. The walled city found at Zheng-zhou (chap. 2) was an important settlement before the

Map of China showing important archaeological sites of the Erlitou culture period, 19th century to 16th century B.C.

founding of the capital at Anyang (ca. 1300 B.C.?). The site discovered at Erlitou, near Luoyang, is earlier still; successive strata there show a primitive Shang culture following closely on levels still apparently Neolithic. Our knowledge of the earlier phases of the Bronze Age has come chiefly from ongoing excavations at Erlitou and Zhengzhou. The distinctive traits that connect the cultures found at these sites with the high Bronze Age civilization of Anyang led archaeologists to divide the Shang dynasty into a sequence of three successive stages: the Erlitou phase, the Zhengzhou phase, and the Anyang period (or Yinxu phase).

Unfortunately, written records from Erlitou and Zhengzhou are still lacking; no counterpart to the Anyang divination inscriptions has yet been found. Although attempts have been made to identify the two sites with various of the pre-Anyang capitals whose names are preserved in later texts, such identifications remain unconfirmed. In fact, while some scholars take Erlitou to be the city of Bo, capital of the founder of the Shang dynasty, others would make it instead a capital of the still problematical Xia dynasty. In the absence of contemporary writings, both suggestions are only speculative. The archaeologist's decision to call Erlitou a Shang site does not rest on any inscriptional evidence, but only on observable cultural traits that link it with Zhengzhou, and, through Zhengzhou, with Anyang. This continuity seems well enough established to justify calling Erlitou a site of Shang culture, but it cannot settle the political status of the city there.

Whatever the actual identity of the place, excavation has made it clear that Erlitou was no minor settlement, but a city that could well have been a capital. Chief among the architectural remains uncovered was the foundation terrace of a very large palatial enclosure, nearly square and more than one hundred meters on a side. The terrace, which still rises nearly a meter above the surrounding ground, was constructed of successive thin layers of earth rammed almost rock-hard. This rammed-earth technique, which requires a great investment of labor, is the hallmark of Shang building technology, used for foundations and platforms, and for city walls like the one at Zhengzhou.

The rammed-earth terrace at Erlitou was surrounded by a low earthen wall followed for almost its entire length by a roofed enclosure. The only other building within the wall was a large rectangular hall placed in the rear center of the terrace, facing south toward the main gate in the containing wall. Since the buildings themselves were of wood, no trace of them survives today except for their individual rammed-earth foundation platforms and impressions left in the foundations by wooden pillars. Even so, the evidence is sufficient to reconstruct the buildings with some confidence and to establish the Erlitou compound as the forerunner of all later Chinese palace architecture, both as regards the individual buildings and in the south-facing symmetrical plan.

The bronzes and jades so far recovered from Erlitou, including the three objects shown here (nos. 1–3), have all come from the stratum of the palace remains. The recent finds of jade have been unexpectedly rich, while little bronze has been found at the site. The only bronze vessels recovered are four small spouted tripods of the type called *jue*. Unimpressive in themselves, these modest tripods are the earliest bronze vessels yet known from China and thus represent the ancestors of all the vessels in this exhibition.

Bronzes and Jades from Erlitou

Compared with its descendants, the first small *jue* discovered at Erlitou (Fig. 15) seems utterly insignificant. For the historian, however, the importance of this clumsy object is in direct proportion to its primitiveness: here we glimpse for the first time the origins of a bronze-casting industry that is already vigorous and mature in the next period, the Zhengzhou phase (chap. 2); and only through study of these earlier stages can we begin to understand and account for the extraordinary achievements of the Chinese Bronze Age at its height, in the Anyang period.

Awkward as it may appear, however, the *jue* from Erlitou is in several respects a rather sophisticated artifact, and one that displays certain basic features that set the metalworking of the Chinese Bronze Age sharply apart from West Asian traditions. The odd shape, which becomes a standard vessel form in later centuries (nos. 15, 47), speaks of an artistic tradition of decided character. The metal composition, reported to be 92 percent copper and 7 percent tin, is not an accidental alloy but a deliberate bronze and implies all the complex metallurgical knowledge required to mine both metals and win them from their ores. Most important, the *jue* has seams, which show it to have been cast from a mold made in sections—at least four separate parts designed to fit together. This technical point deserves close examination, for it affects profoundly the bronze decoration of succeeding centuries.

In the Bronze Age of Western Asia and Europe, castings of complicated shape were from very early times made by the ingenious lost-wax (*cire perdue*) method. In this procedure, a model of the object to be cast is made in wax and then carefully packed in fine clay; when the clay is baked, the wax runs out, leaving a pottery mold with precisely the cavity required to cast a bronze replica of the original wax model. This elegant shortcut to mold-making has much to recommend it. In particular, it gives the bronze founder the freedom to cast objects of any shape, however intricate. One disadvantage is that the mold is closed, apart from pouring inlets and vents, and its interior cannot be inspected before casting. Only when the mold is broken away from the finished object will the caster learn whether the mold has been properly prepared; if it has not been, he may have to begin all over.

Assembled from sections made separately, the mold for the Erlitou *jue* was made by a different and more direct procedure, one that does not necessarily require a preliminary model of the object that is to be cast. It does require perfectly fitted mold sections, but these can be made without using a model as long as the object to be

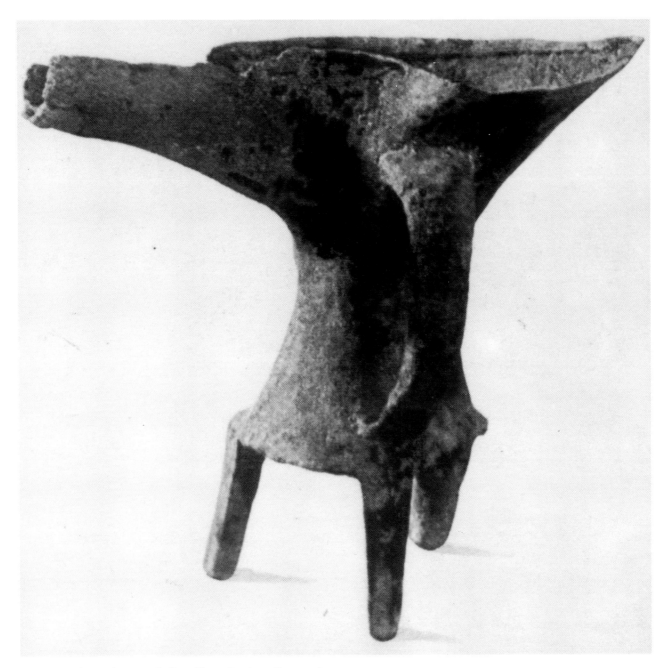

Fig. 15 *Jue* from Erlitou, Yanshi Xian, Henan Province. Photograph after *China Pictorial* 1977/2, p. 22

cast is simple enough in shape; in practice most Shang bronzes are simpler and more symmetrical than the rather odd *jue* tripod. A casting method that employs a mold assembled from fitted sections offers the caster access to the inner surfaces of the mold before the bronze is poured, so that the guesswork inseparable from the lost-wax method is eliminated. Inevitably, though, the section-mold method has the defects of its advantages: one is a restriction to fairly symmetrical shapes. Another is the problem of seams, which will appear in a cast object wherever there are joins in the mold.

These two limitations of the section-mold method are the constraints within which the whole development of bronze art in the Shang period took place. The omnipresent symmetries of the bronze shapes—almost always circular, oval, or rectangular in cross section—reflect the difficulty of constructing section molds for more irregular objects (with or without the help of a model); the lost-wax method is of course free of any such restriction. The equally pronounced symmetries in the bronze decoration are dictated by the sectioning of the mold. If a vessel of circular cross section is to be cast, the *ding* tripod no. 4, for instance, the mold is ordinarily divided vertically into thirds; the three dividing lines will appear as seams on the cast vessel (Fig. 16). (The seams on no. 4 were polished down after casting, except in the decorated band, where they appear as vertical divisions in the frieze.) After the bronze founder has constructed the sections for the mold, he then can add the decoration. As he incises the patterns into each of the three mold sections, the caster will naturally be inclined to make the pattern within a given section complete and self-contained, since

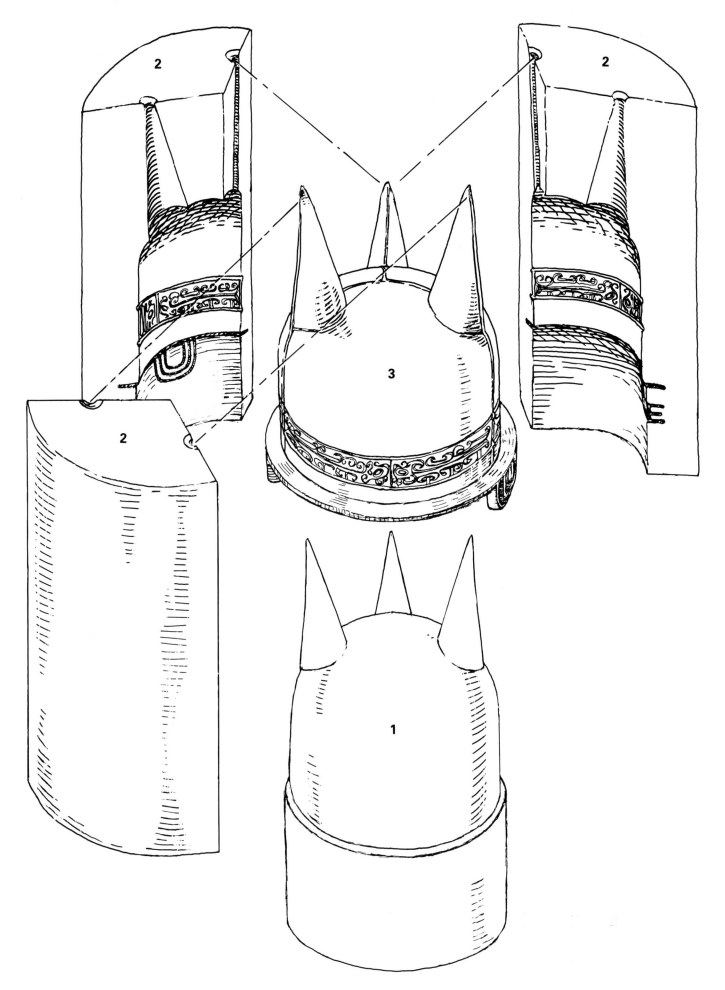

Fig. 16   Schematic drawing of *ding* no. 4, showing piece-mold-casting
assembly: (1) core; (2) mold sections; (3) completed bronze
vessel. Drawing by Phyllis Ward

it will be separated from adjacent sections by a seam. The result is a decorated band that fills the circumference of the vessel with three independent (and in this case identical) units. In later times the decoration of bronzes vastly more elaborate than no. 4 will still be related in the same simple way to the structure of the mold assembly.

At the stage of the most primitive Erlitou *jue* vessel (Fig. 15), decoration has evidently not yet been attempted; the bronze caster has yet to realize that patterns drawn in the mold will emerge as raised lines on the bronze cast from it. But the mold built in sections is already in use, and the discovery will therefore soon be made; for in this method of moldmaking—and not in the lost-wax procedure—the mold surfaces are accessible to the caster and invite decoration. When decoration is added, it will automatically respect the symmetries built into the mold. A first hesitant step in this direction is seen on a more elegant *jue*, also from Erlitou (no. 1); here the simple patterns were carved into only one of the mold sections, on the side opposite the handle (see Fig. 17) At first glance the inevitable seams and the limitation to simple shapes might appear to be grave drawbacks of the section-mold casting method. After surveying the quality and variety attained by the art form to which this casting method gave rise, however, we may be less inclined to view its constraints as defects: for generations of bronze casters they were a stimulus and a challenge.

The same positive contribution of a demanding technology can be detected in the second great art form of Bronze Age China, that of carved jade. "Carved" is not precisely the right word, since this most admirable of minerals is too hard to be cut even by steel tools, and must instead be shaped entirely by means of abrasives. In fact the jade worker's technical repertoire includes little more than sawing, drilling holes, and grinding down surfaces, all done with a tool to which an abrasive is applied. The first step in working a jade pebble or boulder is to saw it into slices, and most of the standard jade forms are shapes emerging from flat slabs—something as true of the Eastern Zhou pendant no. 72 as it is of the blades from Erlitou made a thousand years earlier (nos. 2, 3). As a result the art form is often in essence two-dimensional, giving its principal emphasis to surface and silhouette. On the blade no. 2, the most limited technical means are employed with telling effect: using only a single technique, the lapidary has applied saw cuts in two different ways, first enriching the flat surface with parallel lines and grooves, then sawing the edges to produce a jagged silhouette that is striking and unforgettable.

The crisscross lines that decorate the second blade (no. 3), like the parallel lines of no. 2, could be made with straight saw cuts. Grinding away the stone surface to form other patterns was more difficult. A slight stiffness of line hints that the intricate curves incised on jade figurines

from Fu Hao's tomb (nos. 34–40) were not managed effortlessly even in the Anyang period. The eventual attainment of perfect fluency is documented by the Eastern Zhou pendant no. 72, whose exquisitely shaped plastic curls rise from the surface with an ease and naturalness that deny outright the patient grinding technique required to leave them in relief.

The jade worker's technology does not of course fully account for the shapes of the various artifacts regularly made in jade. These shapes, many of them quite standardized, must have had a variety of different origins. Some objects served perhaps as amulets (nos. 34–40). In later times jades like no. 72 were made as jewelry—albeit jewelry with overtones of magical potency, and therefore appropriate for inclusion in burials. In Shang and earlier, this mortuary function is very much to the fore. Although the two objects from Erlitou may have served some ritual purpose aboveground, they were no doubt intended primarily as funerary offerings or sacrificial gifts to spirits. They are replicas, made in the most precious of materials, of weapons and tools ordinarily made of something more prosaic. The blade no. 2 may conceivably copy a bronze tool, of which one isolated example—a long, blunt-ended ax—was found at Erlitou. The pointed halberd blade no. 10, called a *ge*, copies a much more standard bronze weapon; the *ge* no. 10 comes from a site belonging to the Zhengzhou phase, but examples in both jade and bronze are known from Erlitou as well.

For the other jade from Erlitou, no. 3, the prototype is far more ancient and—like the jade craft itself—reaches back beyond the Bronze Age, into Neolithic times. The blade is an enlarged copy of a Neolithic harvesting knife—too large for use, of course, and of too precious a material, but nevertheless preserving the shape of the Neolithic tool, as well as the perforations along the unsharpened edge that would serve to attach a backing or a grip for the hand. Such replicas of tools, painstakingly ground from jade or other fine stone, took pride of place among the offerings in the richest Neolithic graves. When we find the same shape copied, with still greater finesse, in the Shang period, we are reminded that the working of jade is not in essence a Bronze Age craft at all, but a technology characteristic of the Neolithic; the term "Neolithic" was after all coined in the nineteenth century precisely in order to contrast the polished stone tools of the "New Stone Age" with the chipped tools of the "Old Stone Age" that they replaced.

Indeed, it is only by reference to the Shang inheritance of millennia of Neolithic experience with stone carving that we can explain the most surprising aspect of the recent discoveries made at Erlitou. The products of the nascent bronze industry are of the most obvious simplicity, scarcely hinting at the splendors to come; but the jades are not primitive at all. Their sophistication is nothing less than astonishing.

CHAPTER 1: CATALOGUE ENTRIES

1 *Jue*

First half 2nd millennium B.C. (Erlitou phase)
Found 1975, Erlitou, Yanshi Xian, Henan Province
Height 25.6 cm. (10⅛ in.); length (spout to tail) 31.5 cm. (12⅜ in.);
  weight 0.55 kg. (1 lb. 3 oz.)
Cultural Office of Henan Yanshi Xian

This fastidiously shaped vessel represents a considerable artistic advance beyond its ungainly predecessor from the same stratum at Erlitou (Fig. 15). The compact proportions of the earlier *jue* have given way to an exaggerated fragility: the waist is sharply constricted; spout and tail are drawn out to an extreme slenderness; and the topheavy superstructure is delicately balanced on three long and elegant legs, faintly curved to continue the profile of the skirt. These graceful, mannered proportions, in a vessel type already curiously contrived, bear witness to the Erlitou founder's conscious concern for formal, aesthetic matters.

This concern extended to a careful finishing of the object, and all the casting seams have been polished away. Judging from later examples less perfectly finished, the side seen in the illustration would have required two mold sections meeting at the handle, while the opposite side would have been covered by a single section. In cross section the body of the *jue* is a pointed oval with the pointed ends corresponding to slight creases in the vessel wall; these creases follow the lines of the mold divisions, up the left and right sides of the body to the tips of spout and tail. Besides the three outer sections, the mold assembly included a semicircular or D-shaped solid core occupying the space between the handle and the vessel wall. The two slots in the handle, a feature known from a few other early bronzes, must have been left by pegs that served to hold this core in place during casting. The vessel wall is about 1

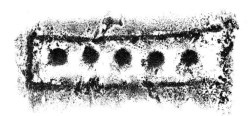

Fig. 17 Rubbing of decor, *jue* no. 1. Courtesy of Cultural Relics Bureau, Beijing

millimeter thick. The rough surface is a light brown varied with dull green areas.

The present *jue* is the earliest decorated Chinese bronze so far known, and its decoration, which appears in a narrow band at the waist on the side away from the handle, was made entirely by casting (Figs. 17, 18). The primitive design consists of five large dots bordered above and below by a pair of thread-relief lines. These elements were drawn with ease in the clay of the single mold section for the far side of the vessel; no attempt was made at this early stage to embellish the two mold sections for the side with the handle.

Although the entire *jue* was made in one casting, its rim seems deliberately to imitate the inward-folded edge that might be expected in a vessel made from sheet metal. This feature, which can also be seen on the *jue* of figure 15, may indicate that the Erlitou bronzes, the earliest known, draw on a still more archaic stage of metalworking, when objects were formed from sheet metal or hammered into shape rather than cast (see entry nos. 4, 5).

The two stubby posts on the rim at the base of the spout,

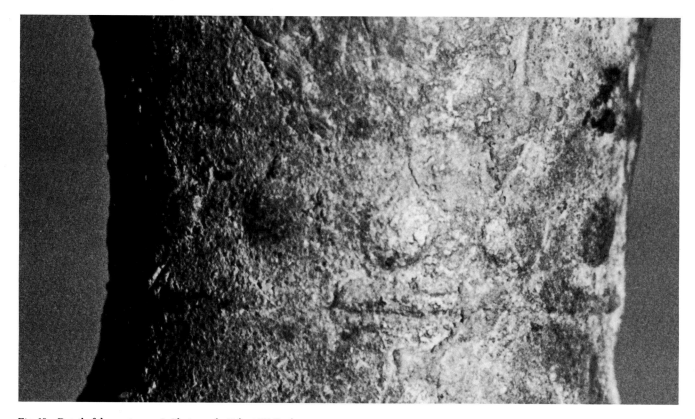

Fig. 18 Detail of decor, *jue* no. 1. Photograph: Robert W. Bagley

triangular in section, may also have originated in some step of fabrication, but whether they are connected with the casting process or were instead retained from some wrought-metal prototype has not been established. The suggestion that they are remnants of pouring inlets for the molten bronze is unconvincing, their location being ill chosen for the purpose. There seems moreover little reason to assume that the *jue* was cast upright, when other vessel types were regularly cast upside down, the legs serving conveniently as inlets and risers. (Casting upside down has the advantage that the core filling the interior of the vessel can be supported from underneath.) It is puzzling that the earliest *jue* known so far, that of figure 15, lacks any trace of the posts.

Whatever its origin, the capped post quickly became a purely decorative feature (shared by the *jia*; see no. 6). This can be established on the evidence of such vessels as nos. 15 and 16, where, far from serving any technical function, the massive caps could be added only by means of a roundabout casting procedure specially devised for the purpose: the caps were cast first, and the vessel cast to them—and cast in the usual upside-down position (see Fig. 35). At their first appearance the posts of *jue* vessels occur in pairs. Only somewhat later are there occasional examples in which a single post sits on a bridge across the spout (e.g., no. 15).

PUBLISHED: *Kaogu* 1978/4, p. 270, pl. 12:1.

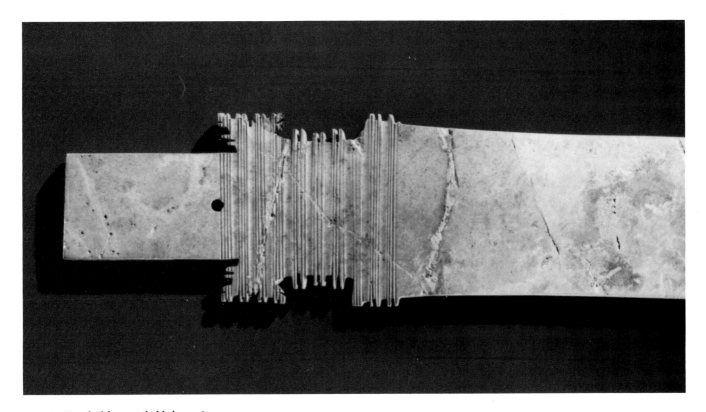

Fig. 19   Detail of decor, jade blade no. 2

2   Jade blade

First half 2nd millennium B.C. (Erlitou phase)
Found 1975, Erlitou, Yanshi Xian, Henan Province
Length 48.1 cm. (19 in.); width 7.8 cm. (3⅛ in.)
Cultural Office of Henan Yanshi Xian

This impressive blade, an outstanding example of a rare shape, was found with nos. 1 and 3 in the stratum of the palace remains at Erlitou. The original color of the stone seems to have been a pale grayish blue flecked with darker blue. Most of the surface is now weathered to a very light tan with white veins and patches of brown, green, and pink. The blade was in seven pieces when discovered and has been restored. Traces of a reddish brown substance adhere to the surface.

The task of extracting a finished object from a block of refractory stone was managed by a series of difficult and time-consuming operations. The blade was designed by drawing its outline on a flat slab sawn from the block. The size and shape of the given piece of jade and its veins and flaws supplied the constraints acting on the design, and the blade no doubt was laid out so as to make best use of the stone. The outline was then cut from the slab. One side of the blade remains perfectly flat and corresponds to the unaltered face of the slab as sawn; the small perforation in the tang was drilled from that side only, and is accordingly conical. On the opposite side the blade was worked down so that its thickness decreases slightly toward the crescentic end, and the crescent itself is ground very sharp. The decorated zone between the blade proper and the tang was made by lightly sawing a series of about forty parallel grooves on each side (see Fig. 19). These are not evenly distributed, but grouped by fours and fives, and the intervals between groups were ground down to a faintly dished profile. The edges of the blade were then notched with deep saw cuts to yield a jagged silhouette, after which the entire surface was polished.

It seems likely that stone blades of the present type derive from a metal ancestor and therefore were unknown before the Bronze Age. The arrangement of the tang with its crosspiece (much elaborated) and perforation suggests that the prototype was hafted transversely, like a *ge* halberd (see no. 10), and was thus some sort of elongated ax. A functional tool or weapon hafted in this way could hardly have been made of stone, given the fragility of so long and

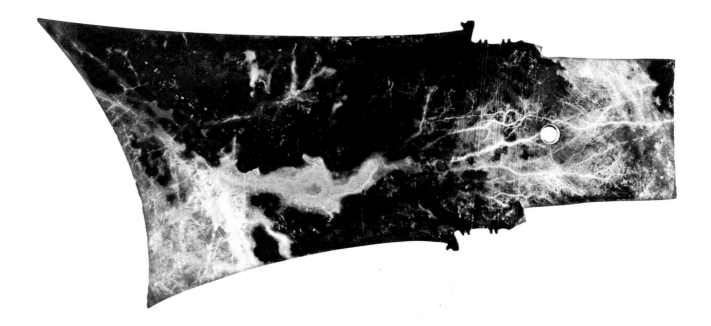

Fig. 20 Jade blade of the Shang dynasty. Provenance unknown. Length 30.8 cm. (12⅛ in.).
Pillsbury Collection, The Minneapolis Institute of Arts, 50.46.310

slender a blade. Although no such metal ax figures among the more standard Bronze Age tool types, a unique example of a long, blunt-ended bronze ax, comparable in proportions to the present blade, was found at Erlitou in the same stratum as the jade (*Kaogu* 1976/4, pl. 5:4). If this bronze implement represents the prototype for the jade, as Jessica Rawson has suggested (verbal communication, March 1979), it would appear that the metal tool fell from use at an early stage, leaving the jade derived from it free to evolve new versions, ever less practical, more refined, and more willful in shape. In the end its resemblance to the original bronze tool, or indeed to any functional object, is even more remote than is the jade *ge* from its own bronze counterpart.

If the prototype of the jade was a bronze tool, it follows that two finds of similar jade blades in local Neolithic contexts in Fujian and Sichuan Provinces are Bronze Age in date, and represent imports or at least influences from more civilized centers in the north. In fact, the blades in question are all typologically more advanced than the one from Erlitou—the most conspicuously archaic example of its type known. The fragmentary blade from Fujian bears some resemblance to a stray find from the Zhengzhou area (*Kaogu* 1959/6, p. 274, fig. 5; *Wenwu* 1966/1, p. 58). The blades from Sichuan have previously been dated as late as Eastern Zhou, but a date toward the end of Shang seems more appropriate (*Wenwu* 1979/2, pp. 30–37). The Sichuan blades are fairly similar to a jade in the Pillsbury Collection, the Minneapolis Institute of Arts (Fig. 20). The incised parallel lines are reduced in number and have been arranged to correspond exactly at their ends with the serrations in the edges; the mechanical precision of this more refined design is distinctly less exciting than the archaic freshness of the Erlitou blade.

Another recent discovery of blades of this type was a Western Zhou intrusion into Neolithic levels of a site in Shenmu Xian, Shaanxi Province (*Kaogu* 1977/3, pp. 154–57, 172, pl. 4). The typical Western Zhou versions from this find are inferior in design to likely Shang examples, including those from Sichuan. An Eastern Zhou blade found a few years ago at Houma in Shanxi is still more routine and simplified (*Wenwu* 1972/4, p. 34, fig. 6:19).

PUBLISHED: *Kaogu* 1978/4, p. 270, fig. 2:1.

3 Jade knife

First half 2nd millennium B.C. (Erlitou phase)
Found 1975, Erlitou, Yanshi Xian, Henan Province
Length 65.2 cm. (25⅝ in.); width 9.6 cm. (3¾ in.); maximum
    thickness 0.4 cm. (⅛ in.)
Cultural Office of Henan Yanshi Xian

The stone of this blade, unlike that of no. 2, is unaltered. Apart from a few areas of lighter green, the color is a dark green mottled with brown. The shape derives from a Neolithic harvesting knife, of which a fine stone example, also with seven perforations, came from a site in Nanjing, Jiangsu Province (Kansas City, 1975, no. 39). In a functional harvesting knife, the perforations along the back edge would have served for attaching a grip. The knife from Nanjing, however, like the present one, shows no signs of wear, and indeed is hardly sharpened; neither blade was made for practical use. They were instead meticulously finished replicas of a tool, meant for ceremonial or mortuary purposes.

The Erlitou blade is an isosceles trapezoid, its longest side ground to a blunt, smoothly rounded edge, the thicker back edge rough and unfinished—the only part of the blade not given a glossy polish. The conical perforations were all drilled from the side illustrated, and the lightly incised decoration is confined mainly to this side. A pair of incised lines runs parallel to three edges of the blade and, with the back edge, defines a smaller trapezoidal area that contains the perforations. The surface of the blade is ground down slightly outside this trapezoid, so that there is a faint downward step just outside the bounding lines (see Fig. 21). At each end of the blade, between the last pair of perforations, there appears a rectangle with an incised network of crisscrossing lines. A confused pattern including a few additional crisscross lines fills the lower corners of the incised trapezoid. The awkward design of these areas and the occasional overshoots of pattern lines elsewhere hint at the extreme difficulty that the execution of such lines entailed for the Erlitou jade worker; the opposite face of the blade dispenses with the patterns, excepting only the pair of parallel lines marking out the trapezoid. The polish of the blade, however, is very fine, and the ends of the knife are superbly shaped and finished, with a row of small teeth along the edge and a delicately formed projecting tip at the lower corner. The blade is broken in two places.

A jade knife only slightly smaller than the present one and made of similar stone is in the Winthrop Collection at the Fogg Art Museum, Cambridge, Massachusetts (Loehr, 1975, no. 210). Judging from its finish, the Winthrop blade is a slightly later piece, the design of the small teeth (which appear only at one end) being extraordinarily refined and delicate. The Winthrop jade is without surface decoration; the crisscross patterns of the present blade are repeated on another large knife, simpler in outline, in the British Museum, London (Rawson, 1980, fig. 59). The shape of this last, conspicuously archaic blade is matched by an undecorated jade knife found at Erlitou in 1967 (*Kaogu* 1975/5, pl. 8:9).

PUBLISHED: *Kaogu* 1978/4, p. 270, pl. 12:3.

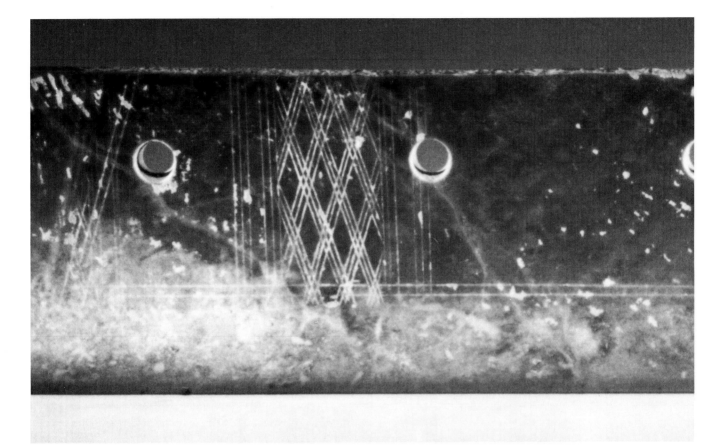

Fig. 21   Detail of incised lines on jade knife no. 3

COLORPLATES 1-11

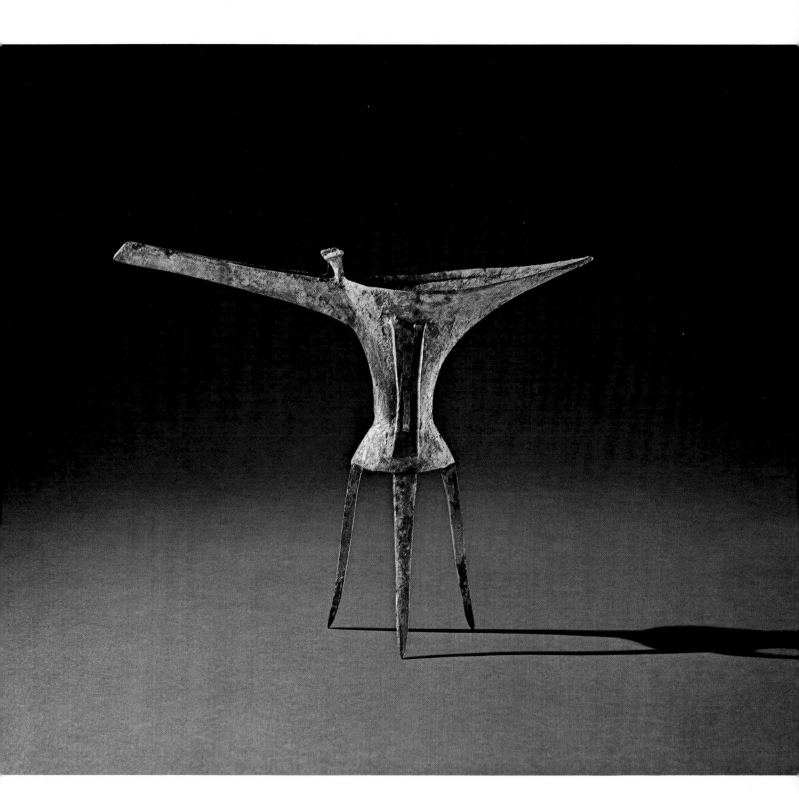

1 *Jue*. First half 2nd millennium B.C. (Erlitou phase). Height 25.6 cm.
(10⅛ in.); length (spout to tail) 31.5 cm. (12⅜ in.); weight 0.55 kg.
(1 lb. 3 oz.)

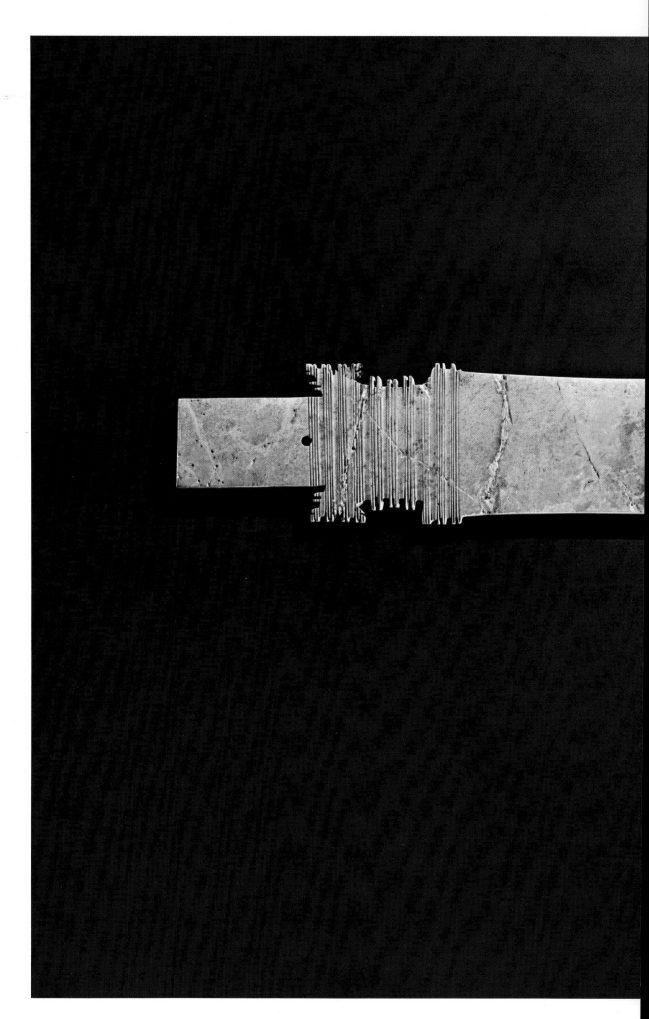

2 Jade blade. First half 2nd millennium B.C. (Erlitou phase). Length
48.1 cm. (19 in.); width 7.8 cm. (3⅛ in.)

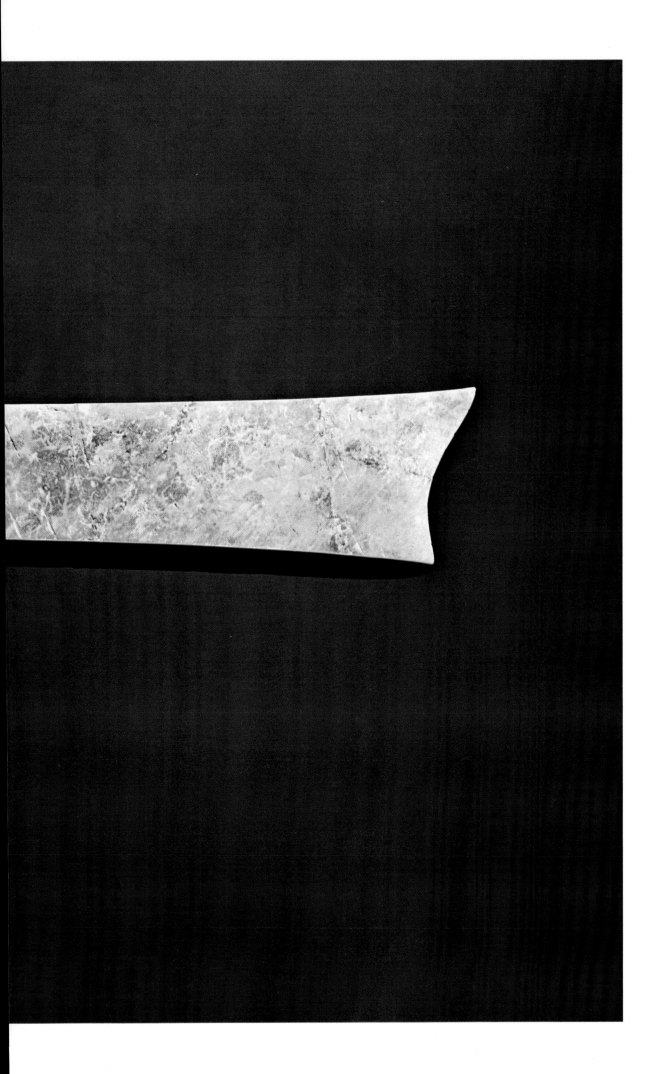

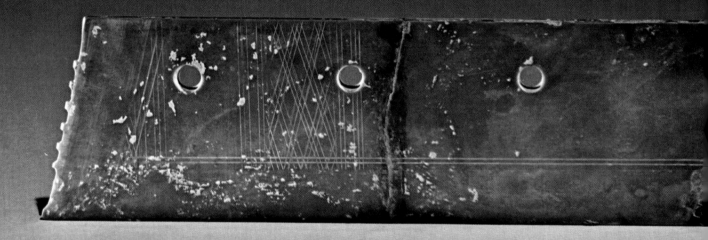

3 Jade knife. First half 2nd millennium B.C. (Erlitou phase). Length 65.2 cm. (25⅝ in.); width 9.6 cm. (3¾ in.); maximum thickness 0.4 cm. (⅛ in.)

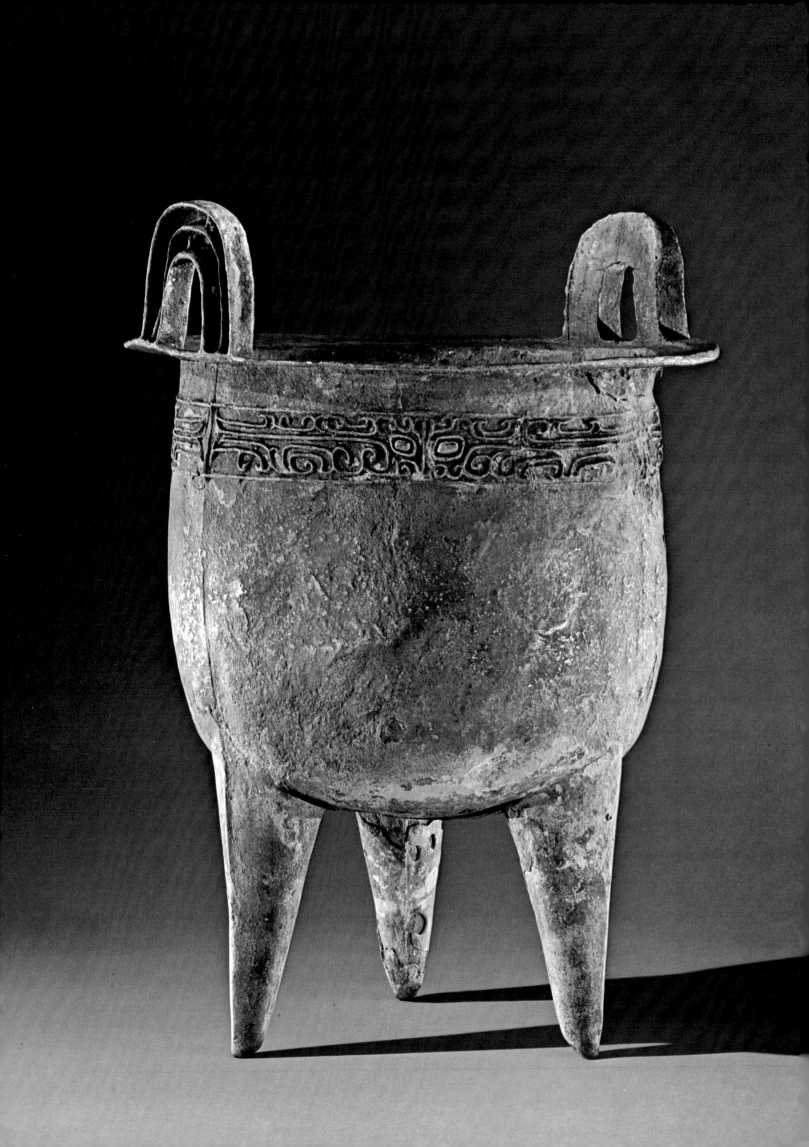

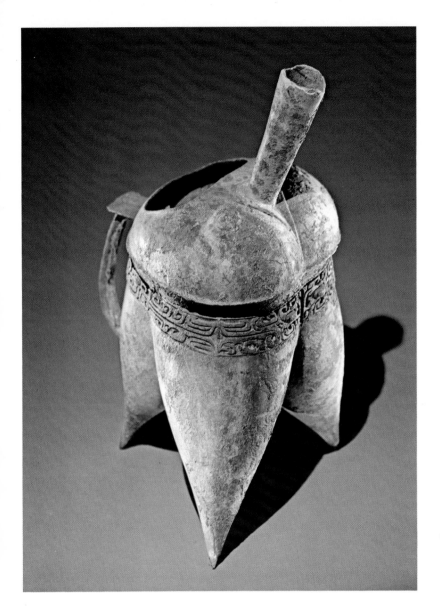

5 *He*. Mid-2nd millennium B.C. (Zhengzhou phase). Height 34.6 cm. (13⅝ in.); weight 1.85 kg. (4 lb. 1 oz.)

6 *Jia*. Mid-2nd millennium B.C. (Zhengzhou phase). Height 30.1 cm. (11⅞ in.); diameter 19.5 cm. (7⅝ in.); weight 2.25 kg. (5 lb.) ▽

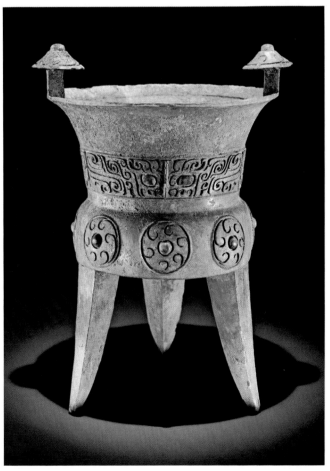

4 *Ding*. Mid-2nd millennium B.C. (Zhengzhou phase). Height 54 cm. (21¼ in.); diameter 40.7 cm. (16 in.); weight 9.6 kg. (21 lb. 2 oz.)

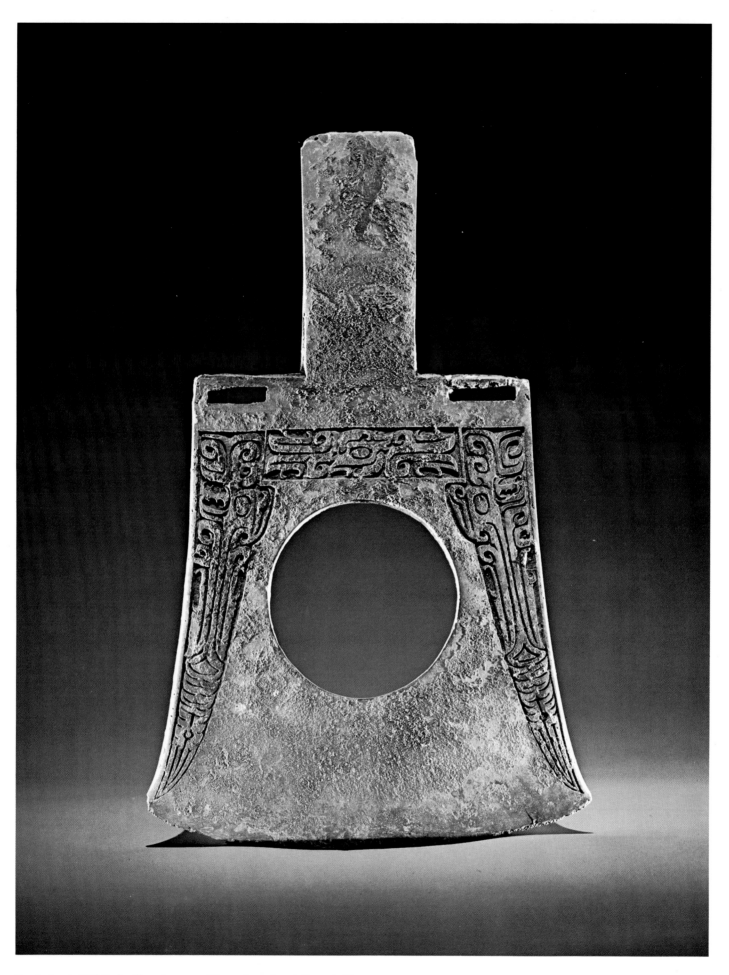

7 Ax (*yue*). Mid-2nd millennium B.C. (Zhengzhou phase). Length 41 cm.
(16⅛ in.); width 25.5 cm. (10 in.); weight 3.85 kg. (8 lb. 8 oz.)

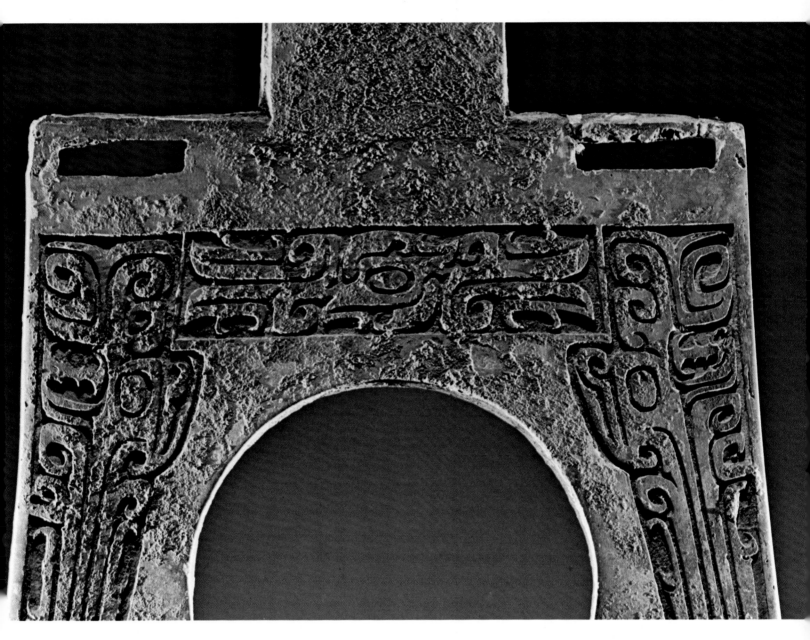

Detail, decoration at join of handle and blade, ax (*yue*) no. **7**

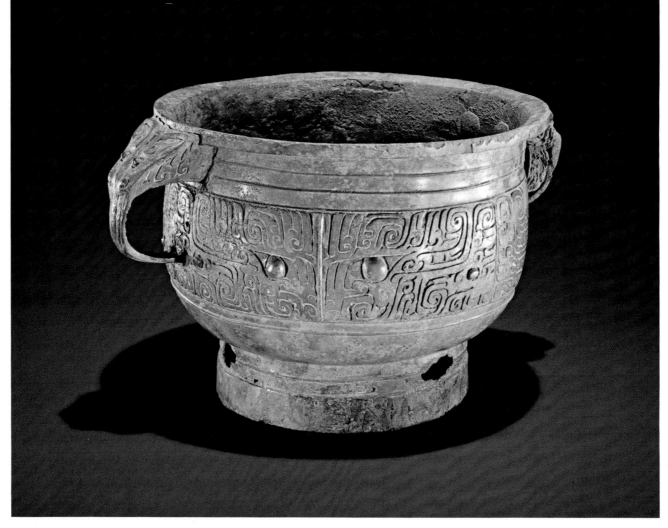

8 *Gui*. Mid-2nd millennium B.C. (Zhengzhou phase). Height 17.4 cm. (6⅞ in.); diameter 24.5 cm. (9⅝ in.); weight 2.8 kg. (6 lb. 3 oz.)

Detail, decor frieze, *gui* no. 8

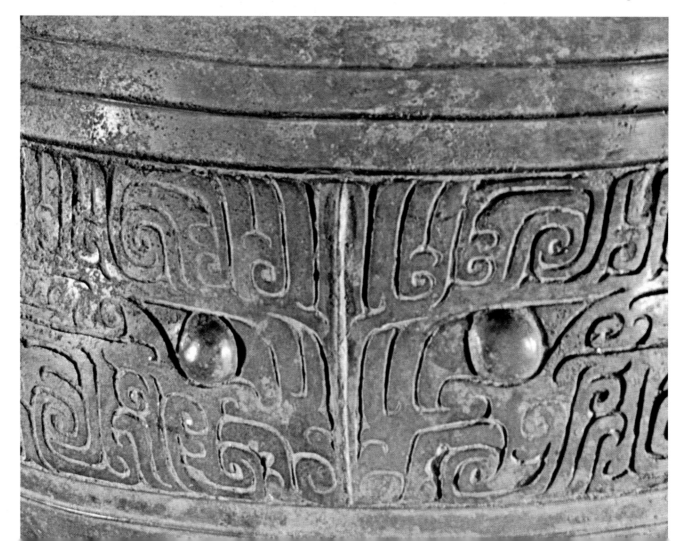

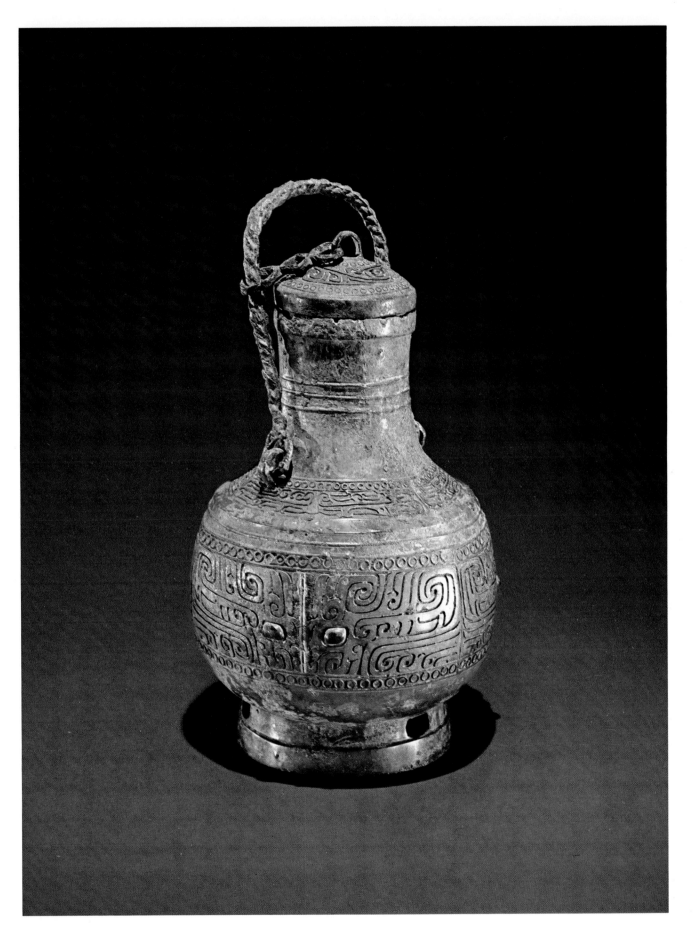

9 *You.* Mid-2nd millennium B.C. (Zhengzhou phase). Height 31 cm.
(12¼ in.); weight 1.7 kg. (3 lb. 12 oz.)

10 Jade *ge* (halberd) blade. Mid-2nd millennium B.C. (Zhengzhou phase).
Length 93 cm. (36¾ in.); greatest width 13.5 cm. (5¼ in.)

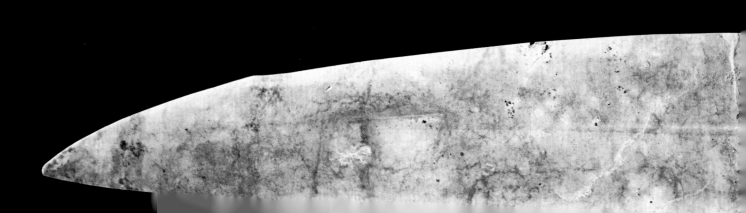

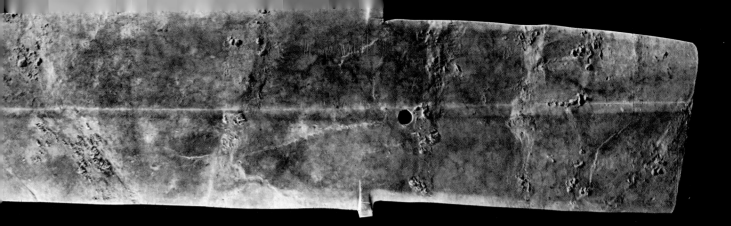

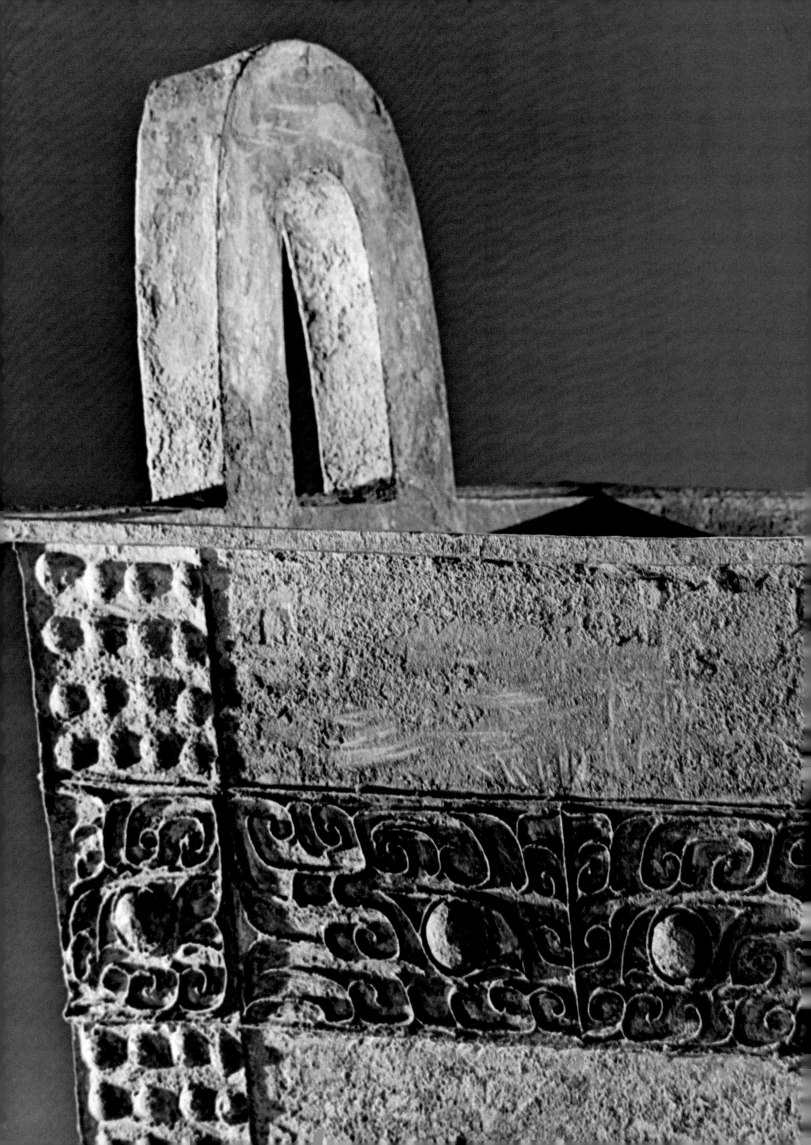

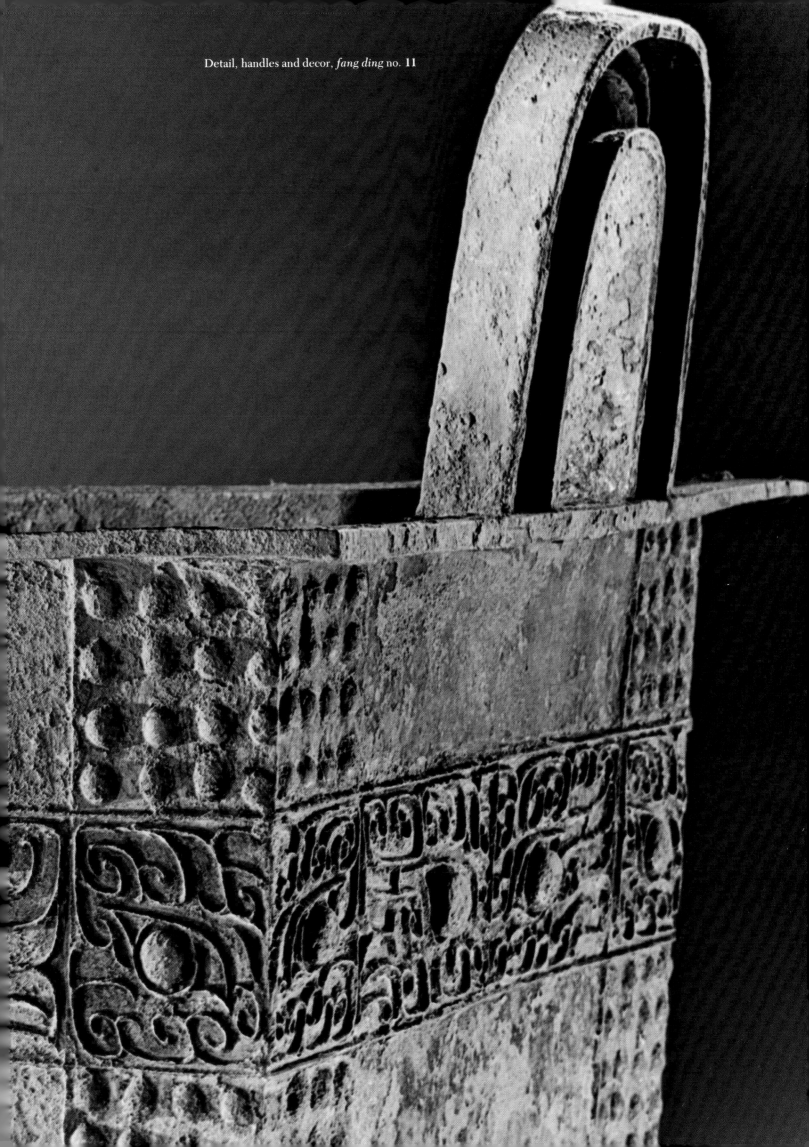

Detail, handles and decor, *fang ding* no. 11

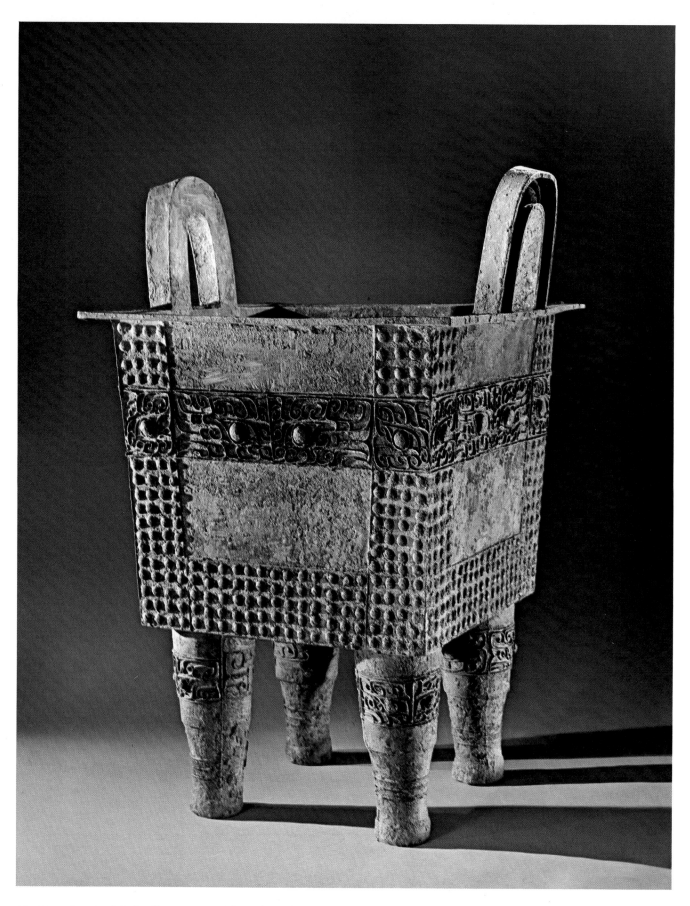

11 *Fang ding.* Mid-2nd millennium B.C. (Zhengzhou phase). Height
100 cm. (39⅜ in.); weight 82.4 kg. (181 lb. 4 oz.)

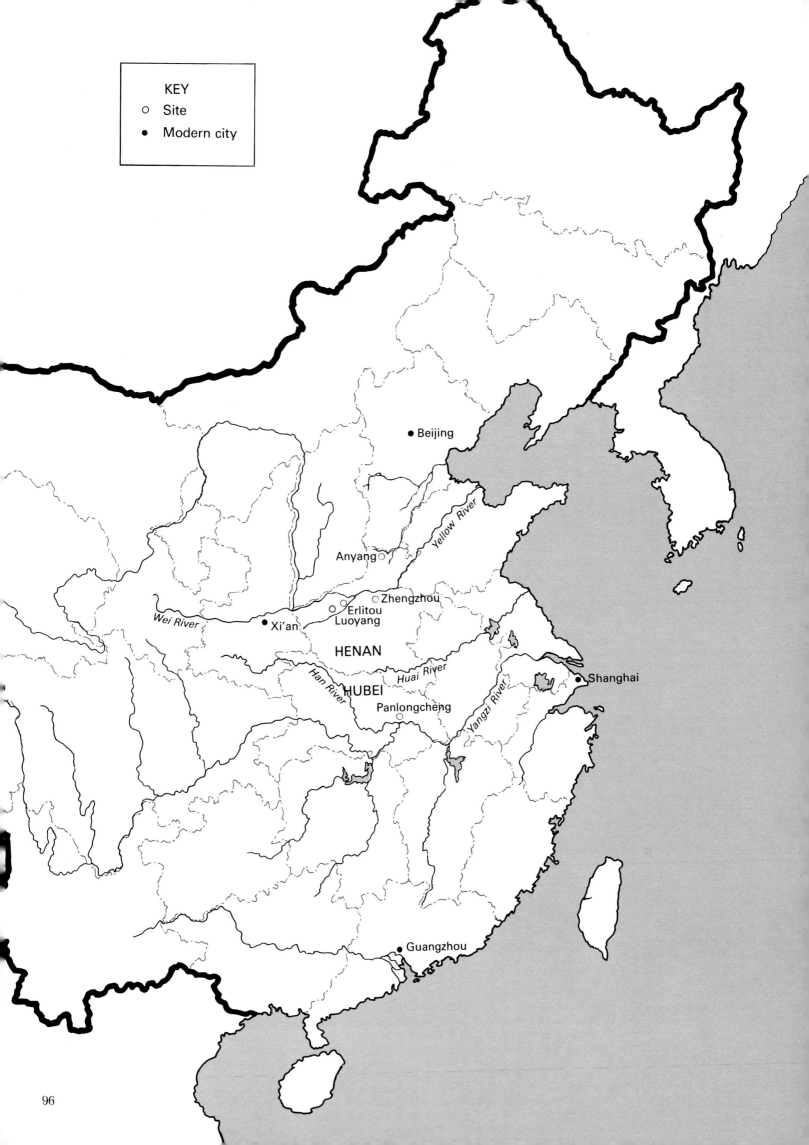

KEY
○ Site
● Modern city

● Beijing

Anyang ○

○ Zhengzhou
○ Erlitou
Luoyang

Wei River

● Xi'an

HENAN

Han River

Huai River

HUBEI

Panlongcheng ○

Yangzi River

Yellow River

● Shanghai

● Guangzhou

96

2 The Zhengzhou Phase (The Erligang Period)

Robert W. Bagley

The civilization whose beginnings are seen at Erlitou came to maturity around the middle of the second millennium B.C., during the period referred to by archaeologists as the Zhengzhou phase. The type site for this phase is located at the modern city of Zhengzhou, 100 kilometers to the east of Erlitou. First excavated in the early 1950s, the Zhengzhou remains include not only palace foundations but also a huge city wall. The scale of the wall is by itself enough to suggest that the city here was of major importance and probably had the status of a capital, but the lack of inscriptions again poses problems of identification. On rather shaky evidence, Zhengzhou has at times been identified with a city called Ao, traditionally supposed to have been the capital during the sixth generation of the Shang kings. More recently, however, speculations that Erlitou might have been a Xia city have been coupled with the suggestion that Bo, first capital of the Shang dynasty, was at Zhengzhou rather than at Erlitou. These conflicting identifications show clearly enough that, without written evidence, only the relative date of the two sites can be taken as securely established. Assignments to specific cities or even to dynasties cannot be taken as fact, particularly when they derive from attempts to combine insufficiently accurate radiocarbon dates with unreliable traditional chronologies. The clumsy terms "Erlitou phase" and "Zhengzhou phase" thus have at least the virtue of being noncommittal.

Excavations in the vicinity of Zhengzhou have brought to light a few scattered remains that resemble artifacts from Erlitou, but it is clear that the main occupation of the site came later, following closely on the uppermost level at Erlitou. The city wall belongs to this period. It is approximately rectangular, with a perimeter of 7.2 kilometers. Rammed-earth foundations of large buildings lie in the northeastern part of the walled enclosure, accompanied by sacrificial burials of human victims; but the exact plan of the Shang city is not known, since it lies in large part beneath present-day Zhengzhou. In places the wall still stands 9 meters high and measures 36 meters thick at the base; the labor required to construct a fortification of these dimensions is the clearest proof of the wealth and power at the disposal of the Shang king. More modest dwellings, along with a variety of workshops, including bronze foundries, lie outside the wall.

Map of China showing important archaeological sites of the Zhengzhou phase (Erligang period) of the Shang dynasty, 16th century to 14th century B.C.

At Zhengzhou bronze vessels were found mainly in a few burials, also located outside the city wall. An exhibition of archaeological finds from the People's Republic seen in the United States in 1974 and 1975 included a large number of these bronzes (Kansas City, 1975, nos. 70–77). At the time, the Zhengzhou finds were of unique historical interest, representing as they did the only substantial group of excavated bronzes earlier than the Anyang period. In the few years since that exhibition, however, many more bronzes of the same phase have been excavated from a variety of new sites. Centering on more recent excavations, the present exhibition includes only one object from Zhengzhou, a newly discovered vessel that in its monumental size surpasses anything else known from its period. It is a *fang ding* (no. 11), one of a pair unearthed by chance at a point some 300 meters west of the city wall. This extraordinary tetrapod vessel shows the technical capabilities of the pre-Anyang founder to have reached a level previously unimagined. It also offers further evidence of the status of the city at Zhengzhou: the cost and difficulty of casting bronzes on such a scale very likely imply a royal patron.

The Zhengzhou phase is represented here not by additional bronzes from Zhengzhou itself, but by objects unearthed at the recently excavated site of Panlongcheng, in Hubei Province (nos. 4–10). The Panlongcheng site is open to more systematic digging than is present-day Zhengzhou, and although Panlongcheng was certainly not so important a city in Shang times, the artifacts recovered there by now probably surpass in quantity the results of years of excavation at Zhengzhou. Stylistically there is nothing to distinguish the bronzes from the two sites, and Zhengzhou and Panlongcheng do not differ culturally in any other respect. There is a city wall at Panlongcheng, considerably smaller than the one at Zhengzhou, but built in the same fashion; and inside it, again in the northeast corner, there are foundations of large wooden buildings. Less important dwellings and graves lie outside the walled precinct.

The cultural uniformity of the Zhengzhou and Panlongcheng remains is not to be taken for granted: Panlongcheng is situated near the Yangzi River, 450 kilometers south of Zhengzhou, in a region that might once have been judged well outside the range of Shang civilization. Furthermore, the Panlongcheng site now appears to be far from unique in this respect. Within the last few years there have come reports of early sites even more distant from the middle reaches of the Yellow River valley, where the early Shang culture presumably had its center. Among the most noteworthy is a find made in Pinggu Xian, in Beijing, represented here by no. 12.

These new discoveries require a revision of earlier notions of Shang history. In the past it was the Anyang site, and particularly the divination inscriptions found there, that shaped our ideas of the Shang empire and of Shang material culture. The excavated parts of the Shang city at Zhengzhou and the still more limited finds from the earlier site at Erlitou both seemed insignificant set next to the wealth and splendor of the Anyang capital. The conclusion, natural enough under the circum-stances, that the Shang state reached the height of its power only in the Anyang period, now seems suspect. The geographic spread of sites culturally indistinguishable from Zhengzhou is apparently far greater than the range of the Anyang civilization.

Anyang became the capital sometime after Zhengzhou and Panlongcheng had experienced a sharp decline in importance, apparently both at the same moment. Archaeologists take the reduced activity at Zhengzhou to define the end of the Zhengzhou phase. We might speculate that the vast territories claimed by the Shang kings at Zhengzhou were ruled through vassal lords; no doubt the more remote areas, less immediately answerable to the central power, with time could grow into statelets more or less independent of the Shang king, whose domain shrank accordingly. When inscriptions of the royal court become available in the Anyang period, they present a picture of an embattled central power, allied with some statelets and at war with others. Among these local powers, alternately vassals and enemies of the Shang, were the Zhou people, who eventually overthrew the Shang state to found a dynasty of their own (chap. 5).

In the archaeological record one piece of evidence for this sequence of events is provided by the first appearance of stylistically provincial bronzes (chap. 3). Bronze finds belonging to the Zhengzhou phase are generally uniform in style, regardless of provenance; as noted above, the "Zhengzhou style" is represented just as well by bronzes from Panlongcheng as by examples from Zhengzhou. This is no longer true in the Anyang period: after the decline of Zhengzhou, outlying regions began to diverge from the artistic tradition of central North China, and the area for which Anyang can be taken as type site is accordingly much smaller. For however short a time, the power of the early Shang state must have made itself felt much more effectively in peripheral areas.

Bronze Technology and Design in the Zhengzhou Phase

Despite its modest aesthetic achievement, the bronze industry at Erlitou was already technically sophisticated enough to serve as the foundation for a vigorous artistic development in the ensuing Zhengzhou phase. The elegantly shaped *jue* no. 1, found at Erlitou in 1975, was cast with a narrow band of very primitive decoration on the side away from the handle. Though it consists of nothing more than a row of five raised dots between a pair of thread-relief lines, the decor of the *jue* shows that the possibility of working the mold surface was appreciated even before the Zhengzhou phase. To this fundamental innovation the Zhengzhou founder added a variety of auxiliary techniques, eventually having at his disposal the full range of casting techniques employed during the remainder of the Shang period. The course subsequently taken by the bronze art was set at this early stage, as the founders began to experiment with cast decoration and to work out the possibilities offered by their distinctive section-mold technology. The dramatic development of the art during the Anyang period did not overstep the confines of technical means and artistic opportunities already recognized and exploited by casters of the Zhengzhou phase.

The technical repertoire of the Chinese metalworker in fact underwent little further expansion for the next millennium. Throughout that time the basis of metalworking technology remained section-mold casting, with decoration made by casting—that is, decoration added by working the mold surfaces, not applied to an object already cast. The first significant exceptions to this rule, inlaid bronzes, do not appear until about the seventh century B.C. (see chap. 8).

During the Shang period, workshop practice insistently favored casting in one pour. The caster took pains to prepare a mold assembly, complete with decoration, that would yield a finished object, with no remaining parts to be joined on or decoration to be added. A few auxiliary techniques for joining separately made parts were used sparingly, only when they could not well be avoided. This strict preference for unitary casting has the important result that Shang bronzes seldom have the look of composites. They were not assembled from independent parts; both shape and decoration emerge together from the mold.

The auxiliary techniques known to the Shang founder nevertheless deserve attention for several reasons. They represent the founder's solution to especially difficult casting problems and thus define the limits of his casting method or of his confidence. At the same time, they serve to introduce the principles that lie behind the much elaborated casting technology of later times. In essence, all are joining methods. They fall into three categories: casting-on, precasting, and ways of joining separate parts that do not rely on casting (welding, soldering, brazing, mechanical joins, and the like).

The third category is the most exceptional. Some techniques that fall under this heading—riveting, for example—may actually have been more common in pre-Shang times (see entry no. 5). Animal heads on the shoulders of Shang vessels were sometimes joined mechanically, probably secured over tenons, the join occasionally strengthened with solder. Handles and other large appendages to a few late Shang and Zhou bronzes were attached with solder. These rare cases apart, Shang joining methods were all special adaptations of the casting process.

Casting-on is the simplest of joining techniques, since it offers an easy way to patch a flawed casting, and it was probably one of the first to be invented. To cast a patch it is necessary only to build a small mold around the hole to be plugged, both inside and outside the vessel. Several small patches can be seen on the very early *ding* no. 4. The remnant of a sprue, the channel through which the bronze flowed into the tiny mold, appears as a raised line in the middle of each patch, where it was broken or filed off after the bronze solidified.

The casting-on method was not confined to patching; where necessary, it could be used to add whole members to an object. In the case of intricate shapes, or for monumental vessels, the Shang master might be persuaded to

make a vessel in several steps. The *fang ding* no. 11 is a good example. The caster evidently distrusted his ability to cast so large a vessel entire, complete with its legs; he instead cast the body of the vessel first, and then cast the legs onto it.

As his expertise grew, the Shang founder was careful to eliminate unnecessary steps. In the Anyang period, even the largest *fang ding* vessels were probably managed without recourse to secondary pours of metal (no. 28). In the same way the *gui* shape, a bowl with handles, in Anyang times was regularly cast in one piece, even though on its first appearance it was made in two steps. The *gui* from Panlongcheng (no. 8), by far the earliest example of its type known, is exceptional in having cast-on handles, neatly locked in place by slight overflows of metal through holes left for the purpose in the side of the bowl. It would seem that the pre-Anyang caster invented this vessel type by adding handles to a bowl—quite literally. But his successors, once equal to the task of constructing the requisite mold assembly, preferred to cast bowl and handles together.

Precasting, the last of the joining techniques, is in principle only a variation of casting-on in which the bulk of the vessel is cast onto a minor appendage. In practice it seems to give neater joins. The precast cap for the post of no. 15 (Fig. 35) was made by itself, then inserted into the mold in which the remainder of the vessel was to be cast. When the vessel was poured, the cap was locked in place. The *you* no. 9 shows a more subtle use of the same precasting technique. Here the imitation rope handle was cast first, then inserted into the mold for the vessel, but inserted in such a way that it would not touch the metal of the vessel. Instead, the loops at its ends interlock with a pair of loops on the side of the *you*, and the handle swings freely.

The advantages of unitary casting and of the section-mold method, which account for the Shang artist's single-minded devotion to his technique, are both aesthetic and practical. As explained in chapter 1, one signal virtue of the section-mold method is the possibility it affords of applying decoration directly to the mold surfaces, before the sections are assembled for casting. On the earliest bronzes of the Zhengzhou phase, cast decor is executed in the simplest of techniques, thread relief. The raised lines of the pattern on the *ding* no. 4 were produced by incising lines in the clay of the mold sections. The pattern applied to each section is complete and self-contained, and the decoration accordingly repeats three times in the circumference of the vessel, once for each section of the mold.

Having learned to decorate his bronzes by decorating the mold, the Shang caster seems to have devoted his full attention to the possibilities of cast ornament. Decoration added to the bronze itself after casting, which plays so large a part in Western metalworking traditions, held no attraction for him. Apart from cleaning and polishing after removal from the mold and the effects of corrosion following burial, Shang bronzes are seen today essentially as they left the mold; the cast surface has not been altered by cold-working the metal. As a result, the de-

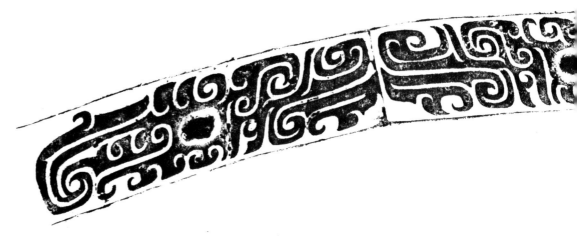

Fig. 22   Rubbing of decor frieze and whorl-circle, *jia* no. 6. Photograph
courtesy of Cultural Relics Bureau, Beijing

signs have a sharp-edged crispness of execution that is foreign to the exacting process of using tools on bronze and that belongs instead to a technique that cuts the design with ease and fluency in clay.

The varieties of ornament that succeeded the simple thread relief of no. 4 were all produced by casting and reflect continual improvements and elaborations of the moldmaking process. The first step beyond thread relief is seen on many bronzes of the Zhengzhou phase (nos. 5–7). Here the raised parts of the decoration are no longer simple lines, but carefully shaped bands of varying widths. The greater expressive possibilities of these modulated lines were immediately exploited to give richer, more forceful designs. The strength and eloquence of the finest examples directly exhibit the virtuosity of the artist, for these qualities are owed entirely to the hand that carved the mold.

The decor patterns, which in hindsight may seem to have grown up almost spontaneously to fill the arc of the mold section, were in reality the product of a minute concern for artistic effects. The direction and coherence that are visible in the evolution of the bronze art can only be explained on the assumption of the artist's intense preoccupation with matters of design. The search for fresh effects at first led to more complicated patterns, which by the end of the Zhengzhou phase approached a labyrinthine complexity (nos. 8, 9, 12). The friezes of decor grew wider, the lines of the pattern narrower and more densely packed. In a study of Shang bronzes published by Max Loehr in 1953, these especially intricate designs were assigned to the third of five stages of evolution (summarized on p. 182 below). Loehr's Style I corre-

sponds to the thread relief of nos. 4 and 11; Style II, to the bold designs with wider, modulated raised strips seen on nos. 5–7. His Style III was reached only toward the close of the Zhengzhou phase (nos. 8, 9, 12).

Although the ornament of each bronze acquires an individual character from the hand responsible for its execution, the patterns nevertheless fall into a very limited number of classes. Leaving aside a few purely abstract design elements of lesser importance, there were during the Zhengzhou phase only two distinct sorts of pattern, either of which could be used to fill a frieze section. One is a vaguely discernible face seen from the front (thus, with two eyes visible). The other is a creature seen in profile, showing only a single eye; it sometimes suggests a bird (no. 5?), but otherwise can be loosely termed a dragon. The face shown frontally is the earlier of the two designs (no. 4), and it remained the principal motif of the bronze art for as long as the Shang artistic tradition survived. We have no knowledge of what it was called or what it may have signified in Shang times, but at a much later date it was given the name *taotie*, and for want of a better this name is still used.

In its earliest forms—there are a few examples still more primitive than the *ding* no. 4—the *taotie* consists of little more than a pair of eyes in the center of the frieze unit (that is, in the center of the mold section). By the time of no. 4, the pattern is already more complicated: symmetrical linear embellishments have been added to fill up the arc of the mold section. Nevertheless, the eyes remain the only definite organic element in the pattern; if a face is to be found in the center of the frieze, it is one that exists more in the imagination of the beholder than in

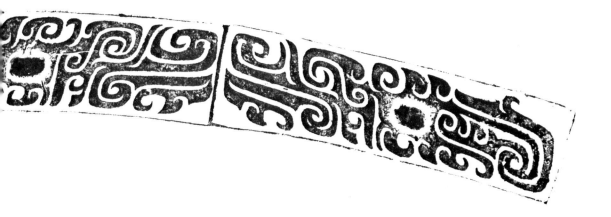

the actual lines drawn on the vessel. Successive generations of bronze casters steadily elaborated the face, adding suggestive organic details, so that while it never turns into a recognizable, real animal, it does constantly grow more persuasively animallike. In a *taotie* like the one seen on the *jia* no. 6 (see Fig. 22, center section), a sympathetic observer will find not only the pair of eyes, but also a nose and, to each side of it, a comma-shaped lower jaw shown in profile.

The appearance of the lower jaw has a special significance. It means that the bronze caster, having at first added a few flourishes merely to fill out the arc of the mold section, has subsequently decided that these embellishments at the extremes of the frieze unit should be connected in some intelligible way with the face in the center. Each end of the pattern unit must then be understood as a body seen in profile, grafted onto the face seen from the front. The lower jaw is the unambiguous sign of this grafting process, because it is shown in profile like the body, rather than in frontal view like the face to which it is attached. It makes the transition from the frontal view of the face to the side view of the body less awkward, and it must appear once for each of the two bodies, on each side of the face. The two bodies and the lower jaw repeated in profile combined with a single upper jaw seen frontally are as yet barely visible on the *jia* no. 6; but they become canonical features of the *taotie* in later times—quite visible on no. 12, vividly present on no. 27.

In this way, a recognizable *taotie* only gradually condenses around the focus provided by the eyes of the earliest patterns; and it is not until the Anyang period, when the art is some centuries old, that these patterns solidify into the familiar, unambiguously corporeal creatures known from the majority of Shang bronzes (no. 32). The history of the motif suggests that Shang decoration is an art of pure design, without any specific symbolism attaching to particular motifs. The later versions of both dragon and *taotie*, with their protean shapes and incessant permutations, would seem to bear out this suggestion, which was made first by Max Loehr (1968).

The animals that condense around single eyes and are therefore seen entirely in profile follow exactly the same development as the *taotie*. They begin as vaguely suggestive ornamental patterns (see no. 6; Fig. 22, left and right sections)—executed with marvelous verve and feeling—and only gradually turn into concrete, recognizably organic motifs. If we call the earliest versions dragons, we can do so only in hindsight; the name is bestowed in recognition of the motifs destined to grow out of them. The ornaments that are to become dragons appear first on two specific vessel types, the *jia* and the *jue*. Both of these shapes have handles that interrupt the decor frieze (see no. 6). Instead of three identical frieze units, the circumference divides naturally into two short units flanking the handle and one longer unit, suitable for a *taotie*, opposite the handle. The two shorter units are at first filled with abstract scrollwork. Later, for the sake of a design more in harmony with the *taotie* in the long frieze unit, each of the shorter units will be supplied with a pattern organized about one eye instead of two; and from this accident it will happen that the creatures into which these ornaments evolve will be shown in profile.

Both dragon and *taotie* patterns participate as frieze units in the same simple, repetitive decor schemes (cf.

the different units in Fig. 22), and alongside them are found entirely abstract designs like that seen on the lid of the *you* no. 9 (see Fig. 28). Like the dragon, the abstract patterns are themselves often formed around isolated eyes, so that both in origin and in ornamental function there is little to distinguish the two. At this stage the dividing line between what is abstract and what is not is quite blurred, and in the end only depends on the absence or presence of a certain organic suggestiveness. All of the patterns, zoomorphic or not, belong to an art of pure ornament, of matchless intelligence and sophistication.

As the patterns of surface ornament grew progressively more complex and elegant, the vessel shapes too were being refined. The relatively thick-walled and solidly proportioned *jia* no. 6 is a far cry from the thinly cast, awkward *jue* vessel from Erlitou (no. 1). The use of clay cores inside the legs of the *jia* made it possible to cast legs of massive proportions, better suited than the spindly legs of the Erlitou *jue* to give the appearance as well as the fact of stable support. The *ding* vessel from Beijing, no. 12, is decorated in Loehr's Style III, and accordingly belongs to the very end of the Zhengzhou phase; in form as well as decoration it is conspicuously more advanced than its Style I predecessor, no. 4. The shape is more compact, and the relative proportions of legs and body seem less accidental, as does the slightly rounded, shallower form of the bowl itself. A continual search for such improvements, in which the bronze caster's attention is directed toward both the surface decoration and the shape on which it appears, is the animating force behind the evolution of the bronze art in the Shang period. The unfailing harmony that exists between shape and decoration is the direct outcome of a method that forms both at once in the casting operation. The shape of the vessel must inevitably reflect the way in which the mold is sectioned, and the decoration, applied to the individual sections of the mold, reveals and even stresses the same symmetries.

CHAPTER 2: CATALOGUE ENTRIES

4 *Ding*

Mid-2nd millennium B.C. (Zhengzhou phase)
Excavated 1974 from Lijiazui M2, Panlongcheng, Huangpi Xian,
  Hubei Province
Height 54 cm. (21¼ in.); diameter 40.7 cm. (16 in.); weight
  9.6 kg. (21 lb. 2 oz.)
Hubei Provincial Museum

To judge from its thread-relief decor and simple shape, this large cauldron is one of the earliest bronzes from the Panlongcheng site. The proportions of the deep bowl and clumsy legs are unsubtle, but the *taotie* designs in the single relief band are vigorously drawn, floridly attractive ornaments. A few small holes in the vessel wall, probably casting flaws, were filled with cast-on patches. The surface, which ranges in color from the predominant dark brown to a light blue, is rough and gritty.

The outer half of the wide everted rim steps up slightly, as though the entire rim had been hammered out and then folded inward to give a smooth edge. This imitation in cast bronze of a feature arising from wrought-metal technology has already been noted in connection with the *jue* no. 1. Rims of this form are common on bronzes of the Zhengzhou phase (nos. 4–6, 11), but seem to disappear toward the end of that period (no. 8).

The vessel was cast in a mold with three vertical divisions; traces of seams run down the sides of the bowl and onto each leg. The structure of the mold assembly and its relation to cast decor are described on pages 70–72, figure 16. The hollow legs are open to the interior of the vessel, so that the cores for the legs could conveniently be made as conical extensions from the main casting core. One of the legs is recast, the new part fitting like a loose shell over the stump of the old. The two handles or "ears" on the rim are also hollow and are braced inside with ribbons of metal. Similar braces can be seen inside the handles of the *fang ding* no. 11; the designs on the outer faces of the handles of much later *ding* vessels (e.g., no. 54) may allude to this early feature. Legs and handles were made hollow presumably in order to conserve metal, and perhaps also to minimize the chance of casting flaws caused by metal shrinkage on solidification of the melt. In later times legs and large handles were cast with individual clay cores that would be permanently incorporated in the finished bronze. Supporting the various cores in proper alignment during casting required considerable refinement of technique, but by sealing the cores inside the bronze the appearance of solid metal could be counterfeited (no. 54).

The positioning of the two handles on the rim relative to the three legs below lends a calculated asymmetry to the *ding* vessel type. The arrangement seen here, common on pre-Anyang vessels, gives way in later times to that of the *ding* no. 52.

PUBLISHED: *Wenwu* 1976/2, pl. 6 (report, pp. 5–46, pls. 2–6);
  Tokyo, 1976, no. 4.

5 *He*

Mid-2nd millennium B.C. (Zhengzhou phase)
Excavated 1974 from Lijiazui M2, Panlongcheng, Huangpi Xian,
  Hubei Province
Height 34.6 cm. (13⅝ in.); weight 1.85 kg. (4 lb. 1 oz.)
Hubei Provincial Museum

This lobed, spouted pouring vessel represents a shape fairly common at sites of the Zhengzhou phase, but rare thereafter. The finely shaped lower part, which imitates hollow-legged pottery tripods of Neolithic times, is covered by a domed lid; a large aperture in the lid is situated just behind the spout. The domed cover is provided with a pair of simple circular eyes in relief, like buttons whose centers rise into tiny conical points, placed on either side of the spout. Seen from above, the lid thus becomes a face, with the spout serving to suggest a nose, and the opening below it a gaping mouth.

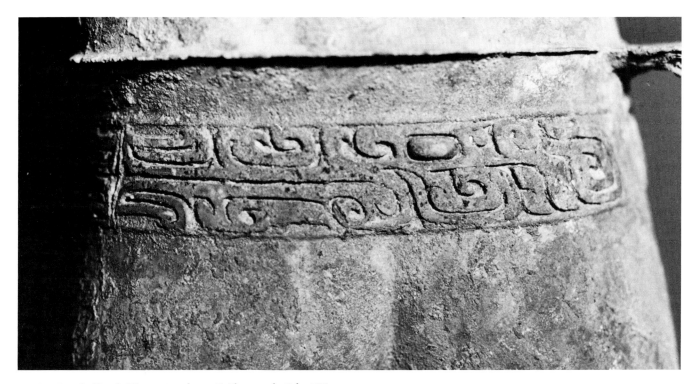

Fig. 23   Detail of band of decoration, *he* no. 5. Photograph: Robert W.
  Bagley

A strap handle runs upward from the lower part of one lobe to the line where the body and cover meet. The single band of decoration, in a sharply cast and handsomely drawn Style II relief, contains a *taotie* and two "dragons"—the latter lacking almost any organic feature apart from the neatly shaped rectangular lozenge that serves for an eye (see Fig. 23). The decor band does not extend under the handle. The opening in the lid has a molded edge, as though it were folded back; part of this edge has been restored. The matte surface is green mixed with brown and yellow. Except for the spout, the vessel seems to have been cast in a single pour. The spout was evidently added in a second operation; a teardrop-shaped puddle at its base belongs to this later pour.

In many respects the *he* shape is uncharacteristic of cast bronzes; its domed cover, for instance, which makes removal of the core after casting very inconvenient, is a feature that would hardly be invented in a founder's workshop. Thus, while the present vessel was made entirely by casting, it offers tantalizing clues to an earlier stage of metal technology that relied less exclusively on the casting process. The lobed lower part imitates an older pottery shape, as already noted. The cover, on the other hand, imitates a wrought-metal object so accurately that it can be used to illustrate the process of manufacture of its prototype. The domed shape is a typical product of the smith's hammering technique, and the tubular spout rolled from sheet metal is equally familiar in wrought-metal traditions. The cover would have been joined to the vessel proper by flaring the edges of both pieces and folding one over the other, a technique known as crimping; the crimped join is meticulously reproduced here. Lastly, the handle of the present *he* has a form typical of wrought-metal vessels, not of cast bronzes. It imitates a composite structure whose horizontal upper section was hammered out from the rim of the vessel and then riveted to the separate strap below. (The lower end of the handle, which need not be so firmly joined to the vessel, would typically have been soldered on or secured by an adhesive. The spout would probably have been attached in the same way.) In China only the *he* vessel has a handle of this form; the simple strap handles of other early bronzes invariably lack the unnecessary horizontal upper part (nos. 1, 6, 15, 16). Among the earliest Shang bronzes the *he* thus stands apart, being uniquely close to some undiscovered wrought-metal prototype of still greater antiquity. Pottery copies of such a prototype, duplicating the domed lid made into a face and the composite handle of the present vessel, are known from a few sites that long predate the Shang period (Bagley, 1977, pp. 196–98). These pottery imitations of metal vessels reveal the existence in China of a developed metal technology long before the earliest bronze vessels known at present (e.g., no. 1).

A bronze *he* slightly more advanced than the present example was found in the tomb of Fu Hao at Anyang (chap. 4); it must already have been an antique at the time it was buried (*China Pictorial* 1978/1, p. 25).

PUBLISHED: *Wenwu* 1976/2, pl. 4:3; Beijing, 1976b, no. 13.

6 *Jia*

Mid-2nd millennium B.C. (Zhengzhou phase)
Excavated 1974 from Lijiazui M1, Panlongcheng, Huangpi Xian, Hubei Province
Height 30.1 cm. (11⅞ in.); diameter 19.5 cm. (7⅝ in.); weight 2.25 kg. (5 lb.)
Hubei Provincial Museum

The body of this vessel—a flared upper part and a short skirt—rests on three stout legs of triangular cross section. A simple strap handle is set directly above one leg; above the other two legs, a pair of small posts with umbrella-shaped caps stands on the rim of the

vessel. The whorl-circle pattern that decorates the post caps appears again in circular bosses on the skirt. The band of Style II decoration, at the narrowest part of the vessel, does not extend under the handle; it consists of a *taotie* unit flanked by two frieze sections whose patterns are organized around single eyes. While the disposition of the decor is thus the same as on the *he* no. 5, the "dragons" flanking the *taotie* on the two vessels have little in common beyond the focal point of the central eye (see Fig. 23). Different hands have moreover imparted quite different characters to these Style II patterns—*taotie* and dragons alike—those on the *he* being tense and energetic, on the *jia* relaxed, fluent, and richly varied. In both cases the casting is exceedingly fine, the sharp-edged relief areas rising cleanly above the vessel wall.

The casting seams, which correspond to the frieze divisions, were polished away from the body of the vessel but are clearly visible on the handle and down the legs. Further seams run from the inner edge of each leg to meet at a point in the center of the vessel bottom. The posts and caps appear to have been cast in the same pour as the rest of the vessel (unlike the larger caps on the *jue* no. 15 and *jia* no. 16). The legs are hollow and open to the interior of the vessel. The smooth surface has a fine light green patination.

The *jia* is one of the most characteristic of Shang vessel types. Nos. 16, 26, and 33 are later versions of the same shape. A few examples significantly earlier than the present one have bulbous hollow legs and sketchy decoration akin to that of the *jue* no. 1.

PUBLISHED: *Wenwu* 1976/2, pl. 3:1; Tokyo, 1976, no. 2.

7 Ax (*yue*)

Mid-2nd millennium B.C. (Zhengzhou phase)
Excavated 1974 from Lijiazui M2, Panlongcheng, Huangpi Xian, Hubei Province
Length 41 cm. (16⅛ in.); width 25.5 cm. (10 in.); weight 3.85 kg. (8 lb. 8 oz.)
Hubei Provincial Museum

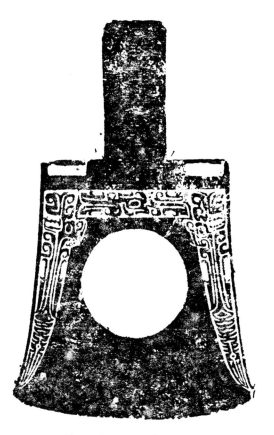

Fig. 24   Rubbing of ax no. 7. After *Wenwu* 1976/2, p. 33, fig. 34

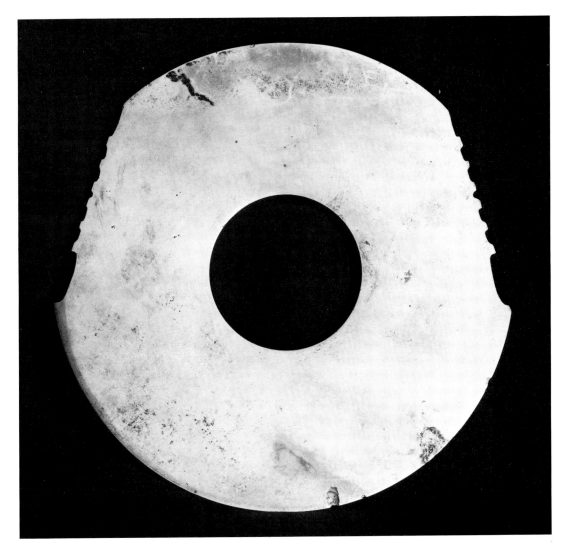

Fig. 25   Jade disk ax of Shang dynasty. Provenance unknown. Diameter 18.1 cm. (7¼ in.). Fogg Art Museum, Cambridge, Massachusetts, 43.50.527

The design of this bronze ax from Panlongcheng stands alone; no other example remotely approaches it in quality. The decoration along three sides of the blade, drawn with easy brilliance and sharply cast, does not rise above the surrounding surface, an arrangement not usual in Style II but probably practical in an ax. The designs themselves are fresh inventions, unknown from other bronzes; elements individually recognizable as eyes and, perhaps, rows of teeth are playfully combined without any attempt at zoological plausibility. The expressive power of the blade resides chiefly, however, in its splendid silhouette, best seen in figure 24. The perfect regularity of the large circular perforation serves to set off the less predictable curves of the cutting edge and sides, investing with the most intense significance an outer perimeter that might otherwise go unremarked. The perforation is a feature that may have been inspired by the central perforations of jade disks. In the Shang period the forms of jade disks and bronze axes seem to show a certain mutual awareness: the jade disk with outer perimeter sharpened for part of its length and trimmed on two sides to resemble an ax is a standard Shang form, though no example in jade quite matches the exact proportions of the Panlongcheng ax in bronze (Fig. 25). Near the rear edge of the blade two rectangular slots on either side of the tang served in hafting the ax. The smooth olive green surface is chipped in places, revealing a bright turquoise color beneath.

With the vessels nos. 4 and 5, this ax formed part of the furnishings of Lijiazui Tomb No. 2 at Panlongcheng. Possibly it played a role in the ceremony of burial, serving to behead the three sacrificial victims that were found in the tomb. The ax no. 23, from a much larger and later tomb, almost certainly had this function.

PUBLISHED: *Wenwu* 1976/2, pl. 5:5; Beijing, 1976b, no. 14.

8   *Gui*

Mid-2nd millennium B.C. (Zhengzhou phase)
Excavated 1974 from Lijiazui M1, Panlongcheng, Huangpi Xian, Hubei Province
Height 17.4 cm. (6⅞ in.); diameter 24.5 cm. (9⅝ in.); weight 2.8 kg. (6 lb. 3 oz.)
Hubei Provincial Museum

This *gui* is the earliest known example of a type common in later times, particularly during Western Zhou (e.g., no. 41). Like other pre-Anyang vessels of circular cross section, it was cast in a mold with three vertical divisions, and its *taotie* patterns accordingly repeat three times in the circumference. No provision was made in this familiar decor scheme for the two handles, which have almost the look of an afterthought. They were in fact cast on in a second operation, locked in place through holes left in the side of the vessel (Fig. 26). Since one handle is located on the seam that separates two frieze units, the handle diametrically opposite had to be set in

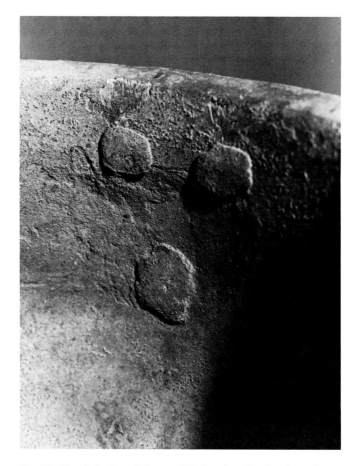

Fig. 26 Detail of *gui* no. 8 showing interior where handle of vessel was attached. Photograph: Robert W. Bagley

the middle of a *taotie*. As a result the arc between two handles contains one and one-half *taotie* units, their placement disconcertingly asymmetrical.

The handles are not the simple straps seen hitherto (cf. nos. 1, 5, 6), but hollow shells with more substantial proportions. The upper end of each handle is shaped into a flattish animal head, the first appearance of a feature standard in later times on many vessel types. The rim is thick and solidly molded, while the foot is very thin. Three irregular perforations in the foot lie on the axes of the vertical seams. Presumably the vessel was cast upside down, and pins passing through these openings served to support the clay core inside the foot (cf. nos. 9, 14). The patination is light green and silvery gray. A large area on one side is repaired.

The decoration of this *gui* offers a fine illustration of Style III motifs at an early stage (see Fig. 27). By comparison with the Style II designs of nos. 5 and 6, the *taotie* has a perceptibly more organic character. The snout and jaws are more easily recognizable, and the jaws are lined with teeth; the eye is elegantly outlined,

with the inner canthus drawn downward in a hook; horns (above the eyes) and bodies (to the side of each eye) have begun to materialize amid the swirl of ornamental lines. Moreover, new motifs are beginning to condense around smaller, isolated eyes set in the lower corners of each frieze unit. Slightly later versions of these new patterns, which eventually become fanciful but well-defined zoomorphs, can be seen on nos. 14 and 16. The growth of such motifs, which become ever more persuasively "real," illustrates the Shang artist's persistent habit of reading organic meaning into ornamental forms, investing them with life and a steadily enhanced zoomorphic character.

No other *gui* quite approaches this archaic example. Certain of its unusual features are however shared by a three-handled *gui* in the Musée Cernuschi, Paris, probably of early Anyang date, whose handles are cast on and rise level with the rim (Elisseeff, 1977, no. 12).

PUBLISHED: *Wenwu* 1976/2, p. 29, fig. 14.

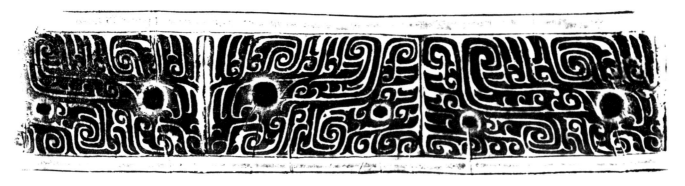

Fig. 27 Rubbing of decor, *gui* no. 8. Photograph courtesy of Cultural Relics Bureau, Beijing

9 You

Mid-2nd millennium B.C. (Zhengzhou phase)
Excavated 1974 from Lijiazui M1, Panlongcheng, Huangpi Xian,
  Hubei Province
Height 31 cm. (12¼ in.); weight 1.7 kg. (3 lb. 12 oz.)
Hubei Provincial Museum

Like the *gui* no. 8, which came from the same tomb, this *you* is the earliest known example of its type. The *taotie* patterns are at about the same stage of elaboration as those on the *gui*, but they appear here with a design on the lid that might be classified as Style II (Fig. 28), and with a narrow abstract band of clumsy thread relief on the shoulder. A detail not seen on the preceding vessels is the generous use of small circles in rows bordering the various decor friezes. The smooth patination has a rich green color.

The vessel is circular in cross section and was cast in a mold with three vertical divisions. As neither handle lies on a mold division, the awkward asymmetry of the *gui* no. 8 is to some extent avoided, and from one side (not illustrated) the *taotie* is presented frontally. Three openings in the foot fall on the lines of the mold divisions. The handle, whose ends interlock with loops on the shoulder of the vessel, was made first and then inserted into the mold for the vessel proper, which was thus cast onto it. Two further operations were required to cast the link to the lid, and the handle to the link. (The order of these operations might of course be shuffled.)

You vessels circular in cross section are known also from the Anyang period, but the classic *you* of Anyang and later times has a pointed oval cross section, and is arranged so that the frieze unit spans the full arc of 180 degrees from one end of the oval to the other (e.g., no. 25). An early *you* only marginally more advanced than the present one was found in 1977 at a site in Pinggu Xian in Beijing (*Wenwu* 1977/11, p. 5, fig. 6:1, p. 7, figs. 19, 20).

PUBLISHED: *Wenwu* 1976/2, pl. 3:2; Tokyo, 1976, no. 3; Beijing, 1976a, no. 3.

10 Ge (halberd) blade

Mid-2nd millennium B.C. (Zhengzhou phase)
Excavated 1974 from Lijiazui M3, Panlongcheng, Huangpi Xian,
  Hubei Province
Length 93 cm. (36⅝ in.); greatest width 13.5 cm. (5¼ in.)
Hubei Provincial Museum

This extraordinary blade is worked from a single piece of jade. The stone is partly altered in composition due to long burial, giving it a warm cream color varied with grayish veins and a few darker patches of brown and gray. The surface was finished to a high polish.

The jade *ge* is based on the bronze *ge* halberd, the characteristic weapon of the Chinese Bronze Age. The blade of the bronze weapon, sharpened on both edges, typically has a slight downward curvature, a tang with a perforation, and a crosspiece between the two to facilitate hafting. The haft of the weapon was perpendicular to the length of the blade, and rested against the crosspiece. In jade, however, the *ge* was made for ceremonial or mortuary purposes. A blade like the present one was too large, too fragile, and too expensive for practical use, and was almost certainly never even hafted. In Shang tombs jade *ge* blades are frequently found in a small pit sunk beneath the coffin; the pit ordinarily contains either a

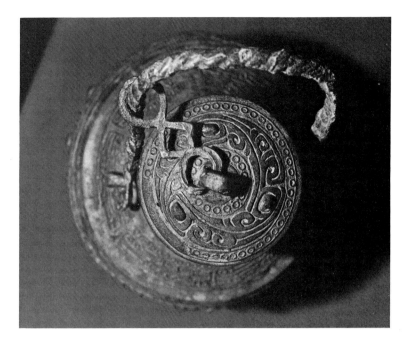

Fig. 28   Detail of lid, *you* no. 9. Photograph: Robert W. Bagley

dog or, in richer tombs, a man, both apparently serving as guardians. At Anyang, and probably at Panlongcheng as well, the *ge* blade regularly accompanies a human guardian. Like other jade *ge* from guardian pits in the Panlongcheng tombs, the present example was found broken in several pieces. The breakage may have been deliberate, serving to "kill" the blade before interment.

Because the jade *ge* did not serve the practical purposes of its bronze prototype, the jade worker was free, within the limitations of a given piece of stone, to arrange and manipulate the various elements of the blade on formal grounds alone. Thus the relative proportions of blade and tang, the degree of curvature, the placement of the median crest, and the size and location of the hafting crosspiece and of the perforation are freely variable; and Shang *ge* blades, which range in size from 3 or 4 centimeters all the way to the 93 centimeters of the present example, show an exceptional variety, each one having a character and personality of its own.

The unsymmetrical outline of the present blade is characteristic of both bronze and jade versions of the *ge*. The lower edge in this case is roughly horizontal, while the upper edge curves downward toward the point. The asymmetry of these curves is given emphasis by the median crest, which is extended illogically beyond the blade proper across the tang of the *ge*, to end at a point above the middle of the butt. This crest is not a simple ridge, but instead a slight bevel introduced between the upper and lower facets of the blade. The edges of the blade are ground very sharp so that near them the stone becomes translucent; the thickness of the *ge* nowhere exceeds half a centimeter. Near the point the taper is momentarily halted by a faint widening on both edges. The inconspicuous ridges at the base of the blade, derived from the hafting crosspiece of the bronze *ge*, are very small and neatly formed. On the side not illustrated, the median crest is less pronounced and runs more nearly axially; the small perforation in the tang is drilled from this side, and all three edges of the tang are sharply beveled. The extreme restraint and understatement of all these details, executed with the utmost precision on an object of such remarkable size, give an air of great austerity and subtlety of expression. It would be difficult to cite another *ge* of equal refinement and power.

PUBLISHED: Beijing, 1976b, no. 15.

11 *Fang ding*

Mid-2nd millennium B.C. (Zhengzhou phase)
Found 1974, Zhengzhou, Henan Province
Height 100 cm. (39⅜ in.); weight 82.4 kg. (181 lb. 4 oz.)
Henan Provincial Museum

This monumental rectangular *ding* vessel is the most imposing bronze yet attributable to the Zhengzhou phase of the Shang period. It was discovered in 1974 in the course of construction work about 300 meters west of the Shang city wall at Zhengzhou. If the source was a tomb, it cannot have been intact. Little was found accompanying the *ding*, the only other bronzes being an undecorated *li* tripod and a second *fang ding* smaller than the first but otherwise almost identical. With the possible exception of a small and primitive *fang ding* found recently in Pinggu Xian, Beijing (*Wenwu* 1977/11, pl. 4:1), the two *fang ding* from Zhengzhou are the earliest examples of their vessel type known. Before the discovery of the Zhengzhou pair, rectangular vessel shapes (signaled by the prefix *fang*) were generally viewed as inventions of the Anyang bronze industry at its height (nos. 27, 28, 32, 33); yet their far earlier appearance in the founder's repertoire of shapes should not be surprising, if we reflect how well adapted they are to the section-mold casting technique: flat mold sections are easy to make and easy to decorate.

According to the excavation report, the *fang ding* was cast in three steps, the handles ("ears") being precast and the legs cast on. There is no sign of precasting, however, and examination of the vessel suggests that ears and body were cast at the same time. Once the upper portion of the vessel was finished, it was supported upside down, and the legs were cast onto it; traces of this step are clear, for in a few places the metal of the legs overflowed onto the decorated side of the vessel above. Openings corresponding to the four legs had been left in the bottom of the vessel, and the legs are open to the interior. The two vertical casting seams on each leg are clearly visible and lie on lines separating the two *taotie* faces. The thread-relief lines are cleanly cast and rise high above the surface. The patination is brownish, with a rough, gritty texture.

The decoration on the body of the *ding* is laid out in a scheme devised especially for the flat sides of the new vessel type. A rectangular central panel, left blank, is bordered on bottom and sides with rows of small round bosses, and above by a frieze of *taotie* designs executed in thread relief. This latter frieze contains one complete *taotie* in the center, its ends coinciding with the ends of the rectangular panel below; while each end of the frieze is filled by the half of another *taotie* that is folded around the corner of the vessel. The two *taotie* faces decorating the upper part of each leg are similar in design, although the one on the back of the leg oddly lacks the raised pupils of the eyes. In all these *taotie* units, only the eyes are rendered unambiguously, though other parts of the creature—horns, nose, jaws, and the two bodies—can be found by a sufficiently imaginative observer. The eyes are shown as large round pupils surrounded by a thread-relief circle itself contained within an almond-shaped outline. This elegantly drawn eye, of which this vessel offers the earliest example in the exhibition, is one of the most pervasive and characteristic of Shang design elements. Later versions in bronze include the mannered configuration seen on the *pou* no. 13; and the motif is ubiquitous in the surface decoration of jades (nos. 36, 39).

The ingenious decor scheme improvised at this early stage for the *fang ding* survived as long as the vessel type itself and recurs twice more in the present exhibition (nos. 28, 54). The *fang ding* no. 28 from Fu Hao's tomb is a direct descendant of the Zhengzhou vessel, in its conspicuous monumentality as well as in decoration. Its decor scheme is refined in a few details (the vessel is stouter in proportions, and the *taotie* frieze is moved up just under the rim); and the decoration is executed in the currently fashionable Style V relief. Though somewhat smaller than the Zhengzhou *fang ding*—it is 79.6 centimeters high—the Fu Hao vessel is much more massive (117.5 kg.); the comparative thinness of the Zhengzhou *ding* is typical of early castings. A slightly later *fang ding* in the same line of descent, the Si Mu Mou *fang ding*, was found in the 1940s in one of the royal tombs at Anyang, at Xibeigang (see entry no. 28). Now in the Historical Museum, Beijing, it is the largest bronze casting known from antiquity, standing 133 centimeters high and weighing 875 kilograms. The last *fang ding* in the exhibition (no. 54), dating to early Zhou times, shows once more the same decoration. The long survival of this ornamental scheme, for at least three centuries, is ample tribute to its precise adaptation to the *fang ding* shape.

PUBLISHED: *Wenwu* 1975/6, pp. 64–68, pl. 1; Tokyo, 1976, no. 1.

3

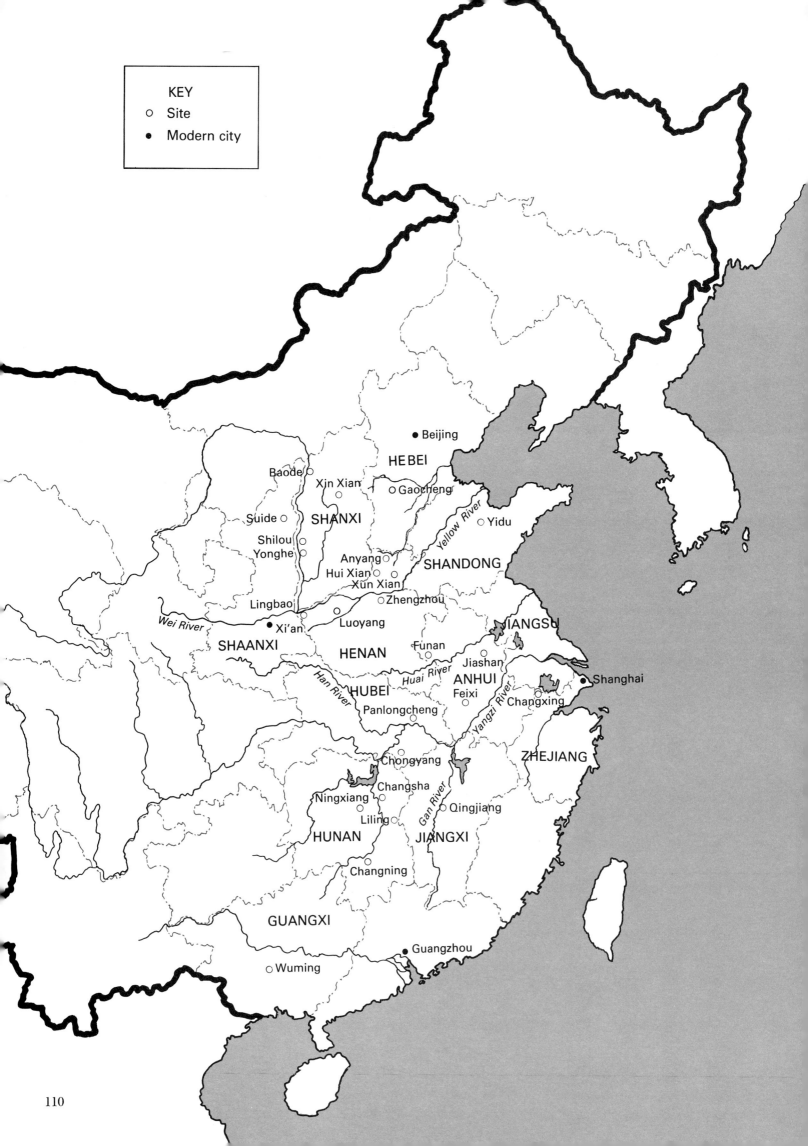

KEY
○ Site
● Modern city

● Beijing

HEBEI

Baode ○
Xin Xian ○
○ Gaocheng

Suide ○   SHANXI
Shilou ○   ○ Yidu
Yonghe ○

Yellow River

Anyang ○
Hui Xian ○   SHANDONG
Xun Xian ○

Lingbao ○   ○ Zhengzhou

Wei River   ○ Luoyang   JIANGSU
● Xi'an

SHAANXI   HENAN   Funan ○

Han River   Jiashan ○
Huai River   ANHUI   ○ Shanghai
HUBEI   Feixi ○
Panlongcheng ○   Yangzi River   Changxing ○

Chongyang ○   ZHEJIANG

Changsha ○
Ningxiang ○   Gan River
Liling ○   ○ Qingjiang

HUNAN   JIANGXI

Changning ○

GUANGXI

● Guangzhou
○ Wuming

110

3 The Appearance and Growth of Regional Bronze-using Cultures

Robert W. Bagley

The early expansion of Shang culture that is implied by the wide geographic spread of pre-Anyang sites disseminated bronze-casting technology over a large area. In so doing, it laid the foundations for regional bronze-using cultures that in time became recognizably distinct from the civilization centered on the Shang court. Little is known at present about these advanced local cultures of Shang times. Systematic excavation of Shang sites in outlying regions is only just beginning, so that at the moment the most revealing, and in fact almost the only pertinent, archaeological evidence consists of scattered finds of bronzes and jades. Some of these objects are imports from metropolitan workshops or faithful copies of imports; others adapt metropolitan forms and technology to the expression of radically different tastes. The wide spectrum of styles encountered in provincial regions must in part reflect the varying strength of the political bond between the Shang court and each local center of power. Areas that had strong ties with the Shang would have kept better in touch with the course of metropolitan fashions.

The present chapter brings together a selection of "nonmetropolitan" bronzes—objects from outside the middle reaches of the Yellow River valley (northern Henan Province). They span about three centuries, from the end of the Zhengzhou phase until the end of the dynasty. Two other objects of nonmetropolitan provenance, nos. 24 and 25, are not discussed in this chapter because they in no way depart from styles associated with the Anyang capital. On the assumption that they may have been imports, made at Anyang and carried elsewhere, they are treated in the next chapter, under the heading of Anyang bronzes.

The earliest bronze industries that are recognizably provincial in stylistic terms go back to a time before Anyang was the capital. In the years following the decline of Zhengzhou, perhaps even earlier, there gradually appeared vessel shapes and decor modes that were unknown at Zhengzhou. While some of these innovations must belong to the "metropolitan tradition," leading to the characteristic Anyang styles, others, usually encountered at sites far distant from Anyang and Zhengzhou, have an individuality that is strictly local. With the pas-

Map of China showing the extent of regional bronze-using cultures during
the Shang dynasty, 15th century to 11th century B.C.

111

sage of time, regional traditions diverged from the widespread stylistic uniformity seen in bronzes from earlier sites. Particularly in the first stages of this process, however, some caution is required in distinguishing "metropolitan" from "provincial."

The progress of the bronze industry in these years can be traced most fully in the rich body of material supplied by a series of recent excavations in the far northeast of the Shang realm. Thus the *ding* no. 12 from a tomb in Beijing provides a starting point for local bronze casting little if at all advanced beyond styles associated with Zhengzhou. Certainly it deserves the epithet "provincial" no more than do the bronzes from Panlongcheng; however remote the find spot, the *ding* is strictly metropolitan in style. The same tomb, however, contained vessels perceptibly more advanced in style. Together with similar bronzes from the same region, like the *pou* no. 13 (and no. 14?), they are well removed from Zhengzhou precedents. The decoration of no. 13 is surely eccentric, and the *pou* shape itself is unknown at sites of the Zhengzhou phase. Here we might begin to suspect the emergence of a local style.

Before adopting this explanation, however, we must face a theoretical difficulty. Since we are uncertain of the locations of the capitals that preceded Anyang, we cannot be confident that these objects from Beijing and Hebei are provincial even in the narrowest geographic sense of the word. The remoteness of the sites from Zhengzhou does not guarantee that novel bronze designs can be taken as provincialisms. Historical sources locate one of the pre-Anyang capitals in southern Hebei, and others nearby. The bronzes from the northeast, nos. 12–14, may well represent the metropolitan tradition at a stage intermediate between Zhengzhou and Anyang.

A few years ago, when the only known Shang sites of any importance all lay within Henan Province, archaeological accounts of the Shang dynasty were written in terms of three sites. Erlitou and Zhengzhou were both large cities in Shang times and are likely to have been capitals, while the status of Anyang was never in doubt, since the oracle inscriptions found there identified it as the last capital of the dynasty. Since the Zhengzhou remains clearly predated the Anyang occupation, and Erlitou was earlier still, it was tempting to conclude that the entire history of the dynasty lay open to view in a sequence of three type sites.

The gradual accumulation of new discoveries has made this simple scheme appear less and less satisfactory. Finds in outlying regions have shown beyond any doubt that, whether adequate for the metropolitan Shang tradition or not, the three sites certainly do not suffice to treat the full range of the Shang civilization. Improved understanding of the Zhengzhou and Anyang sites has now begun to suggest that the scheme is inadequate even to represent the mainstream of the Shang tradition. No doubt there did survive some vestige of a settlement at Zhengzhou in the aftermath of its sudden decline, and an overlap with the early occupation of Anyang is possible. But, as far as the bronzes are concerned, there is a noticeable gap between Zhengzhou and Anyang in the archaeological record, and bronze vessels are virtually the defining artifact of the Shang culture. On present evidence, the major centers for bronze casting, and probably for political life as well, are to be found neither at Zhengzhou nor at Anyang in the years immediately following the Zhengzhou phase.

This hiatus is one that historical accounts might have led us to expect. Tradition has it that the capital of the Shang dynasty was moved five times, the last move being to Anyang. The first two capitals were Bo (Erlitou?) and Ao (Zhengzhou?); the next three have so far not been identified even tentatively with excavated sites. Bronze vessels that make the transition from the latest style current at Zhengzhou to the first typical Anyang products are precisely those found in Hebei (represented by nos. 12–14); related examples have come from a few other places, including several sites in Anhui (cf. nos. 15, 16) and a newly discovered site in the westernmost corner of Henan, in Lingbao Xian. Traditions about the locations of the Shang capitals are fairly well agreed that the center of Shang activity in the time after the move away from Ao and before the move to Anyang lay in the region where Henan, Shandong, and Hebei Provinces meet. Given that one capital may actually have been in southern Hebei, there is every reason to believe that bronzes of this period found in Hebei are not provincial in any sense.

Elsewhere, however, there are unambiguous departures from metropolitan styles in about the same period. Even before Anyang times, the unity of Shang culture, as reflected in the art of the bronzes, was no longer quite perfect. The appearance of the first unarguable stylistic provincialisms indicates that Shang art and technology had established themselves in areas that were far from being under the exclusive domination of metropolitan taste or that perhaps had already lost contact with metropolitan centers.

The rise of a partly independent artistic tradition is best documented in the south, along the course of the Yangzi River through the provinces of Hunan, Hubei, Jiangxi, Anhui, Zhejiang, and Jiangsu. The *ding* no. 17 from Jiangxi is one of the very earliest assertions of a taste at odds with that of northern foundries. The shape, a shallow bowl with flattish legs turned into dragons, is owed to a northern prototype, as is the Style III ornament of the bowl. The openwork treatment of the legs, however, is unexpectedly flamboyant and clumsy (cf. the legs of the Anyang *fang ding* no. 32); while the small figures of tigers cast onto the handles of the *ding* are quite exceptional, technologically as well as stylistically (Fig. 29). Tigers, especially three-dimensional ones, are a motif connected particularly with the south, seen again at a later stage in the four small tigers climbing up the interior of the bell from Hunan, no. 19 (Fig. 36).

Another peculiarity of the southern region is the prominence there of bronze bells and drums. The rather insignificant bells known from Anyang are invariably quite small—easily held in one hand—and usually undecorated. In Hunan, by contrast, monumental clapperless bells, supported stem downward and struck on the outside, are probably the most common of bronze artifact types. The one shown in the exhibition (no. 19), which

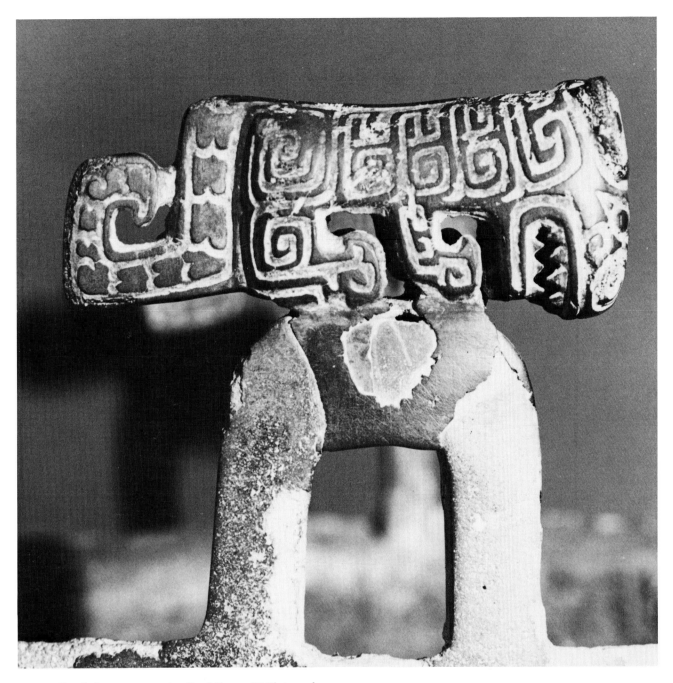

Fig. 29 Detail of tigers cast onto handle of *ding* no. 17. Photograph:
Robert W. Bagley

weighs 154 kilograms, is the largest Shang bell yet discovered. It comes from a cache of five similar bells found in Ningxiang in northern Hunan, a district that has yielded many other important bronze finds, including both the Ge *you* no. 25 and the four-ram *zun* no. 20. Outside Hunan, bells belonging to the same tradition have been unearthed in northern Zhejiang, southern Jiangsu, and southern Anhui.

The bronze drum, no. 18, comes from Chongyang in the southern part of Hubei Province, 200 kilometers northeast of Ningxiang, Hunan Province. With the single exception of an unprovenanced piece in the Sumitomo Collection, Kyoto, it is the only bronze drum known from the Shang period. The Sumitomo drum, which may have come from the same region, is somewhat later in date but

related in style. In the north, bronze drums so far are unknown. Traces of a wooden drum were found in one of the Anyang royal tombs (HPKM 1217), but it was of a different type, being suspended in a frame rather than standing on legs of its own. The prominent role played by large bronze musical instruments in the southern tradition seems to have had no parallel in the north, as Virginia Kane noted in a pioneering article on the southern bronze industry (Kane, 1974–75).

In decoration, too, the drum and bell depart considerably from northern precedents. The drum, which is the earlier of the two, is everywhere embellished with a sparse network of uniformly spaced sunken lines (Fig. 30). On close inspection it will be found that the patterns are loosely drawn versions of the *taotie* face, the paired

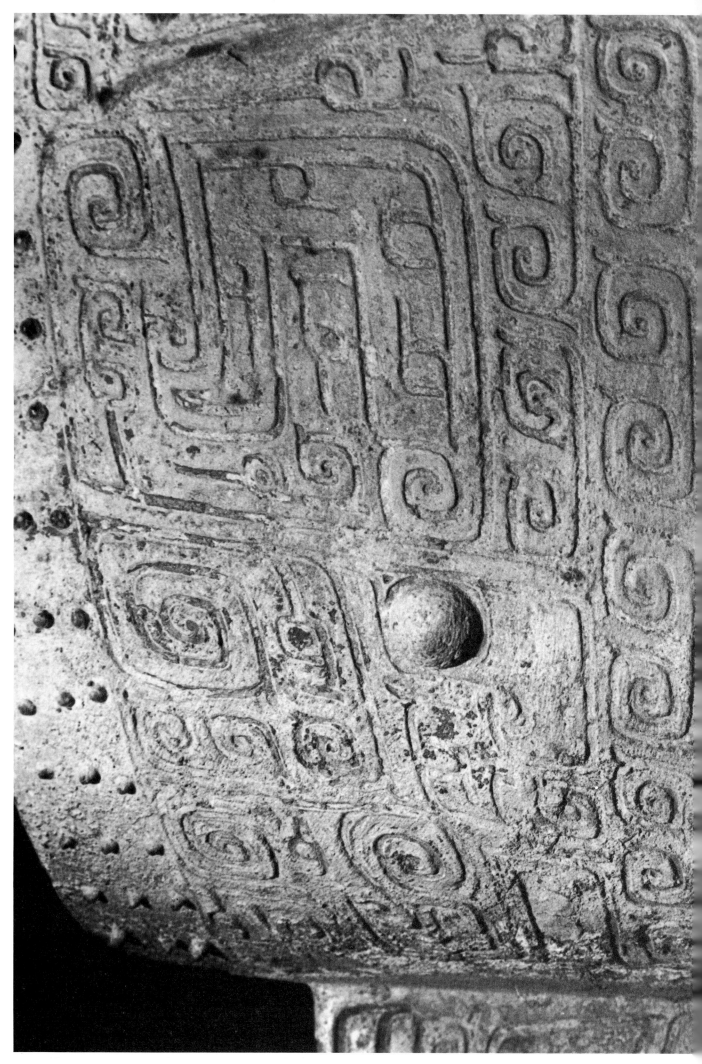

Fig. 30   Detail of decor, drum (*gu*) no. 18. Photograph: Robert W. Bagley

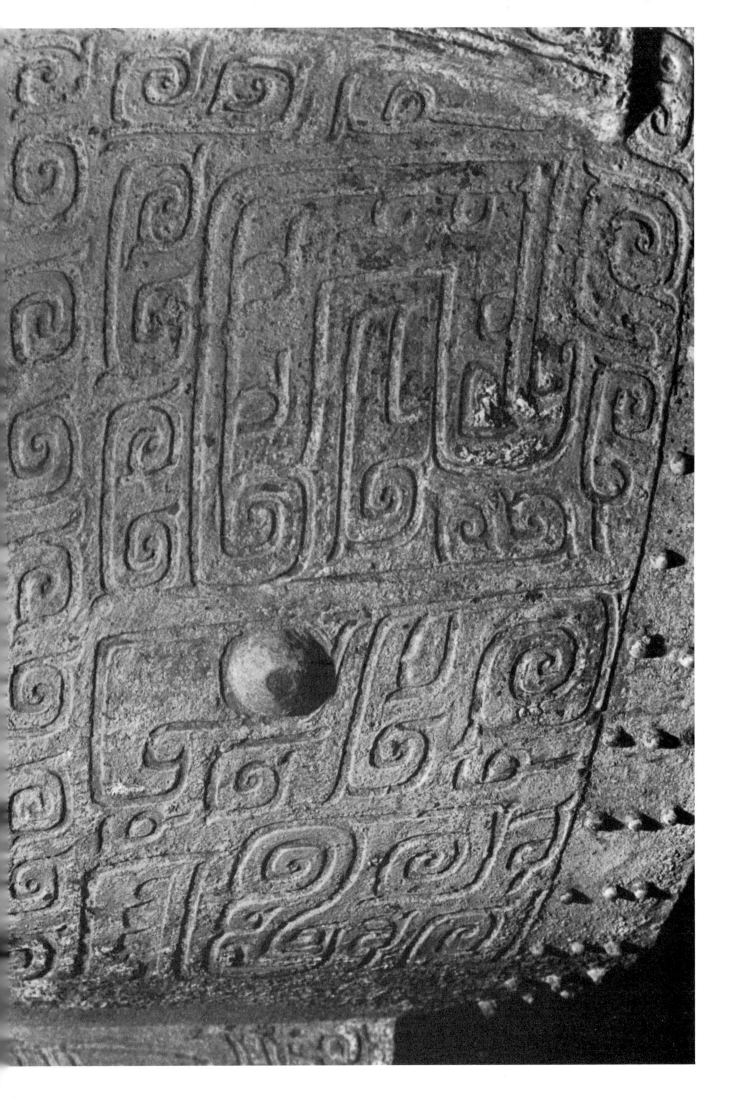

115

eyes alone being raised in relief. In fact, these patterns are based very closely on more conventional Style III *taotie* designs, like that of the *ding* no. 12 from Beijing, but the loose execution and the generous use of spirals as space fillers dilute the motif almost beyond recognition— it is more texture than pattern. Already there is a hint here of something that seems undeniable a little later, that is, that the *taotie* did not have the same absorbing interest for the southern artist that it did for the Anyang master. Too often it is strangely distorted or carelessly allowed to fall apart and dissolve away in meaningless scrollwork.

Both of these fates of the *taotie* can be illustrated by the bell from Ningxiang, Hunan (no. 19). The larger part of the bell is occupied by an extraordinary rendering of the motif, one never seen on northern bronzes and known only from bells of southern type. The *taotie* appears in a high relief formed of heavy ropelike strands with barbed projections and terminations; if it were not for the two eyes, there would be little occasion to interpret the design as a face at all. The filler patterns of loose spirals on the stem of the bell and in the margins surrounding the main design are even less familiar, but they also derive from the *taotie* and in fact represent only the final dissolution of linear designs that on the drum were still recognizably zoomorphic. A few other bells from the same southern tradition, including another found in Ningxiang, are entirely covered with the same neat and regular spirals; the only vestige of the *taotie* spirals is a pair of eyes in high relief. Found at sites scattered all the way from northern Hunan eastward to Shanghai, these bells can be taken as the defining artifact of a distinctive,

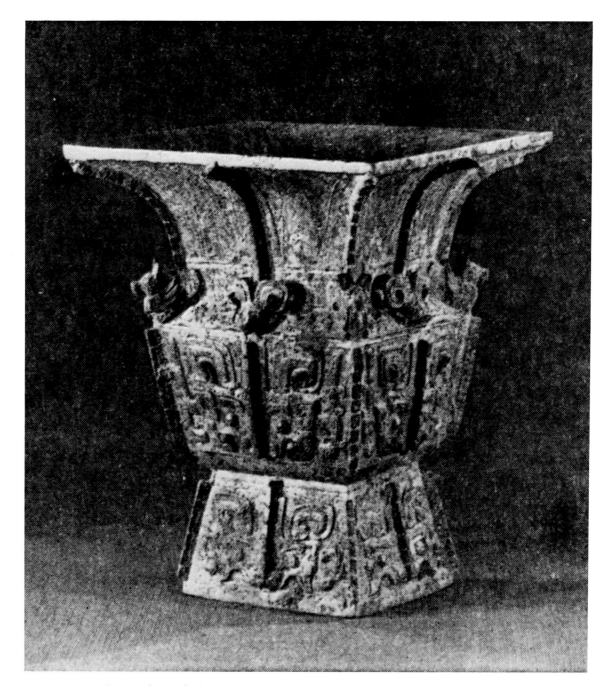

Fig. 31 *Fang zun* from Tomb 5 (tomb of Fu Hao) at Xiaotun, Anyang, Henan Province. Photograph after *Kaogu Xuebao* 1977/2, pl. 19:1

perceptibly alien southern culture. Both the relief designs and the monumental bell as a type belong to a sphere very remote from Anyang.

Though offering more immediately striking proof of southern independence in artistic matters, the astonishing four-ram *zun* (no. 20), also from Ningxiang, Hunan, is in many respects closer to metropolitan sources. In shape it represents an inspired transformation of a standard vessel type, the *fang zun*. At Anyang, small animal figures set on the shoulder of the *fang zun* are employed as minor accents within an abstract, almost architectural scheme (Fig. 31). On the Hunan *zun*, these unessential details have been replaced by a quartet of large rams, whose lifelike three-dimensionality intrudes on and nearly overwhelms the underlying vessel form—a mutation too extreme to be contemplated by the Anyang artist. Other features peculiar to the southern tradition include the snakelike dragons coiled on the shoulder of the vessel, their heads jutting out midway between pairs of rams, and the fresh and lively motif of tall, crested birds seen on the haunches of each ram (see Fig. 38; colorplate, detail, no. 20). Yet even in the context of these unconventional motifs, the influence of Anyang bronze casting remains pervasive. The crested birds are drawn in a smooth low-relief technique that is typical of Anyang bronzes (Style IV), and this technique reappears on the upper part of the vessel, where it is used to render a *taotie* design that cannot be distinguished from Anyang manufactures. Despite their admirable independence of taste, the southern foundries must at least at times have been in close contact with Anyang, attentively following developments at the capital.

The southern provinces were not unique in harboring cultural or political rivals to Anyang. For the most part, however, the bronze finds made elsewhere in China have been too meager and too scattered to give any coherent picture of other provincial traditions. The idiosyncrasies of individual pieces may be extreme, but for the moment they remain in stylistic isolation. This is true in particular of the last two vessels treated in this chapter, nos. 21 and 22, which come from two different sites in the northwest. The *hu* no. 21 is from Shilou in Shanxi Province, a district that has yielded a variety of unusual bronzes in several separate finds. In shape it reproduces a familiar Anyang type (e.g., no. 31), though it is unusual in having a handle. Far more eccentric, however, is its decoration, which does not fall into the usual array of horizontal friezes, but instead fills the entire vessel with a single motif: a large *taotie*, executed in a faintly modeled high relief, faces upward as if to suggest that its mouth is the mouth of the vessel itself.

The second vessel from the northwest, also a *hu*, comes from Suide, Shaanxi Province, 75 kilometers northwest of Shilou (no. 22). Its decoration is conventional enough, and it is rather the shape of the Suide *hu* that is unfamiliar. Instead of having the characteristic flattened-oval cross section of the Anyang type, the body is perfectly round, and the profile is everywhere convex rather than S-curved, steadily narrowing without inflection to the mouth.

The stylistic distinction between metropolitan and nonmetropolitan is not always so clear-cut as in these last two examples. The bronze ax from Yidu Xian, Shandong Province (no. 23), for instance, which dates near the end of the Shang period, in style displays a certain (provincial?) crudity; yet it is difficult to argue that Yidu lay far outside the mainstream of Shang culture. The area in question seems to have been held by an ally or vassal of the Shang king, and excavations there have uncovered large tombs scarcely distinguishable from the royal tombs at Anyang. To decide whether the vassal court nevertheless supported a bronze industry with a style of its own must await a fuller understanding of late bronzes from Shandong, and from Anyang as well.

The oracle inscriptions give the impression that the overlordship of the Anyang court was maintained against the incursions of its neighbors only by incessant military activity. Vassal courts like that at Yidu were often called upon to assist in campaigns against hostile powers. The tribes or statelets capable of threatening or seconding the military might of the Shang were probably equipped with bronze weapons, making use of a metal technology that must have been learned at some earlier stage from the Shang themselves. All of the bronzes described in this chapter, with the possible exception of the earliest (pre-Anyang) vessels, are relics of such rival powers. The stylistic eccentricities discussed here reflect differences of culture and probably at times political differences as well. On the other hand, these variations should not be overstressed. The very occurrence of bronze ritual vessels in outlying regions would seem to signify religious ideas and ceremonial practices held in common; and, like the distinctive Shang metal technology and its potent ornamental style, these were probably acquired in the wake of an expansion of the Shang state that took place earlier, in pre-Anyang times.

12 *Ding*

15th–14th century B.C.? (Zhengzhou-Anyang transition)
Found 1977, Lijiacun, Pinggu Xian, Beijing Metropolitan District
Height 18 cm. (7⅛ in.); diameter 14 cm. (5½ in.); weight 1.25 kg.
(2 lb. 12 oz.)
Beijing Cultural Relics Bureau

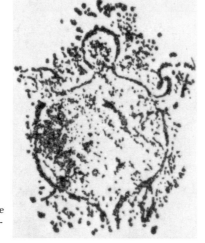

Fig. 32
Rubbing of turtle inside *ding* no. 12. After *Wen-wu* 1977/11, p. 2, fig. 4

This small and engaging vessel is decorated in a single broad frieze containing three *taotie* units. Seams run vertically through the decor frieze, down the legs, and back up the inner sides of the legs to meet in the center of the bottom. The hollow legs are open to the interior. Inside on the bottom a sketch of a turtle appears in very faint thread relief (Fig. 32). Though not executed with quite the same precision and freshness, the ornamental patterns seen here are reasonably close to those of the *gui* and *you* from Panlongcheng (nos. 8, 9; cf. Fig. 33), and the *ding* cannot have been made much later than the end of the Zhengzhou phase. The matte light green of the surface, varied with light brown patches, gives way in places to a smooth lead gray.

The *ding* was recovered from a damaged tomb that contained sixteen bronze vessels, some comparable in date and others a little more advanced (including a *pou* similar to no. 14). The tomb was of canonical Shang form, having a stepped profile, so that the coffin chamber proper was surrounded by a ledge on all four sides (cf. Fig. 11; in the Pinggu Xian tomb one side of this structure had been destroyed). The bronze vessels were found on the ledge. Jades and ornaments of gold—a metal very rare in Shang finds—and one ax blade of iron (presumably meteoritic) were found in the lower part of the tomb. The discovery of an early Shang tomb as far north as Beijing testifies to a wide distribution of Shang civilization in pre-Anyang times.

PUBLISHED: *Wenwu* 1977/11, pl. 3:3 (report, pp. 1–8, pls. 2–5).

Fig. 33   Rubbing of decor, *ding* no. 12. Photograph courtesy of Cultural
Relics Bureau, Beijing

13 *Pou*

15th–14th century B.C.? (Zhengzhou-Anyang transition)
Found 1972, Taixicun, Gaocheng Xian, Hebei Province
Height 27 cm. (10⅝ in.); diameter at mouth 26.6 cm. (10½ in.);
    weight 7.55 kg. (16 lb. 8 oz.)
Hebei Provincial Museum

The unusual and somewhat bizarre puffy high relief in the main register of this *pou* represents a short-lived artistic episode just preceding, and in some ways parallel to, the invention of Style IV. In a design that would otherwise qualify as conventional Style III, high relief is introduced to give emphasis to the principal elements of the *taotie*—horns, nose, bodies, and vestigial jaws (rendered superfluous by the neatly drawn mouth). In this way the *taotie* motif is rescued from submergence in an overwhelming mass of fine details (cf. nos. 14–16). Examples of comparable relief designs have come from Zhengzhou; Panlongcheng; Anyang; and Funan Xian, Anhui Province; all occurring at about the same stage of developed Style III. The same end of making the motifs stand out against subordinate filler patterns is achieved more dramatically by Style IV (see style résumé, p. 182). Once that style had been perfected, Style III high relief designs like the present one ceased to be made.

The designs on the foot and shoulder of the vessel are more conventional Style III, and moreover can easily be recognized as straightforward elaborations of the Style II patterns organized about single eyes—"dragons"—seen on such vessels as nos. 5 and 6. An observer willing to grant that the motif on the foot of the *pou* resembles a bird with an eye, beak, and crest may, proceeding backwards, be persuaded that the motif on the *he* no. 5 (Fig. 23) is also faintly birdlike.

Each third of the circumference, corresponding to one section of the mold, contains four nearly identical pattern units on the shoulder and two on the foot. Although it might be supposed that such identical design units were mass-produced—for instance by stamping from a master pattern—in fact they all differ in details and were executed individually; this seems invariably true of repeated designs on Shang bronzes, stamped patterns appearing only in the latter part of the Zhou period (see chap. 7). The decor is sharply and deeply executed. Slight ridges follow the mold division lines in the main frieze and separate the *taotie* units. The usual three perforations in the foot (cf. no. 14) are absent. The patination is brown and green.

Depressions on the inside wall of the vessel correspond to the raised areas of the *taotie* outside. It is probable that designs like the present one were not carved directly into the mold surfaces, but were executed first on a clay model around which the mold was formed. Only the borders of tiny circles on the shoulder were more conveniently executed directly in the mold.

PUBLISHED: *Kaogu* 1973/5, pl. 2:4.

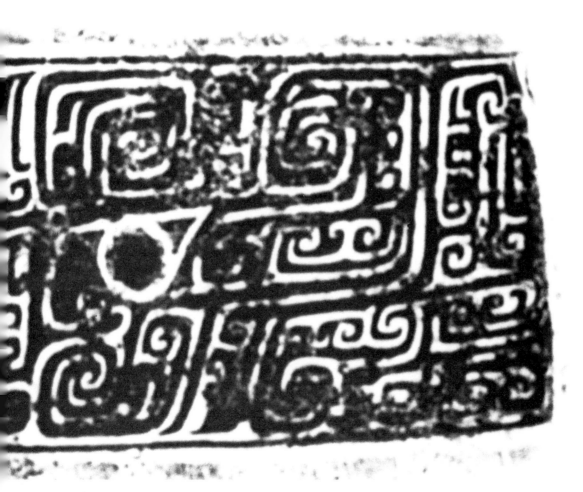

14 *Lei*

15th–14th century B.C.? (Zhengzhou-Anyang transition)
Provenance unknown
Height 52 cm. (20½ in.); greatest diameter 61 cm. (24 in.); weight
    51.2 kg. (112 lb. 10 oz.)
Palace Museum, Beijing

Taking into account the narrow borders above and below the main *taotie* frieze, the decoration of this magnificent vessel comprises five Style III registers. The register on the foot is filled by six small *taotie* units, three bisected by curly flanges; while the patterns on the shoulder, being formed around single, isolated eyes, are identifiable as dragons. The repeated designs in the borders to the main frieze, however, although they too center on small eyes in high relief, seem quite abstract. Indeed, the organic features of all the motifs recede from view in this highly elaborated linear ornament, the regular array of fine quills and swirling lines being interrupted only by the boldly prominent eyes in the friezes. It is chiefly the syncopated arrangement of these eyes, varying in size and recurring at different intervals in different friezes, that is responsible for the somewhat uncanny expression of the vessel.

The *lei* was cast in a three-part mold. Three apertures in the undecorated zone of the foot and three flanges in the decorated portion lie on the dividing lines. The flanges appear to have been cast in the same pour as the vessel proper, but the large and handsome rams' heads overhanging the shoulder were cast on afterward (Fig. 34; colorplate, detail, no. 14). Inside the vessel, neatly defined overflows of metal behind each head lock it in place through two holes in the wall; the overflows take the form of a pair of strips, each about 2 centimeters wide by 10 centimeters long. On the forehead of each ram, between the impressive spiraling horns, stands a small curly flange similar to those on the foot. The space on the back of the ram's head, behind the horns, is occupied by a small Style III *taotie* with flat oval eyes. The surface of the vessel is gray with a greenish brown cast.

This vessel is unprovenanced, although it resembles very closely a smaller *lei* found in 1977 in Pinggu Xian, in Beijing (*Wenwu* 1977/11, pl. 3:1). A Style III *zun* vessel with ornament approaching the same stage of elaboration was found recently at a site in Lingbao Xian, in the westernmost corner of Henan Province (*Kaogu* 1979/1, pl. 6:2). Its massive flanges are immediate forerunners of the smaller and more restrained curly flanges on the foot of the present *lei*. An earlier Style III *lei*, displaying the same motifs in four registers but lacking the flanges and rams' heads, was found some years ago in Jiashan Xian, Anhui Province (*Wenwu* 1965/7, p. 25, fig. 5, p. 26, figs. 9, 10). The wide distribution of these closely related designs would seem to indicate that they belong to the "metropolitan style" of their time.

In current Chinese usage, the name *lei* distinguishes the shape represented by no. 14 from the vessel with convex shoulder called *pou* (no. 13).

PUBLISHED: *Wenwu* 1960/1, p. 4; Tokyo, 1976, no. 19.

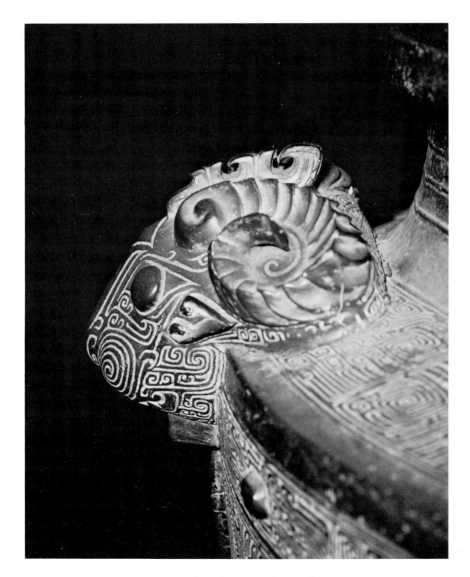

Fig. 34   Detail of ram's head on shoulder of *lei* no. 14. Photograph:
        Robert W. Bagley

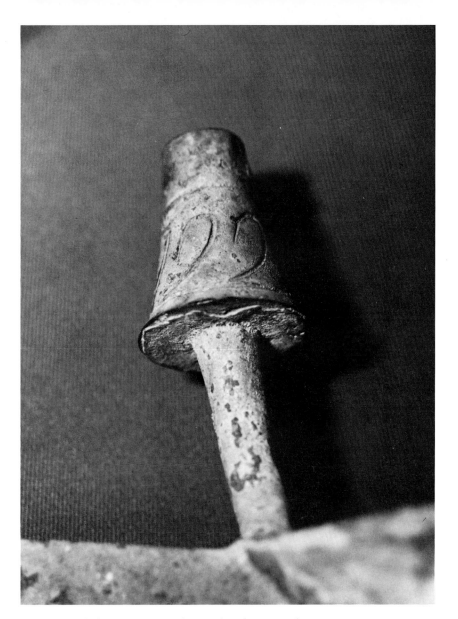

Fig. 35 Detail of post, *jue* no. 15. Photograph: Robert W. Bagley

15 *Jue*

15th–14th century B.C.? (Zhengzhou-Anyang transition)
Found 1965, Feixi Xian, Anhui Province
Height 38.4 cm. (15⅛ in.); length (spout to tail) 21.6 cm. (8½ in.);
  weight 1.7 kg. (3 lb. 12 oz.)
Anhui Provincial Museum

The progress of the bronze art during the Zhengzhou phase is well illustrated by comparing this vessel with the fragile and awkward *jue* from Erlitou, no. 1. In every essential, including the flat bottom and the legs of triangular cross section, the Erlitou *jue* is the prototype; but the decisive proportions and solid, massive casting of the later vessel demonstrate the foundryman's complete mastery of his art in the time that separates the two. The tall and slender body of the Feixi *jue*, circular in cross section, is supported on blade-shaped legs splayed outward. The unusual height of the body, with its two wide Style III friezes, is accentuated by a gradual and restrained flare toward the rim. The inherent asymmetry of the vessel type is stressed by the massive spout, which the modest tail opposite does nothing to balance; and this effect of willful, irrational proportions is enhanced by the almost monumental capped post that forks over the base of the spout.

A seam running around the circumference of the flat bottom reveals a horizontal division of the mold assembly. Correspondingly, the seams visible on the outer faces of the legs are not continuous with those on the body of the vessel, which fall at the divisions between *taotie* units, under the spout and tail. The undecorated area under the handle deprives the *taotie* pattern in the upper register of its eyes and face; by comparison with the designs on the side opposite the handle, the decor of the lower frieze is also somewhat abbreviated, lacking in particular the subsidiary eyes in the lower corners of the pattern unit. Metal overflows show that the post cap was cast separately, probably with its own clay core, and the vessel then cast to it (see Fig. 35). The contrast between the lustrous emerald green patination of the cap and the matte light green of the rest of the vessel shows that the alloys of the two pours were not identical and have corroded differently.

While occasional flat-bottomed *jue* are encountered in Anyang times, this typical vessel shape of the Zhengzhou phase was largely superseded in the Anyang period by *jue* with rounded bottoms, similar to no. 47. Some of these later *jue* are graceful and delicately proportioned, but the majority are routine objects suffering from the standardization of this most common vessel type. Few if any can rival the concentrated force and monumentality of the present vessel.

PUBLISHED: Beijing, 1972a, pl. 40.

16 *Jia*

15th–14th century B.C.? (Zhengzhou-Anyang transition)
Found 1965, Feixi Xian, Anhui Province
Height 54 cm. (21¼ in.); diameter 26 cm. (10¼ in.); weight 7.85 kg. (17 lb. 4 oz.)
Anhui Provincial Museum

The pairing of *jia* and *jue* vessels, both used for offerings of wine, was common in the Shang period. The grave from which this *jia* comes contained a second, matching *jia*, as well as a *gu*; inside each of the two *jia* was a *jue*—no. 15 and its mate. The *jue* and *jia* bear similar Style III friezes, their large post caps were all cast in the same way, and it may be assumed that they were made as a set.

The seams on the body, legs, and underside show that the mold assembly was divided in the same way as that of the earlier *jia* no. 6 from Panlongcheng (thus differing from the horizontally divided mold of the *jue* no. 15). The post caps of the Panlongcheng *jia* were cast integrally, however, and the cores of its legs were made as triangular extensions from the main core inside the vessel. In the present case two separate cores were set in each leg, exposed on the inner faces of the legs. As the cores are no longer in place, the legs have a T-shaped cross section. A heavy fin appears on the seam line down the outer face of the handle. The patination is a soft light green flecked with patches of azurite blue.

Two very similar *jia* were found in 1957 in Funan Xian, Anhui Province, with pairs of *gu*, *jue*, and very large *zun* vessels (*Wenwu* 1959/1, inside front cover).

PUBLISHED: Kansas City, 1975, no. 90.

17 *Ding*

15th–14th century B.C.? (Zhengzhou-Anyang transition)
Found 1975, Qingjiang Xian, Jiangxi Province
Height 30.1 cm. (12⅛ in.); diameter 20 cm. (7⅞ in.); weight 3.35 kg. (7 lb. 6 oz.)
Jiangxi Provincial Museum

This vessel is a distinctly provincial version of a fairly standard type, the shallow *ding* with flat legs in the shape of birds or dragons. The earliest examples of the type, which include one unearthed at Panlongcheng, have the deep bowl of the ordinary *ding* tripod; but the shallow bowl appears already in Style II versions and after the Zhengzhou phase is invariable. The flat legs, ordinarily cast with the rest of the vessel, in the present case were precast, as slight overflows of metal from the bowl onto the legs testify. The small hooked flanges bisecting the three *taotie* units in the decorated frieze, which are similar in design to the curly flanges on the foot of the *lei* no. 14, also appear to have been precast. The tigers on the ears of the *ding*, on the other hand, were cast on, each having been formed in a mold of two sections and secured in place by an overflow of metal locked around the upper part of the ear (see Fig. 29). The different alloys of the separate pours have corroded to different colors, giving a particularly sharp contrast between the smooth dark olive of the tigers and the light brown, fracturing to a powdery light green, of the surface elsewhere.

The precast legs and cast-on tigers are technical oddities seldom if ever encountered on comparable vessels from northern foundries, and they point also to the chief stylistic quirks of the piece. The tiger motif, though it does occur in the north, is associated particularly with the south by virtue of its frequent appearance on bells of southern type (cf. entry no. 19). A small tiger serves as the handle to a bronze lid that was found at Anyang (Li, 1968, pl. 14); paired tigers—but more often dragons—sometimes appear as surface decoration on the outer faces of *ding* handles (nos. 32, 52).

Three-dimensional animal figures perched on *ding* handles, however, seem to be unknown in metropolitan Shang foundries. Paired dragons rendered not as surface decoration but as plastic figures climbing up *ding* handles occur on two famous vessels of the early Western Zhou period, the Tai Bao *fang ding* (Fig. 58) and a *fang ding* in the Nelson Gallery of Art–Atkins Museum, Kansas City, inscribed with a dedication to the second Zhou king (Mizuno, 1959, pl. 92; see also Loehr, 1968, no. 54).

The Style III decoration of the bowl and the tiny flanges are stylistically unexceptional. The legs of the vessel, however, are far removed from northern counterparts, which are simpler in outline, lacking the clear definition of clawed feet and the complicated projections along the animal's back. Metropolitan versions lack also the faint modeling of the animal's bulk attempted here, and are instead more like inarticulate flat slabs—a shape more easily cast in the same mold with the rest of the vessel. Perhaps in the present case the animal intended is not even the usual dragon, but a tiger. The quilled decoration of the body, spirals at the haunches, scale pattern on the tail, and jaws opened wide to a right angle and lined with teeth are conventional enough taken individually, but at the same time they correspond with the features of the tigers cast onto the handles. An unfamiliar chevron pattern executed in sunken lines just above the animal's eye may signify an ear.

The Qingjiang district, south of the Yangzi River on the Gan River, has yielded several early bronzes and much glazed pottery from Shang times, some of it bearing short inscriptions in an eccentric variant of the Shang script. A second, equally unusual

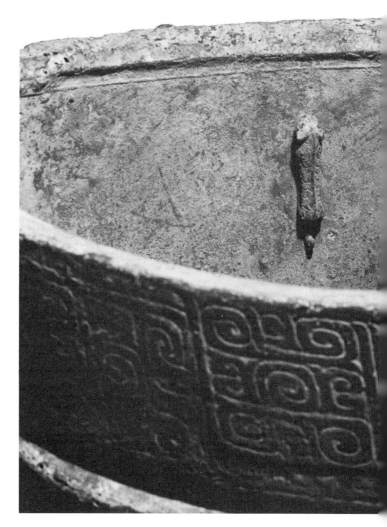

Fig. 36   Detail of tigers on inside wall of bell (*nao*) no. 19.
Photograph courtesy of Cultural Relics Bureau, Beijing

ding found with the present one has bird-shaped legs, and birds atop the handles (*Wenwu* 1977/9, p. 59, figs. 2, 3). Two radiocarbon dates published for a Shang level of the site at Qingjiang Wucheng (source of the inscribed pottery; cf. *Wenwu* 1975/7) calibrate to give calendar dates in the first half of the second millennium, but the reported error is very large (*Kaogu* 1979/1, p. 93).

PUBLISHED: *Wenwu* 1977/9, pl. 6:1.

18 Drum (*gu*)

15th–14th century B.C.? (Zhengzhou-Anyang transition)
Found 1977, Chongyang Xian, Hubei Province
Height 75.5 cm. (29¾ in.); length at top 49 cm. (19¼ in.); weight
    42.5 kg. (93 lb. 8 oz.)
Hubei Provincial Museum

This is only the second bronze drum known from the Shang period; the other is a Style IV example in the Sumitomo Collection, Kyoto (Rong, 1941, vol. 2, p. 514; Kyoto, 1976, p. 2). The two share a number of peculiar stylistic features, suggesting that the Sumitomo drum also came from the south. The diffuse Style III decoration seen here, however, very closely related to typical metropolitan versions of Style III (e.g., no. 12), suggests that the Chongyang drum is much the earlier of the two. Like the *ding* no. 17, it is one of the earliest bronzes of distinctly provincial character.

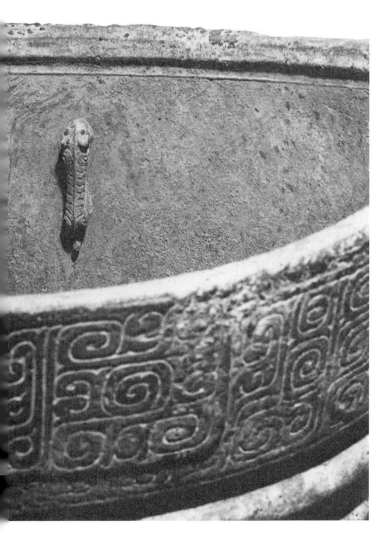

Although the bronze drums evidently imitate a drum made in some other material, the construction of the prototype is not quite clear. Rows of tacks securing the drumheads are indicated, and the heads of the Sumitomo drum imitate the texture of some animal skin, perhaps alligator hide. At the top of the drum from Chongyang sits a hollow saddle-shaped part, perforated at the sides, of unknown purpose; the same element on the Sumitomo drum is turned into a pair of strange birds seated back to back. This curious "saddle" on the Chongyang drum sits in the center of a rectangular patch raised above the surrounding surface; there are signs of casting flaws here, and both the saddle and most of the patch were cast on in a separate pour. The small patch in turn lies in the middle of a much larger patch, raised nearly a centimeter above its surroundings, which covers most of the upper half of the drum. This large area contains one *taotie* face on each side of the saddle, only the two eyes of the *taotie* being set prominently in relief. Smaller "eyes," are, however, distributed around the edges of the large patch as though it, like the drumheads, were tacked in place; the corners of the smaller patch are in the same way secured by four "eyes." The large patch so carefully delineated here figures also in the ornament of the Sumitomo drum. What purpose this feature might have served in a wooden prototype is not obvious. If the prototype was a bronze version, it is conceivable that parts were riveted together, perhaps after removal of the casting core through an opening left in the top. In the present case, however, the core was removed through the underside, which opens out to form the rectangular support of the drum.

The decoration lower on the sides of the drum, below the large patch, is again a large *taotie* face without a body, only the pupils of the eyes in relief (see Fig. 30). The patterns on the support are particularly diffuse and difficult to read, but a careful comparison with the *taotie* just above, on the drum proper, shows them to be the same faces, folded around the corners. The designs on the saddle include still more eyes in relief, belonging to barely legible zoomorphs. The "eyes" in the borders of the two patches, on the other hand, sit in narrow patterned bands adapted from the abstract Style II design seen on the lid of the *you* from Panlongcheng (see Fig. 28).

Except for the recast upper part, the drum was cast in one piece. The vertical seams running down the center of each side and each end divide it into quarters; the mold assembly for the Sumitomo drum was more complex and differently divided. The rather shallow decor patterns appear to have been executed first on a model and then transferred to the mold. The surface is light green and has a matte, powdery appearance. One side is slightly damaged near the top. The sound is still quite nice.

One further instance of a southern bronze drum, set on a stand and with a bird perched on top, comes from a far later period and much further south: it is a drum depicted in the surface decoration of a thoroughly provincial *zun* found in 1964 in Guangxi Province, probably of early Eastern Zhou date (see Fig. 88).

PUBLISHED: *Wenwu* 1978/4, p. 94, pl. 8; *China Pictorial* 1978/9, p. 13.

19 Bell (*nao*)

Anyang period (ca. 1300–ca. 1030 B.C.)
Found 1959, Laoliangcang, Ningxiang Xian, Hunan Province
Height 89 cm. (35 in.); width at mouth 58.5 cm. (23 in.); weight
    154 kg. (338 lb. 12 oz.)
Hunan Provincial Museum

The matte surface of this large bell is green and brown. Inside, about 5 centimeters below the mouth, a pair of small striped tigers climb up each wall (see Fig. 36). Continuous seams run down the

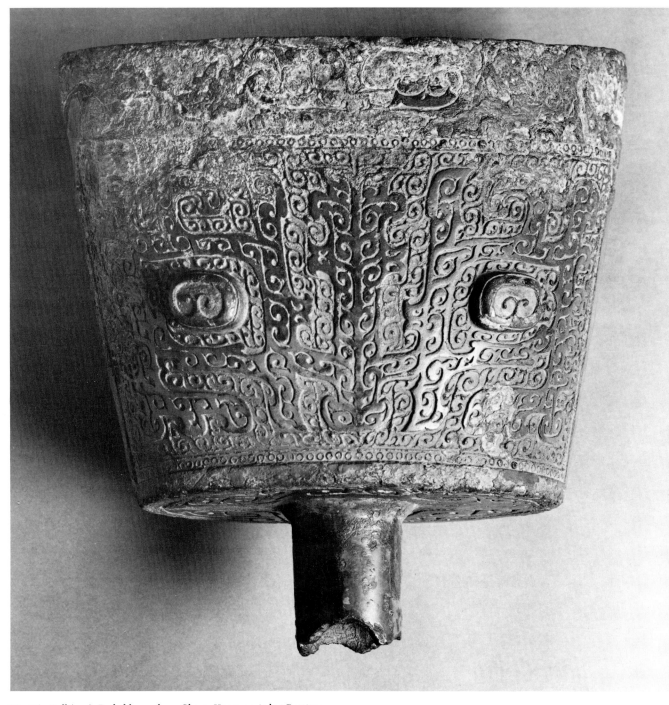

Fig. 37   Bell (*nao*). Probably southern China, Henan or Anhui Province.
The Metropolitan Museum of Art, Purchase, Rogers Fund,
1943, 43.24.2

left and right sides of the bell, across the bottom, and down the stem. The scrollwork patterns that fill the margins around the main *taotie* design extend onto the stem; similar but looser patterns cover the bottom as well. On the bulb of the stem pairs of large eyes and the faint ridges between them suggest that the surrounding scrollwork belongs to a *taotie*, but the scrollwork itself scarcely refers to the face, and elsewhere on the bell has lost all zoomorphic content.

This bell apparently belongs to a group of five discovered in 1959 in Ningxiang Xian, all now in the Hunan Provincial Museum. The bells had been buried neatly arranged in a small pit, four in two rows at the bottom, the fifth above the others, all of them set upright with the stems downward. The sides of all five bells are decorated with the same principal motif, a nearly unrecognizable version of the *taotie* face executed in a relief formed of massive

ropelike strands; but there are interesting variations in the decoration of the margins surrounding this *taotie*. On the present bell the margins are covered with a uniform mesh of scrollwork patterns in sunken line. The margins of the other four bells, however, are more elaborately decorated. In all four cases, the small raised panel in the center of the wide upper margin contains a clumsy but reasonably conventional *taotie* executed in faintly rounded high relief; the panel survives on the present bell, though the *taotie* is omitted. On two of the bells the panel is flanked by a pair of ungainly tigers in the same high relief, facing outward; on the other two, the tigers are replaced by elephants. In each case scrollwork patterns like those seen on the present bell flow uniformly over both the raised animal motifs and the surrounding ground. On one of the bells with elephants, scrollwork decorates even the massive relief parts of the main *taotie* design; the left, right, and lower

124

margins of this bell are further embellished with a procession of fishes and dragons alternating with whorl-circle bosses (Tokyo, 1976, no. 23).

The even distribution of the loose scrollwork patterns on all five bells is a key feature of these provincial bronzes. The patterns betray no awareness of the image-ground distinction of Style IV—all but universal on Anyang bronzes—with its deliberate contrast between densely packed background patterns and sparsely embellished motifs (see style résumé, p. 182). Their even texture instead implies a derivation from the even linear patterns of Style III. In effect this points to an origin in pre-Anyang designs, like that of the drum no. 18. The even linear ornament that remains characteristic of southern bells at a still later stage amounts merely to a retention of these diffuse Style III patterns, arranged as time went on with progressively greater regularity, less variation, and sometimes far more elegant execution. Once having reached complete abstraction, the patterns survived into far later times largely unaffected by succeeding decor styles, appearing for instance on the flat upper surface of the Zhou bell no. 58.

The source of the bold, massive, but curiously incoherent *taotie* that occupies the larger part of all five bells is less obvious. It seems likely, though, that it too originated in *taotie* patterns of the stage represented on the drum (see Fig. 30)—but it came into being by a very different sequence of steps from that which led to complete loss of the image and generated the scrollwork patterns. The intermediaries that stand between the Style III *taotie* on the drum and the version seen on the present bell might be represented by a small bell now in The Metropolitan Museum of Art (Fig. 37). On both the drum and the Metropolitan Museum's bell, the *taotie* is nearly dissolved in a mass of individually meaningless scrolls and volutes; but on the bell some attempt has been made to rescue the motif by setting it in relief (with scrollwork in intaglio) against a ground (with scrollwork in thread relief). However, the choice of areas to set in relief shows little understanding of the anatomy of the Style III *taotie*, or at any rate little fidelity to it. The jaws and nose are raised from the background, though they bear scant resemblance to the originals of those features; but the horn of the *taotie* seems to have been lost altogether, perhaps because it remained sunken while its surroundings were elevated. The thoroughly irrational result is not far from the pattern executed in ropy relief on the present bell. Some confirmation of the intermediate role played by the Metropolitan Museum's bell in this evolutionary sequence is provided by a large bell, resembling the present one, now in the Palace Museum, Beijing (Ecke, 1943, no. 1). The Beijing bell displays the *taotie* in ropelike relief against background areas covered in thread-relief scrollwork identical to the thread-relief ground of the bell in the Metropolitan Museum.

The origin of the ropy relief technique, as distinct from the patterns executed in it, is perhaps to be found in Style III experiments in high relief analogous to that of the *pou* no. 13. A bell with such a design, covered uniformly with loose scrollwork over the raised parts and the ground, is now in the Portland Art Museum (Mizuno, 1959, pl. 112). The large and peculiar eyes of the *taotie* on the present bell, which rise in a sharp-edged plastic spiral, are characteristic of the entire series of these ropy *taotie* designs. On a few other bells, the pair of oddly shaped spiraling eyes survives alone in the midst of a completely abstract ground of regular scrollwork (e.g., an unpublished example unearthed in Ningxiang, Hunan Province; another in Chen, 1955–56, pt. 5, pl. 12:4). From these eventually developed bells with rows of bosses, usually eighteen per side, on a background of regular spirals; a particularly fine example was found in Changxing Xian, Zhejiang Province (Akiyama, 1968, pl. 59; *Wenwu* 1960/7, pp. 48–49).

The composition of one of the bells from the Ningxiang cache has been analyzed, and is reported to be 98 percent copper. So high

a figure suggests that the impurities are only accidental, and that the bell was cast from unalloyed copper. Perhaps tin was temporarily unavailable; whatever the reason, its lack only increases the difficulty of melting and casting, since copper alloyed with tin has a lower melting point and better casting properties. The finished objects show little sign of technical difficulties, however. The size of the present bell—which is about 3 centimeters thick—alone testifies to an awesome technical capacity in southern foundries.

PUBLISHED: *Wenwu* 1978/6, p. 42, fig. 16; *China Pictorial* 1978/9, p. 14. Two reports of the find of five bells give conflicting details of the circumstances: *Wenwu* 1960/10, pp. 57–58; *Wenwu* 1966/4, p. 2. One of the bells decorated with tigers is unpublished. Of the other three, two are illustrated in the *Wenwu* articles cited and in Changsha, 1964, pl. 11; the third and finest of the set, decorated with elephants, appears in Beijing, 1976a, no. 23.

20   Four-ram *fang zun*

Anyang period (ca. 1300–ca. 1030 B.C.)
Found 1938, Ningxiang Xian, Hunan Province
Height 58.3 cm. (23 in.); width at mouth 52.4 cm. (20⅝ in.); weight 34.5 kg. (75 lb. 14 oz.)
Historical Museum, Beijing

Whether considered as a feat of artistic imagination or as a tour de force of casting, this unique vessel seems equally astonishing. It is doubly surprising that so high a level of achievement must be attributed to a provincial foundry rather than to the Anyang capital. The starting point for the design is a standard Anyang vessel type, the shouldered *fang zun*, of which an early example came from Fu Hao's tomb (Fig. 31). A *fang zun* of Anyang style that was found at Changning in southern Hunan, though probably of later date than the four-ram *zun*, might be taken to illustrate the transmission of metropolitan prototypes to the south (*Wenwu* 1966/4, pp. 1–2; Kansas City, 1975, no. 92).

The southern artist's evident willingness to sacrifice the architectural qualities of his Anyang models permitted the essentials of the *fang zun* type to be turned to very different effect. Two principal departures from the design scheme of the Fu Hao vessel were both suggested by the eight animal figures that rest on its shoulders—four birds on the corners and a crested animal head in the center of each side (Fig. 31). Each of the crested animal heads becomes a horned dragon whose snakelike body lies coiled on the shoulder, running left around the corner to end near the next head on the adjacent side of the vessel (see Fig. 38). This unusual motif is known from at least one other spectacular bronze of southern provenance, a *zun* found in Funan Xian, Anhui Province (Akiyama, 1968, pl. 43). The birds on the corners provided the inspiration for the second and more drastic alteration at the hands of the Hunan master: here he substituted rams' heads, and then reshaped the entire lower part of the vessel to depict the legs and forequarters of the rams themselves in a smoothly modeled relief.

The resulting violent distortion of the Anyang vessel shape is amply justified by the brilliance with which so bizarre an idea is carried out, and by the deft ingenuity with which meticulously observed realistic details are expressed within a conventional vocabulary of pure ornament. Nowhere, in fact, do the surface patterns representing details of the rams' heads or bodies stray outside the ornamental repertoire of the Anyang artist. Flanges are neatly adapted to serve as tufted beards, the ankles are ringed with quill-like elements inherited from Style III (see no. 8), and the rearmost quill on each ankle projects backward in relief, as though to represent a lock of hair. The caster has even remembered to include a cleft in the front of each hoof. The rather stereotyped bird designs known from Anyang bronzes offer no parallel to the tall, crested birds that decorate the shoulders of each ram; but this new and attractive motif is nevertheless executed in the familiar Anyang Style IV relief technique (see colorplate, detail, no. 20).

By comparison with the extravagantly inventive lower part, the remainder of the vessel above the shoulder, also executed in Style IV, is quite conventional (see Fig. 47). The only real departure from the Anyang idiom lies in the flanges, whose intaglio designs are drawn with unusual elegance and regularity. They moreover include one amusing detail found only on the upper part of the *zun*, at the very bottom of the flange in the middle of each side: by the simple addition of a tiny eye and bill, the lower end of the flange is transformed into the silhouette of a small duck facing downward (see Fig. 38). This conversion of a flange into a bird is a recurrent theme in the southern bronze industry, and connects the four-ram *zun* with a group of three unprovenanced *pou* vessels in the Sumitomo Collection, Kyoto; Nezu Art Museum, Tokyo; and Freer Gallery of Art, Washington, D.C.; on which the flanges are turned into rows of ducks.

Two other unusual bronzes, one in the British Museum and one in the Nezu Art Museum, are related to the four-ram *zun* by the ram motif itself. These two vessels are conventionally referred to as *zun*, although the shape is contrived from the forequarters of two rams, standing back to back and supporting the upper part of a *hu* vessel between them. One of the two is thought to have been found near Changsha in Hunan Province.

It is difficult without recourse to scientific examination to specify exactly how the four-ram *zun* was cast, but several important steps of the process have left clear traces. The dragons' heads that project from the shoulder were cast onto the vessel in separate pours; the joins are visible in slight overflows of metal onto the body of each dragon. The same unusual method of attachment was employed to cast the similar dragon heads on the *zun* from Funan Xian, Anhui Province. The rams' heads, on the other hand, were cast integrally with the vessel; vertical seams pass down their faces and onto the flanges below. Only the horns and ears of the rams were precast and inserted into the mold for the rest, as slight metal overflows again reveal. One or two minor cast-on repairs of flaws appear to be ancient; the detail otherwise is uniformly sharp and superbly cast. The surface has a fine, lustrous blackish patination.

The four-ram *zun* was found in spring 1938 by peasants digging in hilly country a few kilometers northwest of Huangcai, Ningxiang. In 1963 Gao Zhixi, director of the Hunan Provincial Museum, located the finder of the vessel, who described the find spot and vouched for his account by producing a small fragment broken from the rim of the *zun*. The region around Huangcai has yielded a number of important Shang bronzes, including the bell no. 19 and the *you* no. 25, but all have been stray finds. Nothing of great importance was found in preliminary excavations of a small habitation site at Huangcai, reported in 1963 (*Kaogu* 1963/12, pp. 646–48). In 1974 the site was reexcavated, but no report has yet been published.

PUBLISHED: *Wenwu* 1959/10, p. 4; *Kaogu* 1963/12, p. 648; Tokyo, 1976, no. 18.

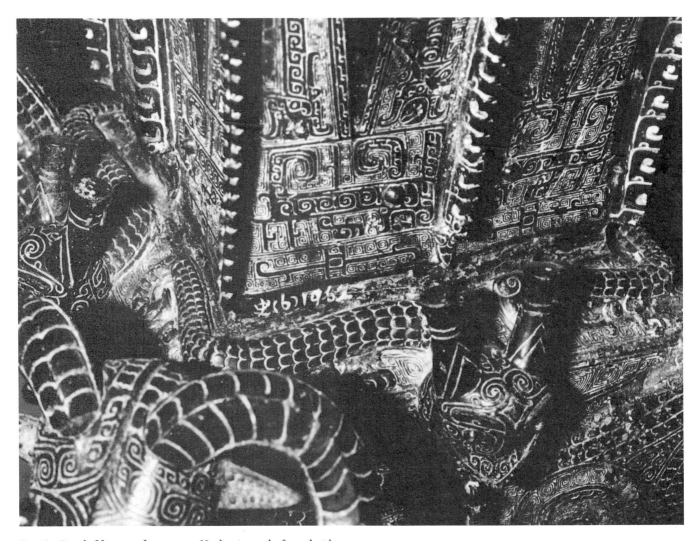

Fig. 38   Detail of four-ram *fang zun* no. 20, showing neck of vessel with Style IV mask and vessel shoulder with snakelike horned dragon. Photograph: Robert W. Bagley

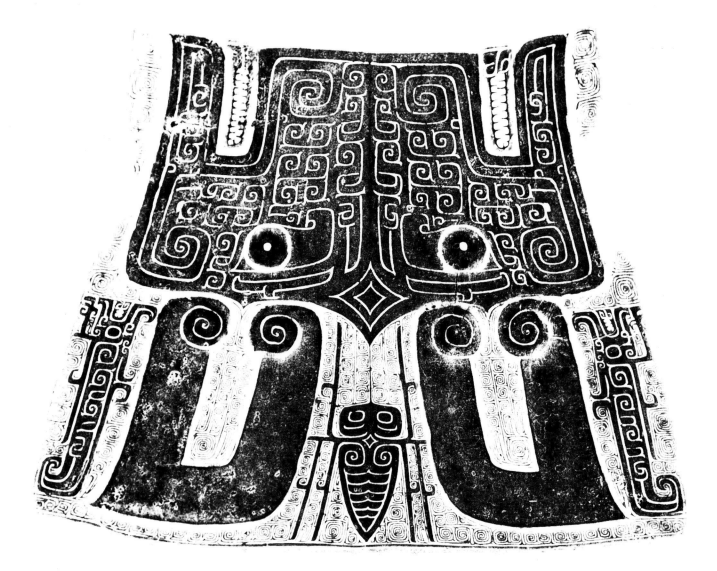

Fig. 39 Rubbing of decor, *hu* no. 21. Photograph courtesy of Cultural Relics Bureau, Beijing

21 *Hu*

Anyang period (ca. 1300–ca. 1030 B.C.)
Found 1959, Shilou Xian, Shanxi Province
Height 42 cm. (16½ in.); weight 4.6 kg. (10 lb. 2 oz.)
Shanxi Provincial Museum

Each side of this oddly decorated *hu* is filled entirely by a single *taotie* face turned mouth upward (see Fig. 39). The lower jaw is, as usual, seen in profile and doubled so that the mouth edged with teeth is repeated on either side of the broad snout. The face is covered with sparsely incised volutes, which, with the elegantly outlined eyes, recall Style III formulations (cf. no. 13). Lower down, however, the tall U-shaped horns of the *taotie* are seen against the dense *leiwen* spirals of Style IV. Between the two horns appears a cicada with long tendrillike appendages; on the other side of each horn a small upended dragon faces in the same direction as the *taotie*. Both the *taotie* and its horns are raised slightly above the surrounding surface, and corresponding depressions are visible on the inside walls of the *hu*. The loose volutes embellishing the face reappear in a narrow band encircling the foot of the vessel. Vertical casting seams run down the sides. The patination is rough and dark green, scaling away in places to reveal a dark gray beneath.

The S-curved profile and oval body of the Shilou *hu* copy the standard Anyang *hu* shape (e.g., no. 31), but the latter ordinarily lacks a handle, having instead a pair of vertical lugs set on the sides at the narrowest part of the body. The handle seen here, terminated with triangular, horned dragon heads and decorated for its full length with a simple pattern of repeated diamonds, seems to derive from early pear-shaped *you* vessels; one example of this vessel type, from a large tomb at Anyang, Wuguancun, was included in the previous exhibition of archaeological finds (Kansas City, 1975, no. 81).

The only *hu* comparable to the one from Shilou is a nearly identical vessel in the Avery Brundage Collection, Asian Art Museum, San Francisco, somewhat finer in execution, that differs in having the more usual vertical lugs instead of a handle (Umehara, 1964, pl. 95).

The Shilou *hu* comes from a richly furnished grave discovered in 1959. The grave was damaged, but the guardian pit usual in Shang tombs was still discernible (see entry no. 10). Many of the fourteen bronze vessels found in the tomb are eccentric in decoration or unfamiliar as types. They include a *gu* shaped like no. 46, and an unparalleled horn-shaped covered casket that was exhibited in the United States in 1974–75 (Kansas City, 1975, no. 88). Also numbered among the tomb furnishings were a few other bronze artifacts, as well as objects of bone and jade; and the occupant of the tomb wore gold ornaments. Judging from the objects illustrated in the report, the burial dates early in the Anyang period. It is the richest of a long series of bronze finds made in the vicinity of Shilou; related artifacts have also been found recently about 50 kilometers to the southwest, in Yonghe Xian (*Kaogu* 1977/5, pp. 355–56). From the oracle inscriptions we learn the names of a host of statelets that were situated in southern Shanxi and northward along the Shanxi-Shaanxi border, including two formidable enemies of the Shang king, Guifang and, a little to the south, Qiangfang. Deducing the precise location of these tribes from the evidence of the inscriptions is exceedingly difficult, but Guifang may have lain somewhere in the vicinity of Shilou and the neighboring Suide site in Shaanxi (see entry no. 22).

PUBLISHED: *Wenwu* 1960/7, p. 50, fig. 4 (report, pp. 50–52); Tokyo, 1976, no. 12. For reports of finds at Shilou, see Bagley, 1977, p. 212 n. 109.

22 *Hu*

Anyang period (ca. 1300–ca. 1030 B.C.)
Found 1965, Suide Xian, Shaanxi Province
Height 31.3 cm. (12⅜ in.); weight 2.7 kg. (6 lb.)
Shaanxi Provincial Museum

This slender, round-bodied vase is decorated only sparingly, in narrow bands on the foot and below the mouth. The design on the foot originates in the pattern of eyes and diagonals seen on the lid of the Panlongcheng *you* (see Fig. 28). The main frieze, bordered at its lower edge by pendant triangles filled with *leiwen* spirals, contains a pair of *taotie* faces. The *taotie* are reminiscent of Style II formulations (cf. nos. 5, 6), but the Style II motif has been much simplified, the patterns left and right of the face being organized into a neat array of regular spirals and thereby deprived of any zoomorphic content. This particular derivative of Style II seems to belong early in the Anyang period, a dating supported by the other twenty-one bronzes of the hoard from which the *hu* came. Three bowstring lines above the *taotie* frieze are interrupted by a pair of small lugs, V-shaped in section, pierced vertically and decorated with sketchy *taotie* faces. Two apertures in the foot, roughly square and 1 centimeter on a side, are aligned with the lugs above. The surface is mottled bright green.

Quite distinct from the more usual *hu* with its S-curved profile and oval cross section (nos. 21, 31), *hu* of this shape are very rare. A single example reproduced in a line drawing in the catalogue of the Qing imperial collection is of special interest on account of its inscription; the vessel has V-shaped lugs like those seen here, though its decoration is more advanced (Liang, 1751, 18/1). The inscription includes a clan sign that Li Xueqin reads as Qiang, and identifies with the tribe or statelet called Qiangfang (Li, 1959, p. 80). On the evidence of oracle inscriptions, Qiangfang is thought to have been situated near the southern end of the Shanxi-Shaanxi border, and thus a little to the south of Suide Xian, source of the present *hu*. It is noteworthy that the Shang finds made at Suide, at Shilou just across the river (cf. no. 21), and further north in Xin Xian and Baode Xian, Shanxi Province (*Wenwu* 1972/4, pp. 62–68, back cover) have included objects with affinities to the so-called "Ordos style," implying contact with nomadic populations in the northwest border region. Tribes like Qiangfang and Guifang are presumed to stand somewhere between the fully civilized Shang on the one hand and the barbarian nomads of inner Asia on the other. The numerous bronze vessels found at Suide and in central and northern Shanxi Province suggest that the populations of this region were rather more civilized than has generally been allowed.

PUBLISHED: *Wenwu* 1975/2, p. 86, fig. 17 (report, pp. 82–87); Xi'an, 1973, p. 5, no. 6.

23 Ax (*yue*)

Anyang period (ca. 1300–ca. 1030 B.C.)
Excavated 1966 from Tomb No. 1, Sufutun, Yidu, Shandong
    Province
Height 31.8 cm. (12½ in.); width at edge 35.8 cm. (14⅛ in.); weight
    4.7 kg. (10 lb. 5 oz.)
Shandong Provincial Museum

The blade of this large ax is perforated so as to depict a face in openwork—probably a human face, although all the features except the mouth are type forms borrowed from *taotie* designs. The eyebrows and the shield-shaped *taotie* nose are plastic elements rising from the surface of the blade, while the irises are hollow spheres held in the punched-out outline of the eye. The face thus constructed is distinctly uncouth, with an almost barbaric force and vigor. The only other bronze depictions of human faces from the Shang period, which include one on a magnificent ax in the Museum für Ostasiatische Kunst, Staatliche Museen Preussischer Kulturbesitz, Berlin, are modeled as plastic units, to quite different effect (von Ragué, 1970, no. 1). Perhaps the closest parallels to the face on the Shandong ax are to be found in a group of horse frontlets or chariot ornaments unearthed at the early Western Zhou site of Xincun, Xun Xian, Henan Province. In some of these ornaments, which take the form of human or *taotie* faces, the features are made as separate units, probably for attachment to a cloth or leather backing; the hollow hemispherical eyes and grinning mouths seem particularly close to the design seen here (Guo [B.], 1964, pls. 42–45; cf. also *Kaogu* 1976/1, pl. 3:2.)

The ax was found on the entrance ramp of a large cruciform tomb, unfortunately looted before excavation, at Sufutun, Yidu, Shandong Province. There were forty-eight sacrificial victims in the tomb. A second ax that accompanied the first carries an inscription conventionally called the Ya Chou pictogram. Many bronzes with this inscription are known, all of late Shang or early Western Zhou style, and a number of them are thought to have come from robbed tombs in the vicinity of Yidu (*Kaogu Xuebao* 1977/2, pp. 23–34). Possibly the pictogram and the Yidu tombs are associated with a Shang vassal state that survived into the early Western Zhou period. Certain peculiar features of bronzes bearing the Ya Chou pictogram enjoy a brief currency in early Zhou bronze designs.

The patination is a rough dark green. The two hafting slots at the back edge of the blade are similar to those on the much earlier Panlongcheng ax no. 7—an object of far more refined and calculated shape.

PUBLISHED: Beijing, 1972b, p. 123 (with the inscribed ax from the same tomb); Tokyo, 1976, no. 24.

24 Elephant *zun*

Anyang period (ca. 1300–ca. 1030 B.C.)
Found 1975, Liling Xian, Hunan Province
Height 22.8 cm. (9 in.); length 26.5 cm. (10⅜ in.); weight 2.78 kg.
    (6 lb. 2 oz.)
Hunan Provincial Museum

The surfaces of this small elephant-shaped container are crowded with ornament. The profusely varied motifs are rendered in high relief, sharp and delicate in execution and exceedingly forceful in design. A staring dragon head on the shoulder of the elephant has only a short curving body attached to it, below which sits a smaller head with no body at all. Further varieties of dragons are disposed in every conceivable posture on the front legs and the hindquarters, and on the rear legs serve as appendages to small *taotie* faces composed of separate, isolated features—eye, eyebrow, C-horn, jaw, and clawed foreleg. Just behind the opening in the top of the *zun*, a more coherent *taotie* face gazes upward, bisected by the flange that forms the elephant's tail. Two more flanges follow the upper and lower sides of the elegantly curved trunk, while a small tiger with a tiny bird under its tail crawls down from the top of the trunk. Not even the backs of the elephant's ears are left empty, this small space being occupied by birds whose long tail plumes extend in a curve onto the dome of the head. The two bony lobes of the elephant's forehead are embellished with coiled snakes, a feature that is recalled, curiously enough, in the far clumsier elephants that appear as surface decoration on a few early Zhou bronzes (e.g., Fig. 57). All of the high relief ornaments are strongly silhouetted against a background of vigorous *leiwen* spirals, and ingeniously adapted to the contours of the elephant's body. It is a tribute to the sure tact of the Shang artist that the wealth of surface ornament does nothing to detract from the fetching plumpness of this youthful and engaging creature.

The patination is a lustrous emerald green. Unobtrusive vertical seam lines cross the body just in front of the hind legs; a further mold division must have bisected the animal lengthwise on top, while another section formed the undecorated inside faces of the legs and the bottom. A bronze plug fills a small hole on the underside of the trunk, near the base. The *zun* must originally have had a lid, now lost. An elephant *zun* in the Freer Gallery of Art, Washington, D.C., which offers the only close parallel to the present vessel, retains its lid, on which stands a second, tiny elephant (Pope, 1967, no. 40).

The *zun* was found by a farmer in 1975 between Zhuzhou and Liling, southeast of Changsha. No other artifacts were discovered in a later search of the find spot. It has been suggested that this and other bronzes unearthed in Hunan and not associated with tombs, including nos. 19, 20, and 25, were buried as offerings to mountains or rivers. Although the elephant is decorated in what might be regarded as impeccable Anyang style, the only known Shang examples of this exceedingly rare vessel form seem to be associated with the south. The *zun* in the Freer Gallery is thought to have been found in Hunan, while a very large Style IV elephant—standing 62 centimeters high—in the Musée Guimet, Paris (Rong, 1941, vol. 2, p. 369), has eccentric decoration relating it to such quintessentially southern bronzes as the Sumitomo drum (see entry no. 18). The elephant also occurs as a motif of surface decoration on a few southern bronzes, notably on two of the bells found with no. 19, but in this role it is known at Anyang as well.

PUBLISHED: *Wenwu* 1976/7, pp. 49–50, pls. 1, 2; Beijing, 1976b, no. 19.

25 Ge *you*

Anyang period (ca. 1300–ca. 1030 B.C.)
Found 1970, Ningxiang Xian, Hunan Province
Height 39 cm. (15⅜ in.); weight 10.75 kg. (23 lb. 10 oz.)
Hunan Provincial Museum

The somewhat flattened body of this imposing, almost architectural bronze is closely akin to the oval body of the *hu* vessel type (e.g., no. 21). In both the *hu* and the *you*, it serves to establish a preferred frontal viewpoint, and both the structure and the ornament of the *you* are conceived with this preferred viewpoint kept strictly in mind. Set on a high molded foot, the body of the *you* has a richly curved profile that is continued in the tall corniced lid and everywhere emphasized by the formidable flanges, with their barbed projections and deep scorings. The arresting silhouette defined by these flanges is crowned by two massive projecting hooks at the sides of the lid; these hooks dictate the placement of the swing handle over the short axis of the vessel. The subdued ornament of the *you* consists only of vertical ribbing and several varieties of birds, elegantly shaped and set against a background of fine angular *leiwen*. The regular and precise disposition of these motifs reasserts the static symmetry of the shape and avoids superfluous details that might compete for attention. The careless profusion of ornament

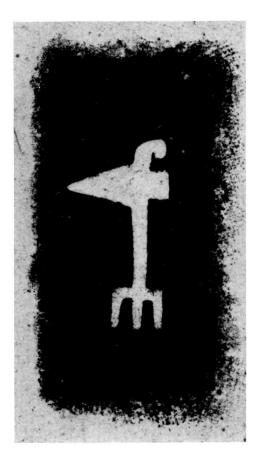

Fig. 40   Rubbing and transcription of
inscription, Ge *you* no. 25. Photograph
courtesy of Cultural Relics Bureau,
Beijing

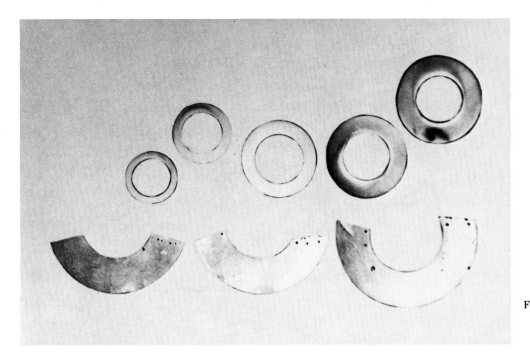

Fig. 41 Some of jade disks found inside Ge *you* no. 25. Photograph courtesy of Cultural Relics Bureau, Beijing

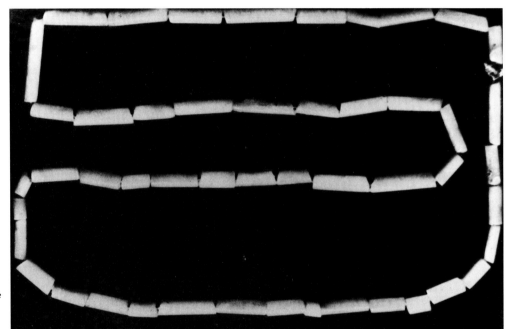

Fig. 42 Some of jade beads found inside Ge *you* no. 25. Photograph courtesy of Cultural Relics Bureau, Beijing

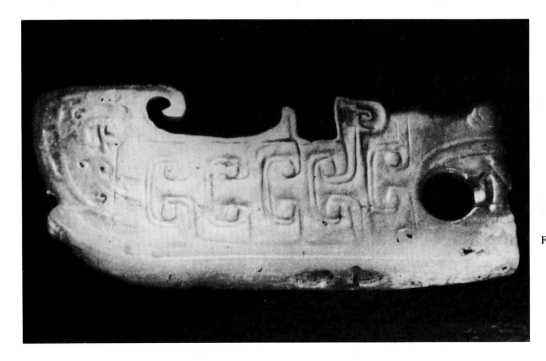

Fig. 43 Jade animal figurine found inside Ge *you* no. 25. Photograph courtesy of Cultural Relics Bureau, Beijing

on an object like the *zun* no. 29, representing an earlier, preclassic stage, makes a sharp contrast with the noble grandeur of the present *you*, the finest vessel of its type known.

Both body and lid of the *you* are inscribed with the single character *ge*, which depicts a *ge* blade, the bronze counterpart of no. 10, mounted perpendicularly in a haft with a pronged foot (see Fig. 40). Possibly the character serves as a name or as the emblem of a clan.

The dark gray green surface of the *you* has the rich luster sometimes described as water patina, which depends on a high proportion of tin in the alloy; the *zun* no. 24 offers another instance. The much brighter green of the handle suggests a composition slightly different from the body and lid; while the handle had to be precast (or cast on) on a separate occasion, the body and lid could have been poured on the same day from the same batch of metal. Analyses have tended to confirm that Shang founders exercised little control over the exact composition of the bronze alloy—as might be expected, since the performance of a ritual vessel does not depend critically on the hardness or other special properties of the metal.

The *you* was a chance find unearthed in 1970. There were no signs of a burial or of any other associated artifacts—except for more than 320 jades found inside the vessel (Figs. 41–43). These include many slit disks, in graduated sizes ranging from about 10 centimeters to 2 centimeters or less; collared disks lightly incised with concentric circles, also in varying sizes, similar to disks from the Anyang tomb of Fu Hao; tubular beads; and a few peculiarly amorphous animal figurines, including a thick flat tiger incised with

unusual, perhaps southern surface patterns. All the jades mentioned are unaltered—having been well protected during burial—and all are a uniform pale green.

This is not the first instance of a *you* used as a repository for jades. A *you* found in 1963 in the same district, Ningxiang Huangcai, contained 1,172 tubular beads (*Kaogu* 1963/12, pp. 646–47, pl. 4: 1, 2). Another *you* is said to have been found in Anhui or Zhejiang Province with fifteen jade beads inside; both the jades and the *you* are now in the Arthur M. Sackler Collections, New York (Umehara, 1933a, 1/73). While all of these vessels are unimpeachably metropolitan in style, it is only at southern sites that *you* used as containers for jade have been found.

A similar but less fine *you* was found in 1965 in Hui Xian, Henan Province (*Wenwu* 1979/7, p. 79). A *you* very likely to be of provincial manufacture was found in 1974 in the far southern province of Guangxi, in Wuming Xian (*Wenwu* 1978/10, pl. 4:2; Beijing, 1978a, no. 34). Both vessels bear short inscriptions.

PUBLISHED: *Wenwu* 1972/1, pp. 6–7; Beijing, 1972b, p. 31; Tokyo, 1976, no. 16.

26 Xi *jia*

Anyang period (ca. 1300–ca. 1030 B.C.)
Found 1968, Wen Xian, Henan Province
Height 37.3 cm. (14¾ in.); diameter 19.6 cm. (7¾ in.); weight 4.3 kg. (9 lb. 7 oz.)
Henan Provincial Museum

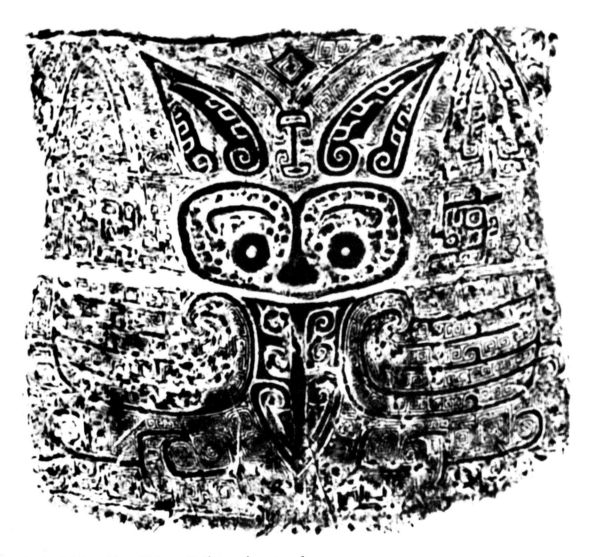

Fig. 44 Rubbing of decor, Xi *jia* no. 26. Photograph courtesy of Cultural Relics Bureau, Beijing

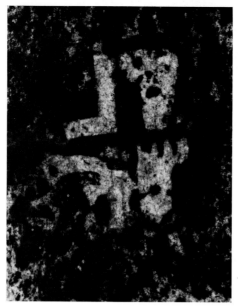

Fig. 45 Rubbing and transcription of
inscription, Xi *jia* no. 26. Photograph
courtesy of Cultural Relics Bureau, Beijing

This small *jia* is distinguished from such predecessors as nos. 6 and 16 by its S-curved body and by its unusual decoration, in which owls replace the more familiar *taotie* patterns (see Fig. 44). Although horizontal lines through the decor hint at a division into two or three separate registers, the owl motif is less amenable to confinement than the *taotie*, and it spreads over the full height of the body without regard to the divisions. The flanges pass unbroken over the first of the horizontal divisions to stop short at the second. The wings of the owl are symmetrically outspread in the lowest zone, in imitation of the doubled body of a *taotie*. The facial mask of the owl, its staring eyes ringed with feathers but also supplied with eyebrows, appears as a plastic unit in the middle zone. In the zone above, finally, the C-horns of a *taotie* are given sharp points to serve as tufts of feathers atop the owl's head. Between these two pointed tufts, the decor includes a configuration that may be a stylized character of the written language; on a very few Shang bronzes, inscriptions are in this way worked into the surface ornament. Although the facial mask of the owl is raised slightly in relief, the decoration otherwise corresponds to Style IV, the principal motifs lying flush with the finely cast *leiwen* background. The ornament continues uninterrupted under the handle.

An inscription of one character appears inside the vessel, in the center of the bottom (see Fig. 45). It shows a pair of footprints next to a pair of right-angled lines, and can be transcribed by the modern graph *xi*. The *jia* was found in what may have been a grave, with twenty-two other bronze artifacts, eight of which are vessels. Of the latter, four are uninscribed, while the remaining four bear the same inscription *xi*, possibly the name of the tomb's owner. None of the bronzes is stylistically outside the range of Anyang bronze casting, and the find might even be taken to typify the contents of a modest Anyang burial. The vogue of the owl as a motif of surface decoration seems largely confined to the earlier half of the Anyang period—it occurs several times among the bronzes from Fu Hao's tomb (e.g., no. 29)—and the Wen Xian bronzes can probably all be dated to that time.

The hollow legs of the vessel are open to the interior. The matte surface is dark green and brown. Traces of a black pigment, often applied to Style IV vessels in order to heighten the contrast between motifs and background, are visible in the sunken parts of the *leiwen* spirals.

PUBLISHED: *Wenwu* 1975/2, p. 90, figs. 8, 9 (report, pp. 88–91); Beijing, 1972b, p. 85.

27 *Fang lei*

Anyang period (ca. 1300–ca. 1030 B.C.)
Provenance unknown
Height 53 cm. (20⅞ in.); weight 29.6 kg. (65 lb. 2 oz.)
Shanghai Museum

This magnificent vessel is discussed in chapter 4. Although its provenance is unknown, it can be taken as typical of the finest bronzes cast in the latter half of the Anyang period, and its style is thoroughly metropolitan. Worthy of special comment is the refined handling of the motifs at this late stage. As also on the *you* no. 25, the elements set in high relief are disposed with extreme clarity against the sharply cast spiral background; and by comparison with earlier relief designs (e.g., nos. 29, 30), the ornament is simple and uncluttered. Nevertheless, the individual motifs are not mere silhouettes raised to a uniform height above the *leiwen* ground. On the contrary, their shapes are elegantly modeled in three dimensions—not in order to depict anything from the animal world, but for purely expressive ends. Horns, tails, and jaws twist suddenly and throw sharp, curved, bladelike edges up into higher relief; *taotie* horns are deeply dished, or layered with overlapping parts; and all the raised surfaces are enlivened with boldly incised spirals and volutes. The confusion that might be expected to result from such intricate detailing is forestalled by the careful spacing and proportioning of the motifs, and by their arrangement in a tightly knit, rigidly symmetrical ornamental scheme.

The large and boldly drawn inscription, cast inside the neck of the vessel, is a work of art in its own right (see Fig. 46). On the left side, a complicated graph is enclosed within a cross-shaped cartouche called a *yaxing*. The two characters on the right, for which various readings have been offered, occur again in the inscription of a *lei* vessel found in 1973 in Kezuo Xian, Liaoning Province (*Kaogu* 1973/4, p. 226, fig. 3:3; *Wenwu* 1973/7, p. 11). It has been suggested, partly on the evidence of oracle texts, that the two characters together form the name of a Shang vassal state situated in the northeast (its territory presumably including the find spot of the *lei* from Liaoning). The owner of the Shanghai *fang lei* would then have been connected with the state, and the graph inside the *yaxing* may be his own name or clan emblem. A few other inscriptions that include the same state name and clan sign are listed in *Kaogu* 1974/6, p. 368.

PUBLISHED: Shanghai, 1964, no. 13; *Kaogu* 1975/5, pp. 274–79, 270 (discussion of the inscription).

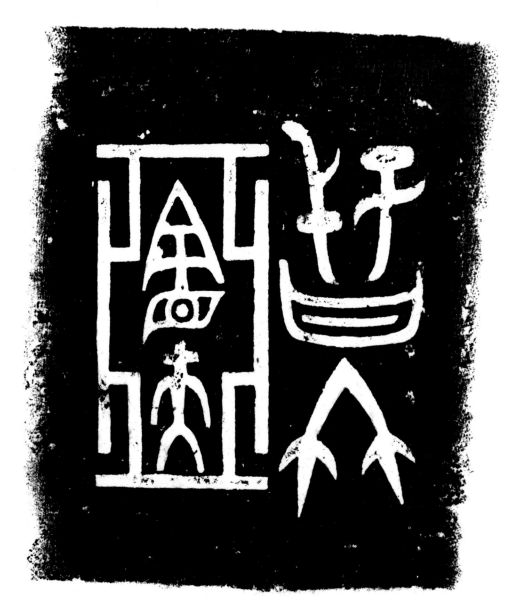

Fig. 46 Rubbing and transcription of inscription, *fang lei* no. 27.
Photograph courtesy of Cultural Relics Bureau, Beijing

COLORPLATES 12-40

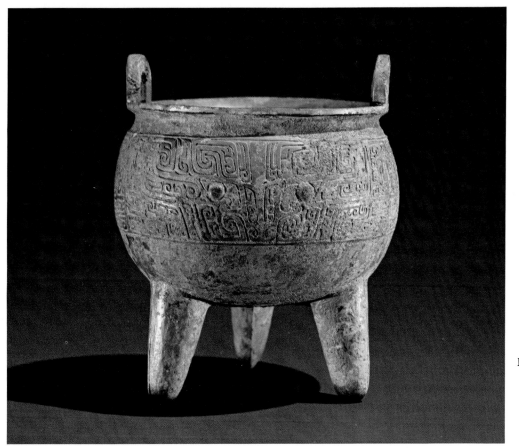

12 *Ding*. 15th–14th century B.C.? (Zhengzhou-Anyang transition). Height 18 cm. (7⅛ in.); diameter 14 cm. (5½ in.); weight 1.25 kg. (2 lb. 12 oz.)

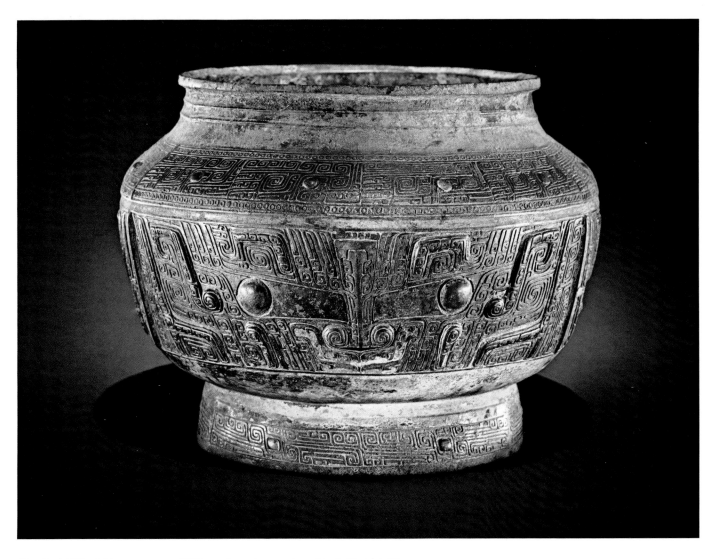

13 *Pou*. 15th–14th century B.C.? (Zhengzhou-Anyang transition). Height 27 cm. (10⅝ in.); diameter at mouth 26.6 cm. (10½ in.); weight 7.55 kg. (16 lb. 8 oz.)

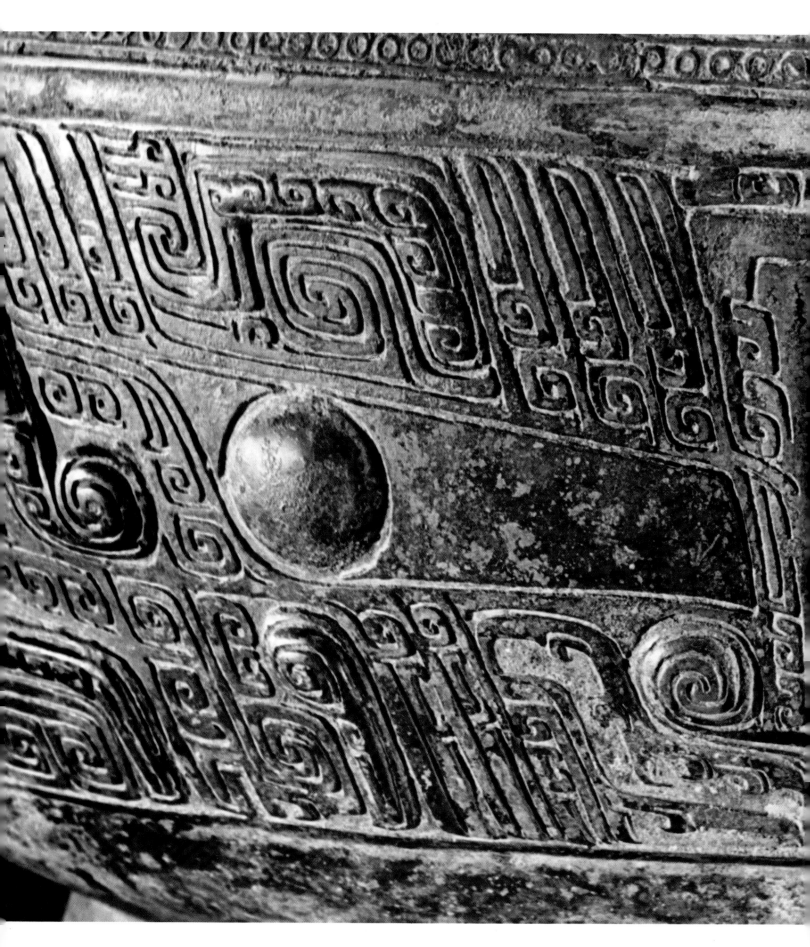

Detail, decor of *pou* no. 13

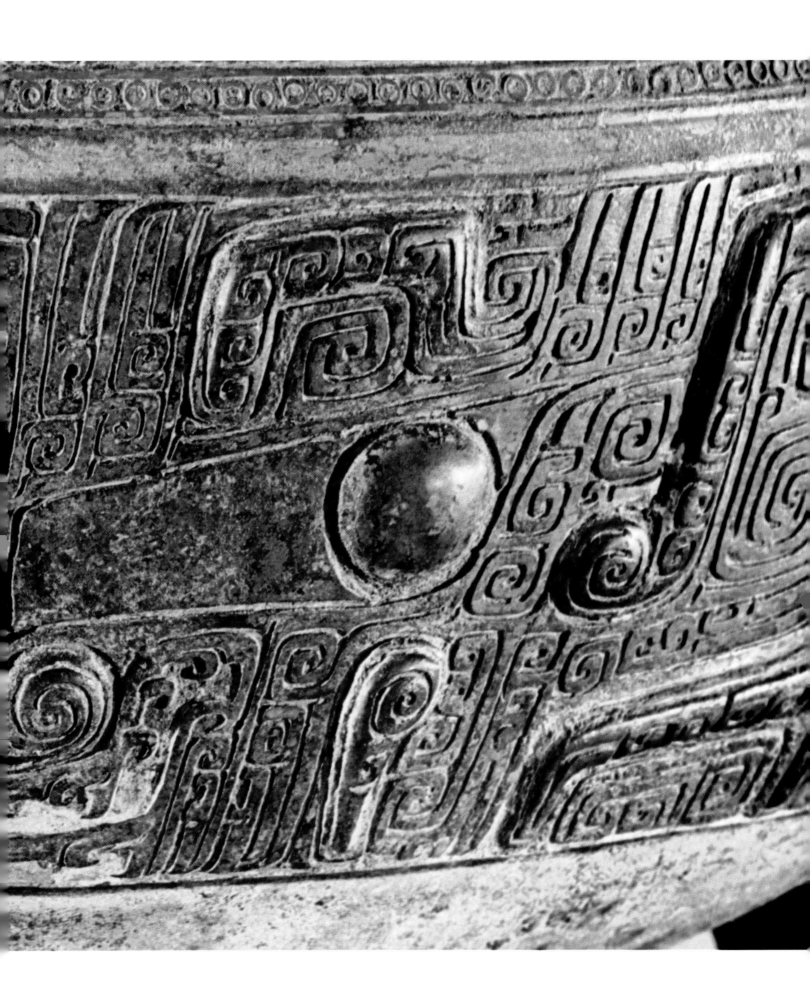

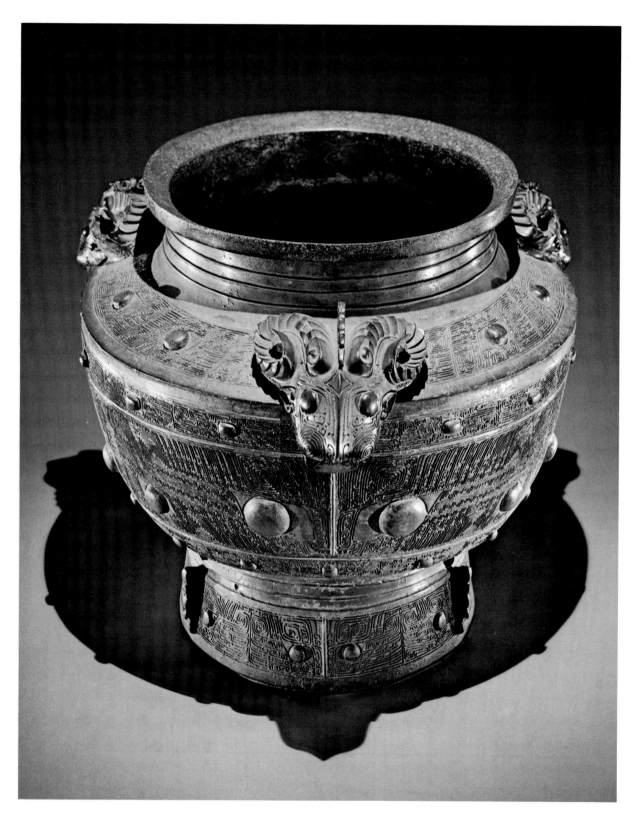

14 *Lei.* 15th–14th century B.C.? (Zhengzhou-Anyang transition). Height 52 cm. (20½ in.); greatest diameter 61 cm. (24 in.); weight 51.2 kg. (112 lb. 10 oz.)

Above, detail of ram's head, *lei* no. **14**.
Below, detail of *leiwen* spirals, *lei* no. **14** ▷

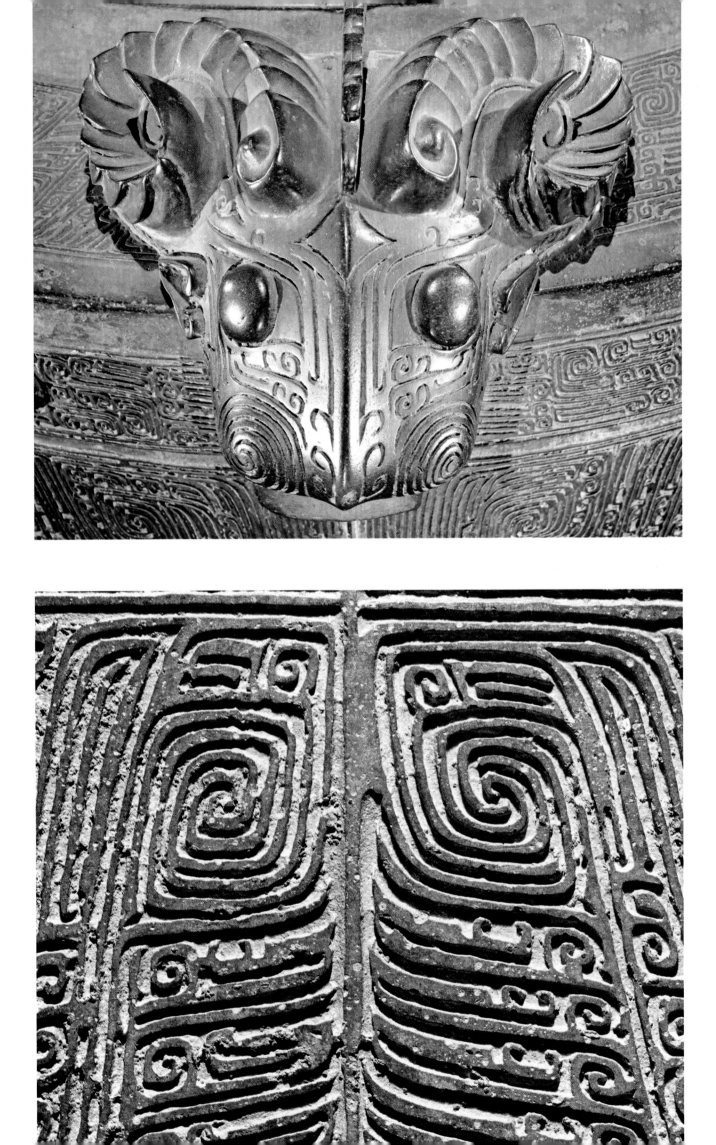

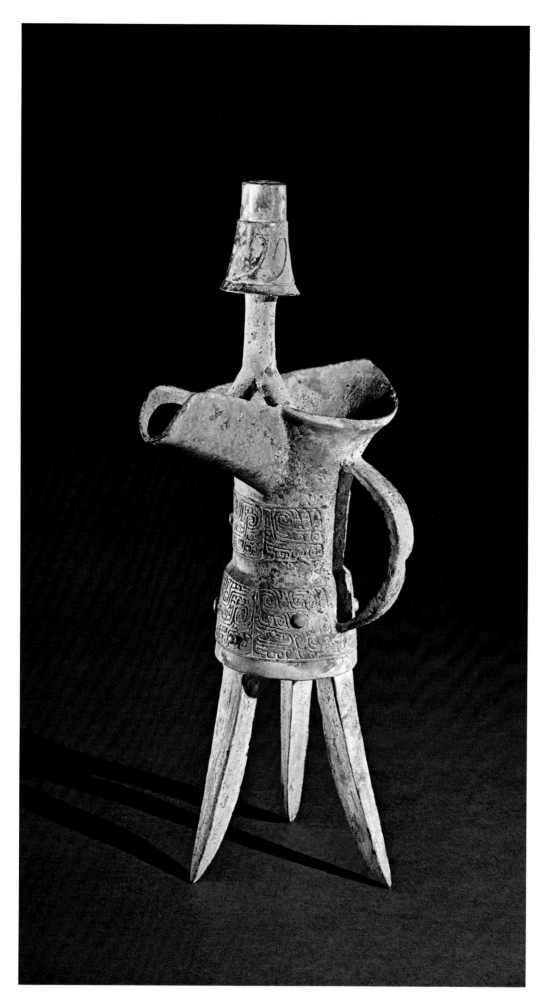

15 *Jue.* 15th–14th century B.C.? (Zhengzhou-Anyang transition). Height 38.4 cm.
(15⅛ in.); length (spout to tail) 21.6 cm. (8½ in.); weight 1.7 kg. (3 lb. 12 oz.)

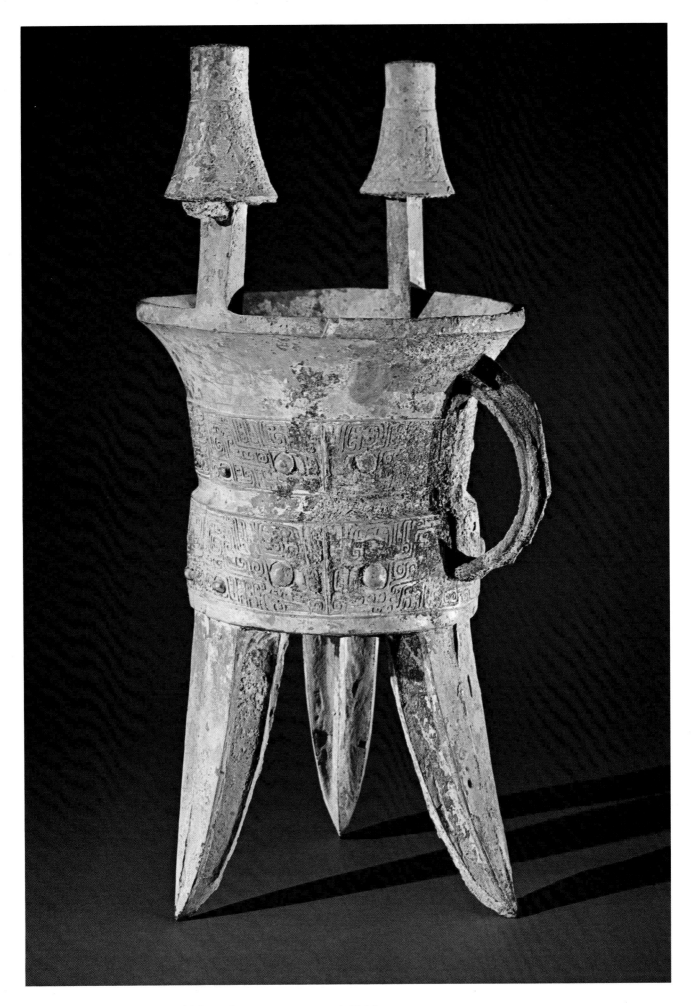

16 *Jia*. 15th–14th century B.C.? (Zhengzhou-Anyang transition). Height
54 cm. (21¼ in.); diameter 26 cm. (10¼ in.); weight 7.85 kg. (17 lb. 4 oz.)

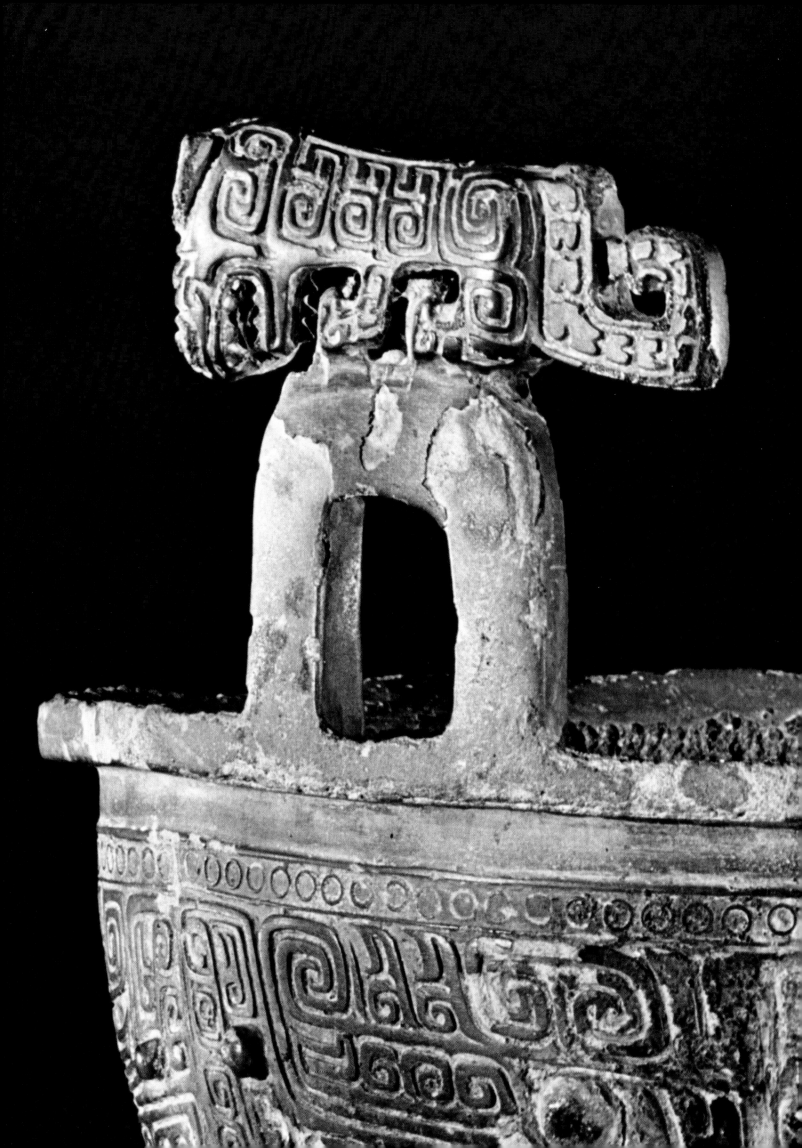

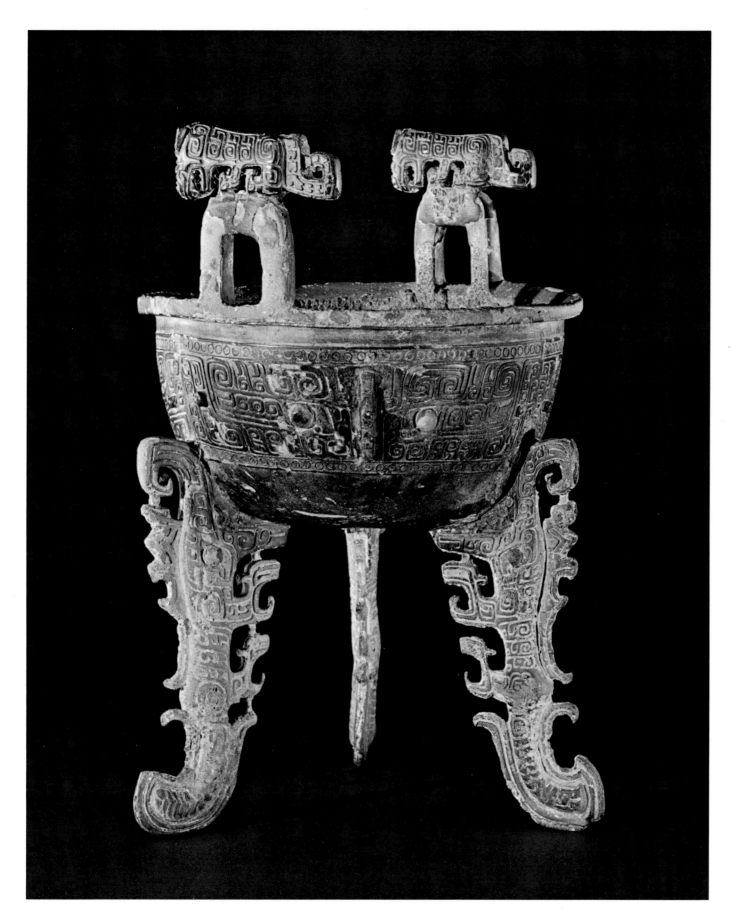

17 *Ding.* 15th–14th century B.C.? (Zhengzhou-Anyang transition). Height
30.1 cm. (12⅛ in.); diameter 20 cm. (7⅞ in.); weight 3.35 kg. (7 lb. 6 oz.)

◁ Detail, handle in the shape of a tiger, *ding*
no. **17**

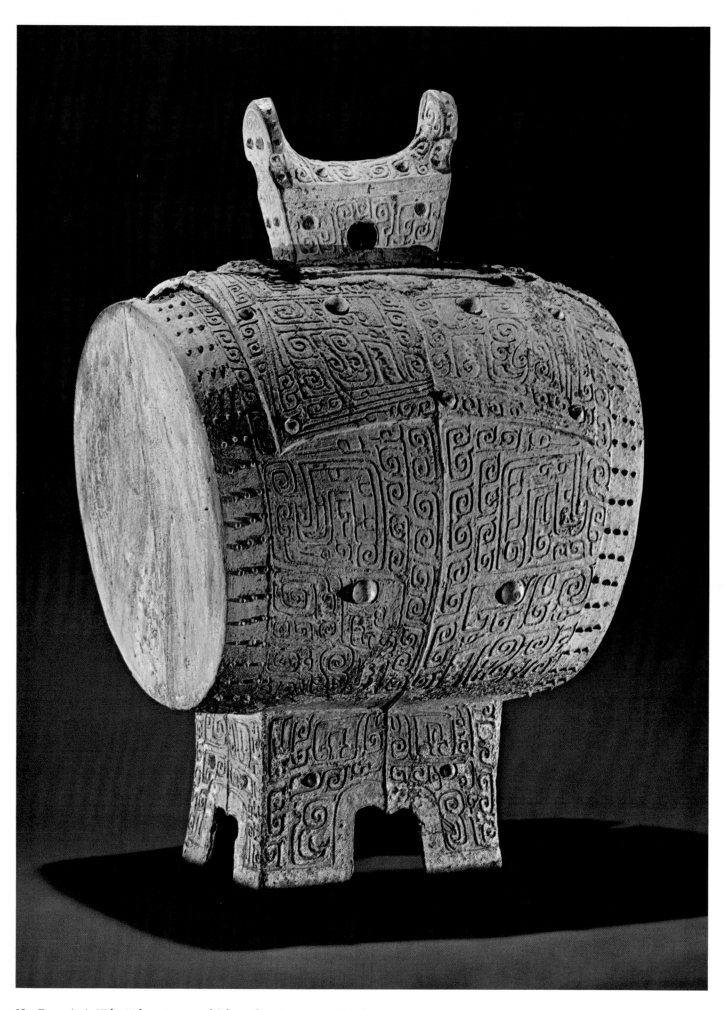

18 Drum (*gu*). 15th–14th century B.C.? (Zhengzhou-Anyang transition).
Height 75.5 cm. (29¾ in.); length at top 49 cm. (19¼ in.); weight
42.5 kg. (93 lb. 8 oz.)

19 Bell (*nao*). Anyang period (ca. 1300–ca. 1030 B.C.).
Height 89 cm. (35 in.); width at mouth 58.5 cm.
(23 in.); weight 154 kg. (338 lb. 12 oz.)

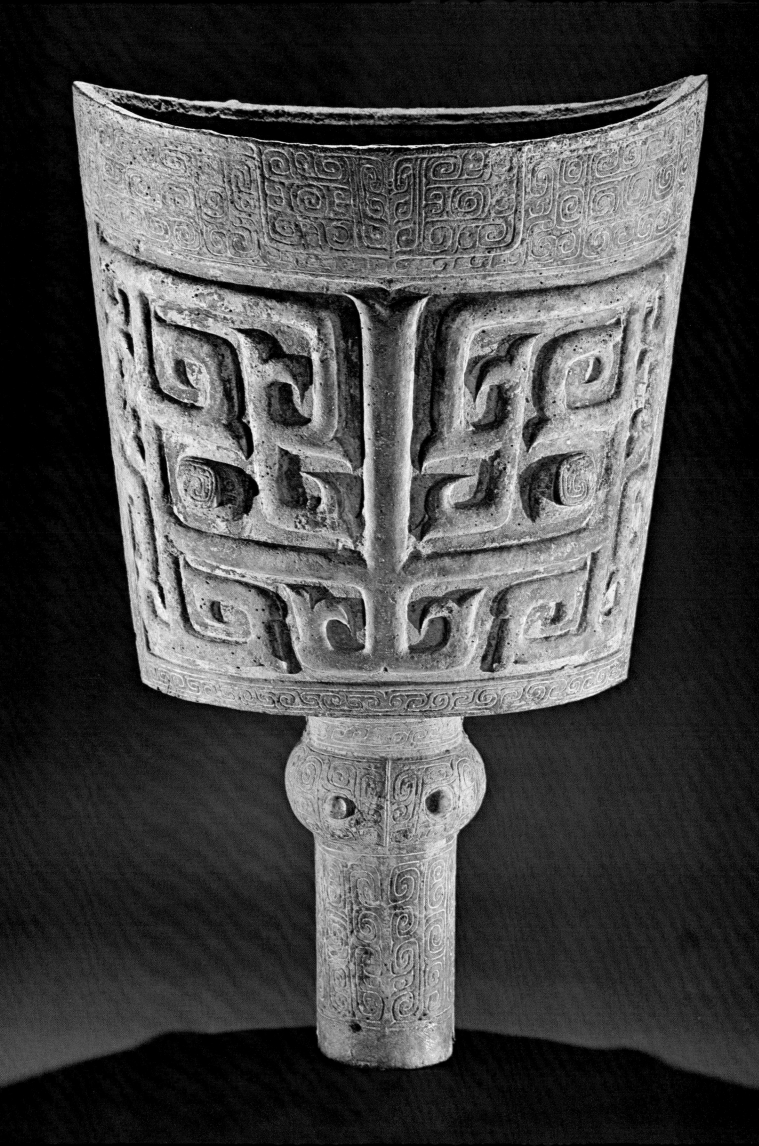

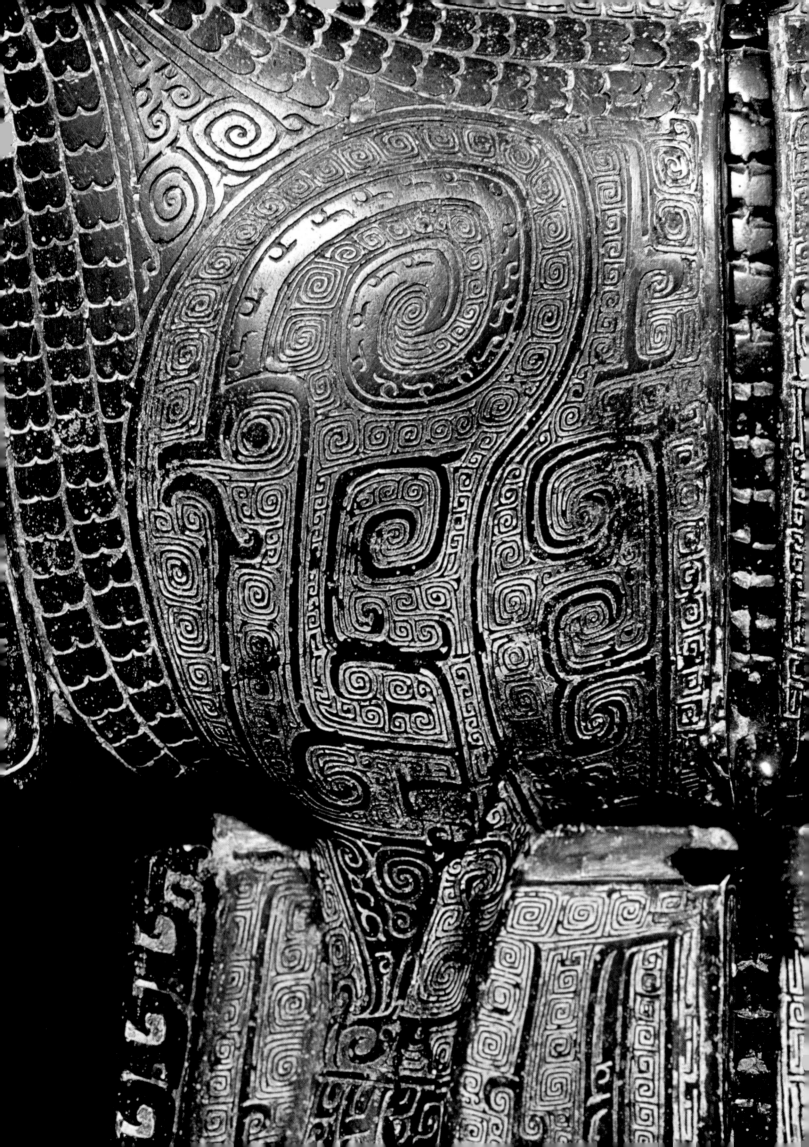

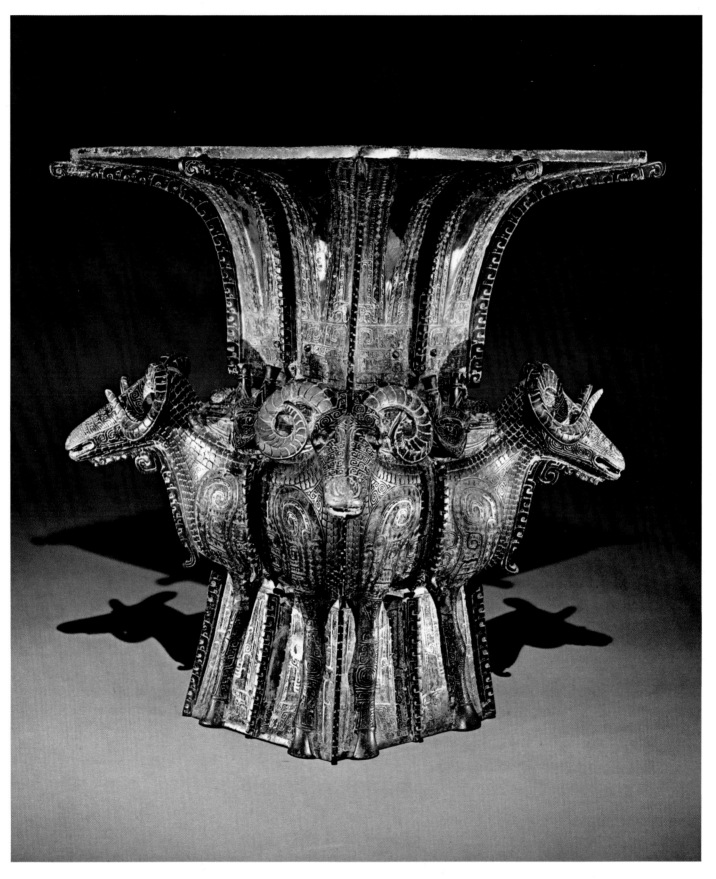

20 Four-ram *fang zun*. Anyang period (ca. 1300–ca. 1030 B.C.).
Height 58.3 cm. (23 in.); width at mouth 52.4 cm. (20⅝ in.);
weight 34.5 kg. (75 lb. 14 oz.)

◁ Detail, decor of four-ram *fang zun* no. **20**

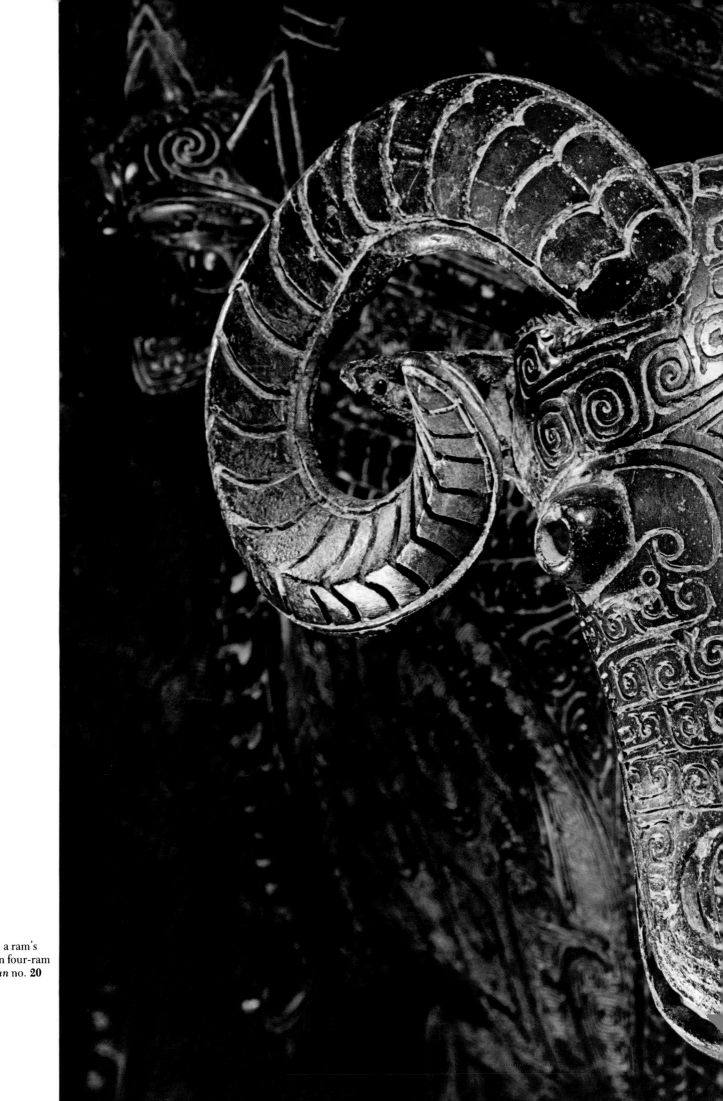

Detail, a ram's
head on four-ram
fang zun no. **20**

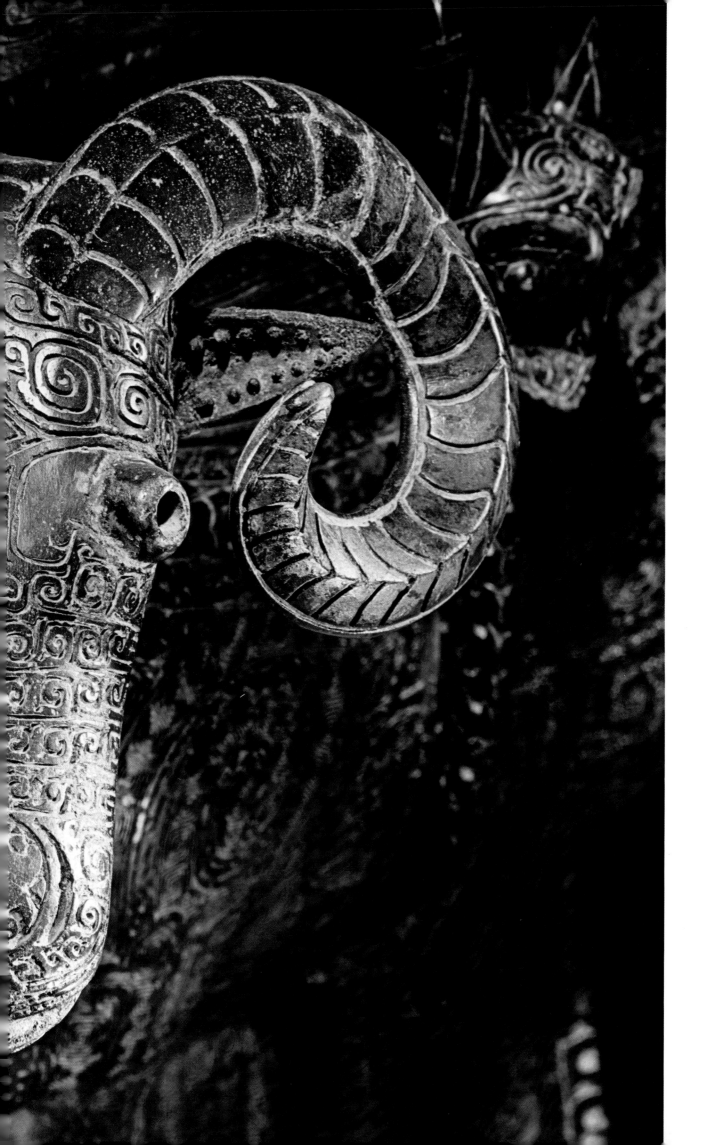

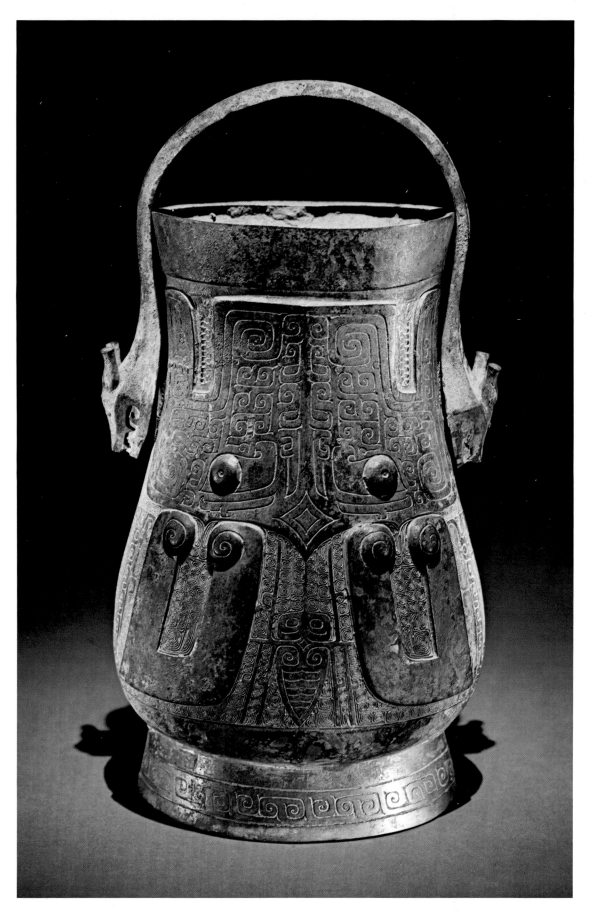

21 *Hu.* Anyang period (ca. 1300–ca. 1030 B.C.). Height 42 cm. (16½ in.);
weight 4.6 kg. (10 lb. 2 oz.)

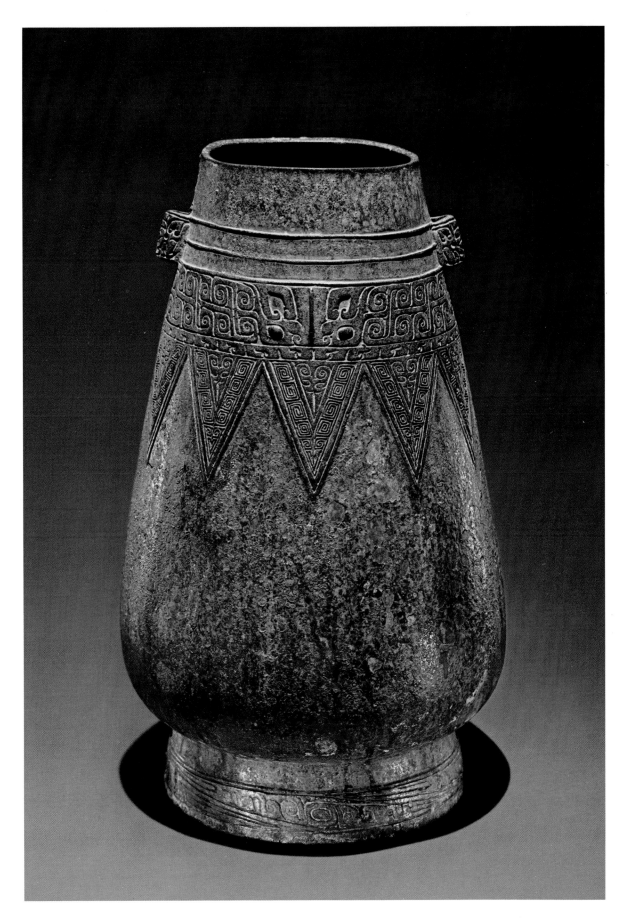

22 *Hu*. Anyang period (ca. 1300–ca. 1030 B.C.). Height 31.3 cm. (12⅜ in.); weight 2.7 kg. (6 lb.)

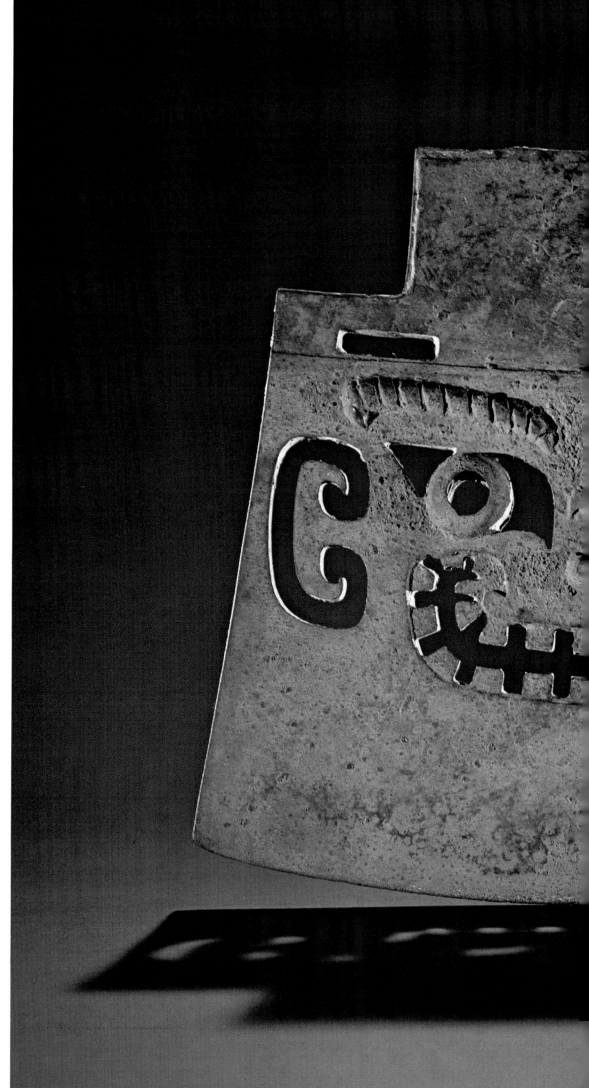

23 Ax (*yue*). Anyang period
(ca. 1300–ca. 1030 B.C.). Height
31.8 cm. (12½ in.); width at
edge 35.8 cm. (14⅛ in.);
weight 4.7 kg. (10 lb. 5 oz.)

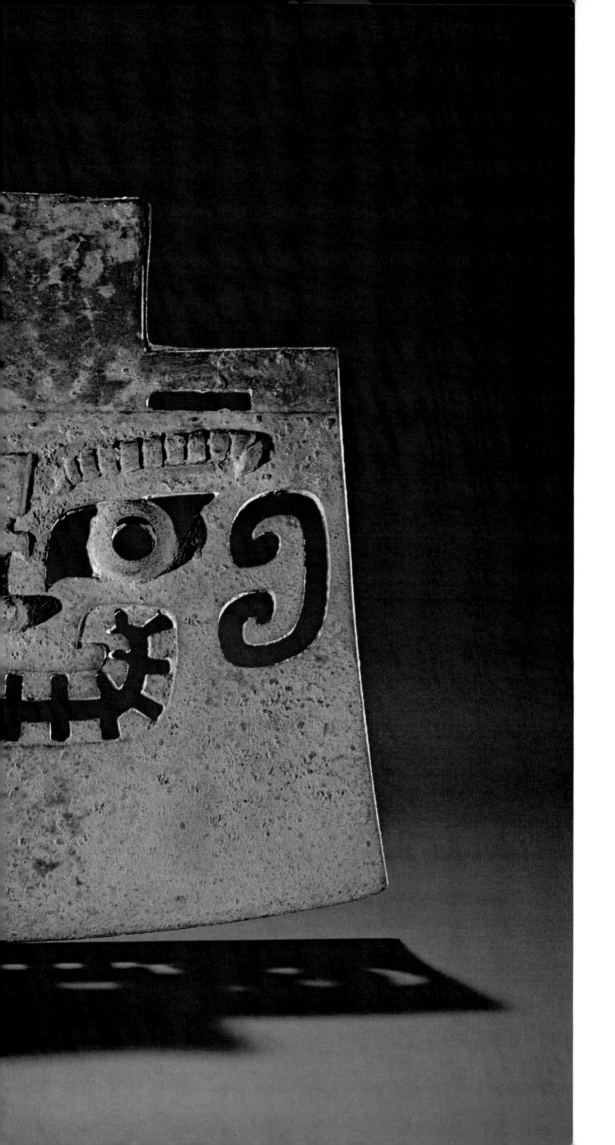

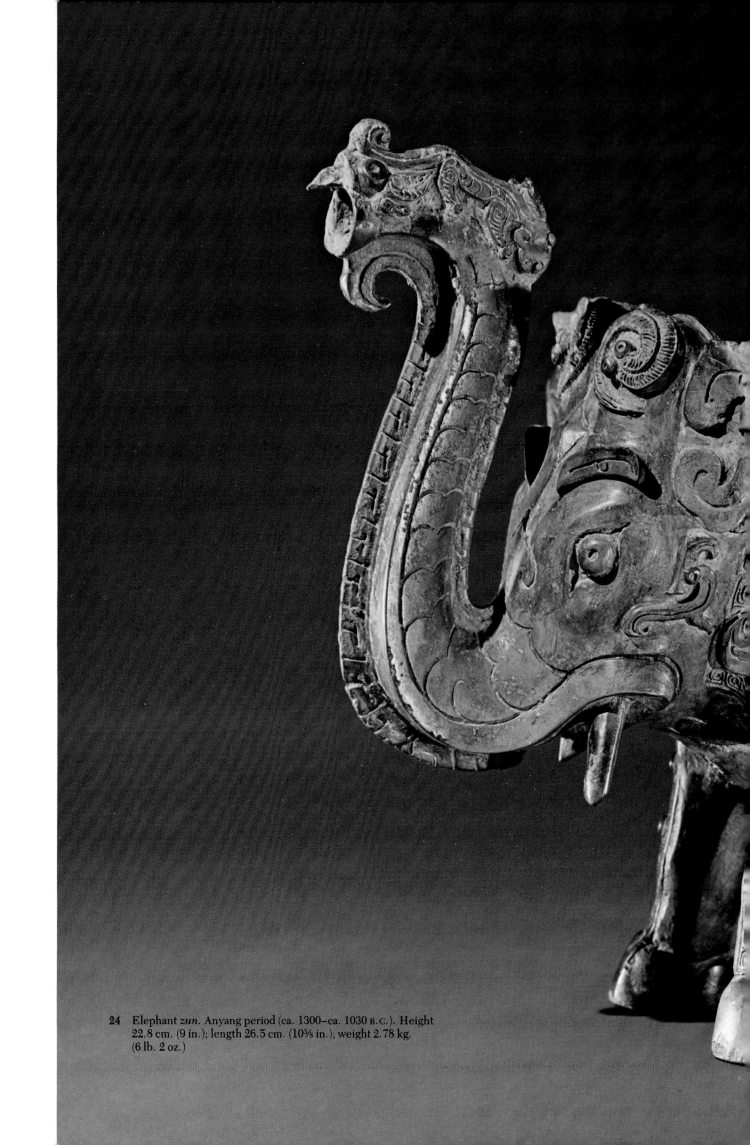

24 Elephant *zun*. Anyang period (ca. 1300–ca. 1030 B.C.). Height
22.8 cm. (9 in.); length 26.5 cm. (10⅜ in.); weight 2.78 kg.
(6 lb. 2 oz.)

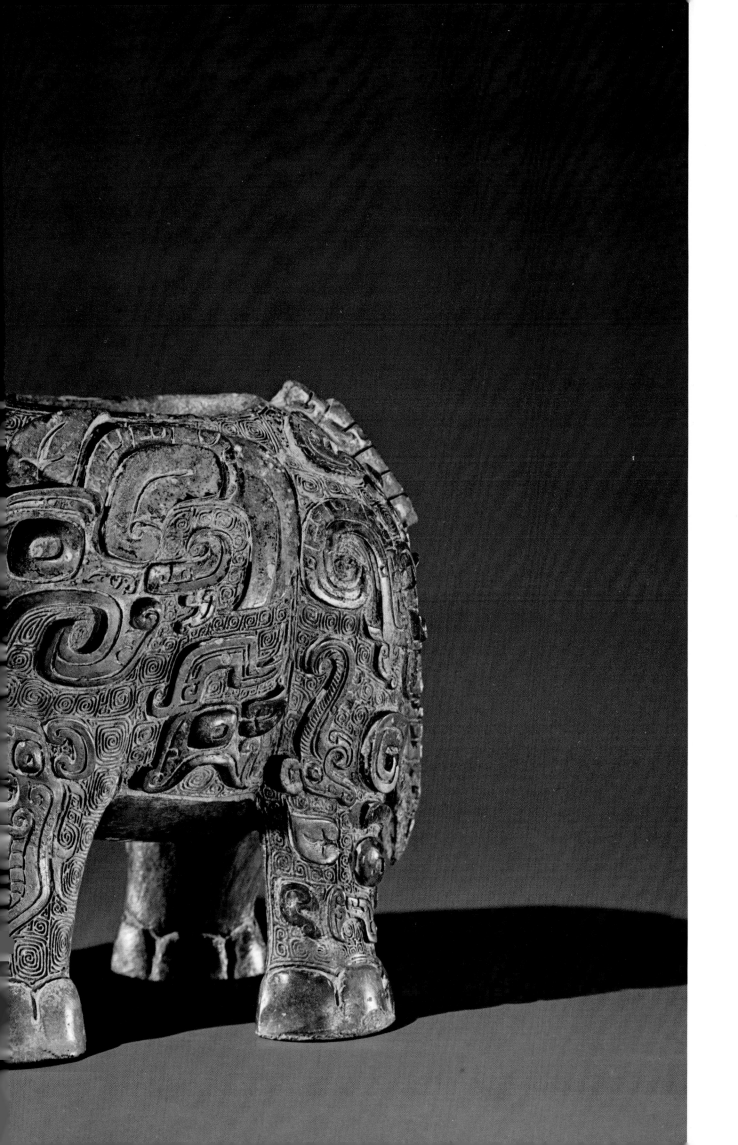

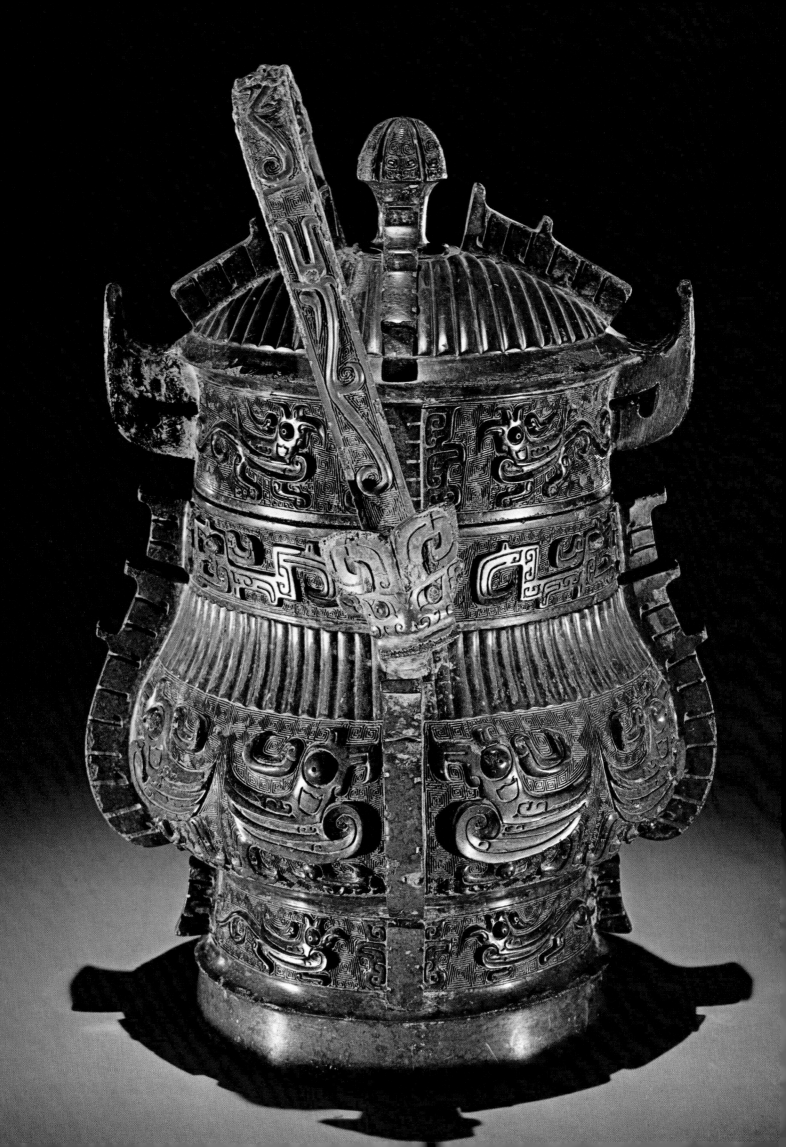

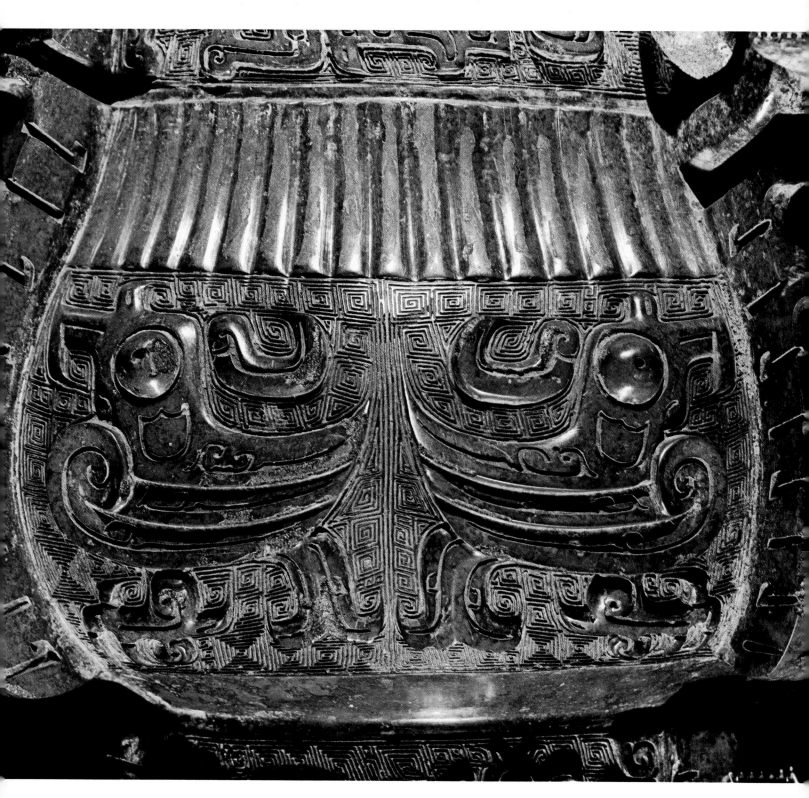

Detail, decor of Ge *you* no. **25**

◁ **25** Ge *you*. Anyang period (ca. 1300–ca. 1030 B.C.).
Height 39 cm. (15⅜ in.); weight 10.75 kg. (23 lb. 10 oz.)

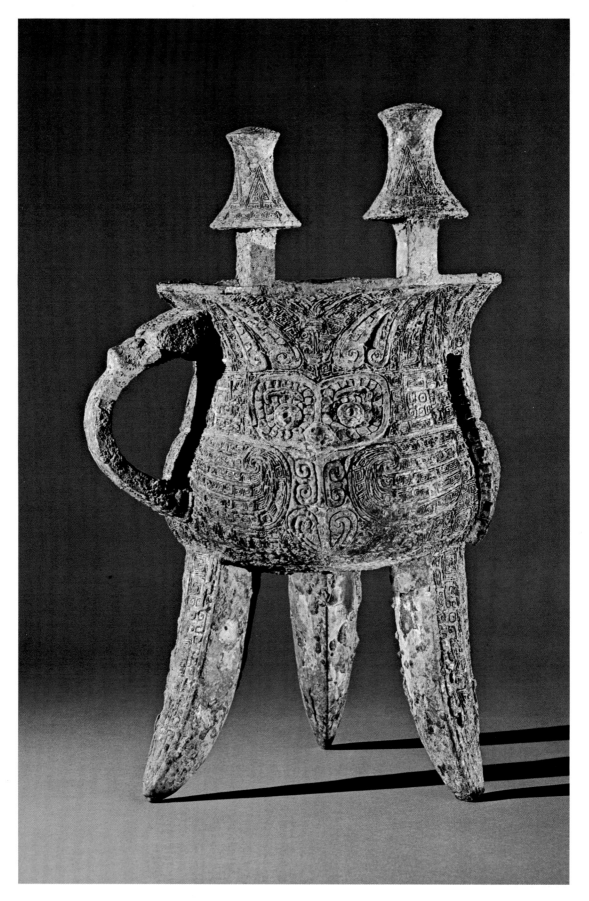

26 Xi *jia*. Anyang period (ca. 1300–ca. 1030 B.C.). Height 37.3 cm.
(14¾ in.); diameter 19.6 cm. (7¾ in.); weight 4.3 kg. (9 lb. 7 oz.)

27 *Fang lei*. Anyang period (ca. 1300–ca. 1030
B.C.). Height 53 cm. (20⅞ in.); weight
29.6 kg. (65 lb. 2 oz.)

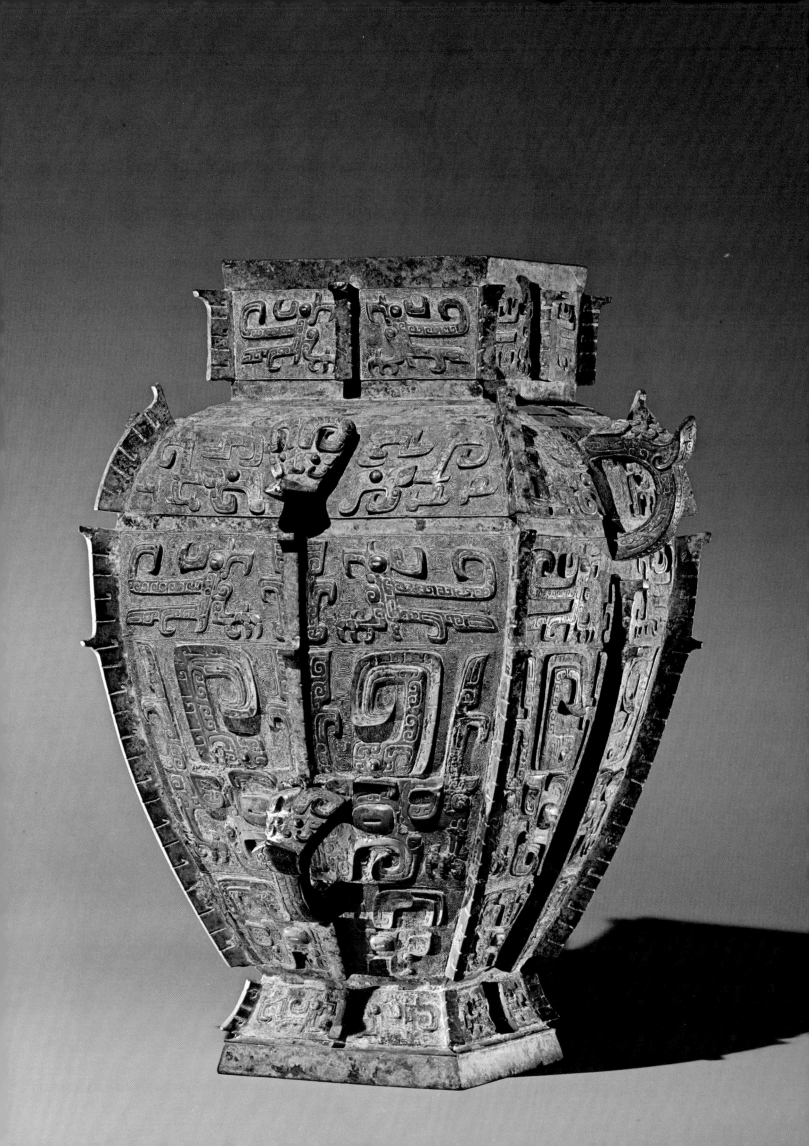

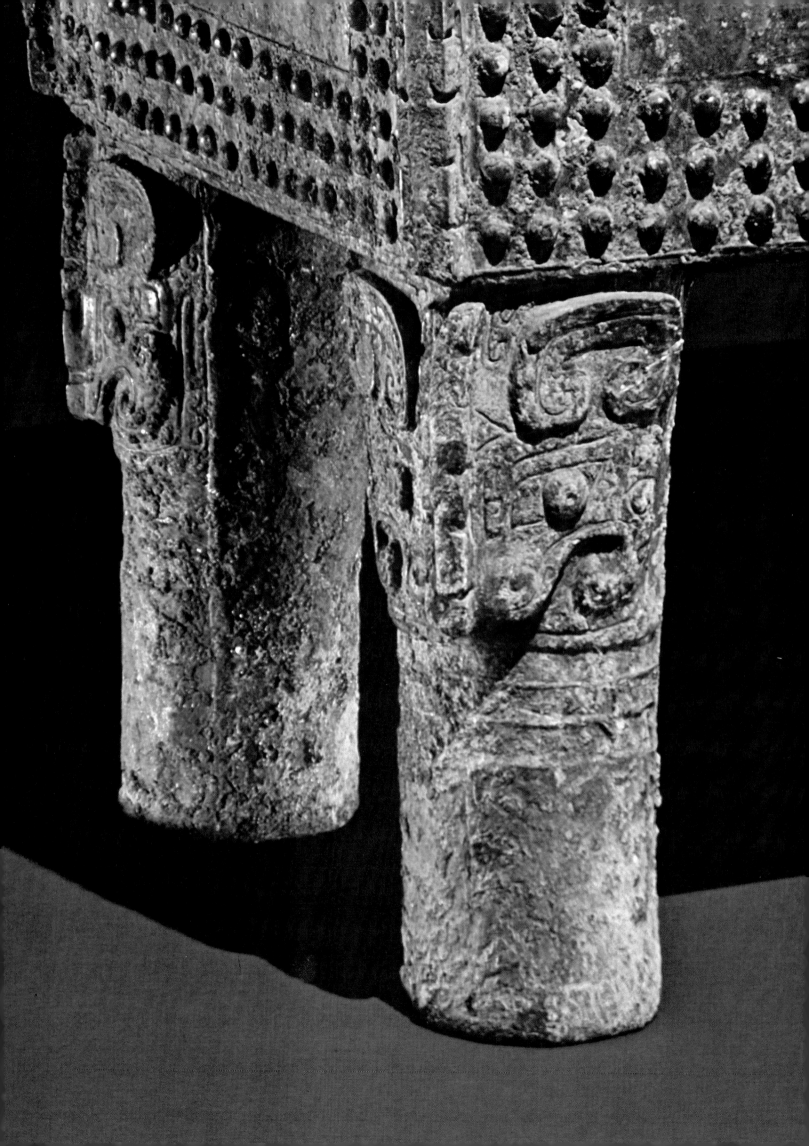

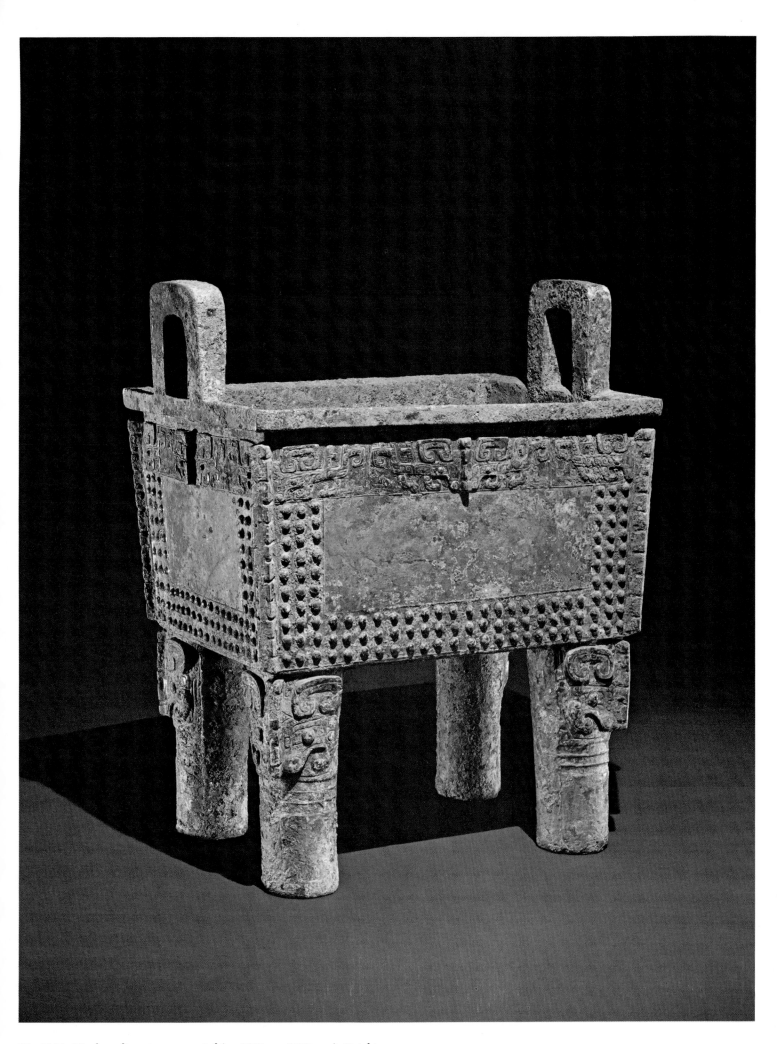

28 Si Mu Xin *fang ding*. Anyang period (ca. 1300–ca. 1030 B.C.). Height
79.6 cm. (31⅜ in.); length and width at mouth 64 x 47.6 cm. (25¼ x
18¾ in.); weight 117.5 kg. (258 lb. 8 oz.)

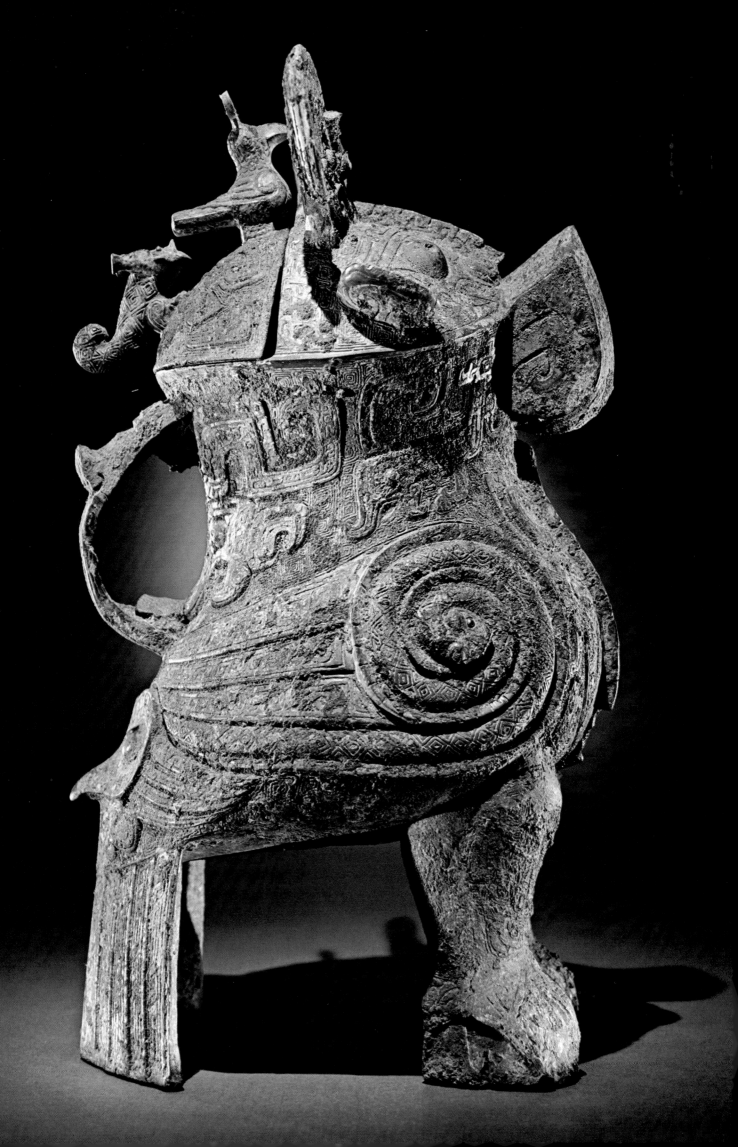

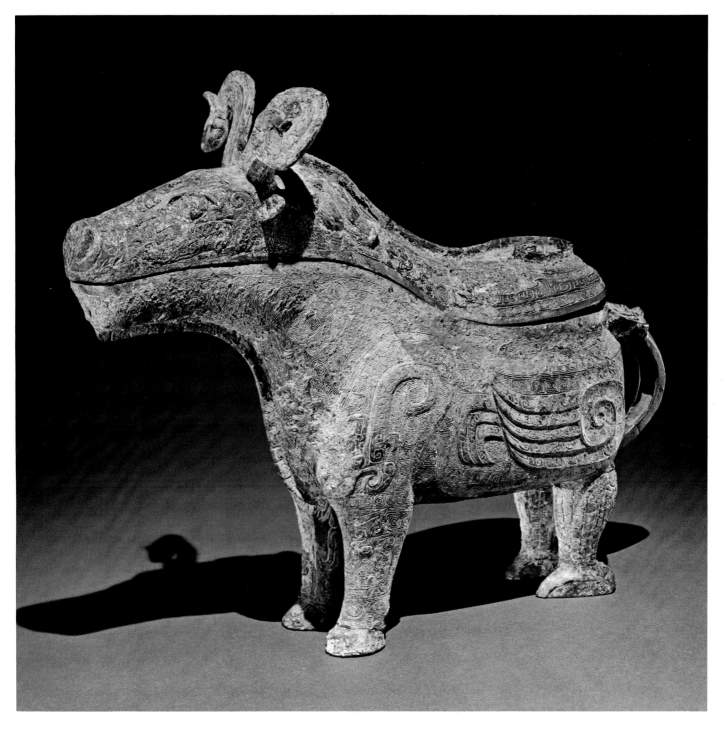

30 Si Mu Xin *guang*. Anyang period (ca. 1300–ca. 1030 B.C.). Height 36 cm. (14⅛ in.); length 46.5 cm. (18¼ in.); weight 8.5 kg. (18 lb. 11 oz.)

◁ **29** Bird-shaped *zun*. Anyang period (ca. 1300–ca. 1030 B.C.). Height 45.9 cm. (18⅛ in.); weight 16.7 kg. (36 lb. 12 oz.)

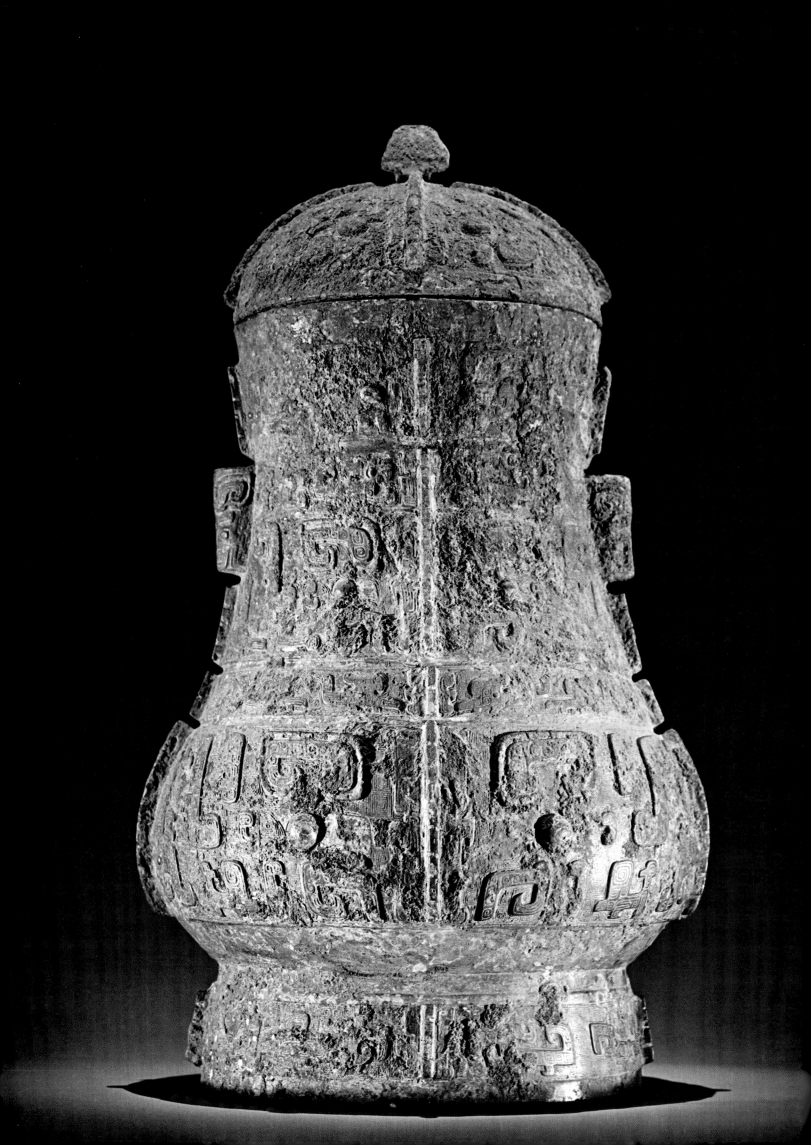

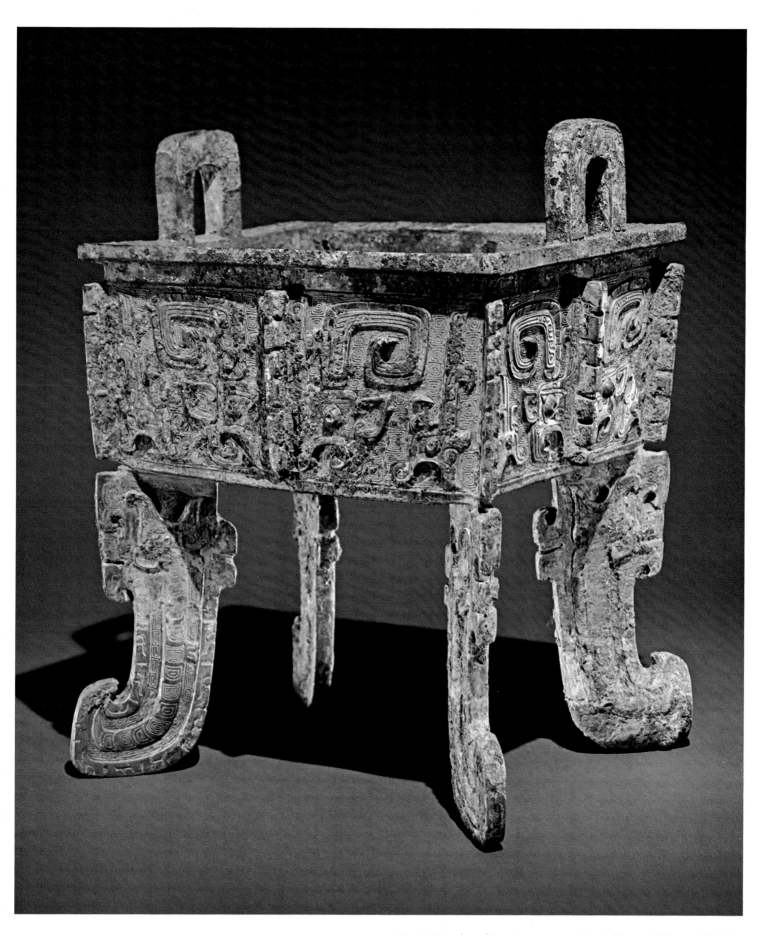

32 Fu Hao *fang ding*. Anyang period (ca. 1300–ca. 1030 B.C.). Height
42.4 cm. (16¾ in.); length and width at mouth 33.3 x 25.1 cm. (13⅛
x 9⅞ in.); weight 17 kg. (37 lb. 6 oz.)

31 Fu Hao *hu*. Anyang period (ca. 1300–ca. 1030 B.C.).
Height 51.5 cm. (20¼ in.); weight 16.8 kg. (37 lb.)

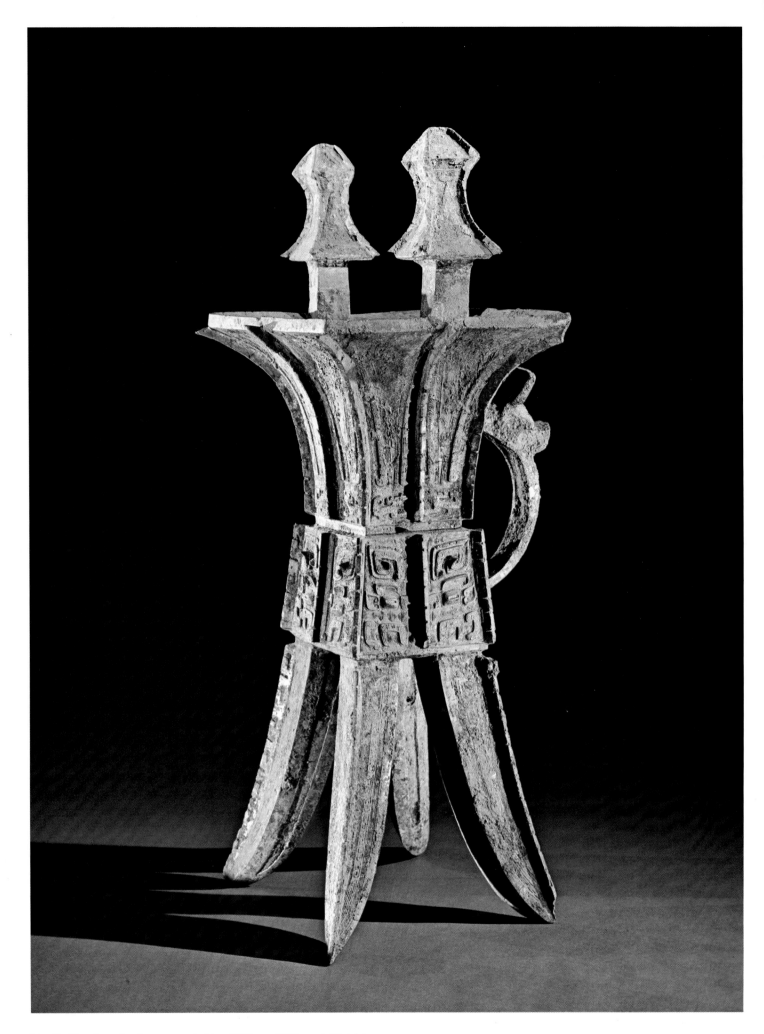

33 Fu Hao *fang jia*. Anyang period (ca. 1300–ca. 1030 B.C.). Height 66.8 cm. (26¼ in.); weight 19.05 kg. (41 lb. 15 oz.)

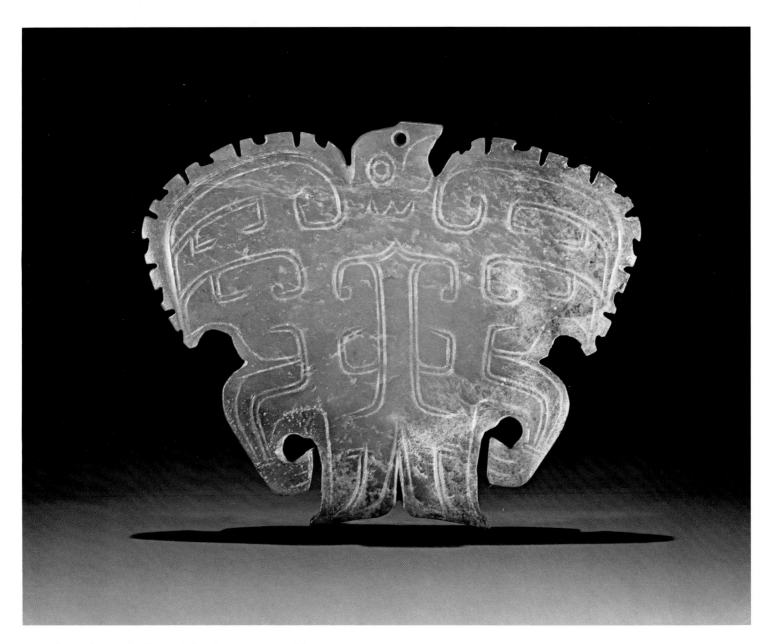

34 Jade pendant in the shape of a hawk. Anyang period (ca. 1300–
ca. 1030 B.C.). Height 6.2 cm. (2⅜ in.); weight 34 g. (1⅕ oz.)

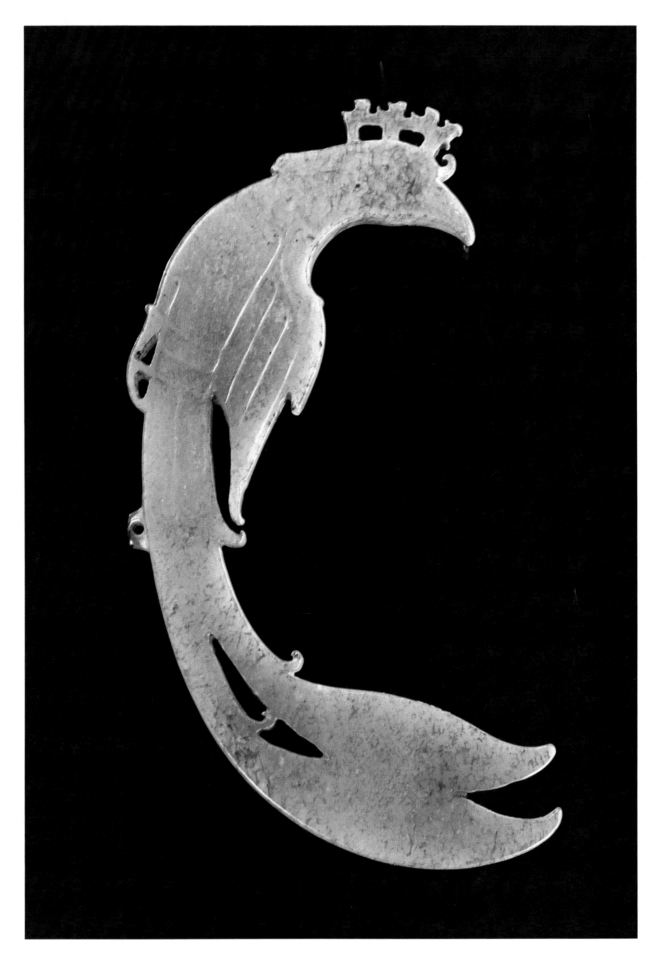

35 Jade pendant in the shape of a plumed bird. Anyang period (ca. 1300– ca. 1030 B.C.).
Length 13.6 cm. (5⅜ in.); thickness 0.7 cm. (¼ in.); weight 87 g. (3 oz.)

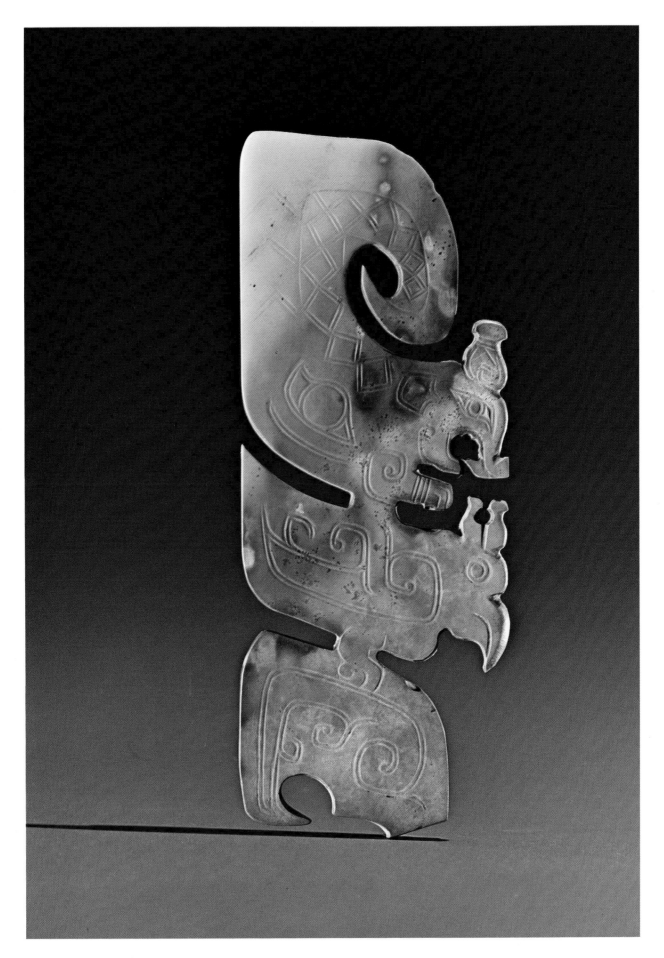

36 Jade plaque. Anyang period (ca. 1300–ca. 1030 B.C.). Length 11.3 cm.
(4½ in.); weight 45 g. (1½ oz.)

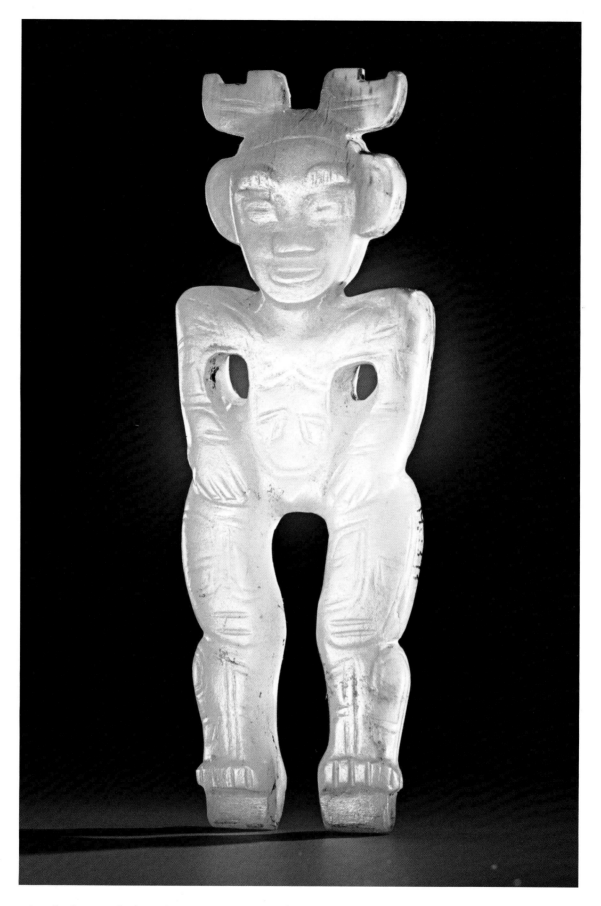

37 Jade plaque in the form of a standing human figure. Anyang period (ca. 1300–ca. 1030 B.C.). Height 12.5 cm. (4⅞ in.); thickness 0.9 cm. (⅜ in.); weight 102 g. (3½ oz.)

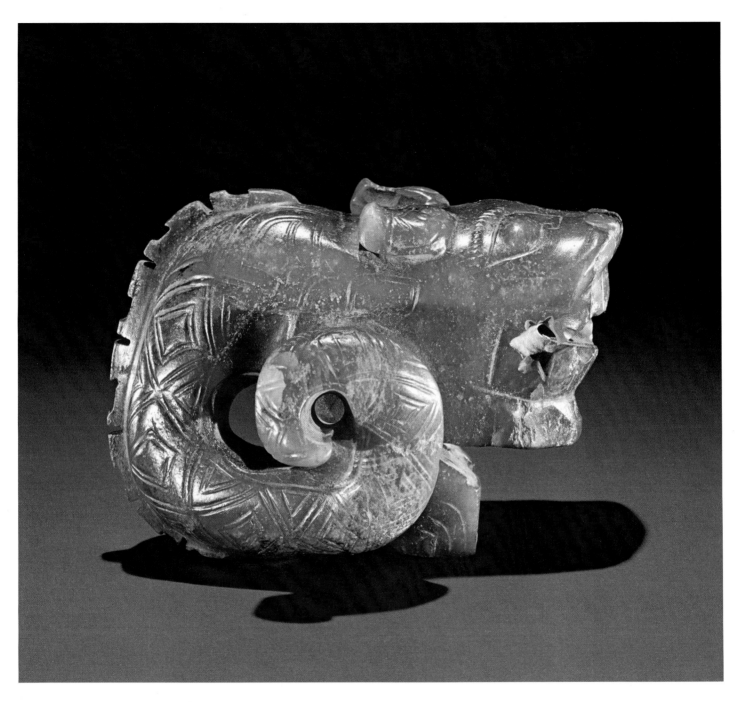

38 Jade dragon. Anyang period (ca. 1300–ca. 1030 B.C.). Length 8.1 cm.
(3¼ in.); height 5.5 cm. (2⅛ in.); weight 228 g. (8 oz.)

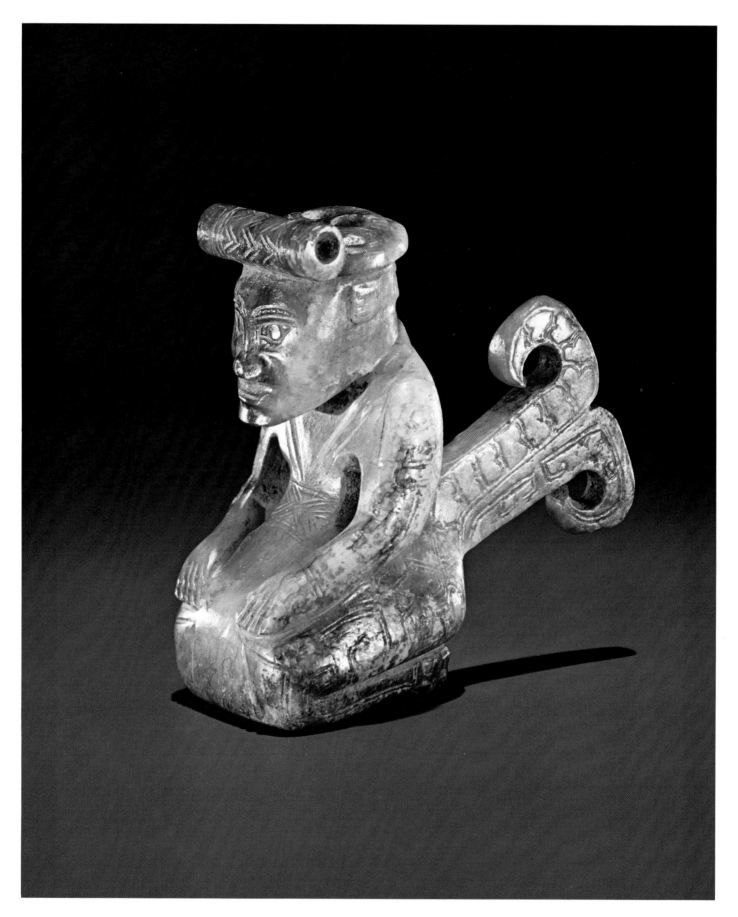

39 Jade figurine. Anyang period (ca. 1300–ca. 1030 B.C.). Height 6.9 cm.
(2¾ in.); weight 136 g. (4¾ oz.)

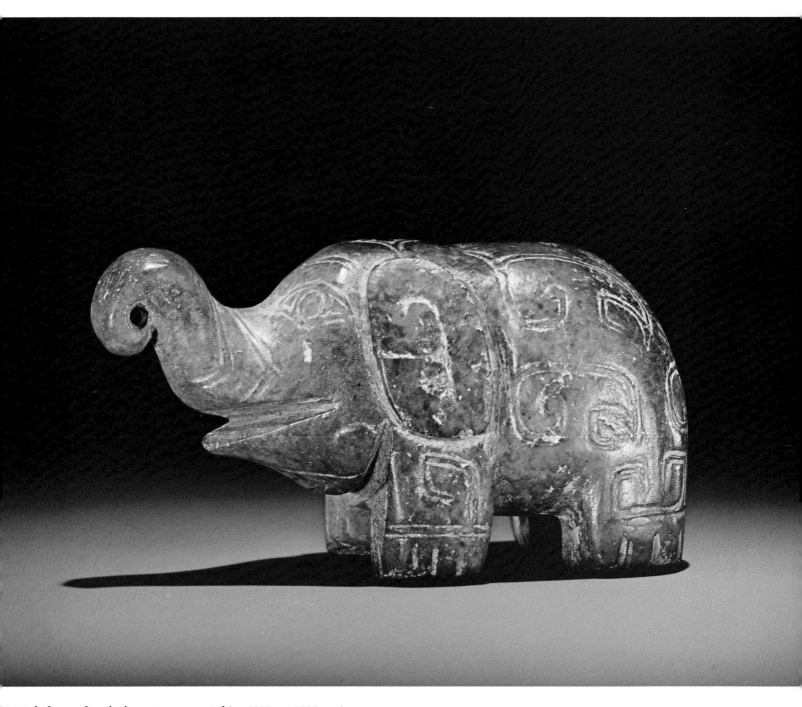

40 Jade figure of an elephant. Anyang period (ca. 1300–ca. 1030 B.C.).
Length 6.5 cm. (2½ in.); height 3.3 cm. (1¼ in.); weight 78 g. (2¾ oz.)

4

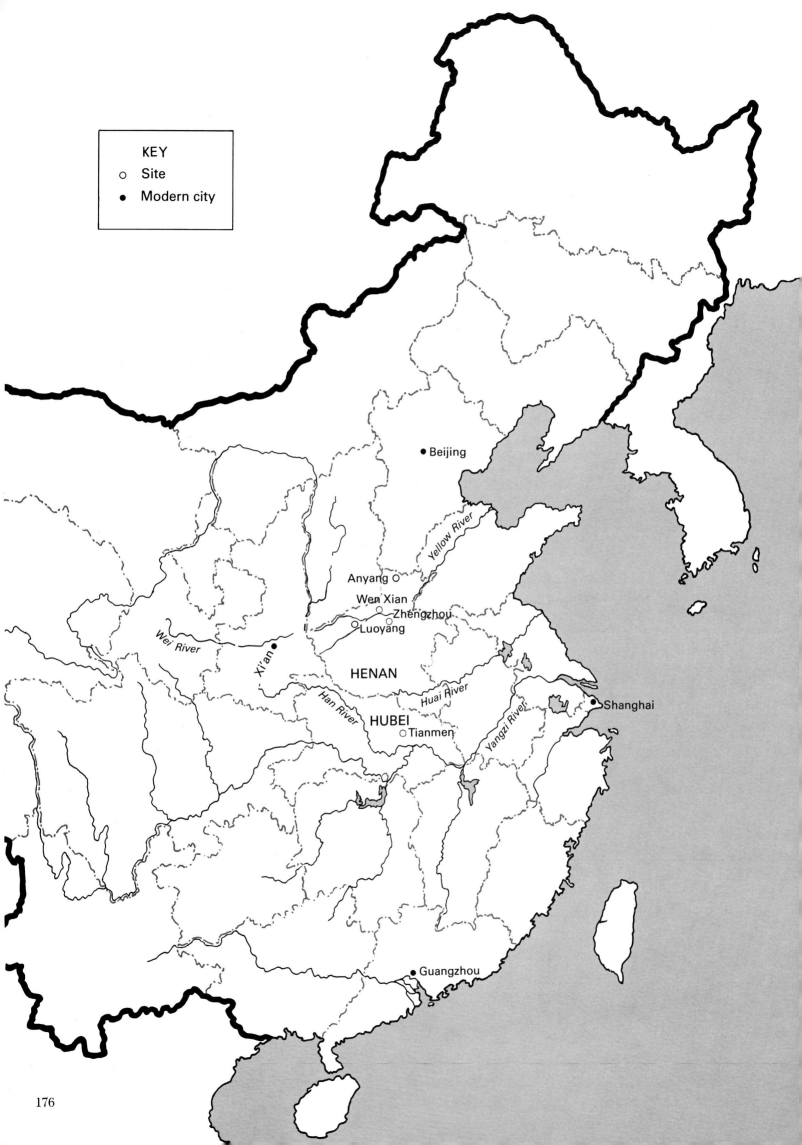

KEY
○ Site
● Modern city

● Beijing

Yellow River

Anyang ○
Wen Xian
○ Zhengzhou
○ Luoyang

Wei River

Xi'an ●

HENAN

Han River

Huai River

HUBEI

○ Tianmen

Yangzi River

Shanghai ●

● Guangzhou

4 The High Yinxu Phase (Anyang Period)

Robert W. Bagley

Tradition has it that the last capital of the Shang dynasty, located near Anyang in northern Henan, was the seat of twelve kings, who ruled there for 273 years. From this period there survive, in the form of the oracle inscriptions, contemporary written records that serve to supplement the brief and sometimes contradictory accounts of Shang history given in later texts. However, the inscriptions so far known confirm the presence at Anyang of only the last nine kings of the twelve named by tradition; no inscribed bones datable to the first three reigns have yet been identified. Moreover, no other remains of any consequence at the Anyang site can be assigned to these first three reigns. The lack may be due only to the fortunes of excavation, since the site is much plundered, damaged by erosion, and far from fully explored; spectacular recent discoveries show well enough what surprises may still lie in store. Nevertheless, present evidence suggests that some considerable time must have elapsed between the decline of Zhengzhou and the first significant activity at Anyang. If Zhengzhou was in fact the capital Ao of traditional history, the time in question would be five generations. As noted in chapter 3, this is a gap that seems to be bridged by discoveries made elsewhere than at Anyang, at the sites, perhaps, of intervening capitals.

Some scholars have actually suggested that Anyang did not become the capital until the reign of Wu Ding, fourth of the traditional Anyang kings. In any case, it is during his long reign, said to have lasted fifty-nine years, that a distinct upsurge of activity at the Anyang site is apparent. A tremendous wealth of oracle inscriptions from Wu Ding's court document an obsessive round of sacrificial observances, in which the bronze vessels surely played a central role. The oracle records also allude to wide-ranging military expeditions, giving substance to the "dynastic revival" that later accounts connect with Wu Ding. His campaigns in the south may well have been aimed at recovering territories lost earlier, at the end of the Zhengzhou phase, when Panlongcheng was abandoned.

One name that occurs especially often in the oracle inscriptions from Wu Ding's court is that of the lady Fu Hao. A royal consort and lady-general, Fu Hao was evidently a person of some character and consequence, mentioned at times as leading military expeditions on behalf of the king and on other occasions as presiding in his name at state sacrifices. Wu Ding repeatedly inquired

Map of China showing important archaeological sites of the High Yinxu phase (Anyang period) of the Shang dynasty, 13th century to 11th century B.C.

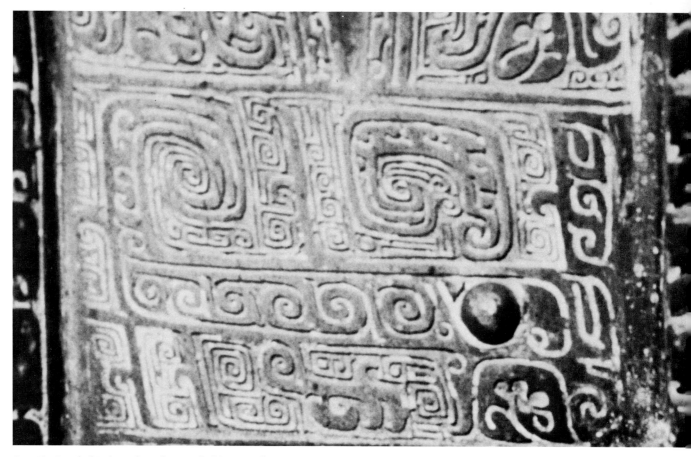

Fig. 47   Detail of Style IV decor from neck of four-ram *fang zun* no. 20.
Photograph: Robert W. Bagley

of the spirits about Fu Hao's childbearing; his special concern in her case may hint that her sons were heirs to the throne.

The most remarkable single find ever made at the Anyang site was the discovery in 1976 of Fu Hao's tomb, intact and undisturbed. The identification of the tomb's occupant was possible because many of the bronzes it contained were inscribed, more than sixty of them with Fu Hao's name (nos. 29, 31–33), others with a posthumous title under which she would have received sacrifice from sons or nephews (nos. 28, 30). Such inscriptions seem never to occur on pre-Anyang bronzes. The brief dedications cast on the Fu Hao bronzes, remarkable for their handsome script, represent the beginnings of a practice that culminated centuries later in the lengthy and increasingly secular inscriptions of Zhou times (chap. 5).

The discovery of Fu Hao's tomb was altogether unprecedented; none of the other major Anyang burials was either intact or assignable to a particular person or reign. The thirteen tombs of royal size found previously near Anyang are clustered in a cemetery area, at Xibeigang, that was reserved exclusively for the tombs and for ceremonies of sacrifice connected with them. The Xibeigang tombs are rectangular pits approached by ramps, usually four ramps sloping down on all sides to the burial chamber. The tomb HPKM 1004, which can be taken as roughly average in size, was 12 meters deep; the pit proper measured 16 by 18 meters, while the overall north-south length, including the ramps, was about 60 meters. The kings buried at Xibeigang were accompanied by sacrificial victims, sometimes in separate satel-lite graves, and occasionally also by chariot burials—including chariot, horses, and charioteer.

The Huan River separates the cemetery at Xibei-gang from a group of building foundations, at Xiaotun, that apparently belonged to the main palace complex of the Shang city. Fu Hao's tomb, surprisingly enough, was not at Xibeigang, but across the river near the Xiaotun palace site. It consisted of a modest rectangular pit without entrance ramps, 8 meters deep and 5.6 by 4 meters on the sides. There were traces of a building, conceivably a mortuary temple, set directly over the tomb, a feature not previously known. The lacquered wooden coffin was enclosed by a larger wooden housing (as also in rich tombs at Panlongcheng) and outside the housing were found sixteen sacrificial victims and six dogs. Despite its unpretentious scale, this grave contained nearly 200 bronze vessels—almost twice the number recovered by archaeologists from all the looted Xibeigang tombs together. In addition, there were well over 200 bronze weapons and tools (tokens, perhaps, of Fu Hao's military career); 600 sculptures and ritual objects of jade and stone; drinking cups of elephant ivory inlaid with turquoise; 500 objects of carved bone; 7,000 cowrie shells (used as money); and the first securely identified bronze mirrors known from the Shang period.

Because the Xibeigang royal tombs had all been plundered before excavation, it has been impossible to establish archaeologically any very useful chronology for the long occupation of the Anyang site. In the absence of such a chronology, it is perhaps inevitable that there should be disagreement about the dating of Fu Hao's tomb. From a conviction that the bronzes in the tomb are

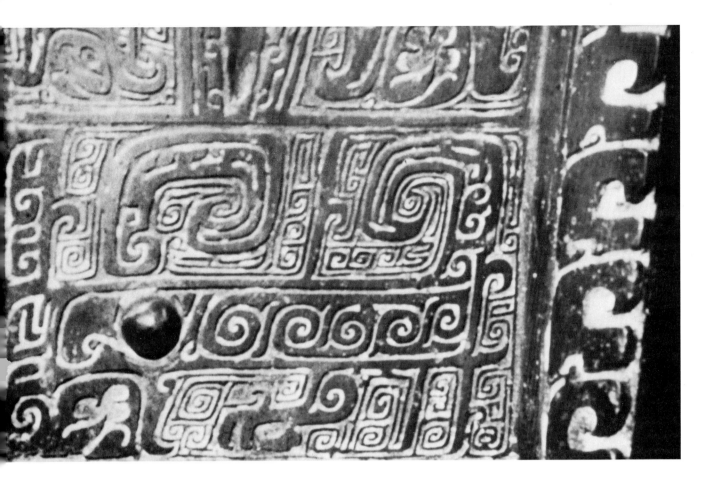

too advanced in style and too accomplished in casting technique to have been made in the early part of the Anyang period, some scholars have suggested that the tomb's occupant was not the consort of Wu Ding, but another person of the same name who would have lived a few generations later. The possibility is one that must be taken seriously. Thorough publication and study of the tomb's contents are only beginning, and, although the early date has so far met with wide acceptance, it may yet prove mistaken.

Nevertheless, recent finds at other sites have helped to establish a context in which an early date for the Fu Hao bronzes seems quite plausible. The level of casting technique required by the monumental *fang ding* from the tomb (no. 28) cannot be regarded as beyond the abilities of the early Anyang founder, if we bear in mind the achievement of Zhengzhou craftsmen in casting the giant *fang ding* no. 11 a century or more earlier. The advances of the intervening century, both stylistic and technical, are best represented by bronzes from sites other than Anyang, as suggested already in connection with nos. 12–16 (chap. 3); the Fu Hao bronzes are not unaccountably distant from these forerunners. Indeed, they could less easily be reconciled with styles current near the end of the Anyang period. It is significant that the tomb's vast inventory of bronzes omits altogether certain vessel shapes that are typical of the latter half of the Anyang period, notably the standard *you* variety represented by no. 25; in a late Anyang tomb of this scale the omission would be inexplicable. As to decoration, high relief execution of surface ornament is characteristic of the Anyang period at large, but within this period the

vigorous and forceful designs of the Fu Hao bronzes seem to belong to a comparatively early phase.

Most of the bronzes from Fu Hao's tomb are decorated in the last two of Loehr's five styles of Shang ornament (see p. 182). Style IV marks a sharp break with the gradual evolution of the earlier decor styles. The diffuse, intricate patterns of Style III, which threaten constantly to dissolve into abstract surface texturing, must finally have seemed to the Anyang artist too ambiguous and too understated. In Style IV, this ambiguity was wholly eliminated. The patterns still remain flush with the surface of the vessel, but the motifs suddenly come into sharp focus, taking on tangible form against an abstract background of dense spirals (Fig. 47). In the process, the design that occupies each frieze unit of a Style III vessel like no. 12 can be imagined as separating into two distinct components, a zoomorphic motif and a neutral background. The *taotie* thereupon ceases to be synonymous with the pattern filling entire frieze units, and becomes instead a well-defined creature displayed against a background, in the frame provided by the frieze unit. In the present exhibition, fully developed Style IV is represented only by the four-ram *zun* discussed in chapter 3 (no. 20; Fig. 38).

The sharp contrast between motif and ground that was introduced by Style IV gave the bronze designs a new force and dramatic clarity, and these were the qualities sought above all others by Anyang artists. Style V was a logical means of placing still greater emphasis on the motif, and its invention followed in short order. The background pattern of spirals, called *leiwen*, remains the same in Style V as in Style IV; but the motifs are now set

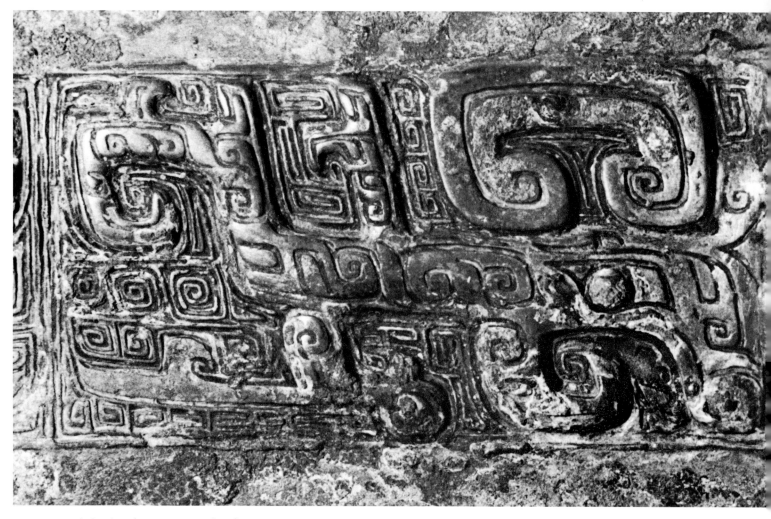

Fig. 48   Detail of Style V decor, Si Mu Xin *fang ding* no. 28.
Photograph: Robert W. Bagley

in high relief against this background. This is the only essential change separating the *taotie* of the four-ram *zun* from its counterpart on the *fang ding* from Fu Hao's tomb (no. 28; Fig. 48).

The Fu Hao bronzes decorated in Style V seem in many cases to represent experiments with the possibilities of the newly invented high relief, and they explore a wide variety of surface treatments. The decor of the bird-shaped vessel no. 29 is an extravagant compound of textures and motifs, ranging from a smooth Style IV on the face of the bird, to the heavy plasticity of the snake coiled on its wing, or even to the half-sculptural owl's face that looks out from a vantage point just above the bird's tail. The vessel's harshly inorganic shape, with its broken silhouette and clumsily aggressive projections, offers an appropriate setting for the lavish display of surface ornament, and the combination achieves an effect of baroque violence. In the case of the four-legged animal no. 30, the same profusion of motifs applied to a less forcefully contrived shape yields an effect merely comical.

The artistic progression that led to these emphatic varieties of surface ornament did not leave the vessel shapes untouched. By comparison with the last two examples, the decor of the *jia* no. 33 is almost subdued; it is confined within strictly compartmented areas of the surface. The ferocious energy of the vessel is owed more to

its heavy flanges, which insistently draw attention to every vertical contour, and to the commanding monumentality of the shape itself. The two earlier *jia* vessels nos. 6 and 16 are landmarks of a steady progress toward dramatically heavier, more angular, and more architectural vessel shapes.

In company with such assertive shapes, the *fang ding* no. 32 may at first glance seem diffident and retiring; in the end it is probably more satisfying. The flat legs of the vessel, curved outward at their lower ends, are not so slight as to be out of proportion to the formidable upper part of the vessel, yet manage to support it with an air of lightness and grace. Next to the unrelieved ponderousness of the *fang ding* no. 28, the exact balance of opposites achieved here is exceedingly impressive.

As Anyang artists learned to judge their effects more precisely, the overstatement that characterizes many of the Fu Hao bronzes was refined away. This is not to say that the bronze vessels became less imposing. On the contrary, the more restrained ornament of the *fang lei* no. 27 speaks with immeasurably greater force than the somewhat bewildering exuberance of the bird-shaped *zun* no. 29 from Fu Hao's tomb: clarity of effect demanded designs less varied and distracting. The relatively simple motifs of the *fang lei* stand out vividly against a *leiwen* ground executed with extraordinary pre-

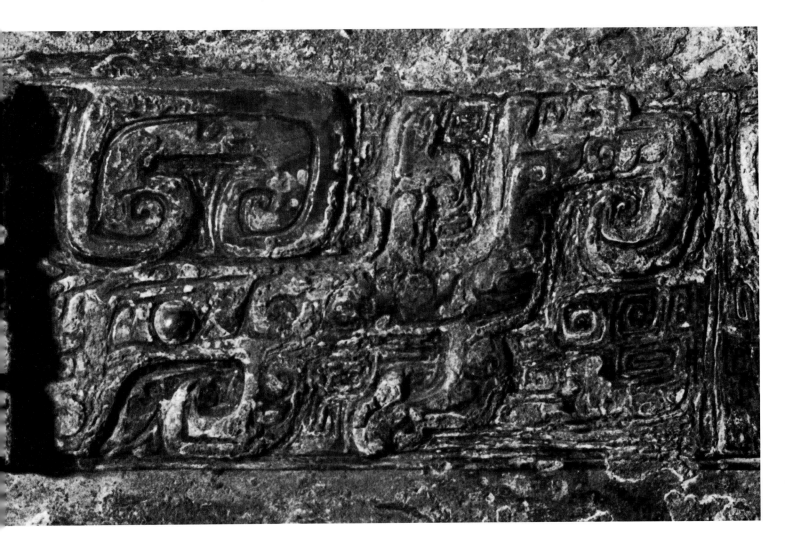

cision and delicacy. Further clarification was achieved by a regular subdivision of the vessel's surface, horizontally by the divisions between friezes and vertically by massive flanges whose weight is carefully measured to accord with the plasticity of the relief ornament; the horizontal divisions receive an additional accent from the breaks in the flanges. The self-contained motifs occupying each separate frieze unit stress yet again the subdivision of the surface; their scale is large enough to animate the shape without overpowering it. The separate contributions of shape, ornament, and flanges to the effect of the whole attain the interdependence and perfect balance that define a classic stage.

Along with the *you* no. 25, the *fang lei* belongs to a classic moment in the history of the bronze art, and the two vessels represent a level of artistic achievement never surpassed. It is no disparagement of their quality to reflect that the subdivision of the vessels by flanges and the almost architectural structures that result take their ultimate origin in the divisions of the section-mold assemblies that were used to cast the earliest bronze vessels of which we have any knowledge (no. 1).

Jades from the Tomb of Fu Hao

The jades found in Fu Hao's tomb include an extraordi-nary array of such familiar Shang forms as axes, disks, and *ge* blades. (No. 10, from Panlongcheng, is an earlier example of a *ge*.) Much more unexpected are the numerous small human and animal sculptures, several of which are shown in the exhibition. By comparison with the extreme refinement characteristic of nonsculptural jades —even those from much earlier times (nos. 2, 3, 10)—the small figures from Fu Hao's tomb must appear curiously awkward and primitive. This is due partly to the difficulty of working so refractory a material as jade; even the simplest of shapes required a formidable amount of sawing and grinding. The tiny elephant no. 40 surely owes some of its charm to the ingenious economy with which the jade worker removed a minimum of material from the original block, evoking his subject with the fewest possible saw cuts and drill holes. The simple rectangular block that was the craftsman's starting point is still to be detected in the stiffly frontal pose and angular shape of the kneeling human figure no. 39; it is even more apparent in the dragon with a coiled tail (no. 38) and the small elephant.

But other factors beyond mere technique may enter into this rigid symmetry, as the elephant-shaped bronze vessel no. 24 serves to suggest; though made in an entirely different material and technique, its simple pose is the same as that of the jade elephant. Admittedly the bronze caster's technique, like that of the jade worker, favors a symmetrical shape, though for different reasons. It is likely, too, that the Shang artist's taste preferred symmetry above the accidental character of any more transient pose. But, beyond these considerations, there is a difficulty of execution that has less to do with the constraints of any particular technique than with the problem of observing and imitating the irregularities of nature. The sculptor's mastery of complex poses is the achievement of later times, represented in this exhibition by the Eastern Zhou rhinoceros no. 93.

The sculptural naiveté of the jade figures should not cause us to overlook the accomplished execution of the incised designs that crowd their surfaces. The technique required to produce flowing linear patterns in reserve, by grinding away the adjacent areas, is exacting in the extreme, but ornamental patterns undoubtedly had a firmer hold on the Shang artist's imagination than the problems of imitating nature, and no effort was spared in their execution. The patterns applied to objects like the dragon and the elephant are adapted to the given form with considerable subtlety and where necessary can serve to supply an eye or define a shoulder or the corner of a jaw. But on the whole their function is nonrepresentational; it is surface embellishment for its own sake, inspired by a sort of *horror vacui*.

The ornamental patterns that make up the decorative vocabulary of the Shang carver appear on sculptural figures and flat plaques alike. The remaining jades from the tomb, nos. 34–37, are for all practical purposes twodimensional. Like most archaic jades, they are worked from slabs rather than blocks of material, and they escape the awkwardness that usually attends the Shang lapidary's essays in three dimensions. The small eagle with outspread wings, no. 34, covered with patterns little different from those seen on the jade figures nos. 38–40, is typical of the Shang artist's overriding concern with flat shapes and surface ornament. The jagged silhouette and the uniform mesh of the surface patterns make only the vaguest reference to wings and plumes, and what representational content they do have is more implied by context than inherent in the patterns themselves. In the case of the plaque no. 36, the surface patterns of necessity must be a trifle more explicit in defining the shapes of a bird and a dragon, for the silhouette of the object is oddly mysterious. The shape is explained once we notice that the piece is recut from a fragment of a broken *ge* blade. Jade was too costly for the smallest piece to be wasted, and the recutting of broken pieces was a regular practice.

By comparison with such typical Shang products as these two, the remaining pair of jades from Fu Hao's tomb stands apart, characterized by a certain crude eccentricity that belongs as much to conception as to execution. The heraldically posed nude human figure no. 37, with its rounded, faintly modeled surfaces, seems not quite reconciled to two dimensions, and its surface patterns are only a clumsy version of those seen on the small eagle plaque. The crescent-shaped bird, no. 35, is still more exceptional in its disquietingly mannered shape and highly polished unadorned surfaces; here the only

markings on the surface, a few parallel hooked lines, are introduced specifically for the purpose of defining the bird's wing. Both of these jades are distinctly foreign to Shang taste, and they are likely to be products of peripheral cultures rather than of the Shang court. The plumed bird, which would be difficult to place or date at all if its provenance were unknown, resembles another found several decades ago in southern Hubei. We are reminded that Fu Hao led campaigns against enemies to the west, northwest, east, and south. The spoils of war may well have included these jades.

Résumé of the Five Styles of Shang Bronze Ornament

Style I (nos. 4, 11).
Thread relief; technically the simplest of relief modes, since it is produced by incising lines directly in the clay of the mold surface. The designs, which quite early include recognizable *taotie* patterns, appear in thin raised lines on a plain background.

Style II (nos. 5–7).
Wider, ribbonlike areas now form the relief pattern: the lines raised above the surface of the vessel are broad, flat, and carefully shaped, having acquired an almost calligraphic modulation. The patterns are still carved in the mold. Style II is the most common relief mode in the Zhengzhou phase (see chap. 2).

Style III (nos. 12–16).
Essentially an elaboration of Style II, with a profusion of fine detail and some new pattern elements (e.g., repeated quill-like formations). Moldmaking technology appears to have been altered at this stage by the introduction of the decorated model: the mold is formed by packing clay around a model of the object that is to be cast, and all or part of the decoration is executed first on the model and then transferred to the mold, instead of being executed on the mold directly. Early Style III designs seem to represent the latest stage of bronze casting at sites of the Zhengzhou phase (nos. 8, 9).

Style IV (no. 20).
A major innovation, and one that makes an abrupt break with the earlier trend toward ever more complex designs. Style IV is characterized by the establishment of an image-ground distinction, which clarifies the intricate patterns developed in Style III. The *taotie* now stands out with new force and vividness. It and the other motifs are set against a very fine spiral background pattern (*leiwen*) that can be shown to derive from reduced and regularized Style III quills and flourishes (Loehr, 1968, p. 50). Tentative versions of Style IV are in evidence already among the bronzes, predominantly Style III, from the Taixicun, Gaocheng, site in Hebei Province (*Wenwu* 1979/6, p. 39, figs. 6:3, 7); these may predate the Anyang period.

Style V (nos. 24, 25, 27–33).
The image-ground distinction of Style IV is maintained and intensified by raising the motifs in high relief against the *leiwen* spiral background.

CHAPTER 4: CATALOGUE ENTRIES

28 Si Mu Xin *fang ding*

Anyang period (ca. 1300–ca. 1030 B.C.)
Excavated 1976 from Tomb No. 5, Anyang, Henan Province
Height 79.6 cm. (31⅜ in.); length and width at mouth 64 x 47.6
    cm. (25¼ x 18¾ in.); weight 117.5 kg. (258 lb. 8 oz.)
Institute of Archaeology, Beijing

This massive *fang ding* is one of a pair; the second vessel is not
inscribed but otherwise identical. In their decoration, royal size,
and even in the fact of being cast as a pair, the vessels from Fu Hao's
tomb inevitably recall the much earlier *fang ding* no. 11, from
Zhengzhou. The decoration, now executed in high relief, is set out
according to the scheme of the Zhengzhou vessel, with *taotie*
pattern units folded over the corners of the vessel as well as at the
centers of the decor friezes. The new plasticity of the ornament is
complemented by heavy vertical flanges and a molded rim on
which stand two solid vertical handles. Like most of the bronzes
from Fu Hao's tomb, the *fang ding* is heavily corroded; the surface
is rough, with a variegated green and reddish brown coloring. The
legs are hollow and open to the interior of the vessel, and appear to
have been cast integrally with it.

    The *taotie* in the decorated frieze is a typical Anyang version of
the motif (Fig. 48). To each side of the face is attached a horizontal
body with a clawed foot and a curving upturned tail. The peculiar
anatomy of this double-bodied creature, which at an earlier stage
was only vague and implicit (cf. no. 11), is now inescapable in the
clear and unambiguous high-relief rendering of Style V.

    The inscription on the inside wall of the *ding* is typical of the
finely written monograms cast in the Fu Hao bronzes (see Fig. 49).
Inscriptions on Shang bronzes are executed in a fancy script quite
distinct from the ordinary writing of the time, more pictorial and
more freely composed and varied (cf. the different versions of the
name Fu Hao inscribed on nos. 29, 31–33). The firm, wiry line must
have been shaped by the moldmaking process, for the inscriptions
look very much as though written in soft clay with a stylus. The
right side of the emblem seen here shows the figure of a kneeling
woman in profile; this is the character *mu* ("mother"). On the left
side are the characters *si* and *xin* (top and bottom respectively). The
meaning of *si* in this context is not settled, but the word *xin* makes
the combination a posthumous title. The inscription thus apparently refers to Fu Hao not by her personal name, used in life, but
by a posthumous name used in sacrifices by her descendants; and
the word "mother" implies that in this case she is addressed by a
son (or nephew, in Shang practice). Hence the vessel was cast for
her funeral by her son or sons. She would not have been addressed
in this way by the king, her husband, who presumably supplied
many of the other bronzes in the tomb.

    The only bronze of Anyang times still larger than this *fang ding*
is the monumental Si Mu Mou *fang ding*, which has not only the
same decorative scheme as the Fu Hao vessel, but also an inscription of precisely the same form referring to a different empress
(*Wenwu Jinghua* 3, 1964, pp. 39–40; *Zhongguo Kaogu Xuebao* 7,
1954; *Wenwu* 1959/12, pp. 27–29; *Kaogu* 1977/1, pp. 14, 21). In this
case the identity of the empress is not certain; there are two
possibilities, according to which the Si Mu Mou *fang ding* would
date either two or four generations later than Fu Hao's time.
Alternatively it has been suggested, somewhat less plausibly, that
the empress in question was another of Wu Ding's consorts, and
this would make the Si Mu Mou *fang ding* more nearly contemporary with the Fu Hao pair.

PUBLISHED: *Kaogu Xuebao* 1977/2, pl. 18 following p. 98; *China
    Pictorial* 1978/1, p. 25. For the second vessel of the pair, see
    Kaogu Xuebao 1977/2, pl. 2:1 following p. 98; *Kaogu* 1977/3,
    pl. 8:4.

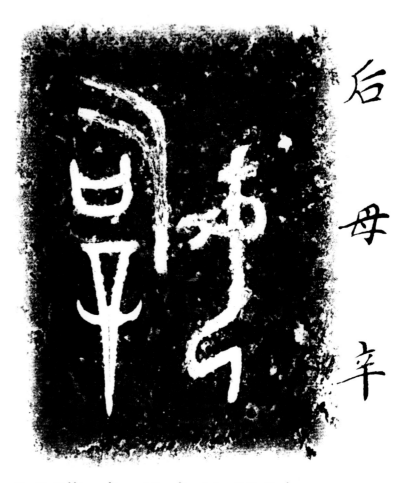

Fig. 49   Rubbing and transcription of inscription, Si Mu Xin *fang
ding* no. 28. Photograph courtesy of Cultural Relics
Bureau, Beijing

29 Bird-shaped *zun*

Anyang period (ca. 1300–ca. 1030 B.C.)
Excavated 1976 from Tomb No. 5, Anyang, Henan Province
Height 45.9 cm. (18⅛ in.); weight 16.7 kg. (36 lb. 12 oz.)
Institute of Archaeology, Beijing

One of an identical pair, this vessel takes the shape of a parrotlike
bird standing on two legs and propped up by its tail. The posture of
the bird, leaning backward slightly and staring almost directly
upward, conveys a stolid energy much enhanced by the bristling
silhouette and vigorously plastic surface ornament. The smoothly
convex face of the bird is framed by a pair of ears projecting on the
sides, a blocky, inward-curving bill in front, and to the rear a pair of
tall, horn-shaped crests. The back half of the domed head is a
removable lid; perched on it are a smaller bird with the same
freestanding crests and a tiny bottle-horned dragon with a curled
tail. Just below this lid, on the vessel proper, is a handle, apparently cast on. Between the handle and the bird's descending tail
feathers appears one of the most unexpected and playful features of
the *zun*, a small owl, reduced to a wide-eyed facial mask joined
directly to stumpy wings with clawed legs. The owl motif appears
on other bronzes from Fu Hao's tomb (no. 30; *Kaogu Xuebao*
1977/2, pl. 19:1 following p. 98), as well as in sculptural form in the
marble figure of an owl excavated from HPKM 1001, an Anyang
royal tomb of about the same period (Umehara, 1964, pl. 135).

    The finer details of the surface ornament are partly obscured
by rough green corrosion, but the profuse decoration makes its
effect little impaired. The *taotie*, the quintessential Shang motif, is
not prominent but nevertheless occurs four times in four different
versions. Under the handle it is seen with a very broad nose and
large, recumbent S-shaped horns extending right and left just
below the rim of the vessel; in this instance the body of the *taotie* is
abbreviated to the merest detail, much smaller than the horns. A

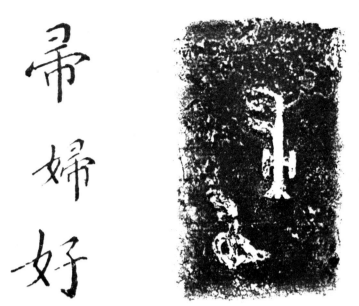

Fig. 50 Rubbing and transcription of inscription, bird-shaped *zun* no. 29. Photograph courtesy of Cultural Relics Bureau, Beijing

plumage, so the upper part is turned into a wing that overlaps the parallel curves of a set of drooping tail plumes. In the same way, the spiral that forms the shoulder of the vessel and marks the front end of the bird's wing is turned into a coiled snake, acquiring in the process an emphatic plasticity. This uninhibited delight in reinterpreting one shape as another—thoroughly characteristic of the Shang artist's flexible imagination—is illustrated once more in the strange motif on the neck of the vessel, to either side of the beak. Toward the front this motif is a bird, shown in profile with beak, crest, and a clawed foot reaching forward from its breast; but toward the rear, the continuation of the bird's body turns into a downward-facing dragon with gaping jaws, a large horn or crest, and a clawed foot of its own.

The underside of the *zun* is undecorated. The hooflike feet of the bird depict grasping claws in relief against an undecorated metal surface. The inscription, consisting of the name Fu Hao, appears on the inside wall of the vessel, just behind the handle (see Fig. 50). The character *hao* is largely obscured by corrosion.

PUBLISHED: *Kaogu* 1977/3, pl. 9:2; *Kaogu Xuebao* 1977/2, pls. 2:2, 19:3 following p. 98; Hong Kong, 1978, no. 17. *China Pictorial* 1978/1, p. 24, illustrates the pair.

second *taotie* covers the surface of the removable lid, this one showing the face broken into several pieces—jaws, eyes, ears, recumbent C-shaped horns, and vestigial body—just as on the *hu* and *jia* from the same tomb (nos. 31, 33). The third *taotie*, filling the breast of the bird, is similarly fragmented, but slightly more unusual in detail; its horns are upturned C-shapes and its jaw is a long descending V. Lastly, the domical face of the bird itself, shorn of its beak and ears, is a thoroughly typical Style IV *taotie* face. The freestanding crests belonging to this face take precisely the form of the *taotie* horns seen in the surface ornament of another bronze from Fu Hao's tomb (*Kaogu Xuebao* 1977/2, pl. 19:1 following p.98).

These crests represent particularly well the element of play in Shang ornament; they are in the form of a many-layered visual pun. The C-shaped horns of the *taotie* suggested to the artist the shape of a dragon, and the dragon duly appears, his head shown in profile with a bottle-shaped horn; but the shape also suits a bird's

30 Si Mu Xin *guang*

Anyang period (ca. 1300–ca. 1030 B.C.)
Excavated 1976 from Tomb No. 5, Anyang, Henan Province
Height 36 cm. (14⅛ in.); length 46.5 cm. (18¼ in.); weight 8.5 kg. (18 lb. 11 oz.)
Institute of Archaeology, Beijing

This ungainly animal is actually a composite: its hind legs, encased in feathers, face backward and belong to an owl whose wings are depicted above on the body of the vessel. The owl's head, however, which ordinarily would appear on the lid, is missing altogether. The full length of the lid is instead occupied by the coiled body of a dragon, whose horned head rises in high relief just behind the

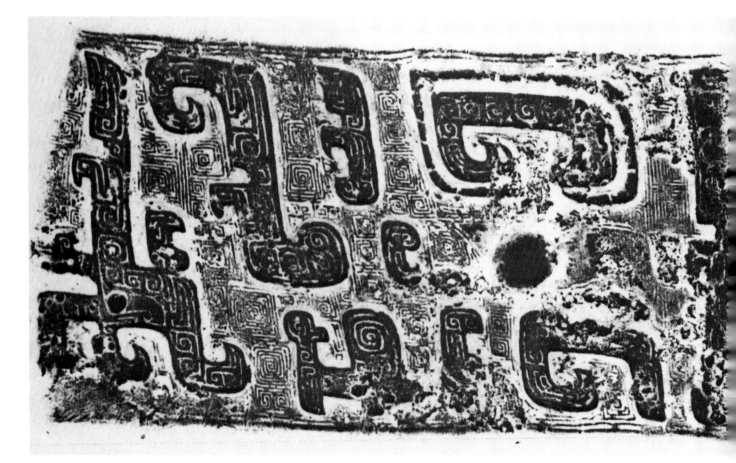

184 Fig. 52 Rubbing of decor frieze, Fu Hao *hu* no. 31. Photograph courtesy of Cultural Relics Bureau, Beijing

upraised horns at the front end. A flange runs along the spine of the dragon; smaller dragons appear on either side of it. Much of the decoration of the vessel is flush with the *leiwen* background, but dragons on the lid and on the forequarters, as well as the owl's wings, are all executed in high relief. The extraordinary treatment of the animal's eyes does not reproduce the familiar type form borrowed from the *taotie* (cf. the eyes of the rams on the *zun* no. 20), but depicts the eyelids much more naturalistically. The nostrils, indicated as sunken crescents, resemble more closely those of the rams on the *zun*. A small hole in the chin serves no obvious purpose. The handle of the vessel is surmounted by a small head with a plump nose and inward-spiraling horns, rather resembling a human face with a headdress. The inscription Si Mu Xin (see entry no. 28) appears in both the lid and body of the vessel (see Fig. 51). Crusty green corrosion obscures much of the decoration; several large breaks have been repaired.

Guang vessels on four legs are very rare; ordinarily the *guang* rests on an oval foot rim (cf. the rectangular *guang* no. 45). A pair of four-legged *guang* later than the present one, in the Freer Gallery of Art, Washington, D.C., and the Fujita collection, Osaka, may be of southern origin (Pope, 1967, no. 45; Mizuno, 1959, pl. 10).

PUBLISHED: *Kaogu Xuebao* 1977/2, pl. 8:1 following p. 98; Hong Kong, 1978, no. 18.

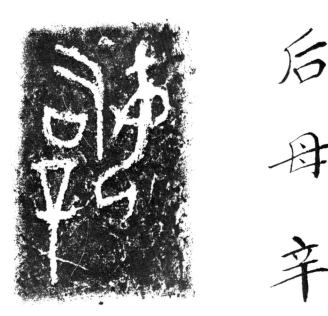

Fig. 51   Rubbing and transcription of inscription, Si Mu Xin *guang* no. 30. Photograph courtesy of Cultural Relics Bureau, Beijing

31   Fu Hao *hu*

Anyang period (ca. 1300–ca. 1030 B.C.)
Excavated 1976 from Tomb No. 5, Anyang, Henan Province
Height 51.5 cm. (20¼ in.); weight 16.8 kg. (37 lb.)
Institute of Archaeology, Beijing

This large vase, oval in section, is decorated in six superposed registers; the domed lid brings another *taotie* into view and might properly be counted as a seventh. The horizontal divisions between the registers are stressed by breaks in the flanges—a refinement missing from many of the Fu Hao bronzes; in one register vertical lugs replace the lateral flanges. The flattened body of the vessel serves to make the entire width of each frieze visible from a single frontal vantage point. The *taotie* arrayed in these friezes are not plastic units, but instead are composed of separate parts individually raised in high relief (Fig. 52). This rendering is similar to that on the square *jia* no. 33; but to the features represented there—eyes, ears, nose, C-horn, jaws, and clawed foreleg—are added further elements standing for the bodies of the *taotie*, while its eyelids are omitted. The raised parts are embellished with intaglio lines slightly less dense than the background *leiwen* spirals. Unfortunately, the decoration is much obscured by dull green and gray corrosion. The *hu* is reassembled from fragments.

The name Fu Hao is cast inside on the bottom of the vessel. The inscription is not repeated in the lid. This vessel is no. 863 of the excavation report (*Kaogu Xuebao* 1977/2, p. 68); a matching vessel, no. 795, is uninscribed (pl. 6:1 following p. 98).

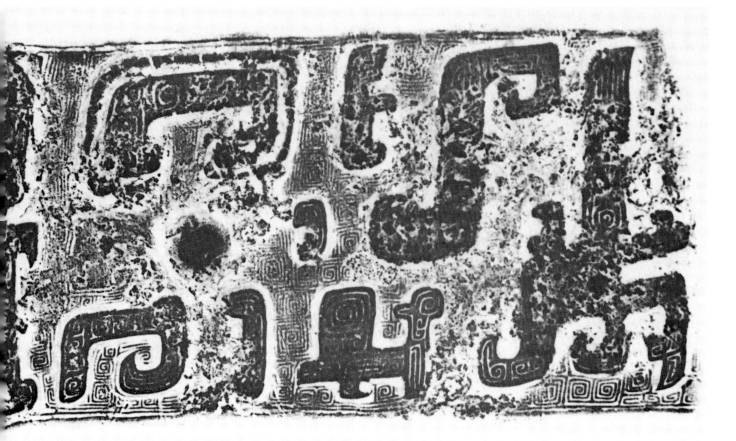

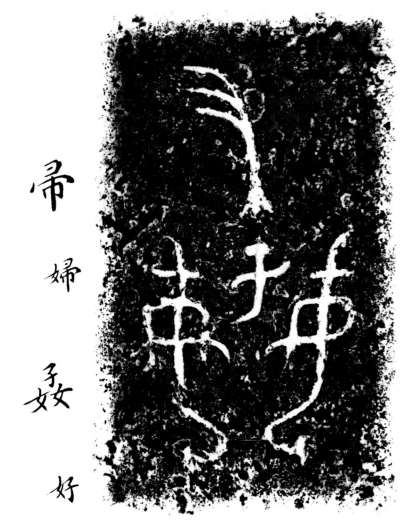

32 Fu Hao *fang ding*

Anyang period (ca. 1300–ca. 1030 B.C.)
Excavated 1976 from Tomb No. 5, Anyang, Henan Province
Height 42.4 cm. (16¾ in.); length and width at mouth 33.3 x 25.1
  cm. (13⅛ x 9⅞ in.); weight 17 kg. (37 lb. 6 oz.)
Institute of Archaeology, Beijing

This graceful and finely proportioned rectangular *ding* vessel is supported by flattish legs in the form of dragons. It is the first example known of a rectangular analogue to the familiar round-bodied *ding* with flat tripod legs (e.g., no. 17) and one of the most satisfying designs among the bronzes from Fu Hao's tomb. The four sides of the vessel are decorated with large *taotie* faces flanked by downward-facing dragons. The motifs are boldly executed in high relief against a background of large, loosely drawn *leiwen* spirals, in draftsmanship very much akin to the *leiwen* on nos. 28–30 from the same tomb. A pair of confronted dragons appears in sunken line on the outer side of each handle. The flanges are heavy and deeply notched, together with the cornicelike overhanging rim contributing an effect of architectural mass and stability.

Inside, on the bottom, the *ding* is inscribed with the name Fu Hao (see Fig. 53). Seam lines following the inner edges of the legs apparently continue along diagonals toward the center of the bottom. The patination is a crusty dark green.

PUBLISHED: *Kaogu Xuebao* 1977/2, pl. 19:2 following p. 98; Hong
  Kong, 1978, no. 16.

Fig. 53 Rubbing and transcription of inscription, Fu Hao *fang ding* no. 32. Photograph courtesy of Cultural Relics Bureau, Beijing

33 Fu Hao *fang jia*

Anyang period (ca. 1300–ca. 1030 B.C.)
Excavated 1976 from Tomb No. 5, Anyang, Henan Province
Height 66.8 cm. (26¼ in.); weight 19.05 kg. (41 lb. 15 oz.)
Institute of Archaeology, Beijing

This square version of the *jia* shape draws on a vocabulary of forms proper to architecture to achieve a convincing monumentality. The boxlike bottom of the vessel proper, decorated with *taotie* faces, is nearly dwarfed by the extraordinarily massive legs and the overhanging flare of the upper section. The architectural air of the whole is accentuated by the massive flanges, applied like moldings to stress vertical lines, and by the firmly molded rim, beyond which the flanges project in tiny points. Flanges are added even to the caps of the posts, which resemble tiny roofs. A three-dimensional animal head at the upper end of the handle has large freestanding horns; the head appears to be devouring a bird, of which only the beak is visible. More explicit renderings of this theme are common at a later stage, on the handles of both Shang and Western Zhou bronzes (cf. nos. 41, 45, 49).

The legs appear solid; presumably cores are sealed inside. The handle and post caps, the latter probably also cored, may have been cast on in separate pours. The name Fu Hao is inscribed inside the vessel, on the bottom (see Fig. 54). The rough corrosion is in various shades of dark green, brown, and blue.

PUBLISHED: *Kaogu Xuebao* 1977/2, pl. 8:3 following p. 98.

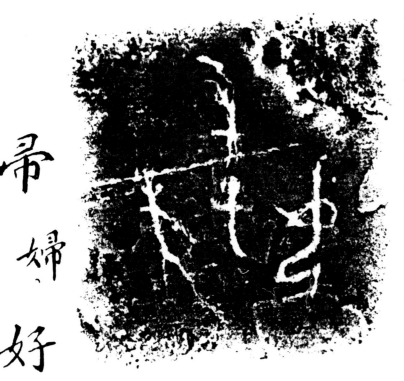

Fig. 54 Rubbing and transcription of inscription, Fu Hao *fang jia* no. 33. Photograph courtesy of Cultural Relics Bureau, Beijing

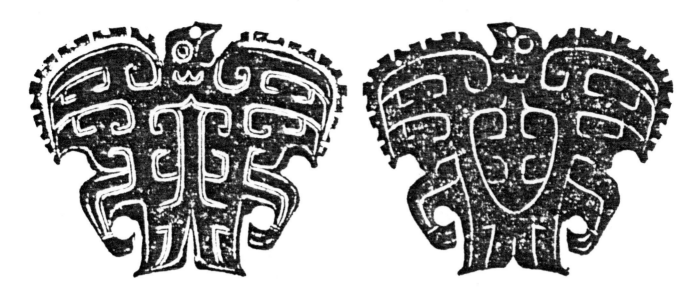

Fig. 55 Rubbing of decor on both sides of jade pendant in the shape of
a hawk no. 34. After *Kaogu* 1977/3, pl. 153, fig. 3:1

34   Jade pendant in the shape of a hawk

Anyang period (ca. 1300–ca. 1030 B.C.)
Excavated 1976 from Tomb No. 5, Anyang, Henan Province
Height 6.2 cm. (2⅜ in.); weight 34 g. (1⅕ oz.)
Institute of Archaeology, Beijing

This pendant, in the form of a hawk with outspread wings, is
perforated for suspension with a small hole through the bird's beak,
drilled from both sides (i.e., biconical). Only the head, its eye
represented by two concentric circles, is seen in profile. The
forward edges of the wings are notched. The surface is covered with
scrollwork patterns executed by incising lines side by side in pairs;
each line of a pair is beveled on the edge away from the other line,
so that the thin strip of material between the two seems to stand in
relief above the surface. On the reverse side the pendant is carved
with similar patterns more carelessly incised in single lines (see
Fig. 55). The translucent stone is a fairly uniform dark green.

PUBLISHED: *Kaogu Xuebao* 1977/2, pl. 33:5 following p. 98.

35   Jade pendant in the shape of a plumed bird

Anyang period (ca. 1300–ca. 1030 B.C.)
Excavated 1976 from Tomb No. 5, Anyang, Henan Province
Length 13.6 cm. (5⅜ in.); thickness 0.7 cm. (¼ in.); weight
    87 g. (3 oz.)
Institute of Archaeology, Beijing

The pale yellow green of this jade verges on white near the top and
is speckled with brown near the bottom. The surface is polished
smooth on both edges and faces, and left almost unembellished;
besides a series of hooked lines defining the wing, there are only a
few faint indications of the bird's eye and the lower edge and hinge
of its jaw. In all cases these are raised lines, formed by grinding
away the surrounding stone. The curved outline of the bird, with
its dripping edges and swollen plumage, is quite extraordinary; the
weight of the tail allows the pendant to be suspended symmetrically from a small perforated nub set midway down the outer
edge of the arc.

The openwork crest on the bird's head, which is only about
half the thickness of the jade elsewhere, calls to mind a few bronzes
likely to be from the south that are decorated with crested birds. A
jade bird very similar to the present one, bent into a circle so that
head and tail touch, was unearthed in Hubei Province, at Shijiahe,
Tianmen (*Kaogu Tongxun* 1956/3, p. 20, fig. 4). It thus seems quite
possible that the bird from Fu Hao's tomb, which in style has
nothing in common with other jades from the tomb, was made in
South China. A third pendant evidently related to these two, now
in the Ernest Erickson collection, New York, depicts a crested bird
whose clawed foot rests on a human head (Salmony, 1963, pl. 11:6).

PUBLISHED: *Kaogu Xuebao* 1977/2, pl. 31:2 following p. 98.

36   Jade plaque

Anyang period (ca. 1300–ca. 1030 B.C.)
Excavated 1976 from Tomb No. 5, Anyang, Henan Province
Length 11.3 cm. (4½ in.); weight 45 g. (1½ oz.)
Institute of Archaeology, Beijing

The outline of this curious plaque suggests that it was recut from a
fragment of a *ge* blade; and in fact the stone is thinnest near the
edges and thickest at the remnant of a median crest near the center.
The upper half of the piece takes the form of a dragon with a paw
extended below its gaping mouth and a large tail arched above it.
Lower down is a small bird, also seen in profile, although two
appendages on its head evidently represent horns seen from the
front. The clawed foot of the bird, drawn in the surface of the jade,
clutches the lowermost segment of the plaque, an irregular piece
that perhaps owes its shape to a break in the stone. Incised double
lines, forming designs like those seen on the hawk no. 34, decorate
the bird's wing and the bottom section, while the body of the
dragon is patterned with diamonds and chevrons. The dragon's
body is also illogically supplied with a large eye set upside down
behind the paw; this favorite Shang design element recurs on the
arms of the kneeling human figure no. 39. The stone is partly
altered and ranges in color from a soft yellow to chocolate brown.
The design is the same on both sides.

PUBLISHED: *Kaogu Xuebao* 1977/2, pl. 33:1 following p. 98.

Fig. 56 Rubbing of both sides of jade plaque in the form of a standing human figure no. 37. Photograph courtesy of Cultural Relics Bureau, Beijing

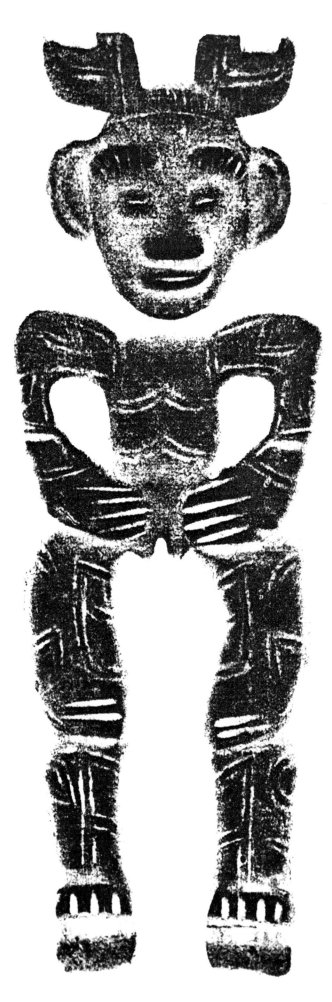

37 Jade plaque in the form of a standing human figure

Anyang period (ca. 1300–ca. 1030 B.C.)
Excavated 1976 from Tomb No. 5, Anyang, Henan Province
Height 12.5 cm. (4⅞ in.); thickness 0.9 cm. (⅜ in.); weight 102 g.
  (3½ oz.)
Institute of Archaeology, Beijing

This fairly thick plaque shows on both sides a human figure symmetrically posed, with two winglike crests on the head and small tabs projecting below the feet as though for insertion into a support of some kind. The stone is a pale translucent gray, partly altered at the tip of one crest and on one ear and shoulder; the surface is not highly polished. Incised lines mark the fingers and toes of the figure, and incised double lines decorate the body elsewhere. The features of the face are not incised, however, but crudely modeled—a wide mouth, flat nose, eyes, and bushy eyebrows. The faces on the two sides differ slightly, and the position of the hands on the hips is also not the same; one side is female, and it is possible that the other is meant to be male (see Fig. 56).

A more crudely shaped but more finely polished figure in the same pose, unambiguously female, is in the Winthrop Collection of the Fogg Art Museum, Cambridge, Massachusetts (Loehr, 1975, no. 118). The posture of the hands on the hips, the prominent eyebrows, the crest on the head, and the suggestion of a tab below the feet all seem to relate the Winthrop piece to the present figure.

PUBLISHED: *Kaogu* 1977/3, pl. 7:4; *Kaogu Xuebao* 1977/2, pl. 27:1 following p. 98.

38 Jade dragon

Anyang period (ca. 1300–ca. 1030 B.C.)
Excavated 1976 from Tomb No. 5, Anyang, Henan Province
Length 8.1 cm. (3¼ in.); height 5.5 cm. (2⅛ in.); weight 228 g.
  (8 oz.)
Institute of Archaeology, Beijing

This compact figurine consists of a massive, blocky head and a small body curled up asymmetrically on the right side; the dragon, which has no hind legs, rests on two forepaws and its tail. On the right side the jade shows dark green; the left side is discolored brown. The eyes of the dragon are executed in a fashion familiar from bronze designs, with the pupil in relief and the outline of the canthus elegantly incised around it. The teeth that line the gaping jaws were formed by repeated drillings, giving a scalloped row of incisors and star-shaped openings in the sides of the mouth. The last coil of the tail is formed by another drill hole, and a biconical suspension hole is drilled in the chin. Running down the dragon's spine is a notched flange resembling the front edge of the wing of the jade hawk no. 34. On either side of the flange the body is covered with nested diamonds in incised double line.

All the essential features of this jade dragon are repeated on the handle of the *hu* no. 21—the gaping jaws, bottle-shaped horns, and nested diamonds patterning the full length of the handle. In a few *you* vessels from the same period, such handles include even the flange seen here running along the dragon's spine.

PUBLISHED: *Kaogu* 1977/3, pl. 6:3; *Kaogu Xuebao* 1977/2, pl. 28:1 following p. 98.

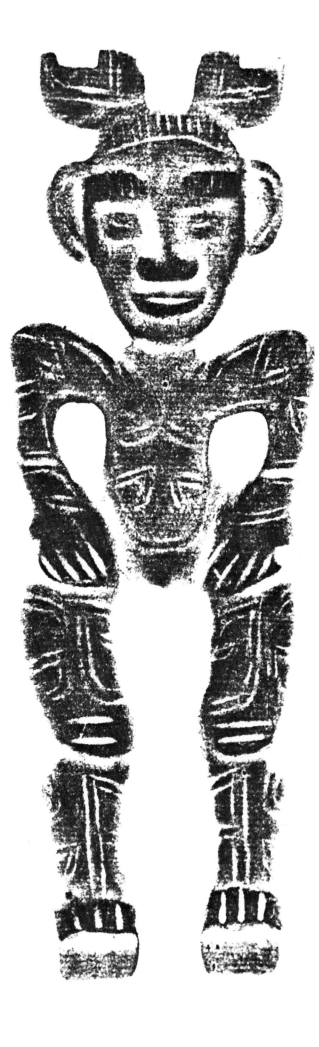

39 Jade figurine

Anyang period (ca. 1300–ca. 1030 B.C.)
Excavated 1976 from Tomb No. 5, Anyang, Henan Province
Height 6.9 cm. (2¾ in.); weight 136 g. (4¾ oz.)
Institute of Archaeology, Beijing

This small figure kneels in the formal seated posture current in China before the introduction of the chair and transmitted from China to Korea and Japan. Several other jade figures from Fu Hao's tomb are seated in the same posture. The person depicted here wears a robe whose lapels cross at the waist under a sash patterned with nested triangles. Drill holes separate the arms and waist. On each arm, just below the shoulder, a single eye is incised. A small snake, its body filled with large scales, decorates the right thigh; on the left thigh, a longer snake extends its body out onto a large flat hooked element that projects behind the left side of the figure, and the snake's tail curls onto the upper hook. The surface patterns yield no clue as to the meaning of this hooked projection. Perhaps it is a decorative elaboration of the end of the sash; but the pattern of the sash as it crosses the back of the figure does not continue onto the rear of the projecting piece, which instead contains only simple incised patterns of single lines. Apart from the eyes on the arms and the two snakes on the thighs, the surface patterns are without any representational content; they consist only of the same incised double-line scrollwork seen on nos. 34, 36, and 40. The stone is partly altered, varying shades of green being mixed with patches of brown. Slight reddish encrustations, seen also on no. 38, may be cinnabar or ocher.

The face of the figure is flat with a jutting chin. The carver's resolute effort to model the features and to round off the transition from the front to the sides of the head was only partly successful; the attempt has left the face with a series of small facets rather than a smoothly modeled surface. The elaborate coiffure consists of a long curl marked with zigzags above the forehead, and a fringe on the sides and rear descending from a band tied round the head. Two interconnected drill holes in the top of the head form a loop for suspension; a third, centrally placed just behind the roll of the hairdo, might have held a plume or some such addition. A few other jade figures from Fu Hao's tomb, which appear by comparison more boyish, have simple, perfectly combed pudding-basin haircuts.

PUBLISHED: *Kaogu* 1977/3, pl. 7:1; *Kaogu Xuebao* 1977/2, pl. 26:3 following p. 98.

40 Jade figure of an elephant

Anyang period (ca. 1300–ca. 1030 B.C.)
Excavated 1976 from Tomb No. 5, Anyang, Henan Province
Length 6.5 cm. (2½ in.); height 3.3 cm. (1¼ in.); weight 78 g. (2¾ oz.)
Institute of Archaeology, Beijing

This small and charming elephant, of jade altered to a dark brown, is one of a pair from Fu Hao's tomb. The final curl of the elephant's trunk is formed by a perforation by which the figurine might have been suspended. The toenails and ears are incised with single lines, but the rest of the decoration is executed in the usual double-line technique. The patterns are purely conventional, and do not differ in any essential from those seen, for instance, on the hawk pendant no. 34. The four stumpy legs were formed by two broad cuts, one from side to side, the other front to back. The ears are set in relief, as is the short fat tail. A small four-pointed star is incised on top of the head.

PUBLISHED: *Kaogu* 1977/3, pl. 6:2; *Kaogu Xuebao* 1977/2, pl. 28:5 following p. 98.

5

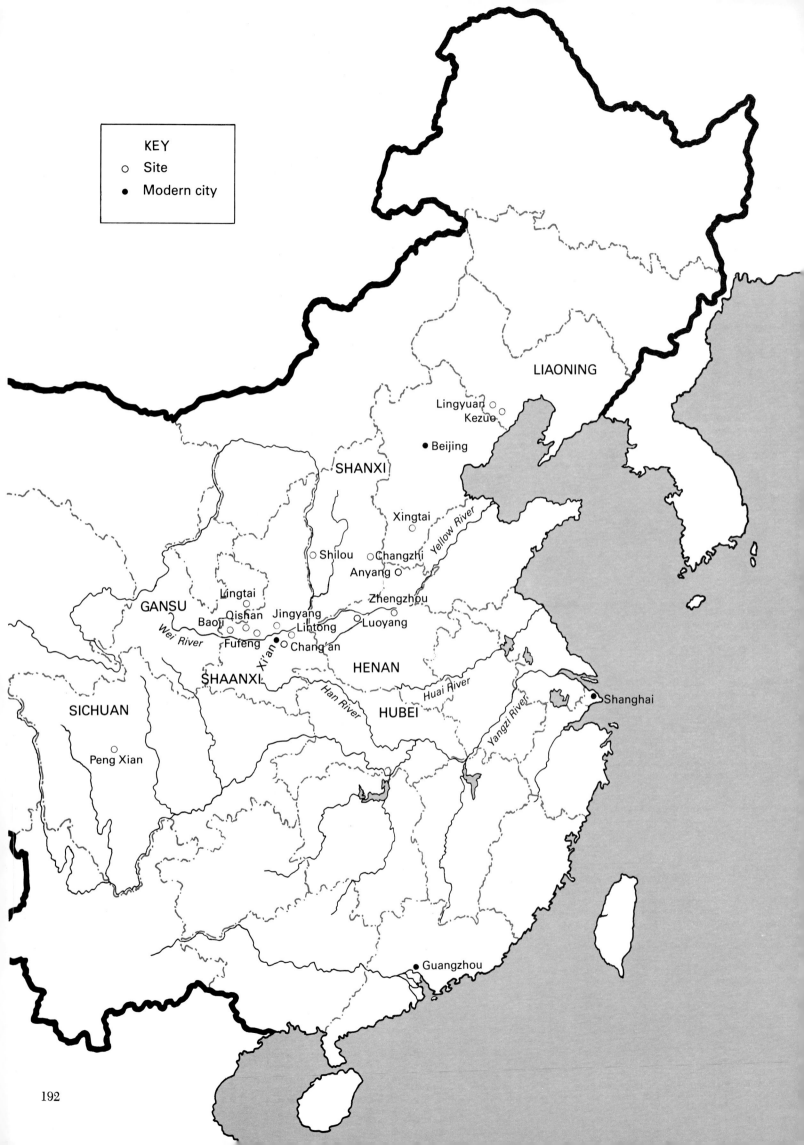

5 The Rise of the Western Zhou Dynasty

Robert W. Bagley

For most of the statelets neighboring on the Shang empire, vassals and enemies alike, our sources of information are limited. The archaeological evidence surveyed in chapter 3 may hint at their cultural attainments and idiosyncrasies. Allusions in the oracle inscriptions of the Shang court supply countless names, together with some clues to the geographic positions of the tribes or states named. As yet, however, there is scant basis for bringing these two sets of facts into correspondence and for associating archaeological finds with recorded names; and beyond what can be gleaned from these two sources, we know almost nothing of the peripheral statelets. Of their histories we have only a dim reflection in the oracle texts, and even that only on the occasions when their activities impinged on the Shang court.

The one exception in this otherwise indistinct historical picture is the Zhou people, who lived toward the end of the Shang dynasty in the Wei River valley of central Shaanxi Province. As far as contemporary documents go, their situation is little different from that of the other statelets; the only sources are archaeological finds and references in the oracle texts. Later historical writings, however, tell a great deal more about the Zhou people. Sometime in the latter half of the eleventh century B.C., the Zhou overthrew the Shang royal house, and in its place founded a dynasty that lasted, in name at least, for eight centuries. To archivists and historians of the Zhou period and of later times, the rise of the Zhou to power and their conquest of Shang were subjects of the most absorbing interest. As a result, while we lack contemporary texts transmitted from the period of the conquest, later writings preserve a wealth of traditions relating both to the early history of the dynasty proper and to the history of the Zhou people before their overthrow of Shang. The texts are often vague or corrupt, and at other times suspiciously full and tendentious in tone, and they contradict each other with a regularity that seems almost calculated. Nevertheless, used with a judicious blend of caution and daring, they provide the basis for a historical reconstruction that seems trustworthy at least in outline. Even if it had no other claim on our interest, this account of the Zhou rise to power would deserve attention as the only picture we have of a peripheral culture being drawn into the orbit of Shang civilization.

Shang culture had reached the Wei River valley in pre-Anyang times, as a recent find of early bronzes at Qishan demonstrates (*Wenwu* 1977/12, pp. 86–87), but

Map of China showing important archaeological sites of the early Western Zhou dynasty, 11th century to 10th century B.C.

193

this area was evidently not then occupied by the Zhou people. The Zhou moved to settle at Qishan only in the reign of the fourth-to-last Anyang king, apparently from somewhere to the north or northeast. In their earlier location they must already have come into conflict with the Shang ruler, for expeditions against a people called Zhou are mentioned several times in the oracle inscriptions of Wu Ding's reign. After his time, however, the Zhou cease to appear in the oracle records; perhaps they were driven temporarily out of range. They are next heard of, on the authority of later texts, on the occasion of their move to Qishan, where they settled and built a city. In so doing they drove from the area another tribe, the Quan Rong, who had been allies of Shang in its wars against Zhou. When the Shang ruler at this time enfeoffed the Zhou chieftain, giving him the rank of a duke, he may simply have been yielding to a situation he was powerless to control. The later histories preserve the names of all the Zhou rulers from this time onward (Table 2), and a few traditions or legends connected with each have also survived.

There are suggestions that it was only at the time of the move to Qishan that the Zhou gave up a nomadic or pastoral way of life. The historian Sima Qian (second century B.C.) says that Danfu—the enfeoffed Zhou duke —"renounced the customs of the barbarians"; while the *Book of Songs*, a collection of poems and folksongs, some of which go back to early Zhou times, describes the building of permanent dwellings and a walled city for the duke at Qishan. It is surely significant that the poem about the construction of Danfu's palace describes foundations made in the typical Shang rammed-earth technique. From this time onward the Zhou assimilation of Shang culture must have been rapid.

From this time, too, the Shang kings must have been increasingly uneasy about the power of their western neighbor. Later texts mention that Danfu's son Jili received lavish gifts from the Shang king and even took a Shang noble lady to wife; they also record that, on a subsequent visit to the Shang court, he was detained and died. The pattern of bribes alternating with force—or treachery—is familiar enough from the dealings of later dynasties with the barbarians.

The next Zhou ruler, Wen Wang, was an equally troublesome vassal, and at one point is supposed to have spent six years in captivity at the Shang court. The histories add that after his release he was reinstated as a vassal with the title Lord of the West (Xi Bo), bestowed on him by the last Shang king. Decisive confirmation of the traditional accounts, showing that Wen Wang was indeed the nominal vassal of the Shang court, has come from the recent discovery of a Zhou palace at Qishan. More than 15,000 oracle bones were found hoarded in the palace, showing that the Zhou rulers practiced divination on a scale hitherto known only from the Anyang court. A few of the bones are inscribed. One of the inscriptions records that Wen Wang offered sacrifice to the father of the reigning Shang king, an act that must surely be interpreted as feudal homage. Another inscription includes the title Earl of the Zhou (Zhou Fang Bo), which can only have been conferred by the Shang king, while still another mentions a visit of the Shang king to the court of his Zhou retainer.

Wen Wang's loyalty was, however, more than a little doubtful. By rights he was entitled to call himself an earl, but the oracle inscriptions from Qishan prove that he was called Wen Wang not only by posterity, but also in his own lifetime, and this use of the title *wang*, "king," amounts to open usurpation of the Shang king's prerogatives. In the light of subsequent events, Wen Wang's move eastward to found a new capital at Xi'an, on the borders of the Shang state, seems equally ominous. The Shang king must no doubt have felt it so.

Sometime thereafter, Wu Wang, the son of Wen Wang, or by some accounts Wen Wang himself, marched farther to the east and overran Shang vassal statelets in southern Shanxi, reaching the vicinity of modern Changzhi, 100 kilometers west of Anyang. The Shang king, his armies exhausted by campaigns at the opposite end of the realm, was unable to stem the Zhou advance. Leading a confederation of tribes from the west and southwest, Wu Wang captured the Shang capital in the twelfth year of his reign. Several texts agree that the battle for Anyang took place on the day *jia zi*, the first day of the sixty-day calendrical cycle; perhaps this seemed to Wu Wang an auspicious day on which to join battle.

Table 2

PREDYNASTIC AND EARLY DYNASTIC ZHOU ROYAL HOUSE

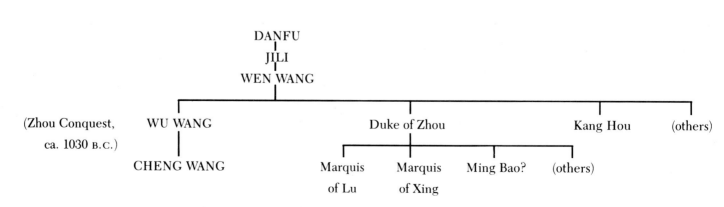

The Shang king died in the ruins of his palace. The central part of the Shang domain, the lands under the direct authority of the Shang court, must have been subdued fairly promptly by the Zhou conquerors. The extension of Zhou rule farther to the east and south was the object of intermittent wars in the reigns of Wu Wang's successors, by means of which the Zhou state conquered or came to terms with tribes and states on the periphery of the Shang domain. The process was slow, and, in the case of the Chu state in Hubei, at least, ended in failure when the fourth Zhou king disappeared with his armies into the south and was not heard from again.

Wu Wang continued to rule from the old Zhou territory in Shanxi after the conquest; it is likely that he felt insecure when too far removed from the neighborhood of his allies. His relatives and other retainers were rewarded for their services with grants of land in the conquered territories, and numerous fiefs were created. The heart of the former Shang state was parceled out to three of Wu Wang's brothers for supervision; their three districts apparently corresponded to administrative units that already existed in Shang times, but the locations of these units can be only vaguely specified. One lay in southern Henan Province; another centered on Zhengzhou. The third brother seems to have had charge of all the northern territories of Shang, probably comprising lands in both Shanxi and Hebei.

Having arranged for the conquered territory to be governed, and no doubt strongly garrisoned, by his three brothers, Wu Wang left a son of the dead Shang king in nominal authority, in order that he might continue the official sacrifices to the ancestral spirits of the Shang royal house. Whether this was only a stroke of policy or whether it represents a genuine awe felt by the Zhou rulers for the Shang deities may perhaps be debated. But there is no denying that Wu Wang and his successors regarded the maintenance of the Shang sacrifices as a matter of the utmost importance, and it seems possible that their own moral right to rule was considered to be at stake.

Wu Wang died seven years after the conquest. After his death, the greatest powers at court seem to have been a pair of dukes, the duke of Shao and the duke of Zhou, both of whom had been given titles and fiefs in reward for services rendered at the time of the conquest. The duke of Shao had been created marquis of Yan; the duke of Zhou, marquis of Lu. The duke of Zhou was a brother of Wu Wang. The duke of Shao was also a member of the Zhou royal clan, but his exact relationship to the royal family is not known.

Wu Wang was succeeded by his son, who reigned as Cheng Wang, but, since the son was a minor at the time of his accession, the duke of Zhou took over the government and ruled as regent. Others among the feudal retainers, his own brothers included, do not seem to have been confident of the duke's good intentions. Satisfied that he intended to usurp the throne, the three brothers of Wu Wang who had been entrusted with the Shang domain, and the Shang prince they were meant to supervise, felt at liberty to revolt. Their rebellion was promptly suppressed by the duke of Zhou, and several of the plotters, including the Shang heir, were executed. Before returning to court, the duke of Zhou was obliged to spend two years campaigning in the Huai River valley in the southeast, against barbarians who had joined forces with the rebellious princes.

The suppression of the revolt signaled a general reshuffling of fiefs. The Shang domain was divided into two portions. One was given as the principality of Song to another member of the Shang royal family, named Qi, who had been found to take charge of the Shang sacrifices. The Song state, located in eastern Henan, was ruled by his descendants and preserved the Shang rites until the state's extinction in 282 B.C. The remainder of the Shang domain was given to another brother of the duke of Zhou, Kang Hou; Wu Wang's supply of brothers seems to have been inexhaustible. Kang Hou became the marquis of Wei, founding a state that survived until the end of the fifth century B.C.

Among the other recipients of fiefs were the sons of the dukes of Zhou and Shao. On becoming regent at Cheng Wang's accession, the duke of Zhou had sent his eldest son to take charge of the fief of Lu, given him by Wu Wang, because he himself was too occupied at court; the first son thus became the marquis of Lu, while the second son remained at court and eventually inherited his father's ducal title. The duke of Shao, who had been made marquis of Yan, apparently followed the same course, remaining at court and sending his eldest son to the Yan fief.

After the regency had continued for seven years, Cheng Wang came of age, whereupon the duke of Zhou relinquished power and became at once the most reverent of subjects. The admiration expressed by historians for this virtuous deed borders on astonishment. The duke of Zhou became a paragon for the moralists of later centuries. Confucius, whose native state was the duke's fief of Lu, on one occasion lamented that his own virtue must have declined because it had been long since the duke of Zhou had last appeared in his dreams. The principal virtue with which Cheng Wang is credited in the histories is his continued reliance on the duke's advice, even after the regency. The duke of Zhou died late in Cheng Wang's reign; the duke of Shao continued to serve at the court of Cheng Wang's successor.

The histories record one other important event in the reign of Cheng Wang. This was the founding of a secondary capital on the site of present-day Luoyang, a step planned by Wu Wang immediately after the conquest. Shortly after the Shang rebellion, Cheng Wang sent the dukes of Zhou and Shao to inspect the proposed site. In either his fifth or seventh year, according to different accounts, the new capital was built, and a son of the duke of Zhou was installed as governor. The city was called Cheng Zhou, a name probably to be understood as "Victorious Zhou."

With its more central location, Cheng Zhou no doubt provided for more effective administration of the empire. Nevertheless, the Zhou rulers continued to reside in their old homeland, at a capital they called Zong

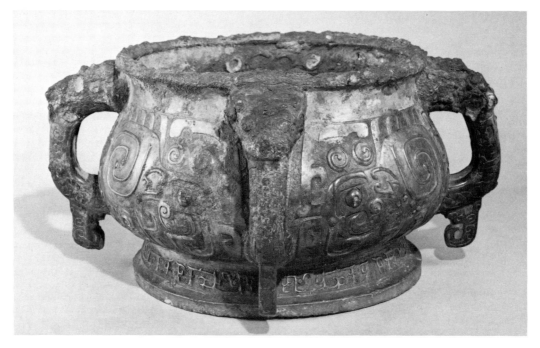

Fig. 57 Xing Hou *gui* from Luoyang, Henan Province. The British Museum, London

Zhou, "Ancestral Zhou," probably to be equated with Danfu's city at Qishan. Only in 771 B.C., when the western part of the empire was overrun by barbarians and the Zhou king killed, was Zong Zhou abandoned. Thereafter, the Zhou kings ruled from their eastern capital, and the second half of the dynasty is accordingly known as Eastern Zhou.

Bronze Inscriptions as Historical Documents

Except at a few points, the foregoing account is based entirely on sources that were written long after the time of the events they describe. Variant traditions exist for many of the details. For instance, some texts mention only two of Wu Wang's brothers as participants in the Shang rebellion; names and genealogies are often hopelessly confused; and it is seldom entirely clear who was enfeoffed where, or in what reign. When two texts do agree on a point, it may be prudent to suspect that they are not independent sources of information, but that one copies the other or that both copy a third; some ostensibly ancient documents are outright fabrications. Thus, while traditional literary scholarship might provide a reasonably convincing picture of Western Zhou history, scarcely a detail of the picture could by itself stand up to close examination.

Fortunately, the evidence of texts can be supplemented by an extremely important historical source not so far mentioned—the corpus of Western Zhou bronze inscriptions. Each of these inscriptions is a contemporary document of the most unimpeachable authority, since we possess the actual bronze vessel on which a Zhou dignitary recorded some event of importance to himself and his family. It would be an exaggeration to say that the bronze inscriptions are sufficient to confirm the historical outline presented above. The surviving inscriptions reflect isolated events, not necessarily those of greatest interest to the historian, and they seldom supply any extended narrative. Furthermore, their language is con-

cise to the point of obscurity, requiring every assistance from the transmitted historical texts in order to be interpreted at all. Nevertheless, the inscriptions can illuminate details here and there in the texts, as well as provide occasional facts of real significance that are missing entirely from later writings. Perhaps more important still, they give us a view of Western Zhou thinking that is not overlaid with later interpretations and refracted by later moralizing, but direct and contemporary: sometimes they record the actual words of the king or his ministers.

Bronzes with lengthy commemorative inscriptions are all but unknown in the Shang period, and their sudden prominence in early Zhou suggests that the bronze art was being diverted to new and more secular purposes after the conquest. Shang bronze vessels were cast, as far as we have any evidence, for use in rituals of sacrifice to spirits. Many, if not most, are uninscribed. Those that are inscribed usually carry nothing more than the name of the owner, or that of his family or clan, and sometimes the posthumous designation of the owner's relative who is receiving sacrifices (see the bronzes from Fu Hao's tomb, nos. 28–33). The short and conventional inscription of the Zhou vessel no. 50 would qualify as lengthy by Shang standards: "This vessel was made by X for his father." Longer inscriptions do appear toward the very end of the Shang dynasty, but only a limited number of examples can be conclusively dated to Shang times.

From the first years of the Zhou dynasty, on the other hand, inscriptions are more common and often conspicuously longer. The purpose for which the bronze vessels were cast is ostensibly the same as before; no. 50 is explicitly dedicated to an ancestor. In the longer inscriptions, however, it is clear that other motivations enter, and they are by no means purely religious. Most often, the bronze texts record benefactions from the king—gifts of money or other valuables, or enfeoffments—and, to the delight of the historian, they sometimes mention the services of the retainer that were the occasion of the king's favor. Bronze vessels were cast, in other words, to commemorate important events in the life of the owner. The founder of a family's fortunes recounts the decisive events of his career, lists in full the gifts of the king that were his reward, and concludes by naming the ancestor for whose sacrifices he has commissioned the casting of the vessel. Presumably the ancestor is thereby notified of his descendant's merit; no doubt the owner's posterity will also be effectively reminded, for as long as the vessel remains on the altar of the family temple. In the course of the Western Zhou period, the longest inscriptions grow ever more prolix and circumstantial. Enormous effort is sometimes lavished on casting long and elegant inscriptions in vessels that have no pretension to artistic quality. In these cases, at least, the bronze vessel serves as nothing more than the vehicle for an inscription; at times we receive the impression that, for the Zhou nobleman, bronze casting was merely the most prestigious form of publication.

Enfeoffments and official charges were the most important occasions for the casting of Western Zhou bronzes, and it is here that the bronze inscriptions make contact with the transmitted historical record. For instance, one of the sons of the duke of Zhou is said to have been enfeoffed at a place called Xing, which some commentators locate at modern Xingtai in Hebei. An inscription on a bronze *gui* vessel in the British Museum states that the vessel was made by the marquis of Xing, for sacrifice to the duke of Zhou (Fig. 57). This celebrated inscription establishes beyond doubt that the lords of Xing were descended from the duke of Zhou. The British Museum *gui* was found in 1921 at Luoyang, site of the secondary capital Cheng Zhou. In 1978 a very similar *gui* was unearthed about 50 kilometers north of Xingtai in Hebei; its inscription names a different owner, but mentions the marquis of Xing as well. This discovery lends some weight to the identification of Xingtai as the location of the Xing fief.

Another renowned *gui* vessel, also in the British Museum, was found in the area of the principality of Wei, where the duke of Zhou enfeoffed his brother Kang Hou after the Shang rebellion. The inscription mentions Kang Hou by name, and the *gui* was evidently made by one of his retainers.

Many inscriptions mention the duke of Zhou in one context or another. The duke of Shao, who held the title of Tai Bao, "Lord Protector," commissioned several particularly imposing bronze vessels, including the Tai Bao *fang ding* now in the Tianjin Art Museum (Fig. 58; *Wenwu* 1959/11, p. 59), and the Tai Bao *gui* in the Freer Gallery of Art, Washington, D.C. (68.29). Several other bronzes bear inscriptions stating that they were cast by his son, the first marquis of Yan, and enough of these have been excavated to leave little doubt as to the location of the Yan state (see below, pp. 199–200).

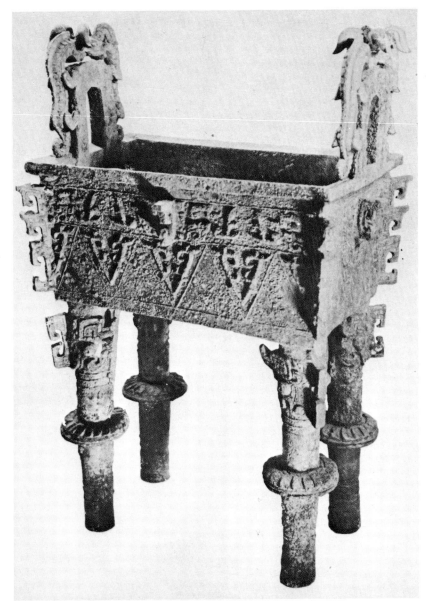

Fig. 58
Tai Bao *fang ding*. Provenance unknown. Tianjin Museum. Photograph after *Tianjin shi yishu bowuguan* (Tianjin, n.d.), p. 13

More important as a historical document than any of these is a bronze *pan* basin with an inscription of 284 characters that was found in 1976 at Fufeng in Shaanxi Province (*Wenwu* 1978/3, pp. 25–34; *Kaogu Xuebao* 1978/2, pp. 139–58). The maker of the vessel, who may have been court historian to the seventh Zhou king, names the first six kings in order, beginning with Wen Wang, and praises each for his notable deeds. The historian recalls, among other things, that the title duke of Zhou was conferred by Wu Wang, and a tactfully vague reference is made to the fourth Zhou king's failure to conquer the Chu state in Hubei. More interesting are passing allusions to campaigns led by Wu Wang against the eastern barbarians, for these are not recorded elsewhere. After reciting the achievements of the kings, the maker of the vessel goes on to recount the history of his own family. It transpires that the ancestor from whom he traces his descent came from a Shang vassal state in Shaanxi Province; the ruler of that vassal state, in Shang times, was none other than the prince Qi enfeoffed after the Shang rebellion in Song for the maintenance of the Shang sacrifices.

Though not so long and informative, the inscriptions of two bronze vessels included in the present exhibition bring us very close to the time of the Zhou conquest, and probably rank as the most remarkable inscriptions of their time yet known. The text cast on the *gui* no. 41 opens with the statement: "Wu Wang vanquished Shang; it was in the morning, on the day *jia zi* . . . ." As usual, the occasion for casting the vessel was not what to us is the central event, the conquest of Shang, but rather a benefaction conferred by the king in connection with the conquest. From the concluding phrases of the inscription, we learn that the maker is named Li, and that he has dedicated the vessel for sacrifices to an ancestor named Tan Gong. The middle part of the inscription, which probably describes the service performed for Wu Wang by Li, is obscurely worded and difficult to interpret; according to one view, it was a divination carried out by Li and pronounced auspicious that persuaded Wu Wang to launch his attack. The inscription goes on to say that the king rewarded Li and that Li commissioned the bronze vessel on the day *xin wei*, the eighth day following the conquest. It is perhaps needless to add that this is the earliest dated bronze known from the Zhou dynasty. It was probably a treasured possession of Li's family for generations. The *gui* was found buried with a hoard of bronzes, some of which date to the very end of the Western Zhou period, so that it must have been kept aboveground for more than two centuries.

The inscription of the *zun* no. 42 is longer, and it gives an exact date for the event it describes, in the fifth year of Cheng Wang. The occasion was the king's audience with one of his retainers, a man named He. He, possibly accompanied by members of his clan, was honored with a moral homily, after which the king made him a present of money in the form of cowrie shells. The money was afterwards used by He to cast the vessel that commemorates the occasion:

It was at the time when the king began the building of Cheng Zhou, and offered a Fu sacrifice in the Hall of Heaven to [his father] Wu Wang. In the fourth month, on the day *bing xu*, the king was in the Jing Hall and exhorted me, saying: "In days past, your late ancestor Gong Shi was able to serve Wen Wang. Wen Wang accepted the great command, and Wu Wang carried out the conquest of the Great City of Shang, announcing it to Heaven with the words: 'I must dwell in the center, and from there rule the people.' Now take heed! You must cherish the memory of the services that Gong Shi rendered to Heaven. Sacrifice to him with reverence!" Our king has indeed a virtuous character, compliant to Heaven, an inspiring example to my own feebleness. When the king had concluded, I, He, was given thirty strings of cowries, which I have used to make this vessel for sacrifices to Gong Shi. This happened in the king's fifth year.

This remarkable inscription provides an exact date for the building of Cheng Zhou, the new capital at Luoyang, and it also confirms the report of later texts that Cheng Wang, in building the new capital, was carrying out an intention already expressed by Wu Wang. In this and in certain other important inscriptions, the absence of any mention of the duke of Zhou has led some scholars to doubt the entire story of his regency during Cheng Wang's minority, but, given the limited and purely negative character of the evidence, the skepticism seems unwarranted. The city of Cheng Zhou figures prominently in another celebrated inscription, on a *fang yi* vessel in the Freer Gallery, that shows an official named Ming Bao being charged with the organization of the city's administrative bureaucracy. According to one interpretation, Ming Bao is the son of the duke of Zhou who was appointed to govern Cheng Zhou.

Even more interesting than any individual fact gleaned from the text cast on no. 42 is the tone of the inscription, with its repeated invocations of the will of Heaven. Implicit in these references is the assertion that the Zhou rulers were commanded by Heaven to overthrow the Shang; here, the implied equation between Gong Shi's services to Wen Wang and his services to Heaven is very striking. The statement that Wen Wang "accepted" Heaven's command, while Wu Wang carried it to fulfillment, accords perfectly with later accounts, in which Wen Wang somehow figures as the author of the conquest and is more to be admired than Wu Wang, who carried it out at the unavoidable but nonetheless deplorable cost of war and regicide. Zhou writers prefer to give credit for the founding of their dynasty to Wen Wang, whose hands were comparatively clean.

The moralistic tenor of the inscription is consistent with the style of certain speeches attributed to Cheng Wang and the duke of Zhou in later texts. Transmitted texts and bronze inscriptions alike give the impression that the early Zhou rulers were deeply conscious that they had usurped the throne, and they were much exercised to justify themselves. By contrast, the oracle bone inscriptions from Anyang give no sign that the Shang kings were ever concerned to assert their legitimacy; the question could hardly arise. Since the principal deities were the spirits of the deceased Shang kings, the living king had a unique and unassailable position, the more so since his line could trace its descent from the vague and mysterious supreme deity, Shang Di; one might almost say that the Shang king was related by blood to the natural order. If the Zhou kings were able to make any similar claim on patron deities of their own, they seem to have derived little comfort from the fact; and the care with which they appointed Shang descendants to maintain the Shang sacrifices suggests that they themselves were quite unable to dismiss or ignore the foundations of Shang legitimacy.

Having dealt with the Shang royal ancestors by endowing their sacrifices, the Zhou rulers seem to have approached the spirit world on more impersonal terms, referring to "Heaven" rather than Shang Di; and they asserted that, because the Shang kings had declined in virtue, Heaven chose to withdraw its protection from them, conferring it on the Zhou house instead: Heaven deliberately shifted its allegiance to a more virtuous line. Thus, when the Zhou kings began referring to themselves as Tian Zi, Son of Heaven, the relationship they claim is, quite literally, adoptive. The Zhou rationale for imperial legitimacy, which was central to Chinese thought in later times, clearly implies that the right to rule is dependent on the moral quality of the ruling house—a claim that it would not have occurred to the Shang king to make. It is extremely interesting to find that this notion of the right to rule bestowed by Heaven is no projection into the past by a later generation of dynastic apologists, but is clearly in evidence from the earliest years of the Zhou dynasty. Inscriptions like that of the *zun* no. 42, by providing a touchstone to authenticate the spirit of later texts, encourage us to have confidence in the substance as well, even when the texts supply information that is not explicitly confirmed by the bronze inscriptions.

Early Zhou in the Northeast: The Yan State

Yan, one of the fiefs created by Wu Wang immediately after the conquest, was given to the duke of Shao. Like the duke of Zhou, the duke of Shao was kept by his duties at court from taking up residence at Yan, and the Yan fief was therefore turned over to his eldest son, who is usually accounted the first marquis of Yan. Beyond this, history supplies almost no information about the state. Little enough is known about the duke of Shao; of his descendants, the marquises of Yan, the Han dynasty historian Sima Qian cannot even provide the names until the very end of Western Zhou. The approximate location of the Yan state, in the far northeast, can be deduced from accounts of the sections of the Great Wall that Yan built in much later times, around the fourth century B.C., when the state enjoyed a transient political importance. In the Western Zhou period, however, Yan must have been remote, threatened on the north by barbarians, and of only limited strategic significance.

Given the altogether trivial role played by the Yan state in traditional accounts of Western Zhou history, its prominence in bronze inscriptions is surprising. Two inscriptions that have long been known supply the name of the first marquis, which is not recorded elsewhere. A *ding* in the Sumitomo Collection, Kyoto, commemorates an honor paid the marquis at the Zhou court in Shaanxi: "When the marquis Zhi of Yan first served in Zong Zhou, the king bestowed twenty strings of cowries on Zhi, which he used to make this vessel for sacrifice to his ancestress." A second *ding* was made by Zhi after the death of his father, the duke of Shao; the inscription says merely, "Vessel made for Father Xin by the marquis Zhi of Yan." A few other inscriptions mention a marquis of Yan, not necessarily the first, without giving his personal name. An interesting pair of covered bowls, unusual both in shape and in decoration, bear the same inscription, "The marquis of Yan made this *yu* for sacrifices during travels." One vessel of the pair is now in the Arthur M. Sackler Collections, New York; the other is in the Metropolitan Museum (49.136.4).

These unprovenanced bronzes connected with the lords of Yan have been joined in recent years by a succession of vessels discovered in the area of the Yan fief. Bronzes from two different localities are shown here (nos. 53–57). The first three, nos. 53–55, come from two separate finds made in the vicinity of Lingyuan in Liaoning Province, north of the Great Wall. The finest vessel of the Liaoning finds, one of the most attractive of all early Western Zhou bronzes, bears the inscription, "The marquis of Yan made this *yu* for food" (no. 53). The style of the vessel is fairly early, and it is possible that the marquis in question is again Zhi, the son of the duke of Shao. It is thus possible that the territory of the Yan fief extended as far north as Liaoning from the beginning, already in the time of the first marquis.

The remaining two vessels, nos. 56 and 57, were found in the southwestern corner of the Beijing Metropolitan District, in Fangshan Xian. Again, several bronzes from Fangshan, including no. 56, are inscribed with the title marquis of Yan. The old literary name for Beijing is Yanjing, or "Yan Capital," and it has always been known that Beijing was a capital of the state in later centuries; but texts differ as to whether it was the site of the capital at the time Zhi was enfeoffed. Since the bronzes from Fangshan are quite early in style, they have been taken by some scholars as evidence that the Yan capital was at Beijing from the earliest years of the fief.

It seems unlikely that Zhou military power, which must have been spread thin in the years immediately following the conquest, could have penetrated as far north as Beijing and Liaoning in the face of any significant opposition. That the Yan region was so early incorporated into the Zhou empire may mean simply that it was already firmly held by a Shang prince, who surrendered to Wu Wang at the conquest. The *ding* no. 12 is evidence that Shang culture had reached as far as Beijing before the Anyang period, and Shang bronzes from Anyang times have been unearthed in Liaoning only a few kilometers from the place where the marquis of Yan *yu* no. 53 was found. Various attempts have been made to identify Shang fiefs or statelets within the territory that later made up the Yan state, some involving inscribed bronzes shown here (see nos. 27, 54). The great scholar Wang Guowei long ago suggested that a Shang vassal state called Pi might have formed part of the territory of Yan after the conquest, pointing out that a *you* vessel found just south of Beijing in the 1890s bears an inscription stating that it was cast by an earl of Pi. Now in the Museum of Fine Arts, Boston, this *you* is very similar to one that was found together with the marquis of Yan *yu* in Liaoning.

It is curious that almost none of the bronzes associated with Yan, either by inscription or by provenance, seem stylistically to belong any later than the time of the third Zhou king. In view of their eccentric decoration, the pair of marquis of Yan vessels now in New York might be difficult to date with any precision, but the Yan cemetery at Beijing from which nos. 56 and 57 come has yielded an almost identical vessel of pottery, found in a burial that the excavators date no later than the third Zhou reign. It is even possible that all of the known inscriptions mentioning a marquis of Yan refer to Zhi, the first marquis. The large number of bronzes known from his time should perhaps be taken as a vague indication of the power or activity of the fief in early Western Zhou, a period for which written history supplies no information. For the two centuries of the Yan state after the marquis Zhi, archaeology and written history are at the moment in better agreement, both preserving an unbroken silence.

Bronze Vessels of the Early Western Zhou Period

As might be expected, Western Zhou bronzes are found in the greatest abundance in the old Zhou territory, in or near the Wei River valley in Shaanxi Province (nos. 41–52). But they are found also throughout the Shang domain, at the secondary capital at Luoyang, in the territories of the various fiefs, and often far beyond. Nearly every province of China has yielded at least isolated examples, though in the south Zhou finds are significantly less common than bronzes of Shang style. In some of the more remote areas, purely local variants of conventional Zhou shapes and ornament are encountered. These few provincialisms aside, however, the immense stylistic variety of early Western Zhou bronzes cannot be explained in terms of neatly circumscribed regional styles. The enormous repertoire of the Shaanxi and Henan bronze casters was current and familiar in every corner of the Zhou domain.

It was the military men above all who were likely to cast bronzes in the early years of the dynasty, and they were certainly the most geographically mobile of patrons, whether campaigning or journeying to and from their fiefs. What this means for archaeology is illustrated by the British Museum's *gui* of the marquis of Xing mentioned earlier: the fief was in Hebei, but the *gui* was found at the Luoyang capital. The case is a common one. Vessels might travel far from their points of manufacture—which in consequence are almost impossible to determine—and in so doing might transmit the latest ideas and fashions to foundries throughout the empire. The unusual *lei* vessel no. 55, from Yan territory in Liaoning, is a case in point. A similar *lei* has been found at the old Zhou capital at Qishan in Shaanxi Province, and two more were unearthed in Sichuan, some 2,000 kilometers from Liaoning.

The *lei* from Liaoning may serve to introduce the distinctly altered character of the bronze art in the first few generations after the Zhou conquest. The classical reserve that survives in even the most assertive of Shang bronzes is here abandoned in an unrestrained display of

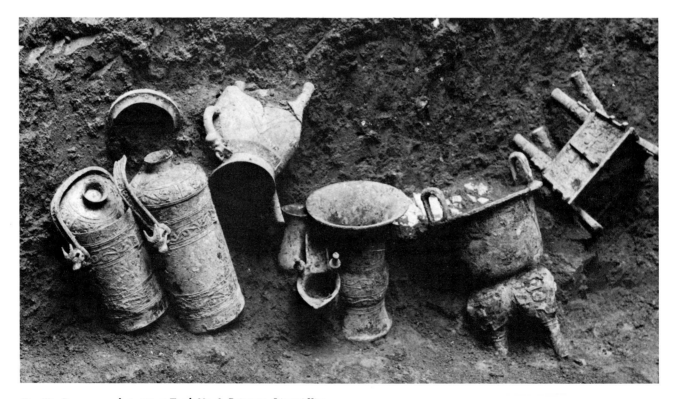

Fig. 59 Bronze vessels *in situ* at Tomb No. 2, Baicaopo, Lingtai Xian, Gansu Province. Photograph courtesy of Cultural Relics Bureau, Beijing

invention. The simplicity of the vessel's shape is offset altogether by the projecting handles, with horned animal heads and pendent rings, and by the profusion of molded high relief ornament—to all of which the lid with its crouching monster adds a touch disquietingly alive.

The same flamboyance is shared by a great many early Zhou vessels; yet within the wide limits set by the strenuous pursuit of striking effects, the variations of style are enormous. The *zun* no. 42, dated to the fifth year of Cheng Wang, strikes a note of undiluted savagery. Its blocky, violently hooked flanges threaten to overwhelm the surface decoration, which only holds its own by dint of a clumsily exaggerated plasticity. The *guang* no. 45 combines the same aggressive flanges with even more extravagant additions to the silhouette, notably the massive projection of the handle from one end and the wing-like crests standing on the lid at the other; yet the rather flowery treatment of the surface ornament is closer in style to that of the *lei* no. 55, and this, together with the *guang*'s more fastidious execution, deprives it of the crude force of the *zun*. The note of heavy emphasis shared by all these vessels can be recognized once more in the *li* tripod from Beijing, no. 56, but here the forms are simpler and bolder, and at the same time handled with a surprising delicacy of proportions.

The range of variation revealed by these four vessels does not exhaust the repertoire of the early Zhou bronze founders. A pair of vessels found in Gansu, just across the Shaanxi border, represents an altogether different but equally prevalent taste (Fig. 59; nos. 43, 44). The decoration is sparse, the shapes are smooth and curvilinear. Set next to the barbaric extravagance of the vessels described above, these two pieces are muted and retiring.

Any more detailed survey of Western Zhou bronzes would only strengthen the impression of diversity. In practice it is not easy to trace the ancestry of each individual stylistic strain, but a number of major sources can be identified. The primary one is Anyang bronze casting, which in its latest phase covered an exceedingly wide range of styles. Even before the end of the Shang period, the Anyang founders had begun to cast softly rounded, sparingly decorated vessels that suggest a deliberate retreat from the architectonic force and angularity of objects like the *fang lei* no. 27; among these austere, rather inexpressive shapes, exact prototypes for the two Zhou vessels from Gansu can be found. At the opposite extreme, the Anyang workshops went on to produce bronzes still more theatrical than no. 27, and these furnished the starting point for the other, more flamboyant side of Zhou taste. A close precursor for the animal rising from the top of the *lei* no. 55—which we might otherwise have been tempted to identify as a typically bizarre Zhou invention—can be found on a magnificent Shang *pou* vessel, now in the Tokyo National Museum, which has a small horned snake coiled on the knob of its lid (Mizuno, 1959, pls. 64, 65). In the same way, much that at first glance seems most characteristically Zhou can in fact be traced to ideas already explored at the Anyang capital.

Zhou artists nevertheless did draw on other sources besides the Anyang inheritance. It is for instance likely that in the years preceding the conquest, Shaanxi bronze casting had given rise to local fashions that survived into the dynastic Zhou period, as a number of scholars have suggested. The chief obstacle to isolating this "predynastic Zhou" stylistic component has been the difficulty of dating bronzes found in Shaanxi; it is not easy to prove that any given piece was made before, rather than just after, the conquest. The bronzes that can be most confidently regarded as predynastic Zhou are too often only inferior copies of familiar Anyang types, without any novelty of style. Despite this difficulty, however, there are strong arguments in favor of a predynastic tradition with a style of its own. It might for instance be suspected that the peculiar motif decorating the shoulder of the *lei* from Liaoning, no. 55, as well as nos. 49–51, had its origins in Zhou territory before the conquest. This strange animal, whose gaping mouth is attached to a body that consists of nothing more than a large, plastically rendered spiral, appears on Zhou bronzes from the first years of the dynasty, while no Shang example is known.

The predynastic Zhou bronze tradition is, by another name, the provincial Shang bronze industry of Shaanxi Province. The special importance of this particular provincial industry lies in the fact that it was incorporated wholesale into the mainstream of metropolitan bronze casting after the conquest. But it probably was not the only provincial contribution to metropolitan Zhou styles. The absorption of Shang neighbor states into the Zhou empire must have brought Zhou artists into contact with a wide variety of regional traditions unknown or unheeded at Anyang, and the sudden mixing of these formerly isolated traditions may partly explain the stylistic complexity of early Western Zhou. There are, for instance, puzzling connections between bronze casting in the southern provinces during the Shang period, and in Shaanxi in Zhou times: after the unique pre-Anyang *ding* vessel from Jiangxi, no. 17, the next occurrence of animals crawling on the handles of a *ding* is on the *fang ding* of the Lord Protector, the duke of Shao, three centuries later (Fig. 58). Moreover, large bells of southern type are the only possible prototype for numerous bells of Western Zhou times, and for their bird- or tiger-shaped flanges (see no. 58). Stylistic peculiarities of a few early bronzes found in Shaanxi hint at contacts between Shaanxi and the south already generations before the conquest (*Kaogu* 1976/1, pp. 31–38, pls. 1–4).

The eccentric *gu* vessel from Shaanxi, no. 46, may conceivably reflect the absorption of another Shang provincial tradition into the Zhou repertoire of styles. With its exaggeratedly slender midpart and uninterrupted curve from foot to rim, this *gu* has no parallel at Anyang. The only similar example comes from the Shang site at Shilou in Shanxi Province, the source also of the exotic *hu* no. 21.

Yet despite all departures from metropolitan Shang bronze casting, the novelty of the earliest Zhou styles is not unlimited. Many Zhou vessels are distinguishable from Shang counterparts only by their inscriptions or provenance; many more represent Zhou variations on Shang themes. In the period following the conquest, what is remarkable is not so much the stylistic independence that is displayed at the outset, but the speed with which the Zhou bronze industry diverged from its Shang sources. Within a few generations the art was transformed.

To some extent this transformation was a result simply of the Zhou caster's selective use of the Shang legacy. His choice of which possibilities to explore and which to neglect was in itself enough to alter the character of the bronze industry and touched on all aspects of the art. In particular, the repertoire of vessel types was drastically affected; a few shapes, like the *gui*, enjoyed special favor, while some of the most standard Shang types all but disappeared (*gu, jia, jue*).

More positive contributions are to be found in the realm of surface decoration and motifs. *Taotie* designs continued in popularity, but the relief treatments and details are often far from any Shang precedent (nos. 41, 42, 45, 52, 54–56). At the same time, a great many new motifs arose to challenge the supremacy of the *taotie*. The coiled animal (nos. 49–51) is one, and its influence can be detected in another typical early Zhou motif that appeared somewhat later: the *gui* no. 57 is decorated with elephants instead of imaginary animals, but the bodies of the elephants are embellished with a spiraling design borrowed from the animal that had no body except the spiral.

Neither of these motifs survived for more than a few generations. Elaborately crested birds were more long-lived and provide many of the most impressive designs from the Western Zhou period. Something of their character can be illustrated by the backward-facing crested dragons seen on the *yu* no. 53 (Fig. 60). Here the surface of the vessel is covered with a uniform mesh of sweeping curvilinear shapes, intricately barbed and plumed, hovering on the dividing line between animal forms and purely abstract ornamental inventions. The blunt, angular hooks of the dragons' crests have no particular resemblance to anything organic, but seem instead to imitate the flange patterns of vessels like no. 42. The body of the dragon is actually birdlike, formed of an inward-curving tail plume overlapped by a much larger wing that rises to the upper edge of the decor frieze.

The casual joining of a dragon's head to the body of a bird is typical of the Zhou artist's attitude toward his motifs at this stage. Neither the dragon nor the bird is of much importance for its own sake; any too precise definition of anatomical parts would jeopardize more important ends. Each motif is valued only insofar as it lends itself to an overriding ornamental purpose and provides a graceful flow of elaborate curvilinear shapes. The sacrifice of the motif to the uniform flow of the relief patterns is most clearly revealed in the decorated band on the foot of the *yu*, where in each quadrant the extended claw of a bird is prolonged into a meaningless ribbon that occupies more space than the bird itself.

The *taotie* motif was subject to the same distortions. In the decor of the *guang* no. 45, the flickering edges of the relief parts serve the same function as the barbs and plumes of the dragon on the *yu*. In each case, something of the clarity and individuality of the motif has been given up in exchange for a florid, richly patterned effect. On the *guang* this decorative uniformity is enhanced by the resemblance in shape between the hooked flanges of the vessel and the hooked borders of the relief areas. In such details we can discern the beginnings of a patternizing tendency that increasingly dominates the bronze art of Western Zhou times and lays the foundation for many of the most influential systems of ornament in the succeeding Eastern Zhou period (chaps. 6, 7).

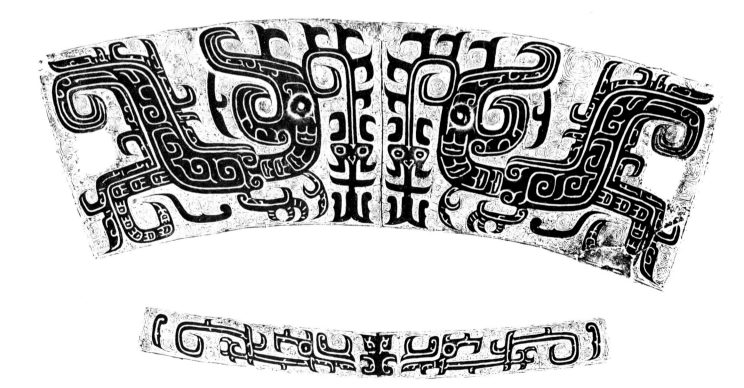

Fig. 60   Rubbing of decor, Yan Hou *yu* no. 53. Photograph courtesy of
Cultural Relics Bureau, Beijing

CHAPTER 5: CATALOGUE ENTRIES

41 Li *gui*

Late 11th century B.C. (first year of Wu Wang's reign)
Found 1976, Lintong Xian, Shaanxi Province
Height 28 cm. (11 in.); diameter at mouth 22 cm. (8⅝ in.);
  weight 7.95 kg. (17 lb. 8 oz.)
Cultural Office of Lintong Xian

The unique importance of this vessel resides in its inscription (see Fig. 61), which alludes to the Zhou conquest of Shang and is dated on the eighth day thereafter (see p. 198). The exceedingly handsome and boldly formed characters of the inscription rank with the finest examples of Western Zhou bronze script, and contrast curiously with the scraggly writing of another celebrated vessel dated to the first Zhou reign, the Da Feng *gui*. Called the Li *gui* after the name of its maker, the present vessel was found in 1976 a few kilometers from the tomb of the First Emperor of Qin. It had been buried in a pit together with four other vessels, a set of thirteen bells, and bronze tools, weapons, and chariot fittings—a total of sixty items. Apart from the *gui*, all the major items of the hoard date to the very end of Western Zhou; the *gui* was thus older by nearly three centuries than the objects interred with it.

As a type the Li *gui* derives from the much earlier handled vessel no. 8, to which it adds a hollow rectangular base cast integrally with the bowl, a feature popular in early Western Zhou. Both sides of the bowl and all four sides of the base are filled by large *taotie* faces set in high relief against a *leiwen* ground. In the four corners on the upper surface of the base, small buffalo heads, resembling those on the handle of the *you* no. 43, are naturalistically modeled in high relief. The circular foot of the vessel is decorated with two species of dragons, one with head facing forward, the other grazing with head lowered; the bodies of both types are edged with flickering borders, an early Zhou fashion more liberally indulged on the *guang* no. 45. Each handle is surmounted by a head with large freestanding horns, apparently engaged in devouring the head of a bird. The wings of the bird appear on the arc of the handle, while its tail feathers descend onto a rectangular pendant below. The cicada filling the space beneath the handle is seen again in the same position on the *guang* no. 45, the *gui* no. 57, and the Xing Hou *gui* of figure 57. The patination is a rough dark green with a few areas of brown. The base is much deformed, its sides bent inward.

The Li *gui* takes its place in a group of dated early Western Zhou bronzes neatly consistent in style. In both shape and decoration it is exceedingly close to a *gui* in the Fogg Art Museum, Cambridge, Massachusetts, made by a Zhou worthy named De (Loehr, 1968, no. 48; Chen, 1955–56, pt. 2, pl. 16, p. 109, fig. 13). This De *gui* is one of two *gui* vessels cast by the same person; the second De *gui* is decorated with coiled monsters rather than *taotie* and is almost identical to the *gui* no. 49 (Chen, 1955–56, pt. 2, pls. 17, 18, p. 109, fig. 12). The dating of the two De vessels depends on the inscription of a third bronze commissioned by De, a *fang ding* now in the Shanghai Museum (Shanghai, 1964, no. 28). The inscription of the *fang ding* mentions a sacrifice to Wu Wang, implying that the vessel was made after his death, presumably in the reign of his successor. The inscription of the first De *gui* seems to refer to the same event; the second *gui*, though it commemorates a different occasion, can plausibly be assigned to the same reign, that of the second Zhou king. Just as the first De *gui* resembles the Li *gui*, the second is very similar to the Da Feng *gui*—the only bronze besides the Li *gui* generally agreed to date to the reign of Wu Wang (Rong, 1941, vol. 2, p. 160, fig. 298; Chen, 1955–56, no. 1). We might on this account suspect that both De *gui* belong early in

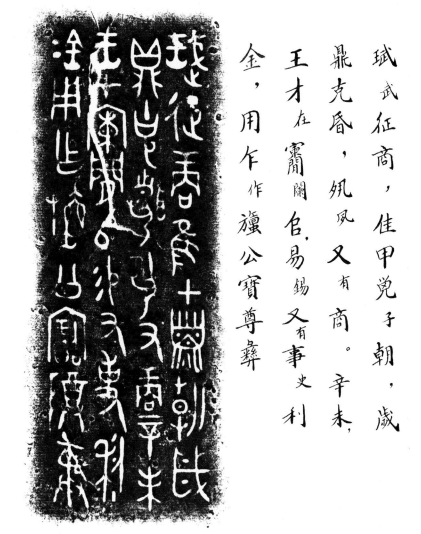

Fig. 61 Rubbing and transcription of inscription, Li *gui* no. 41.
Photograph courtesy of Cultural Relics Bureau, Beijing

Cheng Wang's reign; indeed, in the case of the second De *gui* the inscription does not rule out a date in Wu Wang's time.

PUBLISHED: *Wenwu* 1977/8, pls. 1–3, pp. 1–12. For inscription, see *Kaogu* 1978/1, pp. 58–59; *Wenwu* 1978/6, pp. 77–84.

42 He *zun*

Late 11th century B.C. (fifth year of Cheng Wang's reign)
Found 1963, Baoji Xian, Shaanxi Province
Height 38.8 cm. (15¼ in.); diameter at mouth 28.6 cm. (11¼ in.);
  weight 14.78 kg. (32 lb. 8 oz.)
Shaanxi Provincial Museum

The long inscription of this *zun*, which names the maker, He, and gives a date in the fifth year of the second Zhou king, is sharply and deeply cast, filling the entire bottom of the vessel's interior (see Fig. 62). A tentative translation of the inscription is given on pages 198–199. The vessel was unearthed in 1963 and acquired by the Shaanxi Provincial Museum in 1965, but the inscription of 119 characters, covered by corrosion, went undiscovered until 1975.

The *zun* itself is large and impressive. The thick rim and high molded foot, the boldly plastic *taotie* faces, and above all the heavy hooked flanges, give an effect of overpowering mass and barbaric energy. Although the mouth of the vessel is circular, a cross section of the lower body is square with rounded corners. The consequent flattening of the sides allows the *taotie* face to be displayed almost entirely in the frontal plane, concentrating the forward gaze of its staring eyes. Larger and more forceful than the *taotie* on the foot,

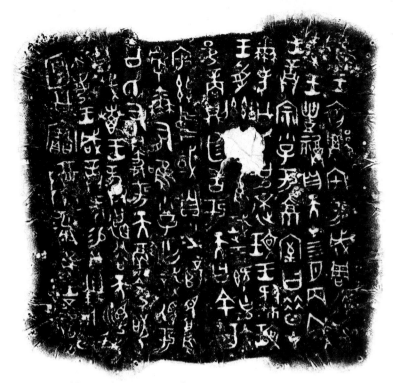

佳
惟
王
初
遷
鄴
宅
于
成
周
，
復
□

珷
武
王
豐
福
自
天
。
才
在
四
月
丙
戌
，

王
誥
宗
小
子
于
京
室
曰
：
昔
才
在

爾
考
公
氏
克
遠
省
玟
文
王
，
肆
肆
玟
文

王
受
茲
大
命
。
佳
惟
珷
武
王
既
克
大

邑
商
，
則
廷
告
于
天
曰
：
余
其

宅
茲
中
或
國
，
自
之
辥
乂
民
。
烏

虖
呼
！
爾
有
唯
小
子
亡
戠
識
，
覞
眂
于

公
氏
有
昏
助
于
天
，
融
徹
令
命
，
敬

享
戈
哉
！
叀
王
龏
恭
德
谷
裕
天
，
順
訓
我

不
每
敏
。
王
成
誥
詰
何
易
錫
貝
卅
朋
·

□
公
寶
尊
彝
·
佳
惟
王
五
祀
。

Fig. 62   Rubbing and transcription of inscription, He *zun* no. 42.
Photograph courtesy of Cultural Relics Bureau, Beijing

the *taotie* in the middle zone has imposing rams' horns that spiral into relief and hooked lower jaws that twist outward from the surface in the same way. Above, a narrow band contains snakes with angular S-shaped bodies; higher still the flanges bisect triangular areas filled with abstract configurations. The motifs in high relief are set against a background of shallow, threadlike *leiwen* spirals.

Vertical seams run down the outside edges of the flanges, which seem to have been cast integrally with the vessel. The blunt upper ends of the two flanges at the sides are cast on, probably repairing flaws in the original casting. The surface is smooth and silvery gray.

PUBLISHED: *Wenwu* 1966/1, p. 4; *Wenwu* 1976/1, pp. 60–66, 93 (discussions of inscription); Beijing, 1972a, pl. 50.

43   Luan Bo *you*

Late 11th–early 10th century B.C.
Excavated 1972 from Tomb No. 2, Baicaopo, Lingtai Xian,
     Gansu Province
Height 29 cm. (11⅜ in.); diameter 12 cm. (4¾ in.); weight
     2.25 kg. (4 lb. 15 oz.)
Gansu Provincial Museum

This and the next vessel were excavated from a cemetery in Gansu Province evidently connected with Zhou fiefs in the area. The two vessels come from the tomb of an earl of Luan (Luan Bo)—a name unknown in historical texts. They have the same inscription, "The earl of Luan made this precious ritual vessel" (see Fig. 63). Judging by the style of the bronzes in his tomb, the earl must have lived at about the time of the second or third Zhou king.

Two narrow bands of ornament decorate the cylindrical body of the *you*, while a third appears on the lid. The bands are bordered with thread-relief lines and filled with confronted pairs of long-tailed birds. The deeply recessed outer face of the handle contains long S-shaped bodies with dragon heads at either end. The terminals of the handle, which engage loops on the body of the *you*, carry finely modeled, fully three-dimensional water buffalo heads. The surface is partly covered with matte green corrosion; elsewhere it is golden brown, very shiny, and only slightly tarnished. The inscription appears inside the vessel proper and in the lid.

The simple, perfectly cylindrical tall *you* is a shape that had appeared already before the end of the Shang dynasty. The present Luan Bo *you* is the smaller vessel of a matched pair, differing only in size, from Tomb No. 2. A similar pair, inscribed with dedications naming an earl of He, came from Tomb No. 1 at the same site. In early Western Zhou and perhaps in late Shang also, *you* seem often to have been cast in pairs of vessels identical except in size. Further examples would include such well-known sets as the two Chen Chen *you* (Fogg Art Museum, Cambridge, Mass., and Hakutsuru Art Museum, Kobe) and the two *you* of the Duan Fang set in The Metropolitan Museum of Art; each of these two pairs is accompanied by a matched *zun* vessel (Rong, 1941, vol. 2, p. 1, fig. 1, p. 281, fig. 536, p. 341, fig. 655, etc.).

PUBLISHED: *Kaogu Xuebao* 1977/2, p. 109, fig. 9:4–7, pl. 9 (report, pp. 99–130).

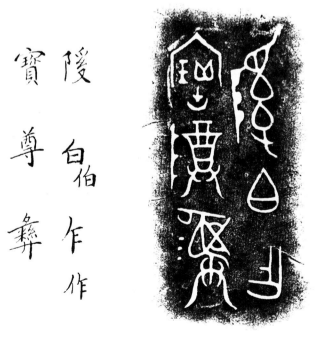

Fig. 63   Rubbing and transcription of inscription, Luan Bo *you* no. 43.
Photograph courtesy of Cultural Relics Bureau, Beijing

44 Luan Bo *he*

Late 11th–early 10th century B.C.
Excavated 1972 from Tomb No. 2, Baicaopo, Lingtai Xian,
  Gansu Province
Height 28.5 cm. (11¼ in.); weight 2.5 kg. (5 lb. 8 oz.)
Gansu Provincial Museum

This vessel was excavated from the same tomb as the *you* no. 43, and inside the lid is the same inscription, "The earl of Luan made this precious ritual vessel" (see Fig. 64). An abbreviated form of the inscription is cast under the handle: Luan Bo *zuo*, "Made by the earl of Luan." The handle, surmounted by a bovine head, is joined by a single link to the lid. The surface is a mottled dull green with a few uncorroded patches.

As a type this tripod pouring vessel derives ultimately from much older *he* vessels, represented by the Panlongcheng *he* no. 5, and it moreover recalls early bronzes in several specific features. The most conspicuous of these is the large zigzag pattern of parallel thread-relief lines decorating the otherwise plain lobes of the vessel; the same pattern is common on pre-Anyang lobed vessels, chiefly *ding*, *li*, and *xian* tripods. The decoration in two narrow bands on neck and lid, shared by many early Zhou bronzes, carries definite allusions to Style III *taotie* patterns, with their rows of parallel quills (cf. no. 17), though the Zhou versions have lost altogether the expressive draftsmanship of the early designs. While at first glance it might seem that these features represent archaisms—deliberate revivals of designs long out of fashion—it is possible that they will prove instead to descend in unbroken sequence from the earlier versions, constituting a simple and unostentatious alternative that coexisted alongside more dramatic and more architectonic Anyang styles.

PUBLISHED: *Kaogu Xuebao* 1977/2, pl. 8:2 following p. 130 (report, pp. 99–130).

45 Qi *guang*

Late 11th–early 10th century B.C.
Excavated 1976 from Storage Pit No. 1, Zhuangbo, Fufeng Xian,
  Shaanxi Province
Height 28.7 cm. (11¼ in.); length 36.5 cm. (14⅜ in.); weight
  7.55 kg. (16 lb. 10 oz.)
Zhouyuan Archaeological Team, Shaanxi Province

The front end of this odd container takes the shape of a knobby animal head with freestanding, winglike horns. The body belonging to this head is nowhere depicted in the surface ornament, however, and the vessel might thus be thought a curious hybrid, combining a relatively minor sculptural part with an otherwise regular and inorganic vessel shape; yet the formidable arched neck of the animal and the intense forward gaze of its bulging eyes come close to animating the entire object.

No part of the *guang* is left unenlivened by relief decoration. In the rectangular side panel a florid *taotie* is elaborated to fill every corner of the available space; spiraling bodies on either side of its broad face set up an effect of swirling movement insistently repeated in the barbed contours of the C-horns and the ubiquitous flickering borders. The same flickering edges surround the sinuous body of a crested, backward-facing dragon in the zone just above the *taotie*, under the pouring channel of the vessel. Smaller dragons on the foot, also facing backward, sport different crests in the form of long tendrils trailing tiny faces—just as on the marquis of Yan *yu* in the principal register (no. 53). On the lid a last pair of dragons touch their foreheads to opposite sides of the central flange, so that seen from above they join to form a *taotie* split down the middle by the flange.

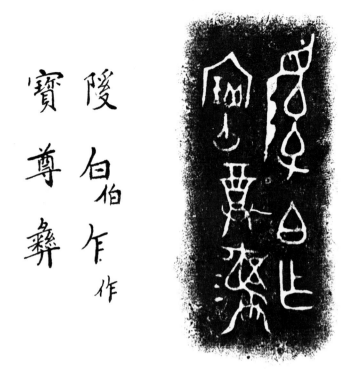

Fig. 64 Rubbing and transcription of inscription, Luan Bo *he* no. 44.
Photograph courtesy of Cultural Relics Bureau, Beijing

The flange on the lid reproduces the blunt hooks of flanges elsewhere on the vessel; at its front end, however, it turns into a small bird perched on the highest part of the lid, and the remainder of the flange might be interpreted as a plumed tail emerging from beneath the bird's wing. At the opposite end of the vessel, another bird, whose beak is shaped like one hook taken from a flange, figures in the zoological riot of the handle. The wing of this bird—on which coils a snake—occupies the arc of the handle, with a small tusked head appearing just below it; from inside the mouth of this head an elephant's trunk emerges (cf. no. 57). The top of the handle takes the form of a larger tusked head with freestanding horns. Similar horns on the rear part of the lid belong to a *taotie* face that stares directly upward. The handle has been broken off and repaired. The patination is a silvery gray.

The *guang* is one of a matched set of three vessels from Storage Pit No. 1, all sharing the same inscription of thirty-nine characters and a clan sign; the other vessels are a *zun* and a *fang yi*. In the *guang* the inscription is cast in both lid and body. In the lid it is arranged in four columns and fitted into the space on one side of the central longitudinal axis (see Fig. 65). In the body the same text is arranged in six columns running from one side of the vessel to the other and thus perpendicular to the columns in the lid. In the lid, but not in the body, the characters are fitted into a neatly ruled grid of clearly marked vertical guidelines and less clear horizontal lines. The inscription identifies the maker of the vessel, a *zuoce* ("annalist") named Qi or Zhe, and can be translated as follows:

> In the fifth month, the king was at X. On the day *mou zi*, he commanded that the annalist Qi give lands to the marquis of Xiang, and bestowed bronze metal and servitors on Qi. In order to extol the king's beneficence, in the nineteenth *si* [annual sacrifice] of the king's reign, I [Qi] have used [the gifts] to make a vessel for Father Yi. May it be treasured forever. [Clan sign.]

The clan emblem that concludes the inscription is formed of a ram's head, the character *mu* ("tree") just above it, and on both sides the character *ce* ("document")—the last element being regularly included in the clan signs of annalists. A number of other vessels from

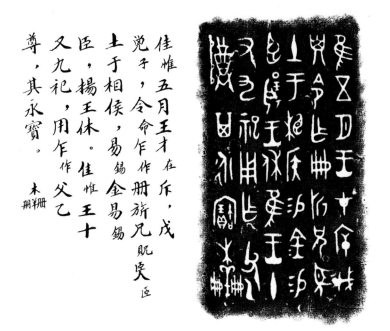

佳惟五月王才在乍，戍
兌子，令令乍作冊旂兄眖奚
土于相侯，易錫金易錫
臣，揚王休。佳惟王十
又九祀，用乍作父乙
尊，其永寶。
木冊羽冊

Fig. 65　Rubbing and transcription of inscription, Qi *guang* no. 45.
Photograph courtesy of Cultural Relics Bureau, Beijing

the hoard (e.g., no. 47), including some far later, bear this clan sign, suggesting that the bronzes in Storage Pit No. 1 represent the accumulated possessions of several generations of the same family (Fig. 78).

　　The bold hooked flanges of the *guang* recall those of the *zun* no. 42, but are less bulky and less aggressive; like the comparatively subdued relief ornament, the flanges function here as subordinate parts in a tidy, carefully compartmented whole. Set next to a bronze so unequivocally Zhou as the *zun*, the *guang* seems rather closer to Shang taste, an impression enhanced by its familiar motifs, conventional relief technique, and fine *leiwen* spirals. In the distinctly "classical" flavor of its design the Qi *guang* joins a well-defined group of early Zhou bronzes, a group that centers on the Ling *fang yi* in the Freer Gallery of Art, Washington, D.C. (Lodge, 1946, pp. 42–47); the matching Qi *fang yi* in fact resembles the Ling *fang yi* closely. Unfortunately, the dating of the entire group has yet to be established. Depending on the interpretation of certain parts of its inscription, the Ling *fang yi* and its relatives have been assigned dates ranging from the second to the fourth

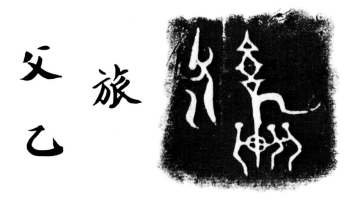

Fig. 66　Rubbing and transcription of inscription, Lü Fu Yi *gu* no. 46.
Photograph courtesy of Cultural Relics Bureau, Beijing

Zhou reign, a span of time corresponding to the end of the eleventh and the earlier half of the tenth century B.C. (cf. Lodge, *op. cit.*).

PUBLISHED: *Wenwu* 1978/3, pl. 3:4 (report, pp. 1–24, 42, pls. 2–8).

46　Lü Fu Yi *gu*

Late 11th–early 10th century B.C.
Excavated 1976 from Storage Pit No. 1, Zhuangbo, Fufeng Xian, Shaanxi Province
Height 25.2 cm. (9⅞ in.); diameter at mouth 13.2 cm. (5¼ in.); weight 0.55 kg. (1 lb. 3 oz.)
Zhouyuan Archaeological Team, Shaanxi Province

This *gu* is one of the rare examples of an ancient bronze that has survived uncorroded. In shape it is no less exceptional, its slender, simply curved silhouette being paralleled only by a *gu* found some years ago at Shilou in Shanxi Province (*Wenwu* 1960/7, p. 50, fig. 3, p. 51, fig. 1). Its decoration, finally, is completely unfamiliar. Confined to the foot zone—as on the Shilou *gu*—it consists of three pattern units, each one an amorphous thread-relief design centered on a single large eye in high relief; these thread-relief elements look distinctly like cloisons meant to receive some sort of inlay material, of which however there is no trace. Since the *gu* was cast in a mold with two vertical divisions, one of the pattern units (that visible in the plate) is bisected by a seam. Above and below the main zone are narrow bands of regular rectangular meanders, resembling Greek fret patterns. These bands contain eyes set on the dividing lines that separate the pattern units of the main register. Additional tiny "cloisons," in stacks of three irregular quadrilaterals, lie on these dividing lines in the main register. The perforations usual in the foot of the *gu* shape are missing. The absence of corrosion may be due to the phenomenon known as cathodic protection, which in this case probably implies a high copper content (Plenderleith, 1956, pp. 189–90).

　　A sharply cast inscription inside the foot consists of a dedication to Fu Yi ("Father Yi") accompanied by a more pictorial graph transcribed as *lü* and taken to be a clan emblem (see Fig. 66). If, despite the differing clan name, this should be the same Father Yi mentioned in the inscription of the *guang* no. 45, it would then be likely that the *gu* also was made by the annalist Qi named in the inscription of the *guang*.

PUBLISHED: *Wenwu* 1978/3, pl. 4:1 (report, pp. 1–24, 42, pls. 2–8).

47　Fu Xin *jue*

Late 11th–early 10th century B.C.
Excavated 1976 from Storage Pit No. 1, Zhuangbo, Fufeng Xian, Shaanxi Province
Height 22.3 cm. (8¾ in.); weight 1.05 kg. (2 lb. 5 oz.)
Zhouyuan Archaeological Team, Shaanxi Province

From the same large hoard as nos. 45 and 46, this vessel is one of the few examples of the *jue* type from the Zhou period. The decoration of birds and vertical ribbing has precedents in late Shang times, notably on the *you* no. 25. Especially typical of Zhou designs, however, is the treatment of the birds under the spout, their shapes reduced to flowing patterns dominated by the long trailing crests. The inscription *zuo* Fu Xin, "Made for Father Xin," appears on the outer side of the (proper) left post; a clan sign, the same as on the *guang* no. 45, appears just below on the rim and side of the vessel (see Fig. 67). The surface is encrusted with powdery bright green corrosion.

PUBLISHED: *Wenwu* 1978/3, pl. 4:2 (report, pp. 1–24, 42, pls. 2–8).

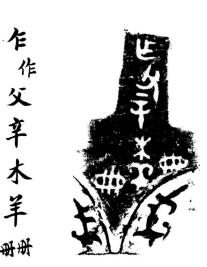

48 Altar table *(jin)*

Late 11th–early 10th century B.C.
Said to have been found 1925 or 1926, Baoji Xian,
Shaanxi Province
126 x 46.6 x 23 cm. (49½ x 18⅜ x 9 in.); weight 47.1 kg.
(103 lb. 10 oz.)
Tianjin Cultural Relics Administration

This large bronze altar table was cast in one piece. There are sixteen rectangular openings in each side, four in each end, and three oval holes in the top over which ritual vessels could be set and perhaps heated. The decoration of elongated dragons is executed on the sides in high relief against a *leiwen* background, and on the top of the table in Style IV, with the dragons flush with the *leiwen* spirals. The surface is a matte dark green.

Only two bronze tables from Shang or Zhou times are known, and both reportedly were found in Shaanxi Province, in Baoji Xian. One table, unearthed in 1901, was accompanied by twelve bronze vessels, a ladle, and a square base for one of the vessels; called the Duan Fang set after its first owner, the group of bronzes and table came intact to The Metropolitan Museum of Art in 1924 (see Umehara, 1933b). The history of this, the second, larger table, for many years lost from sight, is less easy to trace. The first notice of its existence came in 1959, when the Japanese scholar Umehara Sueji published an old photograph that he had been shown during a visit to the Academia Sinica, Taiwan (Fig. 68). The photograph shows an altar table similar to the one in the Metropolitan Museum with a number of bronzes crowded on it. Umehara's inquiries led him to believe that this second altar table and the bronzes on it had been found together in Baoji Xian sometime between 1914 and 1918, and that both table and vessels had passed into the hands of dealers in Tianjin. Many of the very distinctive vessels shown in Umehara's photograph could be identified with objects now in Western collections (the Museum of Fine Arts, Boston; the Freer Gallery of Art, Washington, D.C.; Det Danske Kunstindustrimuseum, Copenhagen; the Albright-Knox Art Gallery, Buffalo; and the Arthur M. Sackler Collections, New York). The whereabouts of the table, however, remained unknown. Since the publication of Umehara's paper, this group has been known as the Second Set from Baoji Xian.

The second altar table recently came to light, having evidently spent the intervening years in a private collection. Now in Tianjin, it was published in 1975 with the information that it was originally found in Baoji Xian at Daijiagou, Doujitai, in 1925 or 1926 (which conflicts with Umehara's information as to the date). With the reappearance of the table, the status of Umehara's "Second Set" has been thrown in doubt. Unlike the smaller table of the Duan Fang set, whose upper surface is plain and unbroken, the Tianjin table has holes in the top with tenoned edges designed to secure the foot rims of three vessels. The fact that all three holes are oval, the two outer ones alike and the central one a trifle larger, implies that the vessels for which the table was designed must all be *you* vessels (or, conceivably, *hu* vessels). None of the vessels shown in Umehara's photograph fits any of the holes. The only likely *you* that will fit is a very large vessel in the Freer Gallery that does not appear in Umehara's photograph (Lodge, 1946, pl. 29; acquired in 1930). At best, therefore, even if we should assume that the vessels in the photograph come from the same tomb as the table, the photograph cannot safely be taken to record the full contents of the tomb, since the three principal vessels associated with the table are missing. A less attractive possibility is that the photograph shows only a group of roughly contemporary vessels collected by a dealer, perhaps in Shaanxi Province, or some other such assortment. In either case, the core of the "Second Set"—the Freer *you* and two companions—remains problematic.

PUBLISHED: *Wenwu* 1975/3, pp. 47–48, pl. 1; Umehara, 1959; Tokyo, 1976, no. 34.

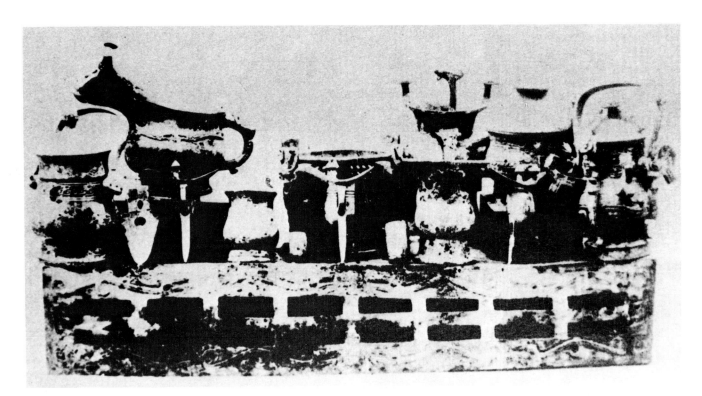

Fig. 68 Set of ritual vessels with altar table from Baoji Xian, Shaanxi Province. Photograph after Umehara, 1959, pl. 1:1

49 Gui

Late 11th–early 10th century B.C.
Found 1971, Gaojiabao, Jingyang Xian, Shaanxi Province
Height 26.5 cm. (10⅜ in.); diameter at mouth 21.5 cm. (8½ in.);
  weight 6.3 kg. (13 lb. 14 oz.)
Shaanxi Provincial Museum

Like the Li *gui* no. 41, this vessel was cast together with its hollow base. The decoration of both vessel and pedestal is dominated by confronted pairs of coiled monsters whose gaping jaws are supplied with pairs of conical teeth projecting sideways from the surface. Below the large eye each of these creatures is equipped with a single clawed foreleg; the body consists only of a coil executed in a very high molded relief. The tusked head surmounting each handle carries upraised horns with hooked edges; a bird's wings are visible lower down, but the rectangular pendant to the handle, usually reserved for the bird's claws and tail feathers (cf. no. 41), is filled instead by a small dragon facing upward, balanced on its tail.

The powerful hooked flanges that separate the two monsters on the bowl of the *gui* are typical of early Western Zhou (cf. no. 42). On top of the pedestal the corners contain small sketchy faces in low relief, composed of eyes, eyebrows, horns, and a curious heart-shaped mouth. The same motif appears on the second De *gui* (see entry no. 41); the close resemblance between the two vessels in fact extends to nearly every detail, suggesting that the *gui* from Gaojiabao might likewise be dated to the first or second Zhou reign.

The *gui* is one of a pair from the same tomb, both reported to be uninscribed. Since the other two similarly decorated vessels from the tomb, the *you* no. 50 and *zun* no. 51, share a one-character inscription, it may be unsafe to assume that all four vessels were cast as a set. On the other hand, not too much importance should be attached to the different flanges and slight differences in execution that separate the *gui* from the *you* and *zun*. It is even conceivable that the inscription of one graph—nearly invisible on the *zun*—is concealed under the dark green corrosion of the *gui*.

PUBLISHED: *Wenwu* 1972/7, fig. 3, inside back cover (report, pp. 5–8); Xi'an, 1973, p. 7, no. 9.

50 Fu Mou *you*

Late 11th–early 10th century B.C.
Found 1971, Gaojiabao, Jingyang Xian, Shaanxi Province
Height 36 cm. (14⅛ in.); weight 6.4 kg. (14 lb.)
Shaanxi Provincial Museum

Together with nos. 49 and 51, this *you* came from a small tomb that contained thirteen bronze vessels, a bronze *ge* blade, and five objects of jade. The burial was oriented north-south and included a guardian pit beneath the corpse, but lacked the stepped profile described in entry no. 12. The bronzes were set near the head and the jades on the breast, all apparently within a wooden housing that survived in traces.

Like the *gui* no. 49, the *you* is decorated with coiled monsters, but the creatures seen here, their lower jaws turned inward, are more firmly shaped than the somewhat puffy versions on the *gui*. Three narrow registers on the *you*, less suitable for the coiled animals, are filled with other motifs. Sinuous dragons are confronted in pairs on the foot and lid, while in the uppermost zone of the body two more dragons come together to share a single three-dimensional head set in the center of the register. The dragons on the foot and lid are edged with flickering borders, and behind each head is a small crest formed of a single eye in the middle of a pronged device. The large shield that stands in bold relief between the coiled animals in the main register is an element that derives

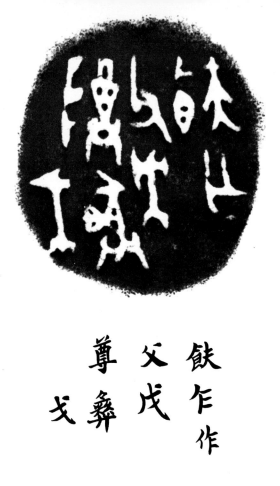

Fig. 69 Rubbing and transcription of inscription,
Fu Mou *you* no. 50. Photograph courtesy of
Cultural Relics Bureau, Beijing

ultimately from the nose of a *taotie* face (cf., e.g., no. 31).

The handle, placed over the long axis of the vessel (cf. no. 25), is decorated with dragons—two heads and two legs attached to each stringy body. The handles end with heads whose large crests or horns have hooked edges, recalling the same feature on the *gui* no. 49. The flanges of both the *you* and the *zun* no. 51 are, however, conspicuously different from those on the *gui*. Solid with blunt projections, rather than openworked and hooked, they are stiff and rather lifeless descendants of the Shang form seen on the *you* no. 25. Their coexistence with the hooked variety appearing on the *gui* is a reminder of the wide range of forms inherited and freely employed by the Zhou artist.

The knob of the lid appears to be cast on, since just beneath it inside the lid a blob of bright, untarnished metal is visible. Curiously, the inscription of the vessel is crowded into this patch of metal and thus was cast with the knob. The result has a makeshift appearance that in an unprovenanced bronze would surely inspire any scholar with doubts of its authenticity; Zhou casters must have been less particular than modern connoisseurs. The inscription (see Fig. 69) reads "X made this precious ritual vessel for Father Mou," followed by the graph *ge* (a halberd). (The name of the vessel's maker is here written as X because the archaic character has no obvious modern equivalent.) This inscription is not repeated in the body of the vessel, which instead contains only a single graph, perhaps a clan emblem, which appears again inside the *zun* no. 51. Perhaps the *you* and *zun* were made originally as a pair inscribed only with this one graph, and the inscription in the lid of the *you* was added later, conceivably by a different owner, in recasting the knob of the lid.

PUBLISHED: *Wenwu* 1972/7, fig. 1, inside back cover (report, pp. 5–8); Xi'an, 1973, p. 10, no. 13.

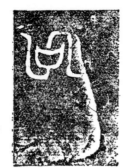

51 *Zun*

Late 11th–early 10th century B.C.
Found 1971, Gaojiabao, Jingyang Xian, Shaanxi Province
Height 31.5 cm. (12⅜ in.); diameter at mouth 22.5 cm. (8⅞ in.);
    weight 4.3 kg. (9 lb. 7 oz.)
Shaanxi Provincial Museum

The inscription of this *zun*, a single graph (see Fig. 70), is shared
with the *you* no. 50 from the same tomb, and the two vessels were
no doubt made as a pair; the surfaces of both are dull green and
brown. The motif of the coiled animal appears here only in the
middle register. The foot is occupied by *taotie* designs, while the
upper part contains a narrow band of angular snakes like those on
the foot of the *gui* no. 49 and eight triangular blades rising to the
rim. The blades are filled with staring faces—two jaws in profile
and two eyes—attached to "bodies" devoid of any organic feature.

Matched sets, usually agreeing in both decor and inscription,
are common in Western Zhou. A *zun* sometimes accompanies a
single *you*, as here, but more often a pair (see entry no. 48). Other
specially favored combinations include *fang yi* and *zun* (see nos. 59,
60); or *fang yi*, *zun*, and *guang* (see entry no. 45). In Shang times,
sets of *jue* and *gu*, *jue* and *jia*, or all three—shapes that disappear in
Western Zhou—are relatively common. Sets combining other vessel types are less often seen. In the Anyang tomb of Fu Hao, the
bronzes seem usually to fall into matched sets of two or more of the
same vessel type rather than of assorted types.

PUBLISHED: *Wenwu* 1972/7, p. 8, fig. 11 (report, pp. 5–8).

52 *Ding*

Late 11th–early 10th century B.C.
Found 1973, Chang'an Xian, Shaanxi Province
Height 78 cm. (30¾ in.); diameter 63 cm. (24¾ in.); weight 85.2 kg.
    (187 lb. 7 oz.)
Shaanxi Provincial Museum

This very large *ding* was found buried in a small pit, where it had
been set inverted over another bronze, a large *yu*. Neither vessel is
inscribed. There were no signs of a tomb or of any other artifacts.
The *ding* belongs to the early Western Zhou period, while the *yu*,
decorated with the wave pattern seen on the Da Ke *ding* (Fig. 79),
dates to the end of Western Zhou; for disparity of contents, this was
the quintessential Western Zhou bronze hoard.

The larger part of the *ding* is covered with a geometric pattern
of interlocked T-hooks, a pattern that occurs already on pre-Anyang bronzes. The register just below the molded rim contains six
taotie, each bisected by a flange, their bodies alternately turning
downward to spiral at the bottom edge of the register, and upward
to fork at the top in a configuration like a fishtail. On the outer faces
of the handles appear confronted pairs of rampant dragons in high
relief. Seam lines are visible on all six flanges, but seams cut
through the T-hook pattern only on the axes of the three legs. The
dark brown surface is overlaid in places with a matte dark green.

PUBLISHED: *Kaogu* 1974/1, pl. 1:1 (report, pp. 1–5, pl. 1); Tokyo,
1976, no. 30.

53 Yan Hou *yu*

Early 10th century B.C.
Found 1955, Machanggou, Kezuo Xian, Liaoning Province
Height 24 cm. (9½ in.); diameter 34 cm. (13⅜ in.); weight 6.45 kg
    (14 lb. 3 oz.)
Historical Museum, Beijing

This *yu* and its inscription have been discussed on page 200. The
vessel formed part of an oddly assorted hoard of sixteen bronzes,
apparently not connected with a tomb, that included both familiar
early Zhou types and such curiosities as a large bronze duck.
(Twelve vessels from the hoard are illustrated in Beijing, 1958, pls.
20–27.) The *yu* is by far the finest vessel of the group, and the only
one mentioning the marquis of Yan in its inscription (see Fig. 71).
The handles, braced at the upper ends by struts from the vessel
wall, appear to have been precast. The surface is dull gray in the
decorated areas and in the interior, but soft light green elsewhere.

The motif of the crested dragon with a bird's body in the
particularly elegant form seen here is quite rare (see Fig. 60). A *gui*
published by Cheng Te-k'un and a paired *you* and *zun* made by one
Jian may perhaps represent slightly earlier and slightly later versions, respectively, of the design (Cheng, 1963, pl. 17b; Watson,
1962, pl. 33b; Kelley, 1946, pl. 23). The two Jian vessels are
provided with hooked flanges of the variety whose outline is imitated by the dragons' crests.

Scholars are not all agreed as to the precise date of this *yu*, and
accordingly it is not certain which marquis of Yan should be assumed to have commissioned it. A date around the third Zhou
reign, however, seems reasonable, and this might still fall within
the period of activity of the first marquis. On the evidence of other
inscribed bronzes, Chen Mengjia takes the personal name of the
first marquis, the son of the duke of Shao, to be Zhi (as assumed
here, above; see Chen, 1955–56, no. 52). Chen's identification has
not gone unchallenged, however, some scholars arguing that Zhi
was a later marquis, or differently related to the duke of Shao.

PUBLISHED: *Wenwu Cankao Ziliao* 1955/8, pp. 16–27; Chen,
1955–56, no. 24.

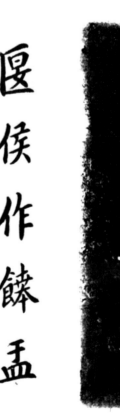

Fig. 71 Rubbing and transcription of inscription,
Yan Hou *yu* no. 53. Photograph courtesy of
Cultural Relics Bureau, Beijing

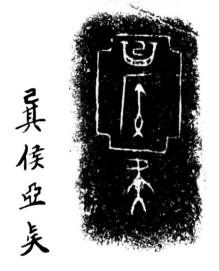

Fig. 72   Rubbing and transcription of
composite pictogram in bottom of Mu Ji *fang
ding* no. 54. Photograph courtesy of Cultural
Relics Bureau, Beijing

54   Mu Ji *fang ding*

11th century B.C.
Excavated 1973 from Pit No. 2, Beidongcun, Kezuo Xian,
    Liaoning Province
Height 51.7 cm. (20⅜ in.); length and width at mouth 40.7 x 30.7
    cm. (16 x 12⅛ in.); weight 31 kg. (68 lb. 3 oz.)
Liaoning Provincial Museum

This *fang ding* was found in a storage pit together with the *lei* no. 55
and four other vessels. It represents a late and somewhat lackluster
variation on the classic decor scheme of the much earlier *fang ding*
vessels nos. 11 and 28. The surface is brown and gray.

    A large composite pictogram is cast in the bottom of the vessel
(see Fig. 72). The bulk of the inscription appears on the inside wall
and consists of twenty-three neatly written characters in four columns, with a twenty-fourth graph centered just below (see Fig.
73). The text, which is peculiarly worded, contains several inde-
cipherable proper names, replaced here by letters of the alphabet:

On the day *ding hai*, A bestowed on the *youzheng* [an official] B
C-cowries at the place Mu, strings with [altogether] two hun-

dred shells. To make known A's generosity, B used [the cowries]
to cast this ritual *ding* vessel for Mother Ji.

The graph C is apparently the place of origin or type of the cowries.
The phrase specifying the quantity might be straightforwardly read
as "two hundred strings of cowries"—but this is a staggering
amount. One hundred strings is the maximum hitherto encountered in Shang and Zhou inscriptions, and most gifts are far smaller.
The reading given above seems warranted by sense if not syntax.
One scholar has proposed instead the reading "one string and two
hundred loose shells"; but this hardly eases the grammar and, if
Guo Moruo is correct in maintaining that a string of cowries held
only ten shells, seems rather less logical (*Kaogu* 1975/5, p. 276).
    The composite pictogram in the bottom of the vessel must
provide some further identification of the owner, the *youzheng* B.
The pictogram includes the familiar *yaxing* cartouche (a rectangle
with the corners removed) and below it a human figure. These two
elements together form an emblem fairly common among late
Shang and early Zhou inscriptions, uninterpretable but sometimes
conventionally read *ya yi*. In some instances the emblem appears
with the *yaxing* left empty. In other inscriptions, possibly later, the
yaxing contains the character *ji* or, as here, the title Ji Hou,
"marquis of Ji"* (Did the "*ya yi*" family acquire a patent of nobility?); examples are known from Anyang (Liang, 1944, 1/8, 1/46).
The title Ji Hou moreover occurs in at least one oracle text, suggesting that the marquis of Ji was a vassal of the Shang court.
    There exist several other bronze inscriptions in which a person
named A figures as donor; in at least one case, the recipient of the
gift writes as his clan sign the same combination *Ji Hou ya yi* seen
here. Yan Wan has argued that these inscriptions are all late Shang
in date, and that the present *fang ding* consequently must have
been cast in Shang times (*Kaogu* 1975/5, pp. 276–77). He goes on to
suggest that the marquis of Ji's fief lay in the northeast (p. 279)—
which might help to account for the fact that the *fang ding* somehow found its way into a hoard of early Zhou bronzes, buried in the
Yan state.

PUBLISHED: *Kaogu* 1974/6, pl. 7:3 (report, pp. 364–72, pls. 1, 6, 7);
    Tokyo, 1976, no. 29.

*This name Ji is not the same graph as the Ji in "Mother Ji" in the body of the
  inscription.

Fig. 73   Rubbing and transcription of
inscription on the inside wall
of Mu Ji *fang ding* no. 54.
Photograph courtesy of Cultural
Relics Bureau, Beijing

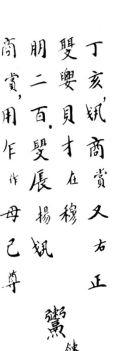

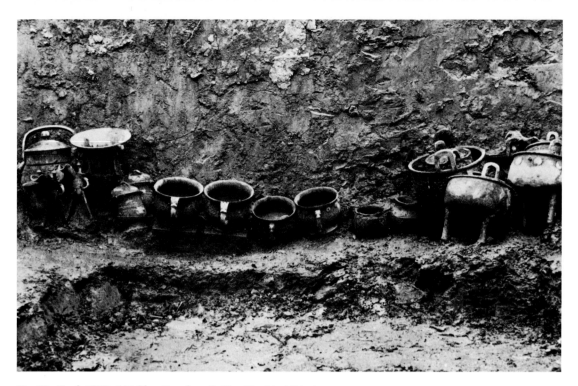

Fig. 74 Tomb M251 at Liulihe, Fangshan, Beijing Municipal District. The Bo Ji *li* no. 56 came from this tomb. Photograph courtesy of Cultural Relics Bureau, Beijing

55 *Lei*

Late 11th–early 10th century B.C.
Excavated 1973 from Pit No. 2, Beidongcun, Kezuo Xian,
    Liaoning Province
Height 45.2 cm. (17¾ in.); weight 8.2 kg. (18 lb.)
Liaoning Provincial Museum

The widest register of this vessel is divided by the vertical seams into quarters, each filled by a large *taotie* unit. Though comparable in design to the *taotie* patterns on the *guang* no. 45, the motif has here been relegated to a distinctly subordinate position. Seen from the front, the central vertical axis separates a pair of *taotie*, instead of bisecting a single one; this off-axis positioning, together with the retiring location of the faces on the lower, inward-curving portion of the vessel, deprives the motif of its usual dominating frontality and weakens its effect. Pride of place is instead taken by the coiled monsters on the shoulder, familiar already from nos. 49–51; while the expression of the vessel as a whole is given by the lid, which takes the form of a coiled, bottle-horned dragon rising menacingly on its forelegs. A pair of handles with pendant rings are set into the shoulder frieze at the sides of the *lei*, and a smaller handle appears lower on the central axis of the side illustrated. The surface is silvery with greenish discolorations.

This vessel was found in a storage pit in Liaoning Province together with the *fang ding* no. 54 and four other bronzes. A group of three large *lei* vessels unearthed in 1959 in Sichuan Province, at Zhuwajie, Peng Xian, included two that are very similar to the present *lei;* in both the Sichuan vessels, however, the dragon on the lid has dramatic upraised crests on its head and a large hooked flange down its back (Beijing, 1972a, pl. 53; *Wenwu* 1961/11, pp. 5, 28–31, front cover). Another vessel of the same type, its lid missing, was found in 1966 in Qishan Xian, Shaanxi Province (*Wenwu* 1972/6, p. 26, fig. 4). A last *lei* related in style to this group is in the Nezu Art Museum, Tokyo (Umehara, 1942, pl. 23). None of the vessels mentioned is inscribed.

PUBLISHED: *Kaogu* 1974/6, pl. 1 (report, pp. 364–72, pls. 1, 6, 7); Tokyo, 1976, no. 28.

56 Bo Ju *li*

Late 11th–early 10th century B.C.
Excavated 1975 from M251, Huangtupocun, Liulihe,
    Fangshan, Beijing Metropolitan District
Height 33 cm. (13 in.); diameter 22.9 cm. (9 in.); weight 8.25 kg.
    (18 lb. 2 oz.)
Beijing Cultural Relics Bureau

The lobes of this tripod are decorated with *taotie* faces, simply and forcefully modeled, with large horns projecting from the surface. The same faces and buffalo horns—features not easy to cast—appear to even more striking effect on the flat lid. In the center of the lid a small loop handle set between the two *taotie* is surmounted by a pair of very realistic buffalo heads modeled in the round. The compact shape of the vessel and the sensitive adaptation to it of extravagantly plastic decoration give an effect of concentrated energy and force without obscuring the delicate proportions; the achievement is almost unique in Western Zhou. One other vessel comparable in style and quality, the Dui Cheng *you* in the Museum of Fine Arts, Boston, can be assigned to the early Western Zhou period on the strength of its resemblance to the Bo Ju *li* (Mizuno, 1959, pl. 88). The matte surface of the *li* has corroded to several shades of green and blue.

This vessel and no. 57 come from two different tombs in a large early Western Zhou cemetery under excavation since 1972 at Liulihe, Fangshan, in Beijing. Traces of a late Shang city wall have been found at the same site. The richly furnished tomb M251 (Fig. 74) contained several bronzes with inscriptions mentioning the marquis of Yan. These include the present *li*, whose inscription reads: "On the day *mou chen*, the marquis of Yan gave Bo Ju cowries, which he used to make this precious ritual vessel for Father Mou." The inscription is cast in the center of the lid, and again in the neck of the vessel proper (see Fig. 75). It is interesting to notice that the cyclical character *mou* used to form the posthumous title for Bo Ju's father is the same as the character that designates the day, *mou chen*, on which the gift of cowries was made. There is good evidence that the posthumous title of an ancestor specified the day on which he regularly received sacrifice;

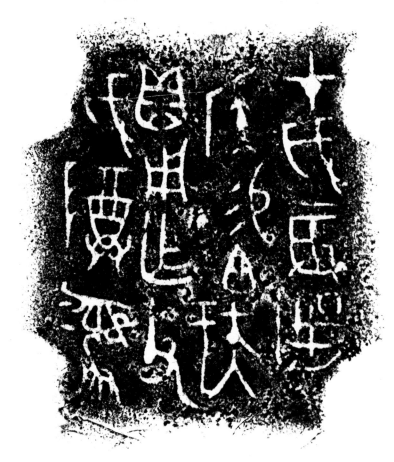

Fig. 75 Rubbing and transcription of inscription, Bo Ji *li* no. 56.
Photograph courtesy of Cultural Relics Bureau, Beijing

the correspondence here might also not be accidental.

Recent excavations at Shanwanzi, Kezuo, Liaoning Province, have unearthed a *xian* vessel apparently cast by the same person who commissioned the present *li*. Its inscription reads *Bo Ju zuo bao zun yi*, "Bo Ju made this precious vessel" (*Wenwu* 1977/12, p. 24, fig. 3; p. 32, fig. 52).

PUBLISHED: *Wenwu* 1978/4, pp. 26–27, figs. 14, 15; Tokyo, 1976, no. 27.

57 Yi Gong *gui*

Late 11th–early 10th century B.C.
Excavated 1974 from M209, Huangtupocun, Liulihe,
    Fangshan, Beijing Metropolitan District
Height 27 cm. (10⅝ in.); diameter 20.5 cm. (8⅛ in.); weight 5 kg.
    (11 lb.)
Beijing Cultural Relics Bureau

The principal motif decorating this *gui* is—judging by its trunk—an elephant, but the anatomically gauche creature seen here owes nothing to earlier and more successful depictions of elephants, being instead pieced together from a variety of other motifs (see Fig. 76). A *taotie*'s horn or crest serves it for an ear, and the jaw and eye are type forms equally old. It is to other motifs, too, that we must turn for an explanation of the odd hooked elements that project behind the elephant, and also in front where they meet the central flange; and the hooked bladelike ornaments supplying the elephant's legs are equally arbitrary adaptations from earlier forms. Finally, the chief impetus behind the assembly of these parts must come from the coiled monster seen on nos. 49–51; the presentation of the elephants in confronted pairs is the same, as is the relief technique, and a precise allusion to the older motif appears in the raised spiraling lines that mark the elephant's body. We might thus be tempted to view the elephant's sudden appearance in fully developed form as an attempt to rationalize the motif of the coiled monster by converting it to the semblance of a real animal. The new motif occurs with little variation on a series of early Zhou vessels, of which the most famous is the marquis of Xing *gui* seen in figure 57; another example, also mentioning the marquis of Xing in its inscription, was found in 1978 in Hebei Province, in Yuanshi Xian (*Kaogu* 1979/1, pl. 8:4).

The present *gui* came from the tomb M209 in the Western Zhou cemetery at Liulihe, Beijing (see entry no. 56). It bears only a short inscription, cast in the center of the lid and repeated in the center of the bowl: "Bo made this *jiu* [*gui*] for Yi Gong" (see Fig. 77). The rough matte surface of the *gui* is variegated blue and green.

The vessel stands on four legs in the form of elephant trunks, the trunks issuing illogically from the mouths of elephantlike tusked heads. Two of these heads are set on the foot rim of the vessel; the other two are placed at the bottoms of the large, bird-shaped handles (cf. no. 45). The *gui* on legs seems to have been a fashion largely confined to early Western Zhou. Typical versions have four handles and are supported on long pendants that descend from the handles, as, for example, the Chen Chen *gui* in the Fogg Art Museum, Cambridge, Massachusetts, and the Ban *gui* in Beijing (Rong, 1941, vol. 2, p. 162, fig. 302; *Wenwu* 1972/9, pp. 2–13; *China Pictorial* 1978/9, p. 14, which shows the Ban *gui*, much restored). A two-handled *gui* excavated from M53 in the Beijing cemetery where the present vessel was unearthed rests instead on three feet in the shape of rampant tigers attached beneath the foot rim (*Kaogu* 1974/5, pl. 8:2); later in Western Zhou, *gui* are often supplied with diminutive feet on the foot rim. None of these variants could be said to attain any great structural eloquence.

PUBLISHED: Tokyo, 1976, no. 26; Beijing, 1976a, no. 27.

212

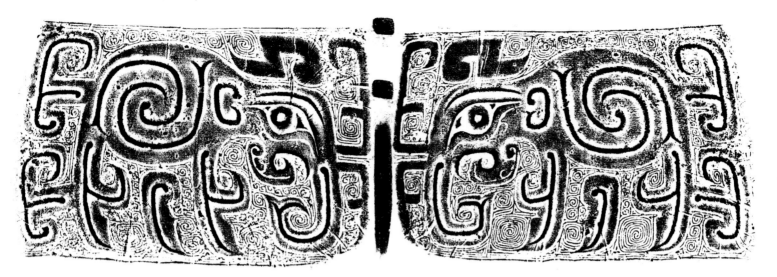

Fig. 76   Rubbing of decor, Yi Gong *gui* no. 57. Photograph courtesy of
Cultural Relics Bureau, Beijing

公 白
尊 伯
簋 乍

白
作
乙

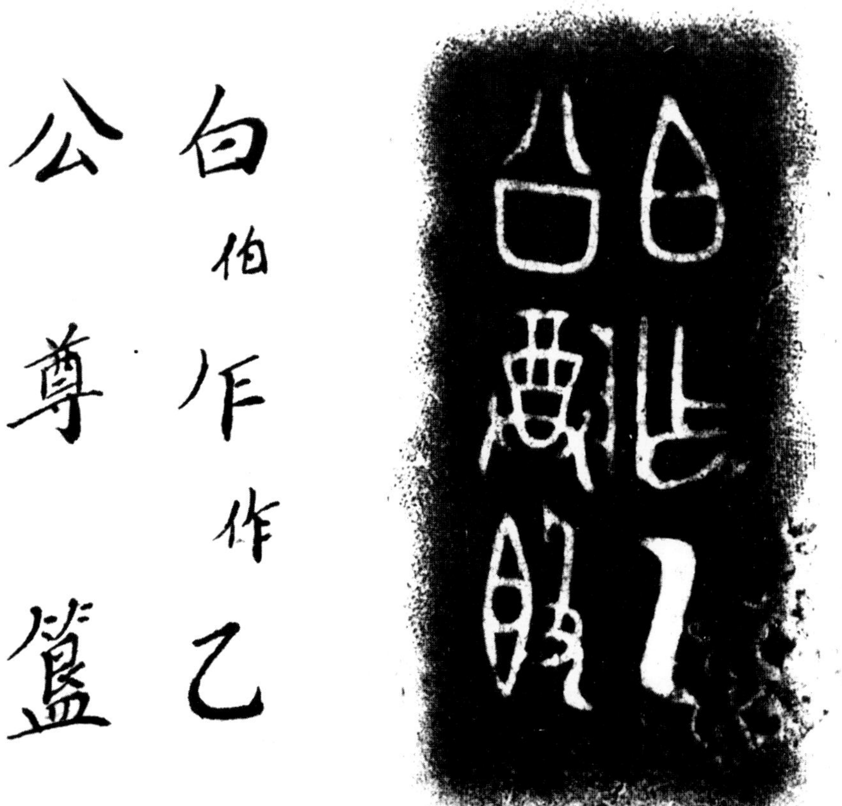

Fig. 77   Rubbing and transcription of inscription, Yi Gong *gui* no. 57.
Photograph courtesy of Cultural Relics Bureau, Beijing

COLORPLATES 41-63

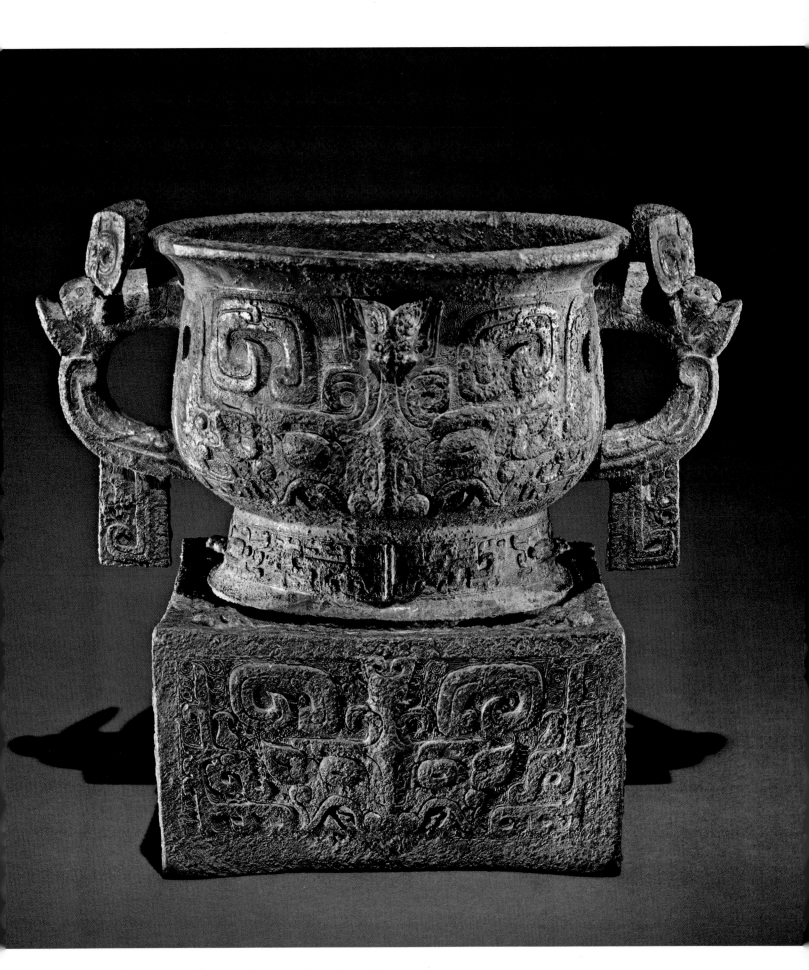

41 Li *gui*. Late 11th century B.C. (first year of Wu Wang's reign). Height
28 cm. (11 in.); diameter at mouth 22 cm. (8⅝ in.); weight 7.95 kg.
(17 lb. 8 oz.)

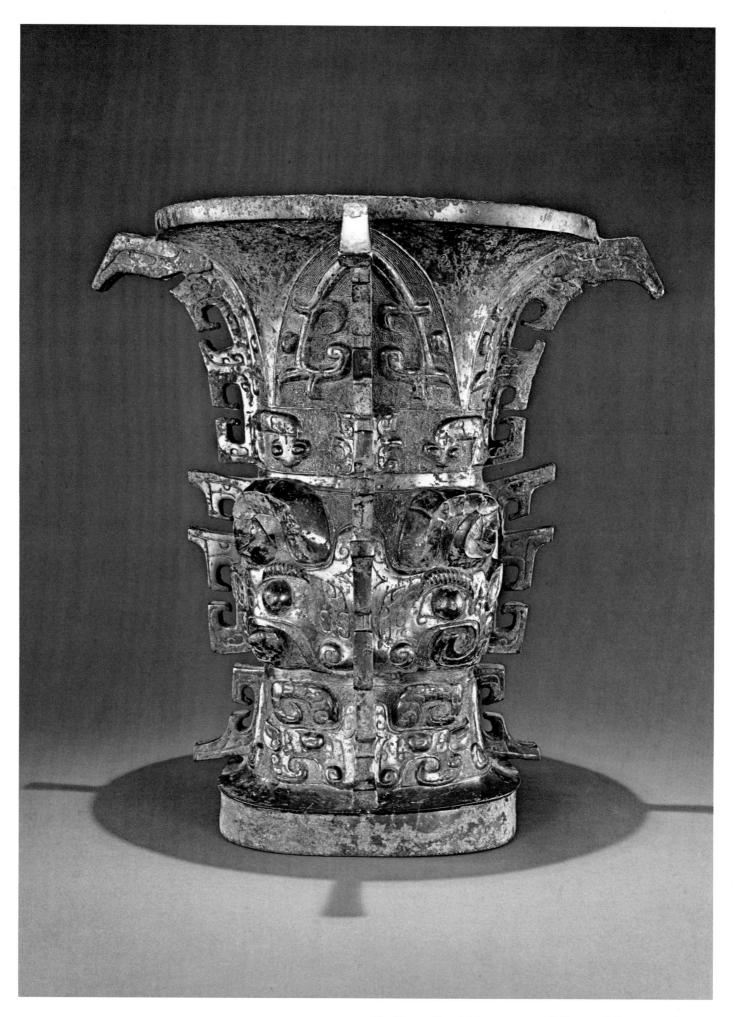

42 He *zun*. Late 11th century B.C. (fifth year of Cheng Wang's reign).
Height 38.8 cm. (15¼ in.); diameter at mouth 28.6 cm. (11¼ in.);
weight 14.78 kg. (32 lb. 8 oz.)

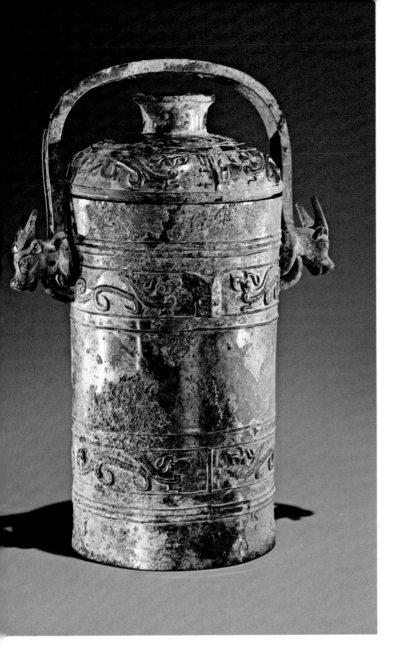

43 Luan Bo *you*. Late 11th–early 10th century B.C. Height
29 cm. (11⅜ in.); diameter 12 cm. (4¾ in.); weight 2.25
kg. (4 lb. 15 oz.)

44 Luan Bo *he*. Late 11th–early 10th century B.C. Height
28.5 cm. (11¼ in.); weight 2.5 kg. (5 lb. 8 oz.)

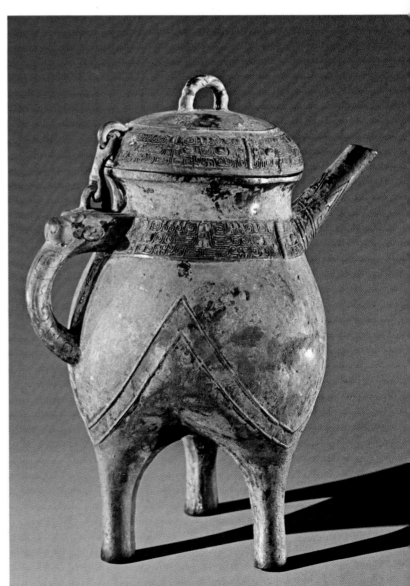

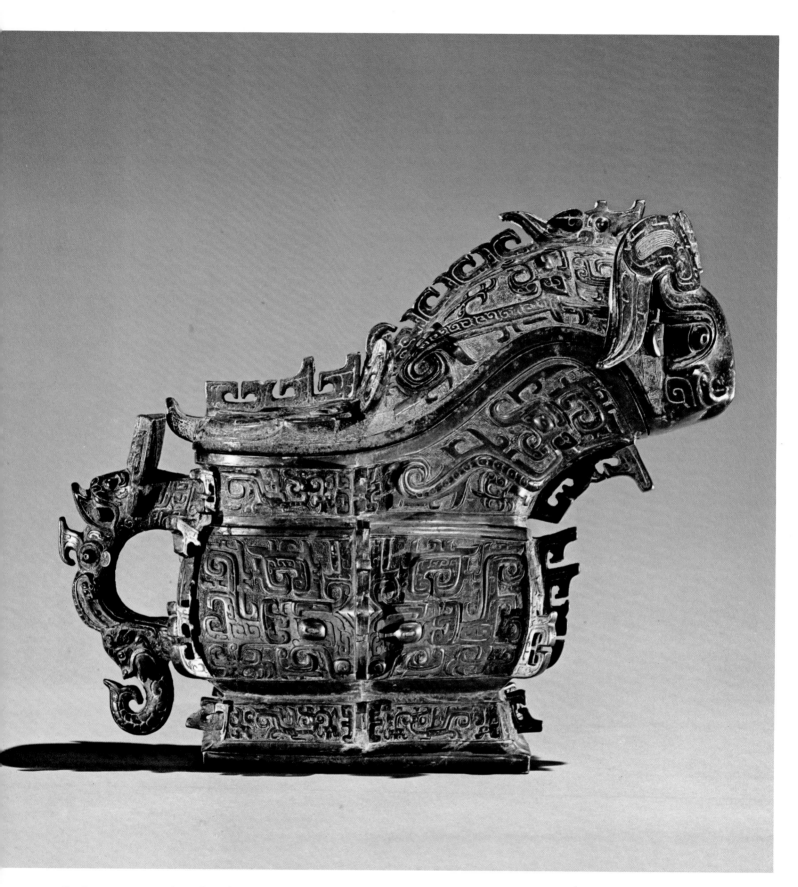

45 Qi *guang*. Late 11th–early 10th century B.C. Height 28.7 cm. (11¼ in.); length 36.5 cm. (14⅜ in.); weight 7.55 kg. (16 lb. 10 oz.)

46 Lü Fu Yi *gu*. Late 11th–early 10th century B.C. Height
25.2 cm. (9⅞ in.); diameter at mouth 13.2 cm. (5¼ in.);
weight 0.55 kg. (1 lb. 3 oz.)

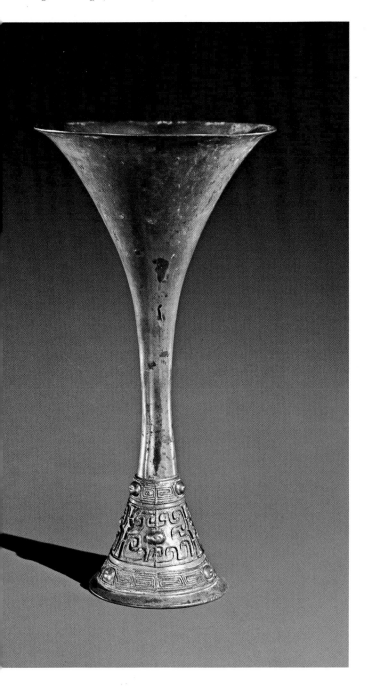

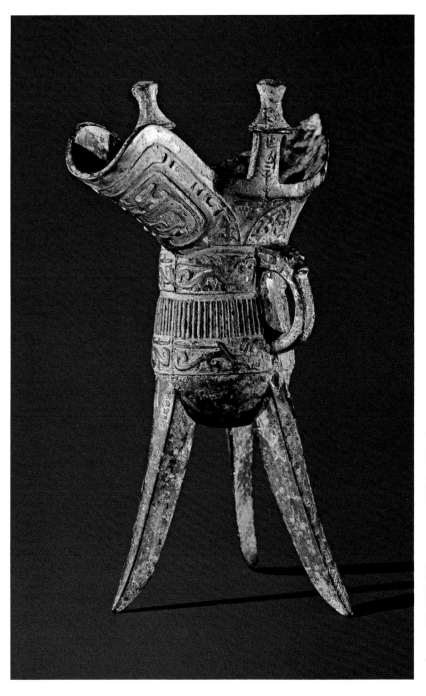

47 Fu Xin *jue*. Late 11th–early 10th century B.C. Height
22.3 cm. (8¾ in.); weight 1.05 kg. (2 lb. 5 oz.)

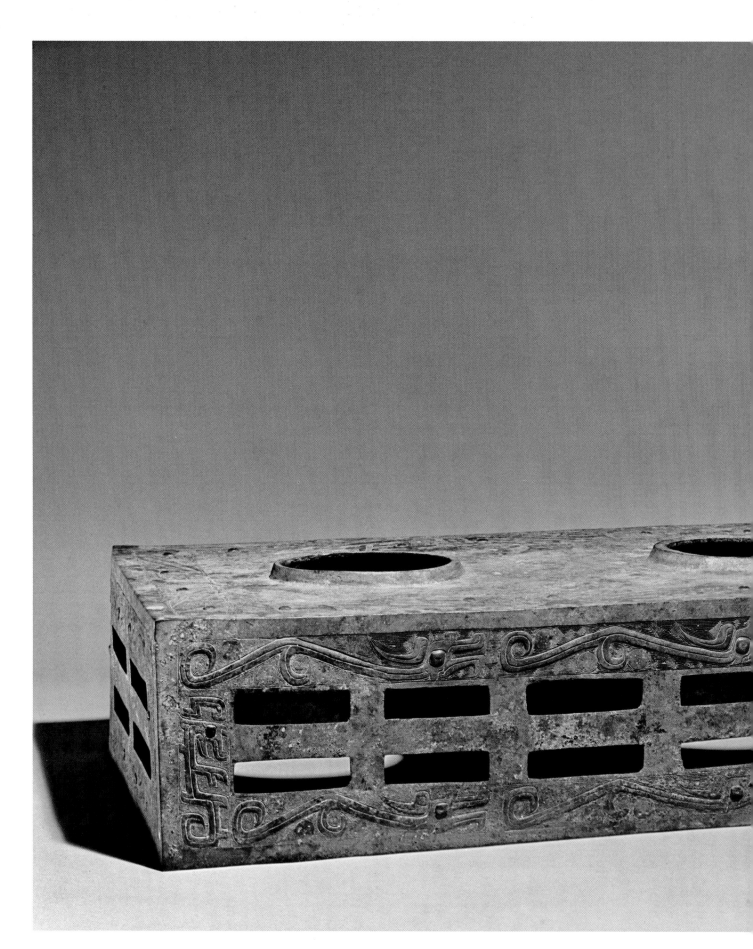

48 Altar table (*jin*). Late 11th–early 10th century B.C. 126 x 46.6 x 23 cm.
(49½ x 18⅜ x 9 in.); weight 47.1 kg. (103 lb. 10 oz.)

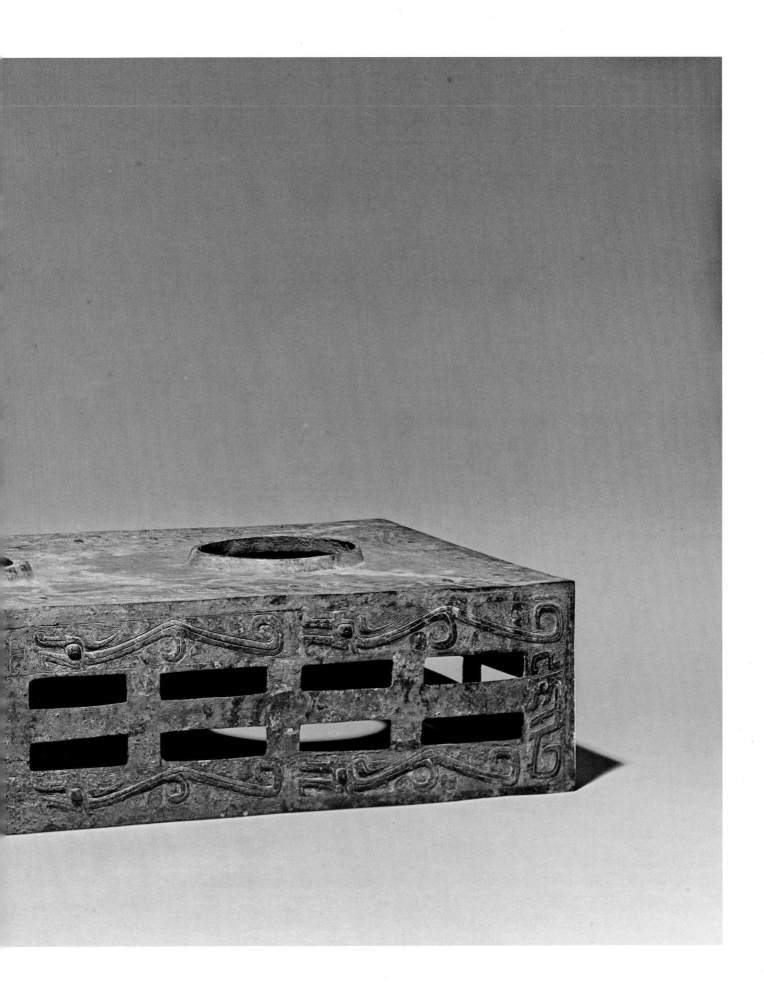

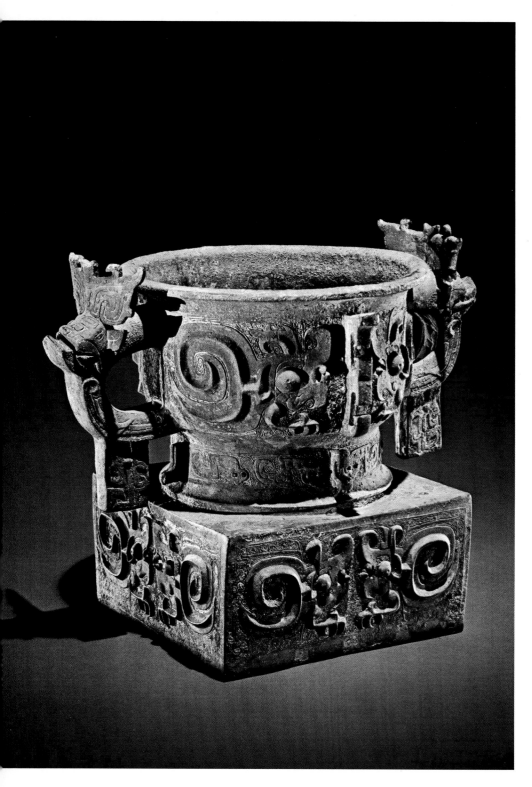

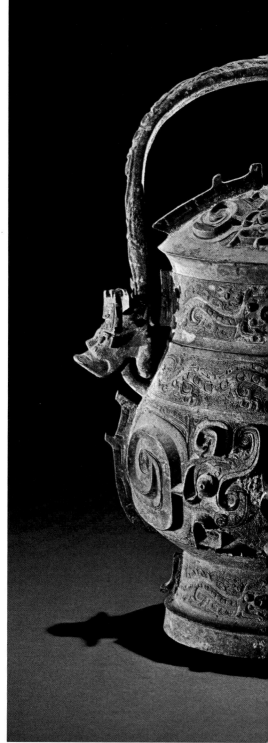

49 *Gui.* Late 11th–early 10th century B.C. Height 26.5 cm. (10⅜ in.); diameter at mouth 21.5 cm. (8½ in.); weight 6.3 kg. (13 lb. 14 oz.)

50 Fu Mou *you.* Late 11th–early 10th century B.C. Height 36 cm. (14⅛ in.); weight 6.4 kg. (14 lb.)

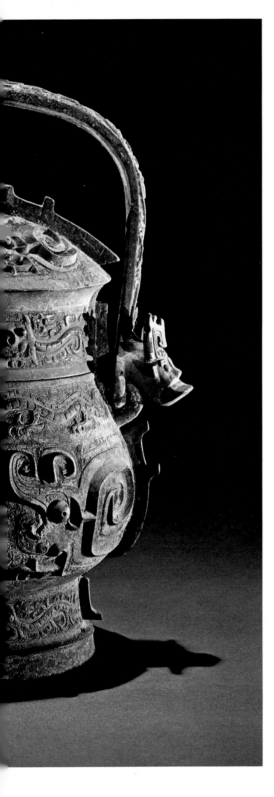
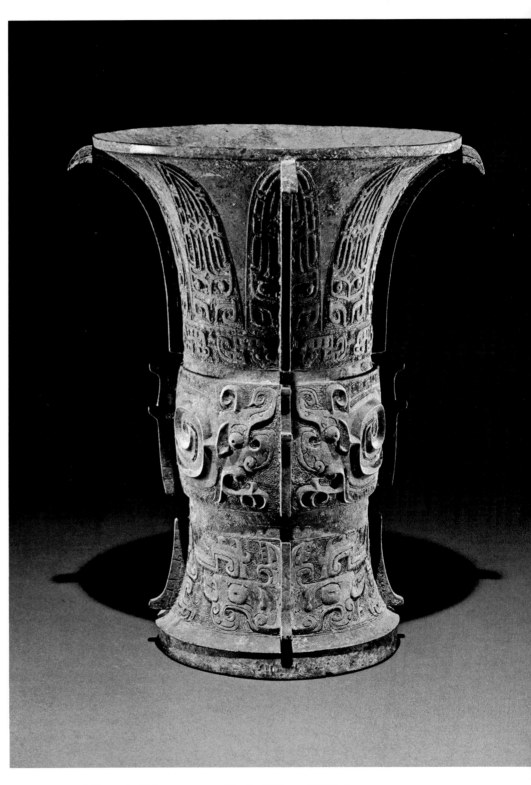

51 *Zun*. Late 11th–early 10th century B.C. Height 31.5 cm. (12⅜ in.);
diameter at mouth 22.5 cm. (8⅞ in.); weight 4.3 kg. (9 lb. 7 oz.)

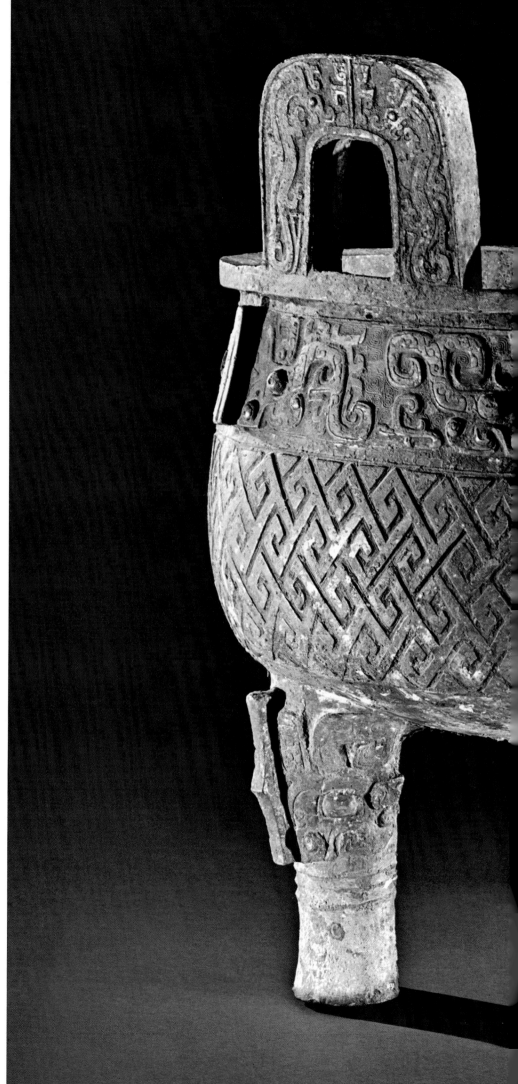

52 *Ding.* Late 11th–early 10th century B.C.
Height 78 cm. (30¾ in.); diameter 63 cm.
(24¾ in.); weight 85.2 kg. (187 lb. 7 oz.)

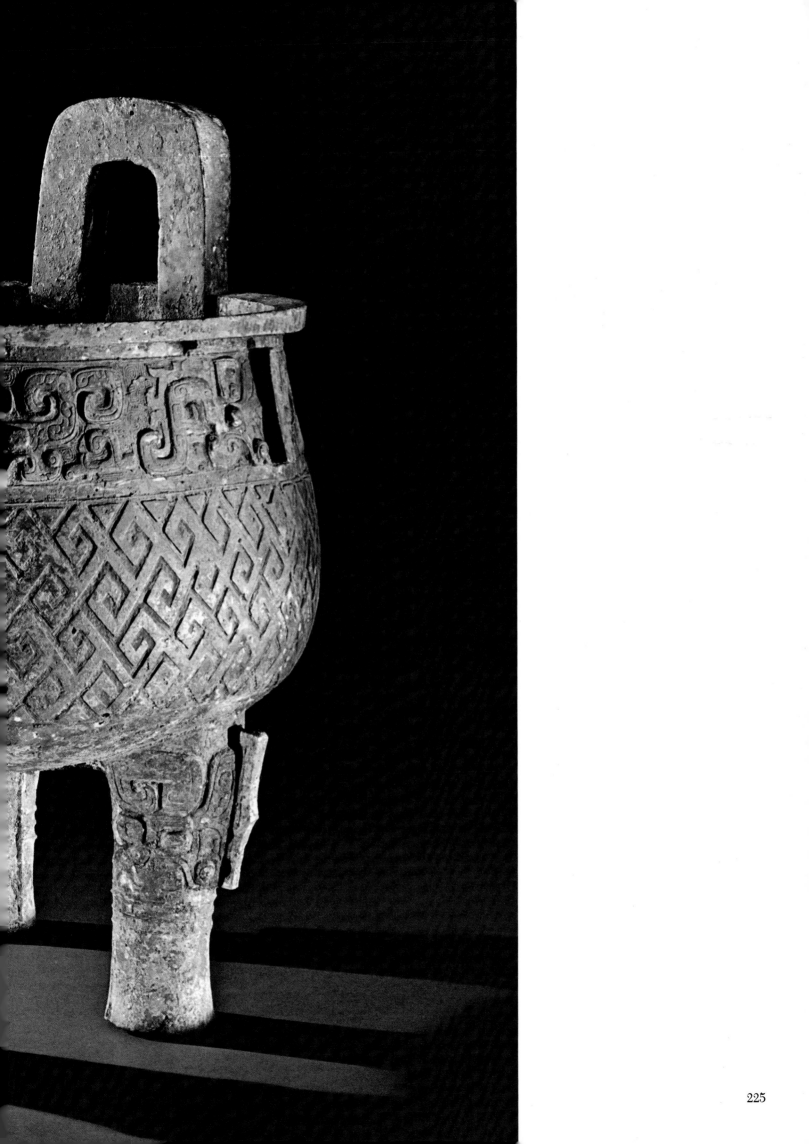

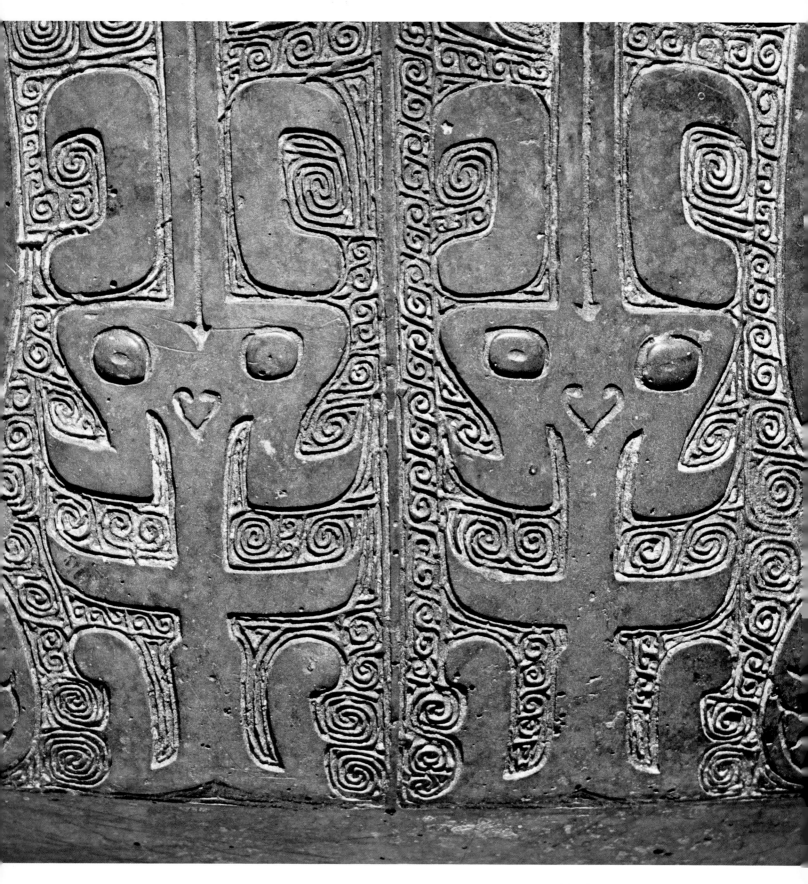

Detail, bird plumage decor of Yan Hou *yu* no. **53**

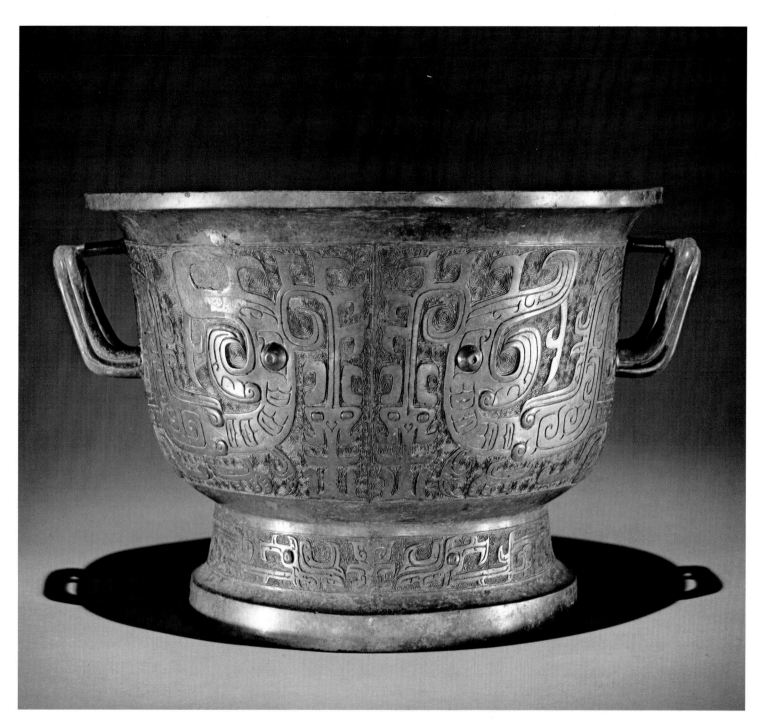

53 Yan Hou *yu*. Early 10th century B.C. Height 24 cm. (9½ in.); diameter
34 cm. (13⅜ in.); weight 6.45 kg. (14 lb. 3 oz.)

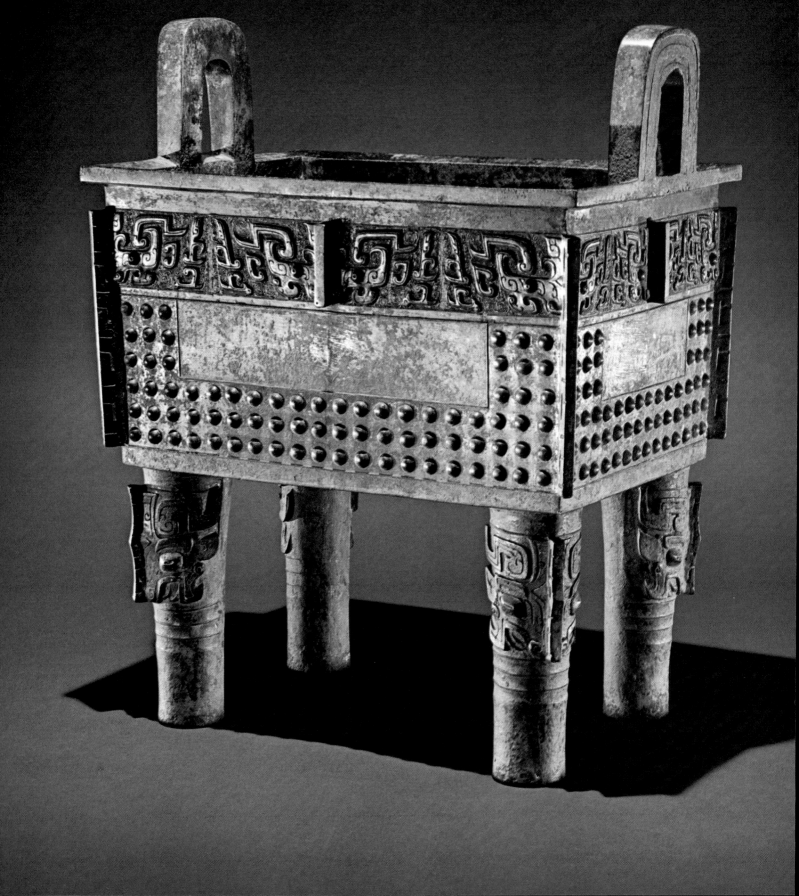

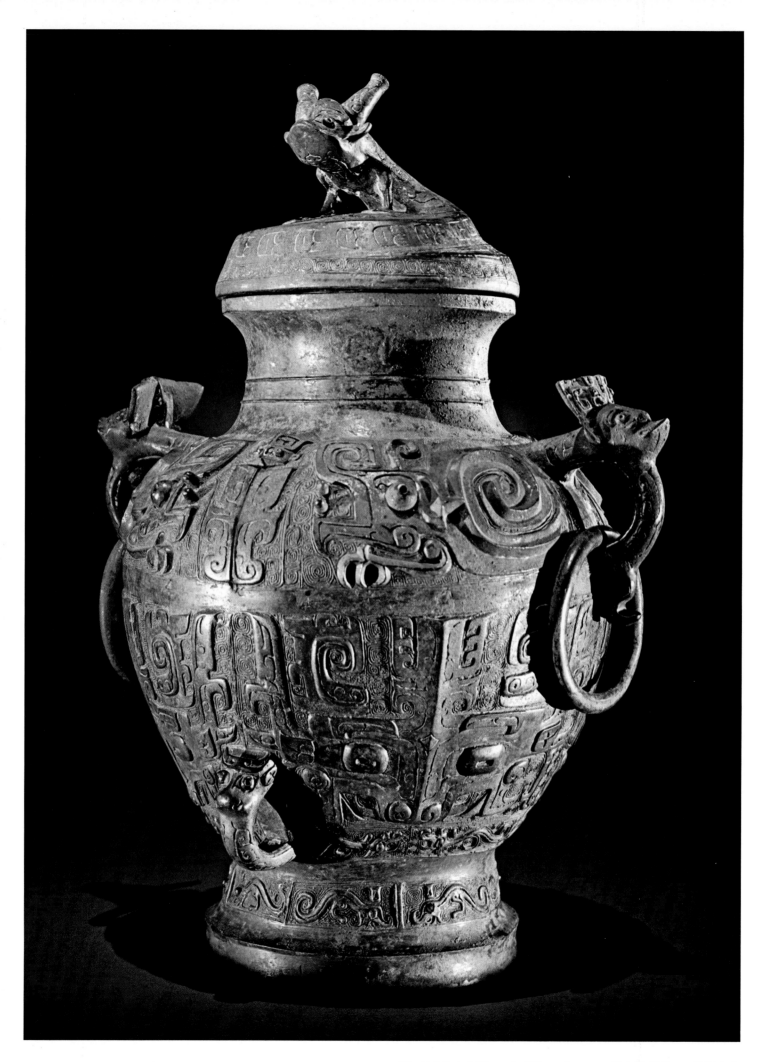

54 Mu Ji *fang ding.* 11th century B.C. Height 51.7 cm. (20⅜ in.); length and width at mouth 40.7 x 30.7 cm. (16 x 12⅛ in.); weight 31 kg. (68 lb. 3 oz.)

55 *Lei.* Late 11th–early 10th century B.C. Height 45.2 cm. (17¾ in.); weight 8.2 kg. (18 lb.)

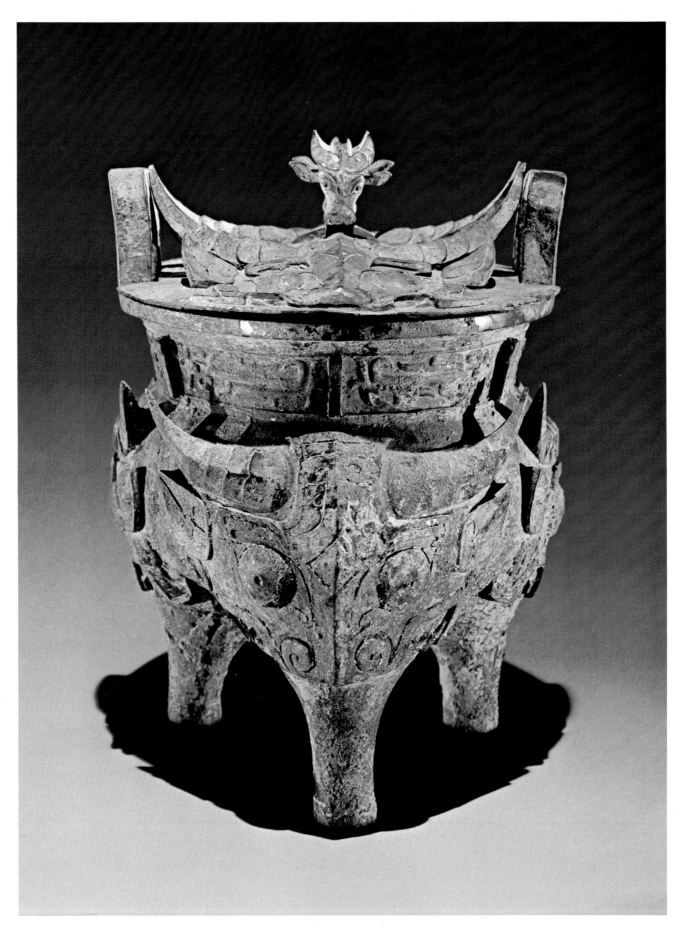

56 Bo Ju *li*. Late 11th–early 10th century B.C. Height 33 cm. (13 in.);
diameter 22.9 cm. (9 in.); weight 8.25 kg. (18 lb. 2 oz.)

57 Yi Gong *gui*. Late 11th–early 10th century B.C. Height 27 cm.
(10⅝ in.); diameter 20.5 cm. (8⅛ in.); weight 5 kg. (11 lb.)

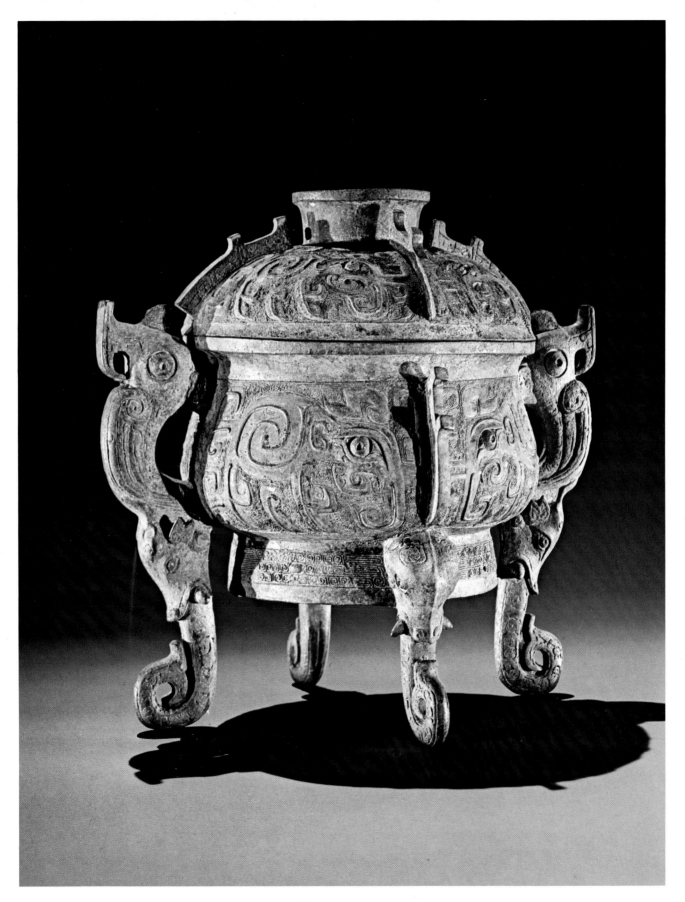

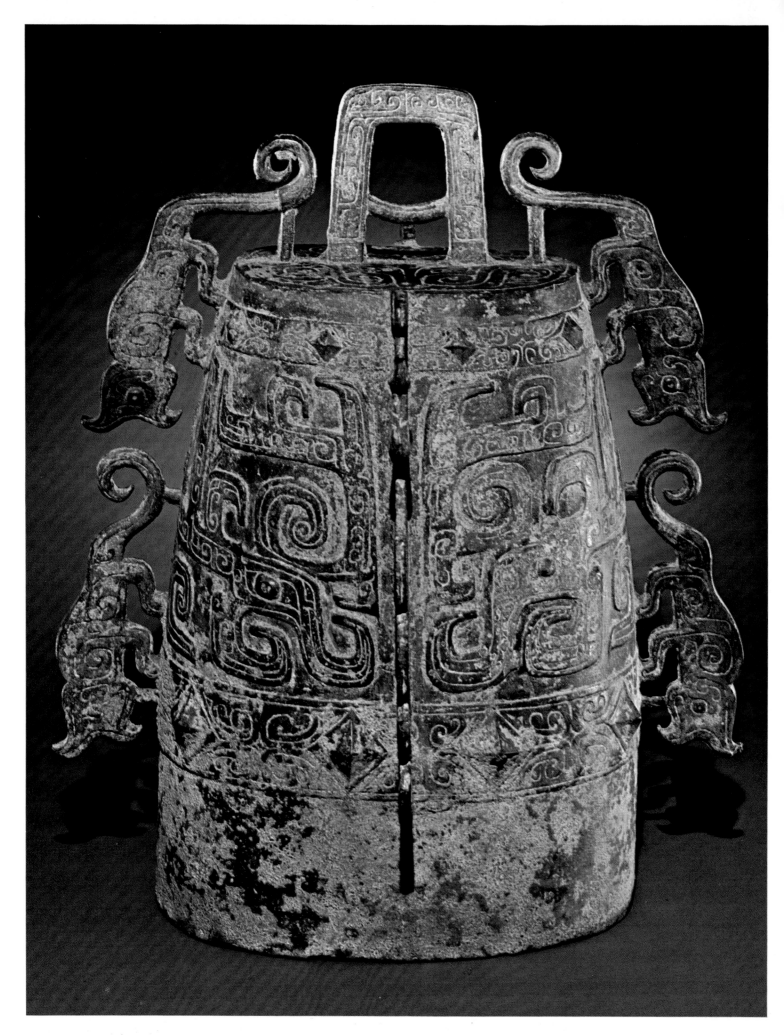

58 Bell (*bo*). Late 10th–early 9th century B.C. Height 42 cm. (16½ in.);
weight 11.54 kg. (25 lb. 6 oz.)

Detail, flange in the shape of a tiger, bell (*bo*) no. **58** ▷

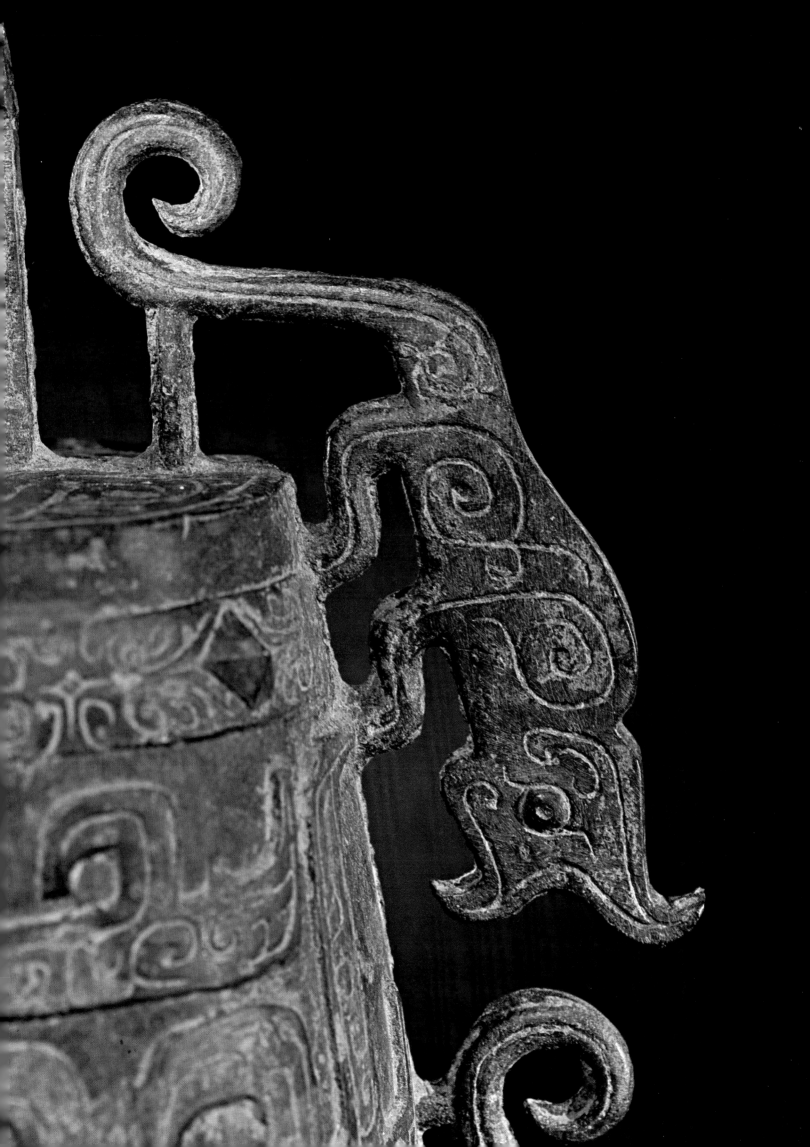

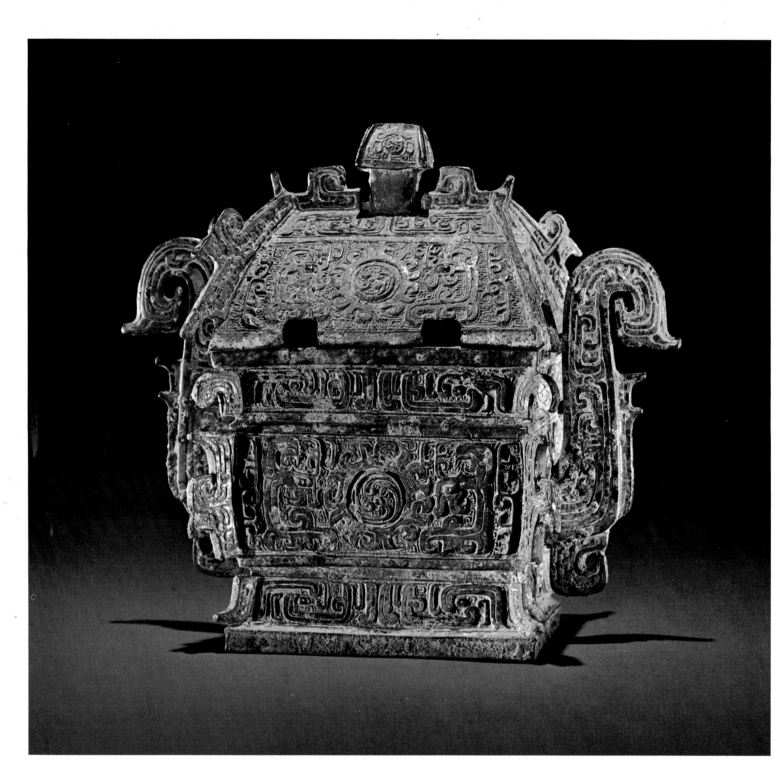

59 Li *fang yi*. Late 10th–early 9th century B.C. Height 18.2 cm. (7⅛ in.);
weight 2.05 kg. (4 lb. 8 oz.)

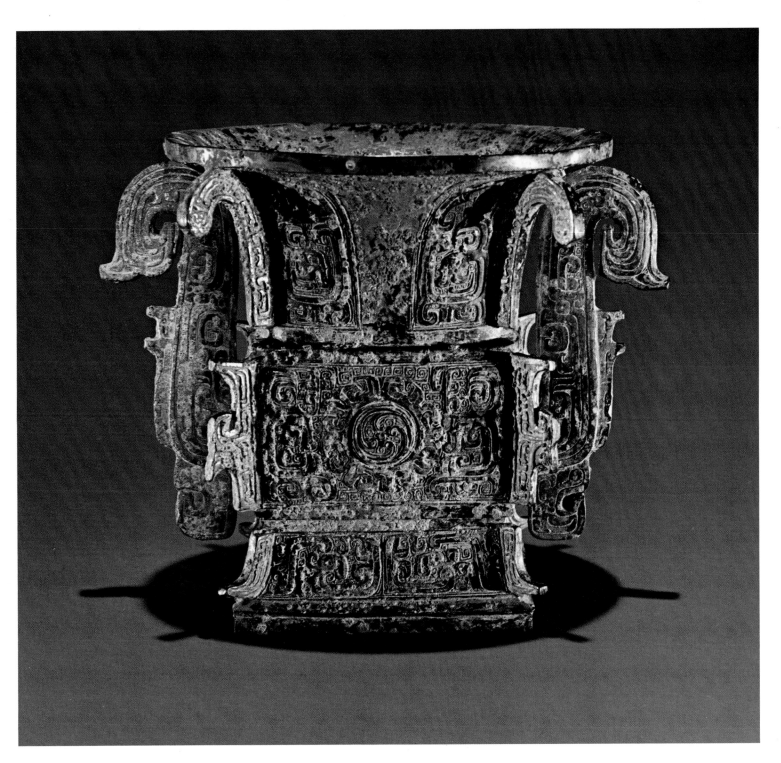

60 Li *fang zun*. Late 10th–early 9th century B.C. Height 17.4 cm. (6⅞ in.);
weight 2.75 kg. (6 lb.)

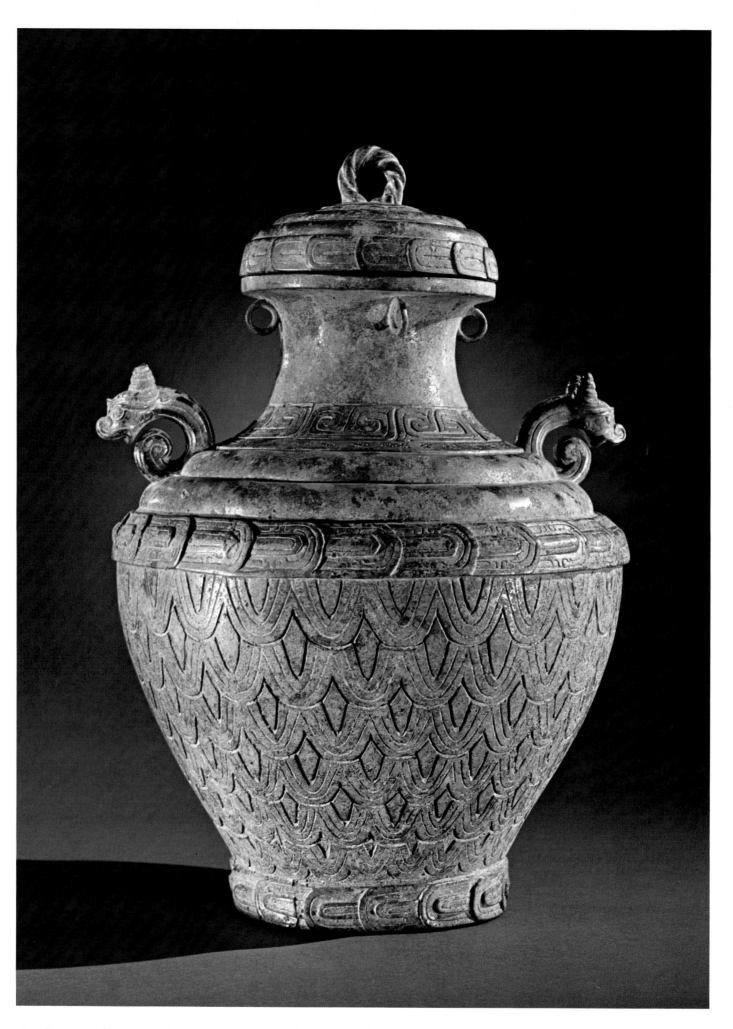

61 Zhong Yi Fu *ling*. Late 10th or 9th century B.C. Height 44 cm. (17⅜ in.); weight 14.43 kg. (31 lb. 12 oz.)

62 Zeng Zhong You Fu *hu*. 8th century B.C. Height ▷ 66 cm. (26 in.); weight 31.85 kg. (70 lb. 1 oz.)

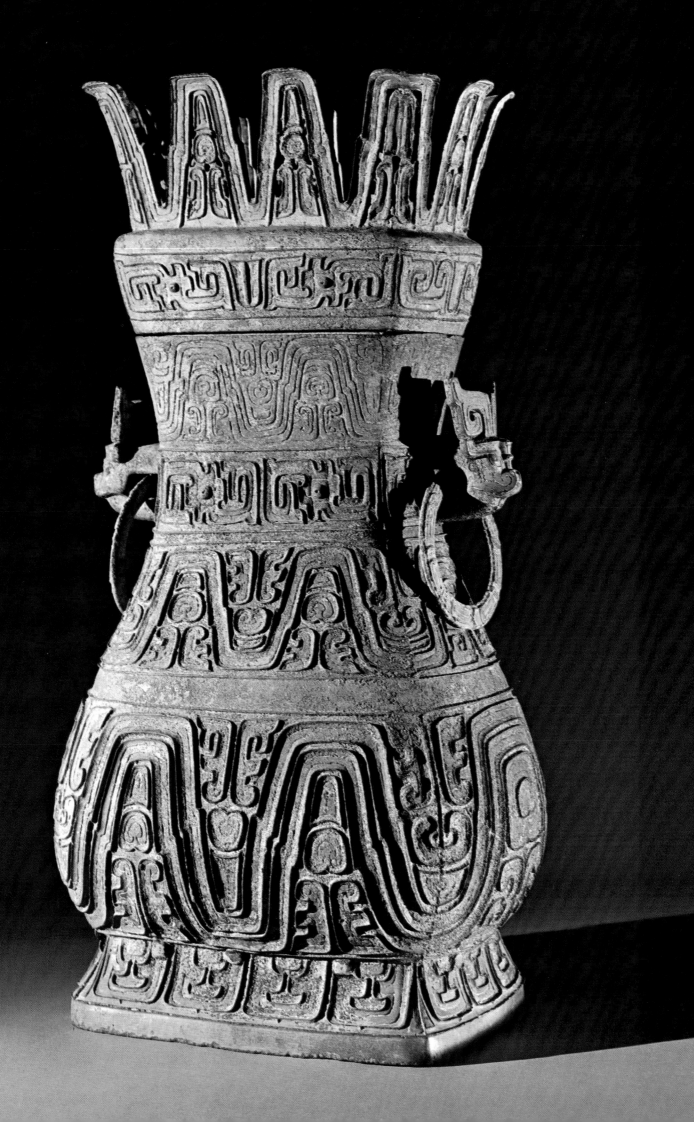

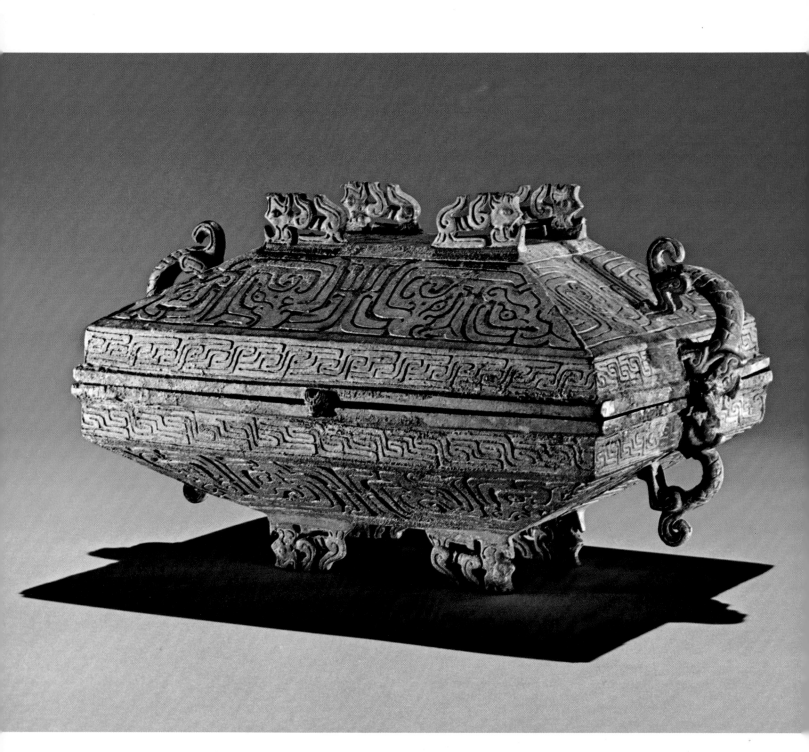

63 *Fu.* 8th century B.C. Height 17.5 cm. (6⅞ in.); length 26.7 cm.
(10½ in.); weight 4.25 kg. (9 lb. 6 oz.)

6

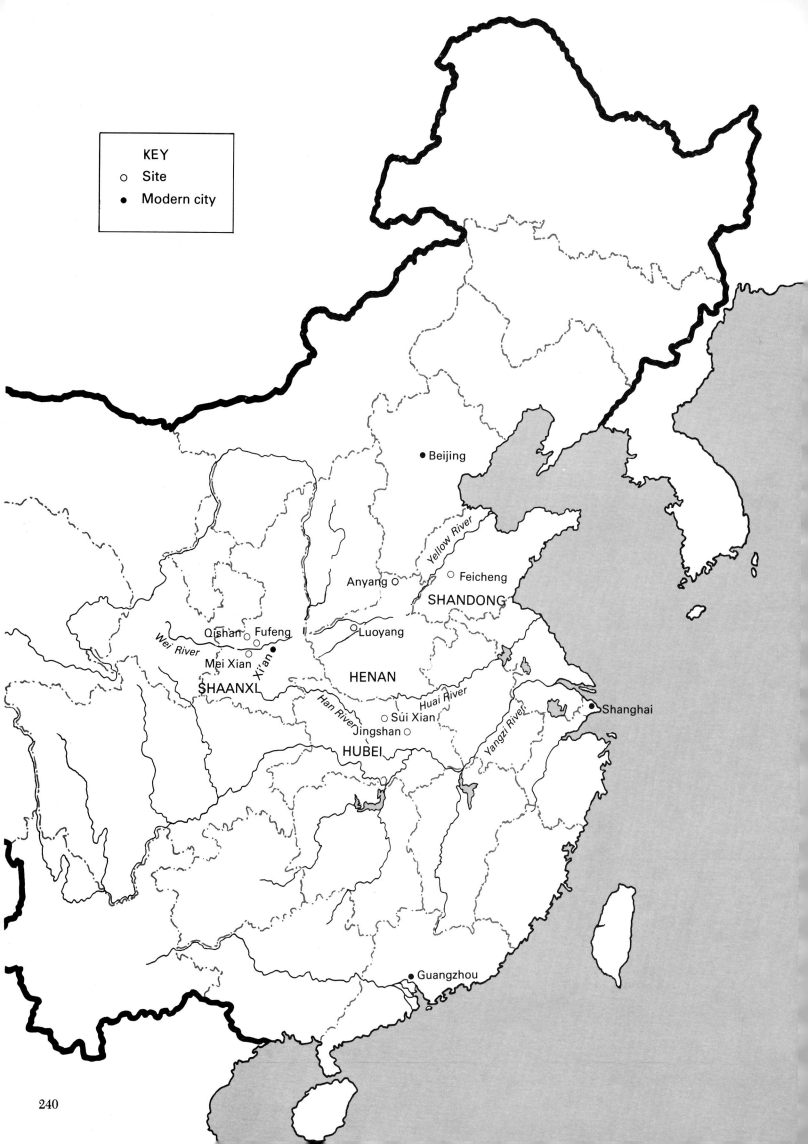

KEY
○ Site
● Modern city

● Beijing

Yellow River

Anyang ○   ○ Feicheng

SHANDONG

Qishan ○   ○ Fufeng

Wei River

Mei Xian ○
○   ● Xi'an

○ Luoyang

HENAN

SHAANXI

Han River

Huai River

○ Sui Xian

Jingshan ○

HUBEI

Yangzi River

● Shanghai

● Guangzhou

240

6 Transformation of the Bronze Art in Later Western Zhou

Robert W. Bagley

The countless grants of land with which the first Zhou kings rewarded their allies and retainers put the administration of the conquered Shang territories into the hands of hereditary lords who owed their advancement to the royal house but who ruled in their own names. At first the central government seems to have been strong enough to compel the allegiance of the provincial lords. The early Zhou bronze inscriptions often record visits to court paid by loyal vassals, who were duly rewarded and retired home to cast bronzes. Less frequently they record tours of inspection made by the king, followed by the same result. With the passage of time, however, the vassals grew less dependent on the support of the Zhou king, and ties of blood alone were scarcely adequate to insure their loyalty to the royal house. It was eventually the pressure of a century of barbarian attacks from the north that brought about the collapse of the central government. When the Zhou king was killed and his capital sacked in 771 B.C., however, the invaders were barbarian tribes allied with two of the king's own vassals. Although a son of the king was able to reestablish the Zhou court at the secondary capital, Cheng Zhou, at Luoyang, the power once exercised by the Western Zhou kings was never recovered, and the history of the Eastern Zhou period is accordingly not the history of a dynasty, but of a large number of independent states.

The destruction of the Shaanxi capital and the forced abandonment of the ancestral Zhou homeland may help to explain why so many of the bronzes found in that region come not from graves, but from large hoards or storage pits. Fleeing before the invading nomads, noble families must have collected and buried their most valuable—and heaviest—possessions in the vain hope of returning someday to recover them. Storage Pit No. 1 at Zhuangbo, Fufeng, from which came nos. 45–47, contained a total of 103 bronzes, of which 74 were inscribed (Fig. 78); many bear what seems to be the clan sign of a single family. The bronzes from the pit span virtually the entire Western Zhou period, so that some of them were heirlooms already centuries old when they were interred. The contents of this one hoard would probably suffice to write the history of Western Zhou bronze vessels.

Map of China showing important archaeological sites of the later Western Zhou dynasty, 9th century to 771 B.C.

241

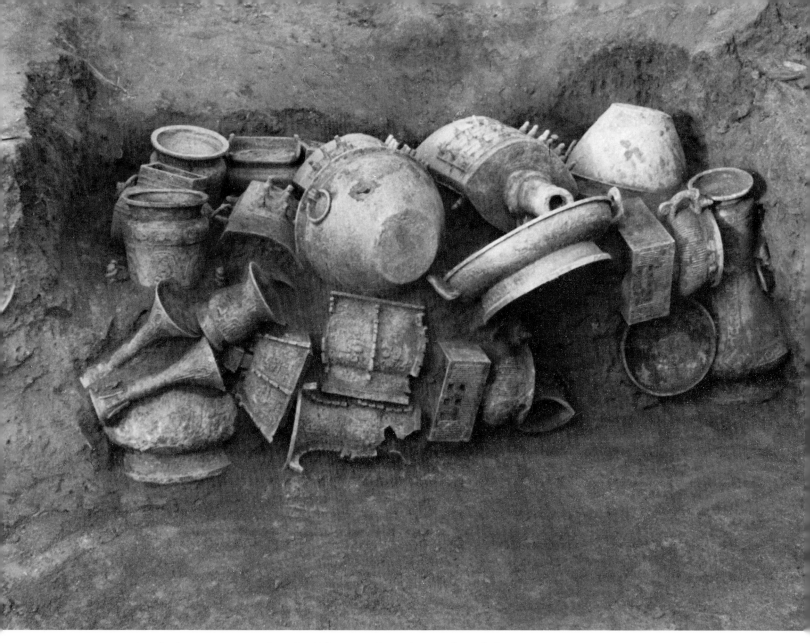

Fig. 78   Storage Pit No. 1 at Zhuangbo, Fufeng Xian, Shaanxi Province, from which
came nos. 45–47. Photograph courtesy of Cultural Relics Bureau, Beijing

The earliest phase of that history has been outlined in chapter 5. By the end of the dynasty, the patternizing tendency whose beginnings were remarked in such early vessels as nos. 45 and 53 had led to the nearly complete elimination of Shang motifs and decorative principles from the bronze art. On the marquis of Yan *yu*, no. 53, the subordination of individual motifs to a large-scale effect of flowing movement and patterned uniformity is already evident. This is so particularly in the decorated band on the foot of the vessel, where the motif of a small bird is encumbered with inorganic additions, needed only to fill out the frieze unit with an uninterrupted flow of broad curvilinear shapes.

The tendency for organically meaningful parts to be suppressed and for inorganic appendages to overwhelm the original motif was carried ever further in the bronzes that succeeded the marquis of Yan *yu*. By the stage of nos. 59 and 60, the dragons set on either side of a central medallion in the main register have dwindled to florid ornaments whose only unmistakably organic element is the head. Yet these graceful creatures are at least still recognizable as dragons; the same cannot be said for the designs in the registers above and below the main one, although they, too, derive from originally zoomorphic motifs. Here the transformation has gone much further, and the single eye remaining in the midst of a pair of interlocked C-shapes is not sufficient to draw the disconnected parts together into anything recognizably organic.

The final stage of this process of dissolution can be represented by the simple pattern of repeated recumbent C-shapes encircling the neck of the *ling* vessel no. 61. These purely abstract design elements are all that is left of the birds, dragons, and *taotie* that once filled the narrower decor friezes of early Zhou bronzes; through intermediaries like those on the vessel pair nos. 59 and 60, all three motifs dissolve into the same indistinguishable ribbons. Western Zhou bronze art, which began with a bewildering stylistic diversity, ends in something approaching unison.

But this elimination of Shang motifs and styles

should not be viewed only in negative terms. The effect of restless movement that arises from the barbed and spiraling shapes on the marquis of Yan *yu* no. 53 represents a deliberate departure from the stability and static monumentality of Shang designs, and one that in time led to an art based on wholly altered decorative principles. By the end of Western Zhou, the symmetrical, rigidly compartmented designs that arose from the Shang method of section-mold casting had been discarded. No longer content with the designs allowed by those constraints, the Zhou artist by degrees broke free from the dictates of technology and habit. Even so simple a design as that on

the *ling* no. 61 represents something fundamentally new, not so far seen on any vessel here: it is a design that does not respect the divisions of the mold assembly. The narrow bands of overlapping scales, lying in one direction on foot and lid and in the other direction on the widest part of the body, renounce the bilateral symmetry of earlier designs for the sake of a faint but undeniable hint of movement.

On the *ling* the new motifs, or rather pattern elements, are employed in a decor scheme that is kept simple and restrained. One of the most famous vessels from the same period, the Da Ke *ding*, shows that more

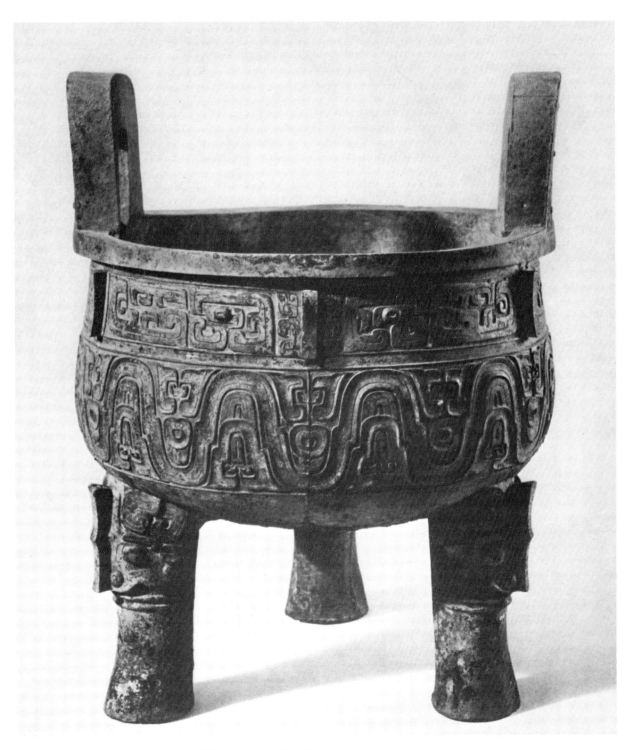

Fig. 79 Da Ke *ding*. Shanghai Museum. Photograph after Shanghai, 1964, vol. 1, pl. 47

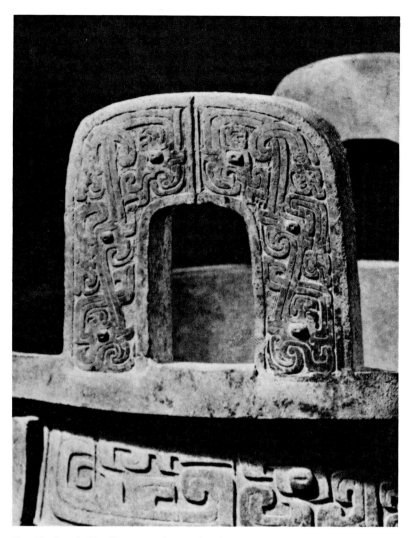

Fig. 80 Detail of handle, Da Ke *ding* in Shanghai Museum. Photograph after Shanghai, 1964, vol. 2, p. 40

dramatic effects might also be achieved (Fig. 79; Shanghai, 1964, no. 47). The possibility of movement is here exploited to the full by a bold wave pattern that sweeps unbroken around the entire vessel—without any allowance made for the mold divisions, which must cut across the pattern six times. The wave pattern is one of the most inspired inventions of the ninth century B.C. and accounts for many large and stately vessels from the end of Western Zhou and the beginning of Eastern Zhou (no. 62).

The Da Ke *ding* also illustrates one other invention of the ninth century, one that was destined to prove most fertile in succeeding centuries. The outer faces of the two handles bear a complicated network of interwoven dragons, a total of ten on each handle (Fig. 80). (Six large ones, with eyes in high relief, are easily found; the remaining four are smaller.) The pattern is concocted with the utmost ingenuity. The first and second of the large dragons share a single ribbonlike body, while the snout of the second is prolonged to double as the body of the third. In this design the most important feature is the overlapping of crests and bodies; the surface patterns seen here are, by implication at least, three-dimensional, since the body of one dragon can pass above or below another. Bearing in mind that the artist of late Western Zhou was restricting himself more and more to abstract or near abstract patterns, in which the surface treatment is uniform and the intrinsic interest of the motif is negligible, the invention of interlaced designs represented a sorely needed enrichment of the grammar of decoration. The possibilities of two-dimensional surface patterns must have seemed disappointingly limited, and the wave pattern is in fact the only one that achieves any real distinction in late Western Zhou. The possibilities of interlace, on the other hand, are boundless—an assertion justified equally by the Alhambra, the Book of Kells, or the bronzes of Eastern Zhou.

CHAPTER 6: CATALOGUE ENTRIES

58 Bell (bo)

Late 10th–early 9th century B.C.
Provenance unknown
Height 42 cm. (16½ in.); weight 11.54 kg. (25 lb. 6 oz.)
Shanghai Museum

Four odd sets of flanges divide this bell into quarters. Those on front and back take the form of a series of hooks and loops surmounted by a crested bird (Fig. 81), while the lateral flanges have been transformed into a procession of flat tigers. Each quarter of the bell's surface is decorated with a large downward-facing dragon head; the dragon's body has dwindled to an inarticulate appendage less conspicuous than the hooked crest lying against its forehead. Narrow borders above and below the dragons are studded with small pyramids. Unlike the earlier bell no. 19, which was mounted stem downward, this bell is equipped with a loop for suspension; both varieties, distinguished in Chinese as nao and bo, existed in Shang times. The top of the bell is covered with sparsely applied intaglio scrollwork. The surface is dark gray with some light green incrustation.

This is one of three closely related unprovenanced bells in the Shanghai Museum; there are further examples in a few other collections. The distinctive tiger- and bird-shaped flanges of these bells are undoubtedly based on the flange patterns of provincial Shang bronzes, for instance a small bell now in the Arthur M. Sackler Collections, New York (Tch'ou, 1924, pl. 7). In the absence of excavated examples, however, it is uncertain whether the Zhou versions are also southern provincialisms, or whether the Shang provincial type had by Zhou times been absorbed into the mainstream of metropolitan bronze casting. An unpublished bell similar to the present one, now in the Hunan Provincial Museum, is thought to have been unearthed in Hunan and might have been cast there. On the other hand, the ornamental motifs on the verge of dissolution into uniform ribbons seem to reflect the ruling decorative trends of metropolitan Zhou foundries. The dragons seen here in fact differ little from those on a very large bell reportedly found in 1890 in Qishan Xian, Shaanxi Province (Wenwu 1972/6, pp. 14–16, pl. 1). The bell from Qishan, on which the flanges have become an elaborate filigree of intertwined dragons, has a long inscription naming its maker, who was the same official Ke responsible for casting the Da Ke ding (Figs. 79, 80). While the resemblance between the Ke bell and the one from Shanghai leaves unresolved the question of a possible provincial origin for the latter, it does at least establish a date: the Ke bronzes belong to the ninth century, and the Shanghai bell cannot be much earlier.

PUBLISHED: Shanghai, 1964, no. 63; Tokyo, 1976, no. 45. See also Kane, 1974–75, pp. 85–88.

59 Li fang yi

Late 10th–early 9th century B.C.
Found 1956, Licun, Mei Xian, Shaanxi Province
Height 18.2 cm. (7⅛ in.); weight 2.05 kg. (4 lb. 8 oz.)
Shaanxi Provincial Museum

Every available space on this tiny fang yi is covered with curvilinear patterns. The ornaments, derived chiefly from dragons, are reduced to hooked ribbons nearly uniform in width, each with a sunken median groove. In the main zones on body and lid the patterns are still recognizable as dragon pairs flanking large circular

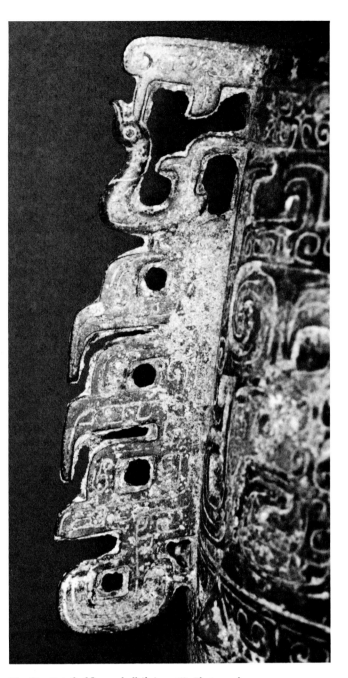

Fig. 81 Detail of flange, bell (bo) no. 58. Photograph: Robert W. Bagley

medallions, but in the subsidiary friezes the only remaining organic elements are barely discoverable eyes. The ruffled borders to the medallions copy earlier flange patterns (nos. 41, 45). The fluent curves of the surface ornament are reiterated in the intaglio patterns on the clumsy flanges, and on the ostentatiously unfunctional trunklike arms projecting from the sides of the vessel. More convincing on a few earlier and finer castings, the arms seem sadly out of place on these small and poorly cast vessels; their flamboyance has become an empty gesture.

The interior of the vessel is divided into two compartments by a partition; on one side two apertures are cut in the edge of the lid to accommodate ladles in the two compartments. The projecting arms appear to have been precast. The surface is light brown and dark gray with spots of powdery green. The inscription, which entirely fills the lid, is repeated on the bottom and sides of the interior of the vessel (see Fig. 82). The same inscription appears on the matching zun no. 60.

PUBLISHED: See entry no. 60.

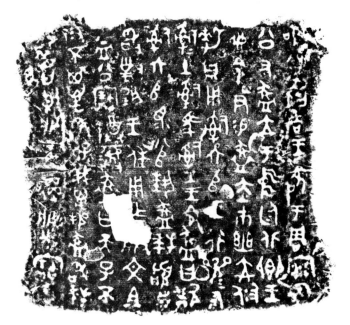

唯八月初吉王各格于周廟穆
公又佑盠立位于中廷北鄉向王
冊令命尹易錫盠赤巿幽亢黄攸
勒曰用嗣司六師王行參有
嗣司嗣司土徒嗣司馬嗣司工空王令命盠曰瓶
嗣司六師梁八師毲盠拜頴首
敢對毲揚王休用乍朕文且祖
益公寶尊彝盠曰天子不
段遘不丕其基萬年保我萬邦盠散拜
頴首曰剌烈朕身遟賡朕先寶事

Fig. 82 Rubbing and transcription of inscription, Li *fang yi* no. 59.
Photograph courtesy of Cultural Relics Bureau, Beijing

60 Li *fang zun*

Late 10th–early 9th century B.C.
Found 1956, Licun, Mei Xian, Shaanxi Province
Height 17.4 cm. (6⅞ in.); weight 2.75 kg. (6 lb.)
Shaanxi Provincial Museum

In ornament, patination, and inscription this vessel agrees with the matching *fang yi* no. 59. The two belong to a set of four vessels connected by long inscriptions concerning their maker, a man named Li. In addition to the present *zun* and *fang yi*, a second, slightly larger *fang yi* carries the same inscription, dated in the eighth month. A vessel in the shape of a horse, also made by Li, has a different inscription, dated in the twelfth month.

The text cast in the first three vessels, 106 characters long, fills the bottom of the *zun* and extends up the inside walls (see Fig. 83).

It describes a ceremony at court, in the course of which Li is invested with certain posts and charged with duties by the king. Judging by the large number of similar inscriptions known from the latter part of Western Zhou, the event was a routine one, the setting and protocol of the ceremony were highly formalized, the symbolic gifts bestowed by the king were customary and prescribed; and the phrases used to report the investiture, and those spoken by Li, are largely stereotyped:

In the eighth month, in the first quarter, the king came to the Zhou Temple. The duke of Mu led Li into the Middle Court, to stand facing north. The king commanded the attendants to present Li with scarlet cloth, black jade, and a bridle, saying: "By these tokens, govern the Royal Officers and the Three Minis-

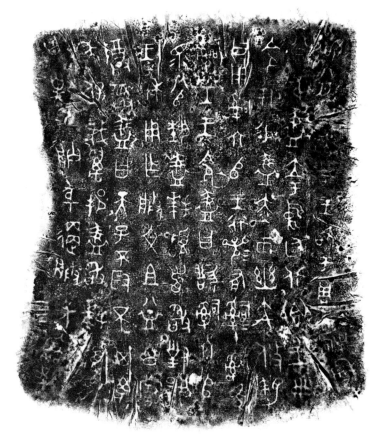

唯八月初吉，王各格
于周廟。穆公
又佑盠立位
于中廷，北鄉向
王冊令命
尹易錫盠赤巿、幽亢黄、攸勒，曰：
用嗣司六師
王行，參有嗣司、嗣司
土徒、嗣司馬
嗣司工空。
王令命盠曰瓶嗣司六師
梁八師毲。
盠拜頴首，敢對揚
王休，用乍
作朕文且祖益公寶
尊彝。盠曰：
天子不段遘不丕其基、萬
年保我萬邦。盠散拜頴首
曰：剌烈
朕身，遟賡朕先寶事。

Fig. 83 Rubbing and transcription of inscription, Li *fang zun* no. 60.
Photograph courtesy of Cultural Relics Bureau, Beijing

ters—the Seneschal, the Master of Horse, and the Master of Artisans." The king commanded Li, saying: "For the time being, take charge of the lieutenants of the Six Regiments [the army of the West] and of the Eight Regiments [the army of the eastern capital, Cheng Zhou]." Li bowed to the floor and made bold to answer that he would proclaim the king's trust by casting precious vessels for his gentle ancestor Yi Gong. Li said, "The Son of Heaven's works defend our empire everlastingly! I prostrate myself before him and vow to be worthy of my forebears' faithful service."

It is difficult to overlook the discrepancy between the evident magnitude of the posts and responsibilities conferred on Li, and the paltry bronzes cast in honor of his investiture.

The inscription of the horse-shaped *zun* mentions at one point an individual named Shi Ju—very probably the same Shi Ju who commissioned a small *fang yi* similar to no. 59 and now in the Shanghai Museum (Shanghai, 1964, no. 58; Shirakawa, 1965, nos. 237, 238). The Li and Shi Ju vessels can all be dated to the late tenth or early ninth century, but there is no agreement among scholars as to the identity of the king who figures so prominently in all their inscriptions.

PUBLISHED: With no. 59 and the horse-shaped *zun*, *Wenwu* 1957/4, pp. 5–9; Beijing, 1960, pp. 18–20, pls. pp. 46–56; Beijing, 1961, pls. 43, 44. For identification of the various titles and officers named in the inscription and for a few obscure passages, see *Wenwu* 1957/5, p. 70; *Wenwu* 1957/6, p. 69; *Wenwu* 1957/7, p. 58; *Wenwu* 1957/8, pp. 52–53; *Kaogu Xuebao* 1957/2, pp. 1–6; *Kaogu* 1958/1, pp. 90–91: Shirakawa, 1965, vol. 2, nos. 268–70.

61   Zhong Yi Fu *ling*

Late 10th or 9th century B.C.
Said to have been found 1890, Qishan Xian, Shaanxi Province
Height 44 cm. (17⅜ in.); weight 14.43 kg. (31 lb. 12 oz.)
Shanghai Museum

This *ling* vessel, one of an identical pair in the Shanghai Museum, reportedly belonged to a hoard of more than 120 bronzes unearthed in 1890 in Shaanxi Province. The hoard is said to have included the Da Ke *ding* of figure 79, the Ke bell mentioned in entry no. 58, and also a number of *ding* tripods inscribed by the same person, Zhong Yi Fu, who cast the present *ling*. The Zhong Yi Fu *ding* vessels, some of which are now in the Shanghai Museum and the Palace Museum, Beijing, are typical late Western Zhou tripods, undecorated except for a single band of repeated scales just under the rim (e.g., Luo, 1935, 1/22).

The same scale pattern, ubiquitous in late Western Zhou, is used with more imagination on the unusual and attractive pair of *ling* vessels. On the foot, lid, and widest part of the vessel appear narrow bands in which the scales are plastically rendered and overlapping; a flatter version of the pattern covers most of the remaining surface. On the shoulder are set two small animal heads with conical, spiraling horns. Apart from these heads, the only remnant of the rich zoomorphic imagery of earlier times appears in a narrow band of decoration on the neck of the vessel and another encircling the loop on top of the lid; and in both cases the animal patterns have been reduced to mere ciphers. The surface of the *ling* is slightly rough, matte, and bright blue green, with a few silvery patches.

The inscription of sixteen characters is cast in a circle around the shoulder, just below the band of abstracted zoomorphs (see Fig. 84). It reads "Zhong Yi Fu made this *ling* for use on travels; let sons and grandsons treasure and use it forever." The concluding formula, which becomes increasingly common in bronze inscrip-

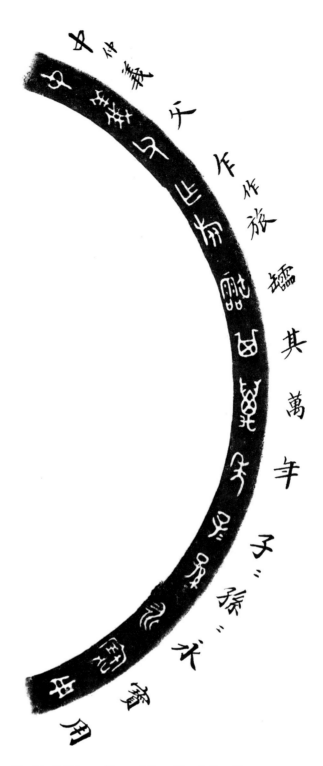

Fig. 84   Rubbing and transcription of inscription, Zhong Yi Fu *ling* no. 61. Photograph courtesy of Cultural Relics Bureau, Beijing

tions during the course of Western Zhou, accords well with the frequent discovery of hoards of Zhou bronzes spanning a wide range of dates (see nos. 41, 45, 52). Apparently the vessels were indeed long used by sons and grandsons before eventually finding their way into the ground.

Although in shape the present vessel resembles the *lei* type of earlier times (e.g., no. 55), its inscription calls it a *ling*. A slightly later vessel of the same type, found in Sui Xian, Hubei Province, in a group of bronzes associated with the Zeng state (see chap. 7), is also self-named a *ling* (*Wenwu* 1973/5, pl. 4:3, p. 22, fig. 3). Its inscription, which mentions an earl of Zeng, runs around the neck, as here.

PUBLISHED: Shanghai, 1964, no. 59; Tokyo, 1976, no. 47.

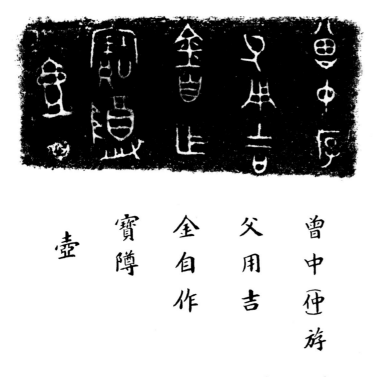

Fig. 85 Rubbing and transcription of inscription, Zeng Zhong You Fu *hu* no. 62. Photograph courtesy of Cultural Relics Bureau, Beijing

62 Zeng Zhong You Fu *hu*

8th century B.C.
Found 1966, Jingshan Xian, Hubei Province
Height 66 cm. (26 in.); weight 31.85 kg. (70 lb. 1 oz.)
Hubei Provincial Museum

The ornament of this stately vessel is dominated by the slow uninterrupted horizontal movement of large undulating ribbons, filling three registers on the body and repeated in the freestanding crown on the lid. The highest frieze on the vessel proper displays the pattern of ribbons, and the filler elements above and below them, as flat grooved bands. Elsewhere, however, the surface acquires a rich plasticity from the dished profile given both the ribbons and the filler motifs. Two narrow registers, one on the lid and one on the vessel at the level of the handles, contain recumbent S-shaped elements punctuated with eyes, executed in the same plastic technique. The handles, surmounted by crested animal heads, carry pendant rings whose decoration of overlapping scales calls to mind the preceding *ling* vessel, no. 61. The lid is perhaps misnamed, since it does not close the vessel; behind the fringe of the crown it is open to the interior. The rough surface has a rich blue green patination. The handles, which were precast, have a slightly different olive green patina.

This *hu* is one of a pair identically inscribed from a hoard of ninety-seven bronzes found near Jingshan in Hubei Province. The style of the vessels is consistent with a date around the eighth century, but whether they belong just before the end of Western Zhou or just after is not certain. A total of six bronzes in the Jingshan cache bear inscriptions naming sons of a marquis of Zeng. These and other inscriptions from recent finds in Hubei and southwest Henan have helped to establish the location of the Zeng state (see pp. 252–53, bibliography). The inscription of the present *hu*, cast in the lid and repeated in the neck of the vessel, reads, "You Fu, second son of [the marquis of] Zeng, used bronze to make this precious ritual *hu* vessel" (see Fig. 85).

PUBLISHED: *Wenwu* 1972/1, pls. 5, 6, p. 75; *Wenwu* 1972/2, pp. 47–53, pls. 9, 10; Beijing, 1972b, pls. 71–73 (several bronzes from the hoard).

63 *Fu*

8th century B.C.
Found 1963, Feicheng, Shandong Province
Height 17.5 cm. (6⅞ in.); length 26.7 cm. (10½ in.); weight 4.25 kg. (9 lb. 6 oz.)
Shandong Provincial Museum

The two parts of this vessel are nearly identical halves, so that the lid can be inverted to serve as a second container standing on legs of its own. Handles at the ends of each half take the form of three-dimensional tigers with arching striped bodies. The legs of the vessel are small, wispy dragon silhouettes, their snouts to the ground. Each set of four legs bounds a horizontal rectangular area filled by an enlarged and flattened version of the abstract recumbent S-shaped motif (see Fig. 86) seen in two narrow registers on the *hu* no. 62. The patterns elsewhere are equally flat, but the motifs on the sloping sections of the vessel are not abstract. Each of these areas contains a pair of independent pattern units formed of dragons. On the long sides of the vessel the units consist of two heads at opposite ends of a single body; on the shorter sides only one head is attached to each body. The broad grooved ribbons composing these dragons are curved and distorted to fill the entire surface uniformly. The even, swirling texture thus obtained was the artist's chief end, while individual motifs served him as nothing more than raw material. The designs stand in a direct line of descent from the patterned versions of zoomorphic motifs that evolved in the course of Western Zhou, but the present *fu* was probably made after the end of that period. At any rate its textured decoration based on dragon units offers a foretaste of the dominant modes of ornament of early Eastern Zhou (see chap. 7).

One of a pair, this vessel was found with ten other bronzes, including two *hu* vessels whose inscriptions name a marquis of Chen (see p. 253). The rough patination is in varying shades of green, blue, and brown. The corrosion carries imprints of a woven material that was in contact with the vessel during burial.

PUBLISHED: *Wenwu* 1972/5, pp. 9–11, pl. 6:3; Tokyo, 1976, no. 49.

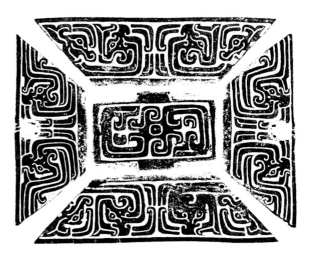

Fig. 86 Rubbing of decor, *fu* no. 63. Photograph courtesy of Cultural Relics Bureau, Beijing

7

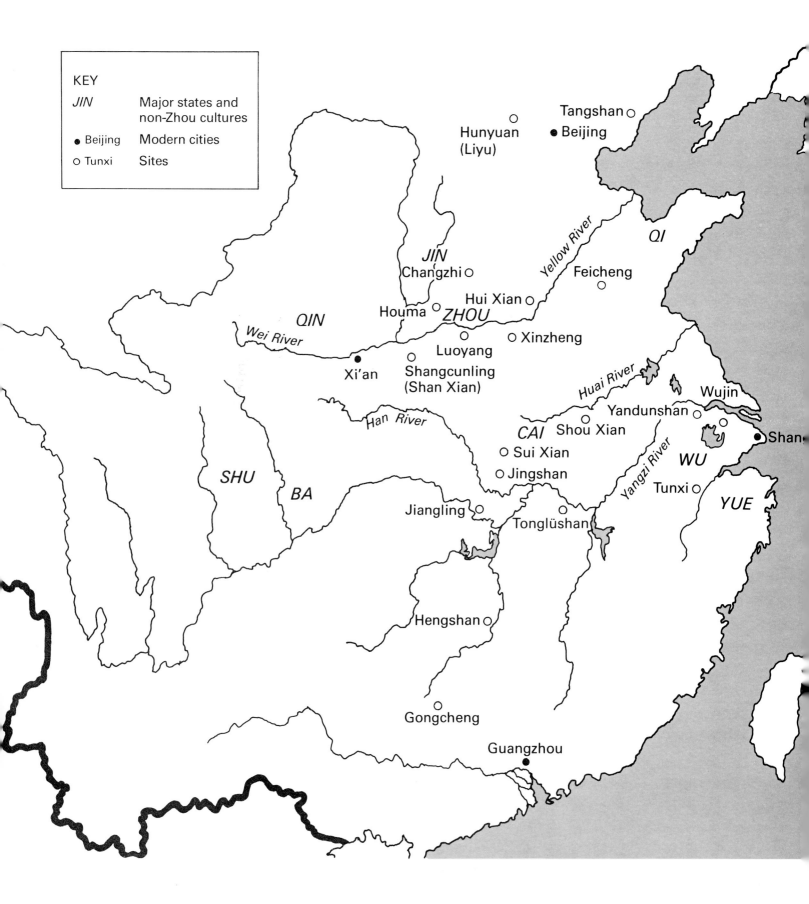

KEY

JIN   Major states and
          non-Zhou cultures

● Beijing   Modern cities

○ Tunxi   Sites

Tangshan ○

Hunyuan
(Liyu) ○

● Beijing

QI

Yellow River

JIN

Changzhi ○

Feicheng ○

Houma   *ZHOU*

Hui Xian ○

QIN

Wei River

Xinzheng ○

Luoyang ○

Xi'an ●

Shangcunling
(Shan Xian)

Han River

Huai River

Wujin ○

Yandunshan ○

CAI Shou Xian ○

Sui Xian ○

WU

Shan

Jingshan ○

Yangzi River

Tunxi ○

SHU

BA

YUE

Jiangling ○

Tonglüshan ○

Hengshan ○

Gongcheng ○

Guangzhou ●

7 New Departures in Eastern Zhou Bronze Designs: The Spring and Autumn Period

Jenny F. So

In 771 B.C. the Zhou capital, located near modern-day Xi'an, fell to marauding nomads descending from the Ordos region of northwest China. The Zhou king was killed, and his son fled east to the secondary capital at what is today the city of Luoyang. This marked the end of the period known to historians as Western Zhou. With the removal of the court to Luoyang, the eastern city became the principal capital of the dynasty, and the dynasty became known as Eastern Zhou. The Zhou court never returned to Xi'an, and Luoyang remained the seat of the Eastern Zhou kings until 256 B.C., when their greatly diminished domain was annexed by the expanding power of the Qin state, under the leadership of Qin Shihuangdi, the First Emperor of Qin. Of greater historical importance, however, is the date 221 B.C., since in that year the Qin armies brought about the final unification of China and founded the Qin dynasty. The 550 years of the Eastern Zhou period are subdivided into two successive periods. The earlier, traditionally known as the Spring and Autumn period (770–476 B.C.), is named after the *Spring and Autumn Annals of the State of Lu*, the official chronicle of Confucius' home state, although the book actually records events only from 722 to 481 B.C. The subsequent Warring States period (475–221 B.C.) drew its name from the *Discourses of the Warring States*, a series of philosophical and theoretical tracts on the ideal system of alliances needed to maintain a stable balance of power among the numerous contending states of the time.

Politically, the Eastern Zhou period saw an accelerated decline of the central government—a process that began in the reigns of the last Western Zhou kings—and a corresponding increase in the power of the feudal states and local princes. The royal domain around the eastern capital at Luoyang continued to dwindle as the territories of the neighboring states expanded. The Eastern Zhou kings possessed little actual power, becoming ceremonial figureheads to whom the increasingly powerful and ambitious feudal lords paid merely nominal allegiance. Dominant at first were the states in the north and east of China, especially Jin and Qi, which declined with the rise

Map of China showing principal states and important archaeological sites of the Spring and Autumn period of the Eastern Zhou dynasty, 770 to 476 B.C.

of the states of Qin and Chu in the west and south during the latter half of the period. In the end, Qin, whose territory lay in the original home of Western Zhou power near Xi'an, emerged victorious. It absorbed the rival states one by one and overcame its last opponent, Chu, in 221 B.C., thus bringing an end to a long period of strife and political instability in China.

The weakening of central authority during Eastern Zhou and the rise of powerful local governments greatly affected the realm of the ritual bronze vessel and the bronze-casting industry. Sets of bronze vessels were commissioned by local princes in increasing numbers, tokens of their desire to usurp the royal rights by practicing similar religious and courtly rituals. Bronze vessels were put to more secular uses at this time, for banquets and festivities at home and at war, as diplomatic tokens of good faith, and as dowries in important marriage contracts. The richly inlaid bronzes from the latter half of the period (see chap. 8) were coveted not only by the feudal princes, but also by members of the newly prosperous merchant class, who valued them mainly as beautiful objects that would grace their households and enhance their social positions.

Regional bronze-producing centers, only intermittently active in earlier periods (chap. 3), now expanded to meet the growing demands of local lords and began to flourish on a much larger scale, often producing bronzes with a distinctly local character. Regional artistic traditions began to play an ever greater part in the formulation of the Eastern Zhou bronze style and must be regarded as one of the major contributing forces behind the endless variety and freshness seen in all the arts of the period. One tradition that had a pervasive influence on the art of Eastern Zhou is native to the Chu state in the south. This is the art of painted lacquers (not represented here), an art based on color contrasts and the dynamic, sweeping movements of the brush. Artistic impulses of a different nature entered China through continual contact with the nomadic cultures distributed across the vast Central Asian steppes north and west of the Great Wall. These include a growing interest in the representation of real animals and a delight in richly inlaid articles of war and personal adornment, such as the belt hook (no. 76). Jade-working techniques reached breathtaking heights, and beautifully carved jades were a major artistic achievement of the time (no. 72).

One might suppose that the cultural differences that distinguished the various states—especially prominent in the arts of Chu—would receive further emphasis from the political disunity of the times, ultimately dividing China into separate artistic and cultural spheres. But this did not happen. Instead, improved communications encouraged a lively interchange of artistic ideas, resulting in an unparalleled flowering of the arts. As trade prospered, articles of bronze, jade, lacquer, and embroidered silk traveled up and down the country along crowded waterways and a growing network of roads. Some of these goods penetrated as far as Central Asia, where a Chinese mirror and a piece of embroidered silk used to decorate a saddlecloth were found among the furnishings of a tomb

dating to the fourth century B.C., of a nomad chieftain, frozen high in the Altai Mountains.

Although nominally the Bronze Age ended in the sixth century B.C., with the appearance of the first iron implements, iron came only gradually into common use, and it never challenged bronze in the realm of art. Iron was first used primarily for agricultural tools, for which bronze was too precious. As experience with the metal grew, it was adapted for the production of superior weapons, notably the long sword. In contrast to the development of Western metallurgy, iron technology in China seems to have relied principally on cast rather than forged iron. In the West, where forging was known far earlier (fifteenth century B.C.), casting remained unknown until the Middle Ages. China's early use of cast iron no doubt reflects a long-standing mastery of large-scale bronze-casting techniques.

China during the Eastern Zhou period presented a picture of bustling artistic, technological, and economic activity. The brilliant, kaleidoscopic nature of the arts is its most eloquent and colorful reflection. The forces that favored political unification contributed at the same time to the spread of regional artistic traditions. These, in turn, were slowly incorporated into the greatly expanded territory that was to become the basis of a large unified country during the Qin and Han dynasties.

The Bronze Vessel and Eastern Zhou Politics

The shift in political power from the royal Zhou court to the feudal lords is well documented archaeologically by numerous rich finds associated with smaller states that flourished during the early decades of the Eastern Zhou period. A major excavation carried out between 1956 and 1957 at Shangcunling in western Henan uncovered 234 tombs and 3 horse-and-chariot burials. A total of 181 bronzes were found, some bearing inscriptions referring to a prince of Guo. These inscribed bronzes suggest that the burials formed part of a royal cemetery belonging to the petty state of Guo. According to historical records, Guo was annexed by its more powerful neighbor, the state of Jin, in 655 B.C., thus providing a *terminus ante quem* for all the bronzes from the site. Although some of the bronzes are likely to have been made several generations before the state's annihilation, perhaps as early as the last years of the Western Zhou period, some should fall within the first hundred years of Eastern Zhou, and so form a basis for the study of ritual bronze vessel types and decoration in this transitional period. Most of the bronzes show strong ties with the late Western Zhou tradition in both type and decoration. Only a few items of personal regalia, such as a small round mirror decorated on the back with crudely drawn tigers and a mountain horse, offer a glimpse of the nomadic culture in the Ordos region whose bearers were immediately responsible for the fall of the Western Zhou capital in 771 B.C.

In spite of the archaeological significance of the Guo state excavations, the generally undistinguished ritual bronzes from this find give a scarcely flattering picture of the artistic achievements of the period. Another hoard of ninety-seven bronzes excavated in 1966 from a site at Jingshan in Hubei Province yielded vessels from the same period, but of markedly higher quality. One superb example is the large *hu* no. 62. This impressive vessel is one of a pair whose inscriptions record that they were cast for a marquis of Zeng. Two states by the name of Zeng are mentioned in the *Spring and Autumn Annals*. One was located in the east in Shandong Province; the location of the second is less certain, but it is thought to have been somewhere in the vicinity of southern Henan Province. Three more finds were made between 1970 and 1972, one at a site in southwest Henan and two in Hubei, all consisting of bronzes inscribed with the names of various marquises of Zeng. These sites stretch down the Han River basin from the southwest border of Henan into the adjoining region of Hubei Province, strong evidence that a Zeng state must have flourished in this region.

The bronzes from these finds are all close in style to those from the Guo burials, and they are likely to be equally close in date. One historical source suggests that the state of Zeng and another neighboring statelet were formed during Western Zhou, when members of the Zhou royal clan were enfeoffed to rule over the barbaric nomads west of the royal domain. Ironically, when the state of Zeng joined forces with its neighbor in a punitive campaign against the excesses of the last Western Zhou king, the two sought help from these same nomads, who then proceeded to sack the Western Zhou capital, murdering the Zhou king and driving the Zhou court to Luoyang. The rich finds belonging to early rulers of the Zeng state suggest that Zeng's political ambitions must have risen significantly at the opening of the Eastern Zhou period.

The history of the Zeng state has been extended into the early years of the Warring States period by an even more recent excavation. In May and June of 1978, a large tomb of the fifth century B.C., also belonging to a marquis of Zeng, was uncovered near Sui Xian in Hubei Province, where an earlier find of Zeng bronzes was made in 1970. The 1978 excavation disclosed an enormous array of bronzes, astonishing in quantity and even more in quality, and included the largest set of bronze bells known to date—a total of sixty-five bells of graduated sizes, suspended on an L-shaped, three-tiered stand of bronze and wood. The tomb also yielded brilliantly painted lacquered vessels and animal sculpture, exquisitely carved jades, and even vessels of solid gold. The succession of Zeng rulers seems to have weathered the changing political climate admirably, maintaining their status into the fifth century B.C., when they shrewdly pledged allegiance not to the Zhou king, but to their more formidable neighbor in the south, the state of Chu. The state of Zeng, whose existence was hitherto recorded, outside of historical texts, only in the inscriptions on a handful of unprovenanced vessels, begins to take on greater substance as excavations reveal something of its geographical context, political status, and artistic character.

While the contents of the inscription on the marquis of Zeng *hu* (no. 62) still reflect their ritual functions inherited from Western Zhou, other bronzes from the same period begin to display a different, more secular character. Together with the bronze *fu* no. 63 and eight other bronzes were unearthed a pair of wine vessels with inscriptions indicating that they were made to accompany the daughter of a marquis of Chen in marriage. Since the petty state of Chen is known to have been in Henan Province, while this set of eleven bronzes was found in Shandong, the marriage is likely to have been between the weaker Chen state and its stronger neighbor, the state of Qi. A somewhat later example is represented by the large bronze *yu* basin (no. 64), which carries a twenty-six-character inscription, indicating that the vessel was made as dowry for the second daughter of the marquis of Qi. The territory of the Qi state occupied much of present-day Shandong and adjoining regions along the coast, but this vessel was found just outside the Eastern Zhou capital of Luoyang. This suggests a marriage alliance between the powerless Zhou domain and the prominent state of Qi.

The plight of the weaker principalities—the royal Zhou domain included—caught up in the intense power struggle of the stronger states often made such marriages a political necessity during the Spring and Autumn period. Nowhere is this more poignantly illustrated than in the fate of the small state of Cai. The tomb of a marquis of Cai was discovered at Shou Xian, Anhui Province, in 1955, and among the 486 bronzes unearthed was a large basin closely resembling no. 71. The inscription of the basin states that it was made by the king of Wu (reigned 514–496 B.C.) for his daughter's marriage, presumably to the marquis of Cai, since it was buried with him. Another inscribed vessel from the tomb mentions an earlier marriage, this time between a Cai princess and the king of Wu. A small state originally located in southeast Henan, Cai was throughout its history harassed constantly by the expanding Chu state in the south. The alliance between Cai and Wu, then a rising power in the east, that is documented by these inscribed vessels, must have been Cai's attempt to insure Wu's support in the event of Chu aggression. The temporary efficacy of the alliance was demonstrated by their joint victory over Chu in 505 B.C. Chu's power was not so easily checked, however, and in 494 B.C. it overran Cai territory, forcing the marquis of Cai to flee eastward and seek refuge with Wu at Shou Xian. When Wu itself was destroyed by its eastern neighbor in 473 B.C., the Cai royal house was left unprotected, and the line was finally extinguished in 448 B.C., when the last surviving marquis was murdered by Chu. It is all the more remarkable, in view of its precarious position, that a small state such as Cai should have possessed the lavish array of carefully inscribed bronze vessels and musical instruments preserved in this one tomb. The proliferation of such bronzes among even the most humble of feudal princes reflects the growing importance of the bronze vessel as political symbol, as the feudal princes attempted to usurp royal prerogatives and functions by engaging in similar rituals and ceremonies themselves.

Western Zhou Tradition and Eastern Zhou Bronze Decoration

The increased demand for ritual bronzes by the numerous feudal dignitaries led to a decline in quality, a tendency, however, already evident toward the end of the Western Zhou period. Yet the finest works of the period, represented by nos. 62 and 63, are far from mediocre, rivaling even the greatest masterpieces of the preceding century. In its simplicity and statuesque monumentality, the marquis of Zeng *hu* (no. 62) finds an adequate parallel only in a large tripod, the Da Ke *ding*, of the ninth century B.C. (Fig. 79). The continuous wave pattern that decorates both vessels is a late Western Zhou invention, a bold departure from the static symmetry in surface decoration that was *de rigueur* since the Shang period. It is also clear from this comparison that the bronzes from the earliest years of Eastern Zhou are often hardly distinguishable from their late Western Zhou counterparts, and precise dates of manufacture are therefore often almost impossible to determine. While the events of 771 B.C. no doubt marked a significant break in China's political history, they seem to have had a less immediate impact in art.

The graceful rhythm of the wave pattern apparently had considerable appeal; not only was it widely adopted in the early decades of Eastern Zhou, but a simplified and schematized version of it, seen on the *yu* no. 64, is found on bronzes as late as the sixth century B.C. Bronzes decorated in this manner are often correspondingly outdated in shape and are usually associated with nobles of the state of Qi, as is the basin no. 64. The Qi state, under the leadership of its greatest ruler, Duke Huan (685–643 B.C.), was the first of five hegemons to come to power in the Spring and Autumn period. In his staunch support for the sacred authority of the Zhou kings, he was also the most traditional. By deliberately choosing established Western Zhou shapes and ornaments for their ritual bronzes, the dukes of Qi gave concrete expression to their political conservatism. What is not expressed is the artistic imagination of the time (see nos. 65–71). The conservatism of the Qi bronzes became, in fact, an artistic *cul-de-sac* in which the vitality of a decorative trend is exhausted by repetition. The total absence of decoration on bronzes produced by Qi during the subsequent Warring States period speaks eloquently enough of the loss of interest caused by a moribund tradition.

While the wave pattern is essentially a late Western Zhou design, that on the *fu* no. 63 is more characteristic of early Eastern Zhou, and, unlike the wave pattern, it plays a more vigorous role in the subsequent development of Eastern Zhou bronze decoration. The design typically involves large dragon motifs, symmetrically arranged. The dragons' bodies are in broad, flat bands with narrow grooves running their entire lengths. The rhythm they set up is slow and deliberate, at times graceful and almost dancelike. These smooth, flowing patterns are closely linked with bronze designs from late Western Zhou, where a similarly even surface effect is generated by continuous, ribbonlike bands (see nos. 58, 59, 60). The heads of the dragons in the early Eastern Zhou designs—

seen in profile, with elongated, upturned muzzles and curled lower jaws each with a spiral jaw hinge—also derive from Western Zhou prototypes, represented here by the bell no. 58 and the still earlier *yu* no. 53. A characteristically early feature of the dragons in the center of this *fu* is the greatly elongated muzzle, vaguely reminiscent of an elephant's trunk. This form recalls the similar trunklike appendages of the late Western Zhou *fang yi* no. 59 and *fang zun* no. 60; but early in the Eastern Zhou period, it was displaced by the shorter, more tightly rolled muzzles of the dragon heads attached, curiously, at the tail end of the motif on the *fu*.

The decoration of the *fu* represents the beginning of a continuous development that culminated in the uniform surface treatment of no. 68. The large, meandering dragon units were progressively reduced in size, while interlacing and overlapping became more common (no. 67). In the end, a new design, based on a repeated application of greatly reduced and simplified units, was created, its zoomorphic ancestry apparent only in the circular "eyes" of each unit (colorplate, detail, no. 68). This stage was reached in the seventh century B.C. and reigned for a time as the overridingly popular style in bronze decoration.

Regional Traditions and Eastern Zhou Bronze Design

The examples so far described (nos. 63, 64, 68), whether stylistically conservative or progressive, belong essentially to the mainstream of late Western Zhou designs. But local traditions and cultures were active outside the Central Plains, the heartland of Chinese civilization, and it is to their fresh and unconventional approach to bronze forms and decoration, often deeply rooted in and affected by the particular character of the local culture, that we owe some of the most exciting ritual artifacts from this period (nos. 65, 66). Bronze vessels with provincial features are known as early as the Shang period, and the incentive for their production then, as in the Eastern Zhou period, must partly be a political one. In this respect, provincialism in Eastern Zhou may be taken to be the culmination, on a much enlarged scale, of a trend begun during Shang.

At the present time, knowledge of these provincial centers is still fragmentary, with large gaps in their history for which we have scarcely any material. Our understanding of Shang provincial bronzes has been greatly enhanced by recent finds (see chap. 3), the most interesting of which came from south and southeast China (nos. 15–20). Perhaps it is significant that the first substantial remains of ancient copper mining and smelting activities were found here as well. In 1974, a large copper mine with elaborate underground timber structures was uncovered at a site appropriately named "Copper-green Hill" (Tonglüshan) in southeast Hubei Province. The remains show both mining and smelting techniques to have been surprisingly sophisticated, and the site appears to have been active over a long period of time. The mining implements were of both bronze and iron, suggesting that the mine might have been abandoned some time in the late Spring and Autumn period or even in the Warring States period. It is much more difficult to date its earliest use, but pottery remains at the site suggest activity as early as the late Western Zhou period.

As in the Shang period, quality alone is no guide for identifying provincial bronzes, since local castings, though at times rough and awkward (nos. 17, 65), can also be of superb quality (nos. 20, 66). Provenance is not dependable either, for vessels might frequently be exported to the provinces from metropolitan centers (nos. 24, 25, 68, 69). Stylistic criteria—including decorative features, form, and idiosyncrasies of technique—remain the most effective.

The shallow basin on three wheels from the eastern province of Jiangsu (no. 65) is outspokenly provincial in every respect. Of particular interest is the decoration around the exterior of the basin, which has no prototype in bronze but is a pattern commonly found impressed on contemporary pottery vessels from the area. Approximately 50 kilometers northwest of Wujin, where the Jiangsu basin was found, a rich site dating to late Western

Zhou times was excavated in 1954 at Yandunshan. Some of the bronzes from the Yandunshan site were also locally manufactured, suggesting that this area must have been producing bronzes for several centuries by the time the Jiangsu basin was made. The Yandunshan find was also unusually rich in remains of glazed and impressed pottery, pointing to a highly developed ceramic industry in the region. This explains, to a large degree, the use of pottery designs on bronze vessels produced in the locality.

The small wine container from Hengshan, Hunan Province (no. 66), presents an even more striking picture of the regional bronze-casting industries that blossomed during the early half of the Eastern Zhou period. The vessel shape is traditionally and characteristically Western Zhou and is rarely found in Eastern Zhou sites in the Central Plains. In the outlying regions, however, vessels of this shape decorated with clearly local motifs are known from late Western Zhou and Eastern Zhou sites, notably in Anhui, Jiangsu, Hunan, and Guangxi Provinces. Thus, the shape of the vessel alone indicates that

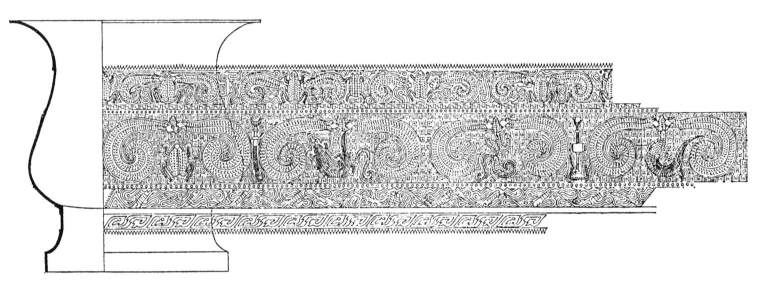

Fig. 87 a & b   Drawings of decor on two *zun* from Gongcheng, Guangxi Province. After *Kaogu* 1973/1, p. 32, fig. 5

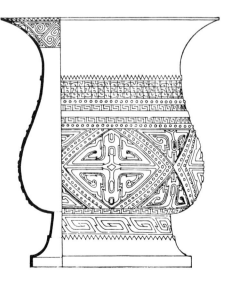

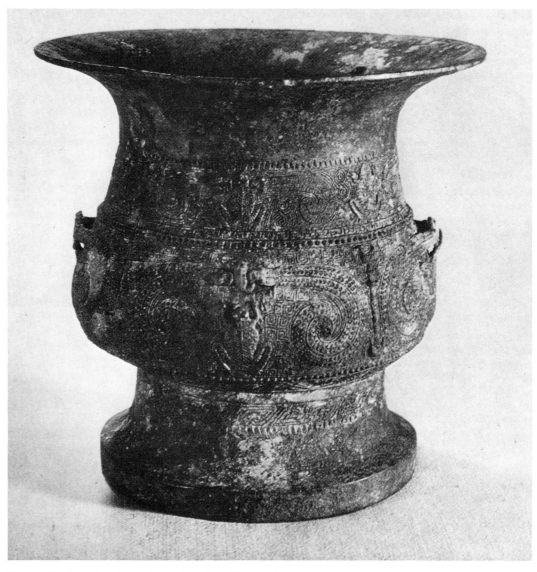

Fig. 88 *Zun* from Gongcheng, Guangxi Province. Photograph after Beijing, 1978a, pl. 44

the regional workshops were at least a century or two behind the fashion set in contemporary metropolitan foundries.

It is the surface decoration of no. 66, however, that speaks most convincingly for the vessel's local manufacture. The dense arrangement of irregularly placed wormlike creatures on four shieldlike elements as main design has no counterpart in either contemporary or earlier traditions of central China. The wormlike creatures appear again inside the flaring mouth, but in ordered pairs, facing each other with heads raised as if in polite tête-à-tête. A further local link is furnished by two similarly shaped vessels from a Spring and Autumn period site at Gongcheng, Guangxi Province, excavated in 1971. One has a design of similar wormlike creatures in pairs (also against an irregular meander ground), with a frog between their heads (Figs. 87a, 88). These are also in lively relief, the frogs at the top of the main design also standing clear above the surrounding surface, just like the creatures on the rim of no. 66. The design on the second Gongcheng vessel (Fig. 87b) is totally abstract, its main decor frieze virtually duplicating the geometric motif on

the neck of the Hengshan vessel, while its foot ring carries an identical meander band. All three vessels have sharp zigzag borders at the top and bottom registers of the neck and foot.

Like the Hengshan vessel, the Gongcheng bronzes are of remarkable quality, scarcely to be anticipated from the southwest at this early date. Similarity in the carving of the design suggests that they might have been manufactured by the same Hunan workshop that produced no. 66, though modifications in design motifs might have been made to suit the Guangxi patrons. This group of material with shared peculiarities in design poses questions about the relationship between the local cultures in southwest China and the Chu culture in Hunan during the early centuries of the Eastern Zhou period that only further evidence can answer.

Metropolitan Tradition and Local Character in Eastern Zhou Bronzes

The magnificent vessel from Xinzheng, Henan Province, no. 67 falls somewhere between the original inventions of

256

regional workshops and the steadfast followers of tradition in the metropolitan centers. Part of an accidental find made in the summer of 1923 by a landowner sinking a well in his fields, this monumental *fang hu* and its companion vessels remain among the most spectacular and important of Eastern Zhou bronzes. The name "Xinzheng" has long since been synonymous with a style of decoration especially prominent on the bronzes from the find, one characterized by repeated units of tightly interlocked zoomorphic motifs that produce a smooth, even surface texture (no. 68). While the site name has come to be associated with this specific variety of bronze design, the finds at Xinzheng actually included a much wider range of decorative styles. The Xinzheng hoard was dispersed during the 1930s and 1940s; a small number went to Taiwan, and most of the pieces are now divided between the Historical and Palace Museums in Beijing.

The styles of the over one hundred bronzes from the hoard span late Western Zhou to early Eastern Zhou (eighth to seventh centuries B.C.). Most fall into decorative trends descended from the Western Zhou tradition and are encompassed by the designation "Xinzheng style." A smaller group of monumental vessels, including a round *lei* and two pairs of *hu* on animal supports (one is no. 67) defy classification, and should perhaps be interpreted as local manipulations of a traditional form. A square brazier and a bizarre bronze beast treading on coiled serpents, reminiscent of lacquered wooden grave guardians familiar from Chu tombs, are local inspirations. These are probably the latest objects from the hoard.

The *fang hu* no. 67 is probably the most outstanding object from the find. Its shape is clearly derived from a traditional type in use during the early years of the Eastern Zhou period, and even the elaborately petaled crown on the lid is not unprecedented (cf. no. 62). Most striking, however, is the unapologetic manner in which its traditional silhouette is almost completely overwhelmed by a profusion of curvilinear animal forms—the large and imposing feline handles; four smaller, winged creatures climbing the rounded corners of the low-slung belly; two small interlaced bird-dragons on the broad faces of the neck; an elegant crane rising in flight from the lid; and a pair of large felines with antlerlike horns at the base. Although the shape of the vessel is essentially simple, the result could hardly be further removed from the sedate prototype no. 62. The vessel appears disturbingly alive: the creatures at the bottom seem ready to walk away with their burden, and even the surface decoration contributes to the general feeling of bustle.

The restless appearance of the Xinzheng *hu* is paralleled only by the equally impressive bronzes from the tomb of the marquis of Zeng at Sui Xian, Hubei Province, dating to the fifth century B.C. Two of the most significant features of the Xinzheng *hu*, the prominent dragon handles and the animal supports, are repeated on the vessels from this site. Also common to both finds is the singular devotion to deeply undercut and spiraling relief elements. The spiraling elements on the Sui Xian bronzes often terminate in a trumpet-shaped quatrefoil, a feature virtually duplicated on the horns of the winged creatures on the belly of the Xinzheng *hu* (no. 67). Furthermore, the most remarkable of the Sui Xian bronzes, among them the set of sixty-five bells with a stand, and an extraordinary, ornate *zun* inside a shallow basin (Fig. 89), are all characterized by decoration with an unsurpassed emphasis on energetic writhing forms, deeply undercut to produce a teeming surface.

The Xinzheng and Sui Xian finds are over a century apart, but the stylistic connection between them is astonishingly close. The bronze monster from Xinzheng suggests Chu associations, and it has been proposed that the tomb in fact belonged to a Chu prince. The marquis of Zeng had close relations with Chu, and the largest of the sixty-five bells found at Sui Xian was a gift from the king of Chu. Perhaps the common denominator between these unusual bronzes will be discovered someday in the art of Chu.

While the unconventional features of the Xinzheng *hu* (no. 67) are clearly regional, the location of manufacture is not immediately apparent. Unlike the Jiangsu *pan* (no. 65), with its outspokenly original shape and crude workmanship, or the Hunan *zun* (no. 66), with its archaic form and unique decoration, the Xinzheng *hu* shows a definite, if eccentric, relationship to current metropolitan traditions in both its shape and surface decoration. The technical excellence of the *hu* and of its Sui Xian counterparts is so astounding that, if they are products of a local workshop, it must have been at least the equal of metropolitan workshops in every respect.

A large early sixth-century tomb excavated in 1961 at Shangmacun, Houma, in Shanxi Province, yielded a large *hu* that is clearly related in type and decoration to the monumental *hu* pairs from Xinzheng, especially in its use of projecting zoomorphic elements at the rounded corners (Fig. 90). But the overall appearance of this *hu* is considerably more restrained, the restless curvilinearity is frozen and hardened, and even the large handles are simplified to heads of dragons, though still with elaborate shieldlike horns. Systematic excavations at Houma since 1959 have shown it to be the site of a major Eastern Zhou bronze foundry of exceptional artistic standards, with a large-scale operation and a relatively long period of activity. The Xinzheng *hu* need not have been the product of the Houma workshops, but the similarities with the Shangmacun, Houma, *hu* strongly suggest that there were, at least, close contact and a ready exchange of ideas between the metropolitan workshops and more distant regions.

Vessels like nos. 65, 66, and 67 compel us to recognize two categories of regionalism in Eastern Zhou bronzes. The first is represented by nos. 65 and 66, whose outlandish provincialism leaves them in geographical isolation as fascinating but strictly local eccentricities. The second is represented by no. 67, which transfigures traditional bronze forms and designs with an unpredictable combination of unusual features with conventional ones. As might be expected, this category poses the greatest problems for determining place of manufacture. More important, it offers the best sense of the lively exchange of artistic ideas between local and metropolitan traditions, and the complicated process of adaptation and transformation of the metropolitan tradition into the repertoire of each region. To regional bronzes of both categories we owe the immense variety and freshness that typify the art of the Eastern Zhou period and that chiefly distinguish it from the more homogeneous Shang and Western Zhou industries.

The Bronzes from Liyu and the Houma Foundry

The summer of 1923 brought to light another major find of Eastern Zhou bronzes, this time from the small village of Liyu in northern Shanxi Province, about 75 kilometers south of the Great Wall. The hoard was discovered and excavated by a local peasant. When the local authorities were informed of the find, they took charge of most of the bronzes. Many of these are now kept in the Shanghai Museum. Not all the bronzes were surrendered, however, and those withheld from the government were purchased by a French merchant, M. L. Wannieck, who was traveling in the vicinity at the time. Wannieck's acquisitions were taken to Paris and exhibited at the Musée Cernuschi in 1924, and later dispersed among Western collections.

The exhibition includes three superb examples from the Liyu find (nos. 68–70). They offer some indication of the stylistic variety of the hoard, which ranges from the ubiquitous seventh-century design of no. 68 to the more advanced late sixth- to early fifth-century ones of nos. 69 and 70. Like Xinzheng, the site name "Liyu" has been used to designate a particular decorative style common to most, but by no means all, of the bronzes from the find. This so-called Liyu style, of which no. 69 is a mature example, is characterized by horizontal friezes of large interlaced dragon configurations in varying degrees of

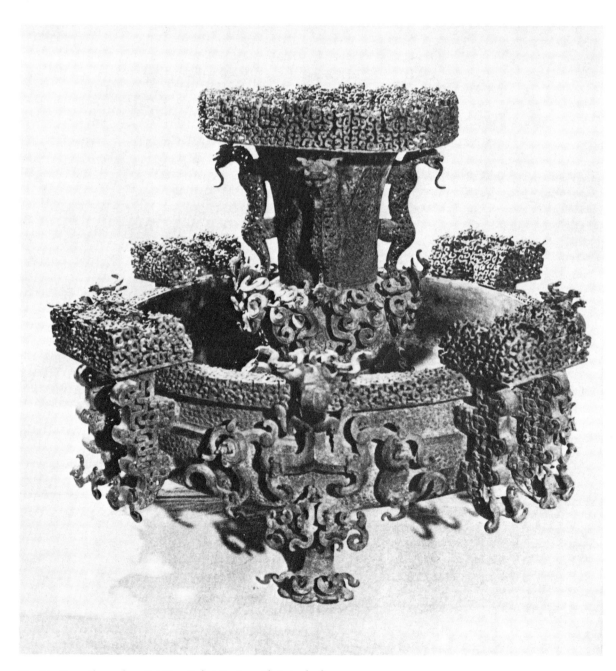

Fig. 89 *Zun* with *pan* from Sui Xian, Hubei Province. Photograph after *Zhongguo Meishu* 1979/1, p. 64

relief against a plain ground. The interlacery is accompanied by great textural variety, achieved through a profusion of motifs in which geometric filler ornaments (such as spirals, meanders, and oblique striae) occur side by side with more descriptive motifs, such as scales, feathers, granulation, rope, and cowries. Some Liyu bronzes even carry thoroughly realistic animals rendered plastically, such as ducks, fish, reclining buffalo, and various feline animals.

In general, vessels with highly sculptural decoration, created by abundant layering and overlapping in the interlacery, are the latest within the style (no. 69). The earlier forms of interlace, not represented here, were less elaborate and flush with the bronze surface. In the course of this evolution, the comma-shaped relief elements came to dominate the designs, obscuring the zoomorphic character of the dragons and masks, which eventually were submerged in a sea of feathered, striated, and meander-filled curls. The dense surface of raised curls on the large fifth-century basin (no. 71) illustrates the final transformation of the Liyu motifs, and the beginning of an entirely new type of design commonly associated with bronzes from the Warring States period, particularly mirrors. Both inscribed and archaeologically datable examples of this style suggest that the change must have already begun by the end of the sixth century B.C. Until now, the design on this basin has been interpreted as an early example of the "Huai style," a name coined by the Swedish archaeologist Orvar Karlbeck, who was the first to study bronzes in this style. Karlbeck mistakenly interpreted this design of teeming curls in relief as a strictly local development peculiar to Chu bronzes from the Huai River basin in Anhui Province. The name "Huai" is retained here for convenient reference; the style was, however, widespread and altogether metropolitan in character.

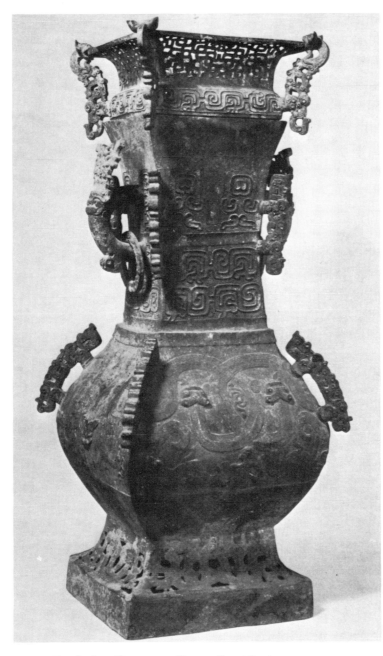

Fig. 90 *Fang hu* from Shangmacun, Houma, Shanxi Province.
Photograph after Kansas City, 1975, no. 117

At the height of their development, the Liyu designs enjoy a distinction to which few Chinese bronze decor styles can lay claim—a consistently high level of workmanship, especially in the precise execution and perfect casting of the fine filler motifs. This points clearly to improved decorative skills and advanced casting techniques of the period. It is the brilliant high point in the history of Eastern Zhou bronze decoration, and, as it happens, it is also the final expression of the characteristically Chinese practice of executing all designs in the mold. The prevailing decorative style of the subsequent Warring States period relies heavily on the cold-working technique of inlaying precious metals and semiprecious stones into the cast bronze, a method that is, by contrast, unmistakably foreign in character.

Decades after their discovery, the Liyu bronzes were still regarded as embodiments of a local stylistic bias, peculiar to the northernmost border of Shanxi and heavily influenced by the nomadic culture in the Ordos region beyond the Great Wall. But, in 1936, numerous bronzes decorated with similar interlaced dragons were excavated from two adjacent sites in the vicinity of Hui Xian, Henan Province, in the heart of metropolitan China. In 1955, more bronzes in a similar style were found at Changzhi in southeast Shanxi. Two years later, comparable examples were unearthed during excavations at the Sanmenxia region in western Henan.

Final confirmation of the metropolitan character of the Liyu style came with a series of excavations carried out between 1956 and 1961 at the site of an Eastern Zhou city at Houma in southwest Shanxi. Just outside the city at Houma, the excavators found the remains of a large foundry with over 1,000 decorated mold and model fragments, many duplicating designs known from the Liyu bronzes. Three large bone workshops and several pottery kilns and workshops were also found nearby, and the entire area was strewn with the remains of what must have been flourishing industries. To the north stand the remains of an Eastern Zhou city, complete with rammed-earth city wall, a defensive moat, and a large palatial structure raised on an earthen platform. The site has been identified with the ancient capital of the Jin state, which was moved there in 584 B.C., at the height of Jin power, and which remained its capital until the Jin territory was divided among the three princely states of Han, Zhao, and Wei in 450 B.C. The height of productivity for the workshops at Houma is likely to coincide with this period, from the sixth to early fifth century B.C., although workshops may have been active in the area before this time.

It is clear from this discovery that the foundry at Houma was a major manufacturing center for bronzes in the so-called Liyu style, and that what was formerly thought to be a regional style was actually the product of a large metropolitan workshop. Between 1959 and 1961, further excavations at Changzhi, east of Houma, yielded more bronzes in this style, while elaborate pottery imitations of bronzes in the Liyu style formed part of the finds made in 1962 at the site of the ancient capital of Yan in Hebei Province. It now appears not only that the Liyu

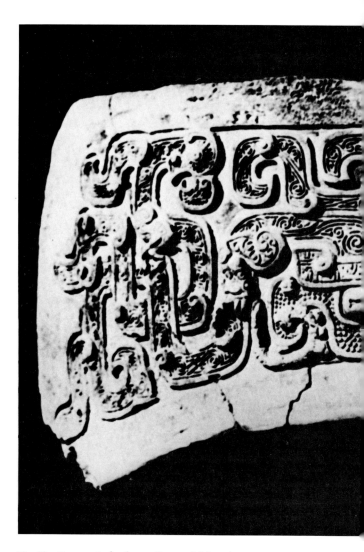

Fig. 91 Fragment of a clay casting model from bronze foundry at Houma, showing Liyu motif. Photograph courtesy of Cultural Relics Bureau, Beijing

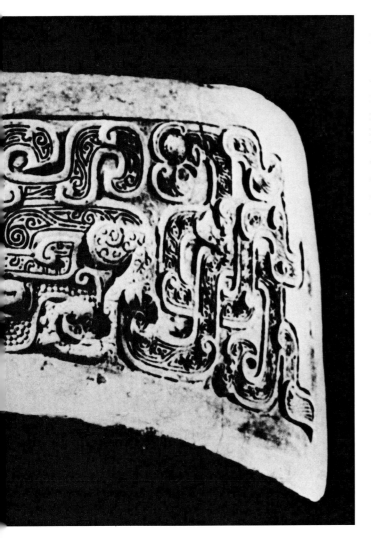

bronzes were metropolitan products, but also that their particular decorative style was popular in many parts of China during the sixth and early fifth centuries B.C.

The Houma excavations are an important key to our understanding of the bronze-casting industry in the Spring and Autumn period. Not only were the different industries—bone carving, ceramics, and bronze casting—carried on in separate workshops, but even the bronze-casting industry itself was specialized, with some workshops limited to the production of only a single type of object. Bronzes were manufactured at Houma in an enormous variety of types, ranging from ritual vessels of all shapes and sizes, to bells, horse and chariot fittings, mirrors, belt hooks, and even bronze coins.

The countless mold fragments found at the site show that the section-mold method was still the dominant technique, while fragments of intricately decorated models show that the section molds were generally made and decorated by forming them around a model, which was itself reusable (Fig. 91). Among the decorated models are many well-preserved rectangular pieces, each corresponding to one design unit that is repeated many times on the finished bronze article. These are evidently master stamps used to prepare molds for casting. Instead of following the time-consuming method of decorating each mold section individually, as Shang and Western Zhou bronze masters did, the Houma craftsmen seem to have used extensively the much more efficient technique of stamp impressing the decorations in the mold sections. This technique must have arisen in response to the rapid commercialization of the bronze industry during the Spring and Autumn period, when both specialization and mass production were needed to meet the states' increasing demands for bronze articles of war, of ritual panoply, and of personal adornment. The invention of the decor stamp at this point might also have been directly linked to the development of designs like the Xinzheng pattern (seen on the *li ding* no. 68), for standardized units readily lend themselves to stamped repetition. The decor stamp continued to be widely popular in the Warring States period, when it was frequently used to produce the ground pattern on the backs of bronze mirrors, another commodity traded throughout China and occasionally even beyond.

The Houma bronze masters must also have been familiar with the technique of inlaying metals and semi-precious stones on bronze, for model fragments showing the stiff geometric designs commonly associated with early Warring States inlaid bronzes were also found at the site (Fig. 92). Other fragments contain pictorial scenes like those on the *hu* no. 91; still others include a host of more realistic human and animal figures (Fig. 93). The extraordinary variety among the fragments shows that the bronze industry at Houma was not only highly organized and commercially successful, but also that it encompassed a wide range of decor techniques—traditional (section-mold casting), newly invented (stamping), and foreign (inlaying). Its major stock-in-trade was bronzes with the Liyu dragon interlace, but it apparently also produced bronzes with pictorial and inlaid decorations, both representing radical departures from the long-established tradition of bronze designs.

An important factor in the originality of the Houma foundry is to be found in its borrowings from the Animal Style of the steppe nomadic cultures in the northwest. Here, Liyu may have played an intermediary role: the covered tazza (*dou*) no. 70 from the hoard is most suggestive in this connection. Its shape is typically Chinese and is frequently encountered at sites throughout China. The casting of no. 70 is equal to the best metropolitan workmanship, and certainly well within the capabilities of the Houma foundry. Yet neither the freely drawn hunting scene nor the technique of inlaying with copper is particularly Chinese. Inlays of turquoise are known in the Shang period, but metal inlays of copper, gold, or silver are a strictly Eastern Zhou phenomenon. On the other hand, such lively animal designs and hunting scenes, as well as colorful inlays, are common in the art of the nomadic tribes that roamed the Central Asian steppes during the first millennium B.C., the best known being the Scythians of the eighth to fourth century. Similar hunting-style, copper-inlaid bronzes have been excavated at other border sites in northern Hebei, all close to the Great Wall and all reasonably open to nomadic infiltrations.

The essence of the Eastern Zhou creative genius, however, lies in the Liyu interlaced dragons themselves, which represent the primary and most vigorously inventive style in China from the sixth to early fifth century. Even so, many of its motifs were influenced by, or borrowed from, the more representational art of the steppes. This foreign element is visible in whole motifs, such as the realistically conceived three-dimensional animals or the rope and cowrie bands, but equally in the suggestive naturalism of the furry, feathery, and scaly textures. Nevertheless, these motifs are transformed and Sinicized in the Liyu decorative scheme as they are set in subtle juxtaposition to create not straightforward depictions but a purely ornamental arrangement of elegant forms, graceful rhythms, and exciting textures. The boldness with which these novel features are exploited in a strictly decorative context reflects the self-confidence that only a long-established ornamental tradition can boast. Next to the superb integration of form and decoration in the Liyu designs, more outspoken inventions like the Xinzheng *hu* (no. 67), dazzling though they may be, appear awkward and somewhat bizarre.

Since the technical procedures of the bronze and jade industries are utterly different, it is only natural that the two crafts should have been largely stylistically inde-

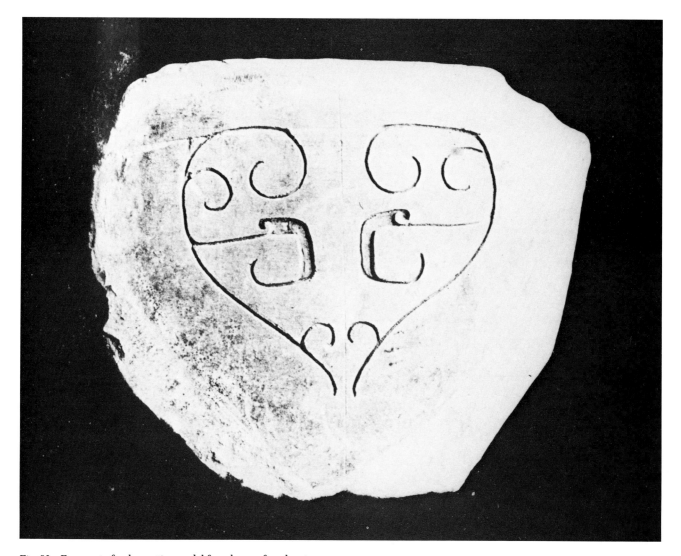

Fig. 92 Fragment of a clay casting model from bronze foundry at Houma, showing inlay motif. Photograph courtesy of Cultural Relics Bureau, Beijing

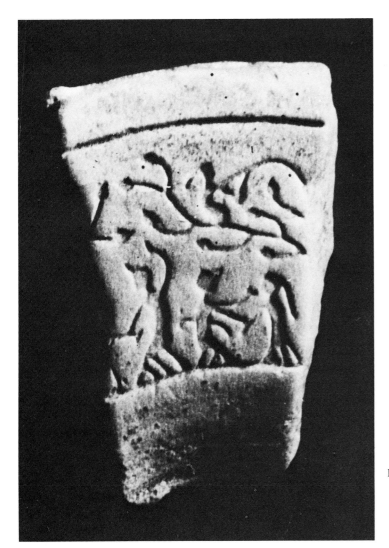

Fig. 93 Fragment of a clay casting model from bronze
foundry at Houma, showing pictorial motif.
Photograph courtesy of Cultural Relics
Bureau, Beijing

pendent throughout their developments. In this regard, the large jade pendant (no. 72) is particularly interesting as evidence of unusually active exchange between the different art forms during the Spring and Autumn period. The reclining deer, and the dense surface decoration of plastic C-curls interspersed with incised striae can all be found in the Liyu bronze repertoire. The small circles among the C-curls are lingering traces of the eyes on once recognizable dragon heads, originally depicted in profile as a standard surface pattern but now completely lost in a sea of densely packed, plump relief curls. The total disappearance of the earlier surface pattern of dragon heads was a direct consequence of elevating the C-curls in relief. The curls are brought so much to the fore that they begin to exist as independent decorative shapes, changing a formerly zoomorphic design of dragon heads into an abstract pattern of plastic C-curls. This development follows the same course taken by the Liyu dragons in bronze when they were transformed into the Huai style decoration of dense relief curls. Excavated examples suggest that jades with dense plastic C-curls existed as early as the mid-sixth century B.C.; if so, it is possible that the earlier stylistic transformation in jade decoration might have been instrumental in provoking the similar change that occurred in bronze.

The jade pendant no. 72 expresses in every detail the advances in jade-carving technique made since the Shang period. Shang and Western Zhou designs were created chiefly by incision (nos. 2, 3, 34–40) and were characteristically two-dimensional and linear. The relieved surfaces, seen most clearly on the middle three sections of the pendant, are an Eastern Zhou innovation and a major technical feat. To produce a smoothly modeled, evenly rounded shape in the surface of a piece of jade, the carver had to grind away the surrounding material slowly and carefully. It is the outstanding technical achievement of the Eastern Zhou lapidary that he could have produced these gently undulating surfaces with such astonishing control and precision, and with no trace of the painfully laborious process that was involved. The mastery displayed in the shaping of the relief elements of the design on the pendant is evident in every other detail as well. The incised linear decorations flow with elegance and ease; the execution of the minute striations is exquisitely fine; and the reclining deer, though still two-dimensional, is shaped with far greater naturalism than its blocky Shang predecessors. With the rich, pearly luster of its highly polished, subtly rounded surface, the pendant no. 72 is an eloquent expression of the sophisticated tastes and high aesthetic standards of the time.

CHAPTER 7: CATALOGUE ENTRIES

64 Qi Hou *yu*

Eastern Zhou (6th century B.C.)
Found 1957, Luoyang, Henan Province
Height 46.4 cm. (18 in.); diameter 75 cm. (29½ in.); weight 75 kg. (165 lb.)
Luoyang Municipal Museum

This large food container is an isolated find, discovered buried in the slope of the Wang Shan, about 3 kilometers north of the Eastern Zhou capital, Luoyang. An inscription cast inside the basin was not noticed until 1974 when cleaning and repairs uncovered twenty-six characters executed in an elegantly slender script (see Fig. 94):

> The duke of Qi of the Jiang family made this precious *yu* vessel for his second daughter in marriage. May it give her long life for ten thousand years, physical well-being always, and may generations preserve and use it forever.

The vessel's inscription and provenance suggest a marriage contract between Qi and the royal Zhou clan. At least two such marriages were recorded in history, in 603 B.C. and in 558 B.C. Both the overall thread-relief wave pattern and the secondary decorative features of handle and movable ring favor a date from the seventh to early sixth century, but since vessels associated with Qi are noted for their conservative designs, the vessel may date from the mid-sixth century as suggested by the report (*Wenwu* 1977/3).

Similar inscriptions appear on a set of three undecorated vessels now in The Metropolitan Museum of Art—a *dui*, an *yi*, and a *pan* (Chen, 1977, nos. A284, A825, A830). These inscriptions indicate that they were made by a duke of Qi (also of the Jiang family) for the marriage of his eldest daughter. The connection between the Luoyang and the New York vessels is unclear since neither inscription names the duke, although the clan mentioned is the same. Typologically, however, the New York vessels suggest a date later than the Luoyang basin. In any case, they cannot be later than 379 B.C. when the ruling duke of the Jiang clan was deposed by a high minister from another clan.

The wave pattern of the Luoyang basin is found on several uninscribed vessels, notably four identical pedestaled *gui* vessels, now distributed among the collections of the Palace Museum, Beijing (Beijing, 1976a, no. 54), the Asian Art Museum, San Francisco (Lefebvre d'Argencé, 1977, pl. 40), The Cleveland Museum of Art, and the fourth without its lid in the St. Louis Art Museum (Kidder, 1956, pl. 23). They also have similarly ornate, composite animal handle designs, particularly the feature of a small tiger with curled tail climbing up the base of each handle. Two such *gui* vessels were formerly in the von Lochow collection and were first published in 1942, when they were dated on stylistic grounds to the sixth to early fifth centuries B.C. (Loehr, 1942, pp. 227–34). Their

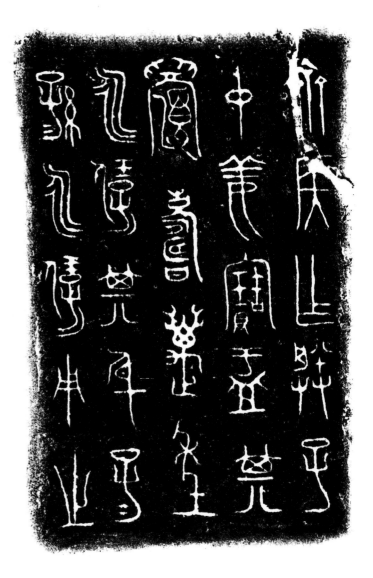

齊侯乍作朕子
中仲姜寶盂，其子
眉壽萬年，
永保其身，子
孫＝永保
＝用之＝

Fig. 94 Rubbing and transcription of inscription, Qi Hou *yu* no. 64.
Photograph courtesy of Cultural Relics Bureau, Beijing

relationship with the Luoyang vessel further supports a sixth-century date for the group.

Both the *yu* and the pedestaled *gui* are characteristic Western Zhou types (see nos. 41, 49, 53) and are rarely encountered in the Eastern Zhou repertoire of shapes. The Luoyang *yu*, however, combines the silhouette of the traditional *yu* (cf. no. 53) with the four handles normally found on the typical Eastern Zhou *jian* basin (cf. no. 71), so that if it were not self-named *yu* in the inscription, it might reasonably be taken for a *jian*.

The vessel is massive and thick-walled, its surface now covered with a light blue green patina overlaid with a fine layer of brownish earth. There is a large repair at the rim just above the inscription, and the foot ring is also damaged.

PUBLISHED: *Wenwu* 1960/4, p. 87; *Wenwu* 1977/3, pl. 3 (discussion of inscription, p. 75).

65 Shallow basin (*pan*) on three wheels

Eastern Zhou (6th–5th century B.C.)
Excavated 1957, Yancheng, Wujin, Jiangsu Province
Height 15.8 cm. (6¼ in.); diameter 26 cm. (10¼ in.); weight 1.65 kg.
  (3 lb. 10 oz.)
Historical Museum, Beijing

This striking vessel is classified as a *pan* only by virtue of its shallow bowl. Supported on three wheels—the two in front turned slightly inward and the one in back flanked by a pair of birdlike projections—the object suggests a simple cart. No other bronze vessel known alludes in shape to a vehicle, and this is a unique and unprecedented example of its kind; a somewhat similar pottery vehicle from Yugoslavia (second millennium?) stands equally isolated in its European context (Sandars, 1968, pl. 168). Such bold inventions were possible only in regional workshops where local peculiarities could still express themselves unhampered by an established metropolitan tradition.

The provincialism of this vessel manifests itself not only in its shape, but also in surface decoration and manufacture. The design on the birdlike projections suggests a loose interpretation of conventional bronze motifs, while the impressed meanders on the bowl and the small dots lining the birds' crests are decorative motifs common on pottery from the region. The casting is crude, and no attempt was made to polish away seams or to disguise the additional pours of metal that secured the projecting parts to the basin. Even the surface decoration on the bowl is carelessly and irregularly stamped.

Considered in isolation, such a vessel would be extremely difficult to date. Its excavation supplies a secure provenance and related data, but can only hint at its date. The other twelve bronzes found with the basin are similarly provincial in character (Beijing, 1963, pls. 90, 92). Among these, a set of three wine vessels (*zun*) is slightly more familiar (Beijing, 1963, pl. 93; Beijing, 1972a, no. 60). Like no. 66, these *zun* represent a regional Eastern Zhou perpetuation of a Western Zhou vessel type, a trend that seems to have disappeared by the Warring States period. The find also yielded an iron knife and sickle, which suggest a burial date no earlier than the sixth century B.C.

When unearthed, the *pan* was found inverted over two spouted water containers. The almost uncorroded surface of the *pan* retains much of the golden luster of the original bronze (see no. 46 for another exceptionally preserved vessel).

PUBLISHED: *Wenwu* 1959/4, cover, pl. 3:1 (report, pp. 3–5); *Wenwu Cankao Ziliao* 1958/11, p. 80); Beijing, 1961, pl. 58:2; Beijing, 1963, pl. 91; Tokyo, 1976, no. 64; Beijing, 1976a, no. 75.

66 *Zun*

Eastern Zhou (6th century B.C.)
Found 1963, Hengshan, Hunan Province
Height 20.3 cm. (8 in.); diameter 19.5 cm. (7⅝ in.); weight 2.1 kg.
  (4 lb. 10 oz.)
Hunan Provincial Museum

Like no. 65, this *zun* represents yet another regional variation of Eastern Zhou bronzes, with its old-fashioned shape and unique decoration (see pp. 255-56). Its lively main motif has been interpreted as silkworms on mulberry leaves, an unusual design that would reflect local preoccupation with sericulture during the Spring and Autumn period. Indeed, if the richly embroidered silks and woven damasks recently recovered from the early second-century tomb at Mawangdui in Changsha (about 100 kilometers north of Hengshan) are any indication, the silk industry in this region must have been of great scale and sophistication for centuries past. Whatever its meaning, the originality and local character of this design remain undisputed.

In type, this *zun* recalls a number of similarly shaped wine vessels, listed here in two groups according to shape:

A

Zun; Palace Museum, Beijing, late Western Zhou (unpublished)
Zun from Tunxi, Anhui Province; Shanghai Museum; late Western Zhou (*Kaogu Xuebao* 1959/4, pl. 10:1,2)
Zun from Wujin, Jiangsu Province; Historical Museum, Beijing (Beijing, 1972a, no. 60)
Zun from Songjiang, Shanghai; Shanghai Museum (Kane, 1974–75, fig. 40)
Zun from Shou Xian, Anhui Province; Historical Museum, Beijing (Beijing, 1956a, pls. 9:1,2, 13:1)
Zun with *pan* from Sui Xian, Hubei Province; Hubei Provincial Museum (Fig. 89)

B

Zun from Hengshan, Hunan Province (no. 66)
Zun from Gongcheng, Guangxi Province (Fig. 88)

The vessels in group A all have an enlarged waist section, a silhouette characteristic of the Western Zhou *zun* type (see nos. 42, 51). Those in group B typically lack this waist, and have instead a smooth and pear-shaped silhouette. This shape follows a later Western Zhou prototype, represented by an elegant example from the Art Museum, Princeton University (Loehr, 1968, no. 52). The difference in prototypes suggests that the provincial workshops that produced these two groups of vessels followed separate Western Zhou traditions that apparently entered the two regions at different times. The local industries were, however, not totally isolated from each other (as suggested by Kane, 1974–75, p. 97), since motifs like the zigzag border pattern, found on vessels from both the southwest and southeast, hint at contacts between them.

The provincialism of no. 66 lies not only in its shape and decoration, but also in its execution. Unlike no. 65, its casting is bold and crisp, but the slightly rough ductus of the decoration is not found on vessels from metropolitan workshops. This ragged surface quality is shared by the Gongcheng vessels (see pp. 255-56), further supporting the possibility that they might have come from the same workshop.

PUBLISHED: *China Pictorial* 1977/6, p. 23; *Kaogu* 1979/6, pp. 566–67, 553.

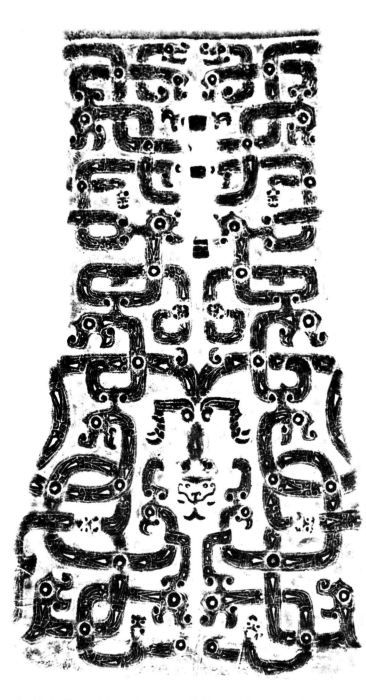

Fig. 95   Rubbing of decor, *fang hu* no. 67. Photograph courtesy of
Cultural Relics Bureau, Beijing

67   *Fang hu*

Eastern Zhou (late 7th–6th century B.C.)
Found 1923, Xinzheng, Henan Province
Height 118 cm. (46½ in.); dimensions at mouth 30.5 x 24.9 cm. (12 x
    9¾ in.); weight 64.28 kg. (141 lb. 7 oz.)
Palace Museum, Beijing

Among the significant features of this monumental vessel (discussed extensively on pp. 256–57), its hybrid character is the most fascinating. The diverse artistic and cultural forces behind its conception are further revealed in the realism of the crane, poised with half-spread wings above an overwhelming flurry of fantastic animal forms and in the surprisingly foreign note of the eight felines crouching with drooped heads around the foot, peculiarly reminiscent of creatures in seventh-century Scythian art (Bunker, 1970, no. 16). The rest of the surface decoration remains traditionally

Chinese, with interlacing bird-dragons on the body (see Fig. 95) and the ubiquitous Xinzheng pattern on the lid and foot ring. The patination is crusty and ranges from dark to bright green.

Four related examples may be added to those discussed on pages 256–57: a pair of bronze *fang hu*, slightly smaller, from the tomb of the marquis of Cai at Shou Xian, dating before the early fifth century B.C. (Beijing, 1956a, pls. 7, 8); and a pair of pottery *fang hu* from the fourth-century Chu tomb at Wangshan, Jiangling, Hubei Province (*Wenwu* 1966/5, p. 37, fig. 10). These four vessels further support the likelihood of Chu influences on these unusually fanciful designs.

The technical achievement of the workshop that produced this *fang hu* is clear in its successful casting of a vessel so large that few bronzes can compare with it in size and quality. A small detail—the spiraling trumpet-shaped horns of the four winged creatures at the belly of the vessel—suggests either very sophisticated section-mold assembly techniques or a different casting procedure altogether, such as the lost-wax method, that allows for irregular, gyrating shapes (see colorplate, detail, no. 67). Lost-wax casting seems even more likely to have been used for the deeply undercut and complicated openwork of the marquis of Zeng bronzes from Sui Xian, Hubei Province (see *Wenwu* 1979/7, pp. 46–48). The designs from Sui Xian are so sophisticated that, if they were indeed cast by the lost-wax method, experience with the technique must date back even further (Fig. 89).

PUBLISHED: Sun, 1937, pls. 100–105; Tokyo, 1976, no. 57; Beijing,
    1976a, no. 56.

68   *Li ding*

Eastern Zhou (6th century B.C.)
Found 1923, Liyu, Hunyuan, Shanxi Province
Height 18.9 cm. (7⅜ in.); diameter 17.5 cm. (6⅞ in.); weight
    2.05 kg. (4 lb. 8 oz.)
Shanghai Museum

The crisp and neatly interlocking units decorating this small tripod are among the finest of their kind (see colorplate, detail, no. 68). The sharp contrast between motif and ground was accentuated by a black substance filling the background, some of which remains along the bottommost register. In most cases, these units were impressed into the clay mold with decor stamps, leaving clear demarcations of the stamp unit on the finished bronze. On this tripod, however, no stamp marks are visible, suggesting that the design was carved by hand into the mold. The interlocking units are identical except for those filling the concentric zones nearest the center of the lid, where each unit becomes more complex, interlocking three instead of two zoomorphs with eyes, in order to accommodate the decreasing circumference of the decor zones at the top. The attention lavished upon such fine details reflects a level of workmanship far higher than commonly encountered on bronzes of this style.

The uniform, virtually abstract design forms a sharp contrast with the three small reclining tigers on the lid. Their poses are relaxed, with front paws folded over each other, hind legs swung toward the front, and long tails drawn out in an elegant curve. As on the other two vessels from the same find (nos. 69, 70), the bronze surface has corroded to a smooth, light green patina.

PUBLISHED: Shang, 1936, pl. 4; Shanghai, 1964, no. 68.

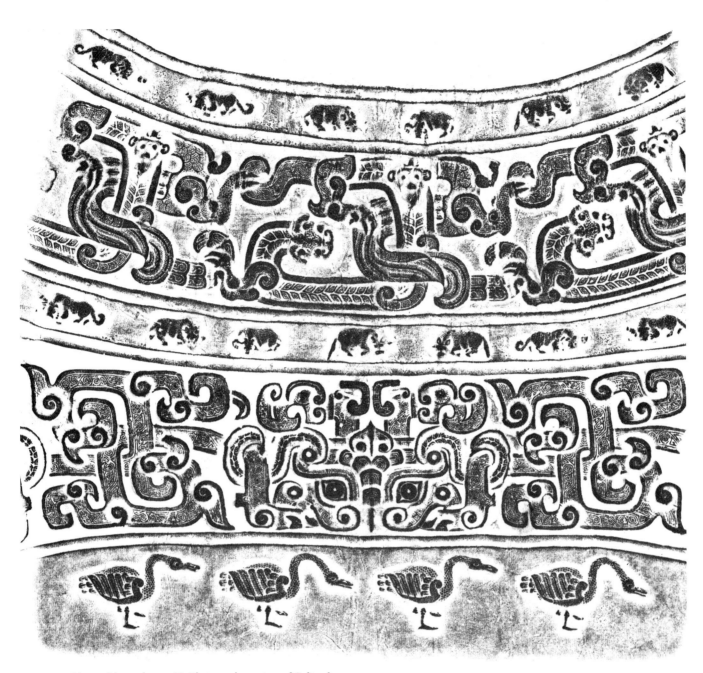

Fig. 96   Rubbing of decor, *hu* no. 69. Photograph courtesy of Cultural Relics Bureau, Beijing

69   *Hu*

Eastern Zhou (early 5th century B.C.)
Found 1923, Liyu, Hunyuan, Shanxi Province
Height 44.2 cm. (17⅜ in.); greatest diameter 25 cm. (9⅞ in.);
   weight 5.77 kg. (12 lb. 11 oz.)
Shanghai Museum

This pear-shaped wine vessel is one of a pair reported to be from Liyu; the mate remains in the Shanghai Museum. The broken stumps on each side of the neck mark the position of handles, presumably feline-shaped (cf. Pope, 1967, pl. 91; Yetts, 1939, pls. 16, 17). According to Ma Chengyuan, curator of bronzes at the Shanghai Museum, the missing handles and a lid are now in a Paris collection. Otherwise, this vessel is remarkably well preserved, covered by a light green patina. Two seams running down the sides of the vessel, partially covered by the remains of the handles, indicate that it was cast in a mold made in two sections.

The vessel is decorated in four horizontal registers separated by narrow bands. The first three registers carry identical motifs of a backward C-shaped dragon, its body distinguished by two parallel rows of U-shaped scales overlapping in slight relief. Intertwined with the dragon is an S-shaped, birdlike creature whose head, seen *en face* and alternately upside down, possesses a strangely human quality, and whose body, with granulated scales, is dominated by a long feathered wing (see Fig. 96). This motif is repeated around the vessel, and its scaly, feathery, granulated, and spiraled surfaces are set in low relief against the smooth bronze ground. The birdlike creature is a rare Liyu motif that appears only once again, in higher relief, on the outside of a large rectangular basin in the Palace Museum, Beijing (*Wenwu* 1972/11, pl. 1, p. 61, fig. 2).

The fourth register carries a more typical Liyu composition, a large mask with magnificent coiled horns and a pair of addorsed birds, their heads visible behind the mask (see colorplate, detail, no. 69). The birds' bodies are conceived as spiral-filled bands that disappear behind the mask to emerge below, between its fangs. They then turn upward, passing over and under the horns of the mask to interlace with the body of the neighboring bird (see

Fig. 96). This interlacing unit of mask and birds is repeated four times around the vessel in an unbroken rhythm which has the grace and discipline of classical choreography. As in the other three registers, a myriad of filler ornaments decorates the motifs, which are set in different levels of relief against the plain bronze ground.

Similar designs are abundant among Liyu style bronzes produced at the Houma foundry which were studied by George Weber in an exhaustive catalogue (1973). The most famous example is a pair of similar *hu* vessels, formerly in the Cull collection, now in the British Museum, London, with an inscription dating them to soon after 482 B.C. (Yetts, 1939, pls. 16, 17, pp. 45–75; G. Weber, 1973, pp. 67–81). Also of exceptional quality is a pair of large *jian* basins, one in the Freer Gallery of Art, Washington, D.C. (Lodge, 1946, pl. 30; Pope, 1967, pl. 88; G. Weber, 1973, pp. 82–91), the other in the Pillsbury Collection, the Minneapolis Institute of Arts (Karlgren, 1952, pl. 71); both *jian* are also inscribed and datable before 453 B.C. A comparable *hu* in the Freer Gallery is not inscribed (Pope, 1967, pl. 91). The inscribed examples suggest a date no later than the early fifth century B.C. for the Liyu *hu*.

In low relief against plain bronze on the lowest register is a series of gooselike birds whose long, graceful necks are alternately raised and twisted. The concave foot carries two bands, one a twisted rope, the other a cowrie design; while a plaited rope band in high relief circles the foot ring.

Small reclining animals in high relief are placed regularly around the narrow dividing bands, a feature not uncommon among Liyu bronzes (see no. 68; Shanghai, 1964, no. 72). It is unusual that, in addition to the rather harmless reclining animals on this *hu*, there are such creatures as a tiger with a man in his jaws, a leopard attacking a boar, and a bearlike creature holding another in its mouth. Here, the steppe animal-combat theme has been robbed of its sinister overtones and exploited largely for variety as a quaint miniaturized ornament.

This vessel is one of the best of its kind, its exceptional design and workmanship evident everywhere from the lyrical interlace to each finely executed detail, and from the three-dimensional animal forms to the subtle layered effect created by controlled variations in relief.

PUBLISHED: *Wenwu* 1960/4, pp. 79–80; Shang, 1936, pl. 18; Tokyo, 1976, no. 58; Beijing, 1976a, no. 59.

70 Dou

Eastern Zhou (late 6th–5th century B.C.)
Found 1923, Liyu, Hunyuan, Shanxi Province
Height 20.7 cm. (8⅛ in.); diameter 17.5 cm. (6⅞ in.); weight 1.8 kg. (3 lb. 15 oz.)
Shanghai Museum

The red copper-inlaid animal and human figures decorating this vessel stand out clearly in contrast to the even, light green patina of the plain bronze surface. The figures are randomly and liberally distributed across the surface with a kind of *horror vacui*, and with no indication of setting or spatial relationships. The animals portrayed are not all recognizable species; many are represented as vague types or adorned with imaginary appendages. All of them, however, are marked by large spiral shapes at their haunches, a motif commonly found on animal representations in steppe Animal Style art (see Fig. 97).

The Animal Style connections of this decoration are supported by two *hu* vessels with similar copper-inlaid designs. The first *hu*, now in the Museum für Völkerkunde, Staatliche Museen Preussischer Kulturbesitz, Berlin, carries an inscription saying that the vessel was acquired from the Xianyu barbarians, who became the rulers of the state of Zhongshan during the Warring States period (Kümmel, 1928, pls. 22, 23; C. D. Weber, 1968, fig. 65:a–d). The second *hu* was unearthed at Tangshan, Hebei Province, a border site in northeast Yan territory, on the edge of the steppes (*Kaogu Xuebao* 1953/6, pl. 10; C. D. Weber, 1968, fig. 62:a–f). A third *hu*, in the Asian Art Museum, San Francisco, deserves mention for its superb quality, although the vessel has no inscription and was not scientifically excavated (Lefebvre d'Argencé, 1977, pl. 54).

An unusual inlay process was apparently used for the copper decoration of these vessels. X-ray studies of a large copper-inlaid *hu* with animal decorations in The Metropolitan Museum of Art have suggested to Pieter Meyers of the Museum's research laboratory that its copper motifs were cut from sheet copper and secured between the mold and the core by chaplets. In the subsequent pouring process, the molten bronze flowed around these chaplets, thus locking (or "casting") the copper motifs into place. The innumerable chaplet marks visible throughout this *dou* suggest that it too was inlaid during the casting process, as Charles D. Weber has suggested (1968, pp. 196–97). This technique appears to be restricted to copper-inlaid animal and pictorial style decorations (cf. no. 91), and does not seem to have been used for inlays of gold, silver, or copper in geometric designs, which were hammered into existing depressions in the cold bronze surface (see nos. 73–76, 93).

PUBLISHED: Shang, 1936, pl. 14; Shanghai, 1964, no. 71; Tokyo, 1976, no. 59; Beijing, 1976a, no. 57. For a detailed study of this *dou* and related examples, see C. D. Weber, 1968, pp. 169–83.

71 Jian

Eastern Zhou (early 5th century B.C.)
Reportedly found 1941, Hui Xian, Henan Province
Height 45 cm. (17¾ in.); diameter 73 cm. (28¾ in.); weight 54 kg. (118 lb. 13 oz.)
Cultural Relics Bureau, Beijing

Three identical large basins were reported to have been found with the present one. One of them, now in the Historical Museum, Beijing, bears an inscription that associates the vessel with Fuchai, the last king of the Wu state (reigned 495–473 B.C.). Of the other two basins now in the Shanghai Museum (Shanghai, 1964, no. 76), one apparently also carries an inscription, but the thick incrustations have rendered it illegible. A fourth identical basin carries an inscription similar to that of the Fuchai *jian* but lacks the tiger handles. It was in the Oeder collection, Berlin, but was lost after the Second World War (G. Weber, 1973, pl. 5). Both the inscriptions and the decor style of these basins (see p. 259) support a date no later than the early fifth century B.C. for the group.

Although the surface is heavily encrusted with patches of blue, green, and brownish red patina, the size of this vessel makes it powerful and impressive. The uniform surface decor, a raised comma pattern that covers much of the basin, is offset by the strongly arched silhouette of the tigers climbing up the sides to peer over the brim. The other pair of handles, formed by animal-head loops, carries movable rings decorated with C-curls curiously reminiscent of designs on jade rings of the sixth century B.C. (Guo [B.], 1959, pl. 111:4).

PUBLISHED: Tokyo, 1976, no. 61; Beijing, 1976a, no. 60.

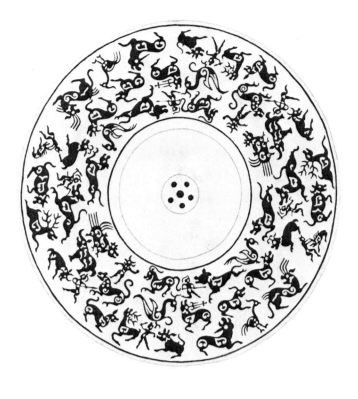

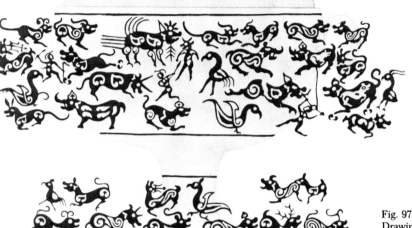

Fig. 97
Drawing of decor, *dou* no. 70.
Courtesy of Cultural Relics
Bureau, Beijing

72 Jade pendant (*huang*)

Eastern Zhou (late 6th–5th century B.C.)
Excavated 1950 from Tomb 1, Guweicun, Hui Xian,
    Henan Province
Length 20.2 cm. (8 in.); maximum width 4.7 cm. (1⅞ in.); weight
    76 g. (2⅔ oz.)
Historical Museum, Beijing

This elegant pendant is composed of seven pieces of jade. They are held together by a narrow bronze strip wrapped in wood and inserted through rectangular perforations in the five middle sections, emerging at each end as gilt-bronze dragon heads that hold the last two sections in their mouths. The jade pieces are alike in quality, semitranslucent grayish white with calcified patches of opaque brown and tan. While most pendants of this type are carved from a single piece of jade, the composite structure here reflects the preciousness of the material: even the smallest fragments of

jade were not wasted, but painstakingly worked and ingeniously assembled.

The surface decorations on the seven sections range from the abstract curvilinear patterns engraved on the two outermost sections, through the virtually abstract dragon heads among C-curls of the three middle sections, to the two large dragon heads of the remaining two sections, and finally to the reclining deer in the center. Such details as the fine striations that border the muzzles and tongues of the large dragons and the tiny circles that form the eyes of the dragon heads in the middle sections are engraved into the subtly convex and finely polished surface of the jade. The gilt-bronze dragon heads are now partially encrusted with a light green patina. Their eyes and temples are inlaid with a black glasslike substance. The pendant is identically carved on both sides. Another piece of jade probably once hung from the small loop at the bottom of the central piece.

PUBLISHED: Beijing, 1956b, pl. 53:2, p. 81, fig. 99; Beijing, 1961, pl. 55:1.

269

COLORPLATES 64-97

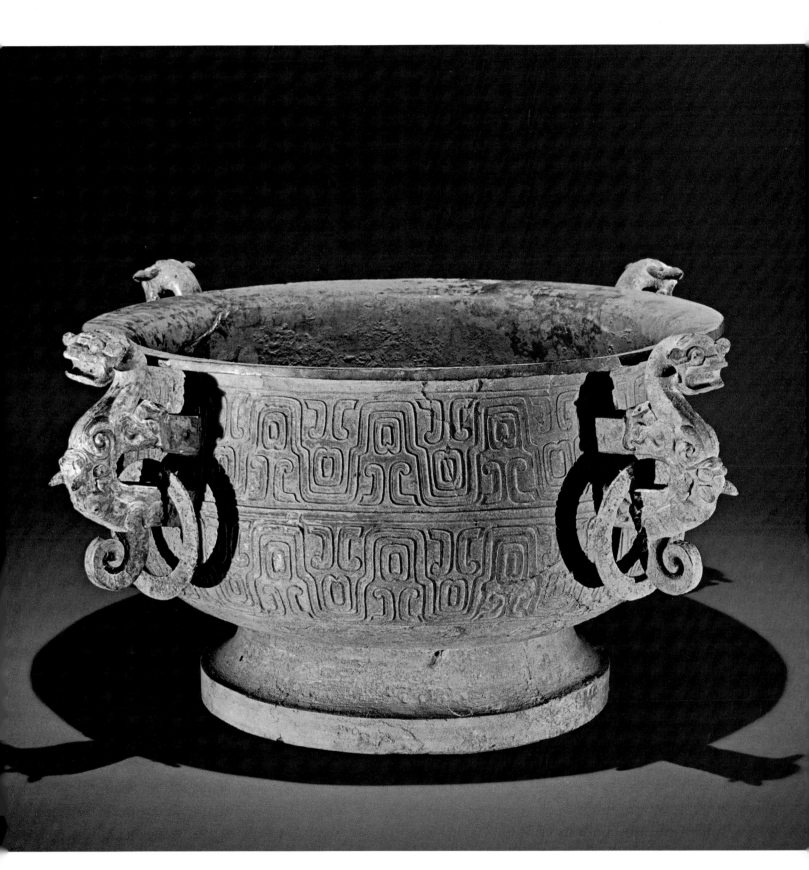

64 Qi Hou *yu*. Eastern Zhou (6th century B.C.). Height 46.4 cm. (18 in.);
diameter 75 cm. (29½ in.); weight 75 kg. (165 lb.)

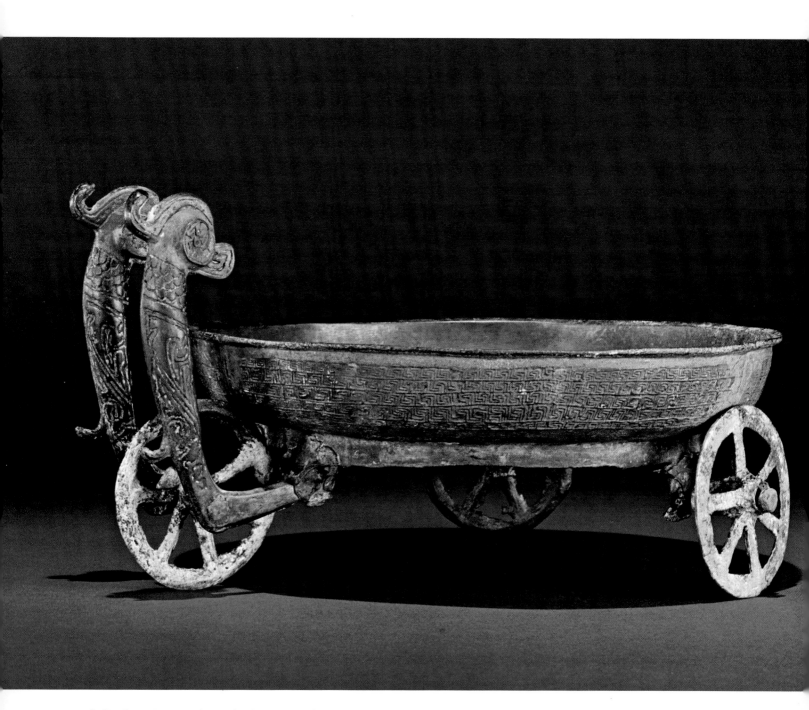

65 Shallow basin (*pan*) on three wheels. Eastern Zhou (6th–5th century B.C.).
Height 15.8 cm. (6¼ in.); diameter 26 cm. (10¼ in.); weight
1.65 kg. (3 lb. 10 oz.)

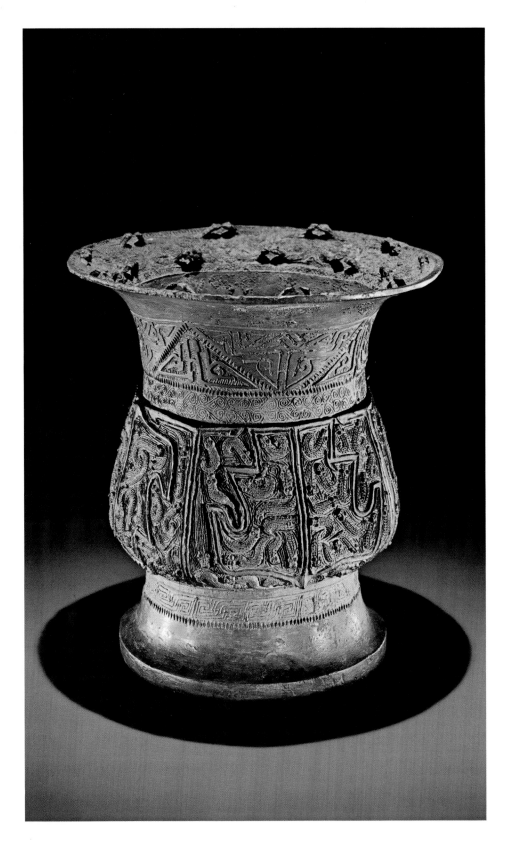

66 *Zun.* Eastern Zhou (6th century B.C.). Height 20.3 cm. (8 in.); diameter 19.5 cm. (7⅝ in.); weight 2.1 kg. (4 lb. 10 oz.)

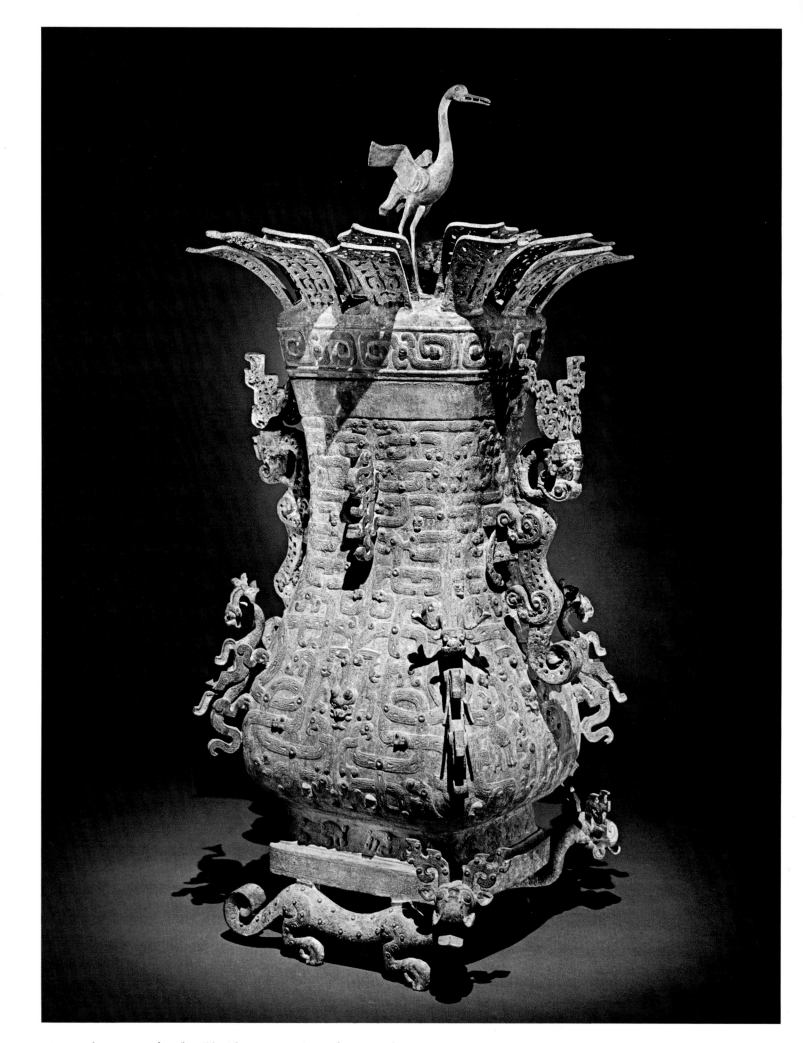

67 *Fang hu.* Eastern Zhou (late 7th–6th century B.C.). Height 118 cm. (46½ in.); dimensions at mouth 30.5 x 24.9 cm. (12 x 9¾ in.); weight 64.28 kg. (141 lb. 7 oz.)

Detail, openwork handle, *fang hu* no. **67**

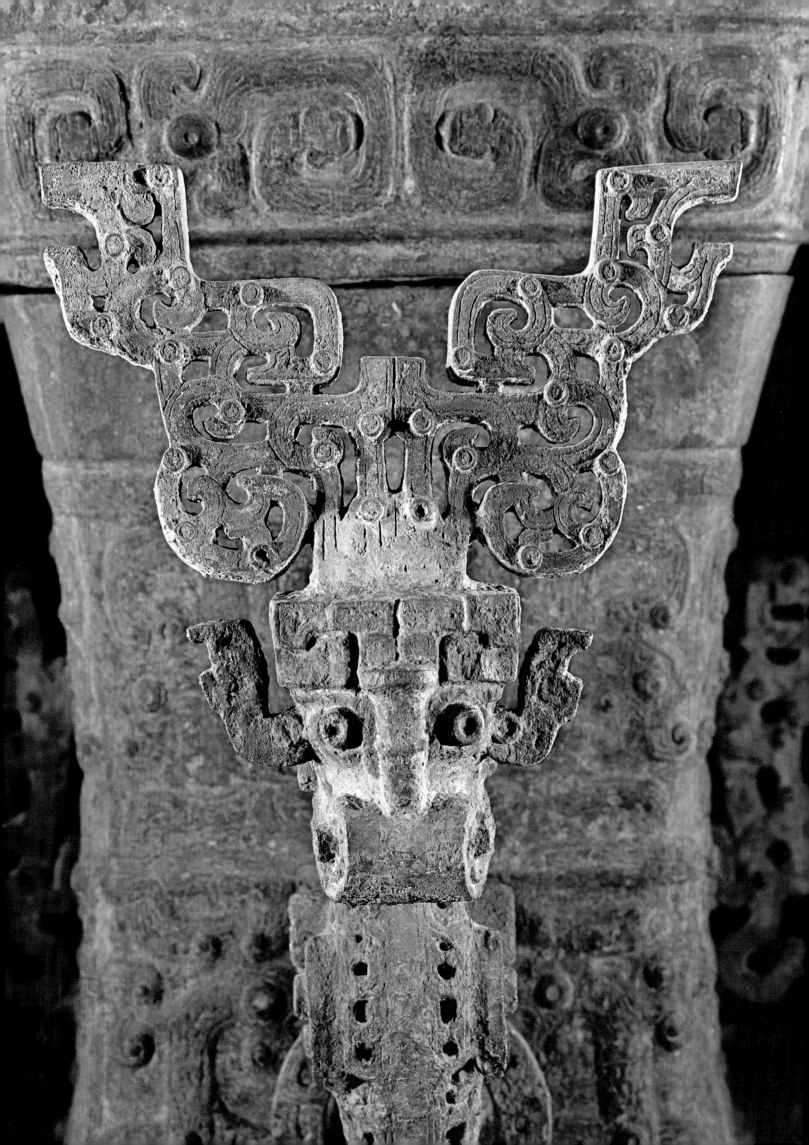

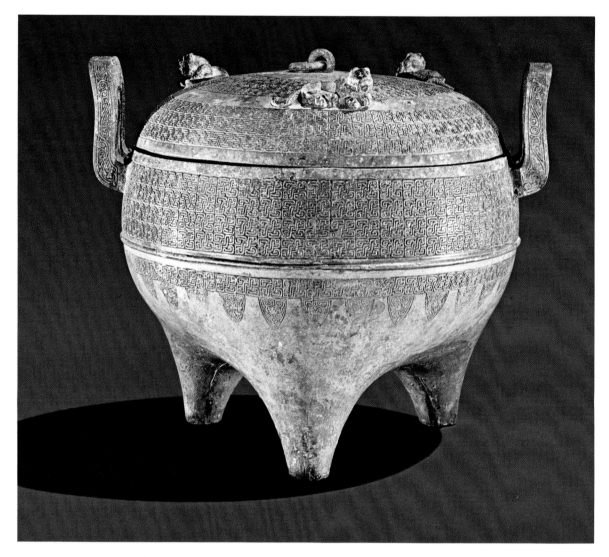

68 Above, *li ding*. Eastern Zhou (6th century B.C.). Height 18.9 cm. (7⅜ in.); diameter 17.5 cm. (6⅞ in.); weight 2.05 kg. (4 lb. 8 oz.).

Detail of decor, *li ding* no. **68**

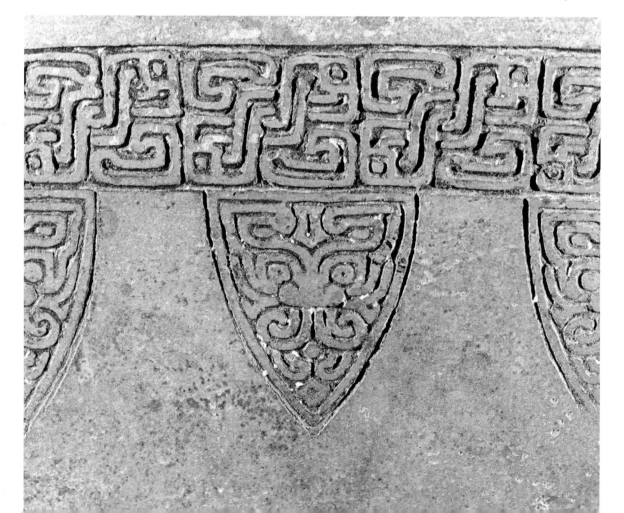

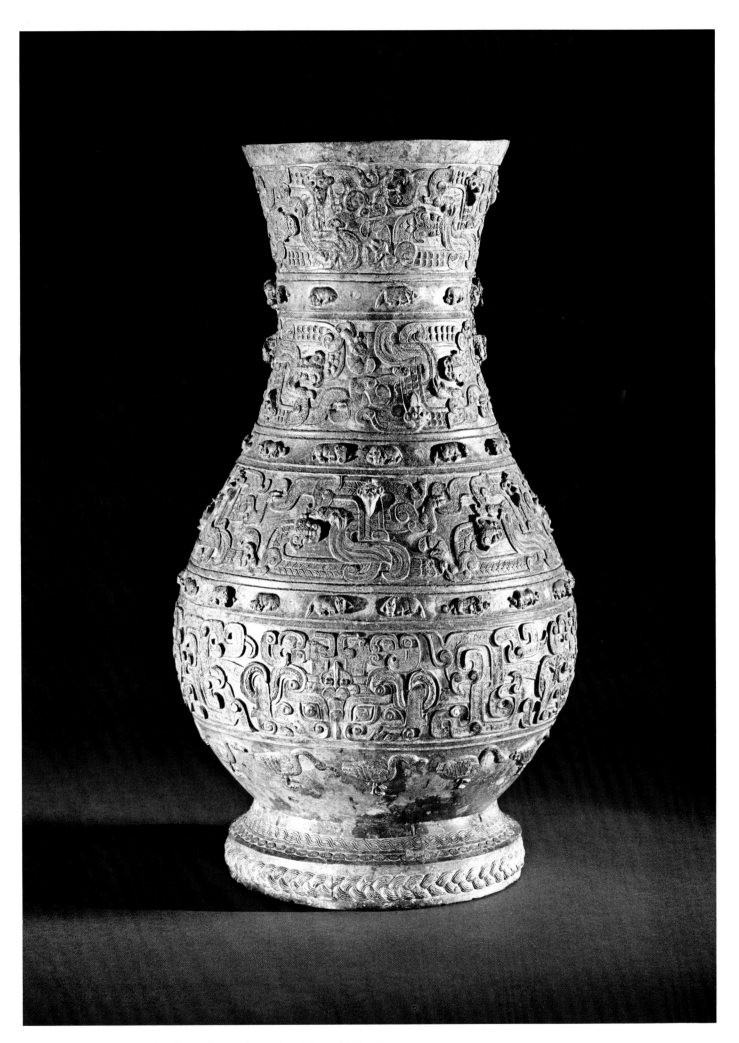

69 *Hu*. Eastern Zhou (early 5th century B.C.). Height 44.2 cm. (17⅜ in.);
greatest diameter 25 cm. (9⅞ in.); weight 5.77 kg. (12 lb. 11 oz.)

OVERLEAF: Detail, decor frieze, *hu* no. **69** ▷

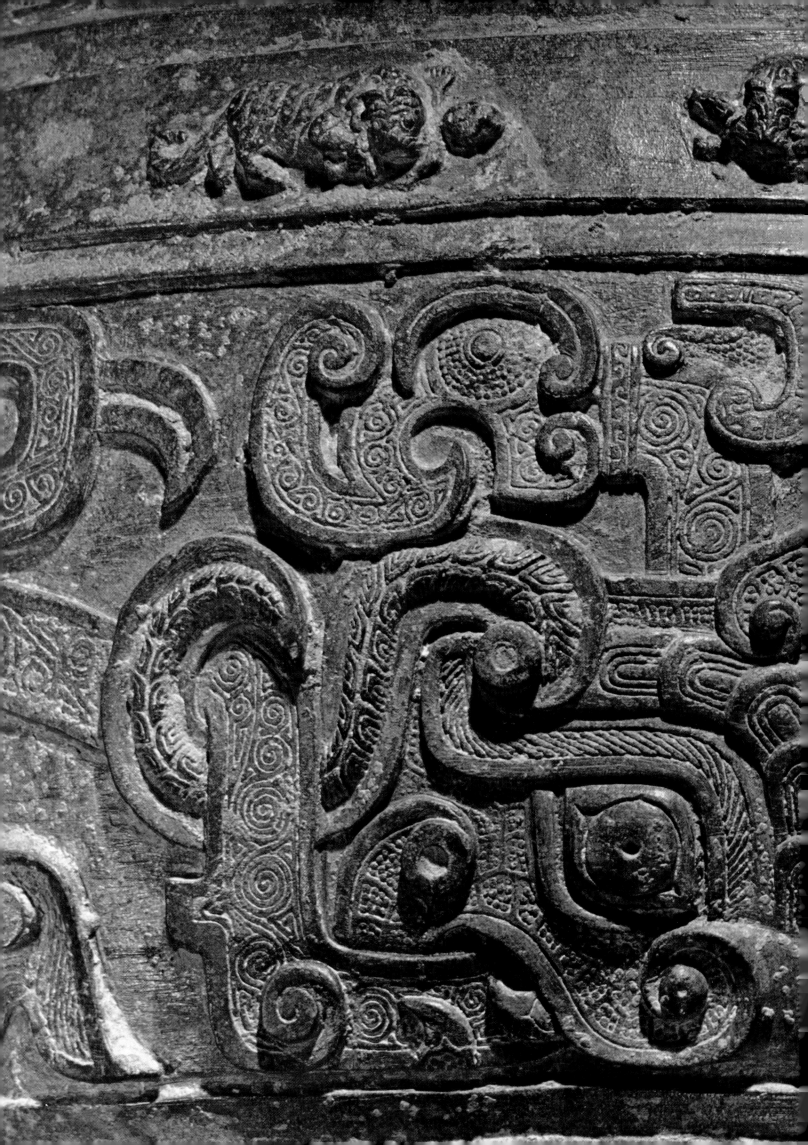

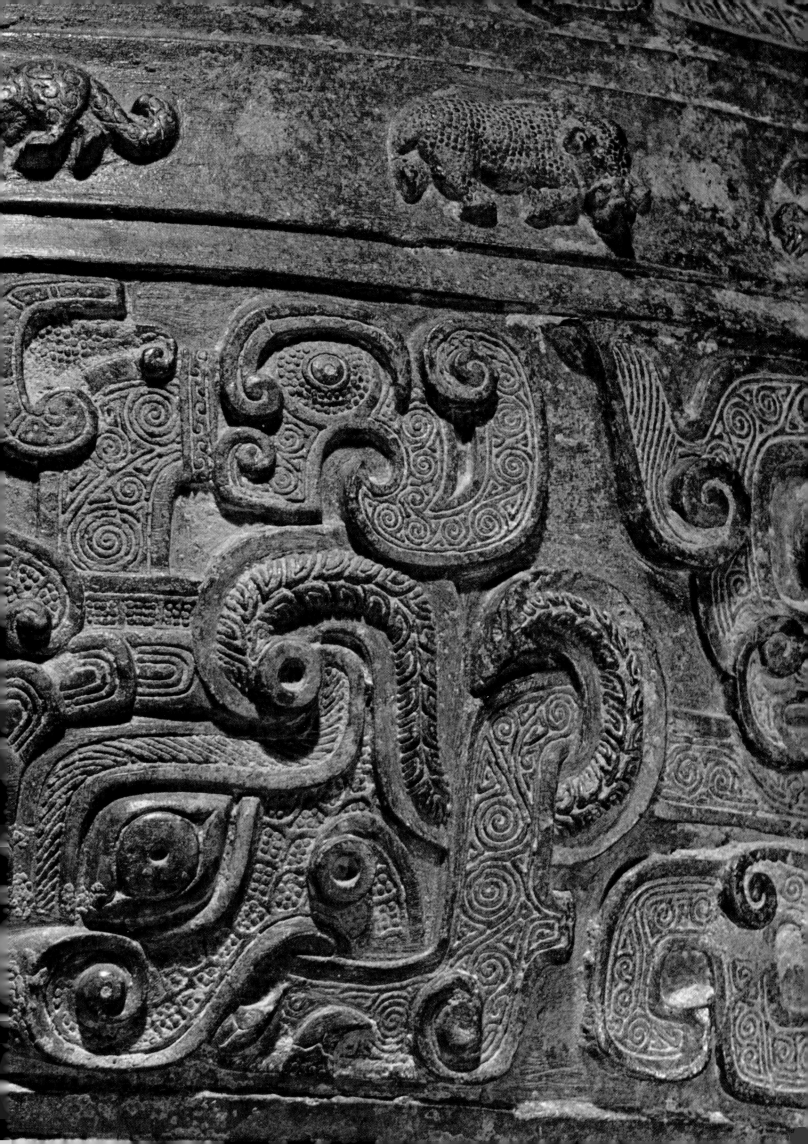

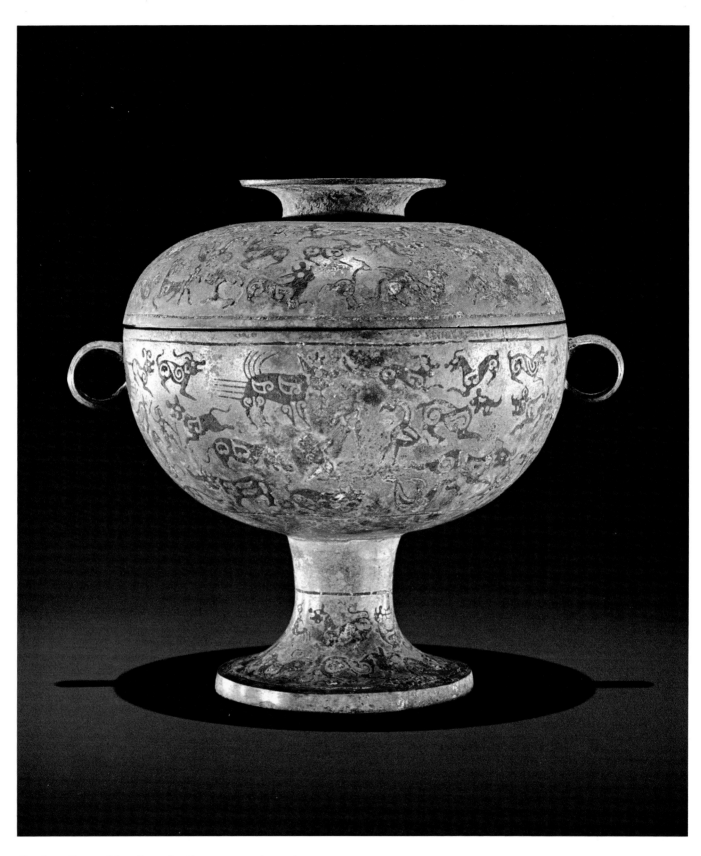

70 *Dou.* Eastern Zhou (late 6th–5th century B.C.). Height 20.7 cm.
(8⅛ in.); diameter 17.5 cm. (6⅞ in.); weight 1.8 kg. (3 lb. 15 oz.)

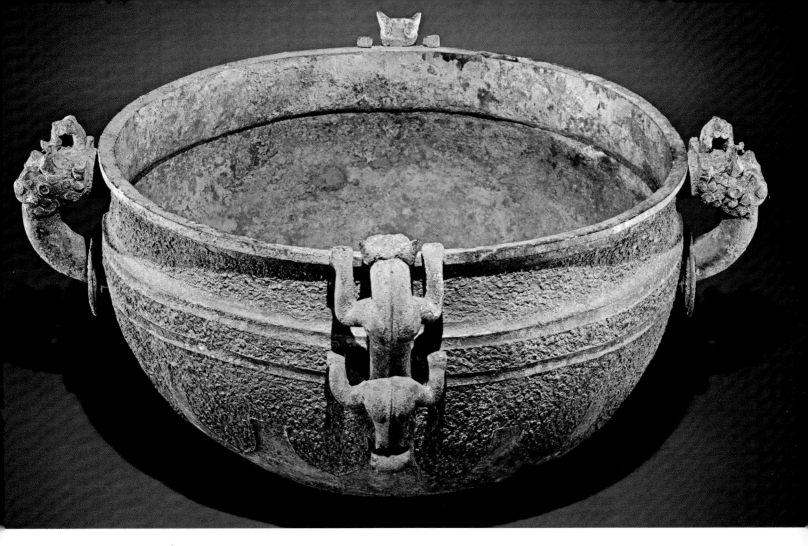

71 *Jian.* Eastern Zhou (early 5th century B.C.). Height 45 cm. (17¾ in.);
diameter 73 cm. (28¾ in.); weight 54 kg. (118 lb. 13 oz.)

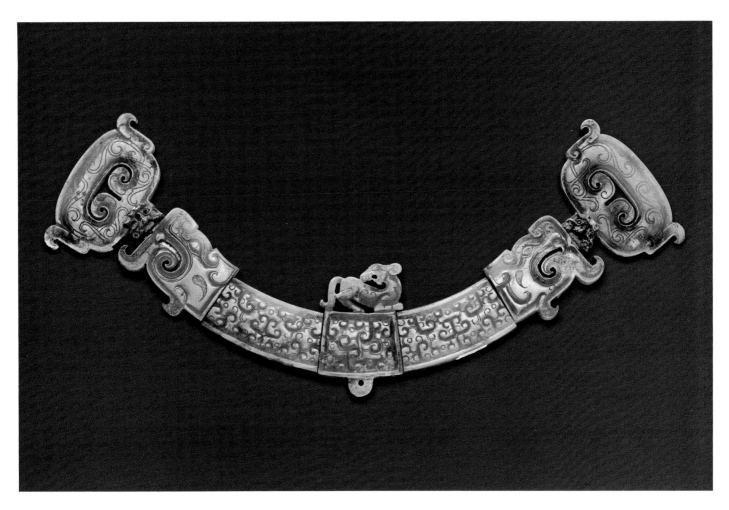

72 Jade pendant (*huang*). Eastern Zhou (late 6th–5th century B.C.). Length 20.2 cm.
(8 in.); maximum width 4.7 cm. (1⅞ in.); weight 76 g. (2⅔ oz.)

73 *Fang hu.* Late Eastern Zhou (4th century B.C.).
Height 53 cm. (20⅞ in.); dimensions at mouth
12.7 x 12.7 cm. (4 x 4 in.); weight 10.4 kg.
(22 lb. 14 oz.)

Detail, inlaid designs on *fang hu* no. 73 ▷

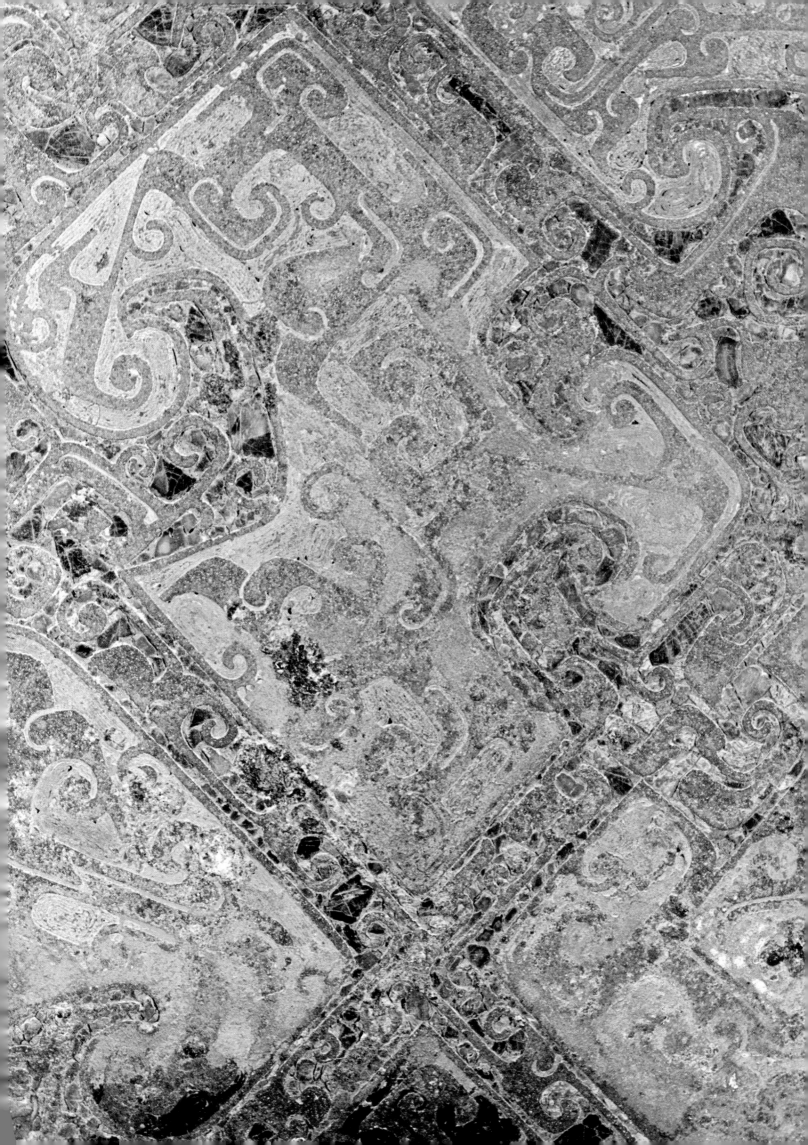

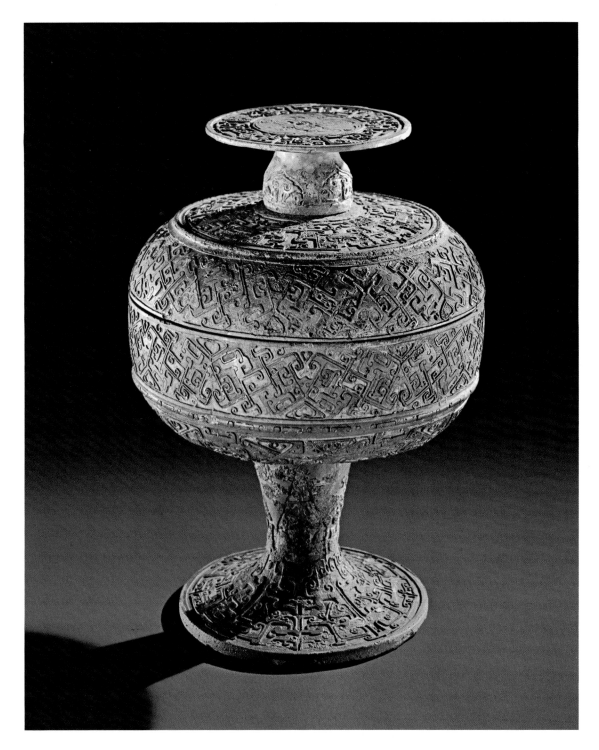

74 *Dou.* Late Eastern Zhou (4th century B.C.). Height 24 cm. (9½ in.);
diameter 16.2 cm. (6⅜ in.); weight 2.3 kg. (5 lb. 1 oz.)

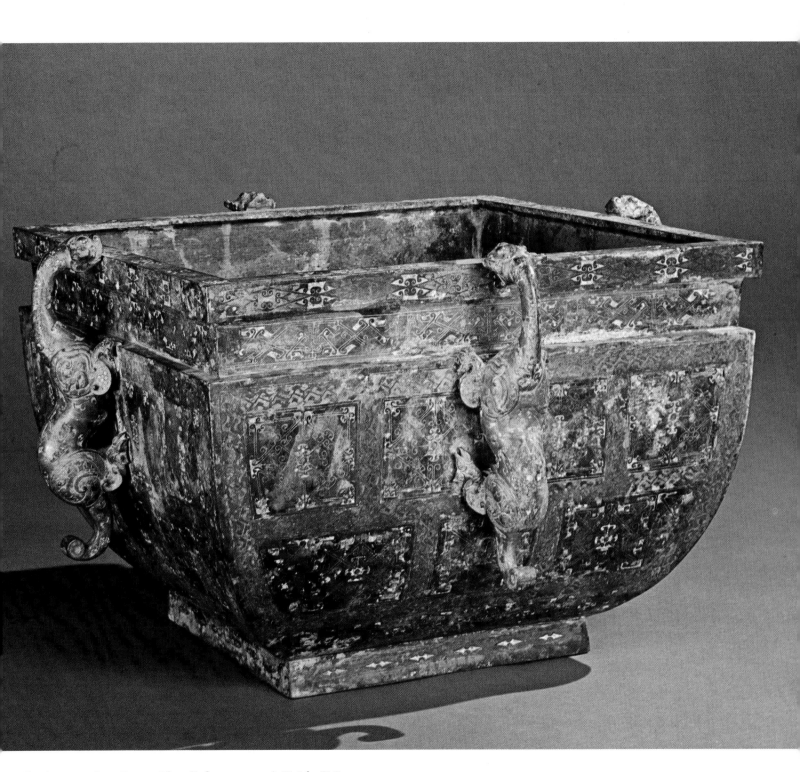

75 *Fang jian.* Late Eastern Zhou (3rd century B.C.). Height 21.6 cm. (8½ in.); dimensions at mouth 30.8 x 30.8 cm. (12⅛ x 12⅛ in.); weight 11.9 kg. (26 lb. 3 oz.)

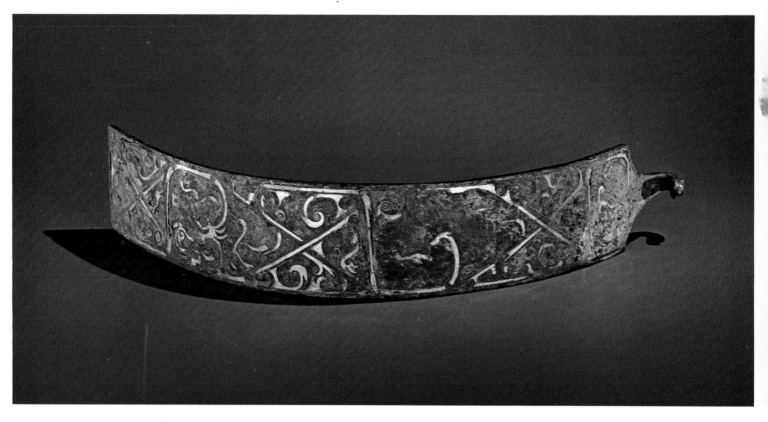

76 Iron belt hook. Late Eastern Zhou (4th century B.C.). Length 48 cm. (18⅞ in.); width 6.5 cm. (2½ in.); weight 0.7 kg. (1 lb. 9 oz.)

78 One of a set of fourteen bells, nos. **77–90** ▷

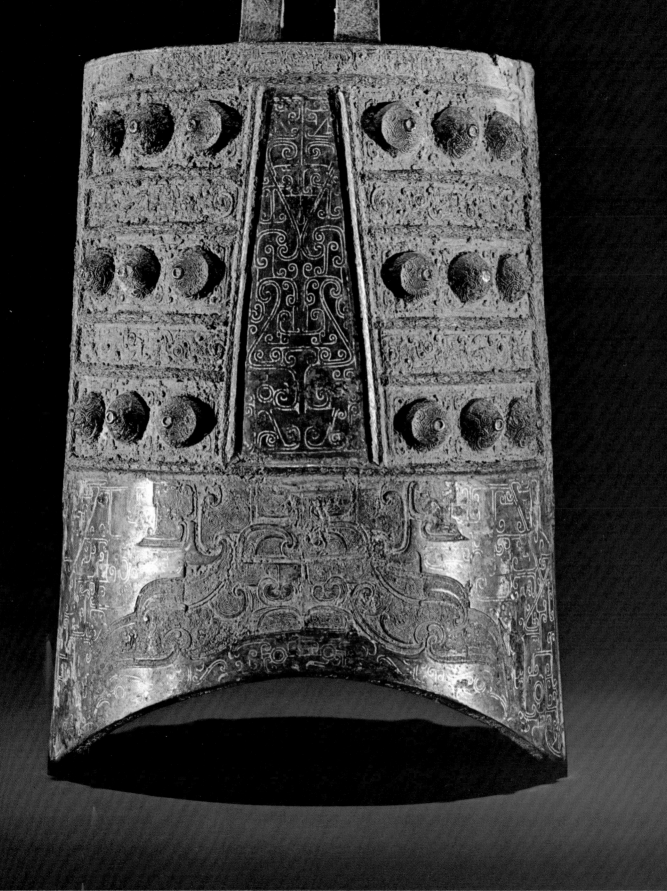

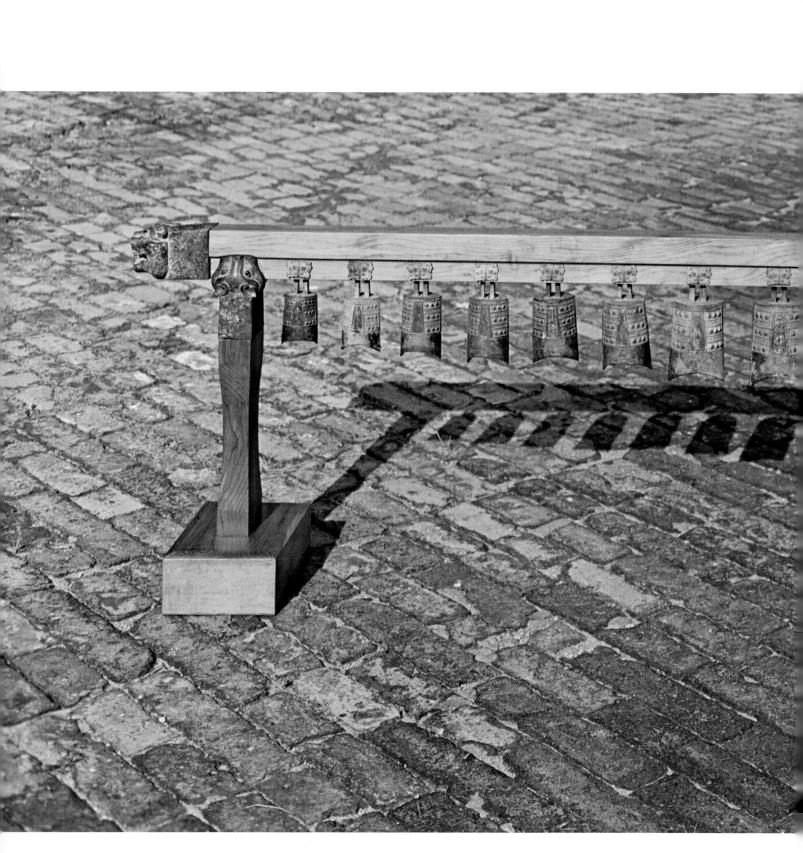

77–90 Fourteen bells. Late Eastern Zhou (3rd century B.C.). Height of largest
bell 27.5 cm. (10⅞ in.); weight 3.05 kg. (6 lb. 11 oz.). Height of smallest
bell 14.6 cm. (5⅝ in.); weight .475 kg. (1 lb. 1 oz.) The wood is a
modern replacement.

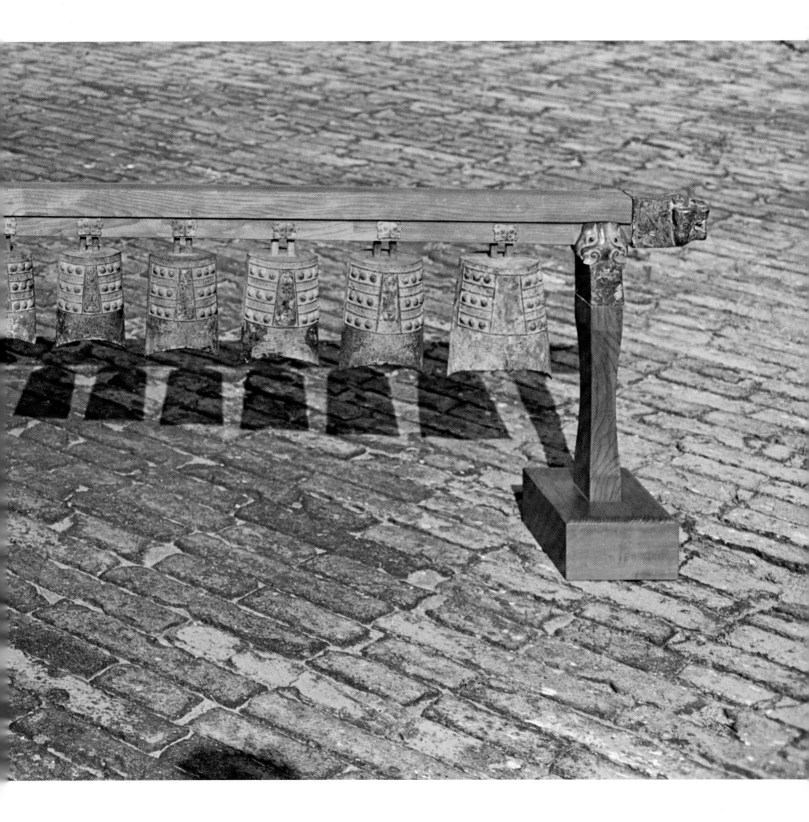

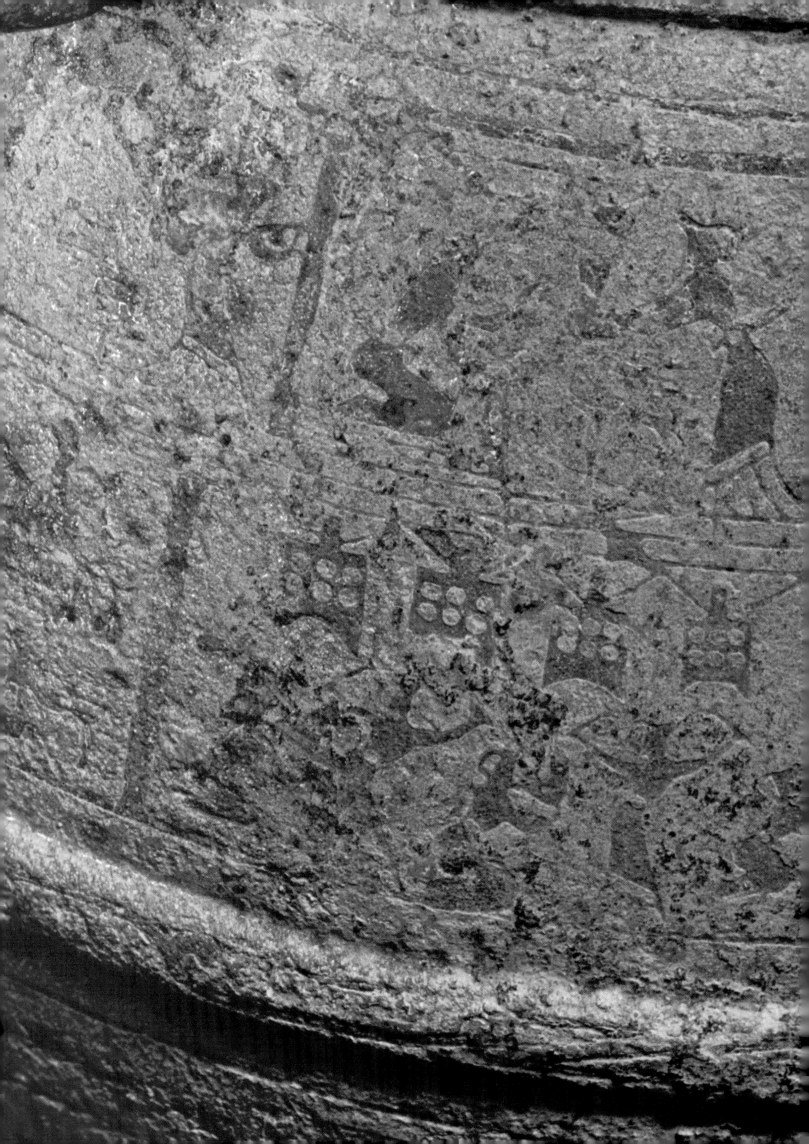

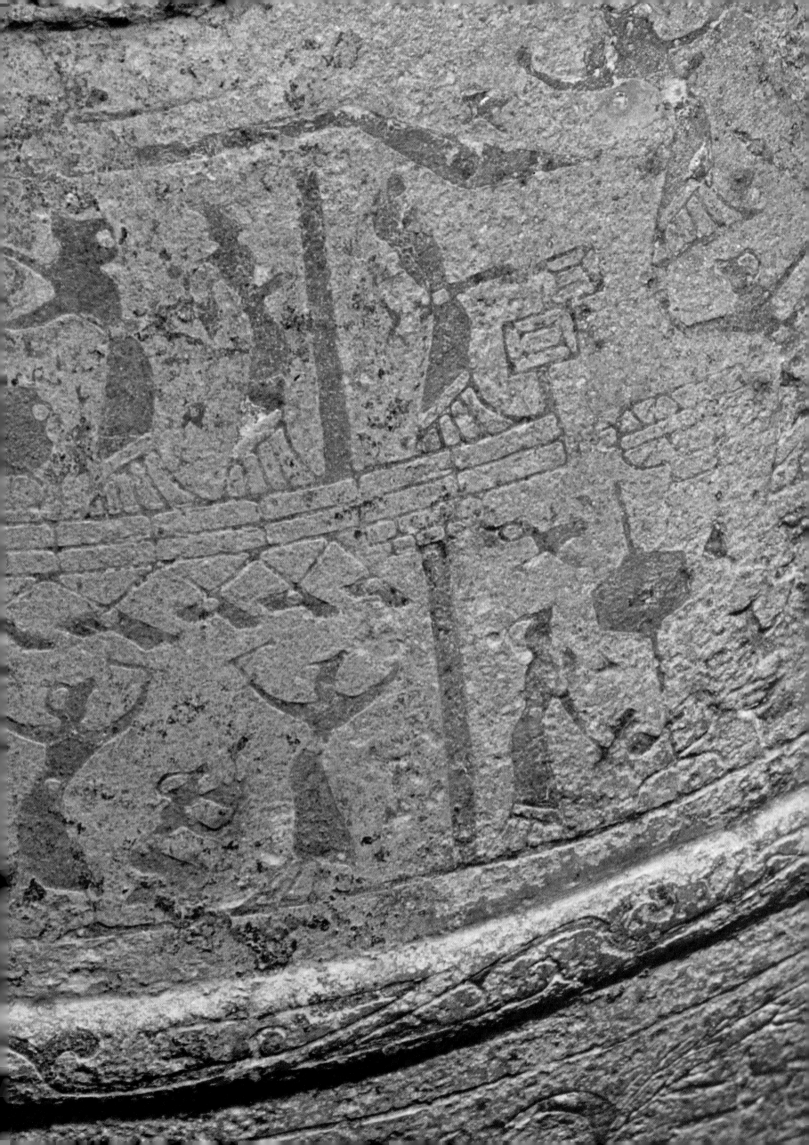

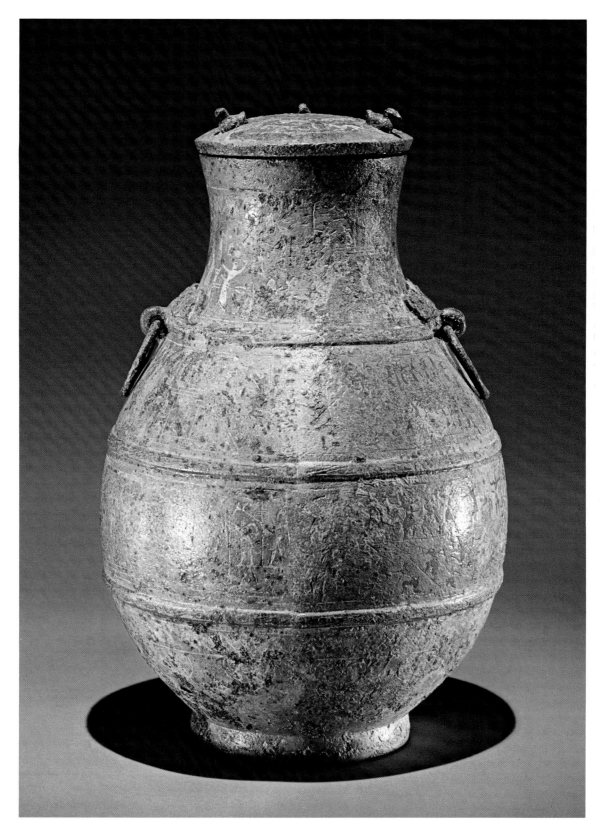

91 *Hu*. Eastern Zhou (late 6th–5th century B.C.). Height 39.9 cm.
(15¾ in.); diameter at mouth 13.4 cm. (5¼ in.); diameter at base
14.2 cm. (5⅝ in.); weight 4.5 kg. (9 lb. 14 oz.)

92 Standard top. Late Eastern Zhou (4th century B.C.). ▷
Height 144.2 cm. (56¾ in.); maximum width 80.3 cm.
(31⅝ in.); weight 50.03 kg. (110 lb. 1 oz.)

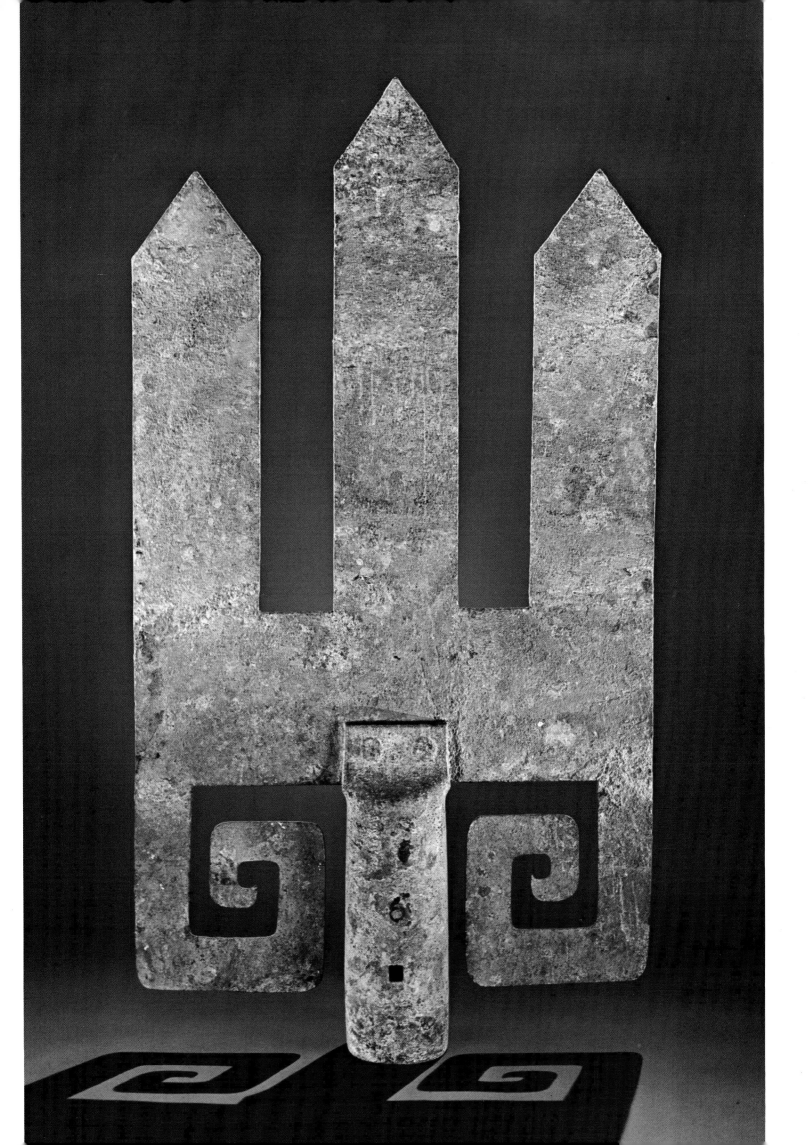

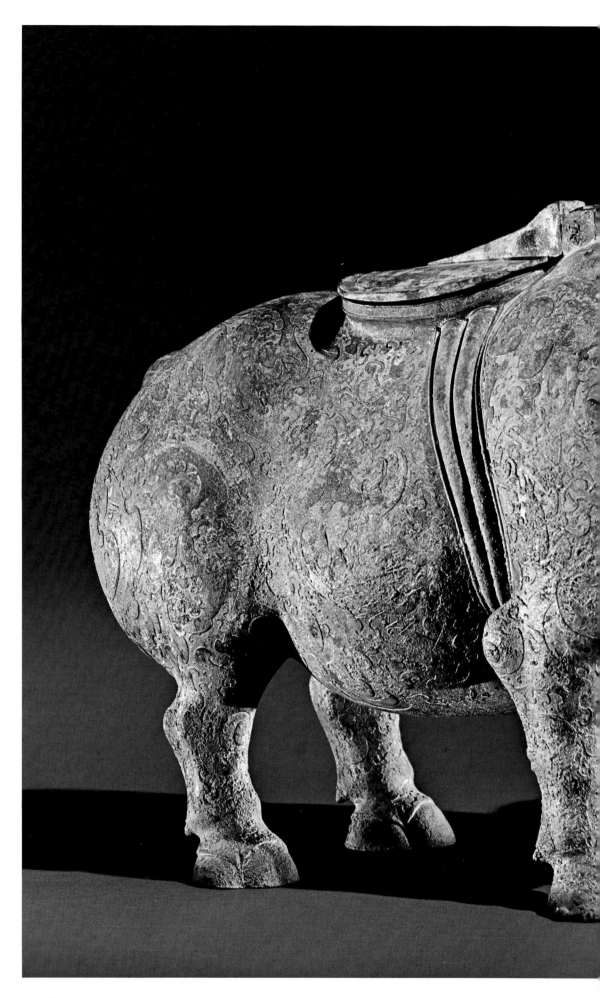

93 Rhinoceros *zun*. Late Eastern Zhou–Western Han (late 3rd century B.C.).
Height 34.1 cm. (13⅜ in.); length 58.1 cm. (22⅞ in.); weight
13.3 kg. (29 lb. 4 oz.)

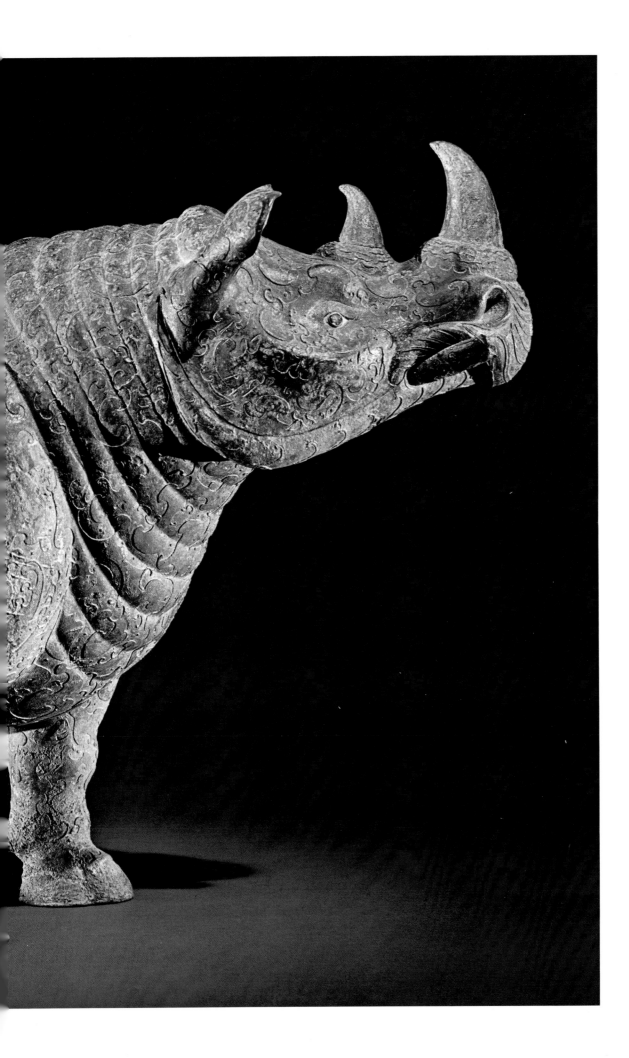

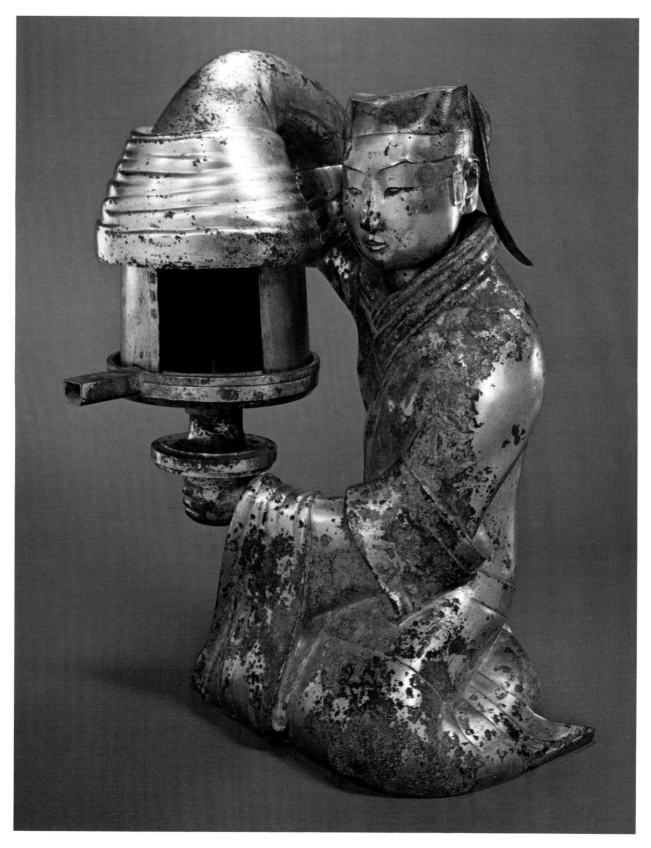

94 Gilt-bronze lamp. Western Han (first half 2nd century B.C.). Height 48 cm.
(18⅞ in.); weight 15.85 kg. (34 lb. 14 oz.). Photograph: Wang Yugui,
Cultural Relics Bureau, Beijing

Detail, young girl holding lamp, gilt-bronze ▷
lamp no. **94**. Photograph: Wang Yugui,
Cultural Relics Bureau, Beijing

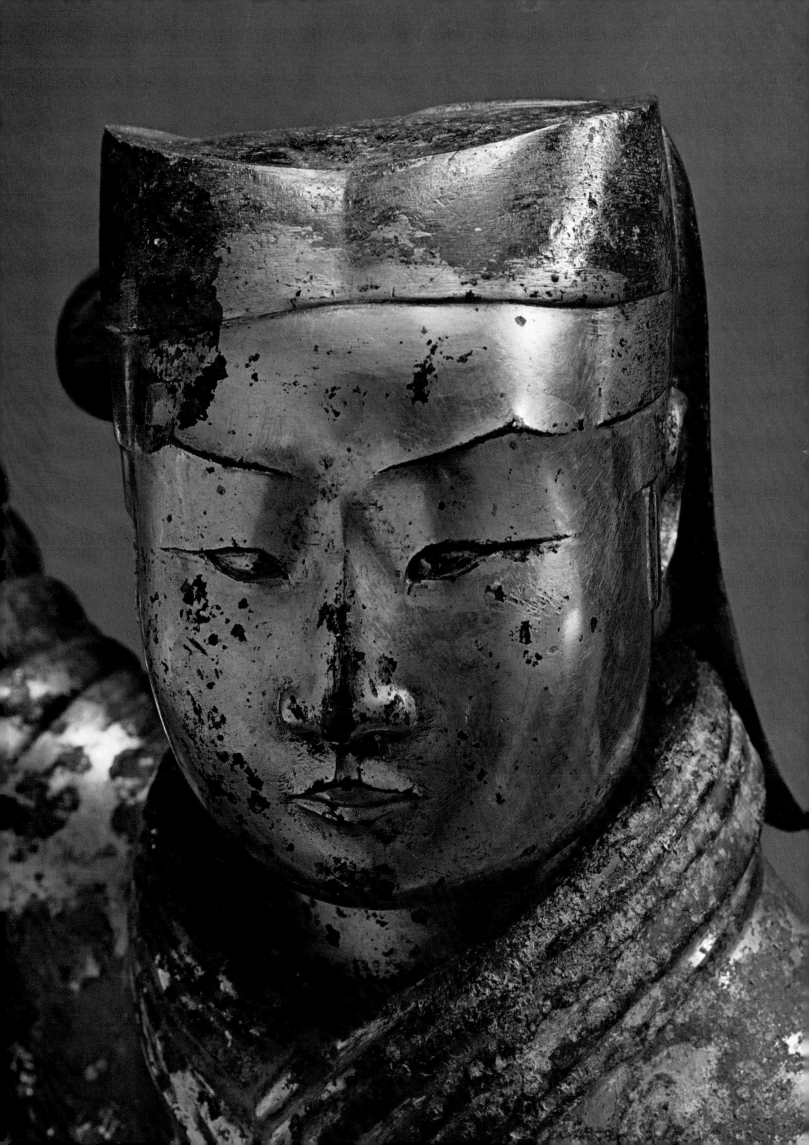

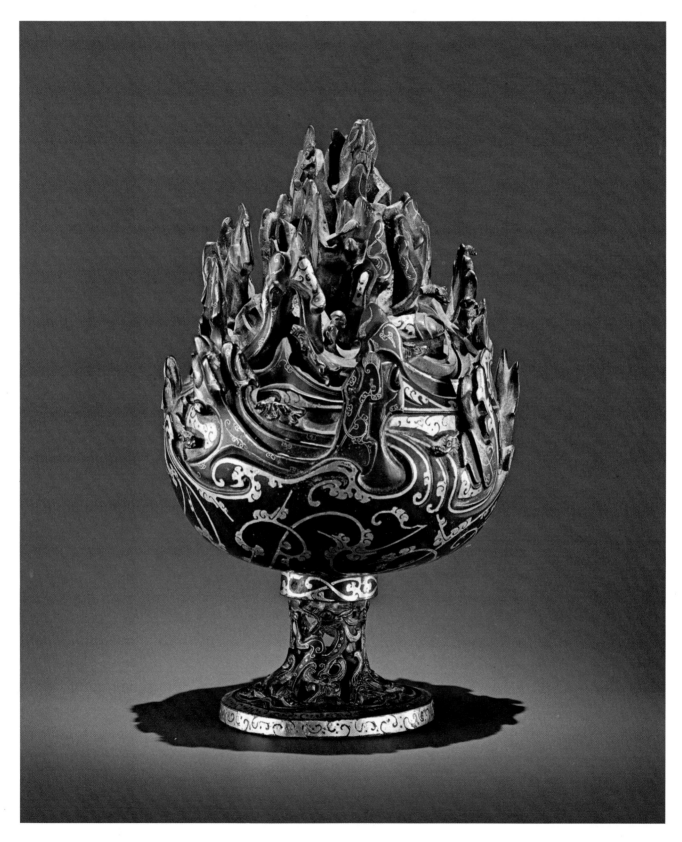

95 Censer. Western Han (second half 2nd century B.C.). Height 26 cm. (10¼
in.); weight 3.4 kg. (7 lb. 8 oz.)

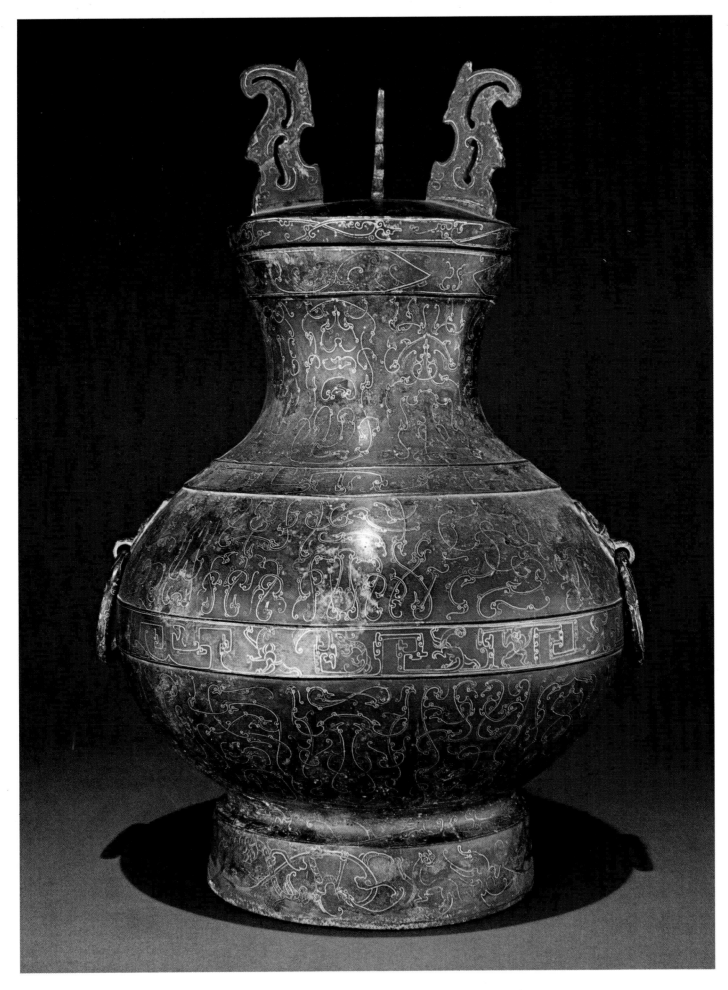

96 *Hu.* Western Han (second half 2nd century B.C.). Height 44.2 cm. (17⅜ in.); diameter 15.6 cm. (6⅛ in.); weight 6.55 kg. (14 lb. 7 oz.)

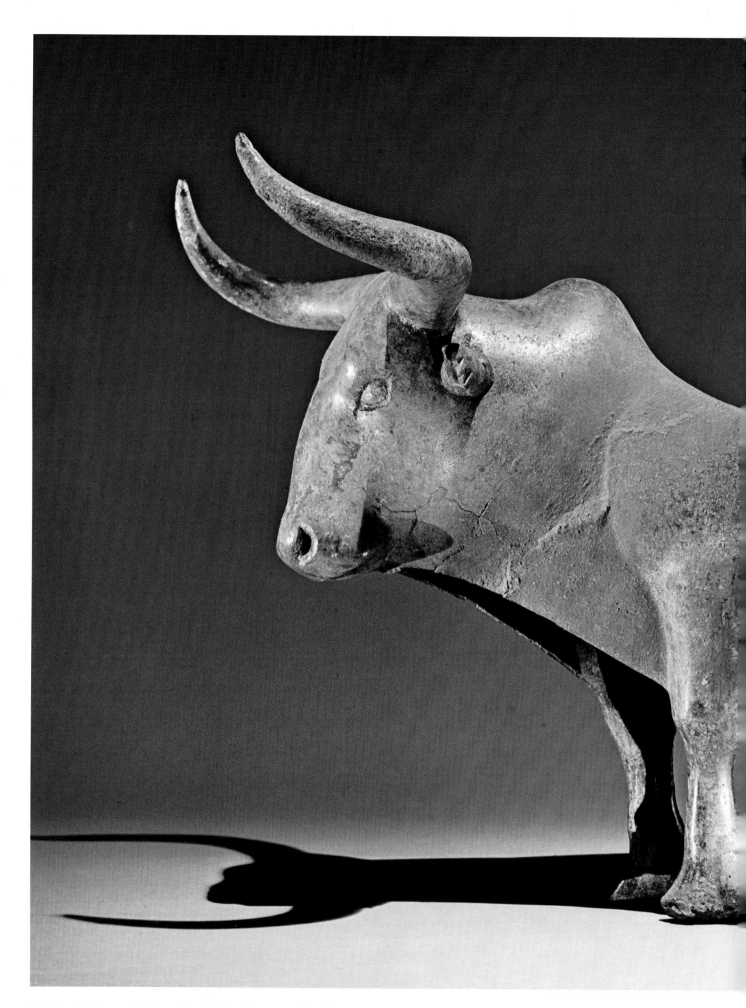

97 Ritual object in the form of two bulls and a tiger. 3rd–2nd century B.C.
Height 43 cm. (16⅞ in.); length 76 cm. (29⅞ in.); weight 12.6 kg.
(27 lb. 11 oz.)

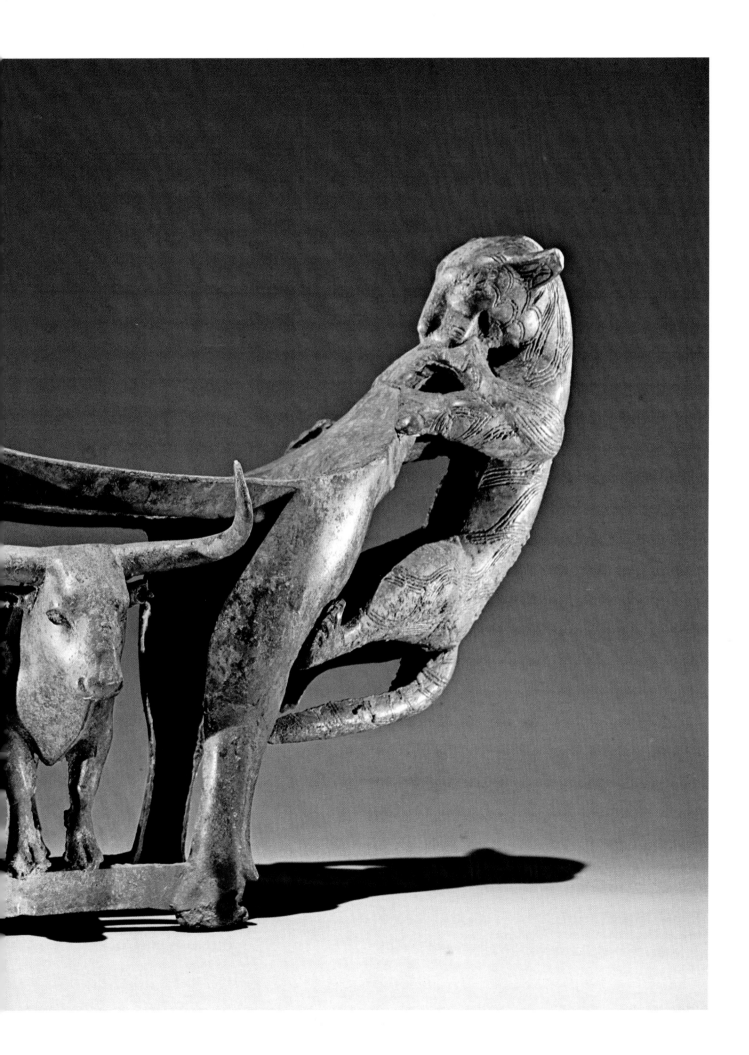

8

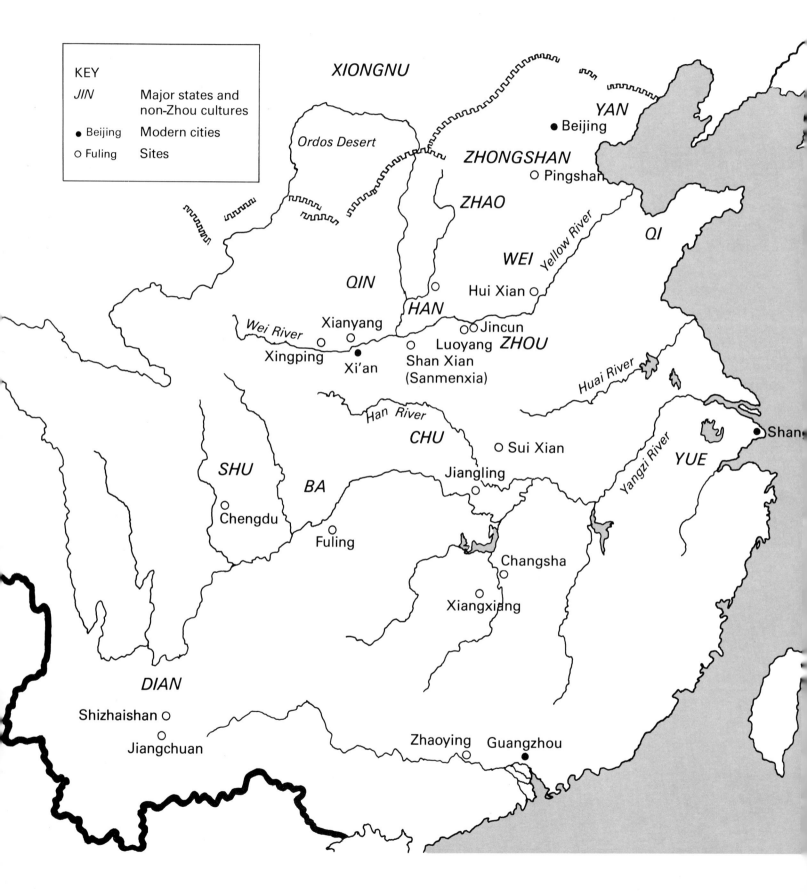

KEY

JIN Major states and non-Zhou cultures

● Beijing Modern cities

○ Fuling Sites

XIONGNU

Ordos Desert

YAN
● Beijing

ZHONGSHAN
○ Pingshan

ZHAO

WEI Yellow River

QI

QIN

Hui Xian ○

Wei River Xianyang
○
Xingping ● Xi'an

HAN
○○ Jincun
○ Luoyang *ZHOU*
Shan Xian
(Sanmenxia)

Huai River

Han River

CHU
○ Sui Xian

Jiangling

YUE
● Shan

Yangzi River

SHU

BA
○
Chengdu

○
Fuling

○
Changsha

○
Xiangxiang

DIAN

Shizhaishan ○

○
Jiangchuan

Zhaoying Guangzhou
○ ●

8 The Inlaid Bronzes of the Warring States Period

Jenny F. So

The regional stylistic differences that were so pronounced during the Spring and Autumn period began to dissolve in the course of the Warring States. This change was largely the result of improved trade and communications, which not only brought the different regions physically closer together, but also served to disseminate new artistic ideas over vast areas. But perhaps the style that appeared early in the Warring States period also played a part in bringing the regions together: its sumptuously inlaid designs, offering an unprecedented and dazzling display of gold, silver, and semiprecious stones, had such universal appeal that the various regions yielded readily to its colorful charm. This style of decoration has come to be known as the Inlay Style, or Jincun style, after the site at Luoyang where, in 1933–34, the earliest group of inlaid bronzes is thought to have been found. Controlled excavations since then have uncovered inlaid bronzes from all parts of China (see nos. 73–93)—from Hebei in the north to Guangdong in the south and from Sichuan in the west to Jiangsu in the east—a territorial distribution far wider than that of the Houma/Liyu bronzes. It is clear that the Inlay Style was the primary decorative style of the fifth to third centuries B.C., and its universal acceptance is an early indication of the cultural unity that foreshadowed the political unification of 221 B.C.

The widespread popularity of the Inlay Style was not achieved overnight. From its beginnings in the sixth century, over a hundred years elapsed before this style of bronze decoration was finally established as the most highly prized decor style throughout China. The history of the Inlay Style and of its conquest of China may be seen in three broad stages. The first spans the period from the sixth century to about 450 B.C.; the second, from 450 to about 350 B.C.; and the last, from 350 to the beginning of the Western Han period.

The first of these stages is represented here by nos. 70 and 91. They are, however, representative of only one type of early inlaid decoration; the other, of far greater consequence in the history of the Inlay Style, is represented by a *hu* from The Cleveland Museum of Art (Fig. 98). Nevertheless, nos. 70 and 91 illustrate two crucial points about the earliest inlaid decoration in China: first, that copper was the first metal to be used as

Map of China showing the principal states and important archaeological sites of the Warring States period of the Eastern Zhou dynasty, 475 to 221 B.C.

305

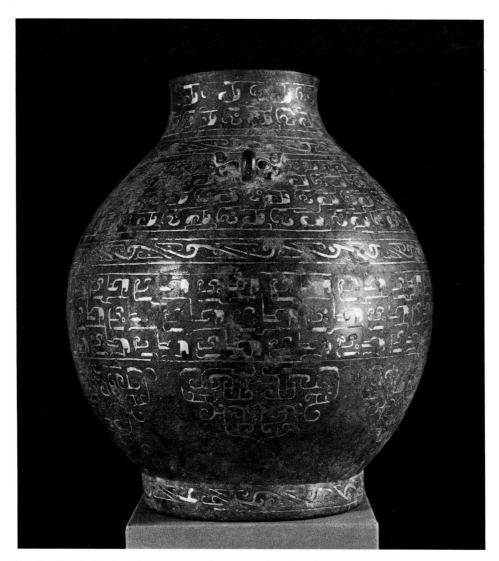

Fig. 98   *Hu* inlaid with gold. Provenance unknown. Purchase from the
J. H. Wade Fund, The Cleveland Museum of Art, 29.984

an inlay (the use of gold sheets applied over bronze, known in the seventh-century bronzes from Xinzheng, is not technically inlay); and, second, that the idea of inlaying with metal was foreign to China, and was acquired from the West through the nomadic cultures of the Central Asian steppes—the immediate source for the Animal Style motifs of no. 70.

Although the Chinese adopted from the West the idea of inlay, they did not borrow the technique without modification. In West Asian workshops, casting ordinarily played no essential role in the inlay process; the designs were applied to the cold surface of an undecorated bronze. The Chinese craftsman, however, with his traditional reliance on the casting process, obtained the same result by casting depressions in the bronze to receive the inlay, a practice verified by model fragments from the foundry site at Houma (Fig. 92). The distinction apparent a millennium earlier between the Chinese preference for casting and the usual Western method of cold-working thus holds up even in the era of inlaid bronzes, and in a context of artistic borrowing. Clearly, what the Chinese bronze master valued was not a set of new techniques, but the exciting possibilities afforded by the

introduction of color to the hitherto monochromatic bronze surface.

The Animal Style motifs that were borrowed along with the idea of inlay quickly proved to have little appeal for native Chinese taste, and they were soon replaced by more familiar subjects, such as the pictorial scenes on the *hu* no. 91. Neither variety of decoration enjoyed any lasting popularity, and the geographical distribution of copper-inlaid bronzes is limited. The muted contrasts of copper against bronze soon gave way to richer inlays of gold, turquoise, and malachite, arranged in abstract ornamental patterns derived from more familiar bronze motifs (colorplate, detail, no. 73). Examples from this early stage of inlaid designs, represented by the Cleveland *hu* (Fig. 98), are relatively rare, and so far attested in metropolitan China only, mainly by excavations at Changzhi in Shanxi Province, and at Luoyang and Hui Xian in Henan Province.

The brilliant ornamental inventions that were to come from this modest beginning belong to the second stage of inlaid designs, beautifully illustrated by the complex, purely abstract patterns of nos. 73 and 74. The superb *fang hu* no. 73, inlaid with copper and malachite, comes from the 1956–57 excavations at Sanmenxia in western Henan and dates between 400 and 350 B.C. Each face of the *fang hu* is crossed by a series of diagonals, forming a symmetrical network. A profusion of small, endlessly varied spiraling elements are crowded into the interstices of the basic diagonal grid (colorplate, detail, no. 73). Both the main diagonals and the intervening spirals form the pattern, which is cast in the bronze and set off by an inlaid background. The inlay in the spaces between the crossed diagonals is copper, originally red but now corroded to a bright blue green, while the diagonals are further emphasized by the addition of dark green bits of malachite. In the perfectly smooth finished surface, patterns are formed by the contrasts of color between bronze and the inlay materials, rather than by the use of relief. Whether the design is in the cast bronze (no. 73) or in the inlays themselves (no. 76), color remains the primary decorative feature. The complete loss of the inlay materials from the covered *dou* no. 74 has left its design, essentially similar to that of no. 73, nearly illegible, despite the unintended compensating effect of relief.

As the Inlay Style matured, the appeal of its rich, brocadelike surface increased, and inlaid bronzes of the second stage are accordingly found over an area that extends beyond metropolitan China to Hebei in the north, Shandong in the east, and Hunan in the south. The third stage, beginning about 350 B.C., is best understood in terms of two parallel developments, one dominant in metropolitan China—that is, Henan and southern Shanxi—the other, in the south.

The first of these developments, a direct outgrowth of the preceding stages, is represented at the highest level of quality by the *fang jian* no. 75, which, like no. 73, comes from the Sanmenxia area in western Henan. Here, the design remains abstract and geometric, but it is executed with a combination of airy lightness and mathematical control that makes the richness of no. 73 seem heavy and effusive. The rarefied design of no. 75 is complemented by the precision and refinement of the inlays themselves: the gold lines have a wiry thinness, the turquoise accents (some now lost) are minute and calculatedly placed. Even the bodies of the four felines climbing up the sides of the vessel are exquisitely inlaid, their sinuously curving silhouettes relieving the austere angular shape and rigid paneled design of the vessel. The precious inlay materials, the modest size of the vessel, and the surpassingly elegant design give the *fang jian* an almost jewellike delicacy.

From this time, the inlaid bronzes of the metropolitan tradition show a tendency toward ever greater refinement. The character of the later designs is well illustrated by a large *fang hu* from Xi'an, dating to the last decades of the Warring States period, that was included in the 1974–75 exhibition of archaeological finds from the People's Republic (Fig. 99). The basic symmetrical design of the earlier *fang hu* no. 73 survives here almost unchanged, but the rich profusion of the earlier design has yielded to a draftsmanlike precision of fine gold-inlaid lines, and its rough energy has been muted and controlled by an exacting restraint.

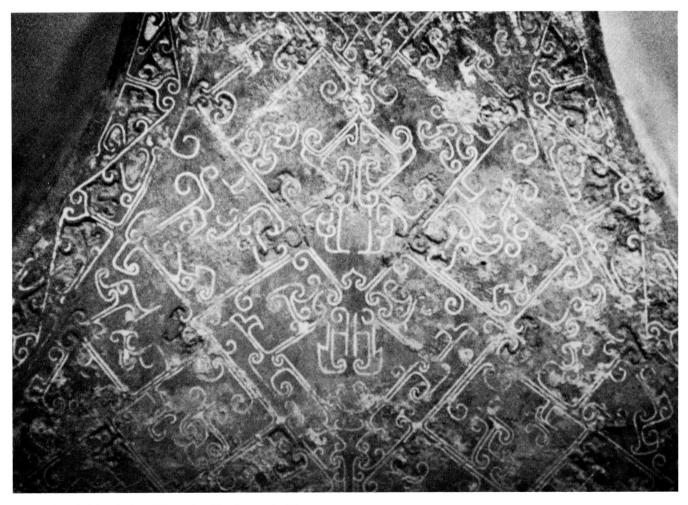

Fig. 99 Detail of *fang hu* from Xi'an with gold and turquoise inlays. Photograph after Kansas City, 1975, no. 201

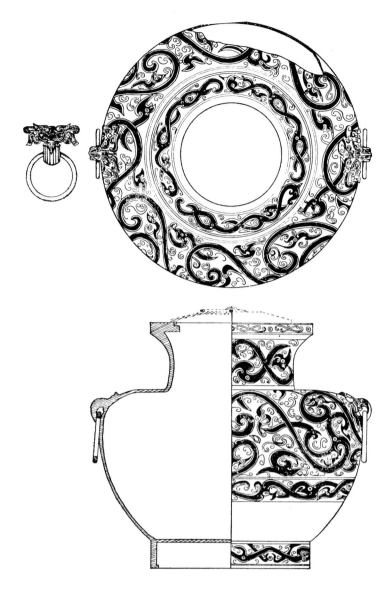

Fig. 100 Drawing of *lei* with silver and lacquer inlays from Zhaoqing, Guangdong Province. After *Wenwu* 1974/11, p. 71, fig. 5

The introduction of a new, dynamic curvilinear style demonstrates that regional artistic traditions still played key roles in the art of the Warring States period, although regional distinctions were already beginning to blur. Since the southern arts of painted lacquers and luxurious silks were coveted by metropolitan patrons, the new bronze designs were also welcomed with enthusiasm. As a result, bronzes of both metropolitan angularity and lacquer-inspired fluidity are found throughout China, so that neither style can justifiably be characterized as regional. Proof of this broad appeal is to be found in the set of fourteen bells from the border region of Sichuan in the west, with their delicate gold inlay (nos. 77–90), and the bronze *lei* inlaid with silver and red lacquer—a rare, probably local combination—that was excavated in 1972 on the outskirts of Guangzhou in Guangdong Province (Fig. 100).

In its sources and permutations, the history of the Inlay Style reflects something of the dynamic vigor and sophistication of the Warring States period as a whole. Its beginnings were inspired by foreign contacts. Its adaptation to the Chinese sphere was subject to a variety of molding forces—a brief flirtation with pictorial designs, a strong and enduring metropolitan tradition of pure ornament, and the seductive elegance of the rising lacquer and textile industries of the south. The underlying unity shared by even the most distinctive manifestations of the style is epitomized by the richly colored and patterned surfaces, in which the worldliness of the period finds an apt expression.

The Secularization of the Bronze Vessel

The splendor and sensuous appeal of inlaid decoration marks the final separation of the bronze vessel from the solemn realm of ritual. It is the culmination of a trend begun in Western Zhou, when the bronzes seem often more political than religious in function, if not at times expressions of family vanity. In the Spring and Autumn period, purely secular motives are sometimes avowed by inscriptions; even so, a vessel cast to commemorate a wedding that unites princely houses may still partake both of the religious and the political (see chap. 7). In the Warring States period, however, the bronze vessels occupied as important a place in the wealthy man's home as they did in the ancestral temple. The religious spirit that pervades Shang vessels and that can still be felt in the solemnity of the eighth-century marquis of Zeng *hu* (no. 62) has evaporated from these luxury objects. No other decorative style could better suit the new social and secular role of Warring States bronzes than the sumptuous elegance of the Inlay Style.

In keeping with their new role in society, most bronze vessels of the Warring States period lack significant inscriptions. The longest inscriptions, some over four hundred characters in length, appear on a few bronzes excavated in 1978 from the late fourth-century tomb of the king of Zhongshan and are unprecedented in the Warring States period. They may reflect a somewhat

The third inlay stage saw a second line of development, moving in parallel with the metropolitan designs, but associated particularly with inlaid bronzes of southern provenance. In contrast to the stiff geometric designs typified by no. 75, it is a style of free-flowing curvilinear patterns, occasionally combined with zoomorphic motifs of dragons and birds, represented by the large gold- and silver-inlaid belt hook no. 76 from a fourth-century Chu tomb in Jiangling, Hubei Province. Despite the shared emphasis on color, a design like that on the belt hook has more in common with the painted designs on lacquered wooden objects from Chu tombs of the fourth and third centuries than with those of nos. 73 and 75. Both the inlaid and the painted designs have a graceful fluidity generated by sweeping curves and many spiraling, tendrillike terminations. The new qualities must have been inspired by the growing popularity of the painted lacquers, and, as might be expected, the earliest such designs in bronze are encountered primarily at southern sites.

overzealous acculturation by the Di barbarians who ruled the Zhongshan state. When inscriptions do occur on Warring States bronzes, they normally record only prosaic matters, such as the year of manufacture, name of the workshop or craftsman, and, more frequently, the weight of bronze used and the capacity of the vessel. Even the Zhongshan king's bronzes follow this common practice.

The Western Han bronzes from the second-century B.C. tombs of Prince Liu Sheng and his wife, Dou Wan, stand at the climax of this secularizing trend, when even religion seems to serve only the most mundane aspirations of its devotees. A representative selection of objects from their tombs, including Dou Wan's jade burial suit, was shown in the 1974–75 exhibition of archaeological finds from the People's Republic. Not included in that exhibition were the *hu* no. 96, the lamp no. 94, and the gold-inlaid incense burner no. 95. The profusion of wiry curvilinear configurations on the *hu* proves on close examination to be writing, executed in a highly stylized script (called "bird script" because each configuration contains birdlike elements). Clearly, this elaborate script, decipherable only to the trained eye, performs above all a decorative function. Nevertheless, when transcribed, the inscription reveals sentiments that are typical of the social elite of Western Han times as well as indicative of the purely secular role of the bronze vessel. Demonstrating a preoccupation with worldly pleasures and otherworldly hopes, all familiar to us from historical texts and philosophical writings of the time, the inscription wishes on the prince endless banquets, good health, long life, and immortality (see entry no. 96). The design of the gold-inlaid incense burner from his tomb alludes to the legendary Isle of the Immortals, which stood amid the turmoil of the Eastern Sea. This glittering image of the utopia of Taoist myth, a paradise of eternal youth and happiness, must have served Liu Sheng in his hopes to approximate immortality in his earthly existence.

The Rise of Representational Art

The colorful inlaid bronzes of the fifth to third century constitute the last brilliant episode in the history of Bronze Age ornament in China. The Warring States period witnessed intensified activity in an art form that was to replace the bronze vessel as the major artistic achievement of the first millennium A.D.: the art of representation, in both sculpture and painting. The surge of archaeological activity in China in the past few decades has not only greatly enriched our understanding of the ornamental tradition of the ritual bronze vessel. It has also brought to light hitherto unsuspected achievements, most notably an art of monumental sculpture dating back to at least the end of the third century B.C., revealed by the excavations begun in 1974 at the mausoleum of the First Emperor of Qin (see chap. 10).

Even in the Shang period, human and animal images appeared alongside purely abstract ones (see nos. 24, 34–40), but their rarity shows that such depictions represented a minor artistic concern of the time. Expressive forms and beautiful patterns took precedence over representational meaning, and it is to the realm of ornamental art that the greatest achievements of the Bronze Age artist belong. In sharp contrast, ancient civilizations in the West concentrated on representation from the first, both in sculpture and in two-dimensional pictorial scenes. Perhaps it is significant that the deities of civilized Mesopotamia were personified in myth and portrayed in art, while those of the Shang dynasty in China remained shadowy and were never depicted.

Viewed in this light, the early fifth-century *hu* from Sichuan (no. 91), with its stiff, naive pictorial scenes, takes on a special historical significance. With a group of similarly decorated bronzes it represents one of the earliest known Chinese attempts at pictorial art, when the artist first began to grapple with the problem of portraying a three-dimensional space on a two-dimensional surface. The solution offered here is simple and primitive: the various scenes of archery, duck hunting, music making, banqueting, and land and sea battles are set next to each other with no regard for spatial relationships. The scenes resemble line diagrams, and each individual scene functions more like an elaborate pictograph to be *read* for its contents than as a convincing pictorial evocation of the event.

This sudden appearance of pictorial scenes in bronze decoration might have been indirectly inspired by contacts with the Animal Style art of the steppes. Dating from the same period as the *hu* no. 91 is a group of vessels whose Animal Style decoration is clearly linked with that of the steppes (see chap. 7: Liyu). The lid and the bottom register of no. 91 carry animal designs identical to those found on copper-inlaid bronzes from Liyu (cf. no. 70) and other regions close to the Great Wall. Perhaps uncomfortable with the strange vocabulary of animal forms, the Chinese soon found a more interesting substitute in these scenes of rituals, festivities, and battles, which were closer to their own everyday experiences.

Steppe Animal Style art had an even more immediate impact on the development of sculpture in China. While nos. 70 and 91 remain as scattered hints of steppe infiltrations, extensive concrete evidence came only recently with excavations at Pingshan Xian in Hebei Province. The excavations, begun in 1974 and completed in June 1978, uncovered numerous burials, the two largest of which belonged to the rulers of the small state of Zhongshan. Two of the most outstanding objects from these royal tombs are the gold- and silver-inlaid tiger stand (Fig. 101) from the tomb of a Zhongshan king who was buried around 310 B.C., and the three-pronged standard (no. 92) from the tomb of a king who lived a generation or so earlier.

During the Warring States period, the state of Zhongshan was ruled by the Di tribe, nomads who were originally located on the western borders of Shaanxi and who had been harassing China's northern and western borders since the seventh century. In the sixth century B.C., other tribes, descending from farther west, drove the Di eastward to Hebei, where they were constantly pressured by northern Chinese states seeking to expel

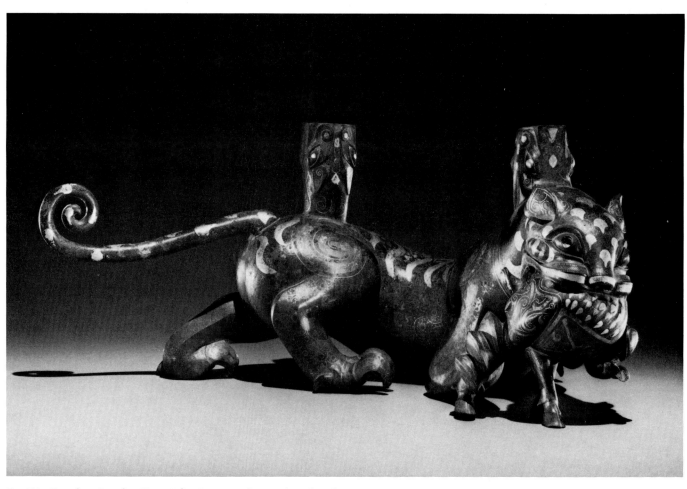

Fig. 101   Tiger from Pingshan Xian, Hebei Province. Photograph: Seth Joel

them from Chinese territory. Finally, by the early fourth century, the Di rulers managed to settle in the region around Pingshan Xian, site of their last capital, by enlisting the support of the state of Wei (even becoming its vassal for a time). The Di suffered a last defeat in 296 B.C. at the hands of the Yan state, which overran their territory and expelled their leaders. Although the Di were not true mounted nomads of the Central Asian steppes, they nevertheless shared cultural traits with nomadic groups to their north and west with whom they must have been in constant contact. Thus, for a period of almost three hundred years, from the sixth to early third centuries B.C., a seminomadic tribe with a steppe cultural background lived in the midst of Chinese territory. The Di must have been heavily Sinicized by interactions with their more sophisticated Chinese neighbors, but no doubt they contributed something in return. The contents of the Zhongshan kings' burials document both their steppe origins and their adopted culture.

The brutally simple form of the large standard top (no. 92), one of a set of six, is hitherto unknown in China. Its origin was probably nomadic, where similarly crudely fashioned standard tops must have formed part of the chieftain's regalia—silent but persuasive emblems of his overpowering authority. The Di tribe's link with the steppe cultures is expressed further in animal sculpture, especially by the forceful image of a tiger caught in the act

of crushing a deer, which is contorted in pain in the tiger's jaws and front paw (Fig. 101). Encounters between predator and victim were a favorite Animal Style motif. A superb example is a gold plaque from the collection of Peter the Great, now at the State Hermitage Museum, Leningrad, which depicts a lion-griffin attacking a horse, whose hindquarters are shown twisted in typical steppe manner (Fig. 102).

Remarkable works of Warring States sculpture, such as the rhinoceros (no. 93), must have been inspired by outstanding objects like the tiger. But, compared with the tiger, the rhinoceros appears unusually tame and unmistakably Chinese. While this can partly be accounted for by the rhinoceros's stiff pose (the mere hint of movement in its slightly turned head is insignificant beside the dramatic swing of the tiger's body), it is, in fact, no less realistically modeled than the tiger. The heavy folds of the skin at its neck, the lumbering weight of its body, and the bony structure of its head and legs are all convincingly rendered with great plastic substance. What distinguishes the rhinoceros from the tiger is rather the distinctly Chinese attention to a richly ornamented surface. The entire body of the rhinoceros is draped with a dense pattern of cloud scrolls once inlaid with gold. Unlike the inlaid gold stripes on the tiger's body, which perform a descriptive as well as a decorative function, these cloud scrolls are exclusively ornamental, flowing with utter disregard for organic structure over the folds of the neck and head, body, and legs. The rhinoceros becomes an apt illustration of a unique characteristic of the early development of sculpture in China—the paradox created by the new desire for realistic depiction and the entrenched habit of ornamentation.

The tension between these two contradictory forces reached a masterful resolution in the incense burner of the second century B.C. from Liu Sheng's tomb at Mancheng, Hebei Province (no. 95). The censer represents the Isle of the Immortals of Taoist myth: the island is the conical top, depicted with numerous fingerlike peaks; the bowl is the Eastern Sea, its swirling currents expressed by the sweeping scroll pattern inlaid with gold. Although these cloud scrolls belong to the same category of abstract ornamental forms as those on the rhinoceros's body, they are here more than mere surface decoration. By virtue of context and layout, the cloud scrolls—mere ornaments on the body of the rhinoceros—acquire a representational meaning on the censer. Without losing their beauty as ornaments, the gold-inlaid motifs have become the essential elements of an evocative realistic image. This elegant blending of form, meaning, and decoration in the Mancheng censer is a grand invention that belongs at once to the era of ornament, now drawing to a close, and to the emerging age of representational art in China.

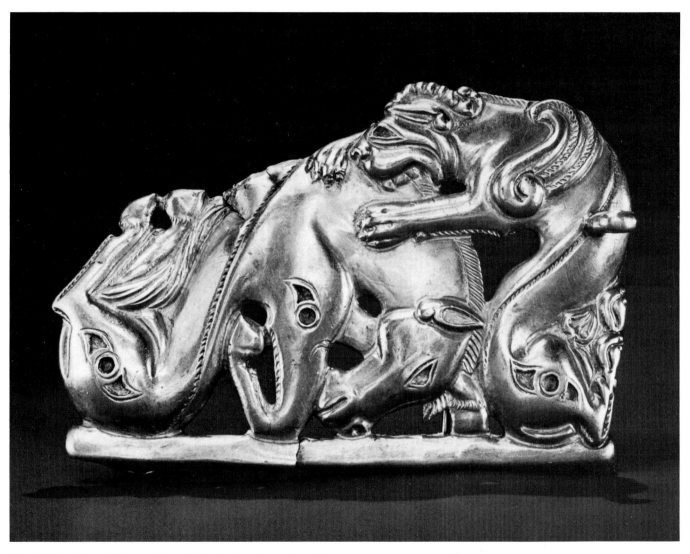

Fig. 102   Scythian gold plaque of lion-griffin attacking a horse. Animal
Style, 5th–4th century B.C. Siberian Collection of Peter I.
State Hermitage Museum, Leningrad. Photograph: Lee Boltin

311

CHAPTER 8: CATALOGUE ENTRIES

73 *Fang hu*

Late Eastern Zhou (4th century B.C.)
Excavated 1957, Shan Xian, Henan Province
Height 53 cm. (20⅞ in.); dimensions at mouth 12.7 x 12.7 cm.
   (4 x 4 in.); weight 10.4 kg. (22 lb. 14 oz.)
Historical Museum, Beijing

Each face of this square wine vessel is decorated by an identical design of geometric elements arranged symmetrically down a central axis. The neck and body designs are clearly distinguished from each other, the former dominated by horizontals and verticals, the latter by a system of crossed diagonals with occasional outcroppings. The angular framework on the neck and the diagonal grid on the body are emphasized by the dark green of inlaid malachite chips. The large intervening spaces are broken by a myriad of hooked motifs in bronze set against a background inlaid with tightly coiled copper strips (see colorplate, detail, no. 73). The copper, originally reddish brown, has corroded green. The vessel is well preserved; its patina ranges from light to bright green with large patches of azurite.

The technique used to apply the copper inlay to this vessel is typical for bronzes from the first and second stages of inlaid decorations (see chap. 7). Narrow ribbons of copper were packed tightly against each other, wedged into the cast depressions of the vessel surface, and then hammered and burnished to give the effect of a smooth sheet. This laborious process was superseded in the next stage, when the more usual method was to cut sheets of metal to fit the shape of the area to be inlaid (no. 95). But the older technique was not abandoned altogether; the gold ground of the *fang jian* no. 75, from about 300 B.C., was applied in tightly coiled gold strips.

The mate of this magnificent vessel forms part of the Meyer Bequest in the Freer Gallery of Art, Washington, D.C. (Pope, 1967, pl. 94). The vessels differ only in the allocation of the inlays; on the Meyer *fang hu*, copper coils are inlaid into the diagonal and rectangular grids, and malachite chips fill the grounds of the interstices. Cleaning has made the original color contrast between the reddish copper and the green malachite on the Meyer vessel more apparent.

Complete archaeological data related to the Shan Xian *fang hu* has yet to be published, but a likely date can be proposed by comparison with a group of similar vessels, listed here in a modified version of Loehr's sequence (1968, p. 154):

1. Pair of *fang hu*, one in the Albright-Knox Art Gallery, Buffalo (Loehr, 1968, no. 69), the other in the Lidow collection, Los Angeles (Kuwayama, 1976, no. 45).
2. Pair of *fang hu*, no. 73 and its mate in the Meyer Bequest, Freer Gallery of Art.
3. Pair of *fang hu*. One is in the University Museum, University of Pennsylvania, Philadelphia (Umehara, 1936, pl. 95:1). An engraved inscription above the foot ring alludes to an event occurring in either 314 B.C. (Chen, 1977, pp. 138–39) or 279 B.C. (Guo [M.], 1958, p. 220b). The mate, reportedly from Jincun, Luoyang, was collected by Bishop White (White, 1934, pl. 109, no. 248; Umehara, 1936, pl. 95:2); fragments of this vessel are now in the study collection of the Royal Ontario Museum, Toronto.
4. Pair of *fang hu* from Tomb 1 at Pingshan, Hebei Province (*China Pictorial* 1979/5, p. 40). The workshop inscription around the foot is dated to the fourteenth year of the Zhongshan king Cuo, about 309–308 B.C. (*Kaogu Xuebao* 1979/2, pp. 167–68).

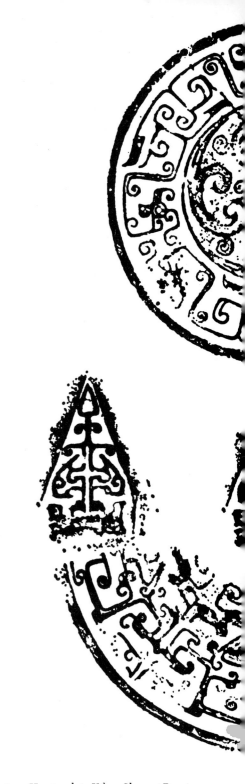

5. *Fang hu* from a Western Han tomb in Xi'an, Shaanxi Province (Fig. 99).
6. Round *hu* from a tomb in Fuling Xian, Sichuan Province, mid- to late third century B.C. (*Wenwu* 1974/5, pl. 2:3, p. 67, fig. 6). The excavation of this vessel lends strong support to the authenticity of the design on a large gold- and silver-inlaid *fang hu* in the Victoria and Albert Museum, London, a suggestion first put forward by Loehr (1968, no. 71), but doubted by Watson (1973, p. 10).

The Xi'an and Fuling Xian designs are clearly third-century examples of the style, illustrating the diverging trends of the time (see pp. 306–8). The pair from Pingshan is securely datable to the last decade of the fourth century B.C. This places the remaining three sets in the fourth century and suggests that Chen's 314 B.C. date for the inscription added to the Pennsylvania *fang hu* is more likely; hence, the vessel itself should date still earlier. The dates for the

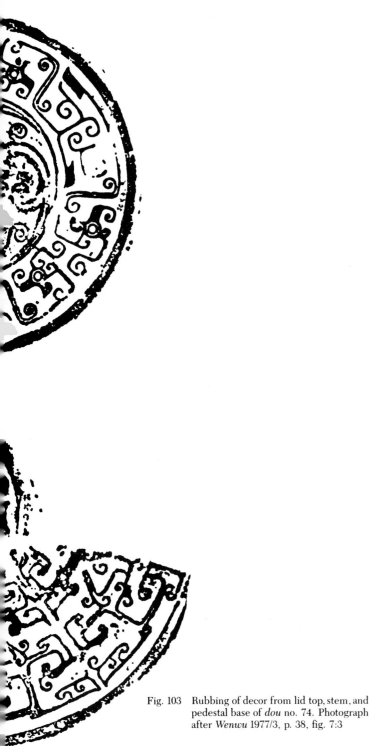

Fig. 103 Rubbing of decor from lid top, stem, and pedestal base of *dou* no. 74. Photograph after *Wenwu* 1977/3, p. 38, fig. 7:3

empty ground which was once filled with inlays of malachite and coiled metal strips, probably copper. The metal inlay is preserved only in isolated places and has corroded to a light green, and malachite chips have fallen off everywhere except in the inside rim of the bowl, where they have been protected by the lid. The central medallion on the flat top of the lid's stem is filled with a blue substance that resembles glass paste. Major repairs have been made on the bowl. The entire surface is covered with a light yellowish green and brown patina.

The decoration on this vessel is an interesting combination of the first and second stages of Inlay Style (see pp. 305–7). The motifs on the stems and bases, as well as on the flat undersides of the bowl and lid, are advanced first-stage designs, simple versions of which are found among the Houma mold fragments (Fig. 92; *Wenwu* 1960/8–9, p. 9, fig. 11 left). The flat top of the lid's stem carries a zoomorphic design of alternately inverted S-shaped dragons that may be recognized by a concentric circular eye, a muzzle in an upswept spiral, and a corresponding backward sweeping spiral for an ear (see Fig. 103). The wide horizontal registers on both bowl and lid bear a second-stage design, also abstract and conceived in confronting units repeated around the vessel, but in a more dynamic arrangement of obliquely crossing and overlapping elements.

Again, the supporting archaeological data published can supply little more than a general Warring States date for this *dou*. But the similarities of its second-stage design with that of the *fang hu* no. 73 suggest a comparable date. The unusual combination of a dynamic, tilted, geometric design with a zoomorphic one occurs on another vessel also regarded as closely contemporary with no. 73, a *dui* inlaid with copper and malachite in the Fogg Art Museum, Cambridge, Massachusetts (Umehara, 1936, pl. 46:1). The central medallions at the top and bottom of the Fogg vessels are decorated with three C-shaped birds, also with concentric circular eyes. A third, less well known example is a *hu* in the Museum of Fine Arts, Boston, with a tilted design similar to that on the present *dou* but arranged in six horizontal registers and inlaid alternately with copper and malachite (Tch'ou, 1924, pls. 33, 34). The second-stage design on the present *dou*, with its constantly overlapping elements, is more complex than any of these examples cited. The glass-paste inlay on the *dou* is another new departure, and reflects an expanded repertoire of inlay materials that were to include crystal, jade, and glass in the third and second centuries B.C.

PUBLISHED: *Wenwu* 1977/2, pl. 1:2, 1:4, p. 4, fig. 11:2; *Wenwu* 1977/3, p. 38, fig. 7:3, p. 49, fig. 52 (report, pp. 41–53); Beijing, 1972a, no. 74; Tokyo, 1976, no. 70; Beijing, 1976a, no. 65.

Meyer and Shan Xian *fang hu* should therefore fall about 350 B.C. or before, while the Buffalo and Lidow pair might date as early as the beginning of the fourth century B.C.

PUBLISHED: *Wenwu Cankao Ziliao* 1958/11, inside cover, bottom right (report, p. 78); Beijing, 1976b, no. 43; Tokyo, 1978a, no. 42.

74 *Dou*

Late Eastern Zhou (4th century B.C.)
Excavated 1965, Xiangxiang, Hunan Province
Height 24 cm. (9½ in.); diameter 16.2 cm. (6⅜ in.); weight 2.3 kg. (5 lb. 1 oz.)
Hunan Provincial Museum

The *dou* is a grain or food container whose cover often serves as a second container when inverted. The cast design is set against an

75 *Fang jian*

Late Eastern Zhou (3rd century B.C.)
Excavated 1975, Sanmenxia, Shan Xian, Henan Province
Height 21.6 cm. (8½ in.); dimensions at mouth 30.8 x 30.8 cm. (12⅛ x 12⅛ in.); weight 11.9 kg. (26 lb. 3 oz.)
Henan Provincial Museum

Unlike the inlays of nos. 73 and 74, the gold and turquoise on this exquisite vessel serve both to highlight a pattern cast in the bronze —a rectangular grid—and provide the pattern themselves in the inlaid panels defined by the grid. This distinction between ground and pattern, inlay and bronze, becomes less obvious in the decorated registers at the top of the vessel, where both the inlaid areas and the cast forms in bronze assume equal weight as patterns. The inlays also form the pattern on the bodies of the four long-necked felines that climb up the sides to peer over the edge. The bronze surface is covered with patchy green patina. Most of the fine gold

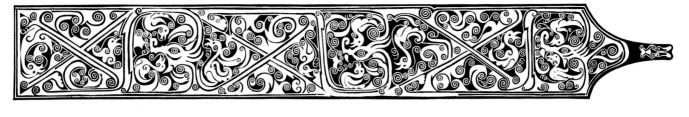

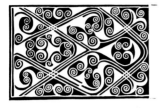

Fig. 104 Drawing of inlaid design on both sides of iron belt hook no. 76. Courtesy of Cultural Relics Bureau, Beijing

inlay has been preserved, but much of the turquoise has fallen from its place.

The similarities between this *fang jian* and the Xi'an *fang hu* (see p. 307) extend even to such details of motif as the series of petal shapes that hang at the bottom of the design. The same motifs appear on the *hu* from Fuling Xian, Sichuan Province, and the *fang hu* in the Victoria and Albert Museum, London (see entry no. 73). A date in the third century should therefore also apply to this vessel.

The *fang jian* is a rare type among Eastern Zhou bronzes. The few known examples include:

1. *Fang jian* from the tomb of the marquis of Cai at Shou Xian (Beijing, 1956a, pl. 14:3) that has two movable ring handles and copper-inlaid animal decorations.
2. Pair of *fang jian* from the tomb of the marquis of Zeng at Sui Xian, Hubei Province (*Wenwu* 1979/7, pl. 7:2, p. 24, fig. 36), both with twelve feline handles, three on each side, and a comma pattern in high relief arranged in panels, and both containing a square wine vessel that emerges from a fitted opening in the middle of the flat cover.
3. *Fang jian* reportedly from Jincun, Henan Province, now in the Royal Ontario Museum, Toronto (Toronto, 1972, no. 60). Each side of the Toronto *fang jian* carries a paneled comma pattern in low relief and simple zigzag designs inlaid with turquoise, copper, and gold in the top two horizontal registers. The stumps projecting from the center of each side mark the position of handles, presumably like those on the Sanmenxia vessel. It also has an openwork flat cover with a square opening in the middle.

The Sanmenxia *fang jian* is the latest in this series.

The Sui Xian examples indicate the function of this rare type. They clearly served as wine warmers or coolers, and form a set with square vessels (*fang lei* or *fang hu*) that are the wine containers. This explains the flat cover on the Toronto *fang jian*, and in addition suggests that the Sanmenxia *fang jian* and the *fang lei* found with it might be a set (*Wenwu* 1976/3, pl. 3:2). The Sanmenxia set, however, is considerably smaller than the others.

PUBLISHED: *Wenwu* 1976/3, pl. 3:4, p. 52, fig. 1 (report, pp. 52–54); Tokyo, 1976, no. 73; Beijing, 1976a, no. 73.

76 Iron belt hook

Late Eastern Zhou (4th century B.C.)
Excavated 1965 from Tomb 1, Wangshan, Jiangling, Hubei
Province

Length 48 cm. (18⅞ in.); width 6.5 cm. (2½ in.); weight 0.7 kg. (1 lb. 9 oz.)
Hubei Provincial Museum

The only cast-iron object in the exhibition, this strongly arched rectangular belt hook is lavishly inlaid with gold and silver in a design composed of three dragons and eleven birds in a sea of curvilinear and spiraling configurations. The inlay covers even the end sections of the underside, as well as the tops of the two buttons, with abstract geometric patterns (see Fig. 104). The interplay between the inlaid motifs and the cast-metal ground is so complex that it is virtually impossible to distinguish pattern from background. The gold and silver strips are set into precast depressions, the widest areas filled with three or more parallel strips, each approximately 2 millimeters wide. The iron is heavily corroded and the silver tarnished, but the gold has remained brilliant. A large section near the middle has been repaired.

The belt hook as an ornament on a fabric or leather belt was introduced into China by the steppe nomads toward the end of the Spring and Autumn period. The earliest belt hooks are modest in size, and appear to have been produced in quantity by the foundry at Houma (*Kaogu* 1959/5, pl. 4). The present belt hook is the largest known example of its kind, and both its size and weight suggest that it could not have been an ordinary garment accessory, if it was worn at all. Its immense size probably accounts for the two buttons on the underside—a small one near the hook and a larger one toward the opposite end—for most belt hooks have only one button to fasten them to the belt. Iron belt hooks are much rarer than bronze ones, but the fact that they were made at all indicates fascination with the new metal and readiness to explore its potentials, although its limitations were soon realized.

This magnificent belt hook came from a rich Chu tomb discovered near the ancient Chu capital of the seventh to early third centuries B.C. The tomb was originally dated to the fifth century, since it contained an inscribed sword belonging to a king of Yue who reigned from 496 to 465 B.C. (Beijing, 1972a, no. 69; Juliano, 1972, pp. 10–17; Tokyo, 1973, sec. 2). But, stylistically, the bronzes and painted lacquers from the tomb fit better in a fourth-century context. The later date is confirmed by inscribed bamboo slips from the tomb that mention the names of three Chu kings who ruled from 431 to 380 B.C. Furthermore, it has been suggested that the Yue sword may have fallen into Chu hands after the destruction of the Yue state in 334 B.C., so the burial may not have taken place before that date (*Wenwu* 1976/8, p. 67).

PUBLISHED: *Wenwu* 1966/5, p. 48, fig. 20, top; Xi'an, 1973, no. 62; Kansas City, 1975, no. 129.

77–90   Fourteen bells

Late Eastern Zhou (3rd century B.C.)
Excavated 1972, Fuling Xian, Sichuan Province
Height of largest bell 27.5 cm. (10⅞ in.); weight 3.05 kg.
  (6 lb. 11 oz.)
Height of smallest bell 14.6 cm. (5⅝ in.); weight .475 kg. (1 lb. 1 oz.)
Sichuan Provincial Museum

The fourteen bells in this set are identical in shape, with elliptical cross sections and curved openings at the bottom. Each is suspended by a U-shaped loop at the top. The first and largest bell, much repaired, is heavily corroded and not inlaid. The second, third, fourth, fifth, seventh, eighth, tenth, and thirteenth bells carry similar but not identical patterns of fine lines inlaid with gold that run down the smooth bronze surfaces of the middle trapezoidal section and along the narrow edges on each side, and flank the cast design at the bottom. On the second bell, the running spiral pattern of the suspension loop is also inlaid. The five remaining bells carry only cast decorations. The patination ranges from crusty light green to blue green. These clapperless bells were meant to be struck on the outside with wooden hammers.

Pictorial scenes on contemporary or earlier bronze vessels, and the magnificent set of sixty-five bells preserved at Sui Xian, Hubei Province, show that such bells were hung in graduated order from a wooden frame, usually ornamented. In bronze representations, the largest bell always appears at the left of the frame (see colorplate, detail, no. 91); but, with the exception of three bells, the set from Sui Xian is hung with the largest bells at the right of the frame, an arrangement based on their discovery *in situ*. The Sui Xian arrangement is probably more reliable.

Of the wooden frame in the present set, only the two pairs of silver-inlaid tiger-head finials are preserved (Fig. 105). The tigers of the first pair, on the vertical supports of the frame, receive in their gaping mouths the transverse beam, whose ends are capped by the second pair, each with a pearl in bronze between its teeth. The tigers' eyes are inlaid with black glass. The silver-inlaid designs on these finials are more flowing and graceful than those on the bells, although all the designs are characterized by numerous tendrillike terminations. The undersides of the second pair of tiger finials carry crudely engraved, enigmatic signs; the largest signs resemble a bovine mask (see Fig. 106). The same mask occurs inlaid with silver on the underside of one of the finials from the first pair, where it is more carefully arranged with three other emblems familiar from swords and weapons belonging to the Ba tribe, who inhabited the Sichuan region during the Warring States period (*Wenwu* 1974/5, p. 77, fig. 40, bottom). These undeciphered inscriptions are believed to be clan signs, or in some cases a highly eccentric local script.

PUBLISHED: *Wenwu* 1973/1, p. 59, figs. 1, 2; *Wenwu* 1974/5, pls. 1, 2:4, p. 72, fig. 16, p. 77, figs. 39–41, p. 78, fig. 49 (report, pp. 61–80); Tokyo, 1976, nos. 76–89; Beijing, 1976a, no. 78.

Fig. 105   Detail of bronze fitting and finial on bell stand of the set
of fourteen bells, nos. 77–90. The wood is a modern
replacement. Photograph: Maxwell K. Hearn

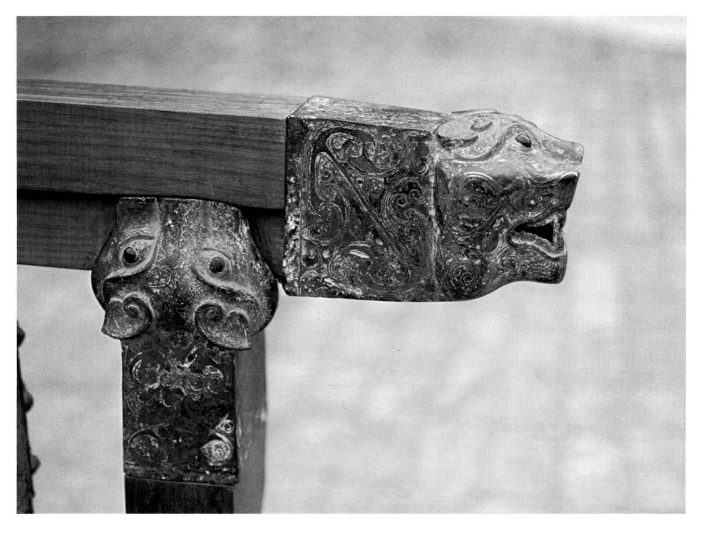

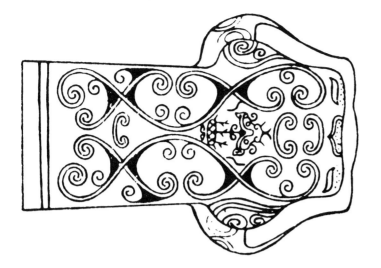

Fig. 106 Drawing of bronze finial on bell stand
showing inlaid decor and inscription.
After *Wenwu* 1974/5, p. 77, fig. 40

91 *Hu*

Eastern Zhou (late 6th–5th century B.C.)
Excavated 1965, Chengdu, Sichuan Province
Height 39.9 cm. (15¾ in.); diameter at mouth 13.4 cm. (5¼ in.);
  diameter at base 14.2 cm. (5⅝ in.); weight 4.5 kg. (9 lb. 14 oz.)
Sichuan Provincial Museum

The heavily encrusted and pitted surface of this wine vessel has a
light gray green patina with patches of blue azurite. The vessel was
cast in a mold of two sections; the seams that run down each side are
partly covered by masked ring holders apparently set over openings left in the vessel. The slightly domed lid is topped by three
squatting ducks familiar from other Liyu style bronzes (Umehara,
1936, pl. 7).

The pictorial scenes that decorate this vessel in four horizontal
registers are inlaid with a substance predominately brownish in
color, but in some places light creamy white. This substance has
been described as "leadlike" (*Wenwu* 1976/3, p. 43). An identical
hu formerly in the Jannings collection, now in the Palace Museum,
Beijing, is thought to have been inlaid with silver, although nearly
all of its inlay is missing (von Erdberg, 1952, p. 18). The bottom half
of a similar *hu* in the Palace Museum, reported to be from the
Chengdu area, is also said to be inlaid with silver (*Wenwu* 1976/3,
p. 47). The common use of copper on such vessels as the *dou* no. 70
would indicate that copper was the most likely inlay. Laboratory
tests on the inlay material in this *hu* should provide a more definite
answer. Whatever the substance, the inlay, corroded and pitted
like the rest of the bronze surface, is so well bonded to the sunken
areas of bronze that it may represent the unusual inlay technique
described in entry no. 70.

The decoration on this *hu* encompasses a wide range of subjects. Each register is set off from the next by a narrow band with a
diagonal and volute pattern that is also inlaid. The scenes on each
register are arranged over half of the vessel surface, corresponding
to one mold section, and repeated on the other half. The top
register shows figures among trees and an archery contest. The
second register includes scenes of a ritual dance with long spears,
musicians playing instruments—bells and chimes suspended from
a frame (see colorplate, detail, no. 91), wind instruments, and a
drum—and a banquet held inside a building while food is cooked

outside. Next to these is another archery contest, followed by
figures hunting wild birds with bows and arrows. The third register
depicts battles on land, with figures scaling a walled fortification,
and on sea, fought from boats with oarsmen and with long banners
trailing in the wind. The lowest register and the lid are both
decorated with freely disposed animals, as on the *dou* no. 70 (see
Fig. 97).

A thorough discussion of each of these scenes appears in the
monograph on pictorial bronzes by Charles D. Weber (1968,
pp. 183–206). However, a new meaning for the scene with figures
among trees in the first register has since been suggested. Instead
of the widely accepted interpretation that the scene represents the
picking of mulberry leaves, an activity related to sericulture, it is
now thought that the scene depicts a ritual selection of mulberry
branches for making bows (*Wenwu* 1976/3, p. 49). This agrees well
with the accompanying archery scenes, and, in a more general
sense, with all the activities in the first two registers—rituals and
festivities related to the peacetime display of martial skills—in
contrast with the actual confrontations in battle depicted in the
third register (*Wenwu* 1976/3, p. 50). The new reading of the decor
scheme gives these pictorial designs an iconographic coherence
and purpose never before acknowledged.

On the second register, next to the scene of bird hunting and
below the archery contest, six figures with birds lined in front of
them are grouped under an arched canopy supported in the middle
by a vertical post, probably a tent in which the bird hunters rest
(see Fig. 107). This unprecedented addition to the standard repertoire of pictorial motifs (not mentioned in the 1968 catalogue by
C. D. Weber) is a graphic illustration of the outdoor life that
accompanied such expeditions, and may reflect a practice learned
from more experienced tent dwellers, the steppe nomads.

The scenes represented on the *hu* are unusually lively by
comparison with similar examples. There is little doubt that the
vessel dates from the early Warring States period, but its place of
manufacture is less certain. It might be a metropolitan product,
since a scene of figures among trees appears on a mold fragment
from the Houma foundry (Fig. 93).

PUBLISHED: *Wenwu* 1976/3, pl. 2 (report, pp. 40–46); *China Pictorial* 1977/6, p. 25; Tokyo, 1976, no. 65; Beijing, 1976a, no. 67.

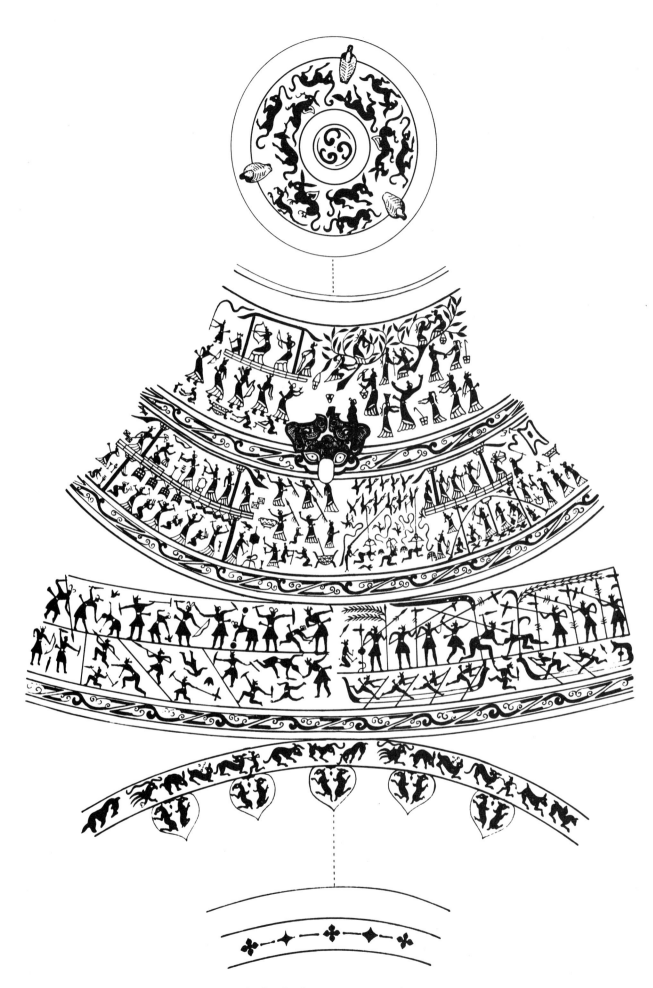

Fig. 107 Drawing of decor, *hu* no. 91. Courtesy of Cultural Relics
Bureau, Beijing

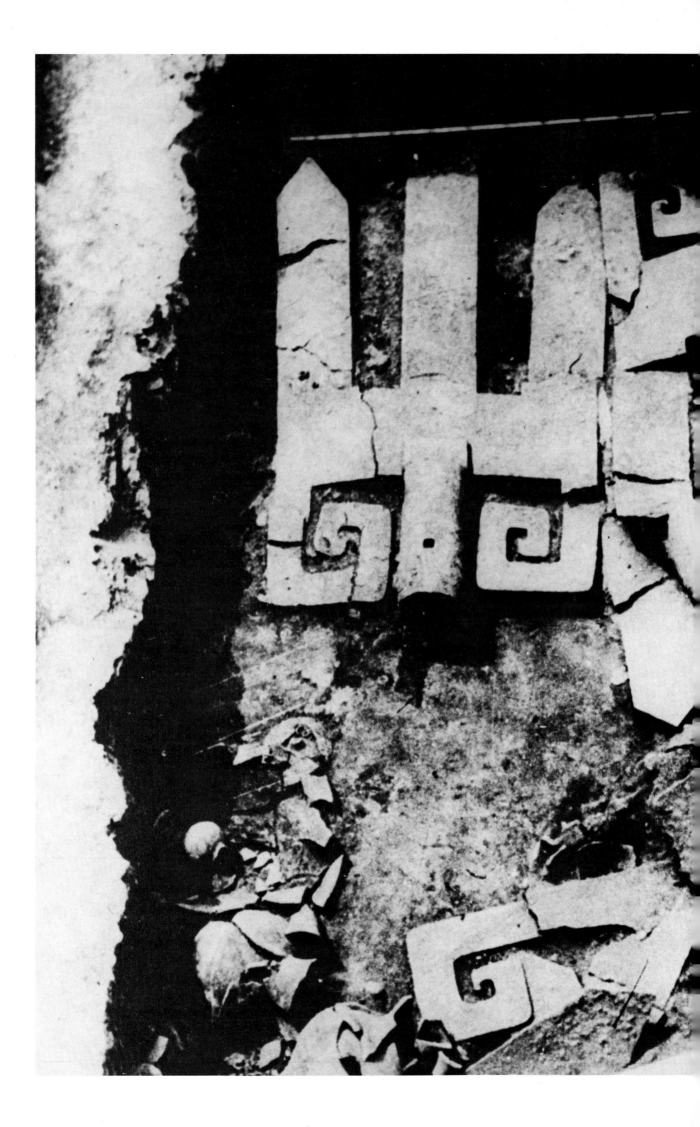

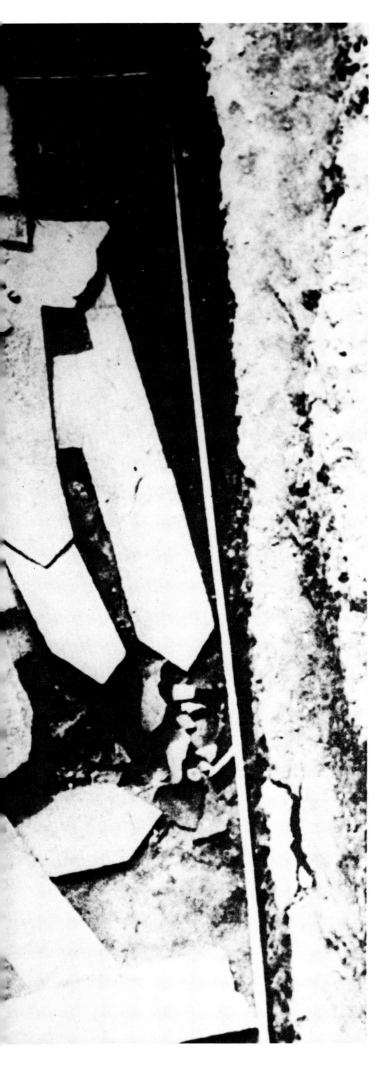

92 Standard top

Late Eastern Zhou (4th century B.C.)
Excavated 1978 from Tomb 6, Pingshan Xian, Hebei Province
Height 144.2 cm. (56¾ in.); maximum width 80.3 cm. (31⅝ in.);
    weight 50.03 kg. (110 lb. 1 oz.)
Hebei Provincial Museum

The set of six large trident-shaped bronzes to which this standard top belongs was found in two burial pits that flank the central chamber of Tomb 6 at Pingshan, Hebei Province. Four whole standards and half of another came from the pit on the eastern side (Fig. 108); another standard and the remaining half came from the western pit. They were buried with remains of a leather tent, bronze tent structures, and many vessels of pottery, bronze, and lacquer. A small portable brazier from the tomb is inscribed with "twenty-seventh year," but the name of the king is not mentioned. Based on this inscription and the similarities between the bronzes from this tomb and those from the tomb of the Zhongshan king Cuo, dating soon after 309 or 308 B.C. (*Kaogu Xuebao* 1979/2, p. 167), Tomb 6 is believed to be the tomb of a Zhongshan king who lived a generation or so earlier (*Gugung Bowuyuan Yuankan* 1979/1, p. 50).

Each trident shape is constructed in two parts: a single sheet of bronze with three projections and involuted angular meanders below is secured into place by two rivets at the head of a hollow pole shaft. The plain bronze surface has corroded to a patchy gray green and blue green. Another group of five trident-shaped bronzes, slightly shorter, heavier set, broader in proportions, and varying in minor details of construction, was found with similar tent remains and weapons in the burial pit of Tomb 1 (*Wenwu* 1979/1, p. 31, fig. 46). Bits of wood still adhere to the insides of their shafts. The immense size, bold forms, and burial context of these sets from Tombs 1 and 6 suggest that they were standard tops, set high on wooden posts outside the chieftain's tent. Visible from long distances and awesome at close range, they are effective emblems of power and reflect dramatically the nomadic, tent-dwelling origins of the Di barbarians, who became rulers of Zhongshan in the Warring States period.

Although there is no adequate Chinese parallel for these magnificent objects, they are intriguingly reminiscent of bronze coffin ornaments unearthed from the late Western Zhou to early Eastern Zhou burials of Guo state princes at Shangcunling (see chap. 7). These ornaments occur in sets of four, are much smaller than those from Pingshan (about one-third their size), but are also characterized by a three-pronged shape (Beijing, 1959b, pl. 50:1). The middle projection is plain and pointed, and those at the sides are conceived as crude bird silhouettes. This section is secured with rivets to a decorated trapezoidal sheet. A similar example appears on the cover of a recent catalogue of bronzes in the Idemitsu Art Gallery, Tokyo (Tokyo, 1978b). A crescent-shaped chariot finial from a Scythian kurgan in the Alexandropol region also has three prongs, surmounted by birds holding bells in their beaks (New York, 1975, no. 90). Both the Shangcunling and Scythian examples are considerably smaller, performed obviously different functions, and cannot rival the Zhongshan standards in power and monumentality. They may, however, share a common origin somewhere in the vast Central Asian steppes.

PUBLISHED: *Wenwu* 1979/1, p. 31, fig. 47 (report on Tomb 6, pp. 10–13; report on excavation, discussions of inscriptions and history, pp. 1–52); *China Pictorial* 1979/3, p. 26, bottom left.

Fig. 108 Bronze trident standard tops *in situ*, Pingshan Xian, Hebei
    Province (cf. no. 92). Photograph courtesy of Cultural Relics
    Bureau, Beijing

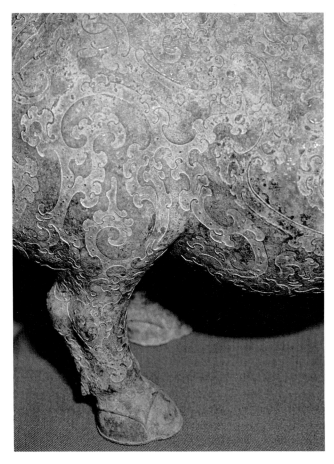

Fig. 109   Detail, rhinoceros *zun* no. 93.
Photograph: Jenny F. So

93   Rhinoceros *zun*

Late Eastern Zhou–Western Han (late 3rd century B.C.)
Found 1963, Xingping Xian, Shaanxi Province
Height 34.1 cm. (13⅜ in.); length 58.1 cm. (22⅞ in.); weight
    13.3 kg. (29 lb. 4 oz.)
Historical Museum, Beijing

This rhinoceros was discovered accidentally by a local farmer plowing his fields at Doumacun in Xingping Xian. It was found inside a large pottery urn packed with soil and buried only one meter deep. Its hollow body contained various bronze objects, including a belt hook and miscellaneous bronze tools, fittings, and weights. There was no sign of a tomb at the site. It appears that the urn held valuables temporarily buried for safety, but never recovered by their owner.

Like the Shang elephant no. 24, this object must have served as a container for wine or other liquids. A narrow tubular spout issues from one side of the rhinoceros's mouth, while the hinged lid on its back allows access to the interior of the vessel. These purely functional features are grafted onto an otherwise realistically modeled sculpture of the animal.

This *zun* and the famous late Shang rhinoceros *zun* in the Asian Art Museum, San Francisco (Lefebvre d'Argencé, 1977, pl. 13), form a delightful contrast. It seems as if the childlike charm and innocence of the earlier rhinoceros have matured over the millennium into the sophisticated self-confidence of the later animal. Both are, however, competent and realistic sculptures. The body of the Shang rhinoceros is plain and undecorated. The Shaanxi rhinoceros, far more sophisticated in modeling, is draped with a dense intaglio pattern of scalloped cloud scrolls (see Fig. 109); these were applied to both lacquers (Loehr, 1967–68, p. 13, fig. 9, 10) and embroidered silks (Beijing, 1973, pl. 126) of the late third to second centuries B.C. On this rhinoceros, however, these abstract ornamental patterns swing around the bronze surface with such energy and vigor that they suggest, in a strange way, the rugged liveliness of the animal, while being beautifully decorative at the same time.

These cloud scrolls were once inlaid, presumably with gold or silver which has not survived. The slightly raised areas between the cloud scrolls are inlaid with gold in short furlike strokes, some of which are still visible (see Fig. 109). The eyes of the animal are inlays of black glass. Only the lid, horns, and the rhinoceros's chest are left plain. The vessel is well preserved; only one ear is a modern repair. The surface is covered with a patina that ranges from light to dark green.

PUBLISHED: *Wenwu* 1965/7, pls. 1, 2, p. 14, fig. 3 (report, pp. 12–13); *China Pictorial* 1977/6, p. 24; Tokyo, 1976, no. 92; Beijing, 1976a, no. 79.

9

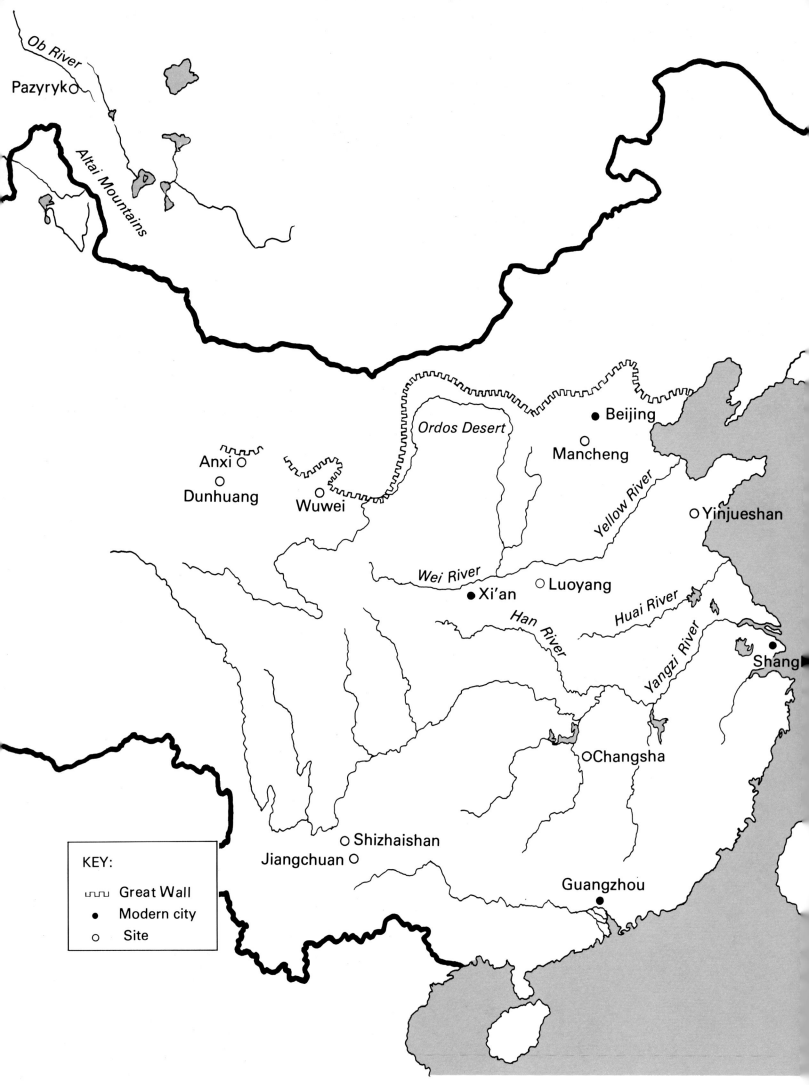

Ob River

Pazyryk

Altai Mountains

Great Wall

Ordos Desert

● Beijing

Anxi

○ Dunhuang

○ Wuwei

○ Mancheng

Yellow River

○ Yinjueshan

Wei River

● Xi'an

○ Luoyang

Han River

Huai River

Yangzi River

● Shang

○ Changsha

○ Shizhaishan

Jiangchuan ○

● Guangzhou

KEY:

ᴨᴨ Great Wall

● Modern city

○ Site

9

The Waning of the Bronze Age:
The Western Han Period (206 B.C.–A.D. 8)

Jenny F. So

The death of Qin Shihuangdi in 210 B.C. and the murder of the legitimate heir by his younger brother signaled the collapse of the Qin dynasty. Peasant uprisings erupted throughout the country, even while the dead emperor was entombed in his magnificent mausoleum (see chap. 10). In 207 B.C., the second Qin emperor was assassinated by his chief minister, who, in turn, was murdered by the new successor to the throne. In the following year, the rebel army, led by the peasant Liu Bang, entered the Qin capital of Xianyang. The third Qin ruler surrendered, and Liu Bang was proclaimed the new emperor of the Han dynasty. He established his capital at Chang'an (modern Xi'an), so founding one of the longest and most colorful dynasties in Chinese history. The Han dynasty continued for over 400 years, ending in 220 A.D. The first half of the period (206 B.C.–A.D. 8), when the capital was at Chang'an, is known historically as Western Han. After a brief interregnum, the Han dynasty reestablished itself at Luoyang in A.D. 25, and the subsequent period from A.D. 25 to 220 is known as Eastern Han.

In literature, the history of the Han dynasty is recorded in the *Shi Ji* compiled by the Han historian Sima Qian (available to Western scholars through the translation by Edouard Chavannes, *Les mémoires historiques de Sse-ma Ts'ien* [1895]). In archaeology, the period is documented by a wealth of material from innumerable sites scattered throughout the country, providing a virtually inexhaustible source for the study of Han history, society, and art. Among the many Han sites discovered in the past twenty years, three stand out in historical, cultural, and artistic importance. These are the tombs of the early second century B.C. at Mawangdui, Changsha, Hunan Province, excavated from 1971 to 1974 (not represented); the tombs dating from the late second century B.C. of the Han prince Liu Sheng and his consort Dou Wan at Mancheng, Hebei Province, excavated in 1968 (nos. 94–96); and the remains of a Dian cultural center at Shizhaishan, Yunnan Province, uncovered between 1956 and 1957 (represented by no. 97, which comes from a Dian site excavated in 1972 at Jiangquan, Yunnan Province, just 40 kilometers south of Shizhaishan). Together, these three excavations present a cross section of Western Han culture and art that ranges from metropolitan sophistication

Map of China showing major sites of the Western Han period, 206 B.C. to A.D. 8

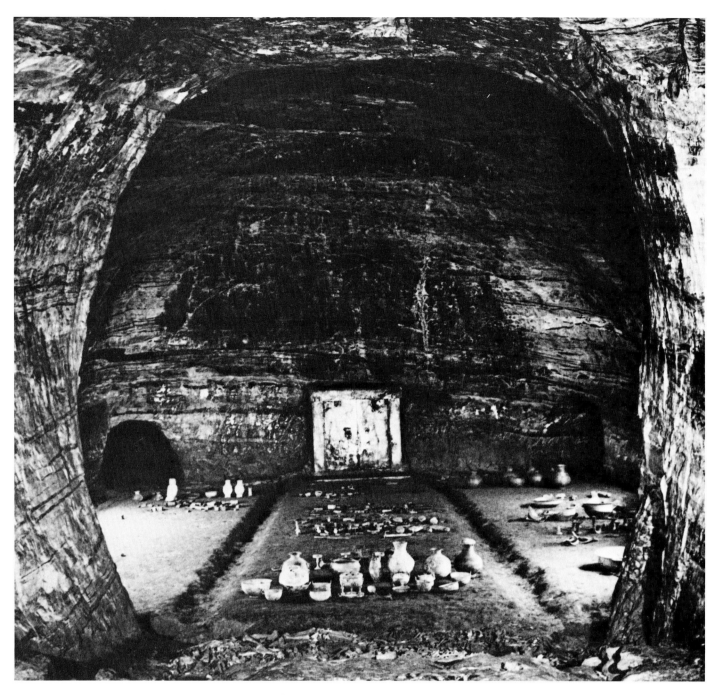

Fig. 110 Entrance to the tomb of Liu Sheng, Mancheng, Hebei
Province. Photograph after Beijing, 1972a, pl. 94

to the rough candor of local expressions.

The Mawangdui and Mancheng burials, though different in location and custom, nevertheless both magnificently demonstrate the prosperity and high artistic achievement reached during the Western Han period. The tombs at Mancheng are elaborately constructed (Figs. 110–112), each resembling an underground palace, with a stable for horses and chariots, a granary for wine and food storage, and a large central chamber for banquets and audiences leading to a private chamber where the prince or his consort was laid, encased in a jade burial suit and set inside a lacquered wooden coffin inlaid with jade. The jade suits alone exemplify the extravagant excesses in which only the ruling class of a prosperous empire could indulge. Prince Liu Sheng's suit was com-

posed of almost 2,500 pieces of jade sewn together with 1,100 grams of gold thread. Dou Wan's jade suit, exhibited in the 1974–75 archaeological exhibition from the People's Republic, consisted of 2,160 pieces of jade and 700 grams of gold thread. In addition, the two tombs yielded a total of almost 3,000 objects of bronze, iron, gold, silver, jade, pottery, lacquer, and silk. Liu Sheng was the stepbrother of Wu Di, one of the greatest Han emperors, whose fifty-four-year reign saw the territorial expansion of the empire, the opening of the Silk Route across Central Asia, and a period of peace and prosperity. The marquis of Dai, his consort, and his son, who were buried at Mawangdui, were only local lords unrelated to the royal clan, but their burial furniture was no less extravagant. The three tombs together yielded over

2,500 objects, most of them handsomely decorated lacquers and exquisitely embroidered silks and damasks, all preserved in nearly pristine condition.

Among the objects found in Dou Wan's tomb is a set of bronze drinking-game chips and inlaid bronze dice, clues to the nature of the frivolous pastimes of the ruling princes. The Mawangdui finds, on the other hand, reveal a more serious and laudable preoccupation of the Han social elite: the tomb of the marquis's son brought to light many texts written on silk, bamboo, or wooden slips. Not all texts are complete, of course, but they include such

classics as the *Yi Jing* (Book of Changes), *Laozi* (a Taoist text), the *Zhanguoce* (Discourses of the Warring States), as well as writings on medicine, an illustrated program of physical fitness exercises, constellation charts, and the earliest surviving maps of China. Another major discovery of a similar nature was made in 1972 at Yinjueshan, Linyi, Shandong Province, where Warring States classics on military strategy and other philosophical tracts were found with burials dating from the second half of the second century B.C. It seems that Qin Shihuangdi's drastic attempts at stifling classical learning by burning texts

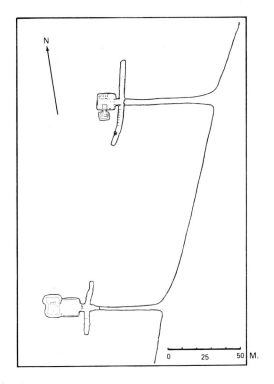

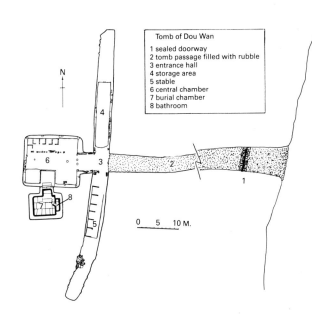

Tomb of Dou Wan

1 sealed doorway
2 tomb passage filled with rubble
3 entrance hall
4 storage area
5 stable
6 central chamber
7 burial chamber
8 bathroom

0 5 10 M.

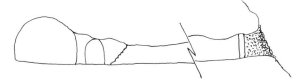

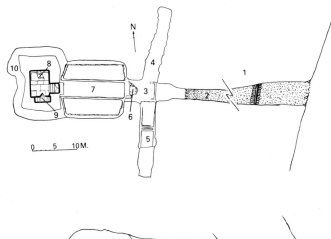

Tomb of Liu Sheng

1 sealed doorway
2 tomb passage filled with rubble
3 entrance hall
4 storage area
5 stable
6 well
7 central chamber
8 burial chamber
9 bathroom
10 encircling corridor

0 5 10 M.

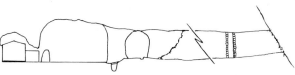

Fig. 111   Plans and elevations of the tombs of Dou Wan (above) and Liu Sheng (below). Drawing by Phyllis Ward after *Kaogu* 1972/1, p. 9, figs. 2, 3

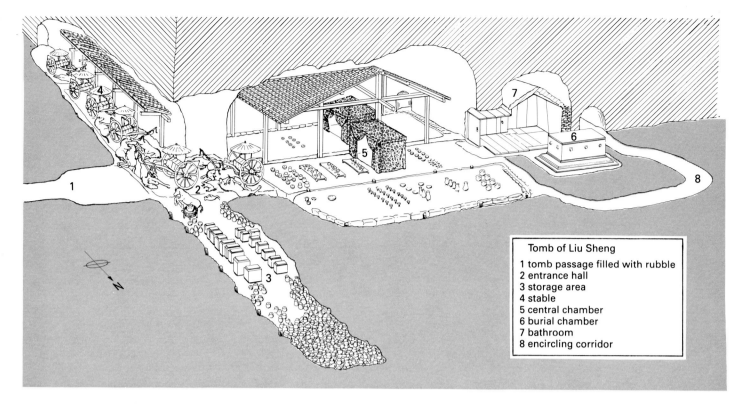

Fig. 112 Cutaway view showing a tentative reconstruction of Liu
Sheng's tomb at the time of burial. Drawing by Phyllis Ward
after Beijing, 1978b, p. 15, fig. 6

Tomb of Liu Sheng

1 tomb passage filled with rubble
2 entrance hall
3 storage area
4 stable
5 central chamber
6 burial chamber
7 bathroom
8 encircling corridor

and burying scholars alive had not only failed, but formed a powerful incentive for the vigorous revival of classical scholarship during the Western Han period. The astounding discovery of these texts at Mawangdui and Yinjueshan illustrates the profound literary involvement of the society that produced one of the richest periods in the history of Chinese literature.

In technology, the furnishings from Mancheng and Mawangdui tell us that, by the Western Han period, the Bronze Age in China was nearing its end. While the Mancheng burials contained large numbers of both bronze and lacquered objects, Tomb No. 1 at Mawangdui (the richest of the three) yielded only a single bronze item—a mirror—from among its over 1,000 objects of lacquer, silk, wood, and bamboo. Bronze was still a luxury metal (the cost of an undecorated bronze basin from Dou Wan's tomb, recorded in its inscription, is estimated to be roughly the same as a working man's wages for one to one and one-half years), but lacquers were even more expensive. A Han dynasty source notes that the price of one lacquered cup is equivalent to that of ten bronze ones. Clearly, the monopoly of bronze as a material for luxury goods was challenged by the beginning of the Western Han period.

In the manufacture of daily tools and agricultural implements, bronze had always been sparingly used, except in weapons where it was used extensively. But even here, this metal was losing ground to another competitor, iron. Among the weapons from Liu Sheng's tomb, the number of iron ones exceeded that of bronze. Furthermore, laboratory tests on a long iron sword buried by his side reveal that the metal is extremely low in carbon content and other impurities, and closely approxi-

mates steel in its metallurgical structure and strength. Greatly improved since its first appearance as crude cast iron in the Eastern Zhou period, iron was to replace bronze in the production of superior weapons during the Han period. At the same time, its low cost continued to make iron the most desirable metal for tools and agricultural implements. From this time on, bronze was used primarily for coins and mirrors. By the Western Han period, the days of the Bronze Age in China were numbered.

With the decline of the Bronze Age in China came the end of the bronze vessel as an art form. The routine shapes and unadorned surfaces of most of the bronze vessels from Mancheng reveal only too clearly that the intense involvement with shapes and surface designs—the essence of the art of the bronze vessel from Shang to Eastern Zhou—had quite evaporated by Western Han. Whether cast in bronze (no. 94), painted in lacquer, or modeled in clay (nos. 98–105), representational themes far outnumber purely ornamental ones. Even a highly decorative Western Han bronze such as the censer no. 95 owes much of its power to its vivid evocation of a realistic image (see chap. 8).

Encounters with foreign cultures, in part responsible for the growing interest in realistic representation and already evident in earlier periods, expanded with the territory of the Han empire. Bronzes decorated in the style of Sarmatian gold with multicolored inlays of semiprecious stones were found among the furnishings from Mancheng. Steppe Animal Style penetrated as far as Chu territory in Hunan, where the common steppe motif of an animal portrayed with twisted hindquarters was considered fitting decoration on one of the coffins from Tomb

No. 1 at Mawangdui (cf. Fig. 102). At the same time, the opening of the Silk Route by Wu Di permitted more Chu lacquers and silks to reach the hands of Hun chieftains in Central Asia, and silks alone traveled as far as the Roman Empire. The legendary "blood-sweating" horses of Fergana and Sogdiana were first imported at this time, and a powerful representation of this high-spirited breed is seen in the "flying horse" from a tomb at Wuwei, Gansu Province, of the second century A.D. (Kansas City, 1975, cover). Buddhist teachings probably first entered China at this time, too, although the earliest Buddhist representations in China date only from the Eastern Han period.

Another aspect of Han territorial expansion is illustrated by the bronze composition of bulls and tiger (no. 97). It came from a recently excavated Dian site in Yunnan Province, in the immediate vicinity of the first large-scale Dian excavation at Shizhaishan. According to the *Shi Ji*, the Dian tribe was an independent barbarian tribe engaged in agriculture and stock rearing in the high mountain region of southwest China. In the late fourth century B.C., a Chu general entered Dian territory and subdued the tribe. Finding his return route blocked by advancing Qin troops, he settled in Yunnan, became a Dian chieftain, and adopted Dian ways. The tribe remained autonomous and was enough of a threat to Han southwest border traffic that Wu Di initiated a series of military campaigns against it during his reign. In 109 B.C., the Dian chieftain finally surrendered. A Han prefecture was established in Yunnan, and the Dian chieftain was reinstated to rule as a Han representative.

Unlike other cultures, Dian neither gained much from its encounter with China nor contributed much to Chinese culture. The excavations at Shizhaishan and other Dian sites show a clear division between the tribe's period of autonomy and its subsequent incorporation into the Han empire at the end of the second century B.C. Tombs belonging to the earlier phase reveal a highly localized culture of complex origins and significant artistic character (see no. 97), while those from after the Han conquest yielded little more than routine Han remains.

The upper limit of the tombs from the early phase is difficult to determine, but it probably dates back at least to the late Warring States period. The artifacts reveal an essentially bronze-using culture with distinct local characteristics. With its geographical isolation high among the hills of southwest China, the only discernible Chinese influence on Dian came from Chu and its southwestern neighbors. The combination of serpents with various animals, a typical Chu motif, is frequently encountered in Dian art, and the bronze drum played an important part in the lives of both Chu and Dian cultures. Such Chu traits in Dian culture seem to support the Chu invasion recorded in the *Shi Ji*.

The greater part of Dian culture, however, was drawn from steppe cultures of Central Asia to its northwest and from peninsular Southeast Asian and Indian cultures to its west and south. Steppe influences would have filtered down the narrow mountain passes of Sichuan, perhaps even through Chu territory. For Chu was apparently equally vulnerable to the allure of steppe

Animal Style motifs during the early Western Han period, while Chu silks and decorative motifs had penetrated nomadic circles in the Altai Mountains as early as the fourth century B.C. Steppe influences would have been largely responsible for the common occurrence of animal combat themes in Dian art, but, in Dian hands, these scenes are stripped of all the splendor of gold and colored inlays and presented with an almost brutal, undisguised realism. From the steppes, too, the Dian tribe must have acquired the knowledge of mounted warfare and the delight in elaborate articles of war and weaponry abundantly evident among their artifacts.

Dian culture probably also came into contact with early cultures in mainland Southeast Asia, even as far as India, judging from the prominence of the bull as a Dian decorative motif (no. 97). An interesting stray find at Jiangquan, where no. 97 was excavated, shows a nude couple in erotic embrace, a motif reminiscent of similar images in early Indian art. Finally, the unusual shape of bronze ritual objects like no. 97, which finds no counterpart in either Chinese or other cultures, reflects the native Dian culture at its most individualistic. To this may be added other types such as cowrie containers— often topped by lively scenes of warfare, ritual sacrifices, weaving and market scenes—innumerable bronze drums, and agricultural implements whose elaborate decoration suggests use in rituals rather than daily functions. A representative selection of such bronzes from Shizhaishan was included in the 1974–75 People's Republic exhibition.

Dian bronze culture before the Han conquest also seems to have been familiar with a metalworking tradition distinct from China's. While lost-wax casting may have been known in China by the early Warring States period (see entry no. 67) and certainly by Western Han times (nos. 94, 95), the method was not widely adopted until much later. Most of the bronzes from Dian sites, in contrast, show fluid modeling of intricate animal and human forms, often in freestanding relief (no. 97), which points to lost-wax casting as their common manufacturing technique. Other characteristically Western habits were also in evidence: metal armor plates and a quiver unearthed at Jiangquan were found to have been hammered from sheet copper and soldered together, another practice rarely encountered in China. The complex form of no. 97 was constructed in a piecemeal manner that is also distinctly un-Chinese: the various animals were first cast separately, then assembled with a liberal use of soldering and additional pours of metal. All this suggests that there must have been a thriving local metal industry in the Dian culture which had learned its craft from other than Chinese sources.

The characteristic features of Dian culture discussed above were to disappear soon after the Han conquest of 109 B.C. Dian tombs that date after the second century B.C. are poor in typical Dian artifacts. Iron implements and weapons began to replace bronze ones, and bronze vessels of the time are usually routine Han types imported from metropolitan China, or rough ceramic ones of equal inconsequence.

CHAPTER 9: CATALOGUE ENTRIES

94 Gilt-bronze lamp

Western Han (first half 2nd century B.C.)
Excavated 1968 from tomb of Dou Wan, Mancheng,
    Hebei Province
Height 48 cm. (18⅞ in.); weight 15.85 kg. (34 lb. 14 oz.)
Hebei Provincial Museum

This gilt-bronze lamp is conceived in the shape of a kneeling young girl, holding a lamp in front of her in her left hand. She wears a simple wrapped robe with generous flowing sleeves, and her hair is smoothed back into a chignon and tied with a trailing sash (Fig. 113). Her right arm is raised above her shoulder, the full sleeve falling to cover the top of the lamp. The brilliantly gilded surface is well preserved with only occasional patches of blue green corrosion.

The lamp held in her left hand has a movable circular base with a small pin in the center for the candle and a handle projecting from the edge. The vertical wall of the lamp consists of two freely sliding semicircular sheets that can be adjusted to control the direction of light and to regulate brightness by changing the size of the opening. The hollow right arm and body of the girl act as funnel and container for the smoke rising from the burning candle, channeling it into the sleeve and trapping it inside the body, to keep the room free from soot. The lamp can be cleaned by dismantling its movable base, walls, and top, and the removable right arm and head provide access to the interior. This elegantly functional design fully reflects the remarkable creativity and mechanical resourcefulness of the artists of the time.

The different owners of this lamp are revealed by engraved inscriptions totaling sixty-five characters, which appear in nine groups distributed throughout the surface. Six groups mention "Yang Xin Jia," and one includes the date "seventh year." "Yang Xin Jia" is believed to be the name of the household of a royal relative, enfeoffed in 179 B.C. and stripped of the title in 151 B.C. when the son was found guilty of treason (Kaogu 1972/1, p. 11; Beijing, 1978b, pp. 46–47). The lamp should therefore date between 179 and 151 B.C., and if the date "seventh year" refers to the actual date of manufacture, the lamp would probably date to 173 B.C., the seventh year of the reign of Wen Di (179–157 B.C.). Since it was not unusual for entire family fortunes to be confiscated at the family's downfall, it is likely that this lamp entered the royal household in 151 B.C. It must have appealed to Empress Dowager Dou, grandmother of Liu Sheng and probably a close relative of Dou Wan, for the remaining groups of inscriptions mention the Chang Xin palace, where the empress dowager lived during her politically influential years in the mid-second century B.C. The lamp, probably presented as a gift to Dou Wan, was eventually buried with her.

The shape of this lamp is unique among Western Han examples, common types of which are also found in the tombs at Mancheng (Kaogu 1972/1, pl. 6:1, 4; Beijing, 1972a, nos. 100, 101; Beijing, 1972b, pls. 2,3). It also ranks among the finest of early Chinese sculptures, whether in bronze, terracotta, or wood. The girl's young face is sensitively modeled, her pose natural, with feet neatly tucked behind and her full, flowing robe draped with substance and decorum. Her timid expression and slightly downcast eyes, her modest attire and humble pose reveal poignantly her position of servitude. Compared to the terracotta kneeling girl found near the mausoleum of Qin Shihuangdi at Lintong, Shaanxi

Province (Fig. 114), this girl from Mancheng possesses a relaxed ease and a psychological realism entirely lacking in the Qin figure from about fifty years earlier.

As in nos. 95 and 97, lost-wax casting must have been employed in the production of this figure; it is a technique that seems to have been increasingly exploited during the Western Han period to meet the demand for highly sculptural and complex shapes in bronze. The gilded surface also represents the most popular bronze decorative technique in Western Han. The technique of fire-gilding appeared during the Warring States period (see no. 72), and its overriding popularity in Western Han is a natural development from the taste for elaborately inlaid surfaces on Warring States bronzes. Compared to inlaying, however, the process of gilding required less time and labor, but its result was no less attractive to the extravagant and worldly tastes of the time. The fluidity of the mercury and gold powder mixture used in gilding also enabled the bronze master to produce painterly designs on bronze (Kelley, 1946, pls. 72–74) with the same ease and dynamism as on painted lacquers, with which the bronze industry had to compete since the late Warring States period.

PUBLISHED: *Kaogu* 1972/1, pl. 1 (see also references, entry no. 95); Beijing, 1972a, no. 99; Beijing, 1972b, pl. 1; Tokyo, 1976, no. 93; Beijing, 1976a, no. 82; Beijing, 1978b, pl. 1.

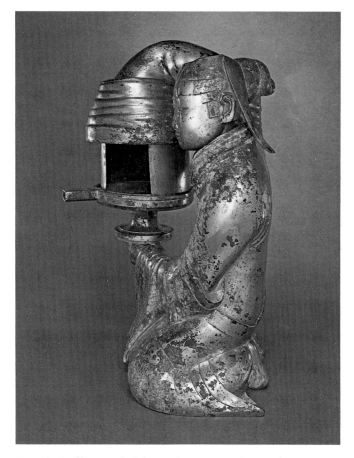

Fig. 113 Profile view of gilt-bronze lamp no. 94. Photograph: Wang Yugui, Cultural Relics Bureau, Beijing

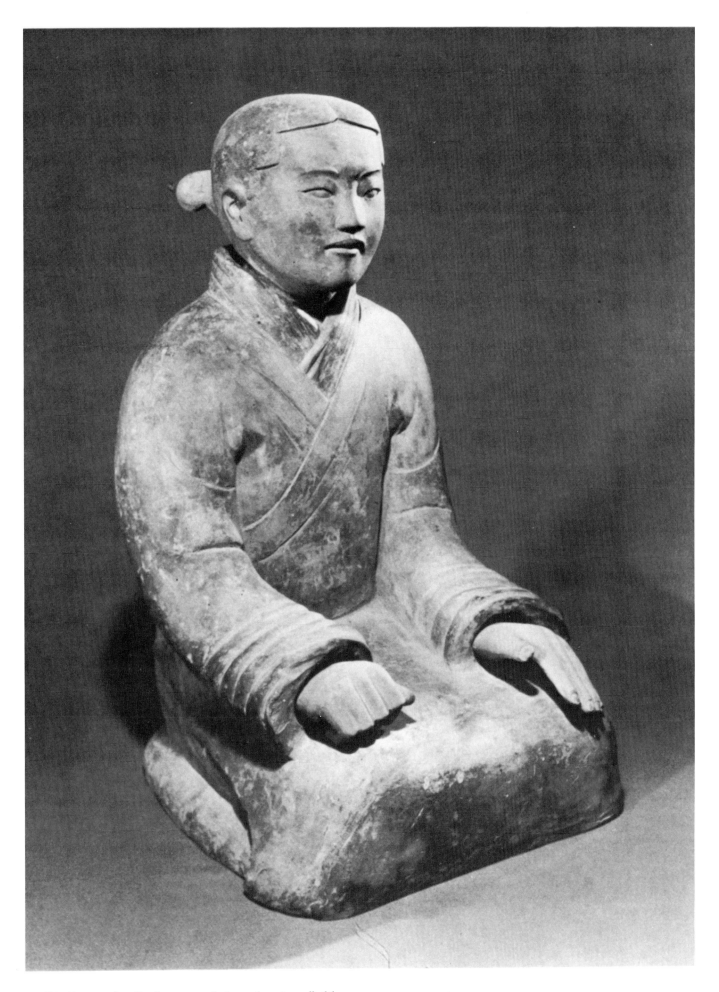

Fig. 114   Terracotta kneeling figure unearthed near the outer wall of the
mausoleum of the First Emperor of Qin, Lintong Xian, Shaanxi
Province. Photograph after Kansas City, 1975, no. 139

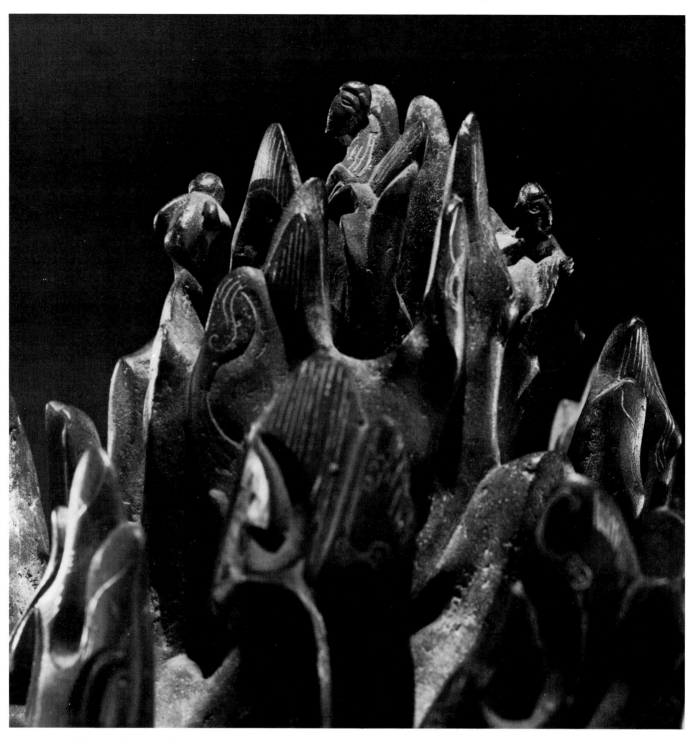

Fig. 115   Detail showing figures amid craggy peaks, censer
no. 95. Photograph: Seth Joel

95   Censer

Western Han (second half 2nd century B.C.)
Excavated 1968 from tomb of Prince Liu Sheng, Mancheng,
  Hebei Province
Height 26 cm. (10¼ in.); weight 3.4 kg. (7 lb. 8 oz.)
Hebei Provincial Museum

Exceptional in design and workmanship, this beautiful incense
burner is also extremely well preserved, with no signs of incrustation, repair, or damage. Its smooth dark gray bronze surface is
marred only by spots of blue green corrosion. The gold inlays, some
of which are thread thin, are virtually all preserved. The censer is
constructed in three parts. A conical top bears irregular, deeply
undercut fingerlike projections that conceal apertures for releasing
the incense. This is set over a deep bowl, also with projections
rising above its rim. The bowl in turn is secured by a crosspin in the
sleevelike top of an openwork stem and base composed of three
dragons. The irregular shapes and deep undercuts that form the
top suggest strongly that the lost-wax method must have been used
in its casting, for no other moldmaking technique could have
produced a form as complex and as sculptural. The same method
might have been employed in the casting of the bowl, which is also
cast integrally with its free-standing elements.

ern Han period, giving its art the eclectic character of a truly cosmopolitan age.

PUBLISHED: *Kaogu* 1972/1, pl. 6:2 (see references, entry no. 95); *Kaogu* 1972/5, pl. 2; Beijing, 1972b, no. 10; Beijing, 1976a, no. 81; Beijing, 1978b, pl. 10.

97 Ritual object

3rd–2nd century B.C.
Excavated 1972, Lijiashan, Jiangquan, Yunnan Province
Height 43 cm. (16⅞ in.); length 76 cm. (29⅞ in.); weight 12.6 kg. (27 lb. 11 oz.)
Yunnan Provincial Museum

This unusual object is a *symplegma* of a tiger, a young bull, and an older bull. The body and head of the larger bull form the major part of the object. Its head is smoothly modeled in the round, with a pair of proudly curved horns and small ears projecting from under them. But its body has been reduced to a saddlelike slab, its back scooped away to form a smooth shallow depression, and its belly removed to allow the young bull, sculpted in entirety, to be placed between its legs. The tiger clutches with all its paws to the hind end of the bull and holds the bull's tail in its teeth. The tiger's body is marked with intaglio stripes. Both bulls are plain, but their bony features are simply and realistically modeled and their sweeping horns magnificently conceived. The patination is an even dark green. Repairs have been made on the neck, the scooped back, and the hind leg of the larger bull.

The cultural and technological significance of this object has been discussed above, page 327. In the piecemeal construction of this object, organic consistency is sometimes sacrificed to production; for example, the bull's tail was cast as part of the tiger rather than the bull, and attached by soldering. Seams present where the horns emerge from the bulls' heads suggest that the horns were also cast separately and soldered on.

The function of this striking object is perhaps its most intriguing aspect. Chinese archaeologists have variously classified it as a low table (*Kaogu Xuebao* 1975/2, p. 131) and as a kind of ritual altar (Beijing, 1976a, no. 86). There is no precedent in either Dian or Chinese contexts that can resolve this question. It was found in one corner of a burial pit, among spearheads and next to bronze drums and fragments of armor (*Kaogu Xuebao* 1975/2, p. 100, fig. 3). This burial association suggests that the object, like the bronze drums, probably served in a ritual related to warfare. Without question, it represents a type unique to Dian culture.

The motif of a tiger attacking a bull from the rear is found on bronze headrests (*Kaogu Xuebao* 1975/2, p. 131, fig. 36, pl. 13:2) and as an ornament on the tubular socket of a bronze tapper (p. 112, fig. 14:2), both from the same find. It evokes a famous West Asian parallel—the reliefs of a lion attacking a bull from the rear that flank the stairway to the audience hall at the sixth- to fifth-century Achaemenian site of Persepolis (Frankfort, 1970, fig. 416).

This object came from Tomb 24 at Lijiashan, the largest of the twenty-seven burials excavated. Since this burial primarily contained typical Dian objects and no Han period Chinese objects, the report has tentatively dated it before the Han reign of Wu Di, midsecond century B.C. or earlier.

PUBLISHED: *Wenwu* 1972/8, pl. 4:1 (preliminary report, pp. 7–16); *Kaogu Xuebao* 1975/2, pl. 14:3 (report, pp. 97–156); Tokyo, 1976, no. 99; Beijing, 1976a, no. 86.

COLORPLATES 98-105

Terracotta figures and horses *in situ*, ▷
Pit No. 1. Lintong Xian, Shaanxi Province.
Photograph: Wang Yugui
Cultural Relics Bureau, Beijing

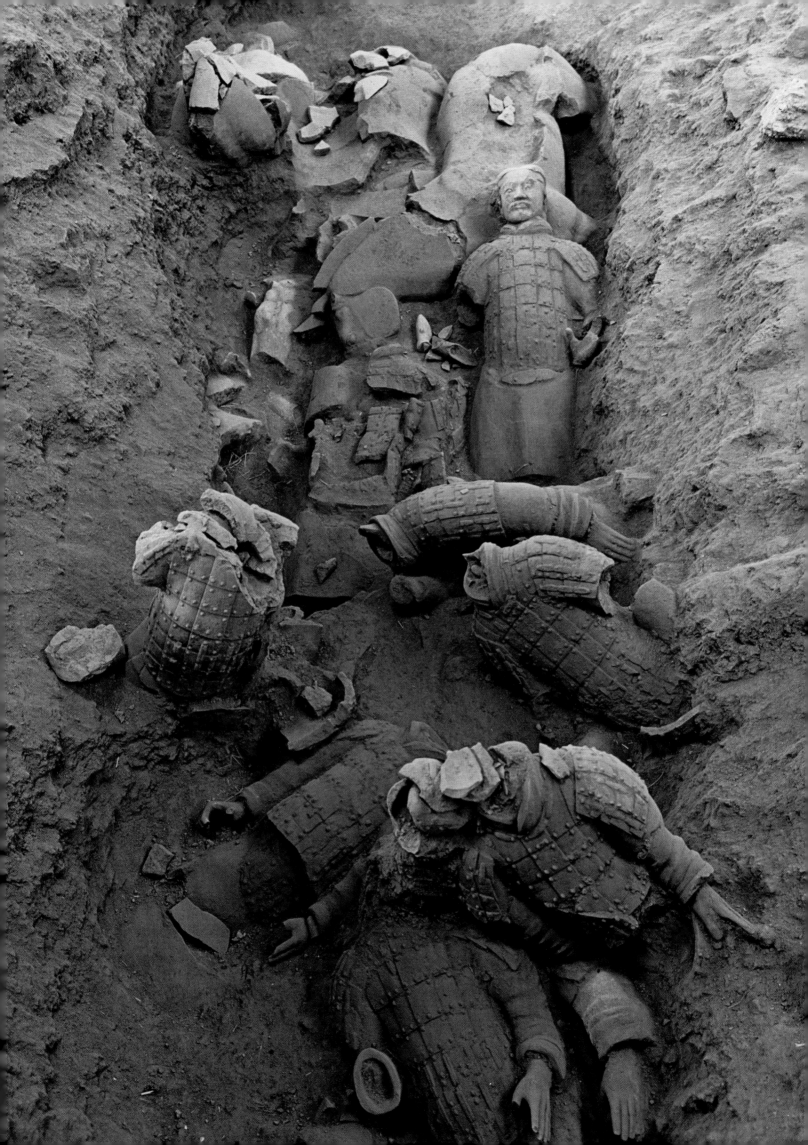

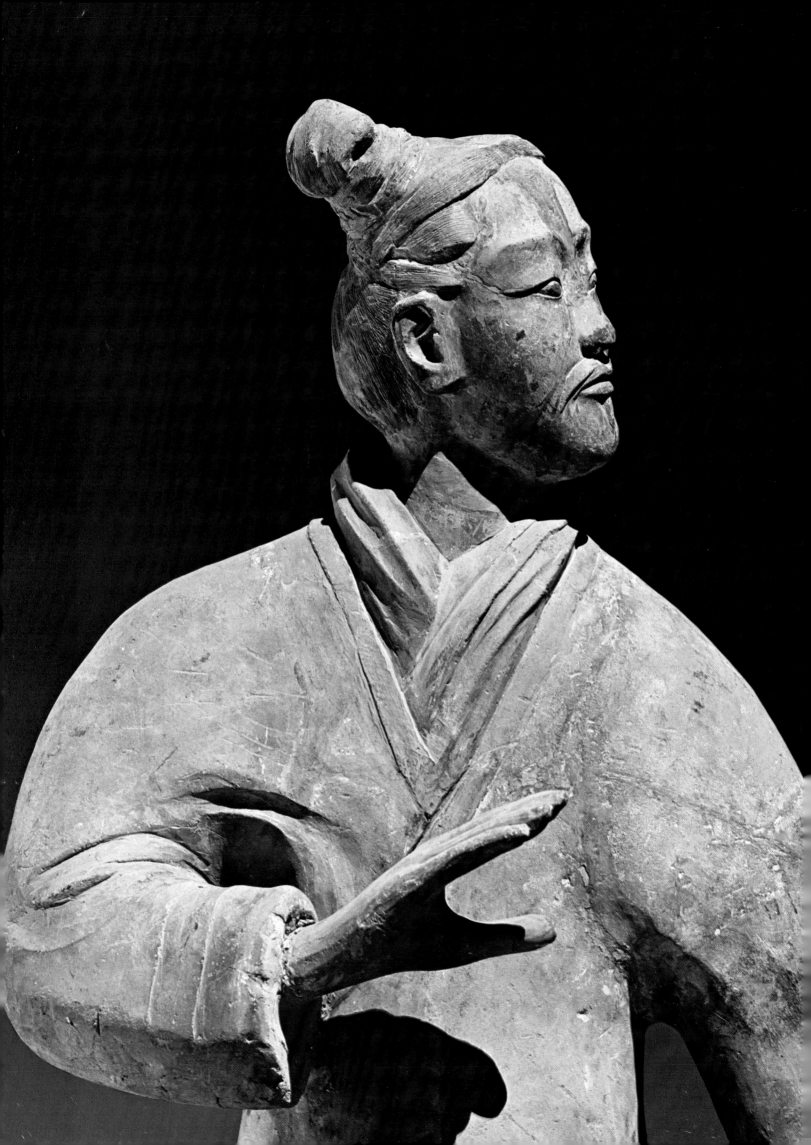

98 Striding infantryman. Qin dynasty (221–206 B.C.).
Height 178 cm. (5 ft. 10 in.)

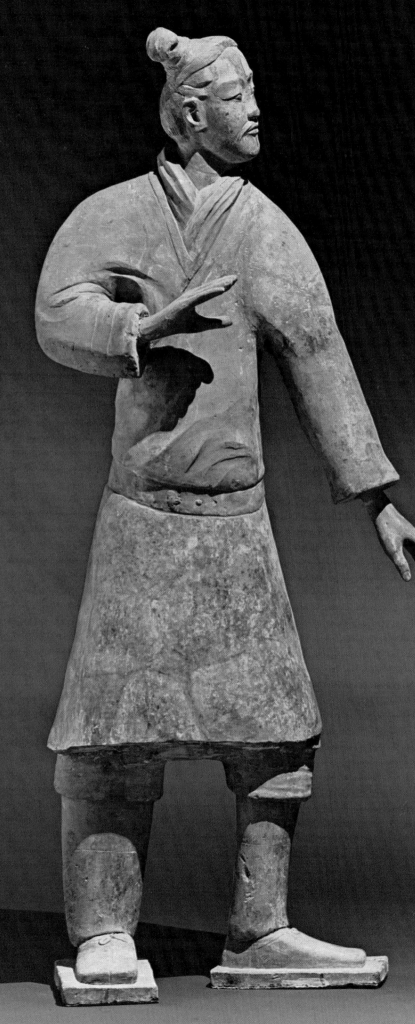

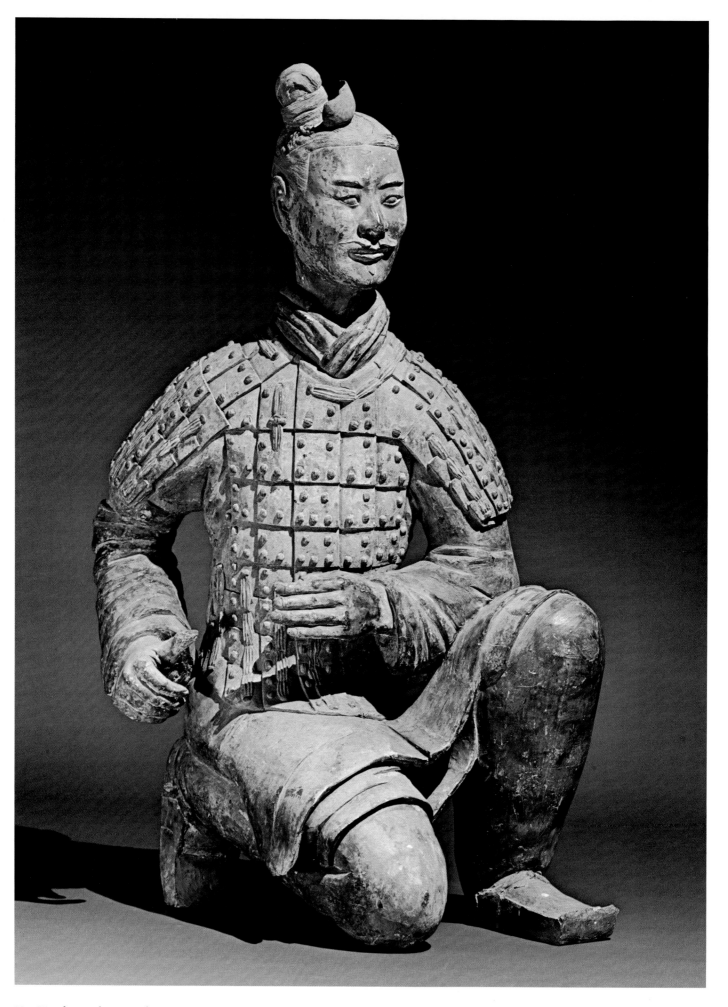

99 Kneeling archer. Qin dynasty (221–206 B.C.).
Height 120 cm. (3 ft. 11 in.)

Detail, kneeling archer no. **99** ▷

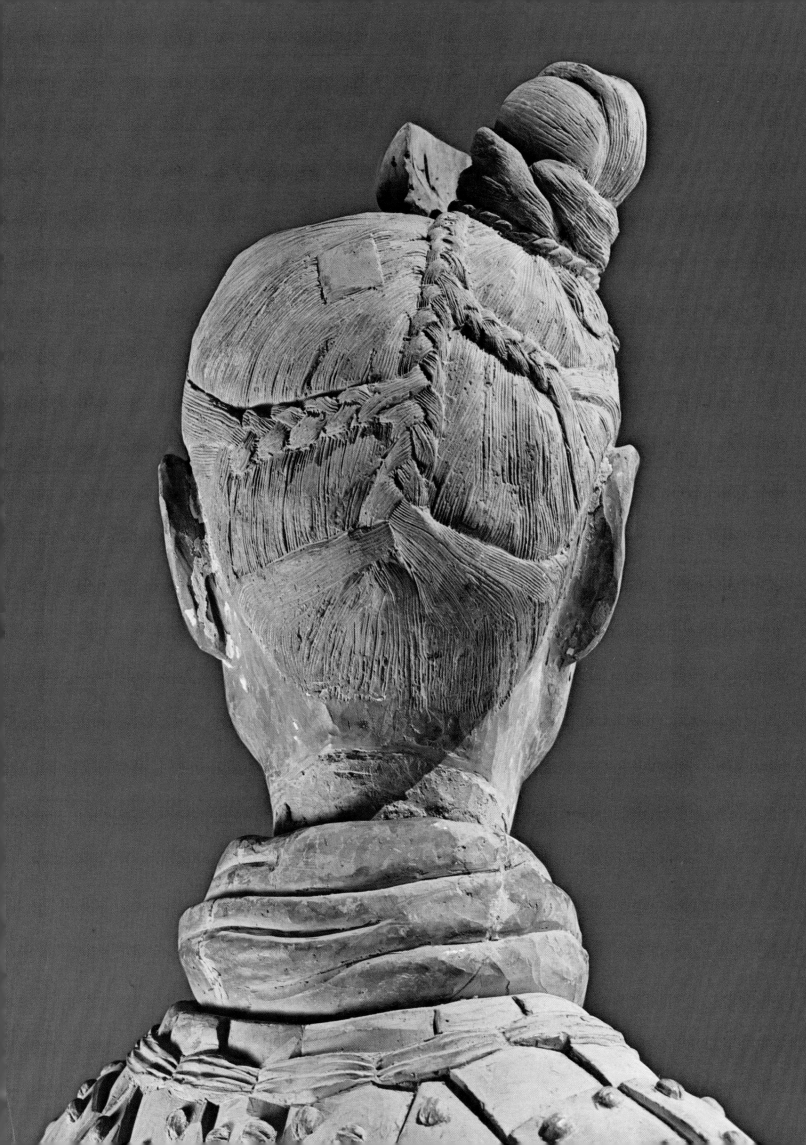

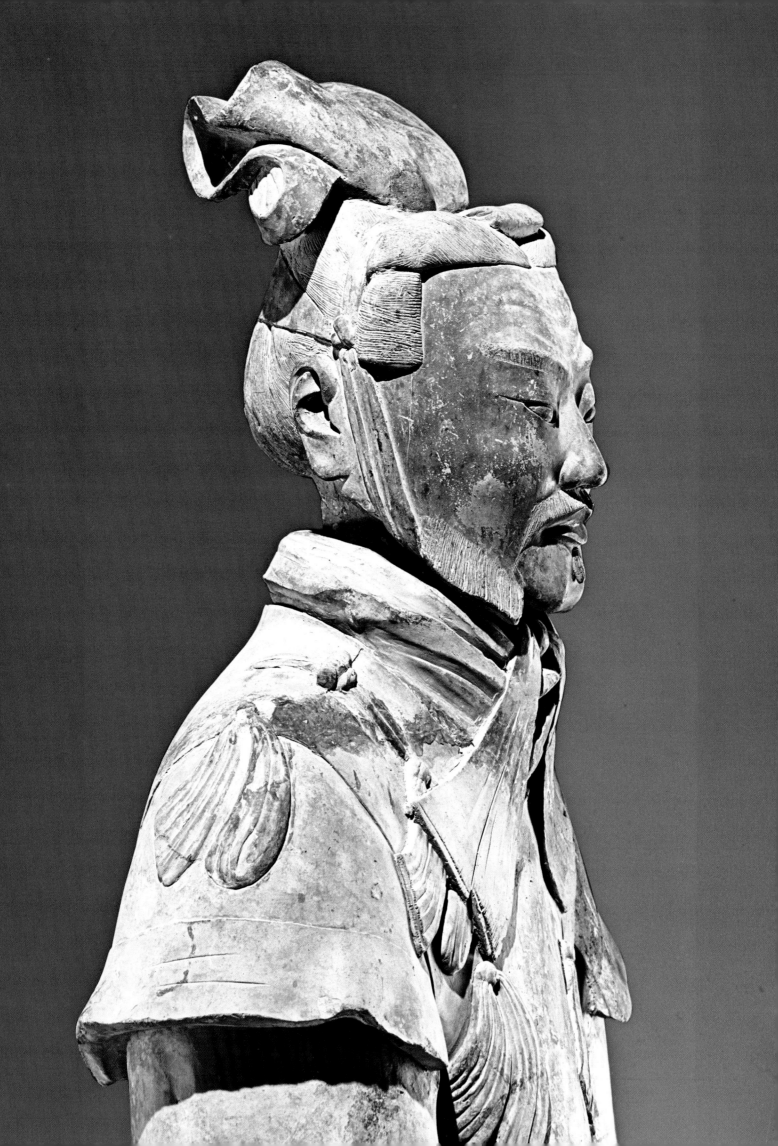

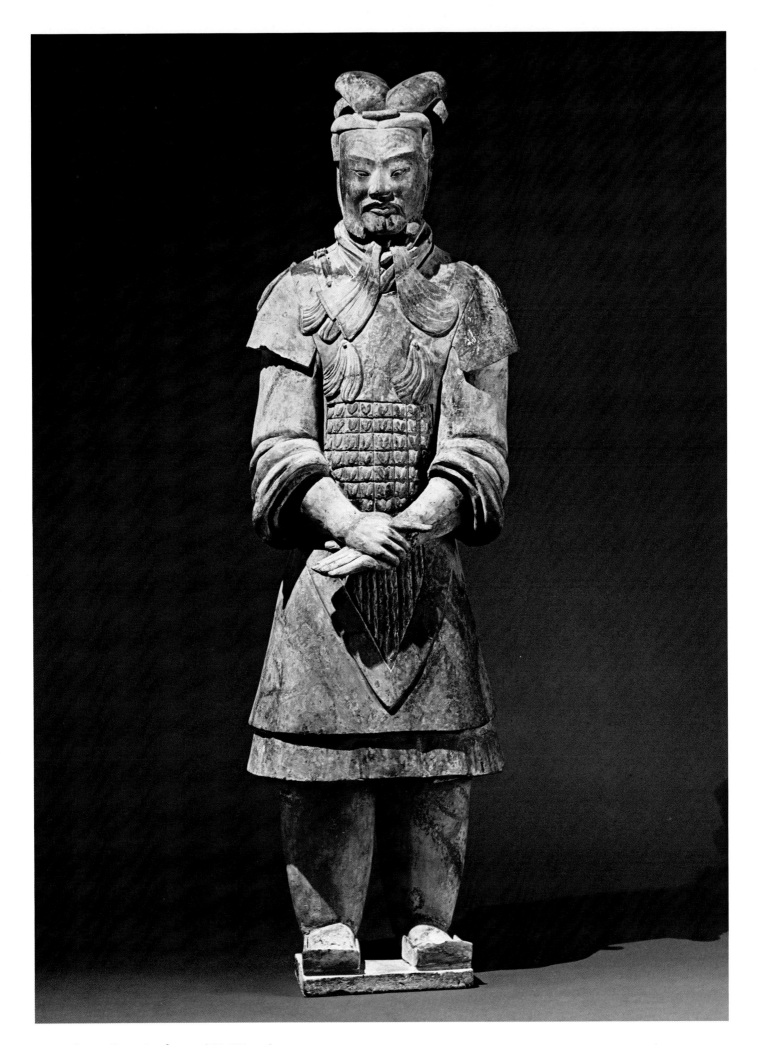

100 Infantry officer. Qin dynasty (221–206 B.C.).
Height 196 cm. (6 ft. 5 in.)

◁ Detail, infantry officer no. **100**

101, 102　Cavalryman and saddle horse. Qin dynasty (221–206 B.C.).
Cavalryman: height 180 cm. (5 ft. 10½ in.). Saddle horse: height
172 cm. (5 ft. 7½ in.); length 203 cm. (6 ft. 7¾ in.)

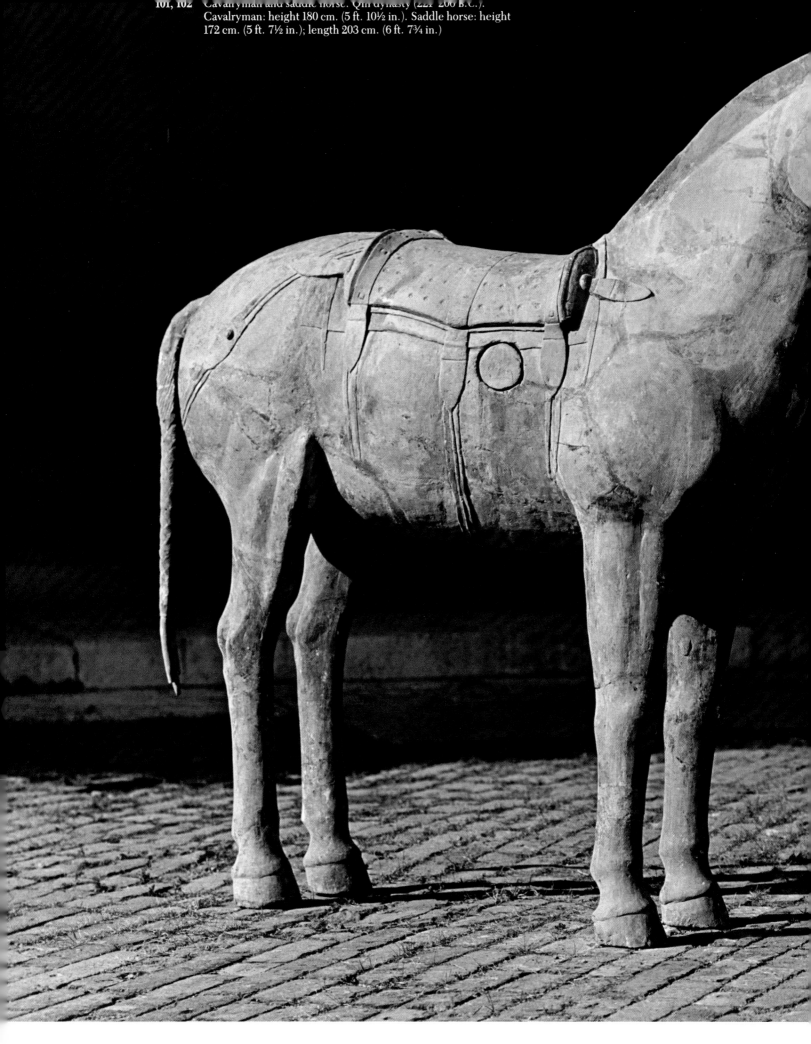

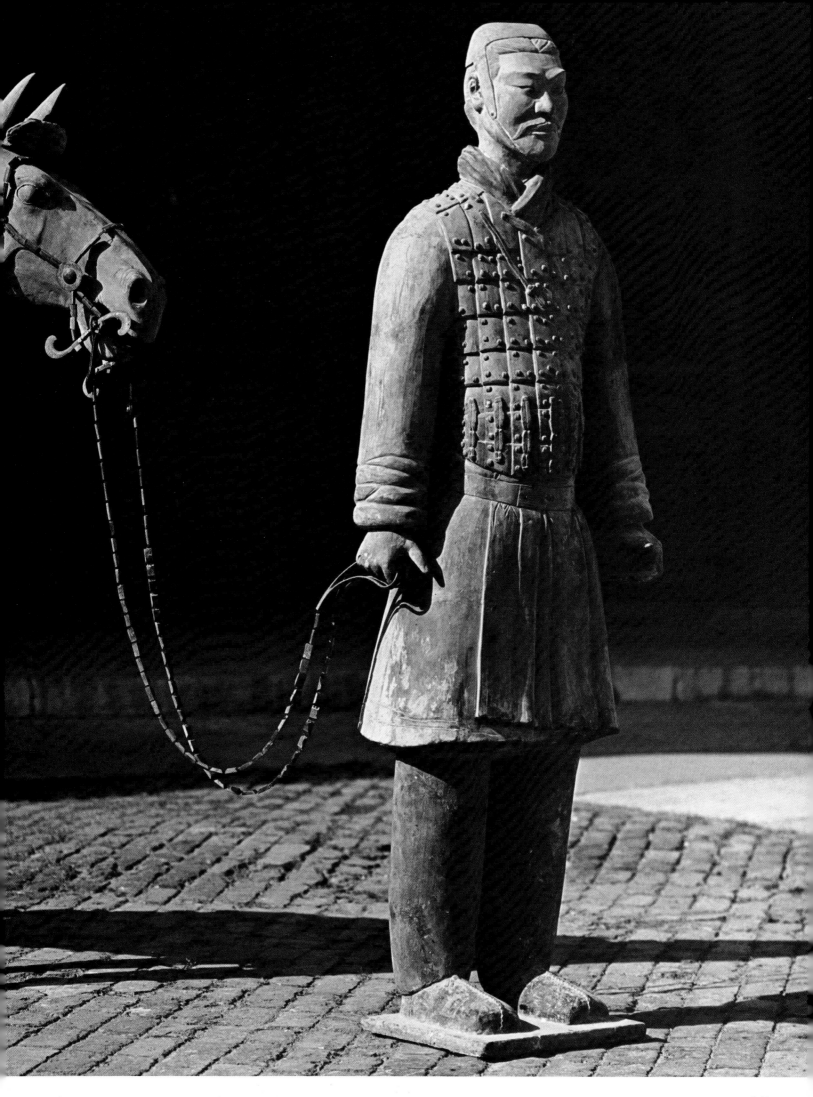

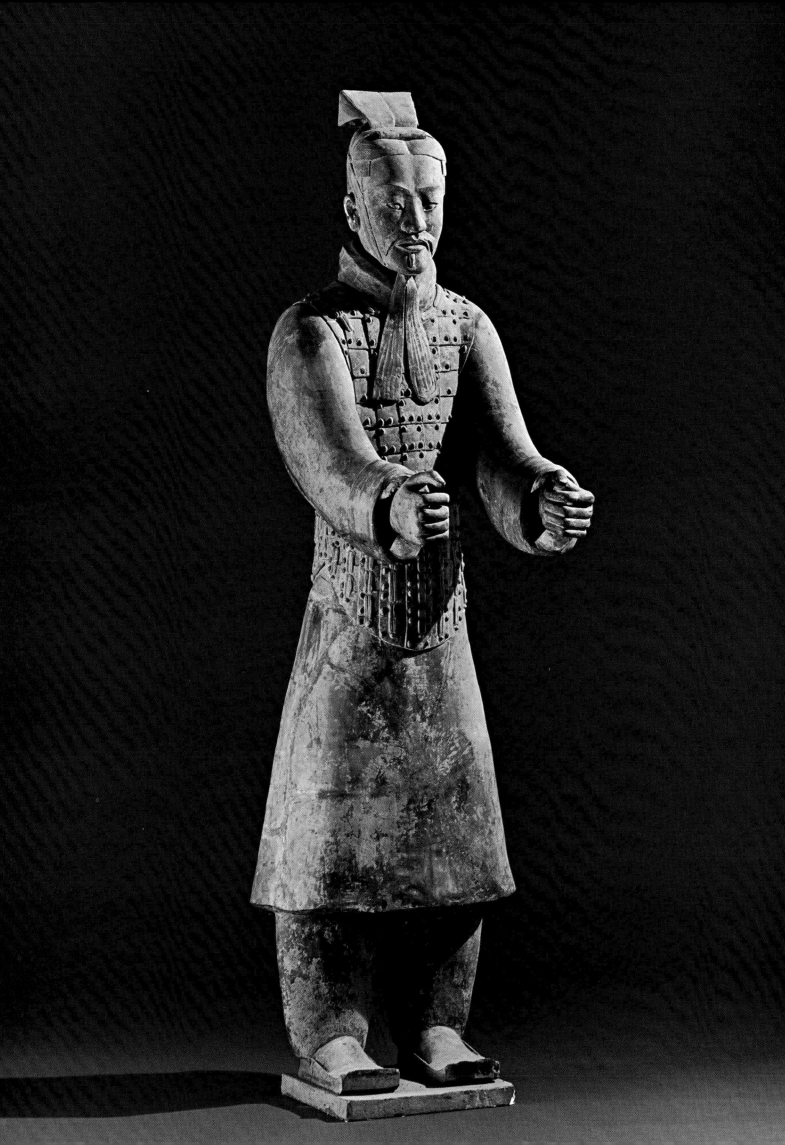

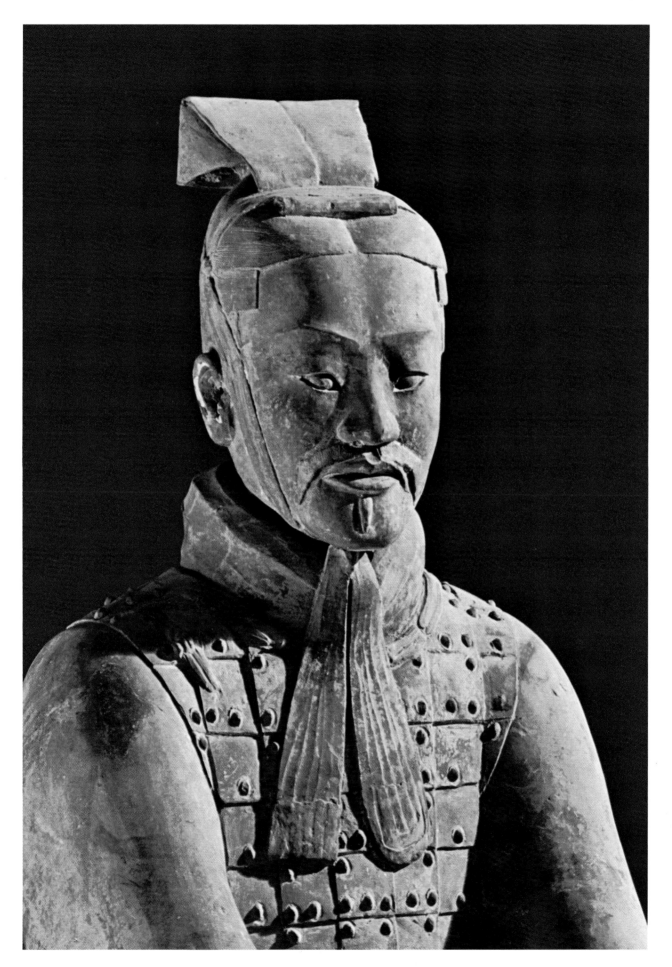

Detail, charioteer no. **103**

◁ **103** Charioteer. Qin dynasty (221–206 B.C.).
　Height 190 cm. (6 ft. 2½ in.)

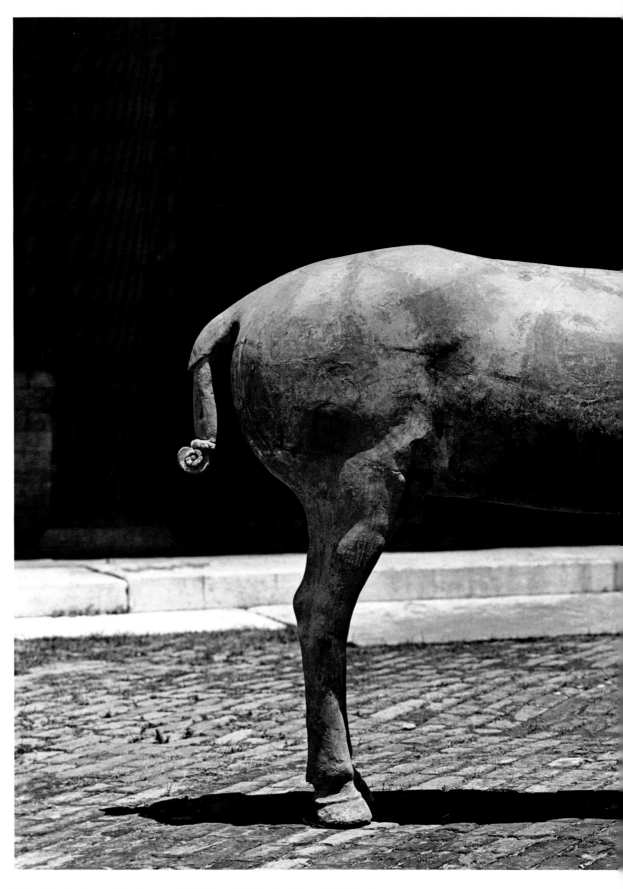

104 Chariot horse. Qin dynasty (221–206 B.C.). Height 171 cm. (5 ft. 7 in.); length 226 cm. (7 ft. 4¾ in.)

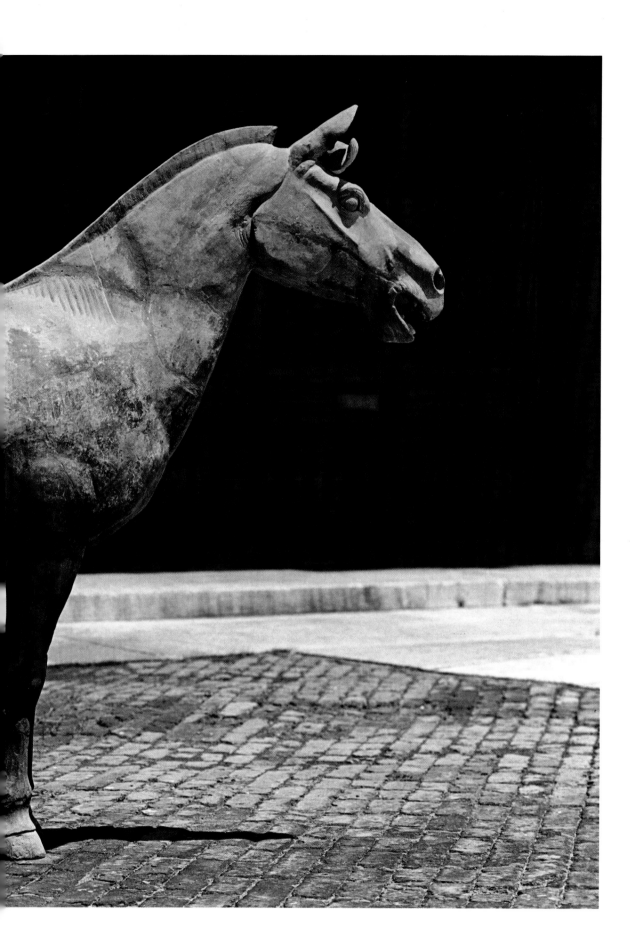

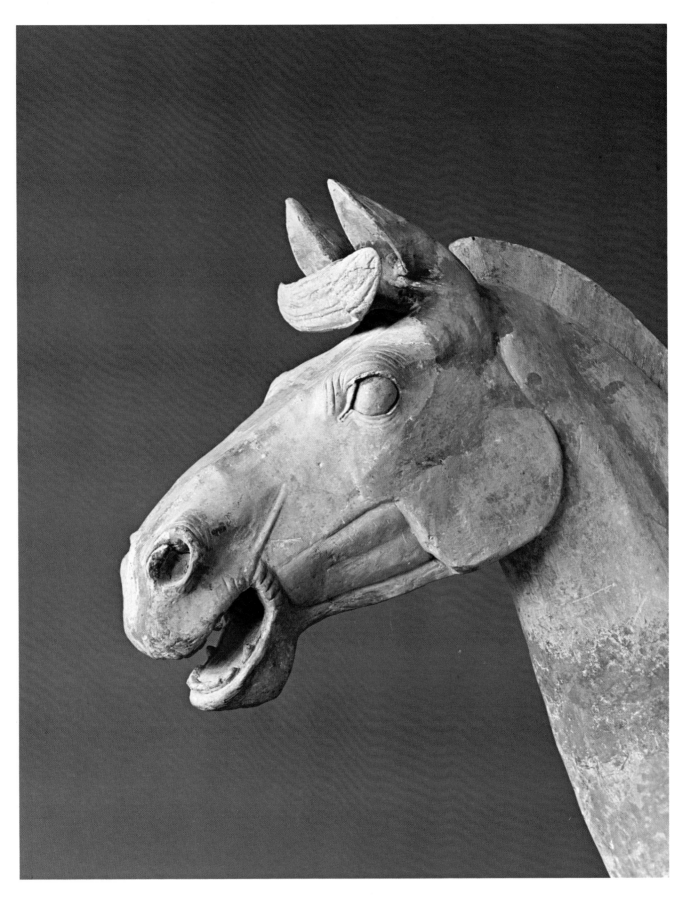

Detail, head of chariot horse no. **104**

Detail, armored infantryman no. **105** ▷

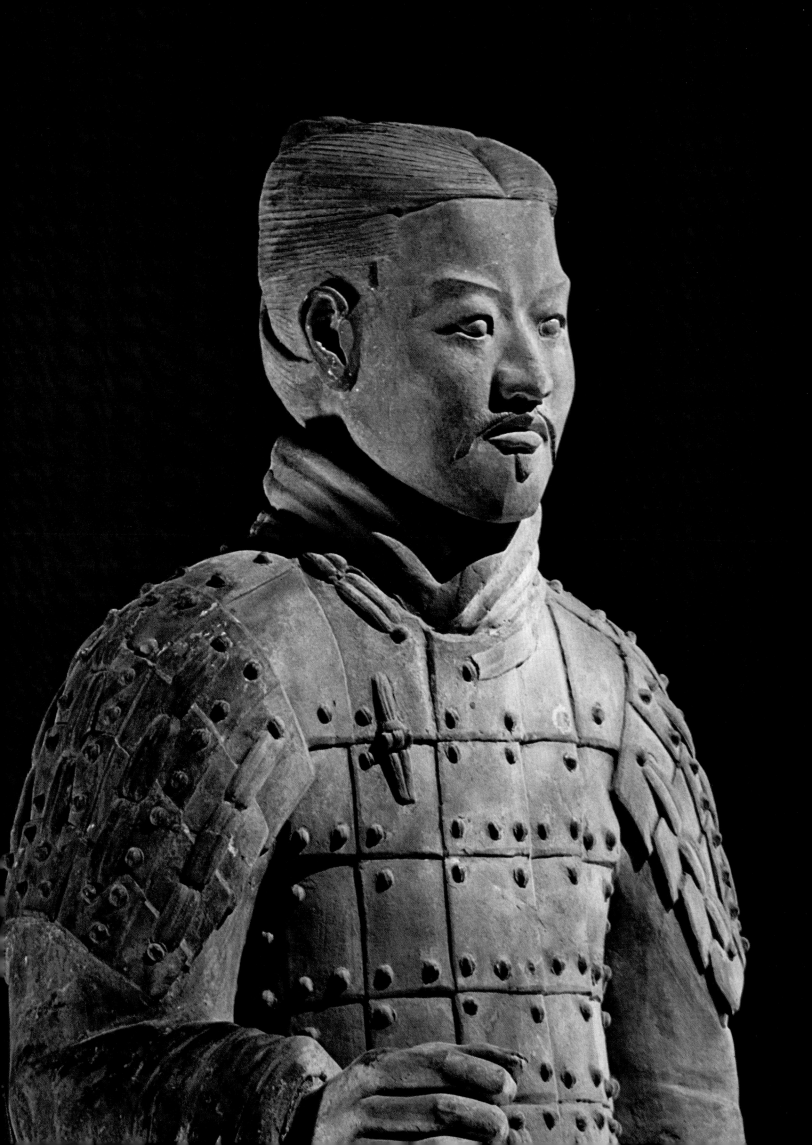

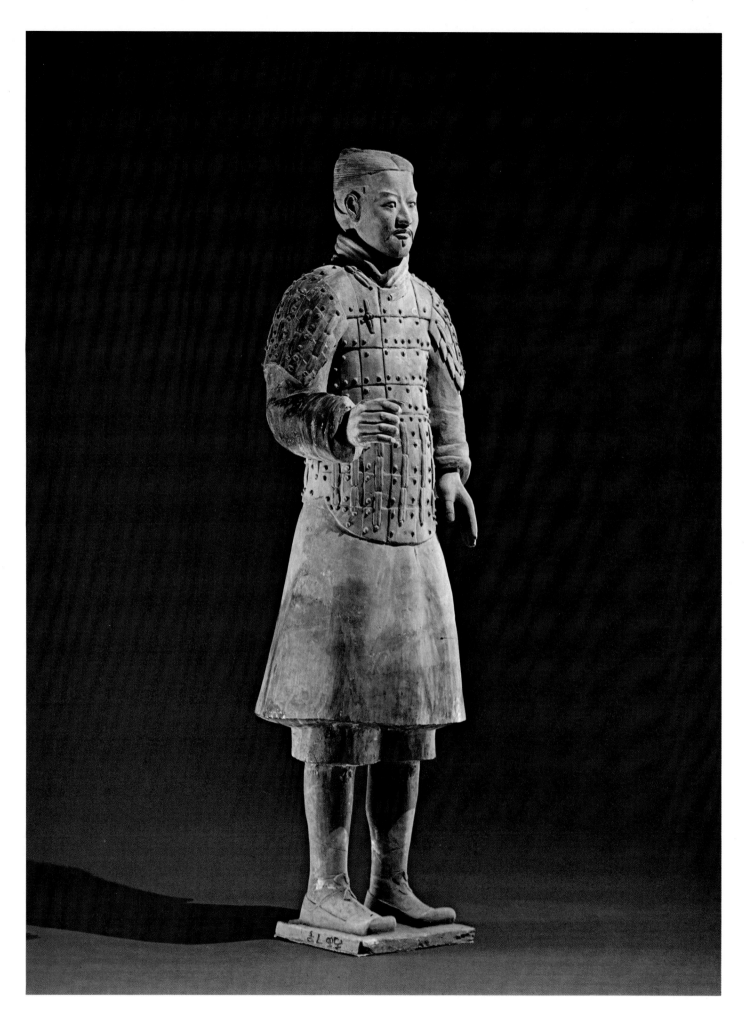

105 Armored infantryman. Qin dynasty (221–206 B.C.).
Height 183 cm. (6 ft.)

10

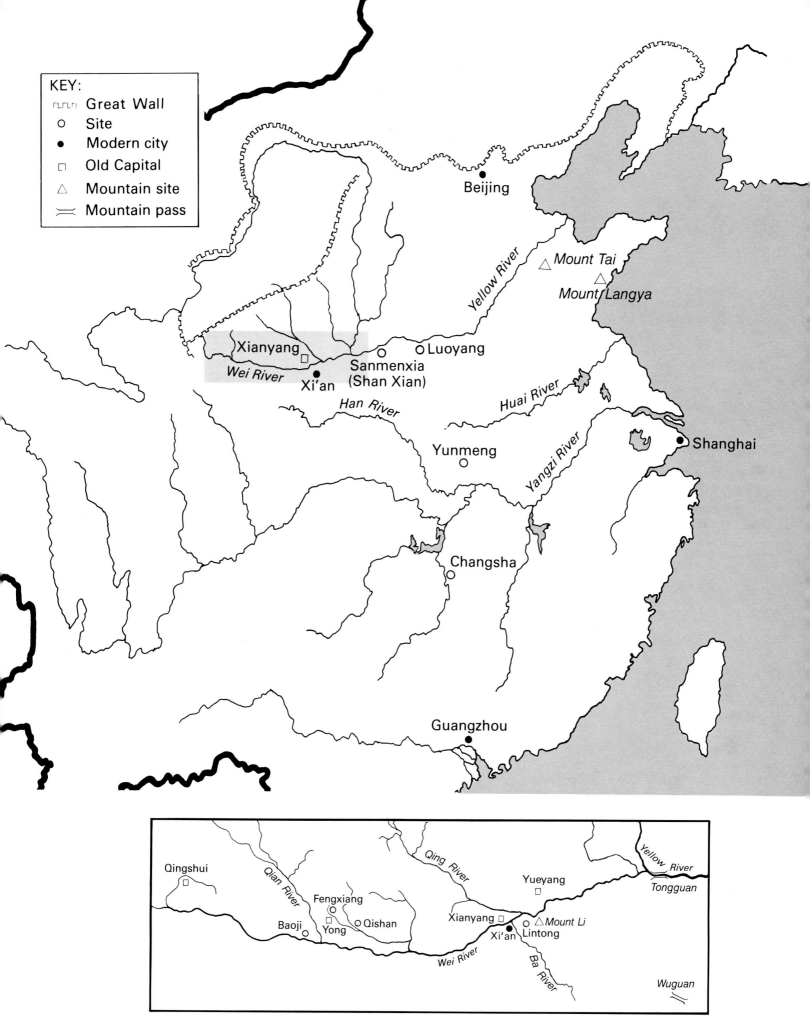

KEY:
- ⊓⊓⊓ Great Wall
- ○ Site
- ● Modern city
- ▫ Old Capital
- △ Mountain site
- ⋈ Mountain pass

Beijing

△ Mount Tai
△ Mount Langya

Yellow River

Xianyang
▫ Luoyang
Sanmenxia
(Shan Xian)
Wei River
Xi'an

Han River

Huai River

Yunmeng

Yangzi River

Shanghai

Changsha

Guangzhou

Qingshui
Qian River
Qing River
Yueyang
Yellow River
Tongguan

Fengxiang
Baoji Yong Qishan
Xianyang ▫
Xi'an Lintong △ Mount Li
Wei River
Ba River

Wuguan

Map of China showing major sites of the Qin state and Qin dynasty, 10th
century to 206 B.C.

10

The Terracotta Army of the
First Emperor of Qin (221–206 B.C.)

Maxwell K. Hearn

In ancient Greek myth Jason and his Argonauts face a band of warriors that spring from dragon's teeth sown in the earth. Today in China the legend of an army that rises from the ground has become a reality, as archaeologists uncover file after file of armed terracotta soldiers buried near the tomb of the First Emperor of Qin. This discovery, made by chance in 1974, is the most important revelation in recent Chinese archaeology. Created over 2,000 years ago as an imperial bodyguard to serve the emperor in his afterlife, the army of some seven thousand life-size soldiers and horses sculpted in clay, painted in brilliant colors, and equipped with real chariots and bronze weapons, bears witness to the military might of China's unifier, Qin Shihuangdi.

The First Emperor of China and the Qin Achievement

China's unification by the ruler of Qin in 221 B.C. had the greatest impact of any event in Chinese political history. Through military supremacy, the self-proclaimed First Emperor brought to an end centuries of internecine warfare and political discord. Just as he connected the many separate ramparts previously erected against nomad incursions to form the 1,500-mile-long Great Wall, politically he welded into a single empire the several states into which the country had been divided. By promulgating a uniform code of law, standardizing currency, weights and measures, and even the written language, and, governing through a nonhereditary, centrally administered bureaucracy, he unified the country under his rule. Although the dynasty itself would end in 206 B.C., less than four years after the First Emperor's death, this unification laid the foundation for China's imperial order of the next two thousand years. While the specific policies implemented under the First Emperor's rule owe their genesis to a long line of able advisors to the Qin throne, it was his ambition that brought the long-sought ideal of a unified Chinese empire to fulfillment.

The First Emperor was crowned King Zheng of Qin upon the death of his father in 246 B.C. Since Zheng was only thirteen years old and too young to rule, his powerful chancellor, Lü Buwei (died 235 B.C.) served as regent until the king came of age in 238 B.C. (*Shi Ji*, 85, pp. 2505–14). Less than a year after assuming the powers of his title, King Zheng had forced his former regent into exile and launched the first of a series of military campaigns. These culminated sixteen years later in the subjugation of all China. Finding himself at thirty-eight the ruler of the entire civilized world as he knew it, he summoned his ministers to devise a new title worthy of his unprecedented accomplishment:

> Insignificant as I am, I have raised troops to punish the rebellious princes; and thanks to the sacred power of our ancestors all six kings have been chastised as they deserved, so that at last the empire is pacified. Now unless we create a new title, how can we record our achievements for posterity? [*Shi Ji*, 6, p. 236; trans. Yang in Li, ed., 1975, pp. 267–68]

In the end he created the new imperial title himself. Combining the words *huang* and *di*, which had previously denoted demigod kings of the legendary past, with the word *shi*, "first," he proclaimed himself Qin Shihuangdi, or "First Sovereign Emperor of Qin." At his direction his successors were accordingly to be titled "Second Emperor," "Third Emperor," and so on for generations without end.

To inspect his new realm and impress his subjects with the grandeur of his reign, the First Emperor initiated a series of imperial tours. During each of these, he visited various sacred mountains where he had stone stelae erected to enumerate the virtues of his rule and proclaim his vision of a universal empire. One stele reads in part:

> In the twenty-eighth year of his reign [219 B.C.]
> A new age is inaugurated by the Emperor;
> Rules and measures are rectified,
> The myriad things set in order,
> Human affairs are made clear
> And there is a harmony between fathers and sons.
> The Emperor in his sagacity, benevolence and justice
> Has made all laws and principles manifest....
>
> Great are the Emperor's achievements,
> Men attend diligently to basic tasks,
> Farming is encouraged, secondary pursuits
>   discouraged,
> All the common people prosper;
> All men under the sky
> Toil with a single purpose;
> Tools and measures are made uniform,
> The written script is standardized;
> Wherever the sun and moon shine,
> Wherever one can go by boat or by carriage,
> Men carry out their orders
> And satisfy their desires;
> For our Emperor in accordance with the time
> Has regulated local customs,
> Made waterways and divided up the land.
> Caring for the common people,
> He works day and night without rest;
> He defines the laws, leaving nothing in doubt,
> Making known what is forbidden.

> The local officials have their duties.
> Administration is smoothly carried out,
> All is done correctly, all according to plan....
>
> The universe entire
> Is our Emperor's realm,
> Extending west to the desert,
> South to where the houses face north,
> East to the East Ocean,
> North beyond Dahsia [Daxia]
> Wherever human life is found,
> All acknowledge his suzerainty,
> His achievements surpass those of the Five Emperors
> His kindness reaches even the beasts of the field;
> All creatures benefit from his virtue,
> All live in peace at home.

> [*Shi Ji*, 6, pp. 244–45; trans. Yang in Li, ed., 1975, pp. 272–73]

The grandiose governmental powers assumed by the First Emperor were expressed in the cultural sphere by an imperial art imposed upon the disparate traditions of the earlier Warring States. Twelve colossal statues cast in bronze are our first evidence in historical accounts of this imperial art in China. Created to glorify the emperor's unification, they presaged, in their magnitude, the stone sculptures of the ensuing Han dynasty: "All weapons of the empire were collected and brought to the capital at Xianyang, where they were melted down to make bells and twelve metal figures [*jin ren*], each weighing 1,000 *dan* [roughly 3.15 M.T.], which were erected in the palace" (*Shi Ji*, 6, p. 239). The last of the twelve colossi were melted down in 190 A.D., but the large-scale terracotta warriors recently discovered near the First Emperor's tomb offer a clue about their appearance. In addition, as an outgrowth of the sculptural traditions of the late Zhou, the pottery figures provide new evidence that by the third century B.C. Qin culture, traditionally regarded as semibarbaric, stood unequivocally within the mainstream of Chinese culture.

Qin Culture

The history of the predynastic principality of Qin bears a remarkable resemblance to the rise of the Zhou state before its overthrow of the Shang dynasty in the eleventh century B.C. Like the Zhou, the forebears of the Qin were originally loyal allies on the western edge of the civilized world. Early in the ninth century B.C. the Zhou monarch rewarded this clan of herdsmen with a settlement called Qin situated in the western marches of present-day Gansu Province. During the next century Qin served as a buffer between Zhou and the nomadic tribesmen to the north and west. In 771, when these tribesmen sacked the Zhou capital, killed the Zhou king and forced his son to flee eastward, the Qin came to the rescue of the royal house. For his aid in protecting the retreating court, the Qin chieftain was ennobled as a feudal lord (*zhuhou*) and given title to all lands west of Qishan (in western Shaanxi Province.) For the first time, Qin opened diplomatic relations with the other feudal states to its east.

Initially, Qin rulers maintained their fealty to the Zhou kings: after Qin troops routed the nomadic tribesmen in 753, they dutifully presented the Zhou royal house with the lands to the east of Qishan. Yet, as the power of the Zhou declined, control over these royal domains was contested by Qin and the neighboring state of Jin, another powerful Zhou feudatory. The decisive engagement came in 645, when Qin captured Duke Hui of Jin (reigned 650–635 B.C.), releasing him only after the Jin had relinquished all claims to the region west of the Yellow River (*Shi Ji*, 5, pp. 188–89). It was from this well-protected territorial base "within the pass" (*guannei*) that during the course of four centuries the Qin launched the successive campaigns that resulted in the conquest of China in 221 B.C.

In spite of Qin's vigorous policy of military expansion, it remained somewhat isolated, both geographically and culturally, from the more tradition-bound states of the lower Yellow River basin. Relatively free of classical conservatism, Qin rulers believed that their success in conquering the region "east of the pass" (*guandong*) rested in their adoption of the newest trend in political philosophy. Beginning in the fourth century B.C., Qin rulers, influenced by a series of able advisors from other principalities, reorganized the state by adhering to a system of thought later called "Legalism."

Most notable among the early advisors to Qin was Shang Yang (also known as Gongsun Yang and as "Lord Shang"; died 338 B.C.) Rejecting traditional rites and customs, Shang Yang sought to make Qin the most powerful of the feudal states by means of a strictly governed, centrally administered society devoted to economic development and military might. According to Shang Yang's egalitarianism, the state alone held the power to reward or punish; aristocrat and commoner were equal before the law. Severely limiting the hereditary privileges of the landed gentry, he created a hierarchy of nonhereditary titles awarded on the basis of military prowess. To remove the Qin ruler from the intrigues of powerful clans and aristocratic cliques, he relocated the capital at Xianyang in 350 B.C. At the same time he reorganized Qin territories into thirty-one centrally administered prefectures. Beneath this bureaucratic superstructure, the population was divided into groups of five to ten persons; within each group every member was made responsible for the actions of fellow members. Anyone who denounced a criminal received the same reward as one who decapitated an enemy soldier; anyone harboring a wrongdoer received the same punishment as one who surrendered to the enemy. A similarly rigorous system of compensations and penalties was applied to the basic economic activities of farming and weaving; those who produced large quantities of grain or silk were exempted from corvée labor, while those who did not—supposedly because of laziness—were impressed into slavery. Such policies, hand in hand with a program for opening up new farmland by resettlement and irrigation, brought impressive results. According to the *Han Shu*, the history of the former Han dynasty, "the territory of

Qin comprised one-third of the empire, and the number of its people did not exceed three-tenths, yet if we were to estimate its wealth, this would be found to amount to six-tenths" (Ban Gu, *Han Shu*, 28b, pp. 6a–7b; trans. Bodde, 1967, p. 4).

Not surprisingly, the success of such policies at the expense of tradition earned Qin the enmity of the other states. Reflecting the great apprehension with which they regarded Qin's ruthless tactics, a noble of Wei reportedly remarked to his king:

> Qin has the same customs as the Rong and the Di [barbaric tribes]. It is avaricious, perverse, eager for profit, and without sincerity. It knows nothing about etiquette [*li*], proper relationships [*yi*], and virtuous conduct [*de xing*], and if there be an opportunity for material gain, it will disregard its relatives as if they were animals. [*Shi Ji*, 44, p. 1857; trans. Bodde, 1967, p. 3]

Nonetheless, its orderly society commanded the respect, and perhaps even the envy, of the Confucian philosopher Xunzi (fl. ca. 280–240 B.C.), who by his visit to Qin about the year 264 B.C. was moved to praise:

> Its frontier defences are precipitous, its geographical configurations are advantageous, its mountains, forests, streams and valleys are excellent, and its natural resources are abundant. Thus in the geographical configurations it is outstanding.
>
> When I entered its frontiers and observed its customs, I saw that its people are simple and unsophisticated. Their music is not corrupting or licentious, and their clothing is not frivolous. They stand in deep awe of their officials, and are people who follow precedent obediently. When I reached the yamens [governmental offices] of its cities and towns, I saw that their officials are dignified and that there are none who are not courteous, temperate, honest, serious, sincere and tolerant. They are worthy officials....
>
> When I entered the capital and observed its great prefects, as they went forth from their doors and entered the public places, or left the public places and returned to their own homes, I noticed that none of them engaged in private business, have partialities, or form cliques. They are high-minded, and there are none who do not have understanding of the common welfare. They are worthy prefects....
>
> When I observed its court, I noticed that in hearing of affairs everything was attended to, and yet in a quiet manner as if nothing were going on. It is a worthy court.
>
> Thus it is no accident, but calculation, which has made [Qin] victorious during four generations....
>
> Nevertheless, it also has disturbing features. Granted that it possesses all of the above characteristics, yet if we compare these with the reputation of a true King, there is no question that [Qin falls] far short. Why should this be? It is because [Qin] has almost no Confucians [*ru*] [*Xunzi*; trans. Bodde, 1967, pp. 9–10]

Xunzi's grudging admiration inadvertently reveals Qin's success at selectively adopting and rejecting schools of thought that originated in the traditional center of culture in the east. This process of assimilation long antedates Lord Shang's reforms of the fourth century B.C. Most noteworthy is the state's use of the Zhou written language and literary traditions. Shortly after the Qin ruler was ennobled in 771 B.C., he began appointing astrologer-archivists (*shi*) to record events. The chronicle they kept, the *Qin Ji* (Qin Historical Records), although no longer extant, provided much of the material for the account of the Eastern Zhou period set down by China's Herodotus, Sima Qian (ca. 145–ca. 86 B.C.; *Shi Ji*, 15, pp. 685–87). The existence of Qin poetry is attested by a collection of ten odes included in the *Shi Jing* (Classic of Poetry). One of the poems, "Yellow Bird," describes the burial of Duke Mu, the ruler who enlarged Qin's domains by defeating Duke Hui of Jin in 645 B.C.; it is traditionally dated to around the year of his death in 621 B.C.

Qin's avid acquisition of Zhou culture is best illustrated by the eastward movement of its own capital and its concomitant adoption of Zhou principles of city planning, architectural construction techniques, and styles of art. The settlement of Qin, established by King Xiao of Zhou (traditionally reigned 909–895 B.C.) represents the earliest focus of the Qin state. Little more than a frontier outpost on the western edge of the Zhou realm, it was situated in the area of modern Qingshui Xian, in eastern Gansu Province. In 762 B.C., the capital moved eastward to the region between the modern cities of Fengxiang and Qishan, both in Shaanxi Province, where it changed locations at least three times during the next century (see map at beginning of this chapter).

Yong, the most important of these earlier capitals (occupied from 667 to 384 B.C.), has recently been identified with the remains of a city and its enclosing wall discovered just south of Fengxiang. Two groups of bronze architectural fittings unearthed inside the walled area are decorated with an all-over pattern of interlaced dragons that corresponds closely, both in style and in casting quality, to that on contemporary bronzes produced within the central states of China (*Kaogu* 1976/2, pp. 103–8, 121–28, pls. 3–5).

In 383 B.C. the capital was again shifted some 170 kilometers eastward to the city of Yueyang, eastern Shaanxi Province. An archaeological survey of this site has found a rectangular rammed-earth wall measuring 2.2 by 1.8 kilometers enclosing a city with major north-south and east-west thoroughfares, workshops, wells, and a system of sewers for drainage (*Wenwu* 1966/1, pp. 10–16; Chang, 1977, pp. 343–44).

The most elaborate cultural remains yet discovered in Qin territory are those of Xianyang. Located on the north bank of the Wei River, just west of modern Xi'an, it served as the last Qin capital from 350 to 206 B.C. During its brief imperial era as the first capital of a unified China, Xianyang enjoyed extraordinary prosperity. In 221 B.C., some 120,000 aristocratic and wealthy families were forcibly resettled there as part of the program to destroy the Zhou feudatories. This influx of wealth and talent must have transformed Xianyang into a truly cosmopolitan environment boasting a large population of accomplished craftsmen and artisan retainers from every region of the country. That year, work was begun on a vast building program.

As each feudal domain was abolished replicas of the feudal lords' palaces were constructed in the hills north of the capital overlooking the Wei River. Such was their extent that the entire area from Yongmen [in the west] to the Jing and Wei Rivers in the east was given over to palaces and pavilions. Connected by elevated avenues and encircling corridors, they were filled with the beautiful women and musical instruments captured from the different states. [*Shi Ji*, 6, p. 239]

The shifting course of the Wei River has obliterated most of the ancient city of Xianyang, but a survey conducted from 1974 to 1975 has revealed the existence of an extensive palace district on the bluffs just north of the Wei River flood plain (*Wenwu* 1976/11, pp. 12–41, pls. 1–3). Extending over 12 kilometers from east to west and dotted with numerous rammed-earth foundations, this district may well correspond to the complex of palaces described in the *Shi Ji* account. A tentative reconstruction of the one palace site excavated shows that the original building was an important three-story structure with symmetrical wings that flanked a ravine and were connected by a bridge. Constructed atop a multilevel earthen platform, the palace was decorated with polychrome murals and carved ceramic tiles, and boasted such amenities as built-in heating stoves in many of its rooms and a system of subterranean drainage conduits.

In 212 B.C. the First Emperor declared his replicas of the feudal lords' palaces too small and ordered the construction of a new imperial residence, the legendary E Pang palace, south of the Wei River in the imperial parklands. So immense was the projected size of the palace that several hundred thousand laborers were conscripted to work there, yet it was still incomplete at the time of the emperor's death in 210 B.C. The vast scale of this and other colossal undertakings, including the construction of the Great Wall and the First Emperor's mausoleum, strained the population to the breaking point. His heir, the Second Emperor, by refusing to halt construction on the palace, even as the empire faced open rebellion, obstinately led his dynasty to utter collapse.

The Site and Symbolism of the First Emperor's Mausoleum

Razed by rebel armies in the same year the Qin dynasty fell, only the elevated foundation of the E Pang palace survives, but its name still lives as the epithet for unbridled luxury. Similarly, the layout of the First Emperor's mausoleum epitomizes his vision of an everlasting world order. As described by Sima Qian, the First Emperor's tomb chamber reproduced in minute detail the universe over which he expected to rule:

From the time the First Emperor first took the throne [in 246 B.C.] work was begun [on his mausoleum] at

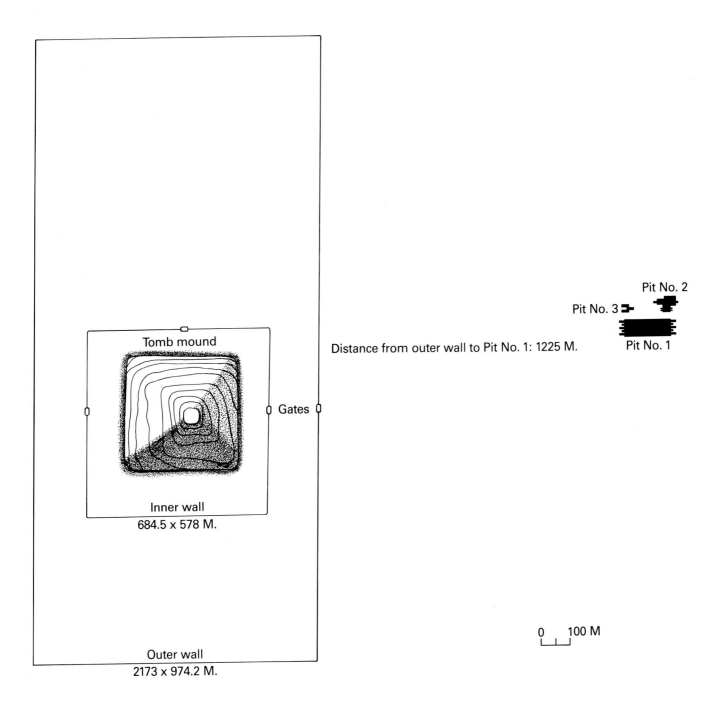

Tomb mound

Inner wall
684.5 x 578 M.

Gates

Outer wall
2173 x 974.2 M.

Distance from outer wall to Pit No. 1: 1225 M.

Pit No. 2

Pit No. 3

Pit No. 1

0   100 M

Fig. 117   Plan of the mausoleum complex of the First Emperor of Qin showing the
tomb mound, inner and outer walls, and position of Pit Nos. 1–3. Drawing by Phyllis Ward
after material supplied by Cultural Relics Bureau, Beijing

Mount Li. After he had won the empire, more than 700,000 conscripts from all parts of the country labored there. The laborers dug through three subterranean streams which they sealed off with bronze in order to make the burial chamber. This they filled with [models of (?)] palaces, towers, and the hundred officials, as well as precious utensils and marvelous rarities. Artisans were ordered to install mechanically triggered crossbows set to shoot any intruder. With quicksilver the various waterways of the empire, the Yangtze [Yangzi] and Yellow Rivers, and even the great ocean itself were created and made to flow and circulate mechanically. The heavenly constellations were depicted above and the geography of the earth was laid out below. Lamps were fueled with whale oil so that they might burn forever without being extinguished .... Finally, trees and grass were planted [on the tumulus] to make it appear like a mountain. [Shi Ji, 6, p. 265]

While this description has not yet been confirmed by modern excavation, it is strongly supported by the tomb site's outward configuration, which functioned as a replica of a palace city and as a diagram of the cosmos (Fig. 117).

At the center of the mausoleum is the tomb mound itself (Fig. 118). Landscaped into a four-sided pyramid of three concentric tiers totaling 43 meters in height, it

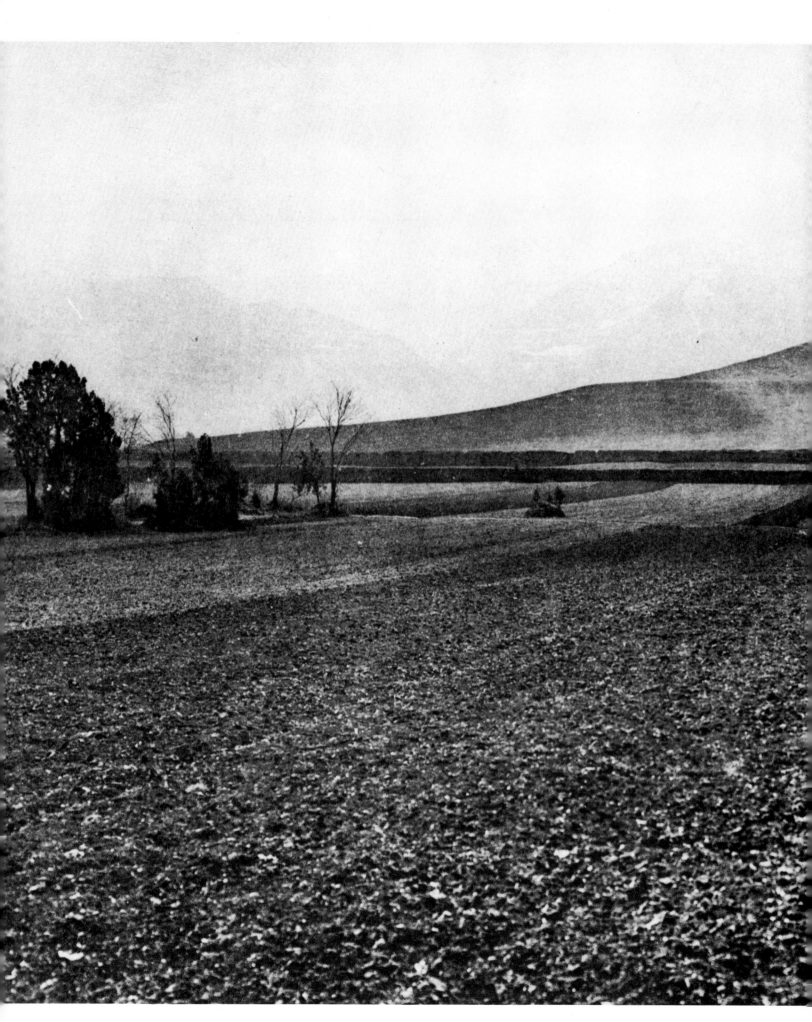

Fig. 118   View of the First Emperor's tomb mound, looking south.
Photograph after Segalen, Voisins, and Lartigue, 1924, vol. I, pl. 1

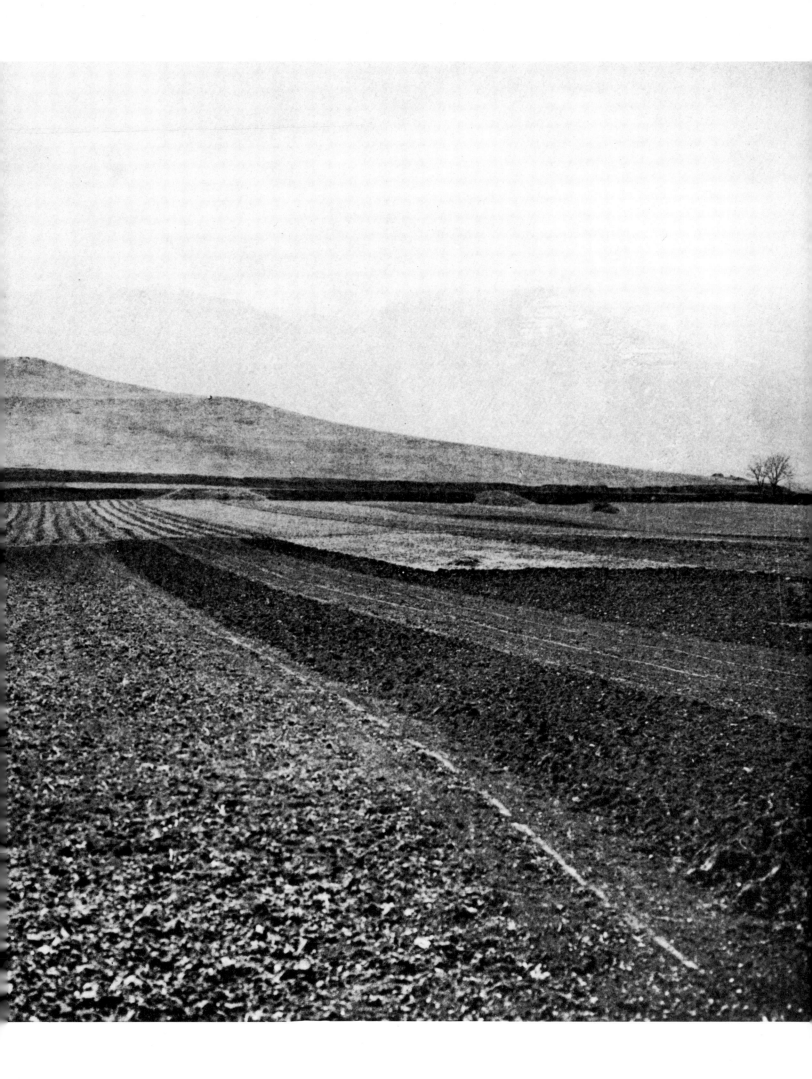

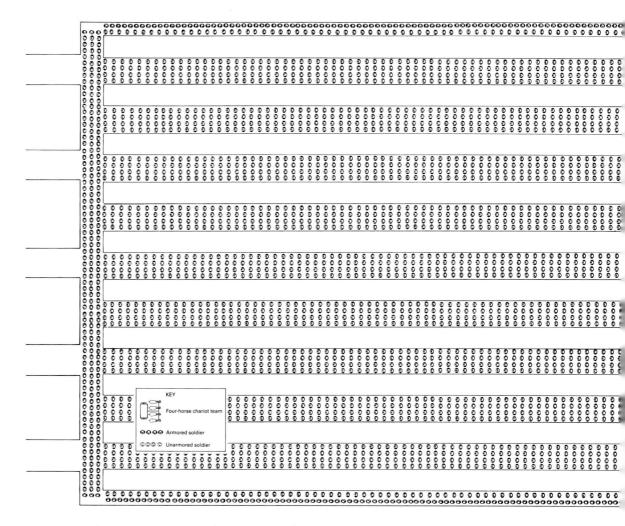

KEY

Four-horse chariot team

⊖⊖⊖⊖ Armored soldier

⊖⊖⊖⊖ Unarmored soldier

Fig. 119 Plan of Pit No. 1, Lintong Xian, Shaanxi Province, showing
a tentative reconstruction of the arrangement of terracotta
figures and wood chariots. Drawing by Phyllis Ward

represents both the apex of worldly power as well as the zenith of Heaven, around which the inner and outer rings of the cosmos revolve. This use of the stars and the celestial order as a metaphor for earthly government has a long tradition in Chinese thinking: "He who exercises government by means of his virtue may be compared to the pole star (*beichen*), which keeps its place while all the stars turn around it" (*Confucian Analects*; trans. Needham, 1959, vol. III, p. 230). During the Han dynasty the number three often signified the realms of Heaven, Man, and Earth, and played an important role in ceremonial structures like the three-level building tentatively identified by its excavators as the Biyong, "Hall of the Circular Moat" (*Kaogu Xuebao* 1959/2, pp. 44–55, pls. 1–10; *Kaogu* 1963/9, pp. 501–15).

The idea of a tripartite division of space is reinforced by the placement of the tomb mound within two walled compounds. With a perimeter wall over 6 kilometers long, the mausoleum's vast outer compound encloses an area equal to a Zhou city, while the inner sanctuary, occupying the compound's southern half, recalls by its placement and size the E Pang palace. Remains of roof tiles and brick pavements, discovered within the northern half of the outer precinct, suggest that it once contained a funerary temple and perhaps a population to

provide for and administer the yearly round of sacrifices. To further maintain harmony with the cosmic order the entire complex was geomantically aligned along the north-south axis formed by Mount Li to the south and the former capital city of Yueyang to the north. Here, again, the mausoleum city duplicates the configuration of the E Pang palace, where historical, geomantic, and astronomical considerations played a part in siting and design:

The First Emperor, feeling Xianyang to be overcrowded and the palaces of the former kings too small, declared: "I have heard that King Wen of Zhou had his capital at Feng and King Wu had his capital at Hao, therefore the area between Feng and Hao is a fit location for an imperial capital." And so, construction was begun on an audience hall and palace complex south of the Wei River in the Shanglin Park. First to be built was the front reception hall, E Pang. From east to west it measured 500 *bu* [over 900 meters], from north to south [over 150 meters]. Ten thousand persons could be seated on its upper level, while there was room in its lower level for flagstaffs [over 15 meters] high. An elevated gallery encircled its perimeter, then extended [southward] from the palace in a straight line to Southern Mountain [Nanshan], the summit of

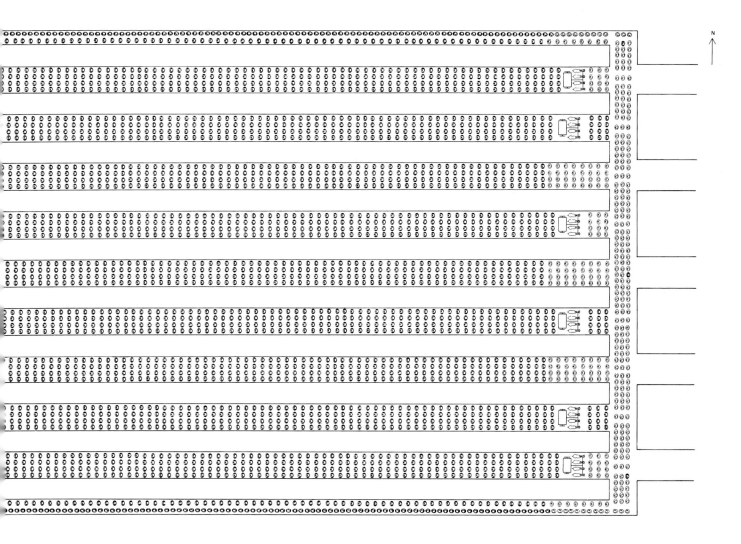

N ↑

which was crowned by a pair of gate towers. A raised thoroughfare also led from the E Pang hall across the Wei linking it with Xianyang [to the north]. Thus [the entire complex] resembled [the configuration of the heavens where] the Celestial Causeway [Gedao] spans the Milky Way joining the Apex of Heaven [Tienji] and the Military Encampment [Yingshi or Shi] constellation. [*Shi Ji*, 6, p. 256]

Another feature of the mausoleum's orientation was its connection with worship of the First Emperor's ancestors by a highway that he ordered built between the mausoleum and the Qin ancestral temple some 50 kilometers to the west. Thus united with his forebears to the west, and anchored between Yueyang and Mount Li to the north and south, only the eastern side remained to be accounted for. There, facing east toward Qin's former enemies stood the First Emperor's bodyguard, sculpted in clay.

The Terracotta Army

Evidence that the area around the First Emperor's tumulus might conceal an entire population of pottery figurines appeared sporadically between 1932 and 1970.

During this time five kneeling figures—probably servants—were discovered at different times inside or near the outer wall of the complex (*Kaogu* 1962/8, pp. 408–11; *Wenwu* 1964/9, pp. 55–56; *Wenwu* 1973/5, pp. 56–67). Ranging from 65 to 78 centimeters in height, each is individually modeled, with head and hands fashioned separately (see Fig. 114).

The kneeling figures thus far discovered have all been found close to the present soil surface and in no discernible pattern, although it has been suggested that they may be attendants accompanying sacrifices to the First Emperor (Thorp, 1979, pp. 119–20). The army of warriors and horses found in 1974, however, was found to have been carefully arranged within several elaborately constructed subterranean chambers. The first of these to have been discovered is located 1,225 meters east of the center of the outer mausoleum wall (Fig. 117). Subsequent excavations have revealed that Pit No. 1 (the Chinese excavators' designation for this underground complex) stretches 210 meters from east to west and 60 meters from north to south. It is estimated to contain some six thousand pottery figures of warriors and horses outfitted with real weapons, chariots, and chariot gear (Fig. 119). Though called a "pit," it is actually a series of eleven parallel trenches or corridors, each measuring

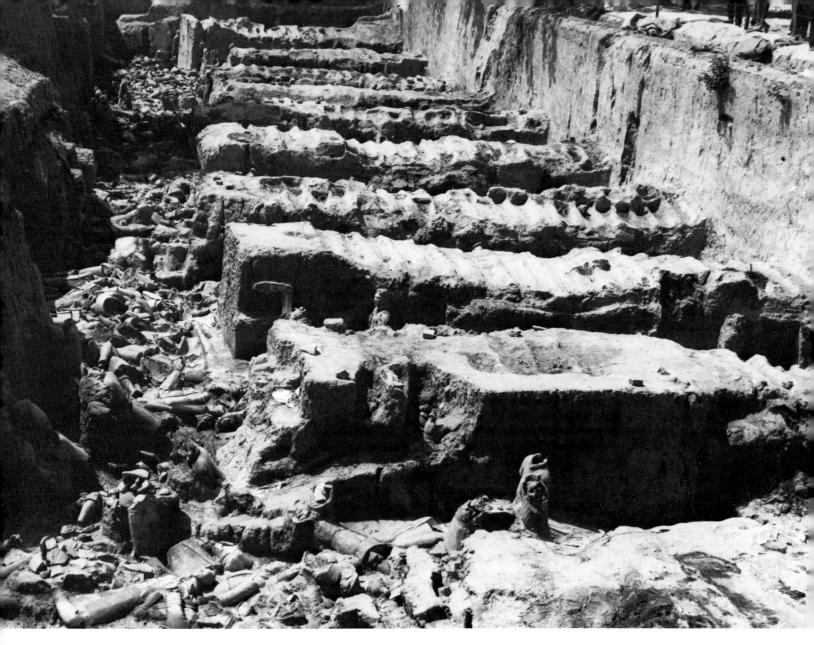

Fig. 120   Eastern end of Pit No. 1, Lintong Xian, Shaanxi Province, looking south, showing
the broad north-south gallery and east-west corridors separated by earthen partitions.
Photograph courtesy of Cultural Relics Bureau, Beijing

about 3 meters wide and over 200 meters long, with broad galleries that run from north to south across the entire width of either end (Fig. 120). The floor, paved in brick, was sunk to a depth of 4.5 meters below Qin soil level. Access was provided by rammed-earth ramps at the east and west ends. Each trench was originally covered by a closely laid roof of thick planks supported by massive wooden pillars and crossbeams that lined each trench, as well as by the earthen walls bordering them. The planks were blanketed by woven fiber mats plastered with clay; the entire network of corridors was then covered by a thick layer of earth. When completed, the interior of each corridor was 3.2 meters high (Fig. 121).

From the amount of soil that filled in these trenches when the ceilings collapsed, the excavators have estimated that there was originally a mound on top of the pit that stood about 2 meters higher than the surrounding soil surface in Qin times. This prominence would have made it an obvious landmark; it is hardly surprising, therefore, that the pit was looted of weapons and burned

not long after it was built. Most likely, the subterranean complex did not outlast the fall of the Qin dynasty in 206 B.C., when the rebel general Xiang Yu is said to have razed the palaces of the Qin capital and desecrated the First Emperor's tomb (*Shi Ji*, 6, p. 275; 7, p. 315; 8, p. 376). Whatever the cause, the pit was filled in and forgotten, preserving intact the entire army of terracotta figures.

From the position of the various figure types and few remaining weapons it is evident that the subterranean complex was designed to accommodate a specific military formation. The wide gallery at the eastern end of Pit No. 1 contains a vanguard unit of unarmored bowmen and crossbowmen, whose long-range weapons would have been the first to be employed in any military engagement (Fig. 119). Behind the vanguard, the formation is subdivided within the eleven long corridors. The narrow outer corridor on either side contains two files of archers; the outer file faces outward, prepared to repulse a surprise attack from the flank, and the inner file faces forward to assist in an assault. Inside these units stands the heart of the army—thirty-six files of infantrymen divided evenly among the nine remaining corridors. All wear armor and carry spears or other close-combat weaponry (e.g., no. 105). Between this body of infantrymen and directly behind the vanguard of bowmen is a specialized unit of six chariots and three unarmored infantry squads. Each chariot, pulled by a team of four life-size pottery horses (Fig. 122), is manned by both a charioteer and a warrior. An advance squad of twelve foot soldiers stands at the front of each chariot. In the three corridors not occupied by a chariot team a squad of thirty-two unarmored spearmen precedes the main body of troops. The rear of the formation is protected by three ranks of armored infantrymen placed at the western end of the pit in the north-south gallery. The last of these faces west as a rearguard. This configuration of warriors follows military prescriptions in such contemporary texts on military strategy as the *Qin hui yao ding bu* and *Liu tao*: "Long-range crossbows in front, halberds behind," "bows are the outer layer, halberds and shields the inner," and "skilled soldiers and strong bows on the flanks" (Dien and Riegel, trans., 1977, p. 100).

In May 1976 a second subterranean complex with warriors (Pit No. 2) was discovered 20 meters to the north of the eastern end of Pit No. 1 (Fig. 123). Whereas Pit No. 1 contains primarily infantrymen, Pit No. 2 holds a smaller complementary force composed largely of chariots and cavalrymen, estimated to number slightly more

than fourteen hundred warriors and horses.

The construction of the second pit is similar to the first; its layout, however, is considerably more complex, reflecting the greater variety of military personnel it contains (nos. 98–104). Four basic units may be distinguished. A projecting rectangular area at the northeast corner of the pit contains a vanguard of archers. It is subdivided into an encircling array of unarmored striding infantrymen (no. 98) and a core of kneeling armored archers (no. 99). The figure of an officer (no. 100), probably the unit commander, once stood at the left rear of the vanguard. Directly behind this advance force are two units composed largely of chariots and cavalrymen. One of these, in which cavalrymen predominate, occupies three northern corridors. The other occupies three considerably longer corridors and is made up primarily of chariot squads, some accompanied by as many as thirty-two infantrymen. The center and right corridors in this unit have four cavalrymen as a rearguard. The left corridor has a large concentration of foot soldiers protecting the rearmost chariot, which is a mobile command post for another officer. The fourth unit, occupying a nearly square area at the southern end of the pit, is divided into eight corridors, each with eight chariots—a total of sixty-four in all.

A smaller, third pit (Pit No. 3) located just to the north of the west end of Pit No. 1 contains only sixty-eight figures. From its position toward the rear of the formation and the large number of "officer" figures found there, it

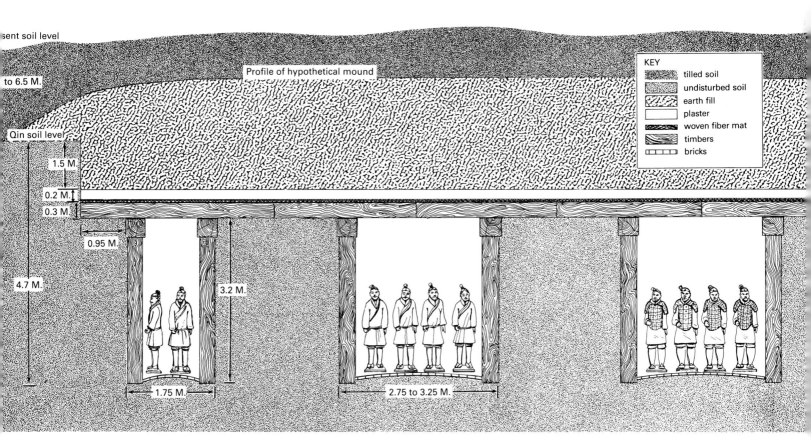

Fig. 121 Cross-sectional view of three corridors of Pit No. 1 showing a tentative reconstruction of their appearance at the time the pit was sealed. Drawing by Phyllis Ward

363

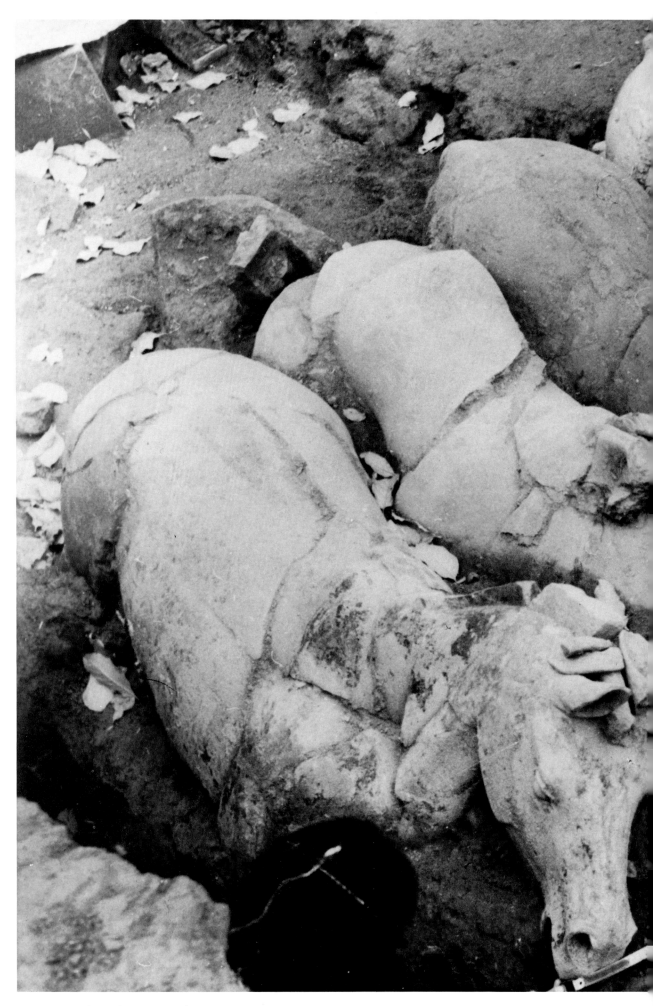

Fig. 122   Four-horse chariot team under excavation in Pit No. 1.
Photograph: Lo Chongmin, Shaanxi Provincial Museum, Xi'an,
Shaanxi Province

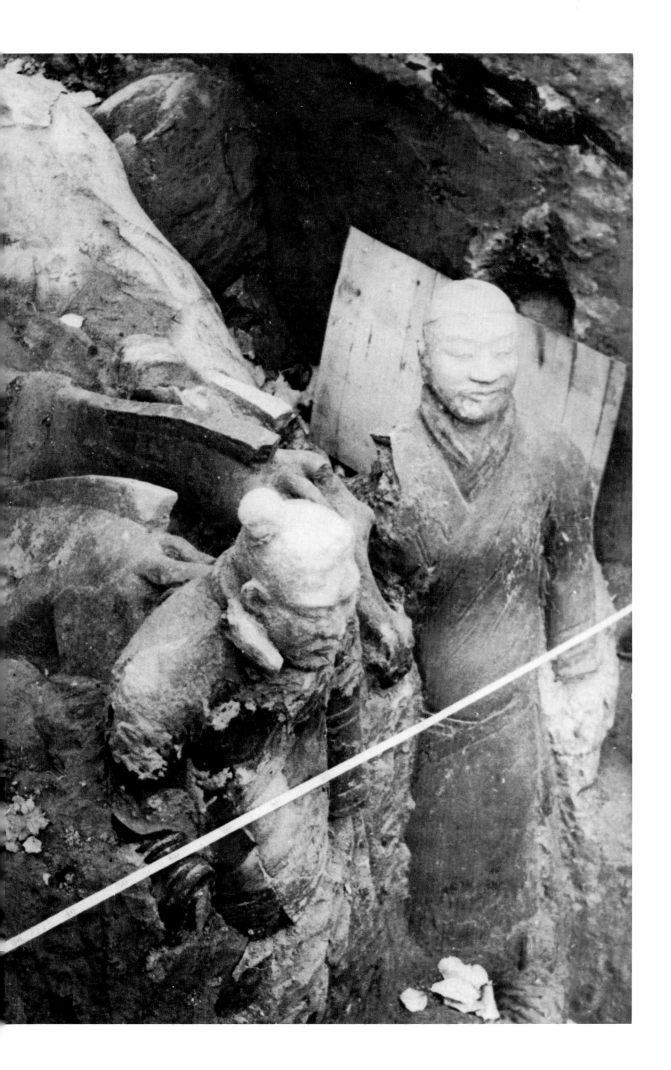

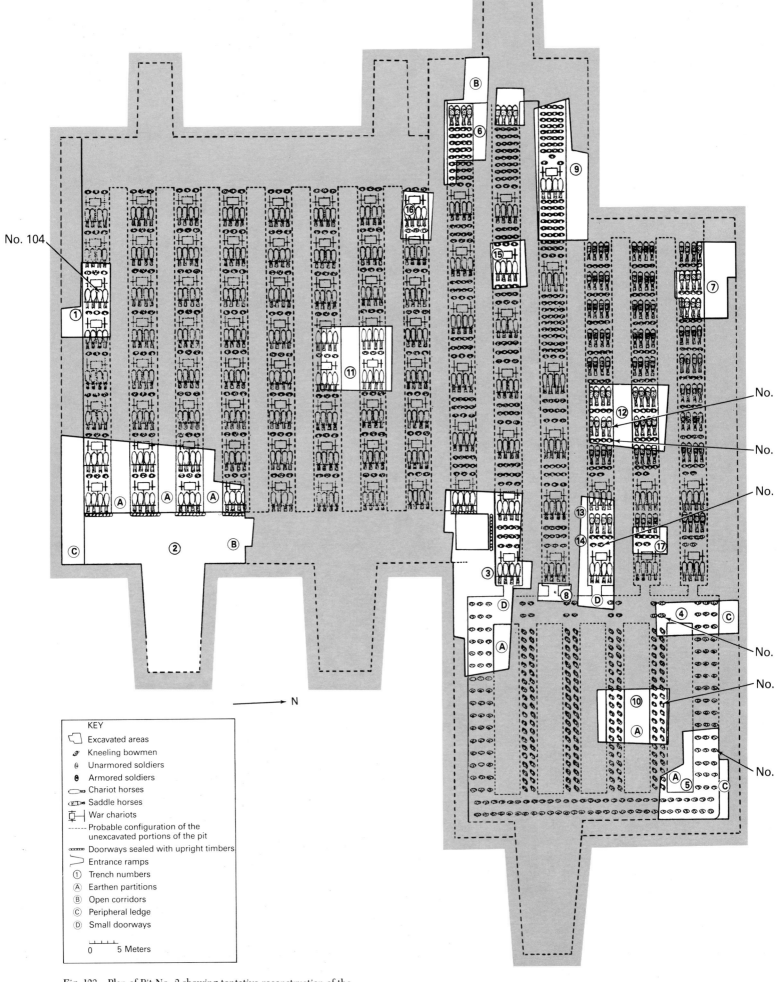

No. 104

No.
No.
No.
No.
No.
No.

N

Fig. 123   Plan of Pit No. 2 showing tentative reconstruction of the
arrangement of terracotta figures and wood chariots. Drawing
by Phyllis Ward after *Wenwu* 1978/5, p. 2, fig. 1

would appear to represent an elite command unit.

A fourth pit, reportedly between Pits 2 and 3, has also been uncovered. Quite empty, it suggests that work on the terracotta army was abandoned before the formation had been completed.

Judging from their various troop types and asymmetrical arrangement it seems logical to assume that Pits 2, 3, and 4 would be balanced by identical units on the south side of the main body of troops represented by Pit No. 1. In that case, vanguard and cavalry units would be in a position to maneuver freely to the front or sides of the less maneuverable chariots and slower moving armored infantrymen held in reserve at the center of the formation for all-out frontal assaults. Test probes have revealed, however, that no such southern pits exist; perhaps the sudden death of the First Emperor and the rapid demise of the dynasty precluded their construction.

The Qin Terracotta Figures as Sculpture

Despite the staggering number of figures required to fill the ranks of this pottery army, warriors and horses were not stamped from molds, but individually modeled. Each body was built up from coils of coarse gray clay, with the hollow torso fully supported by solid columnar legs. Once the desired shape was achieved, the surface was finished with a slip of finer clay. Smaller details—such as elements of armor—were also individually modeled and applied to the surface while the clay was still pliant. Next, the entire assemblage was fired at high temperature and mounted on a prefired base. The hands and heads of the warriors, and the tails and forelocks of horses, were fashioned and fired separately, then attached with clay strips. Finally, each figure was painted in bright colors and fitted with actual weapons or chariot gear.

Arrayed in formation and posed for imperial review, most warriors are shown at attention, their precise stance governed by the kind of weapon they held; others are depicted kneeling or striding, driving a chariot, leading a horse, or poised for hand-to-hand combat. Ordinary foot soldiers range in height from 1.75 to 1.86 meters. Charioteers—such as no. 103, at 1.90 meters—are even taller; the towering commander of the vanguard, no. 100, measures 1.96 meters. For charioteers and officers, height may be a function of rank or importance rather than verisimilitude. This is certainly true for Han two-dimensional figural representations, where important personages are always shown in larger scale than subsidiary characters.

An astounding specificity in uniforms further distinguishes the role of each figure. Excavators have described seven basic types of armor and a wide range of specialized accouterments: caps, belt hooks, leggings, and shoe styles. The varied colors applied to the uniforms may also indicate the several units into which the army was divided. Although the mineral-based pigments applied after firing have largely flaked off, enough has survived to permit archaeologists to present a tentative reconstruction. Among the armored infantrymen in Pit No. 1 (e.g., no. 105), there are at least two color schemes.

One group wore a green robe with lavender patterned collar and cuffs, dark blue trousers, and black shoes tied with red laces; their armor, made of black plates, had white rivets, purple cords, and gold buttons. A second group wore short red coats with pale blue patterned collars and cuffs. Its armor, made of dark brown plates, had red or light green rivets, and orange cords. Faces and hands were painted in flesh tones; eyes were white with black irises; eyebrows, whiskers, and hair were black. The horses were also painted, usually with brown or black for coats, white for hooves and teeth, and red for the insides of ears, nostrils, and mouth.

However gaudy and splendid this spectacle must have been, the individual human quality of the warriors' faces is touchingly personal. Anatomical details are surprisingly lifelike: eyes have been sculpted to give a sense of the eyeballs pressing against the overlying flap of the eyelid; ears have the form of the upper cartilage and earlobe; and even hairstyles show distinct manners of

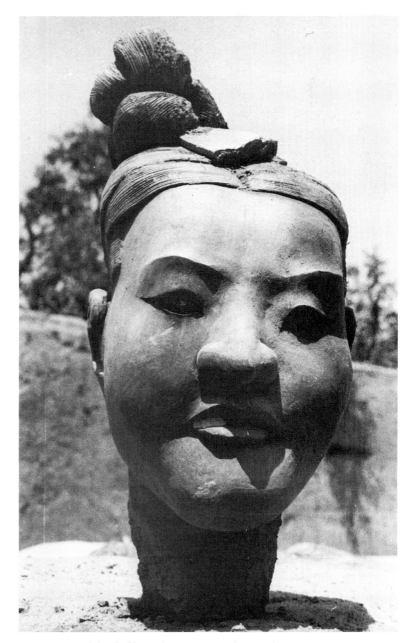

Fig. 124   Detail, head of figure from Pit No. 1. Photograph: Lo Chongmin, Shaanxi Provincial Museum, Xi'an, Shaanxi Province

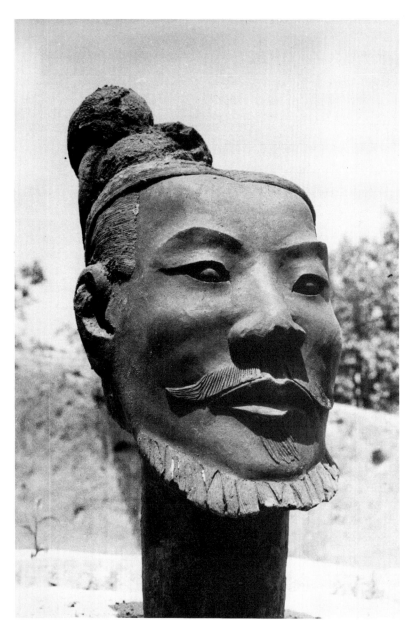

Fig. 125   Detail, head of figure from Pit No. 1. Photograph: Lo Chongmin, Shaanxi Provincial Museum, Xi'an, Shaanxi Province

variations include clean-shaven and full-cheeked visages that appear youthful (Fig. 124) and sharp-nosed, bearded countenances that suggest Central Asian ancestry (Fig. 125). The degree to which such details are used to evoke specific character traits is apparent in the face of the infantry officer (no. 100). Given added prominence by his great height and distinctive uniform, he wears an elaborate coiffure and whiskers that bespeak the dignity of his rank; a furrowed brow testifies to the responsibilities and cares of leadership.

For all their realistic detail the Qin terracotta figures are types rather than portraits. Closer observation reveals that their bodies are not anatomically correct. Heads are attached to the torso by an elongated cylindrical neck. In the same fashion, forearms were frequently telescoped inside the rolled-up sleeves, making the arms appear unnaturally short (e.g., no. 105). Even allowing for the stiff greaves worn by many soldiers, legs are rigid tubes supporting symmetrically arrayed torsos.

The stance of the striding vanguard infantryman (no. 98) represents an attempt to escape this rigid frontality: the head and bent left leg have been turned sideways, imparting a sense of movement; nevertheless, the figure's hips and shoulders remain impossibly frontal. Despite such details as a protruding belly or bent knee, the figure still lacks a sense of the body as a unified organic structure of muscle and bone. The illusion of a contrapposto is more successful in the kneeling bowman from the same vanguard unit (no. 99), where the head, torso, and legs lie in three distinct planes; yet the figure's tubular legs fail to give an impression of the flexed muscles required to maintain the twisted posture.

Despite the representational inaccuracies of the terracotta figures, Qin efforts mark a new level of achievement in naturalistic depiction. Their life-size scale enabled artisans to reproduce garments, hairstyles, and facial features in a comprehensive manner not possible in smaller works. Interestingly, the profusely detailed appearance of the terracotta army reveals the same ardor for minutiae that pervades Qin's precisely defined legal statutes.

The Qin terracotta figures, as the earliest known large-scale sculptures in China, provide new material for the study of Chinese sculptural arts. In addition, they offer graphic illustrations of contemporary treatises on military organization and tactics, giving precise information about battle formations, dress, and armor. Joining an earlier trend in representational accuracy with a new monumentality of scale, these figures reflect developments in the secular arts, arts made expressly for the enjoyment of the living. Their size, variety, and detail may have been further stimulated by the belief that mortuary arts should replicate the world of the living for the dead. By its grandiose conception and thoroughgoing depiction, as well as by the sheer magnitude of its numbers, the pottery army exemplifies the First Emperor's imperial vision, a standard that all later dynasties would strive to emulate.

braiding and of forming topknots (colorplate, detail, no. 99; cf. Fig. 130). So overpowering are the facial expressions, they suggested to the excavators that the First Emperor's entire bodyguard sat for their portraits in lieu of being buried alive. Even if such exacting realism had been intended, most faces do conform to an idealized type that has a high, smooth forehead; crisply molded, angular eyebrows above deep-set eyes; prominent cheekbones; and full nose. By varying hairstyles or applying elegant, trimmed mustaches or chin whiskers, this basic facial type was almost endlessly individualized. Other

CHAPTER 10: CATALOGUE ENTRIES

98 Striding infantryman

Qin dynasty (221–206 B.C.)
Excavated 1976–77 from Trench 5, Pit No. 2, Lintong,
    Shaanxi Province
Height 178 cm. (5 ft. 10 in.)
Shaanxi Provincial Museum

This striding infantryman comes from the leftmost file of warriors in the infantry vanguard of Pit No. 2 (see Fig. 123). From trial digs it is estimated that nearly half of the approximately 252 men in the unit shared this stance. Unlike the vast majority of foot soldiers in the terracotta army that stand in strictly frontal poses, this figure holds an animated stance that recalls a movement in *taijiquan*, the Chinese martial art of shadow boxing. Facing to the side, feet apart, the left arm extended and right arm cocked, the warrior presents a minimal target to oncoming adversaries while keeping his arms ready either to ward off an attacker or to strike a blow. The slight tilt of the head and thrust of the chin heighten the impression of alert readiness implicit in the tensed gesture of the hands and arms. The bent left knee throws the figure's weight forward, adding to the sense of pent-up energy about to be released. Bronze arrowheads found beside these pugilists suggest that they doubled as archers. Unencumbered by heavy suits of armor, such vanguards might be deployed ahead of the main army to observe, harass, or decoy enemy troops prior to any full-scale engagement.

The Qin sculptor's interest in conveying a sense of mass and texture is exemplified by the treatment of this figure's robe, built out at the belly to suggest a heavy fold of drapery overhanging a tightly fastened belt (see Fig. 126). Creases in the material have been made by cutting into the unfired clay surface with a spatula or blade. Other details, such as the belt hook, were fashioned separately from small pieces of clay and were applied to the surface before firing.

PUBLISHED: *Wenwu* 1978/5, pl. 4:2.

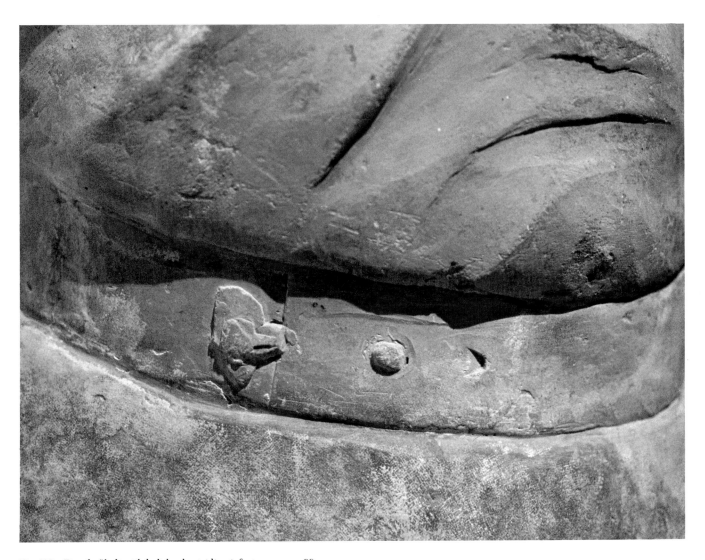

Fig. 126   Detail of belt with belt hook, striding infantryman no. 98.
         Photograph: Maxwell K. Hearn

99 Kneeling archer

Qin dynasty (221–206 B.C.)
Excavated 1976–77 from Trench 10, Pit No. 2, Lintong,
  Shaanxi Province
Height 120 cm. (3 ft. 11 in.)
Shaanxi Provincial Museum

This kneeling archer represents a second figural type belonging to the infantry vanguard of Pit No. 2. An estimated eighty such figures with virtually identical poses are positioned in the four corridors occupying the center of this phalanxlike unit (Fig. 123). In this pose, the right leg is tucked under the body with only the knee and the square toe of the sandal touching the ground. The left leg bends at right angles at the knee with the weight placed squarely on the full surface of the left foot. Although the figure's head and eyes are fixed frontally, the torso is slightly turned to the side, pulled by the two arms, which are flexed as if cradling a bow. Arrowheads, traces of wooden bows, and fragments of swords and scabbards uncovered alongside these infantrymen confirm that they depict archers; some of whom, at least, were also armed with swords.

The trousers, short double-layered robe, and waist-length suit of armor worn by these warriors have been delineated with the utmost care. Note, for example, the armored tunic and epaulettes. Rectangular armor plates—leather or metal in the original—are here arrayed in overlapping rows seemingly fastened together with numerous clay studs that simulate either metal rivets or knotted cords. At the shoulders and curved skirt of the tunic, the plates are strung together by broad laces for added flexibility. A similar lace encircling the neck and secured at the chest by a toggle permitted the collar to be loosened so that it would pass easily over the head.

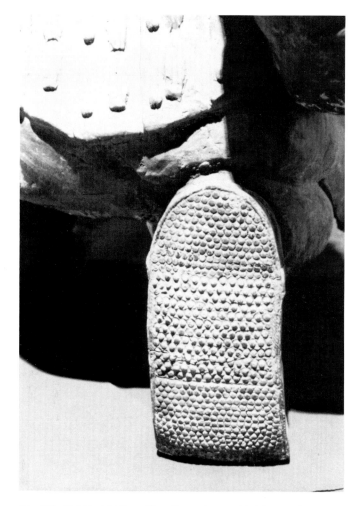

Fig. 127 Detail, right foot of kneeling archer no. 99. Photograph:
  Maxwell K. Hearn

The figure's coiffure is described with the same precision as the uniform. Strands of hair from the temples and back of the head are shown plaited into braids that have, in turn, been wound together with the remaining hair and a piece of decorative cloth to form an elaborate chignon, tied with a cord (see colorplate, detail of hairstyle, no. 99). Traces of red pigment on both this cord and the armor laces, as well as white underpaint on the face, remind us that the realism of such minutely portrayed details was originally further enhanced by the addition of color. Perhaps the most remarkable feature of the exacting portrayal of this figure is not to be found on either the armor tunic or the carefully combed coiffure, but on the sole of the figure's shoe, where even the stippled tread of the sandal has been faithfully reproduced (see Fig. 127).

PUBLISHED: *Wenwu* 1978/5, pl. 4:1; Hong Kong, 1978, no. 37.

100 Infantry officer

Qin dynasty (221–206 B.C.)
Excavated 1976–77 from Trench 4, Pit No. 2, Lintong,
  Shaanxi Province
Height 196 cm. (6 ft. 5 in.)
Shaanxi Provincial Museum

Among the more than two hundred terracotta warriors unearthed from Pit No. 2, two figures are distinguished by their great height, ornate uniforms, and unique poses as commanding officers. One, a chariot-mounted officer, stands at the left rear of the chariot found in Trench 9. The present figure, excavated from Trench 4 at the rear of a corridor of kneeling bowmen, depicts an officer of the infantry vanguard (see Fig. 123). With its furrowed brow, pursed lips, and bony chin set off by side whiskers and goatee, this figure's face captures the dignity and confidence of an experienced military commander. The pyramidlike stance formed by the legs and coupled forearms, once braced by a sword, underscores this impression of authority, projecting an image of unshakable stability. The wide-sleeved double robe and intricate plate-armor tunic are attributes of elevated rank, as is the elaborately folded bonnet secured under the chin by cap strings tied in a flamboyant bow. Smaller bows decorate the front, back, and shoulders of the tunic, which has a waist-length back but hangs down in front in a long tapered apron.

PUBLISHED: *Wenwu* 1978/5, pl. 4:3–5; Hong Kong, 1978, no. 36.

101, 102 Cavalryman and saddle horse

Qin dynasty (221–206 B.C.)
Excavated from Trench 12, Pit No. 2, Lintong, Shaanxi Province
Cavalryman: height 180 cm. (5 ft. 10½ in.)
Saddle horse: height 172 cm. (5 ft. 7½ in.); length 203 cm.
  (6 ft. 7¾ in.)
Shaanxi Provincial Museum

According to Sima Qian, cavalry was first introduced into Zhou China by King Wu Ling of Zhao (reigned 325–299 B.C.). To combat the mounted tribesmen of the steppes threatening the Zhao state's northern frontier, the king ordered his people to practice the nomadic customs of horseback riding and mounted archery, and to replace the long cumbersome Chinese robe with barbarian trousers.

The advent of cavalry revolutionized warfare. During the Shang and most of the Zhou dynasty, chariots were an army's main striking force. The Zhou four-horse chariot was an unwieldy vehi-

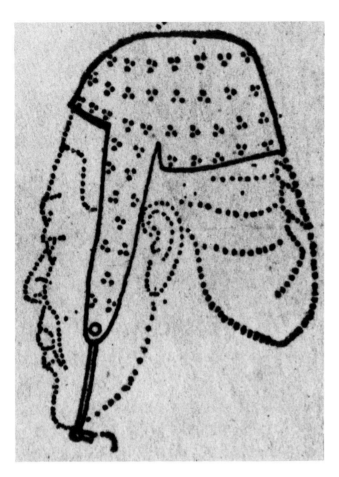

Fig. 128   Drawing of cap worn by cavalrymen like no. 101. After *Wenwu* 1978/5, p. 18, fig. 22:1

cle, however, requiring wide expanses of dry, level ground for its maneuvers, as well as an auxiliary force of infantrymen to protect it from being captured in close-quarter engagements. The cavalry horse was far easier to handle and could be employed in terrain too rugged for wheeled vehicles. Thus, while the chariot remained a symbol of authority and continued to be utilized as a command car, by Han times its role as a tactical weapon had been superseded by the saddle horse. Judging from the almost equal numbers of chariots and cavalrymen in the First Emperor's buried bodyguard, during the Qin dynasty the transformation from chariot-mounted warfare to cavalry was not yet complete. Pit No. 2, for example, contains an estimated 91 chariot teams compared with 116 cavalry troops. Nevertheless, the Qin clearly appreciated the versatility of cavalry. Whereas the chariots in the terracotta army are massed close to the main body of infantrymen, the cavalry troops are deployed in the outside ranks of the formation, a position from which such troops could maneuver freely to the side or rapidly advance to reinforce the infantry vanguard.

The clay cavalrymen stand as if for an imperial review, each rider at attention in front of his mount in ranks of four abreast. The present figure, representative of this figural type, stands with his arms at his sides, the right hand grasping the reins, the left hand half-clenched with the thumb out as if holding a weapon. Since two bronze crossbow trigger mechanisms and the remains of six quivers filled with eighty to one hundred arrows each were discovered in the same trench with this figure, it is likely that he was armed with a crossbow. The figure's uniform is appropriate to his role as horseman. He wears a short robe topped by a brief armor vest, long close-fitting trousers, shoes of stitched leather, and a cap secured by a chin strap. According to the excavation report, such caps were

originally painted reddish brown with a pattern of red dots in groups of three decorating the entire surface (see Fig. 128).

The saddle horse is also at attention, its head erect and legs together, perfectly upright with muscles taut as if awaiting the command to charge into battle. The vitality and animation of the animal almost obscures the remarkable feat of its construction and firing. Weighing well over 230 kilograms, the entire figure was built up of clay coils, the hollow head and torso supported by solid columnar legs. The tail, forelock, and large round plugs located on each flank below the saddle were added later, filling holes that during the firing of the piece served as vents to permit the escape of gas and vapor from the hollow interior. The saddle is fashioned from the same piece of clay as the horse's torso, but it reproduces in detail what must have been leather and metal in the original. Placed atop a saddle blanket and secured by means of a girth and crupper, the saddle is depicted with a seat studded with rivets or knotted cords, a padded pommel and cantle, and even leaf-shaped ornamental flaps and ribbons attached to the sides. There are no stirrups, since that piece of equipage did not become a part of Chinese saddles until after the Han dynasty (see *Wenwu* 1977/10, pp. 27–32).

Originally, each saddle was elaborately painted with red, white, reddish brown, and blue pigments; these have all flaked off the present example. Each horse was also originally equipped with a separate bridle, but only one example, from Trench 14, has been successfully reassembled. This unique bridle has been fitted to the saddle horse in this exhibition. The bronze mouthpiece of the snaffle bit terminates at either end in a ring. These rings ride freely along two S-scroll guides fastened top and bottom to the forward straps of the headstall; two leaf-shaped pendants, one suspended from each bit ring, connect the bit with the reins. Both the headstall and reins are fashioned of bronze wire strung with cylindrical and prismatic stone beads. The reins terminate in bronze hand rings that imitate leather, suggesting that the bridles worn by the terracotta horses were specially crafted from imperishable materials so that they might survive underground forever.

PUBLISHED: Cavalryman in *Wenwu* 1978/5, pl. 3:4; saddle horse unpublished.

103   Charioteer

Qin dynasty (221–206 B.C.)
Excavated 1976–77 from Trench 13, Pit No. 2, Lintong,
   Shaanxi Province
Height 190 cm. (6 ft. 2½ in.)
Shaanxi Provincial Museum

Charioteering was one of the six arts practiced by the aristocratic class in Zhou China. Although Qin laws sought to replace hereditary distinctions with a hierarchy of ranks based on military merit, the imposing stature of this charioteer suggests that the status of chariot-mounted warriors, as might be expected, continued to be higher than that of ordinary foot soldiers. The driver's distinctive bonnet and cap strings, although less elaborate than the headgear of the infantry officer no. 100, further imply elevated rank. The charioteer's uniform, which includes a long robe topped by an armored vest, with broad leggings or greaves and square-toed sandals, is considerably lighter than the suits of other charioteers. A driver found in Trench 1, for example, is protected by thigh-length armor fitted with a high collar, and armor plating that entirely covers his outstretched arms and fists (*Wenwu* 1978/5, pl. 3:1). The charioteer's function is unmistakably defined by his pose: both arms extended toward the front, the fists half-clasped as if grasping reins, thumbs slightly raised, the index and middle fingers separated to control the leather harness straps, which the driver originally held.

Although Pit No. 2 has not been fully excavated, it is estimated that it contains ninety-one chariots, each drawn by four terracotta horses and manned by a driver, one or two armed riders, and in some cases from eight to thirty-two infantrymen. The present charioteer belongs to one of the teams located immediately behind the infantry vanguard (Fig. 123); he is accompanied by one chariot-mounted warrior (*Wenwu* 1978/5, pl. 3:3). Unlike those of Pit No. 1, both the drivers and riders in Pit No. 2 were positioned behind rather than inside of their wooden chariots. Although the wooden chariots have been largely destroyed by fire or decay, enough has survived to give a general idea of the appearance of the Qin war carriage. The chariot body is almost square, 130 to 150 centimeters wide and 120 centimeters from front to rear. A grillwork balustrade 30 centimeters high encloses the front, sides, and part of the rear. The carriage box, which has a thin plank floor, sits atop the crossing of the shaft and axletree; the two wheels have a diameter of 180 centimeters. The four-horse team is connected to the single shaft by a crossbar, to which inverted V-shaped yokes are mounted for the two inner horses, with the two outer horses harnessed to leather traces.

Unpublished.

104 Chariot horse

Qin dynasty (221–206 B.C.)
Excavated 1976–77 from Trench 1, Pit No. 2, Lintong,
   Shaanxi Province
Height 171 cm. (5 ft. 7 in.); length 226 cm. (7 ft. 4¾ in.)
Museum of Qin Figures, Lintong, Shaanxi Province

This example of a Qin chariot horse belongs to the same stocky breed as the terracotta saddle horse no. 102. Of the same height, both horses are characterized by compact bodies, short legs, and broad necks. Despite generic similarities, however, the distinct characters and functions of the two animals are both immediately apparent from their profiles and details of grooming. While the cavalry horse stands erect, the chariot horse strains forward against the reins, giving an impression of bridled power, which is heightened by the taut, angular muscles of his head, the bared teeth, the curled lips, and forward cant of the ears. The tail of the chariot horse, tied up to keep it clear of the harness traces, contrasts with the long, plaited tail of the saddle horse. The original full complement of harness trappings included a yoke, leather reins, and ornamental bridle.

Unpublished.

Fig. 129 Detail of sandals and puttees, armored infantryman no. 105.
   Photograph: Maxwell K. Hearn

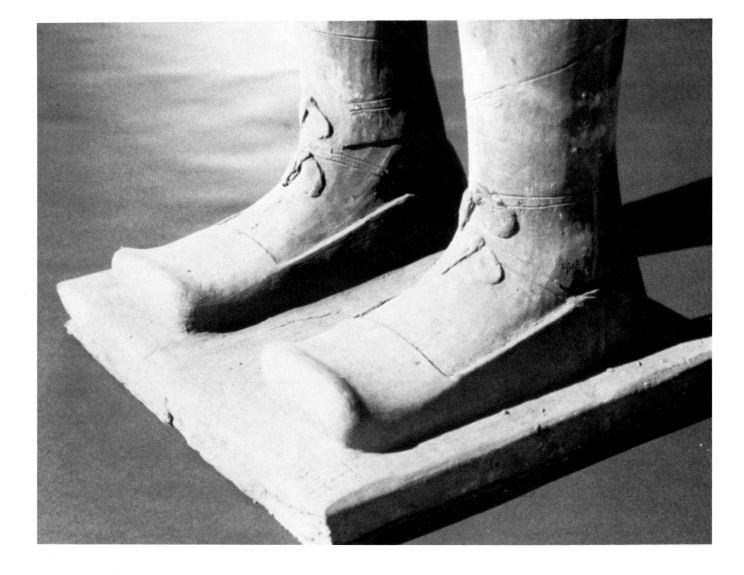

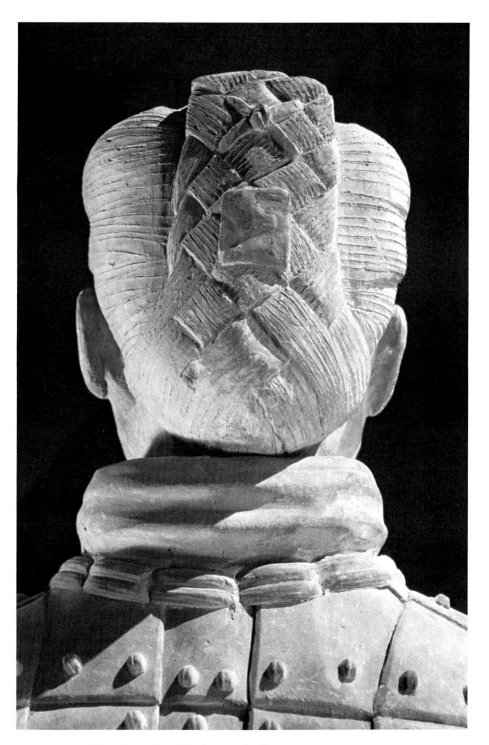

Fig. 130   Detail of coiffure at back of head, armored infantryman
no. 105. Photograph: Maxwell K. Hearn

105   Armored infantryman

Qin dynasty (221–206 B.C.)
Excavated 1974–78 from Pit No. 1, Lintong, Shaanxi Province
Height 183 cm. (6 ft.)
Museum of Qin Figures, Lintong, Shaanxi Province

The vast majority of soldiers in the terracotta army are armored
infantrymen like this foot soldier from Pit No. 1. Judging from the
extended right forearm and its half-clenched fist, this figural type
once held actual spears. A robe topped by an armored tunic,
puttees, and square-toed sandals tied with a cord (Fig. 129) complete the costume of the basic type. In spite of their uniformity in
pose and dress, these pottery figures were not moldmade but
individually sculpted, often with great sensitivity and particularity.

For example, while most warriors from Pit No. 1 have their hair tied
in a bun at the top of the head (colorplate, detail, no. 99), this figure
is depicted with the hair combed into six strands plaited in a flat
braid at the back of the head, where it is secured with a crisscrossed
cord and a square patch of ornament (Fig. 130). The idealized canon
of beauty epitomized by the face recalls the similarly perfected
features of the gilt-bronze lamp in the form of a female servant from
the tomb of Princess Dou Wan (died after 103 B.C.; see no. 94). The
shared preference for smoothly tapering cheeks and chin, deep-set
eyes, crisp, angular eyebrows, and stepped-back hairline along the
temples reveals a remarkable continuity in aesthetic sensibilities
between the artisans working at the mausoleum of the First Emperor and later sculptors of the Han imperial palace.

Unpublished.

Summary of Comments on the Catalogue from the Committee for the Preparation of Exhibitions of Archaeological Relics, People's Republic of China

When the manuscript of the present catalogue was finished, it was sent to Beijing, where it was translated into Chinese, then read and checked for accuracy by the scholars of the Committee for the Preparation of Exhibitions of Archaeological Relics. Since the Committee's comments on the manuscript were received when the catalogue was already in galley proof, only the most essential changes were made. Some of the questions raised in connection with chapters 1 through 9, however, concern alternative interpretations preferred by Chinese scholars, whose methods and approaches sometimes differ from those of Western art historians. It seems appropriate here to summarize and translate in full some of the relevant comments.

The alternative views expressed by the Committee have in some cases already been expressed in the essay by Ma Chengyuan (see above, "The Splendor of Ancient Chinese Bronzes"). For instance, evidence hinting at the possible use of metal in China long before 2000 B.C., the conservative figure given in chapter 1, is reviewed in his essay. The interpretation given there of the bronze designs and of their sequence also differs from that proposed in chapters 1 and 2.

The Committee would have preferred more literal adherence to terminology current in Chinese archaeological publications. The eras referred to in chapters 1 through 4 as the Erlitou phase, the Zhengzhou phase, and the Anyang period are by Chinese archaeologists called the Erlitou culture period, the Erligang period, and the Yinxu period (the last term, strictly archaeological in definition, does not attempt a correlation between the Yinxu-period strata at Anyang and the historical Anyang period). The titles of chapters 1 through 4 have been modified to incorporate these terms.

In chapter 1, the Committee objected to the attempt to relate the bronze decoration to the Shang founder's casting method: "Symmetry and continuity are the most fundamental principles of design and have little connection with the technique of casting in pottery molds. As long as the art follows the standards of design, symmetry is inevitable. On cylindrical shapes, symmetrical patterns are made up of identical design units. The principle of continuity is similar and is often encountered on bronze vessels. In the section-mold method, the designs are carved in the mold. The artist can carve any design he wishes on the mold, and in this respect is not restricted in any way. Symmetrical designs can be seen on both pottery and jades from Erlitou. Neither pottery nor jade is made with molds, and, moreover, the history of carving symmetrical designs in jade must go back far earlier than the decoration of bronzes." In this connection, the Committee noted further that the Erlitou site has yielded a bronze *ge* blade with a zoomorphic design and inlaid with turquoise.

In connection with the remarks in chapter 2 dealing with the greater power and extent of the Shang state in the Zhengzhou phase as compared with the succeeding Anyang period, the Committee stressed that, whatever the political situation may have been, the material culture of the later period was certainly advanced: "History records that before Pan Geng moved to Yin [Anyang], the fortunes of the Shang royal house varied, and that they continued to fluctuate during the Yinxu period. But, from the point of view of the political organization of the slave society and the overall growth of the economy, the material culture of the Yinxu period reveals the extraordinarily high development of China's slave system."

The Committee also had reservations about a few points in the discussion of metalworking techniques given in chapter 2. In connection with the chapter's assertion that the basic casting techniques used prior to Eastern Zhou times underwent little change during the millennium following the Zhengzhou phase, the Committee stressed instead a continuous growth of technology: "History does not stagnate but continues to advance unbroken within its possibilities." The chapter's statement that until Eastern Zhou the bronze decoration was made almost exclusively by casting was qualified by the Committee, which mentioned again the existence of turquoise-inlaid weapons. The Committee also questioned the mention of the use of solder in attaching appendages to certain bronze vessels, a technique whose use has been suggested only in recent years by technical studies carried out in the West.

More fundamental was the doubt expressed about the evolution of the bronze designs outlined in chapter 2: "This kind of 'the earliest' approach is rather one-sided. It is based on the principle that most things develop from simple to complex. In reality, this [*taotie*] is a kind of simplified animal face. There were several different kinds of simplified animal faces used in the early Shang period, some with and some without eyes. This type of design with only two eyes is known from early to late Shang, and even in early Western Zhou." This interpretation of the *taotie* as an animal face is given more fully in Ma Chengyuan's essay above.

In chapter 3 the Committee called into question the interpretive framework used to treat the topic of provincial bronzes. Several statements made in the first paragraph of that chapter were singled out for special attention: "Regional bronze-using cultures . . . in time became recognizably distinct from the civilization centered on the Shang court. Very little is known at present about these advanced local cultures of Shang times. . . . The wide spectrum of styles encountered in provincial regions must in part reflect the varying strength of the political bond between the Shang court and each local center of power." The Committee wrote: "Note the contradictions in the phrases 'recognizably distinct,' 'very little is known at present,' and 'the wide spectrum of styles.' We consider that, in general, no such variation exists, and that the excavated bronzes prove this point. But, if we speak of 'bronze-using cultures,' then local characteristics do exist. 'Cultural influences' and 'political bonds' are disparate concepts; if there is not evidence enough to substantiate it, the connection spoken of in the text is best not mentioned. The chapter goes on to say: 'The stylistic distinction between metropolitan and non-metropolitan is not always so easily made. . . .' This clearly reveals that use of the phrase 'recognizably distinct' is unjustified."

Both in chapter 2 and chapter 3, the Committee questioned the dating of the Pinggu Xian grave (see no. 12) to a time transitional between the Zhengzhou phase (Erligang period) and the Anyang period, preferring to follow the excavation report in assigning this find to the early Yinxu period. The unresolved problem of correlating the archaeologically defined "Yinxu strata" with the historically defined Anyang period gave rise in part to the disagreement in chapter 3. The Committee wrote: "The so-called gap between Zhengzhou and Anyang does not exist in archaeological stratification. Upper Erligang strata contain typical Yinxu remains, while at Meiyuan, Yinxu, strata of Erligang type have been discovered. Relatively few bronzes from this period have been found, but Chinese archaeologists do not believe that there is a gap. The earliest burials from the Yinxu period often contain bronzes in the Erligang style and also later ones, thus indicating that there is no gap."

The Committee adopted a cautious position with respect to the attempt made in chapter 3 to characterize in stylistic terms a local bronze industry in the Yangzi River valley. The chronology of southern bronzes was viewed rather differently from the chapter; instead of a continuous growth from beginnings in the Zhengzhou phase, represented at Panlongcheng, to more advanced bronzes stretching through the Anyang period, the Committee regarded the bronzes found in Hunan as an iso-lated group dating as a whole to the middle of the Anyang period: "At present the nature of the Shang bronzes from Hunan remains difficult to determine: one sort was produced locally, another was imported. Unfortunately, most of these bronzes were not excavated scientifically but were found by chance. So far archaeological workers at the find sites have not encountered any sign pointing to burials. Some assume the finds to be caches. The bronzes far excel most Anyang finds in quality. Because of this, Chinese scholars have adopted a suspicious attitude toward the origins of these bronzes. To date, no trace of the casting of such vessels has been found in Hunan. Indeed, to the contrary, inscriptions like those on the Ge *you* (no. 25) and the Da He *fang ding* from Ningxiang Xian can also be seen on bronzes from the Central Plain. The Ge clan was a major clan in the late Shang and early Western Zhou periods—especially the late Shang—which confirms the origin of these two bronzes. Incidentally, no bronzes comparable to those of the early Shang [i.e., pre-Anyang] period have been found in Hunan, nor have bronzes from the early Yinxu period (before Wu Ding) been found there. A large number of bronzes appear suddenly from about the middle Yinxu period; moreover, none date later than the end of the Shang period. This phenomenon of no predecessors and no descendants deserves serious thought. Given the uncertain sources of these bronzes, to take the discoveries made to date as the basis for a definition of a 'southern' style is neither appropriate nor founded on solid evidence."

In a last comment on chapter 3 the Committee said that the form of the *hu* from Suide Xian, no. 22, "is not really unusual," adding that similar vessels have been found at many places in the Central Plain.

In chapter 5 the Committee objected to the characterization of the Western Zhou state of Yan as remote and of limited importance: "The enfeoffment of Yan stemmed from military considerations, as it played a strategic role in Western Zhou communications with the north and northeast and was also a buffer for the Zhou royal house. It is wrong to say that it was unimportant. In the last thirty years the [ancient] Yan territory has yielded many bronzes, more in fact than any other feudal state, confirming the strength of the rulers of Yan and their vassals."

In connection with the bell no. 58, which the catalogue text seeks to connect with southern bronzes on stylistic grounds, the Committee noted: "The text seems to want to explain the tiger as a southern style of decorative motif; the same point was suggested in chapter 3. In fact, tigers cannot be considered uncommon on typical Shang bronzes, and among jades from Yinxu there are similar sculptures of tigers. To infer from this one point that a certain motif appeared in the south or in the north is perhaps too farfetched."

With regard to the influence of steppe art on North China discussed in chapter 7 in connection with the Houma/Liyu bronzes, the Committee commented: "We must proceed with a concrete analysis of verified facts. Animal designs in either two or three dimensions always played a central role in the decoration of bronzes from the

Shang and Zhou periods; under no circumstances could the dragons on the Sanmenxia *fang jian* (no. 75) be considered to have any connection whatsoever with nomadic art. This sort of decoration is also common on bronzes from South China. Thorough analysis must therefore be required to show [which] animal designs were derived from steppe art. As for the technique of gold and silver inlay, the assertion of a connection with West Asia is also without foundation. The technique of silver inlay was very popular both in Shang and Zhou, as shown not only by bronze vessels but also by articles of lacquer and wood; some chariots still retain much silver inlay. Silver inlay may thus be regarded as an artistic technique special to China. The gold and silver inlay that emerged during the Spring and Autumn period indeed constitutes a new development in artistic technique that arose from a moribund tradition of cast decoration and that had its foundations in China. Moreover, the inlay technique in China is quite individual. Thus, there is no basis for the claim that the silver inlay technique in China originated in the West. [The same points were reviewed in a further comment on the discussion of inlay technique that appears in chapter 8: "This view is unacceptable."] Also doubtful is the view that the so-called hunting-style motifs reflect steppe cultural influences, since it is clearly recorded in history that hunting was a major ritual and sport of the Chinese emperors and lords."

As to the nomadic origins of the rules of Zhongshan proposed by some Chinese scholars and discussed in chapter 8, the Committee stated: "The Zhongshan state of the Warring States period was reestablished by royal Zhou descendants within the territory occupied by the Di. From the long inscriptions executed on the bronze vessels from the tomb [Tomb No. 1], we can see that this ruler was an ardent Confucian: the language of the inscription is classical and sophisticated, and there is nothing 'barbarian' about it. Although among the artifacts there are some having Di characteristics, the greater number are objects from the most classical and best of Central Plains traditions."

With respect to the discussion of the Dian culture of Shizhaishan in chapter 9, the Committee stated: "The excavated tombs of the Dian tribe at Shizhaishan clearly show Chu influence, as demonstrated by innumerable artifacts from these tombs. It is equally clear that the Dian culture is a local culture, but there is as yet no material evidence to enable us to speculate on the relationship between the Dian culture and its Southeast Asian neighbors."

In connection with the *zun* from Hunan (no. 66), the Committee stated that the "misinterpretation of snakes in bronze decoration as silkworms" originated with Rong Geng's *Shang Zhou yiqi tongkao* (Rong, 1941), and went on to observe: "The eyes of silkworms are so totally degenerate that silkworms appear to have no eyes at all. But the snakes of the *zun* all have eyes, a clear indication that they are not meant to represent silkworms. Furthermore, carved jade examples of silkworms from the Shang and Zhou periods are depicted without eyes, like their real-life counterparts. Hence, snake and silkworm motifs should not be confused."

Glossary

安徽 Anhui
安陽 Anyang
隞 Ao

巴 Ba
　 Baijiazhuang
班固 Ban Gu
班殷 Ban *gui*
半坡 Banpo
保德縣 Baode Xian
寶雞鬥鷄臺戴家溝 Baoji Doujitai Daijiagou
寶雞茹家莊 Baoji Rujiazhuang
北辰 *beichen*
北京 Beijing
編鐘 *bianzhong*
柄 *bing*
辟雍 Biyong
鎛 *bo*
亳 Bo
博山爐 *boshan lu*

蔡侯 Cai Hou (marquis of Cai)
長安普渡村 Chang'an Puducun
常寧縣 Changning Xian
長沙馬王堆 Changsha Mawangdui
長興縣 Changxing Xian
長信宮 Changxin palace
長治 Changzhi
臣辰卣，殷 Chen Chen *you*, *gui*
成都 Chengdu
成王 Cheng Wang
成周 Cheng Zhou
陳侯 Chen Hou (marquis of Chen)
崇陽縣 Chongyang Xian
楚 Chu
臀 Cuo

大豐殷 Da Feng *gui*
軑侯 Dai Hou (marquis of Dai)
大克鼎 Da Ke *ding*
石 *dan*

亶父 Danfu
大司空村 Dasikongcun
大汶口 Dawenkou
大冶銅綠山 Daye Tonglüshan
大盂鼎 Da Yu *ding*
德殷 De *gui*
登封王城崗 Dengfeng Wangchenggang
德性 *de xing*
狄 Di
滇 Dian
鼎 *ding*
定王 Ding Wang
帝辛 Di Xin
帝乙 Di Yi
東鄉縣 Dongxiang Xian
豆 *dou*
竇太后 Dou (empress dowager)
竇綰 Dou Wan
端方 Duan Fang
敦 *dui*
自承卣 Dui Cheng *you*
杜嶺 Duling

阿房宮 E Pang palace
二層臺 *ercengtai*
二里崗 Erligang
二里頭 Erlitou

方 *fang*
房山琉璃河黃土坡村 Fangshan Liulihe Huangtupocun
肥城 Feicheng
肥西縣 Feixi Xian
豐 Feng
風胡子 Feng Hu Zi
封建 *fengjian*
鳳翔縣 Fengxiang Xian
汾水嶺 Fenshuiling
缶 *fou*
簠 *fu*
夫差 Fuchai
扶風莊白 Fufeng Zhuangbo

復古	*fugu*	輝縣固圍村	Hui Xian Guweicun
婦好	Fu Hao	湖南	Hunan
福建	Fujian	渾源李峪	Hunyuan Liyu
涪陵縣	Fuling Xian		
阜南縣	Funan Xian	斝	*jia*
阜陽縣	Fuyang Xian	鑑	*jian*
		講解員	*jiangjie yuan*
贛江	Gan River	江陵望山	Jiangling Wangshan
甘肅	Gansu	江川李家山	Jiangquan Lijiashan
藁城臺西村	Gaocheng Taixicun	江蘇	Jiangsu
高至喜	Gao Zhixi	江西	Jiangxi
戈	*ge*	姜寨	Jiangzhai
恭城縣	Gongcheng Xian	見卣、尊	Jian *you, zun*
勾踐	Gou Jian	胶縣三里河	Jiao Xian Sanlihe
觚	*gu*	嘉山縣	Jiashan Xian
關東	*guandong*	嘉祐	Jia You
觥	*guang*	桀	Jie
廣東	Guangdong	集古錄	*Ji gu lu*
廣西	Guangxi	季歷	Jili
廣州	Guangzhou	禁	*jin*
關內	*guannei*	晉	Jin
殷	*gui*	金村	Jincun
珪	*gui* (jade)	涇河	Jing River
鬼方	Guifang	京山縣	Jingshan Xian
鯀	Gun	涇陽高家堡	Jingyang Gaojiabao
椁	*guo*	金人	*jin ren*
虢大子	Guo Da Zi (crown prince of Guo)	金石學	*jinshi xue*
郭沫若	Guo Moruo	金文叢考	*Jinwen congkao*
		爵	*jue*
韓	Han	康侯	Kang Hou
漢朝	Han dynasty	康王	Kang Wang
夯土	*hangtu*	考工記	*Kaogongji*
漢水	Han River	考古圖	*Kaogu tu*
漢書	*Han Shu*	考古研究所	Kaogu Yanjiu Suo
鎬	Hao	喀左北洞村	Kezuo Beidongcun
盉	*he*	喀左馬廠溝	Kezuo Machanggou
河北	Hebei	喀左山灣子	Kezuo Shanwanzi
㵡伯	He Bo (earl of He)	夔	*kui*
河南	Henan		
衡山	Hengshan	罍	*lei*
後岡	Hougang	雷紋	*leiwen*
侯馬上馬村	Houma Shangmacun	鬲	*li* (vessel type)
厚葬	*houzang*	禮	*li*
壺	*hu*	奩	*lian*
淮河	Huai River	遼寧	Liaoning
齊桓公	Huan Gong (duke of Qi)	鬲鼎	*li ding*
黃坡盤龍城李家咀	Huangpi Panlongcheng Lijiazui	李濟	Li Ji
洹水	Huan River	李家咀	Lijiazui
湖北	Hubei	醴陵	Liling
晉惠公	Hui Gong (duke of Jin)	鑫	*ling*
回紋	*huiwen*	靈寶縣	Lingbao Xian

陰陽	*yinyang*	昭王	Zhao Wang	
伊河	Yi River	柞鐘	Zha *zhong*	
懿王	Yi Wang	浙江	Zhejiang	
雍	Yong	政王	Zheng Wang	
永和縣	Yonghe Xian	鄭振鐸	Zheng Zhenduo	
雍門	Yongmen	鄭州	Zhengzhou	
卣	*you*	觶	*zhi*	
幽王	You Wang	旨	Zhi	
盂	*yu*	鐘	*zhong*	
禹	Yu	中國科學院	Zhongguo Kexue Yuan	
元朝	Yuan dynasty	中山	Zhongshan	
元氏縣	Yuanshi Xian	周朝	Zhou dynasty	
鉞	*yue*	周方伯	Zhou Fang Bo	
越	Yue	周公	Zhou Gong (duke of Zhou)	
櫟陽	Yueyang	周原	Zhou Yuan	
禹貢	*Yu Gong*	楚莊王	Zhuang Wang (king of Chu)	
雲夢	Yunmeng	諸侯	*zhuhou*	
雲南	Yunnan	株州	Zhuzhou	
		紫荊山	Zijingshan	
		資料	*ziliao*	
棗陽縣	Zaoyang Xian	琮	*zong*	
曾	Zeng	宗法	*zongfa*	
璋	*zhang*	宗周	Zong Zhou	
趙	Zhao	祖甲	Zu Jia	
朝歌	Zhaoge	尊	*zun*	
昭穆	*zhaomu*	左傳	*Zuo Zhuan*	

Bibliography

A. *Key to Shortened References*

Akiyama, 1968
Akiyama Terukazu et al. *Arts of China, Neolithic Cultures to the T'ang Dynasty: Recent Discoveries*. Tokyo: Kodansha, 1968.

Bagley, 1977
Bagley, Robert W. "P'an-lung-ch'eng: A Shang City in Hupei." *Artibus Asiae* 39 (1977), nos. 3/4, pp. 165–219.

Beijing, 1956a
Shou Xian Cai hou mu chutu yiwu [Remains unearthed from the tomb of the marquis of Cai in Shou Xian]. Beijing: Science Press, 1956.

Beijing, 1956b
Hui Xian fajue baogao [Report on excavations in Hui Xian]. Beijing: Science Press, 1956.

Beijing, 1958
Wu sheng chutu zhongyao wenwu zhanlan tulu [Illustrated catalogue of important cultural relics unearthed in five provinces]. Beijing: Wenwu Press, 1958.

Beijing, 1959a
Yunnan Jinning Shizhaishan gumu qun fajue baogao [Excavation report on a group of ancient tombs at Shizhaishan, Jinning, Yunnan Province]. 2 vols. Beijing: Wenwu Press, 1959.

Beijing, 1959b
Shangcunling Guoguo mudi [The Cemetery of the state of Guo at Shancunling]. Beijing: Science Press, 1959.

Beijing, 1960
Shaanxi sheng bowuguan, Shaanxi sheng wenwu guanli weiyuanhui cang qingtongqi tushi [Illustrations of bronzes in the collections of the Shaanxi Provincial Museum and the Shaanxi Province Committee for the administration of cultural relics]. Beijing: Wenwu Press, 1960.

Beijing, 1961
Xin Zhongguo di kaogu shouhuo [Archaeological harvest of New China]. Beijing: Wenwu Press, 1961.

Beijing, 1963
Jiangsu sheng chutu wenwu xuanji [A Selection of cultural relics unearthed in Jiangsu Province]. Beijing: Wenwu Press, 1963.

Beijing, 1972a
Xin Zhongguo chutu wenwu (Historical Relics Unearthed in New China). Beijing: Foreign Languages Press, 1972.

Beijing, 1972b
Wenhua da geming qijian chutu wenwu, di yi ji [Cultural relics unearthed during the Great Cultural Revolution, vol. 1]. Beijing: Wenwu Press, 1972.

Beijing, 1972c
Changsha Mawangdui yihao Han mu fajue jianbao [A Brief

report on the excavation of Han Tomb No. 1 at Mawangdui, Changsha]. Beijing: Wenwu Press, 1972.

Beijing, 1973
Changsha Mawangdui yi hao Han mu [Han Tomb No. 1 at Mawangdui, Changsha]. 2 vols. Beijing: Wenwu Press, 1973.

Beijing, 1976a
Zhongguo gu qingtongqi xuan [A Selection of ancient Chinese bronzes]. Beijing: Wenwu Press, 1976.

Beijing, 1976b
Zhonghua renmin gongheguo chutu wenwu xuan (A Selection of Archaeological Finds of the People's Republic of China). Beijing: Wenwu Press, 1976.

Beijing, 1978a
Guangxi chutu wenwu [Cultural relics unearthed in Guangxi]. Beijing: Wenwu Press, 1978.

Beijing, 1978b
Mancheng Han mu [The Han tombs at Mancheng]. Beijing: Wenwu Press, 1978.

Bishop, 1927
Bishop, Carl W. "The Bronzes of Hsin-cheng Hsien." *The Smithsonian Report for 1926*, pp. 457–68. Washington, D.C.: The Smithsonian Institution, 1927.

Bodde, 1967
Bodde, Derk. *China's First Unifier: A Study of the Ch'in Dynasty as Seen in the Life of Li Ssu (280?–208 B.C.)*. Repr. ed. Hong Kong: Hong Kong University Press, 1967.

Bunker, 1970
Bunker, Emma C.; Chatwin, C. Bruce; and Farkas, Ann R. *"Animal Style" Art from East to West*. New York: The Asia Society, 1970.

Chang, 1977
Chang, Kwang-chih. *The Archaeology of Ancient China*. 3rd rev. ed. New Haven: Yale University Press, 1977.

Changsha, 1964
Hunan sheng wenwu tulu [An Illustrated catalogue of cultural relics from Hunan]. Changsha, 1964.

Chavannes, 1895–1905
Chavannes, Edouard. *Les Mémoires historiques de Sse-ma Ts'ien*. 5 vols. Paris: Ernest Leroux, 1895–1905.

Chen, 1955–56
Chen Mengjia. "Xi Zhou tongqi duandai" [Dating Western Zhou bronzes]. *Kaogu Xuebao* 1955–56/9–11.

Chen, 1977
Chen Mengjia. *In Shū seidōki bunrui zuroku (A Corpus of Chinese Bronzes in American Collections)*. 2 vols. Tokyo: Kyūko Shoin, 1977. Japanese redaction of *Mei diguo zhuyi*

jieliao di wo guo Yin Zhou tongqi jilu, published anonymously by the Academia Sinica; Beijing: Science Press, 1962.

Cheng, 1963
Cheng Te-k'un. *Chou China*. Archaeology in China, vol. 3. Cambridge: W. Heffer & Sons, 1963.

Dien, trans. 1977–78
Dien, Albert E., trans., "First Report on the Exploratory Excavations of the Ch'in Pit of Pottery Figures at Lin-t'ung *hsien," Chinese Sociology and Anthropology* 10, no. 2 (Winter, 1977/78), pp. 3–50. A complete translation of the excavation report in *Wenwu* 1975/11, pp. 1–18.

Dien, trans., 1979
Dien, Albert E., trans., "Excavation of the Ch'in Dynasty Pit Containing Pottery Figures of Warriors and Horses at Lin-t'ung, Shensi Province," *Chinese Studies in Archaeology* 1, no. 1 (Summer, 1979), pp. 8–55. A complete translation of the excavation report of Pit No. 2 in *Wenwu* 1978/5, pp. 1–19.

Dien and Riegel, trans., 1977
Dien, Albert E.; and Riegel, Jeffrey K., trans. Abstract of *Wenwu* 1975/11, pp. 1–18. *Early China* (1977), pp. 1–18.

Ecke, 1943
Ecke, Gustav. *Sammlung Lochow: Chinesische Bronzen*. 2 vols. Beijing: Fujen Press, 1943–44.

Elisseeff, 1977
Elisseeff, Vadime. *Bronzes archaïques Chinois au Musée Cernuschi*. Paris: L'Asiathèque, 1977.

von Erdberg, 1952
Erdberg, Eleanor von. "A *Hu* with Pictorial Decoration." *Archives of the Chinese Art Society of America* 6 (1952), pp. 18–32.

Frankfort, 1970
Frankfort, Henri. *The Art and Architecture of the Ancient Orient*. 4th rev. ed. Harmondsworth: Penguin Publishing, 1970.

Gettens, 1969
Gettens, Rutherford John. *The Freer Chinese Bronzes, II. Technical Studies*. Washington, D.C.: The Smithsonian Institution, 1969.

Guo (B.), 1959
Guo Baojun. *Shanbiaozhen yu Liulige*. Beijing: Science Press, 1959.

Guo (B.), 1964
Guo Baojun. *Xun Xian Xincun*. Beijing: Science Press, 1964.

Guo (M.), 1958
Guo Moruo. *Liang Zhou jinwenci daxi tulu kaoshi*. 2nd ed. Beijing: Science Press, 1958.

Hong Kong, 1978
Zhongua renmin gongheguo chutu wenwu zhanlan [The Exhibition of Archaeological Finds of the People's Republic of China]. Hong Kong: The Committee for the Exhibition of Archaeological Finds in China, 1978.

Juliano, 1972
Juliano, Annette L. "Three Large Ch'u Graves Recently Excavated in the Chiangling District of Hupei Province." *Artibus Asiae* 34 (1972), no. 1, pp. 5–17.

Kane, 1974–75
Kane, Virginia C. "The Independent Bronze Industries in the South of China Contemporary with the Shang and Western Chou Dynasties." *Archives of Asian Art* 28 (1974/75), pp. 77–107.

Kane, 1975
Kane, Virginia C. "A Re-examination of An-yang Archaeology." *Ars Orientalis* 10 (1975), pp. 93–110.

Kansas City, 1975
The Chinese Exhibition: A Pictorial Record of the Exhibition of Archaeological Finds of the People's Republic of China. Kansas City: Nelson Gallery of Art–Atkins Museum, 1975.

Karlgren, 1952
Karlgren, Bernhard. *A Catalogue of the Chinese Bronzes in the Alfred F. Pillsbury Collection*. Minneapolis: The Minneapolis Institute of Arts, 1952.

Kelley, 1946
Kelley, Charles Fabens; and Ch'en, Meng-chia. *Chinese Bronzes from the Buckingham Collection*. Chicago: The Art Institute of Chicago, 1946.

Kidder, 1956
Kidder, Jonathan Edward, Jr. *Early Chinese Bronzes in the City Art Museum of St. Louis*. St. Louis: City Art Museum of St. Louis, 1956.

Kümmel, 1928
Kümmel, Otto. *Chinesische Bronzen aus der Abteilung für Ostasiatische Kunst an den Staatlichen Museen Berlin*. Berlin: Gesellschaft für Ostasiatische Kunst, 1928.

Kuwayama, 1976
Kuwayama, George. *Ancient Ritual Bronzes of China*. Los Angeles: Los Angeles County Museum of Art, 1976.

Kyoto, 1976
Sen-oku Hakko Kan [Sumitomo Collection]. Kyoto: Benridō, 1976.

Lefebvre d'Argencé, 1977
Lefebvre d'Argencé, René-Yvon. *Bronze Vessels of Ancient China in the Avery Brundage Collection*. San Francisco: Asian Art Museum of San Francisco, 1977.

Li, 1968
Li Ji and Wan Jiabao. *Yinxu chutu qingtong jia xing qi zhi yanjiu (Studies of the Bronze Chia-vessel)*. Nangang, Taiwan: Academia Sinica, 1968.

Li, 1959
Li Xueqin. *Yin dai dili jian lun* [A Brief discussion of Shang geography]. Beijing: Science Press, 1959.

Li, 1975
Li Yu-ning, ed. *The First Emperor of China*. White Plains, N.Y.: International Arts and Sciences Press, Inc., 1975.

Liang, 1751
Liang Shizheng et al. *Xi Qing gu Jian*. Beijing: Ching Neifu Kanben, 1751. An illustrated and annotated catalogue of 1,529 bronzes and other antique objects in the Qing imperial collection.

Liang, 1944
Liang Shangchun. *Yanku jijin tulu* [An Illustrated catalogue of the bronzes in the Yanku collection]. Beijing, 1944.

Lodge, 1946
Lodge, John E.; Wenley, Archibald G.; and Pope, John A., *A Descriptive and Illustrative Catalogue of Chinese Bronzes Acquired during the Administration of John Ellerton Lodge*. Washington, D.C.: The Smithsonian Institution, 1946.

Loehr, 1942
Loehr, Max. "Ein Sockel-Kuei aus der Zeit des K'ungtse." *Monumenta Serica* 7 (1942), pp. 227–34.

Loehr, 1953
Loehr, Max. "The Bronze Styles of the Anyang Period (1300–1028 B.C.)" *Archives of the Chinese Art Society of America* 7 (1953), pp. 42–53.

Loehr, 1967
Loehr, Max. *Chinese Art: Symbols and Images*. Wellesley, Mass.: Wellesley College, 1967.

Loehr, 1967–68
Loehr, Max. "The Fate of the Ornament in Chinese Art." *Archives of Asian Art* 21(1967/68), pp. 8–19.

Loehr, 1968
Loehr, Max. *Ritual Vessels of Bronze Age China*. New York: The Asia Society, 1968.

Loehr, 1975
Loehr, Max. *Ancient Chinese Jades from the Grenville L. Winthrop Collection*. Cambridge, Mass.: Fogg Art Museum, 1975.

Luo, 1935
Luo Zhenyu. *Zhensong Tang jijin tu* [An Illustrated catalogue of the bronzes in the collection of Luo Zhenyu]. Dalian: Moyuan Tang, 1935.

Mizuno, 1959
Mizuno Seiichi. *In Shū seidōki to gyoku (Bronzes and Jades of Ancient China)*. Tokyo: Nihon Keizai Shinbunsha, 1959.

Needham, 1959
Needham, Joseph, et al. *Mathematics and the Sciences of the Heavens and the Earth*. Science and Civilization in China, vol. 3. Cambridge: Cambridge University Press, 1959.

New York, 1975
From the Lands of the Scythians. (The Metropolitan Museum of Art Bulletin 32, no. 5.) New York: The Metropolitan Museum of Art, 1975.

Pirazzoli, 1974
Pirazzoli-t'Serstevens, Michèle. *La civilisation du royaume de Dian à l'époque Han, d'après le matériel exhumé à Shizhai shan (Yünnan)*. Paris: Ecole Française d'Extrême-Orient, 1974.

Plenderleith, 1956
Plenderleith, Harold J. *The Conservation of Antiquities and Works of Art: Treatment, Repair, and Restoration*. London and New York: Oxford University Press, 1956.

Pope, 1967
Pope, John Alexander; Gettens, Rutherford; Cahill, James; and Barnard, Noel. *The Freer Chinese Bronzes, Catalogue*. Washington, D.C.: The Smithsonian Institution, 1967.

von Ragué, 1970
Ragué, Beatrix von. *Ausgewählte Werke Ostasiatischer Kunst*. Berlin: Staatliche Museen Preussischer Kulturbesitz, 1970.

Rawson, 1980
Rawson, Jessica. *Ancient China, Art and Archaeology*. London: Trustees of the British Museum, 1980.

Rong, 1941
Rong Geng. *Shang Zhou yiqi tongkao* [Encyclopedia of Shang and Zhou ritual vessels]. Yenjing Xuebao Zhuanhao, no. 17. 2 vols. Beijing: Harvard-Yenching Institute, 1941.

Salles, 1934
Salles, Georges. "Les Bronzes de Li-yu." *Revue des Arts Asiatiques* 8, no. 3 (1934), pp. 146–58.

Salmony, 1963
Salmony, Alfred. *Chinese Jade Through the Wei Dynasty*. New York: Ronald Press, 1963.

Sandars, 1968
Sandars, N. K. *Prehistoric Art in Europe*. Harmondsworth: Penguin Publishing, 1968.

Segalen, Voisins, and Lartigue, 1924
Segalen, Victor; Voisins, Gilbert de; and Lartigue, Jean. *Mission Archéologique en Chine*. 2 vols. Paris: Librairie Orientaliste Paul Guethner, 1924.

Shang, 1936
Shang Chengzuo. *Hunyuan yiqi*. [Ritual vessels from Hunyuan]. Beijing, 1936.

Shanghai, 1964
Shanghai bowuguan cang qingtongqi [Bronzes in the collection of the Shanghai Museum]. 2 vols. Shanghai: Renmin Meishu Chubanshe, 1964.

Shi Ji
Sima Qian. *Shi Ji* [Historical Records]. 10 vols. (130 juan). Beijing: Zhongguo Shuju, 1959.

Shirakawa, 1965
Shirakawa Shizuka. *Kimbunshū*. 4 vols. Tokyo: Nigensha, 1965.

Soper, 1966
Soper, Alexander C. "Early, Middle, and Late Shang: A Note." *Artibus Asiae* 28(1966), pp. 5–38.

Sun, 1937
Sun Haibo. *Xinzheng yiqi*. [Ritual vessels from Xinzheng]. Beijing: Hunan Tongzhi Guan, 1937.

Tch'ou, 1924
Tch'ou Tö-yi. *Bronzes antiques de la Chine appartenant à C. T. Loo et Cie*. Paris and Brussels: Librairie Nationale d'Art et d'Histoire, 1924.

Thorp, 1979
Thorp, Robert, L. "The Mortuary Art and Architecture of Early Imperial China." Ph.D. diss., University of Kansas, 1979.

Tokyo, 1973
Chūka jimmin kyōwakoku shutsudo bunbutsu ten (Archaeological Treasures Excavated in the People's Republic of China). Tokyo: Asahi Shinbunsha, 1973.

Tokyo, 1976
Chūka jimmin kyōwakoku kodai seidōki ten (Exhibition of Ancient Bronzes of the People's Republic of China). Tokyo: Nihon Keizai Shinbunsha, 1976.

Tokyo, 1978a
Chūka jimmin kyōwakoku shutsudo bunbutsu ten [Exhibition of cultural relics unearthed in the People's Republic of China]. Tokyo: Seibu Bijutsukan and Nihon Keizai Shinbunsha, 1978.

Tokyo, 1978b
Chūgoku kodai no bijutsu [Arts of ancient China]. Tokyo: Idemitsu Bijutsukan, 1978.

Toronto, 1972
Chinese Art in the Royal Ontario Museum. Toronto: The Royal Ontario Museum, 1972.

Umehara, 1933a
Umehara Sueji. *Ōbei shūchō Shina kodō seika* [Ancient bronzes from collections in Europe and America]. 7 vols. Osaka: Yamana & Co., 1933.

Umehara, 1933b
Umehara Sueji. *Henkin no kōkogaku-teki kōsatsu (Etude archéologique sur le Pien-chin, ou série de bronzes avec une table pour l'usage rituel dans la Chine antique)*. Mémoire Tōhō-bunkā gakuin Kyōto Kenkyūsho, vol. 2. Kyoto, 1933.

Umehara, 1936
Umehara Sueji. *Sengoku-shiki dōki no kenkyū (Etude des bronzes des royaumes combattants)*. Mémoire de Tōhō-bunkā gakuin Kyōto Kenkyūsho, vol. 7. Kyoto, 1936.

Umehara, 1942
Umehara Sueji. *Seizansō Seishō, Kodōki-hen (Illustrated catalogue of the K. Nezu Collection. Volume on Ancient Bronzes)*. Tokyo, 1942.

Umehara, 1959
Umehara Sueji. "Sensei-shō Hōkeiken shutsudo no dai ni no henkin" [The Second Set of ritual vessels, *Pien-chin*, from Pao-chi-hsien, Shensi Province]. *Tōhōgaku kiyō* 1(1959), pp. iii–viii, 1–15.

Umehara, 1964
    Umehara Sueji. *Inkyo* (*Yin Hsü, Ancient Capital of the Shang Dynasty at An-yang*). Tokyo: Asahi Shinbunsha, 1964.

Waley, 1960
    Waley, Arthur, trans. *The Book of Songs*. 2nd ed. New York: Grove Press, 1960.

Watson, 1962
    Watson, William. *Ancient Chinese Bronzes*. London: Faber and Faber, 1962.

Watson, 1973
    Watson, William. "On Some Categories of Archaism in Chinese Bronze." *Ars Orientalis* 9 (1973), pp. 1–13.

Weber, C.D., 1968
    Weber, Charles D. *Chinese Pictorial Bronze Vessels of the Late Chou Period*. Ascona, Switzerland: Artibus Asiae Publishers, 1968. Originally published in *Artibus Asiae* 28–30 (1966–68).

Weber, G., 1973
    Weber, George W., Jr. *The Ornaments of Late Chou Bronzes*. New Brunswick, N.J.: Rutgers University Press, 1973.

Wenley, 1948–49
    Wenley, Archibald G. "The Question of the Po-shan-hsiang-lu." *Archives of the Chinese Art Society of America* 3 (1948/49), pp. 5–12.

White, 1934
    White, William Charles. *Tombs of Old Lo-yang*. Shanghai: Kelly & Walsh, 1934.

Xi'an, 1973
    Wenhua da geming qijian Shaanxi chutu wenwu [Cultural relics during the Cultural Revolution in Shaanxi Province]. Xi'an: Shaanxi People's Press, 1973.

Yetts, 1939
    Yetts, W. Perceval. *The Cull Chinese Bronzes*. London: University of London, Courtauld Institute of Art, 1939.

B. *Excavation Reports and Related Materials*

CHAPTER 1

Erlitou:
    Kaogu 1959/11, pp. 598–600
    Kaogu 1961/2, pp. 82–85, pl. 7
    Kaogu 1965/5, pp. 215–24, pls. 1–5
    Kaogu 1974/4, pp. 234–48, pls. 2–5

Identification of the Erlitou site:
    Wenwu 1973/7, pp. 5–14, pls. 2–4
    Kaogu 1978/1, pp. 1–4
    Wenwu 1978/2, pp. 69–71

CHAPTER 2

Zhengzhou:
    Wenwu 1955/10, pp. 24–42
    Kaogu Xuebao 1957/1, pp. 53–73
    Kaogu 1965/10, pp. 500–6
    Wenwu Ziliao Congkan 1 (1977), pp. 1–47
    Soper, 1966

Identification of the Zhengzhou site:
    Wenwu 1961/10, pp. 39–40, and references cited there

Panlongcheng:
    Wenwu 1976/1, pp. 49–59
    Wenwu 1976/2, pp. 5–46
    Bagley, 1977

CHAPTER 3

Lingbao Xian, Henan Province:
    Kaogu 1979/1, pp. 20–22, pls. 6–7

Funan Xian, Anhui Province:
    Wenwu 1959/1, inside front cover
    Akiyama, 1968, pl. 43
    Beijing, 1972a, no. 49

Jiashan Xian, Anhui Province:
    Wenwu 1965/7, pp. 23–26

Gaocheng Xian, Hebei Province:
    Kaogu 1973/1, pp. 25–29, pls. 8, 9
    Kaogu 1973/5, pp. 266–71, pls. 1–3
    Wenwu 1974/8, pp. 42–55, pls. 1, 3, 4
    Wenwu Ziliao Congkan no. 1 (1977), pp. 149–62
    Wenwu 1979/6, pp. 33–56, pl. 6
    Gaocheng Taixi Shang dai yizhi (Beijing: Wenwu Press, 1977)

Qingjiang Xian, Jiangxi Province:
    Wenwu 1975/7, pp. 51–83, pl. 10
    Kaogu 1976/6, pp. 383–91, pls. 7–9
    Wenwu 1977/9, pp. 40–63, pl. 6
    Wenwu Ziliao Congkan no. 2 (1979), pp. 1–13, pl. 5

Yidu Sufutun, Shandong Province:
    Wenwu 1972/1, p. 81
    Wenwu 1972/8, pp. 17–30
    Zhongguo Kaogu Xuebao no. 2 (1947), pp. 167–77

CHAPTER 4

Chronology of the Anyang site:
    Kaogu 1975/1, pp. 27–46
    Kaogu 1977/1, pp. 13–36
    Kaogu Xuebao 1979/1, pp. 1–47
    Kane, 1975

Tomb of Fu Hao:
    Kaogu 1977/3, pp. 151–53 and pls. 5–9
    Kaogu 1977/5, pp. 341–50
    Wenwu 1977/11, pp. 32–37
    Kaogu Xuebao 1977/2, pp. 1–22, 57–98
    China Reconstructs 1977/10, pp. 38–39
    China Pictorial 1978/1, pp. 24–27
    Kaogu 1979/2, pp. 165–70

CHAPTER 5

Bronzes from the Yan state:
    Chen, 1955–56, pt. 2, pp. 94–104, 122–33
    Kaogu 1975/5, pp. 274–79, 270

Zhou oracle bones and palace at Qishan, Shaanxi Province:
    Wenwu 1979/10, pp. 27–50, pls. 4–7

CHAPTER 6

No references

CHAPTER 7

Sui Xian, Hubei Province:
    El popola Cinio 1979/2, pp. 42–45
    China Reconstructs 1979/5, pp. 28–31
    Wenwu 1979/7, pp. 1–52

Tonglüshan, Hubei Province:
  Kaogu 1974/4, pp. 251–56
  Wenwu 1975/2, pp. 1–12

Gongcheng, Guangxi Province:
  Kaogu 1973/1, pp. 30–34

Xinzheng, Henan Province:
  Bishop, 1927

Shangmacun, Houma, Shanxi Province:
  Kaogu 1963/5, pp. 229–45

Liyu, Shanxi Province:
  Salles, 1934

Bronze foundry site at Houma, Shanxi:
  Kaogu 1959/5, pp. 222–28
  Wenwu 1960/8–9, pp. 7–14
  Wenwu 1961/10, pp. 31–32
  Kaogu 1962/2, pp. 55–62

CHAPTER 8

Pingshan Xian, Hebei Province:
  Wenwu 1979/1, pp. 1–52
  China Reconstructs 1979/1, pp. 40–44
  Gugong Bowuyuan Yuankan 1979/1, pp. 39–50
  Gugong Bowuyuan Yuankan 1979/2, pp. 81–96
  Kaogu Xuebao 1979/2, pp. 147–84
  China Pictorial 1979/3, pp. 22–27
  China Pictorial 1979/5, p. 40
  Wenwu 1979/5, pp. 43–50

Tomb No. 1, Mawangdui, Changsha, Hunan Province:
  Beijing, 1972c
  Kaogu 1972/5, pp. 37–42
  Kaogu 1972/6, pp. 48–58
  Kaogu 1973/1, pp. 43–61
  Kaogu 1973/2, pp. 118–27
  Kaogu 1973/4, pp. 247–57
  Beijing, 1973

Tomb Nos. 2 and 3, Mawangdui, Changsha, Hunan Province:
  Kaogu Xuebao 1974/1, pp. 175–87
  Kaogu 1975/6, pp. 344–48

Kaogu 1979/3, pp. 273–74
Wenwu 1974/7, pp. 39–48, 63
Kaogu 1975/1, pp. 47–57, 61
Wenwu 1976/1, pp. 18–31
Wenwu 1978/2, pp. 1–9
Kaogu 1979/2, pp. 171–73

Mancheng, Hebei Province:
  Kaogu 1972/1, pp. 8–18
  Kaogu 1972/2, pp. 39–50
  Kaogu 1972/3, pp. 49–53
  Kaogu 1972/5, pp. 49–52
  Beijing, 1972b
  Beijing, 1978b

Dian culture in Yunnan:
  Beijing, 1959a
  Wenwu 1972/8, pp. 7–16
  Kaogu Xuebao 1975/2, pp. 97–156
  Pirazzoli, 1974

CHAPTER 10

Kneeling terracotta figures found in the vicinity of the mausoleum of Qin Shihuangdi:
  Kaogu 1962/8, pp. 407–11, 419
  Wenwu 1964/9, pp. 55–56
  Wenwu 1973/5, pp. 66–67
  Kansas City, 1975

Terracotta warriors and horses discovered in March 1974 east of the mausoleum of Qin Shihuangdi (Pit No. 1):
  Wenwu 1975/1, pp. 44–51
  Wenwu 1975/11, pp. 1–30
  Kaogu 1975/6, pp. 344–39
  China Pictorial 1975/11, pp. 22–25
  Tokyo, 1976, nos. 122–30
  Dien and Riegel, trans., 1977
  Dien, trans., 1977–78

Terracotta warriors and horses discovered in May 1976 north of Pit No. 1 (Pit No. 2):
  Wenwu 1978/5, pp. 1–19
  Dien, trans., 1979

Composition by Zimmering & Zinn Typography
Composition of Chinese characters by Asco Trade Typesetting, Ltd.
Color separations by Chanticleer Co., Inc.
Printing by Case-Hoyt
Binding by American Book–Stratford Press, Inc.